Reading & Language

INSIDE

LANGUAGE · LITERACY · CONTENT

PROGRAM AUTHORS

David W. Moore

Deborah J. Short

Michael W. Smith

Alfred W. Tatum

Josefina Villamil Tinajero

Acknowledgments

Grateful acknowledgment is given to the authors, artists, photographers, museums, publishers, and agents for permission to reprint copyrighted material. Every effort has been made to secure the appropriate permission. If any omissions have been made or if corrections are required, please contact the Publisher.

Photographic Credits

Cover: Submerged Alligator, Andrew Masur.
Photograph © Andrew Masur/Flikr/Getty Images.

Acknowledgments continue on page 684.

For product information and technology assistance, contact us at
Cengage Learning Customer & Sales Support, 888-915-3276

For permission to use material from this text or product, submit all requests online at **www.cengage.com/permissions**
Further permissions questions can be emailed to
permissionrequest@cengage.com

National Geographic Learning | Cengage Learning
1 Lower Ragsdale Drive
Building 1, Suite 200
Monterey, CA 93940

Cengage Learning is a leading provider of customized learning solutions with office locations around the globe, including Singapore, the United Kingdom, Australia, Mexico, Brazil, and Japan. Locate your local office at **www.cengage.com/global**.

Visit National Geographic Learning online at **ngl.cengage.com**
Visit our corporate website at **www.cengage.com**

Printer: Quad Graphics, Versailles, KY

ISBN: 978-12854-37101

Printed in the United States of America
19 20 21 22
10 9 8 7

Contents at a Glance

Reviewers

We gratefully acknowledge the many contributions of the following dedicated educators in creating a research-based program that is appealing to and motivating for middle school students. In addition to the contributors listed below, we also thank the many teachers, students, and administrators whose feedback over the last several years helped shape the original program and this updated program.

Dr. René Saldaña, Jr., Ph.D.
Texas Tech University

Dr. Saldaña teaches English and education and is a widely published trade book writer. His books include *The Jumping Tree* and *Finding Our Way: Stories*. His stories have also appeared in anthologies such as *Guys Write for GUYS Read*, *Face Relations*, *Every Man for Himself*, and in magazines like *Boy's Life* and *READ*.

Teacher Reviewers

Idalia Apodaca
English Language Development Teacher
Shaw Middle School
Spokane, WA

Pat E. Baggett-Hopkins
Area Reading Coach
Chicago Public Schools
Chicago, IL

Judy Chin
ESOL Teacher
Arvida Middle School
Miami, FL

Sonia Flores
Teacher Supporter
Los Angeles Unified School District
Los Angeles, CA

Brenda Garcia
ESL Teacher
Crockett Middle School
Irving, TX

Margaret Jan Graham
Montford Middle School
Tallahassee, FL

Susan Harris
Department Head Language Arts
Cobb Middle School
District - Leon
Tallahassee, FL

Kristine Hoffman
Teacher on Special Assignment
Newport-Mesa Unified School District
Costa Mesa, CA

Patricia James
Reading Specialist
Brevard County
Melbourne Beach, FL

Dr. Margaret R. Keefe
ELL Contact and Secondary Advocate
Martin County School District
Stuart, FL

Julianne Kosareff
Curriculum Specialist
Paramount Unified School District
Paramount, CA

Lore Levene
Coordinator of Language Arts
Community Consolidated School
District 59
Arlington Heights, IL

Kathleen Malloy
9th Grade Coordinator and Reading Coach
Godby High School
Tallahassee, FL

Natalie M. Mangini
Teacher/ELD Coordinator
Serrano Intermediate School
Lake Forest, CA

Laurie Manikowski
Teacher/Trainer
Lee Mathson Middle School
San Jose, CA

Patsy Mills
Supervisor, Bilingual-ESL
Houston Independent School District
Houston, TX

Juliane M. Prager-Nored
High Point Expert
Los Angeles Unified School District
Los Angeles, CA

Patricia Previdi
ESOL Teacher
Patapsco Middle School
Ellicott City, MD

Dr. Louisa Rogers
Middle School Team Leader
Broward County Public Schools
Fort Lauderdale, FL

Rebecca Varner
ESL Teacher
Copley-Fairlawn Middle School
Copley, OH

Hailey F. Wade
ESL Teacher/Instructional Specialist
Lake Highlands Junior High
Richardson, TX

Cassandra Yorke
ESOL Coordinator
Palm Beach School District
West Palm Beach, FL

Program Authors

David W. Moore, Ph.D. Arizona State University

Dr. Moore taught high school in Arizona public schools before becoming a professor of education. He co-chaired the International Reading Association's Commission on Adolescent Literacy and has published research reports, articles, book chapters, and complete books including *Developing Readers and Writers in the Content Areas, Teaching Adolescents Who Struggle with Reading*, and *Principled Practices for Adolescent Literacy.*

Deborah J. Short, Ph.D. Center for Applied Linguistics

Dr. Short is a co-developer of the research-validated SIOP Model for sheltered instruction. She has directed scores of studies on English Language Learners and published scholarly articles in *TESOL Quarterly, The Journal of Educational Research, Language Teaching Research*, and many others. Dr. Short also co-wrote a policy report: *Double the Work: Challenges and Solutions to Acquiring Language and Academic Literacy for Adolescent English Language Learner*s.

Michael W. Smith, Ph.D. Temple University

Dr. Michael Smith has won awards for his teaching both at the high school and college level. He contributed to the Common Core State Standards initiative by serving on the Aspects of Text Complexity working group. His books include *"Reading Don't Fix No Chevys": Literacy in the Lives of Young Men, Fresh Takes on Teaching Literary Elements: How to Teach What Really Matters About Character, Setting, Point of View, and Theme*, and *Oh, Yeah?! Putting Argument to Work Both in School and Out.*

Alfred W. Tatum, Ph.D. University of Illinois at Chicago

Dr. Tatum began his career as an eighth-grade teacher and reading specialist. He conducts research on the power of texts and literacy to reshape the life outcomes of striving readers. Dr. Tatum's books include *Reading for Their Life: Re-Building the Textual Lineages of African American Adolescent Males* and *Teaching Reading to Black Adolescent Males: Closing the Achievement Gap.*

Josefina Villamil Tinajero, Ph.D. University of Texas at El Paso

Dr. Tinajero consults with school districts to design ESL, bilingual, literacy, and biliteracy programs. She has served on state and national advisory committees for standards development, including English as a New Language Advisory Panel of the National Board of Professional Teaching Standards. Dr. Tinajero has served as president of the National Association of Bilingual Education and the Texas Association of Bilingual Education.

Imagine the Possibilities

GUIDING QUESTION What makes an idea powerful?

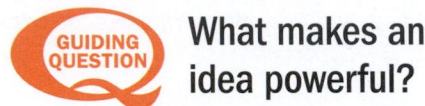

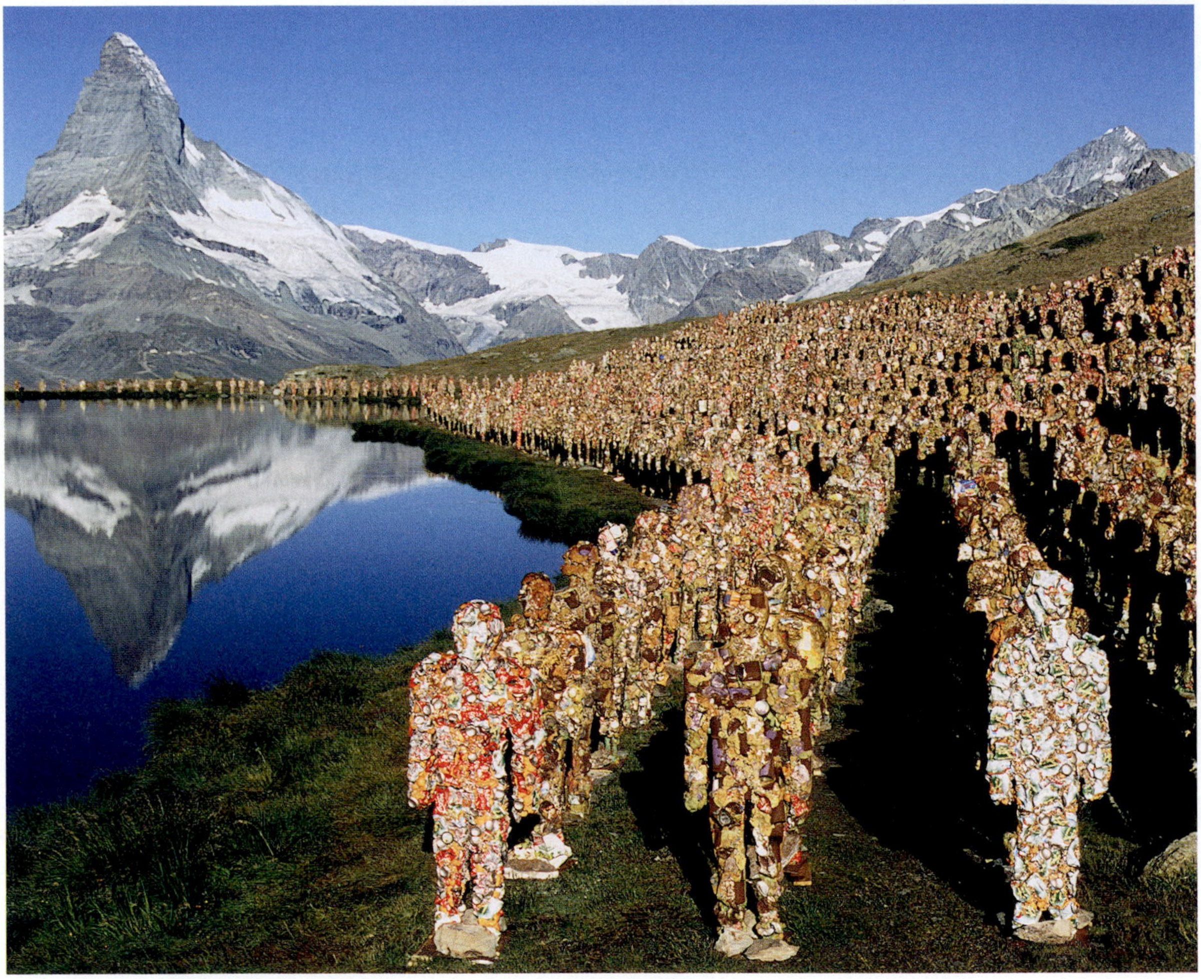

Writing ✏

▶ **Paragraph**
Problem-and-Solution, Chronological Order, Spatial-Order, Compare-and-Contrast

Pages 1W–65W

Play to Your Strengths

GUIDING QUESTION How should people use their talents?

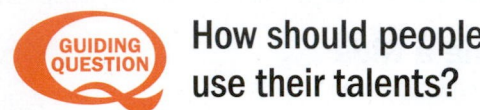

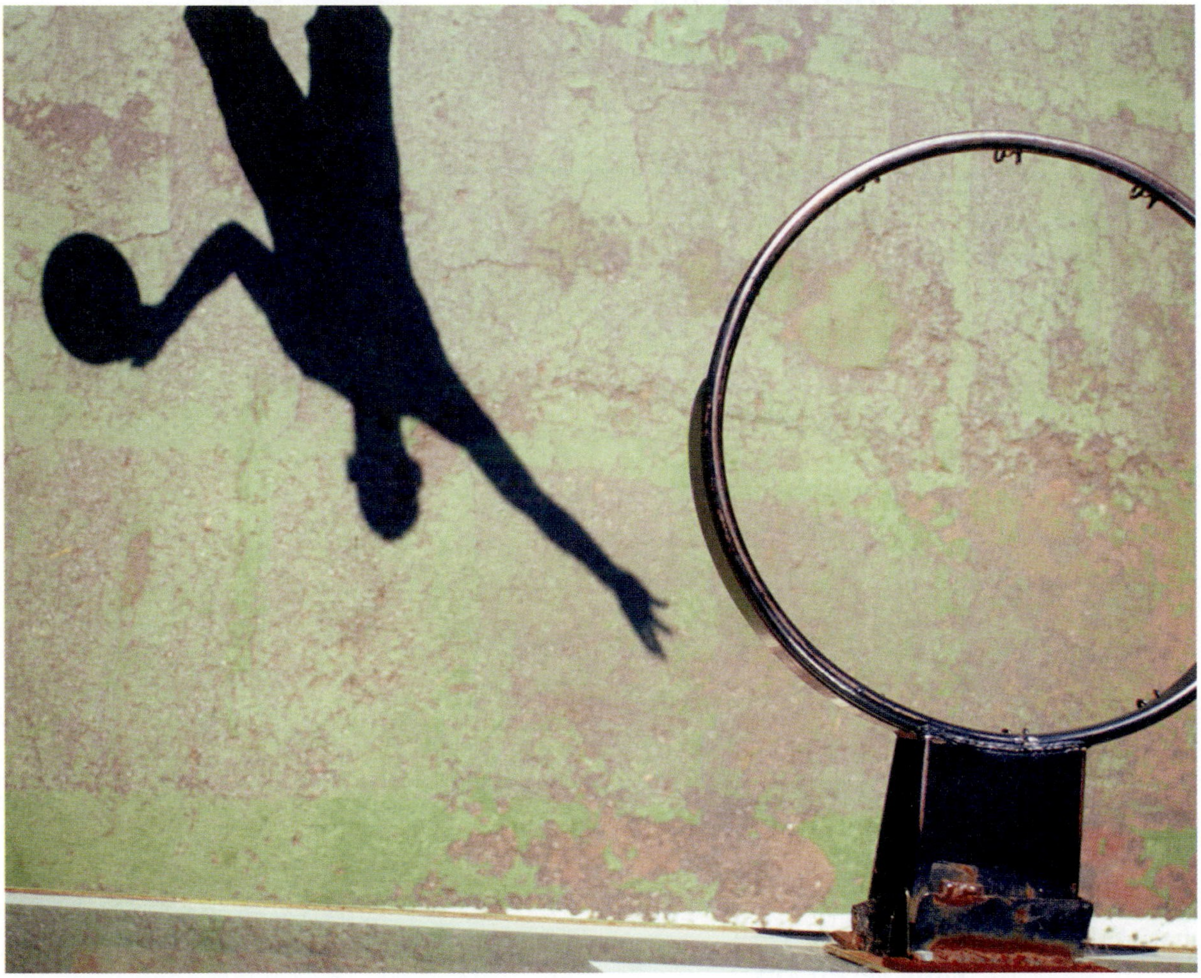

Writing 🖊
▶ **Personal Narrative**
▶ **Short Story**

Pages 66W–107W

A NEW
Chapter

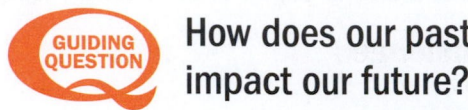 **How does our past impact our future?**

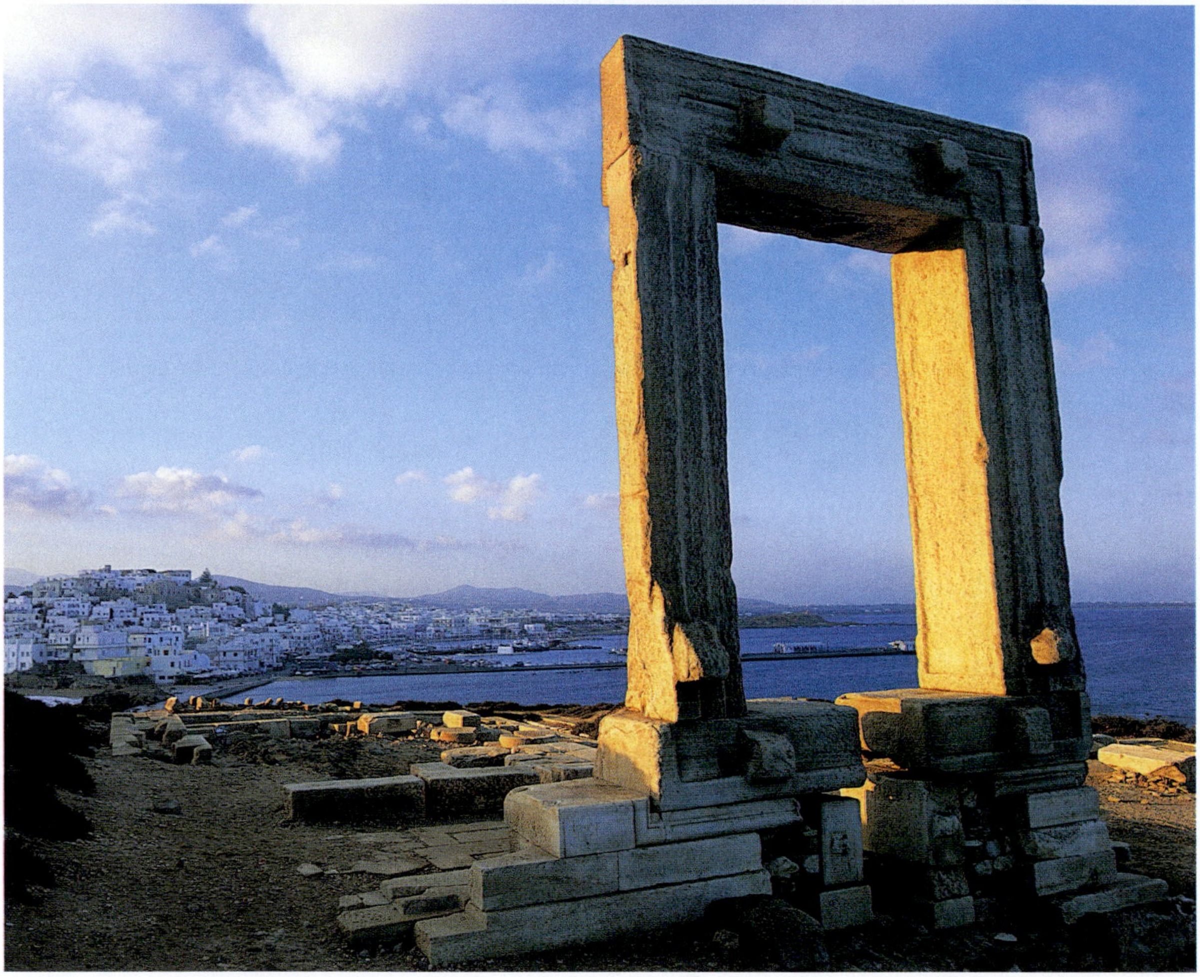

Unit 3

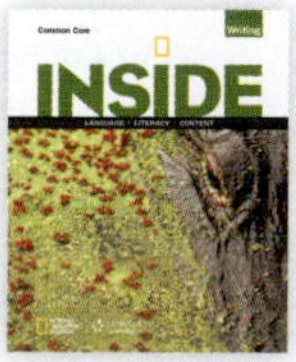

Pages 108W–149W

Writing

▶ **Realistic Short Story**
▶ **Cause-and-Effect Essay**

Every **Body** Is a
Winner

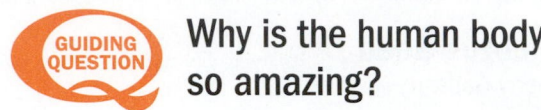

Q GUIDING QUESTION

Why is the human body
so amazing?

Writing
▶ **Research Report**

Pages 150W–227W

Close
Encounters

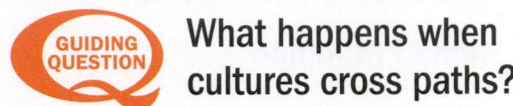 **GUIDING QUESTION** What happens when cultures cross paths?

Writing ✎
▶ Story Scene
▶ Literary Response

Pages 228W–269W

TO THE
RESCUE

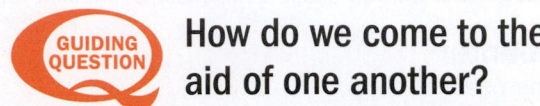

GUIDING QUESTION How do we come to the aid of one another?

Writing ✏
► **Summary Paragraph**
► **Letter to the Editor**
► **Business Letter**

Pages 270W–307W

MORE THAN A GAME

GUIDING QUESTION

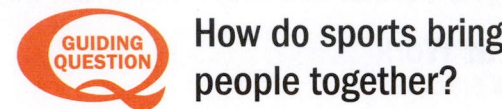

How do sports bring people together?

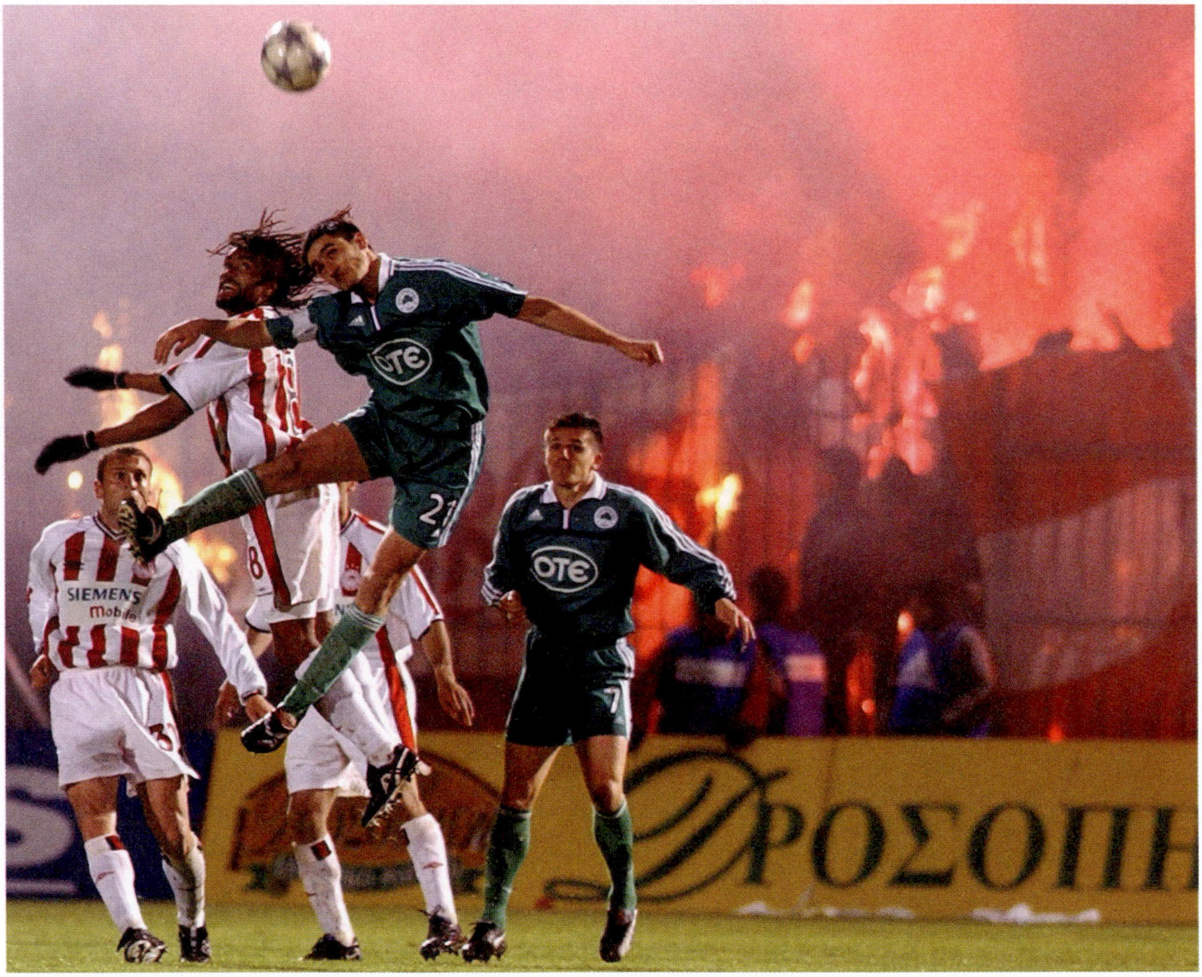

Writing ✏

▶ **Paragraphs in Chronological Order**
▶ **Biography**

Pages 308W–349W

GLOBAL WARNINGS

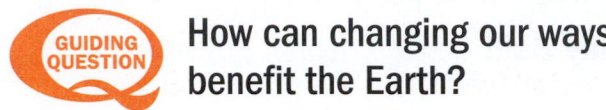

GUIDING QUESTION How can changing our ways benefit the Earth?

INSIDE

Writing ✎
▶ Public Service Announcement
▶ Persuasive Essay

Pages 350W–389W

Genres at a Glance

INFORMATIONAL TEXTS

Imagine
the Possibilities

What makes an idea powerful?

READ MORE!

Content Library
Building Tiny Transistors
by Glen Phelan

Leveled Library
Amelia Earhart: Free in the Skies
by Robert Burleigh
Rosa Parks
by Maryann N. Weidt
A Library for Juana
by Pat Mora

Web Links
myNGconnect.com

◄ An army of trash figures by artist Ha Schult
makes viewers consider the impact of human
activities on the world we live in.

Focus on Reading

Reading Strategies

Reading strategies are thinking tools that help you better understand texts. Use reading strategies before, during, and after you read.

Plan: How It Works

To plan, first preview what you will read. Look at headings, visuals, captions, and boldface words to determine what the text is about. Next, set a purpose for reading. What do you hope to learn? Finally, predict what you think the text will be about. As you read, look for information to confirm, or check, your predictions.

▶ **Plan**
Preview, set a purpose, and predict what the text is about before reading it more carefully.

Plan: Practice Together

Preview and set a purpose for reading "National Youth Contest." As you read, predict what will happen next. Confirm your predictions during and after reading.

National Youth Contest

The Unionville Youth Group will compete in the National Problem Solvers Contest in Chicago, Illinois. First, the club must raise the funds needed for airfare to the competition. Only two months remain to raise $2,000. Luckily, the club has many events planned to accomplish their goal.

Strategy in Action
❝ The title and first sentence tell me the text is about a contest, so I expect to learn more about it. Yes, the text is about what a club has to do to compete in the contest. ❞

Monitor: How It Works

To monitor means to keep track of, or check on, something. Monitor as you read to make sure you understand the text. Stop if something is unclear or confusing, then reread or read ahead to clarify ideas and vocabulary. Think about what you already know to help you better understand new words and ideas.

Strategy in Action
❝ I'm not sure what *funds* means. Reading ahead, I see it must be money. ❞

Monitor: Practice Together

Reread "National Youth Contest." Tell a partner where you stopped to reread or read ahead. Explain how you figured out new words or ideas.

▶ **Monitor**
Notice confusing parts in the text and reread or read on to make them clear.

Visualize: How It Works

When you visualize, you create pictures in your mind to help you understand what you read. Look for words that **describe** how things look, sound, smell, taste, and feel. Use this information to imagine the people, places, and events in the text.

Visualize: Practice Together

Read "A Little Help from Friends." As you read, stop and create mental images. After you read, discuss what you visualized with a partner. Explain how your imagination helped you understand the text.

A Little Help from Friends

Eileen Rios knew her lawn was out of control. Since breaking her foot last fall, the 70-year-old had trouble taking care of her property. All that changed last Saturday morning when twenty students from Weber Middle School's Community Outreach Club chose Mrs. Rios's yard as their monthly project.

"I woke up to the sound of shovels. It was a wonderful surprise!" commented Mrs. Rios.

The group spent several hours pruning, weeding, and mowing. The results of their labor were evident. Ruby red roses and bright yellow daisies are once again visible around the porch, and everyone shared baskets of vegetables picked from the garden.

Determine Importance: How It Works

When you determine importance, you identify the most important points or main ideas and add details that support these ideas. A good way to determine importance is to summarize the text, stating the most important ideas about the topic.

Determine Importance: Practice Together

Reread "A Little Help from Friends." As you read, look for the main idea and record it on the Main-Idea Chart. Add details to support the main idea. After reading, summarize the main idea and share your summary with a partner.

▶ **Visualize**
Picture the sights, sounds, smells, tastes, and touch of what the author describes.

Strategy in Action
" I imagine the sound of clinking metal from the shovels, and I can picture those brightly colored flowers. "

Strategy in Action
" It seems the main idea is that the Community Outreach Club cleaned Mrs. Rios's yard. "

▶ **Determine Importance**
Focus on the author's most significant ideas and information.

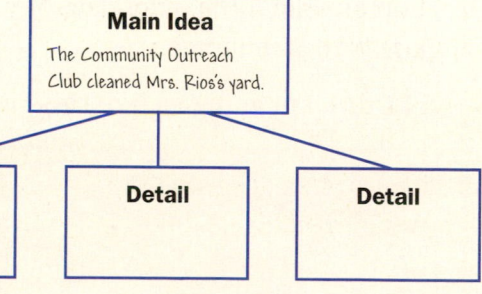

Main Idea
The Community Outreach Club cleaned Mrs. Rios's yard.

Detail
Group spent several hours working.

Detail

Detail

Main Idea-Chart

Focus on Reading

Ask Questions: How It Works

As you read, ask questions about what the author is trying to tell you. Asking questions helps you to learn and clarify information, and to understand or figure out what is important. Use words such as *Who? What? When? Where? Why?* and *How?* to ask questions about the text.

Look for answers by rereading or reading on in the text. Sometimes the answers are right there. Sometimes you may need to search different parts of the text. For some answers, you need to analyze what the author is thinking.

▶ **Ask Questions**
Ask and answer questions to help you connect with what you read.

Ask Questions: Practice Together

Read "A Good Fit." Pause to ask a question as you read. Use the text and visuals to answer your questions.

A Good Fit

Last week, the school opened an after-school fitness club in the gym. The club focuses on all types of fitness training, but the program begins with weight training.

I went in to see what it was all about. Coach Allen said that weightlifting is helpful for staying fit, but we should do it correctly to avoid injuries.

Coach then explained that each day we would warm up before lifting. This will lessen the chance of straining a muscle. After that, a good workout that exercises key muscle groups takes no more than 20 to 30 minutes.

I think I'm going to like this fitness club. It's a good fit!

Strategy in Action
" When I read that you should lift weights correctly to avoid injuries, I wonder what kinds of injuries might happen."

Make Connections: How It Works

To make connections, put together information in the text with what you know outside of the text to increase your understanding. As you read, you make connections to your personal experiences. You can also connect a text to other texts you have read and to what is going on in the world.

Make Connections: Practice Together

Read "Students Helping Students." Connect the text to your own experiences and what you have read or learned about young people who help others. Tell a partner about the connections you made and how they helped you understand the text.

▶ **Make Connections**

Combine your knowledge and experiences with the author's ideas and information.

Students Helping Students

Last September, 12-year-old Kadir Ahmed noticed that his school's tutoring center didn't have enough tutors. Many of the students who came in before or after school couldn't get help. So Kadir formed a team of student volunteers. They created online lessons for math, reading, and science. Kadir's free service is called Tutoring Aid. Nearly 200 students have used the service since it was created.

Strategy in Action

" I read the school did not have enough tutors. I think this is a problem because I know how much tutoring can help. "

Make Inferences: How It Works

When you make inferences, you put together clues from the text with what you already know to figure out what the author means.

I read *"So Kadir formed a team of student volunteers."* **+**

I know *it's a lot of work to organize and lead others.* **=**

And so *I think Kadir is a hard-working, confident leader.*

▶ **Make Inferences**

When the author does not say something directly, use text clues and what you know to figure out what the author means.

Make Inferences: Practice Together

Read "Students Helping Students" again. As you read, look for ideas in the text that are not fully explained. Use your own experience and knowledge to make inferences about what the author means but does not directly state.

Focus on Reading

Synthesize: How It Works

Reading is like putting together a puzzle. To **solve** the puzzle, you combine ideas and information from the text to form a bigger picture. This process is called synthesizing. When you synthesize, you draw conclusions, compare information across texts, and form generalizations. You form new understandings about the overall meaning of the text.

When you draw conclusions, you combine what the writer says with related facts and what you know. You combine this information to make a statement about the topic. When you form generalizations, you take ideas from the text, compare them to what you already know, and form an idea that applies to more than one situation.

▶ **Synthesize**
Bring together ideas you learn from texts and combine them into a new understanding.

Synthesize: Practice Together

Read "My Pets." Use text evidence from the selection and your own experience to draw conclusions, form generalizations, and compare across texts as you read.

My Pets

I love animals, but living in an apartment with a strict "No Pets Allowed" rule made my dream of having one seem nearly impossible. I say *nearly* because I'm not one to give up easily on important things. That's why I volunteered at the local animal shelter. It's been amazing to love not just one but many animals.

I work most days after school. Between playing with the cats and walking the dogs, I'm very busy. Last week, we even cared for a few ferrets. My favorite part of the job is helping people adopt pets. I know I can't bring one home with me, but it sure feels great to see so many people find new best friends. In the end, I feel like the luckiest girl alive.

Strategy in Action

" I read that the narrator doesn't give up easily. She also finds a way to be with animals. So, I conclude that she is a determined person."

Strategy in Action

" I read that many people find new animal friends. I know that many people adopt pets. I think it is true that many people have animal friends."

Academic Vocabulary
- **solve** (solv) *verb*
  When you **solve** a problem, you find the answer to it.

Read "A Farewell Celebration." Use the reading strategies you've been practicing before, during, and after reading to help you understand the selection.

A Farewell Celebration

Saying goodbye is hard, especially when the person has meant so much to so many. What is a fitting farewell? Hear the story of how one school said goodbye to a much-loved leader.

Marc hung the last poster and breathed a sigh of relief. Looking around the gym, he felt the weight of all the planning and preparation slip away. The place looked great! He could hardly believe it had all started with his little idea.

Last school year had started with Mr. Summers, the principal, announcing his retirement. He meant so much to the school and the students. Everyone was sad to hear he planned to leave, and everyone had big ideas for how to say goodbye. Shortly after the announcement, a group of teachers and parents organized a meeting to plan a fitting celebration.

Almost a hundred people attended. Marc had gone, too. He had an idea he wanted to share. It had been just a little idea really, something he thought Mr. Summers might like. Entering that meeting room, Marc remembered feeling so small. How could anyone possibly be interested in what he had to say? Finding a chair near the back, Marc sat and listened as idea after idea was presented. He liked many of the suggestions he heard, but none seemed to really excite the group. Most involved a great deal of money and work.

Finally, Marc found the courage to stand and share his idea. He thought everyone could work together and create a "museum exhibit" in the gym. Different groups could make displays showing the contributions Mr. Summers had made to the school throughout his career.

The room grew quiet for a few minutes. Marc looked around, worried that people might laugh. Instead, he found everyone looking thoughtful. Slowly, smiles began to spread across the faces of parents, teachers, and students alike. His idea sparked a lively discussion that lasted another hour as different people shared ideas for displays.

By the end of the meeting, a list of twenty exhibits was made and a date was set for the installation.

Now that day had arrived. The hard work had paid off. Marc could hardly believe his eyes. On one side of the gym hung old photographs from Mr. Summer's first year at the school. He looked so different! Another section was dedicated to all the school improvements he had overseen and helped raise funds for, including a slideshow of added classrooms and computers and science equipment.

Marc's favorite display was the one showing pictures of all the fun activities Mr. Summers did with students. The pictures were framed with brightly colored streamers of red, white, and blue. Marc was even in one picture. His class had invited Mr. Summers to build bridges with them for a project. The two had been partners. The picture showed Marc and Mr. Summers accepting the prize for the strongest and tallest bridge.

That picture turned out to be one of Mr. Summer's favorite parts of the exhibit, too. He was grateful for the hard work that went into the celebration. He thanked everyone, especially Marc, for making his retirement so special. The school even decided to keep parts of the exhibit. They now hang in the main hallway as a tribute to a great principal and a great little idea.

Focus on Vocabulary

Use Word Parts

Many English words are made up of parts. Often you can figure out a word's meaning by looking at the parts.

EXAMPLES

The prefix *mis-* means "wrong."

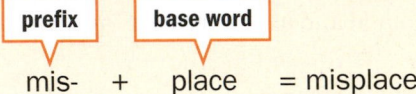

mis- + place = misplace

Misplace means "put in the wrong place."

The suffix *-ion* means "state of."

perfect + -ion = perfection

Perfection means the "state of being perfect."

Sometimes two base words combine to make a new <mark>compound</mark> word.

tooth + brush = toothbrush

How the Strategy Works

When you read, use word parts to figure out a word you don't know.

1. Look closely at the word to see if you know any of the parts. If you see two base words, think about the meaning of each one.
2. Do you see a prefix or a suffix? If yes, cover it.   **misuse**
3. Think about the meaning of the base word.
4. Uncover the prefix or suffix, and think about its meaning.
5. Put the meanings of the word parts together to understand the whole word. Be sure the meaning makes sense in the text.

Use the strategy to figure out the meaning of each underlined word.

> How does an <u>invention</u> help you? It makes your life easier. For example, typing on a computer instead of writing by hand solves the problem of reading sloppy <u>handwriting</u>. Computers can also correct words you <u>misspell</u>.

Strategy in Action

" I see the suffix *–ion*. I'll cover it. There is the base word *invent*. I know *–ion* means 'state of.' So *invent* + *-ion* means 'state of being invented.' "

☑ **REMEMBER** Use word parts to figure out an unknown word.

Academic Vocabulary
- **compound** (**kom**-pownd) *adjective*
  When something is a **compound**, it is made of two or more parts.

Practice Together

Read this passage aloud. Look at each underlined word. Find the word parts. Put their meanings together to figure out the meaning of the underlined word.

Some Word Parts

Suffix: *-ful* means "having the qualities of"

Suffix: *-ous* means "full of"

Into the Air

Orville and Wilbur Wright were <u>courageous</u> men. Instead of staying safe on the ground, they looked to the sky. In the late 1800s and early 1900s, they tried to build a machine that would fly. They used equipment from their bicycle factory. They called their machine the <u>airplane</u>.

Their early tries weren't always <u>successful</u>, but the men learned from their mistakes.

▲ **The Wright Brothers, in Kitty Hawk, North Carolina, 1903**

On December 17, 1903, they finally got their machine to fly. Orville stayed in the air 12 seconds, and Wilbur's flight lasted 59 seconds.

Try It!

Read this passage aloud. What is the meaning of each underlined word? How do you know?

Invention Convention

Sandra could not wait to get home. Her mind raced with ideas. She held tightly to the *Invention Convention* application Mr. Worth had given her. Sandra remembered how much fun her older brother had had with this <u>marvelous</u> assignment. Now it was her turn to create a <u>useful</u> gadget from things she found around the house.

Mr. Worth had said a <u>successful</u> invention fixed a common problem but did not require lots of money. After school, Sandra hurried to her basement and began digging through boxes for possible materials. She uncovered a <u>typewriter</u>, some wire, a plastic container, and several <u>lightbulbs</u>. Materials in hand, Sandra set off in search of a problem to solve.

SCIENCE ARTICLE

HITCHING a Ride

by Rebecca L. Johnson

Build Background

Connect

Survey Imagine that you can see what an ocean animal sees. Which animal would you choose? Ask your classmates.

Meet Greg Marshall

Greg Marshall discovered how to put a camera on sharks and other animals. Now we can see what animals see.

Digital Library

myNGconnect.com
View the video.

▲ An ocean animal explores the sea.

Language & Grammar

Ask and Answer Questions

CD

Look at the photo and listen to the questions and answers. Then play the question game by asking and answering the questions.

PICTURE PROMPT

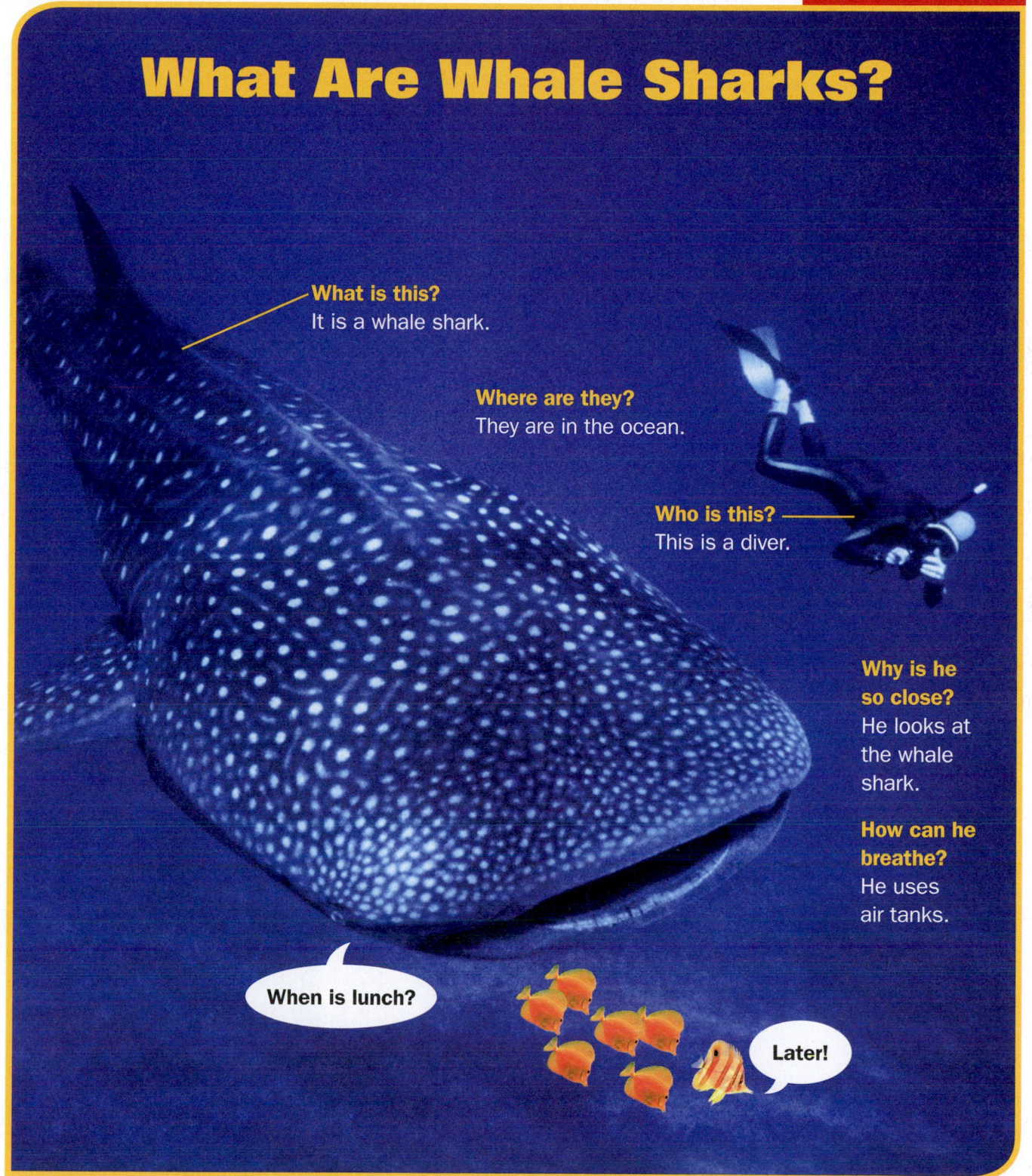

What Are Whale Sharks?

What is this?
It is a whale shark.

Where are they?
They are in the ocean.

Who is this?
This is a diver.

Why is he so close?
He looks at the whale shark.

How can he breathe?
He uses air tanks.

When is lunch?

Later!

Use Different Kinds of Sentences

There are four kinds of sentences. Start every sentence with a capital letter. Each kind of sentence has a different purpose. Use the end mark that fits the purpose.

Kinds of Sentences	Examples
1. Statement Make a **statement** to tell something. End with a period.	Sharks are fish. There are about 350 different kinds of sharks.
2. Question Ask a **question** to find out something. End with a question mark.	Are sharks dangerous? How big are sharks?
3. Exclamation Use an **exclamation** to express a strong feeling. End with an exclamation point.	Sharks have a lot of teeth! I am scared of sharks!
4. Command Give a **command** to tell someone what to do. End with a period.	Swim away from sharks. Do not shout near a shark.

Practice Together

Listen to each sentence. Write the mark that goes at the end on a card. Then tell what kind of sentence it is. Make up another sentence of the same kind.

1. Where do sharks live ⎯⎯
2. Some sharks are huge ⎯⎯
3. Go to the aquarium to see sharks ⎯⎯
4. Sharks hear sounds far away ⎯⎯
5. Do sharks have bones ⎯⎯

Try It!

Write each sentence, and add the end mark. Then tell what kind of sentence it is. Write another sentence of the same kind.

6. Are all sharks dangerous ⎯⎯
7. Read this book about sharks ⎯⎯
8. Sharks can smell things a mile away ⎯⎯
9. What do sharks eat ⎯⎯
10. Sharks are cool ⎯⎯

▲ Great white sharks are scary!

▲ This is a black tipped shark.

▲ Are hammerhead sharks dangerous?

Ask a Friend

ASK AND ANSWER QUESTIONS

There are more than 300 kinds of sharks in the ocean. What do you want to learn about them? Look at the photos. With a partner, ask and answer questions.

▲ Leopard shark

▲ Nurse shark

▲ Whale shark

Plan your questions. Think about what you want to learn. Write six questions, one for each question word.

> Where can I see a shark?
> How big is a shark's fin?

Then ask a partner your questions. Listen to your partner's question. Find answers to your partner's questions. When you and your partner are ready, share your answers.

HOW TO ASK AND ANSWER QUESTIONS

1. When you want information, you ask questions. Start your questions with *Who, What, When, Where, Why,* or *How.*

2. When you answer questions, you give information.

> What do you know about sharks?

> They are older than dinosaurs!

USE DIFFERENT KINDS OF SENTENCES

Think about the kinds of sentences you will use to ask and answer questions. Questions ask for information. Your answers are statements, exclamations, or commands.

> What can sharks eat? (Question)
> They eat small fish. (Statement)
>
> Why is a shark's mouth so big? (Question)
> Because it has so many teeth! (Exclamation)
>
> How can I learn more about sharks? (Question)
> Read a book. (Command)

Prepare to Read

Learn Key Vocabulary

Study the Words Use the steps below.

1. Pronounce the word. Say it aloud several times. Spell it.
2. Rate your word knowledge.
3. Study the example. Tell more about the word.
4. Practice it. Make the word your own.

Key Words

attach (u-**tach**) *verb*
▸ page 18

When you **attach** something, you stick it to something else. Use tape to **attach** a poster to your wall.
Related Word: **attachment**

captive (**kap**-tiv) *adjective*
▸ page 21

A **captive** animal is not free to leave. Animals in cages are **captive**.
Related Word: **captivity**

challenge (**chal**-unj) *noun*
▸ page 22

A **challenge** is something that is hard to do. It is a **challenge** to run a race.
Related Words: **challenger, challenging**

experiment (ik-**sper**-i-ment) *verb* ▸ page 23

When you **experiment**, you try an idea. You can **experiment** in science class.
Related Word: **experimentation**

invention (in-**ven**-chun) *noun* ▸ page 18

An **invention** is something that is made for the first time. The telephone is an **invention** to let people talk.
Base Word: **invent**

record (ri-**kord**) *verb*
▸ page 18

When you **record**, you make a copy. The singer **records** her song in a studio.

scientist (**sī**-un-tist) *noun*
▸ page 19

A **scientist** studies things in nature. This **scientist** uses a microscope.
Base Word: **science**

test (test) *verb*
▸ page 20

When you **test** something, you try it. You should **test** your flashlight to see if the batteries work.

Practice the Words Make a Study Card for each Key Word. Then compare your cards with a partner.

> **record**
> **What it means:** to make a copy
> **Example:** I <u>record</u> my favorite TV show.
> **Not an example:** I watch a TV show.

Study Card

Plan, Monitor, and Ask Questions

Plan Look over the text before starting to read. Predict what you think might happen or what you might learn. Set a purpose for reading.

Monitor When you don't understand something, reread the text or read on to clarify ideas.

Ask Questions Stop and ask questions to check your understanding.

Look Into the Text

Hitching a Ride

Brightly colored fish swirled around Greg Marshall as he glided over the reef. He checked his air supply. It was almost time to end the dive. Then he saw the shark. It was swimming right toward him. The shark came closer, and closer…

Greg held his breath as the shark swam past. That's when he saw the remora on the shark. A remora is a long, skinny fish…

Plan: I think this text will be about swimming with fish.

Monitor: I'm not sure why Greg Marshall would need to check his air supply.

" When I read on, I see he is diving. The air supply must be the air left in his tank. "

Practice Together

Begin a Reading Strategies Log Use a Reading Strategies Log to show how the strategies help you understand the text. The first row shows how one strategy helped one reader. Reread the passage and add to the Log.

Text I Read	Strategy I Used	How I Used the Strategy
Page: 17 **Text:** Brightly colored fish swirled around Greg Marshall as he glided over the reef.	☑ Plan ☐ Monitor ☐ Ask Questions ☐ _____	To plan my reading, I predicted that the story would be about swimming with fishes.

Science Article

A science article is a type of nonfiction. It tells about real people, places, and events that are related to a science topic, such as an experiment or an observation.

Often, you will see **section headings** that tell what each part of the text is about. One way to preview a text is to read each heading before you read the text. You can monitor as you read to make sure you understand new or unfamiliar ideas. Ask yourself questions about ideas you do not understand to learn new information and figure out what is important in the text.

Look Into the Text

heading

Scientists Ask Questions

A whale comes out of the ocean. Then it arches through the air and disappears below. What does it do after it dives out of sight?

That's a good question. It is a problem scientists have tried to work out for years. <u>Studying animals like whales and sharks isn't easy.</u> They can dive deeper than divers in scuba gear.

▲ Remoras hitch a ride on a shark.

HITCHING
a Ride

by Rebecca L. Johnson

Brightly colored fish
swirled around Greg Marshall
as he glided over the reef. He
checked his air supply. It was almost
time to end the dive. Then he saw the
shark. It was swimming right toward him.
The shark came closer, and closer . . .

Comprehension Coach

Greg held his breath as the shark swam past. That's when he saw the remora on the shark. A remora is a long, skinny fish. It has a structure on its head that looks like a suction cup. This allows it to **attach** to other fish.

Greg could not stop thinking about what he had seen after **the dive**. He wondered if a camera could be stuck to a shark, like a remora. If he could figure out how to do that and get the camera back, he'd see the ocean **from the shark's point of view**. The "hitchhiking" camera would go where the shark went. It would **record** what the shark saw and did.

Greg's idea became an **invention** called Crittercam. Crittercam is a camera that shows us the secret lives of ocean animals. It's a way to swim with them without scaring them.

Key Vocabulary
attach *v.*, to connect
record *v.*, to film an event
invention *n.*, a new tool or product

In Other Words
the dive his swim underwater
from the shark's point of view like the shark sees it

▲ With a flip of its tail, a whale dives.

Scientists Ask Questions

A whale comes out of the ocean. Then it arches through the air and disappears below. What does it do after it dives out of sight?

That's a good question. It is a problem **scientists** have tried to work out for years. Studying animals like whales or sharks isn't easy. They can dive deeper than divers in **scuba gear**. They can swim faster than small **submarines** can travel. Scuba divers and submarines can also scare ocean animals. They might act in **unnatural** ways.

▲ Humpback whales jumping out of the ocean

Key Vocabulary
scientist *n.*, a person who studies how nature works

In Other Words
scuba gear clothing and tools made for diving
submarines underwater ships
unnatural strange

Look Into the Text

1. **Viewing** Look at the photos of the whales. Would it be easy or hard to learn about them from a boat? Why?
2. **Paraphrase** In your own words, describe Crittercam. What does it **record**?
3. **Cause and Effect** What caused Marshall to make Crittercam?

Changes in Crittercam
design, 1987–2000 ▶

1987　　　　**1988**

Marshall Invents Crittercam

Greg started building Crittercam in 1987. He began by taking apart a video camcorder. He took out all the parts he didn't need. He **got down to** the camera's basic parts. He placed those parts in a **waterproof metal tube**.

The tube was made so that water would flow smoothly around it. The smooth Crittercam would create less drag for the animal wearing it. Imagine how hard it would be to swim wearing a backpack. That's drag!

The tube also had to be strong. It would probably get bumped as an animal wearing it searched for food.

First Try

Greg made his first prototype of Crittercam. A prototype is a **model**. The first Crittercam model looked like a toy rocket. It had little fins on the sides.

Then Crittercam had to be **tested**. Greg plunged the prototype into a full bathtub to test it for leaks. He made sure that it was buoyant. That meant the camera would float. It needed to float because Greg had to get the camera back when it was done taking pictures.

The camera couldn't be too buoyant. Then it would make the animal wearing it rise in the water. Crittercam had to be like a remora. It had to be smooth and nearly weightless underwater.

Key Vocabulary

test *v.*, to try something
in order to learn about it

In Other Words

got down to saved, kept
waterproof metal tube tube that
water cannot enter
model small copy of something else

1991 **1994** **1997** **2000**

The next step was to test the prototype on an animal. What kind of animal? Something small and easy to handle. Probably not a shark! Greg chose a **captive** turtle in Central America.

Greg carefully strapped Crittercam onto the turtle's shell. The turtle slid into the water of its tank. Greg watched closely. What would the turtle do?

How the Crittercam looks today ▶

Look Into the Text

1. **Steps in a Process** What was the first step in making the Crittercam? How did Marshall **test** it?
2. **Inference** Why did Marshall use a **captive** turtle with the prototype?
3. **Compare and Contrast** How are the Crittercams from 1987 and 2000 alike and different?

The turtle swam around. Greg was happy. The turtle dived down and bobbed up to the surface. It didn't pay any attention to the camera on its back. The first big **challenge** was **overcome**.

Greg kept improving Crittercam. He got a lot of help from his team. They tested it on wild turtles in the Caribbean Sea in 1989.

Greg made harnesses to hold Crittercam in place on the turtles' shells. A harness is a type of strap. Greg put the harnesses on when the turtles came **ashore** to lay eggs. The harnesses didn't work on the first attempt. The turtles slipped out of them when they went underwater. Greg lost eight Crittercams before he made a harness that worked.

The first fish to wear Crittercam was a captive nurse shark. Greg watched the shark swim around its tank. He could tell that the camera was causing too much drag. So it was **back to the drawing board**. Crittercam got smaller and sleeker. It got better each time it was rebuilt.

◄ Crittercam on a turtle

Key Vocabulary

challenge *n.*, a task that is difficult

In Other Words

overcome finished, completed
ashore out of the water; to the beach
back to the drawing board time to try again

Attaching Crittercam

Greg later went to work for National Geographic. Other people joined him to study ocean animals using Crittercam. The Crittercam team **experimented** with everything from walruses to whales. The team learned something new from each experiment.

One **goal** was to attach Crittercam in ways that were safe for each animal. The team first tried attaching Crittercam to a shark by poking metal tags into its skin. Later the team used a **clamp**. The clamp held the camera on the shark's top fin. No poking was needed.

▲ The Crittercam team safely harnessed, or attached, the camera to a walrus.

▼ The Crittercam harnessed to a hippopotamus

Look Into the Text

1. **Conclusion** How could Marshall tell that Crittercam was causing too much drag on the nurse shark?
2. **Summarize** How did Marshall improve Crittercam after **experimenting** with it each time?

Removing Crittercam

Greg's team has also found **creative** ways to get the cameras off of animals.

Some animals hop onto ice or land to rest. People then unclip their harnesses to get the cameras.

Seals and sea lions often come out of the sea to **sun** themselves. The Crittercams glued to their fur can be easily removed. What if **traces** of glue are left behind?

They'll disappear when the animals go through a molt. That's when they naturally shed their fur and grow a brand new coat.

The team has also made a tether out of a thin strip of metal that **dissolves**. This rope can tie a camera to an animal. Crittercam pops free when the tether dissolves.

Greg hoped Crittercam would help scientists learn about ocean animals in a new way. And it certainly has! ❖

▼ Marshall attached a Crittercam to a furry sea lion with glue. The glue will disappear when the animal molts.

In Other Words
creative clever, interesting
sun warm
traces small amounts
dissolves slowly disappears in water

Crittercam Expeditions Around the World, on Land and in the Sea

Chichagof Island, Alaska: 2002, 2003
Grizzly Bear

Grizzly bears aren't as unfriendly as they look—to other bears. After the team released this grizzly with the Crittercam, it joined a mom and her two bear cubs. Surprisingly, the bears napped together and even shared meals!

Svalbard, Norway: 1997
Bearded Seal

Cameras showed three-week old bearded seal pups exploring the sea floor alone. They used their noses and flippers to dig in the sand. Scientists still need to learn more, but they think the babies may have learned this from their mom.

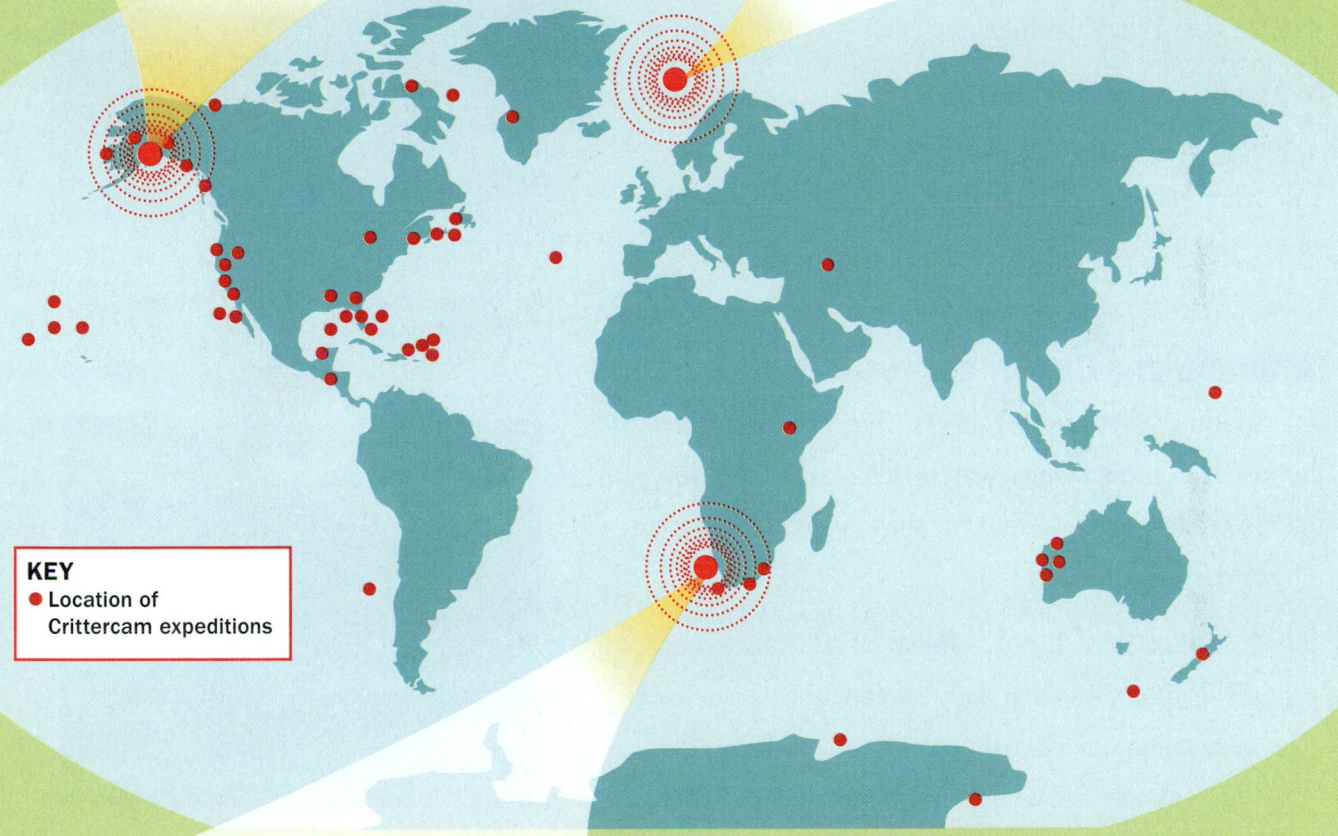

KEY
- Location of Crittercam expeditions

🔺 **Interpret the Map** What do the red dots represent?

False Bay, South Africa: 2004, 2005
Great White Shark

Crittercam found that great white sharks don't seem to mind sharing their space with other great whites. Maybe these sharks are friendlier with each other than we thought!

Look Into the Text

1. **Explain** How do the **scientists** get the cameras off the animals?
2. **Compare Details** What did Crittercam show about grizzly bears and great white sharks? What do these animals have in common?
3. **Judgments** Was Marshall's project a success? How do you know?

CRITTERCAM TO THE RESCUE

Some scientists thought Crittercam wouldn't work. Others worried that it might even harm animals. But the Crittercam team has proved that the cameras are safe. And we've learned a lot about ocean animals along the way. Here are just a couple of the things we now know about ocean animals thanks to Crittercam.

The Great White Mystery

The world of a great white shark comes into view with Crittercam. The shark's head moves slowly from side to side. What is it doing?

What Crittercam Found The shark is hunting. Exactly how the shark is hunting is an important discovery. It looks for **outlines** of fish or seals. The great white shark speeds up to attack when it spots a shape!

▲ Crittercam is tethered to the shark's dorsal, or top, fin.

A Whale of a Question

Sperm whales are fast divers. They can also travel hundreds of meters underwater. This makes them very hard to follow. It's not hard for the Crittercam! So what did the camera discover?

What Crittercam Found These whales talk to each other. They use clicks and high squeals to communicate. They also communicate using whistles and deep "huffing" sounds. The whales **groom** each other. They bump into each other hard enough to knock off pieces of loose skin.

▲ A sperm whale surfaces. The whales dive deep in the ocean to find food.

In Other Words
outlines the shapes
groom clean and brush

A Big Problem

The Hawaiian monk seal has large brown eyes and **bristly whiskers**. These features make it look a lot like a big, lazy dog. But unlike dogs, the monk seal is endangered. There are only 1,200 to 1,300 of them left in the wild.

Monk seals spend most of their time in shallow water around **coral reefs**. Laws set aside these areas for the seals. This will protect them from harmful people or activities. Yet the number of monk seals keeps shrinking.

What the Crittercam Found Seals spend a lot of time in shallow water. Scientists thought that's where seals must catch their food. The Crittercam showed this is not true. Seals do not feed in shallow water. They hunt for crab and eel in deeper water. They may also look for octopus and other big fish there.

Thanks to Crittercam, scientists now know how important deep water is to the monk seal. Now we can also help monk seals get protection in deeper waters.

The Crittercam allows Marshall and his team to follow the monk seal into deep water. ▶

In Other Words
bristly whiskers short, wiry hair on its face
coral reefs areas where coral grows

Look Into the Text

1. **Paraphrase** Tell in your own words what Crittercam showed when it **recorded** whales.
2. **Evaluating Sources** Is Crittercam a good **source** for information about monk seals? Why or why not?

Diving for Dinner

The Crittercam team is deep in the bitter cold of Antarctica. It is working here with scientists. They are studying what the world's largest penguin eats. The emperor penguin looks like he is dressed in a fancy suit for a dinner party. But no one really knows just where these penguins eat their meals. That changes when the Crittercam **catches it all on film!**

Scientists already know that emperor penguins make "yo-yo" dives when they search for food. They dive down for several dozen meters. Then they **zoom** up near the surface and back down again. Finally, they come up for air. But when were they catching their fish? Was it deep in the water? Was it near the surface? Crittercam has the answer!

What the Crittercam Found

The Crittercam team attached the cameras to the penguins using special harnesses. Each penguin wore a camera like a backpack. When the birds were ready, they dove into the sea through holes in the ice.

The team learned that the penguins dive down and then turn to look up at the ice overhead. Against the bright white of the ice, they can easily spot their favorite fish. They go up to grab a meal. Then they go down again for another look at the ice. The penguins make a few of these food-finding trips. Then the penguins pop out of the water with stomachs **bulging full of** fish.

The Crittercam team also strapped cameras pointing in the other direction on some penguins. Why? So they could find out what was happening behind the penguins. The reason for this is because scientists wondered if penguins fish on their own or in groups. What did they find out? These penguins dine alone!

▲ Crittercams on emperor penguins

In Other Words
catches it all on film records their actions
zoom go quickly
bulging full of fat with

Look Into the Text

1. **Explain** Tell how an emperor penguin finds it food.
2. **Details** What did the scientist learn by putting Crittercam on backwards on some of the penguins?

Connect Reading and Writing

CRITICAL THINKING

1. SUM IT UP Use your Reading Strategies Log to summarize the selection to a partner.

Text I read	Strategy I used	How I used the strategy
Page: 17 Text: Brightly colored fish swirled around Greg Marshall as he glided over the reef.	☑ Plan ☐ Monitor ☐ Ask Questions ☐ _____	To plan my reading, I predicted that the story would be about swimming with fish.

Reading Strategies Log

2. Describe and Explain Tell a partner about the Crittercam. Explain why the **invention** was such a **challenge** to make and use. Use details from the selection to support your ideas.

3. Speculate Why do you think Marshall **experimented** with different ways to **attach** the camera to different animals?

4. Compare Think about your survey. To what animal would you **attach** the Crittercam now? Why? Compare your responses.

READING FLUENCY

Intonation Read the passage on page 638 to a partner. Assess your fluency.

1. My tone never/sometimes/always matched what I read.

2. What I did best in my reading was _____ .

READING STRATEGY

What strategy helped you understand this selection? Tell a partner about it.

VOCABULARY REVIEW

Oral Review Read the paragraph aloud. Add the vocabulary words.

_____ wanted to know what sea animals do underwater. It was a real _____ to find out. The _____ sea animals in zoos do not live in very deep water. So the scientists _____ a camera to wild sea animals. The cameras _____ what the animals did underwater! Scientists continue to _____ and _____ new ways to use their _____ to help animals.

Written Review Imagine you are a **scientist** trying to find out how birds build their nests. What kinds of **challenges** would you have? Write a paragraph about it. Use five vocabulary words.

 **WRITE ABOUT THE** GUIDING QUESTION

Explore New Possibilities
Asking questions leads to **inventions** and new possibilities. Do you agree or disagree? Write your ideas. Reread the selection to find support for your ideas.

Connect Across the Curriculum

Use Compound Words

Academic Vocabulary
- **compound** (**kom**-pownd) *adjective*
  When something is **compound**, it is made of two or more parts.

What Are Compound Words? A **compound** word is made by combining two base words.

Follow these steps to figure out the meaning of a **compound** word.

1. Find the base words. **waterproof** = **water** + **proof**
2. Figure out the meaning of the base words.
   water = a liquid, as in ocean water
   proof = able to keep something out
3. Put the meanings of the base words together to figure out what the word means. A **waterproof** camera keeps water from getting inside.

Analyze Compound Words Figure out the meaning of each word.

1. hitchhiking, p. 18
2. backpack, p. 20
3. bathtub, p. 20
4. underwater, p. 20
5. outlines, p. 26
6. overhead, p. 28

Research/Speaking

Study an Endangered Species

HEALTH & SCIENCE

Academic Vocabulary
- **research** (rē-**surch**) *verb*
  When you **research** something, you look for information about it.

An endangered species is a type of animal or plant that may not be able to survive. With a group, use online and print resources to **research** an endangered species.

1 **Gather Information** Answer these questions:
   - Why is the animal considered an endangered species?
   - How do people try to protect and save the animal?

2 **Discuss as a Group** Imagine you are in charge of a group to help an endangered species. What would you do to help protect and save the species? Why? Use details and examples from your **research**.

Ask and Answer Questions

Role-Play With a group, act out a news conference with scientists who study animals. Some students ask questions as the reporters. Other students answer questions as scientists. Use different kinds of sentences when asking and answering questions. Trade roles.

> How can sperm whales talk?

> They use clicks and other sounds.

Write About New Ideas

Study the Models When you write, you want to keep your readers interested. Use different kinds of sentences to do this.

JUST OK

> Greg Marshall, the inventor of Crittercam, had problems attaching Crittercam to ocean animals. I wanted to know more about how Crittercam worked with other animals. I checked National Geographic's Web site to learn how it was attached to a brown bear cub. With the camera, we can see what the bear sees and does. I even saw the bear catch a fish. I wonder why people study bears. Greg Marshall thinks that when we learn about animals, we work harder to protect them.

This writer only uses statements. The reader thinks: **"This is really boring!"**

BETTER

> Greg Marshall, the inventor of Crittercam, had problems attaching Crittercam to ocean animals. How did it work with other animals? Check out National Geographic's Web site to learn about how it was attached to a brown bear cub. It was a lot of work to get Crittercam on. But with the camera, we could see what the bear sees and does. I even saw the bear catch a fish! Why do people do so much work to study bears? Greg Marshall thinks that when we learn about animals, we work harder to protect them.

This writer uses different kinds of sentences. The reader thinks: **"This is very interesting!"**

Add Sentences Think of two sentences to add to the BETTER model above. Be sure to use different kinds of sentences.

WRITE ON YOUR OWN Write about something you learned about animals. Pay attention to the kinds of sentences you use.

REMEMBER
- Use a **statement** to tell something. It ends with a period.
- Use a **question** to ask something. It ends with a question mark.
- Use an **exclamation** to express a strong feeling. It ends with an exclamation point.
- Use a **command** to tell someone what to do. It ends with a period.

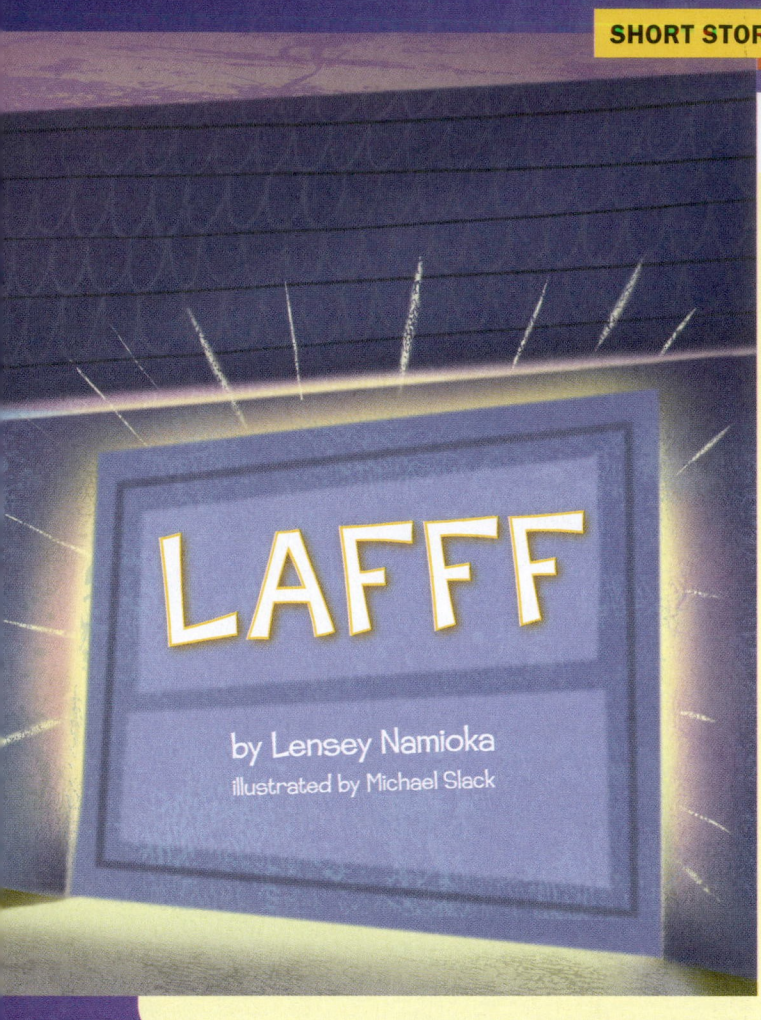

LAFFF

by Lensey Namioka

illustrated by Michael Slack

SELECTION 2 OVERVIEW

- **Build Background**

- **Language & Grammar**
  Express Ideas and Feelings
  Use Nouns

- **Prepare to Read**
  Learn Key Vocabulary
  Make Connections, Make Inferences, Visualize

- **Read and Write**
  Introduce the Genre
  Short Story
  Focus on Reading
  Make Connections, Make Inferences, Visualize
  Critical Thinking
  Reading Fluency
  Read with Expression
  Vocabulary Review
  Write About the Guiding Question

- **Connect Across the Curriculum**
  Vocabulary Study
  Use Prefixes
  Literary Analysis
  Analyze the Main Problem in Plot
  Language and Grammar
  Express Ideas and Feelings
  Writing and Grammar
  Write About Time Travel

Build Background

See Inventions Through Time

Quickwrite Time travel has fascinated people for years. But what would a time machine look like? Writers, artists, and inventors have all come up with ideas about what a time machine looks like. What's yours?

Connect

Quickwrite Imagine you invent a machine that lets you travel through time. You can visit any place in the past or in the future. Write a paragraph about where you will go. Why do you want to go to this place?

Digital Library

myNGconnect.com
View the video.

◄ The term "time machine" was first seen in H. G. Wells's book *The Time Machine*, published in 1895.

Express Ideas and Feelings

CD

Look at the picture. Where is the boy? What is he thinking? How does he feel? Listen to the song, and then sing along.

SONG

A Trip to the Past

It's amazing. It's fantastic.
I've landed in the Late Jurassic.
Dinosaurs have come to meet me.
They sniff and stare and soon will
    start to get me.

I stay mellow. I act cheerful
Even though I'm feeling fearful.
I'm afraid, but I don't show it.
I hate to think of what will happen
    once they know it.

So

"Good bye fellows. Glad to meet you.
Once I'm gone I won't forget you.
There's no more I need to see here.
Now that I know it's not too safe
    for me to be here!"

1 TRY OUT LANGUAGE
2 LEARN GRAMMAR
3 APPLY ON YOUR OWN

Use Nouns

A **noun** names a person, place, thing, or idea.

Idea	I want to travel to another **time** .
Person	My **friend** wants to travel, too.
Thing	She wants to see the first **telephone** .
Place	I want to go to the **hospital** where I was born!

- A singular noun names one idea, person, thing, place.

  EXAMPLES   time, friend, telephone, hospital

- A plural noun names more than one idea, person, thing, place.
- To make most nouns plural, add -**s**.

  EXAMPLES   time**s**, friend**s**, hospital**s**, telephone**s**

- If the noun ends in **s**, **z**, **sh**, **ch**, or **x**, add -**es**.

  EXAMPLES   class**es**, buzz**es**, dish**es**, box**es**

Say each example word. Listen to how the sound at the end is different for each plural.

Practice Together

Tell if the noun in the box names a person, place, thing, or idea. Say the plural form of the noun. Then say the sentence, and add the plural noun.

1. | friend | My _____ and I made a model of a time machine.
2. | box | We used _____ to make the main structure.
3. | junkyard | We found parts at different _____.
4. | bench | There are even three _____ to sit on.
5. | inch | Our time machine is 84 _____ tall!

Try It!

Tell if the noun in the box names a person, place, thing, or idea. Write the plural form of the noun on a card. Then write the sentence, and add the plural noun.

6. | year | We wish we could go to different _____.
7. | bench | What will parks and _____ look like in 3000?
8. | car | What will _____ use for fuel?
9. | parent | What were our _____ like when they were young?
10. | dream | We will never know, but we have our _____!

▲ We all have different ideas about how a time machine would look.

Take a Trip in Time

EXPRESS IDEAS AND FEELINGS

Imagine that you are stepping into a time machine. Where will you go?
Tell a partner about your trip. Tell how you feel and why you feel that way.

> I see a lot of buttons and handles. I feel nervous! Which button do I push first?

HOW TO EXPRESS IDEAS AND FEELINGS

1. To express ideas, tell what you see.
2. To express feelings, tell how you feel. Tell why.

To get started, make a storyboard. Show the place you go. Show the people you meet. Show how you feel. Use your drawing to tell a partner about your trip.

USE SPECIFIC NOUNS

When you tell your story, give details to express your ideas and feelings. Use nouns that give your partner a clear picture of the people, places, things, or ideas that you tell about.

NOT CLEAR			CLEAR
person	► family	► parent	► my mom
place	► house	► room	► family room
thing	► something in a box	► birthday gift	► skateboard
idea	► celebration	► party	► birthday party

Not Precise: I travel to the future to see a celebration.
Someone in my family gives me something in a box.
The party is in our house.

Precise: I travel to the future to see my birthday party.
My mom gives me a skateboard.
The party is in our family room.

Prepare to Read

Learn Key Vocabulary

Study the Words Use the steps below.

1. Pronounce the word. Say it aloud several times. Spell it.
2. Rate your word knowledge.
3. Study the example. Tell more about the word.
4. Practice it. Make the word your own.

Key Words

backward (bak-**wurd**)
adverb ▶ page 42

To move **backward** is to move toward the back. You can move some chess pieces **backward**.
Antonym: **forward**

concentrate (**kon**-sun-trāt) *verb* ▶ page 52

When you **concentrate**, you think about what you do. You have to **concentrate** when you read.
Synonym: **think**

convince (kun-**vints**) *verb* ▶ page 44

When you **convince** someone, you cause the person to agree with you. The woman tries to **convince** her husband that she has a good idea.

destination (des-tu-**nā**-shun) *noun* ▶ page 49

A **destination** is a place you plan to go. The **destination** for our summer vacation is New York City.

forward (**for**-wurd) *adverb* ▶ page 42

To move **forward** is to move ahead or to the front. A sign can tell you to move **forward**.
Antonym: **backward**

future (**fyū**-chur) *noun* ▶ page 47

The **future** is a time that has not yet happened. Tomorrow is in the **future**.
Antonym: **past**

genius (**jēn**-yus) *noun* ▶ page 40

A **genius** is someone who is very smart. A **genius** named Thomas Edison invented the lightbulb.

machine (mu-**shēn**) *noun* ▶ page 41

A **machine** is a tool made of parts that does some kind of work. You can make clothes with a sewing **machine**.

Practice the Words Make a Vocabulary Chart for the Key Words.

Word	backward
Synonym	reverse
Definition	to move toward the back
Sentence or Picture	Mom drives the car backward to park.

Vocabulary Chart

Make Connections, Make Inferences, and Visualize

Make Connections As you read, connect the text to your own experiences, to other texts you have read, and to your knowledge of the world.

Make Inferences Sometimes information in a text is suggested rather than stated. You can figure out what the author means by combining clues from the text with what you already know.

Visualize Use details from the text to help you create mental images. Words that describe how things look, smell, sound, taste, or feel can help you visualize people, places and events.

Look Into the Text

Inference:
The author wants me to know that movies make geniuses look a certain way.

In movies, geniuses have frizzy white hair, right? They wear thick glasses and have names like Dr. Zweistein.

Peter Lu didn't have frizzy white hair. He had straight hair, as black as licorice. He didn't wear thick glasses, either, since his vision was normal.

" **Based on what I read and what I know, I think the speaker is suggesting that Peter Lu is a genius.** "

Practice Together

Begin a Reading Strategies Log Use a Reading Strategies Log to show how the strategies help you understand the text. The first row shows how one strategy helped one reader. Reread the passage and add to the Log.

Text I Read	Strategy I Used	How I Used the Strategy
Page: 40 **Text:** frizzy white hair, thick glasses	☐ **Make Connections** ☐ **Make Inferences** ☑ **Visualize** ☐ _____	I pictured a genius as an older person whose hair would be white and frizzy. It helps me see how Peter isn't the typical genius.

Reading Strategies Log

Short Story

A short story is a type of fiction. Fiction is about people, things, and events that are not real. The people or animals in a story are called characters. The characters act out the events in the story.

You can use sensory details to visualize the characters, setting, or events of a story. Picturing the details can make it easier for you to make connections to what you already know or have read before. Visualizing may also help you infer information that the author does not directly tell you.

Look Into the Text

Then on Halloween he surprised us all. As I went down the block trick-or-treating, dressed as a zucchini in my green sweats, I heard a strange, deep voice behind me say, "How do you do?"

I yelped and turned around. Peter was wearing a long black Chinese gown with slits in the sides. On his head he had a little round cap, and down each side of his mouth drooped a thin long mustache.

LAFFF

by Lensey Namioka

illustrated by Michael Slack

In movies, **geniuses** have frizzy white hair, right? They wear thick glasses and have names like Dr. Zweistein.

Peter Lu didn't have frizzy white hair. He had straight hair, as black as licorice. He didn't wear thick glasses, either, since his vision was normal.

Peter's family, like ours, had **immigrated** from China, but they had settled here first. When we moved into a house just two doors down from the Lus, they gave us some good advice on how to **get along** in America. I went to the same school as Peter, and we walked to the school bus together every morning. Like many Chinese parents, mine made sure that I worked very hard in school.

In spite of all I could do, my grades were nothing compared to Peter's. He was **at the top** in all his classes. We walked to the school bus without talking because I was

Key Vocabulary
genius *n.*, a person who is very smart

In Other Words
immigrated moved here
get along live; be successful
at the top very successful

a little scared of him. Besides, he was always deep in thought.

Peter didn't have any friends. Most of the kids thought he was a nerd because they saw his head always buried in books. I didn't think he even tried to join the rest of us or cared what the others thought of him.

Then on Halloween he surprised us all. As I went down the block trick-or-treating, dressed as a zucchini in my green sweats, I heard a strange, deep voice behind me say, "How do you do?"

I **yelped** and turned around. Peter was wearing a long black Chinese gown with slits in the sides. On his head he had a little round cap, and down each side of his mouth drooped a thin long mustache.

"I am Dr. Lu Manchu, the **mad** scientist," he announced, putting his hands in his sleeves and bowing.

He smiled when he saw me staring at his costume. It was a scary smile, somehow.

Some of the other kids came up, and when they saw Peter, they were impressed. "Hey, neat!" said one boy.

I hadn't expected Peter to put on a costume and go trick-or-treating like a normal kid. So maybe he did want to join the others after all—at least some of the time. After that night he wasn't a nerd anymore. He was Dr. Lu Manchu. Even some of the teachers began to call him that.

When we became too old for trick-or-treating, Peter was still Dr. Lu Manchu. The rumor was that he was working on a fantastic **machine** in his parents' garage. But nobody had any idea what it was.

One evening, as I was coming home from a baby-sitting job, I cut across the Lus' backyard. Passing their garage, I saw through a little window that the light was on. **My curiosity got the better of me**, and I peeked in.

In Other Words
yelped yelled in surprise
mad crazy, evil
My curiosity got the better of me I really wanted to know what was happening

I saw a booth that looked like a **shower stall**. A stool stood in the middle of the stall, and hanging over the stool was something that looked like a great big showerhead.

Suddenly a deep voice behind me said, "Good evening, Angela." Peter bowed and smiled his scary smile. He didn't have his costume on, and he didn't have the long, droopy mustache. But he was Dr. Lu Manchu.

"What are you doing?" I squeaked.

Still in his strange, deep voice, Peter said, "What are *you* doing? After all, this is my garage."

"I was just cutting across your yard to get home. Your parents never complained before."

"I thought you were spying on me," said Peter. "I thought you wanted to know about

I saw a booth that looked like a shower stall.

my machine." He **hissed** when he said the word *machine*.

Honestly, he was beginning to frighten me. "What machine?" I demanded. "You mean this shower-stall thing?"

He **drew himself up** and narrowed his eyes, making them into thin slits. "This is my time machine!"

I **goggled** at him. "You mean . . . you mean . . . this machine can send you **forward** and **backward** in time?"

"Well, actually, I can only send things forward in time," admitted Peter, speaking in his normal voice again. "That's why I'm calling the machine LAFFF. It stands for Lu's **Artifact** For Fast Forward."

Key Vocabulary
forward *adv.*, toward the front
backward *adv.*, toward the back

In Other Words
shower stall place to stand to take a shower
hissed sounded scary
drew himself up stood up straight
goggled looked
Artifact Object, Tool

Look Into the Text

1. **Character's Viewpoint** Does Angela think Peter is a <mark>genius</mark>? How do you know?
2. **Explain** Why does Peter name the machine LAFFF?
3. **Word Choice** Which words or phrases does the author use to make Peter sound scary?

Of course Peter always won first prize at the annual statewide science fair. But that's **a long way from** making a time machine. Minus his mustache and long Chinese gown, he was Peter Lu.

"I don't believe it!" I said. "I bet LAFFF is only **good for a laugh**."

"Okay, Angela. I'll show you!" hissed Peter.

He sat down on the stool and twisted a dial. I heard some bleeps, cheeps, and gurgles. Peter disappeared.

He must have done it with mirrors. I looked around the garage. I peeked under the tool bench. There was no sign of him.

"Okay, I give up," I told him. "It's a good trick, Peter. You can come out now."

Bleep, *cheep*, and *gurgle* went the machine, and there was Peter, sitting on the stool. He held a red rose in his hand. "What do you think of that?"

I blinked. "So you produced a flower. Maybe you had it under the stool."

"Roses bloom in June, right?" he demanded.

That was true. And this was December.

"I sent myself forward in time to June when the flowers were blooming," said Peter. "And I picked the rose from our yard. Convinced, Angela?"

It was **too hard to swallow**. "You said you couldn't send things back in time," I objected. "So how did you bring the rose back?"

But even as I spoke I saw that his hands were empty. The rose was gone.

Key Vocabulary
convince *v.*, to prove something to someone

In Other Words
a long way from not as hard as
good for a laugh a joke
too hard to swallow unbelievable

"That's one of the problems with the machine," said Peter. "When I send myself forward, I can't seem to stay there for long. I **snap back** to my own time after only a minute. Anything I bring with me snaps back to its own time, too. So my rose has gone back to this June."

I was finally convinced, and I began to see **possibilities**. "Wow, just think: If I don't want to do the dishes, I can send myself forward to the time when the dishes are already done."

"That won't do you much good," said Peter. "You'd soon pop back to the time when the dishes were still dirty."

In Other Words
snap back return
possibilities how I could use
 LAFFF to get what I wanted

Too bad. "There must be something your machine is good for," I said. Then I had another idea. "Hey, you can bring me back a piece of fudge from the **future**, and I can eat it twice: Once now, and again in the future."

"Yes, but the fudge wouldn't stay in your stomach," said Peter. "It would go back to the future."

"That's even better!" I said. "I can enjoy eating the fudge over and over again without getting fat!"

It was late, and I had to go home before my parents started to worry. Before I left, Peter said, "Look, Angela, there's still a lot of work to do on LAFFF. Please don't tell anybody about the machine until I've got it right."

A few days later I asked him how he was doing.

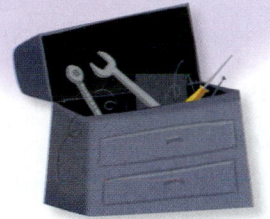

"There must be something your machine is good for," I said.

"I can stay in the future time a bit longer now," he said. "Once I got it up to four minutes."

"Is that enough time to bring me back some fudge from the future?" I asked.

"We don't keep many sweets around the house," he said. "But I'll see what I can do."

A few minutes later, he came back with a spring roll for me. "My mother was frying these in the kitchen, and I **snatched** one while she wasn't looking."

I bit into the hot, crunchy spring roll, but before I finished chewing, it disappeared. The taste of soy sauce, green onions, and bean sprouts stayed a little longer in my mouth, though.

It was fun to play around with LAFFF, but it wasn't really useful. I didn't know what a great help it would turn out to be.

Key Vocabulary
future *n.*, a time that has not yet happened

In Other Words
snatched quickly took

Look Into the Text

1. **Summarize** How does Peter **convince** Angela that LAFFF works?
2. **Describe** Tell about the problems Peter has with the **machine**.
3. **Conclusion and Evidence** Peter and Angela want to be friends. Give two details that support this.

Predict
**Angela has an exciting idea for using LAFFF.
Will Peter agree to it?**

Every year our school held a writing contest, and the winning story for each grade got printed in our school magazine. I wanted desperately to win. I worked awfully hard in school, but my parents still thought I could do better.

Winning the writing contest would show my parents that I was really good in something. I love writing stories, and I have lots of ideas. But when I actually write them down, my stories never turn out as good as I thought. I just can't seem to find the right words, because English isn't my first language.

I got **an honorable mention** last year, but it wasn't the same as winning and showing my parents my name, Angela Tang, printed in the school magazine.

The **deadline for** the contest was getting close, and I had a pile of stories written, but none of them looked like a winner.

Then, the day before the deadline, *boing,* **a brilliant idea hit me**.

I thought of Peter and his LAFFF machine. I rushed over to the Lus' garage and, just as I had hoped, Peter was there, tinkering with his machine.

"I've got this idea for winning the story contest," I told him breathlessly. "You see, to be certain of winning, I have to write the story that would be the winner."

"That's obvious," Peter said dryly. "In fact, you're **going around in a circle**."

"Wait, listen!" I said. "I want to use LAFFF and go forward to the time when the next issue of the school magazine is out. Then I can read the winning story."

After a moment Peter nodded. "I see. You plan to write down the winning story after you've read it and then send it in to the contest."

In Other Words
an honorable mention a special
  award
deadline for last day to enter
a brilliant idea hit me I thought
  of a great idea
going around in a circle not
  making sense

I nodded eagerly. "The story would *have* to win, because it's the winner!"

Peter began to look interested. "I've got LAFFF to the point where I can stay in the future for seven minutes now. Will that be long enough for you?"

"I'll just have to work quickly," I said.

Peter smiled. It wasn't his scary Lu Manchu smile, but a nice smile. He was getting as excited as I was. "Okay, Angela. **Let's go for it.**"

He led me to the stool. "What's your **destination**?" he asked. "I mean, when's your destination?"

Suddenly I was nervous. I told myself that Peter had made many time trips, and he looked perfectly healthy.

Why not? What have I got to lose—except time?

I took in a deep breath. "I want to go forward three weeks in time." By then I'd have a copy of the new school magazine in my room.

"Ready, Angela?" asked Peter.

"As ready as I'll ever be," I whispered. *Bleep*, *cheep*, and *gurgle*. Suddenly Peter disappeared.

What went wrong? Did Peter get sent by mistake, instead of me?

Then I realized what had happened. Three weeks later in time, Peter might be somewhere else. **No wonder** I couldn't see him.

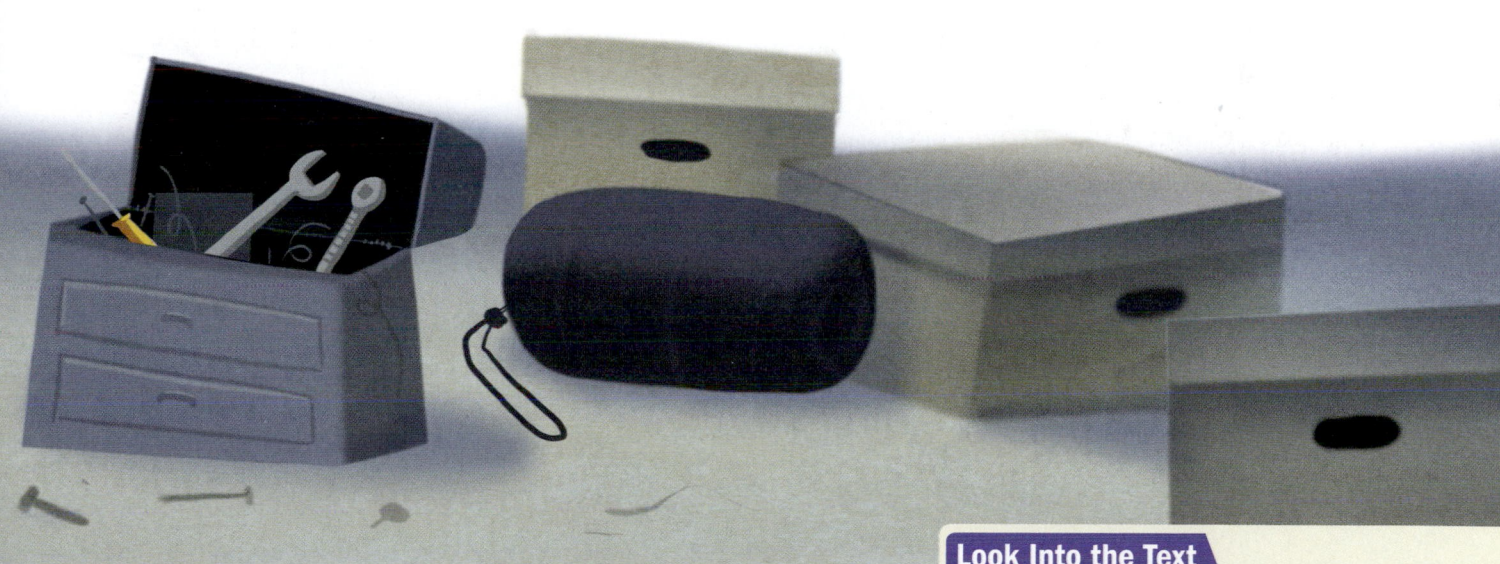

Key Vocabulary
destination *n.*, the place a person is going to or traveling to

In Other Words
Let's go for it. Let's use LAFFF to send you to the future.
No wonder That was why

Look Into the Text

1. **Explain** What is Angela's plan?
2. **Confirm Prediction** Did Peter agree to Angela's plan? Was your prediction correct? Explain.
3. **Character** Angela wants to win the contest to show her parents she is good at something. What does this show about her?

There was no time to be lost. Rushing out of Peter's garage, I ran over to our house and entered through the back door.

Mother was in the kitchen. When she saw me, she stared. "Angela! I thought you were upstairs taking a shower!"

"Sorry!" I panted. "No time to talk!"

I dashed up to my room. Then I suddenly had a strange idea. What if I met *myself* in my room?

Argh! It was a spooky thought.

There was nobody in my room. Where was I? I mean, where was the I of three weeks later?

Wait. Mother had just said she thought I was taking a shower. Down the hall, I could hear the water running in the bathroom.

Okay. That meant I wouldn't run into me for a while.

I went to the shelf above my desk and frantically **pawed through the junk** piled there. I found it! I found the latest issue of the school magazine, the one with the winning stories printed in it.

How much time had passed? Better hurry.

The shower had stopped running. This meant the other me was out of the bathroom. Have to get out of here!

Too late. Just as I started down the stairs, I heard Mother talking again. "Angela! A minute ago you were all dressed! Now you're in your robe again and your hair's all wet! I don't understand."

In Other Words
There was no time to be lost.
 I had to hurry.
Argh! Oh no!
pawed through the junk looked
 through my things

I shivered. It was scary, listening to Mother talking to myself downstairs. I heard my other self answering something, then the sound of her—my—steps coming up the stairs. In a panic, I **dodged** into the spare room and closed the door.

I heard the steps—my steps—go past and into my room.

The minute I heard the door of my room close, I rushed out and down the stairs.

Mother was standing at the front of the stairs. When she saw me, **her mouth dropped**. "But . . . but . . . just a minute ago you were in your robe and your hair was all wet!"

"See you later, Mother," I panted. And I ran.

Behind me I heard Mother muttering, **"I'm going mad!"**

I didn't stop and try to explain. I might go mad, too.

It would be great if I could just keep the magazine with me. But, like the spring roll, it would get carried back to its own time after a few minutes. So the next best thing was to read the magazine as fast as I could.

It was hard to run and flip through the magazine at the same time. But I made it back to Peter's garage and plopped down on the stool.

At last I found the story: the story that had won the contest in our grade. I started to read.

In Other Words
dodged ran
her mouth dropped she was very surprised
"I'm going mad!" "I feel crazy!"

Language Background
Some English word meanings change over time. For example, *mad* in Old English means *crazy* or *silly*. Old English was the language used in England before the year 1100. In modern American English, *mad* usually means *angry*.

Suddenly I heard *bleep*, *cheep*, and *gurgle*, and **Peter loomed up** in front of me. I was back in my original time again.

But I still had the magazine! Now I had to read the story before the magazine popped back to the future. It was hard to <mark>concentrate</mark> with Peter jumping up and down impatiently, so different from his usual calm, collected self.

I read a few paragraphs, and I was beginning to see **how the story would shape up**. But before I got any further, the magazine disappeared from my hand. So I didn't finish reading the story. I didn't reach the end, where the name of the winning writer was printed.

That night I stayed up very late to write down what I remembered of the story. It had a neat plot, and I could see why it was the winner.

I hadn't read the entire story, so I had to make up the ending myself. But that was okay, since I knew how it should come out.

The winners of the writing contest would be announced at the school assembly on Friday. After we had filed into the assembly hall and sat down, the principal gave a speech. I tried not to **fidget** while he explained about the contest.

Suddenly I was struck by a dreadful thought. Somebody in my class had written the winning story, the one I had copied.

Key Vocabulary
<mark>concentrate</mark> *v.*, to think very hard

In Other Words
Peter loomed up I could see Peter standing
how the story would shape up what the story would be about
fidget move around

Wouldn't that person be declared the winner, instead of me?

The principal started announcing the winners. **I chewed my knuckles in an agony of suspense**, as I waited to see who would be announced as the winner in my class. Slowly, the principal began with the lowest grade. Each winner walked **in slow motion** to the stage, while the principal slowly explained why the story was good.

At last, at last, he came to our grade. "The winner is . . ."

Look Into the Text

1. **Plot** Tell what happens when Angela travels to the **future**.
2. **Character's Viewpoint** How does Peter feel about Angela cheating to win a contest? How can you tell?

He stopped, slowly got out his handkerchief, and slowly blew his nose. Then he cleared his throat. "The winning story is 'Around and Around,' by Angela Tang."

I sat like a stone, unable to move. Peter nudged me. "Go on, Angela! They're waiting for you."

I got up and walked up to the stage in a daze. The principal's voice seemed to be coming from far, far away as he told the audience that I had written a science fiction story about time travel.

The winners each got a notebook **bound in imitation leather** for writing more stories. Inside the cover of the notebook was a ballpoint pen. But the best prize was having my story in the school magazine with my name printed at the end.

Then why didn't I feel good about winning?

After the assembly, the kids in our class crowded around to congratulate me. Peter **formally** shook my hand. "Good work, Angela," he said, and winked at me.

That didn't make me feel any better. I hadn't won the contest fairly. Instead of writing the story myself, I had copied it from the school magazine.

That meant someone in our class—one of the kids here—had actually written the story. Who was it?

My heart was **knocking against my ribs** as I stood there and waited for someone to complain that I had stolen his story.

Nobody did.

As we were riding the school bus home, Peter looked at me. "You don't seem very happy about winning the contest, Angela."

"No, I'm not," I mumbled. "I feel just awful."

In Other Words
bound in imitation leather that looked like it was covered in leather
formally politely
knocking against my ribs beating very fast

"Tell you what," suggested Peter. "Come over to my house and we'll discuss it."

"What is there to discuss?" I asked glumly. "I won the contest because I cheated."

"Come on over, anyway. My mother bought a fresh package of humbow in Chinatown."

I couldn't turn down that invitation. Humbow, a roll stuffed with barbecued pork, is my favorite snack.

Peter's mother came into the kitchen while we were munching, and he told her about the contest.

Mrs. Lu looked pleased. "I'm very glad, Angela. You have a terrific imagination, and you deserve to win."

"I like Angela's stories," said Peter. "They're original."

It was the first **compliment he had ever paid me**, and I felt my face turning red.

After Mrs. Lu left us, Peter and I each had another humbow. But I was still miserable. "I wish I had never started this. I feel like such a jerk."

Peter looked at me, and I swear he was enjoying himself. "If you stole another student's story, why didn't that person complain?"

"I don't know!" I wailed.

"Think!" said Peter. "You're smart, Angela. Come on, **figure it out**!"

In Other Words
compliment he had ever paid me nice thing he had ever said about me
figure it out use the clues to tell what really happened

Me, smart? I was so overcome to hear myself called smart by a genius like Peter that I just stared at him.

He had to repeat himself. "Figure it out, Angela!"

I tried to concentrate. Why was Peter looking so amused? **The light finally dawned.** "Got it," I said slowly. "*I'm* the one who wrote the story."

"The winning story is your own, Angela, because that's the one that won."

My head began to go around and around. "But where did the original idea for the story come from?"

"What made the plot so good?" asked Peter. His voice sounded unsteady.

"Well, in my story, my character used a time machine to go forward in time . . ."

"Okay, whose idea was it to use a time machine?"

"It was mine," I said slowly. I remembered the moment when the idea had hit me with a *boing.*

"So you s-stole f-from yourself!" sputtered Peter. He started to roar with laughter. I had never seen him break down like that. At this rate, he might **wind up being** human.

When he could talk again, he asked me to read my story to him.

I began. "'In movies, geniuses have frizzy white hair, right? They wear thick glasses and have names like Dr. Zweistein . . .'" ❖

About the Author

Lensey Namioka visiting Beijing, China, 1992.

Although **Lensey Namioka** (1929–) studied to be a mathematician, telling stories was what she enjoyed doing the most. When she was eight years old, she wrote her first story about a woman warrior. Many of her stories describe experiences of children and young adults learning new languages and moving to new countries.

In Other Words

The light finally dawned. I finally understood.

My head began to go around and around. I felt confused.

wind up being start to seem

Look Into the Text

1. **Confirm Prediction** Was your prediction correct? Why doesn't Angela admit she cheated?

2. **Inference** Why does Peter "roar with laughter"?

Connect Reading and Writing

Vocabulary
backward
concentrated
convinced
destination
forward
future
genius
machine

CRITICAL THINKING

1. SUM IT UP Have students share their Reading Strategies Log with a partner and use it to summarize the story.

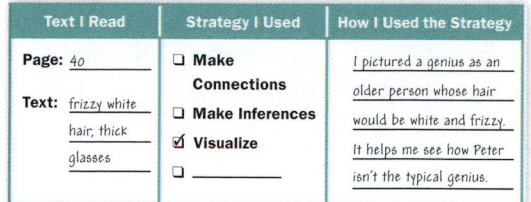

Text I Read	Strategy I Used	How I Used the Strategy
Page: 40 Text: frizzy white hair, thick glasses	☐ Make Connections ☐ Make Inferences ☑ Visualize ☐ _____	I pictured a genius as an older person whose hair would be white and frizzy. It helps me see how Peter isn't the typical genius.

Reading Strategies Log

2. Draw Conclusions Why does Peter continue to act like the mad **genius** Dr. Lu Manchu after Halloween? How do others react?

3. Explain Why did Angela have to **concentrate** so hard to read the story she took from the **future**?

4. Make Judgments Think about what Angela did to win the contest. Are you **convinced** that it was fair? Why or why not?

READING FLUENCY

Expression Read the passage on page 639 to a partner. Assess your fluency.

1. My voice never/sometimes/always matched what I read.

2. What I did best in my reading was _____ .

READING STRATEGY

What strategy helped you understand this selection? Tell a partner about it.

VOCABULARY REVIEW

Oral Review Read the paragraph aloud. Add the vocabulary words.

I dreamed I saw an ad in a magazine. It asked questions such as: *Are you a scientific* _____? *Can you invent a* _____ *to take you* _____ *and* _____ *in time?* When I woke up, I _____ myself to try it! My time machine would go to a planet in 2090. My _____ was Mars. But no matter how hard I _____, I could not think of a way to travel into the _____ . So I just went back to sleep!

Written Review Imagine you could go **forward** or **backward** in time. Write a postcard to a friend about your **destination** . Use five vocabulary words.

WRITE ABOUT THE GUIDING QUESTION

Explore the Imagination
Think about this question: How could a time **machine** change the world or the **future**? Reread the selection to add to your own ideas.

Connect Across the Curriculum

Vocabulary Study

Use Prefixes

Prefix	Meaning
en-	to give
im-	into, inside, not
un-	not

Academic Vocabulary
- **analyze** (a-nu-līz) *verb*
  When you **analyze** something, you study it closely.

What Are Prefixes? A **prefix** is a word part that is added to the beginning of a word. It changes the meaning of the base word.

1. **Analyze** the meaning of each word part.
2. Combine the meaning of each part to figure out the word meaning.

> The prefix *dis-* means "the opposite of." So, disappear means "the opposite of appear."

Figure Out Word Meanings Work with a partner. Find each word below in the selection. Then use the two steps and the chart to figure out the meaning.

1. immigrated, p. 40   2. enjoy, p. 47   3. unable, p. 54   4. unsteady, p. 56

Literary Analysis

Analyze the Main Problem in Plot

Academic Vocabulary
- **solve** (solv) *verb*
  When you **solve** a problem, you find the answer to it.

Many stories tell about a problem that a character needs to **solve**. Often the character's actions affect or change the plot. Think about the problem in the text below. How do Peter's actions affect the plot and **solve** the problem?

> Most people thought Peter didn't care about having friends, but he did care. He wanted people to know that he was just like everyone else.
>
> On Halloween he dressed up as a mad scientist. The other kids were surprised to see him dressed up, and they were very impressed. They realized that he did things like normal kids did.

Identify Problem and Solution You can make a Problem-Solution Chart to analyze how a character's actions shape the plot. Compare it to the text.

What Is the Problem?	How does the character solve it?
Peter wants people to know that he's a normal kid.	He dresses up in a cool Halloween costume to impress everyone.

Make a Problem-Solution Chart Make a chart like the one above. Use it to tell a partner about Angela's problem and how her actions help **solve** it.

Express Ideas and Feelings

Role-Play With a partner, role-play the characters in "LAFFF." Take turns telling what you see, how you feel, and why you feel this way. Use words, facial expressions, and body movements to show how you feel. Use nouns to make your ideas clear. Remember to use a singular noun for "one" and a plural noun for "more than one." Trade roles.

> Peter showed me a rose from the future! I was shocked!

Write About Time Travel

Study the Models To make your writing interesting, use nouns that say exactly what you mean. Use the correct form of singular and plural nouns to make your ideas clear.

JUST OK

> I saw a <u>thing</u> about time travel to the past. A <u>man</u> made a car that took him to a different time. A <u>person</u> used the car to go to the past. He saw <u>stuff</u> and <u>places</u>. He borrowed some <u>clothes</u>.

These <u>nouns</u> are not specific. The reader thinks: "What 'thing' did the writer see? Who is the 'person' who used the car? What 'stuff' did he see?"

BETTER

> I saw a <u>science fiction movie</u> about time travel to the past. An <u>inventor</u> made a car that took him to <u>1955</u>. A <u>teenager</u> used the car to go to the past. He saw a <u>Ford Thunderbird convertible</u> and an <u>ice cream parlor</u>. He borrowed a <u>Letterman jacket</u>.

The writer made the passage better with specific <u>nouns</u>. The reader will have a better picture.

Add Sentences On a separate piece of paper, write two more sentences to add to the BETTER paragraph. Use the correct forms of singular and plural nouns.

WRITE ON YOUR OWN Write about what you might see if you traveled to the past. Use specific and clear nouns. Use a singular noun for *one* and a plural noun for *more than one*.

REMEMBER
- To make most nouns plural, add **-s**.
- If the noun ends in *s, z, sh, ch,* or *x,* add **-es**.

▲ What would you see if you traveled to the past?

Kids ARE INVENTORS, TOO

by Arlene Erlbach

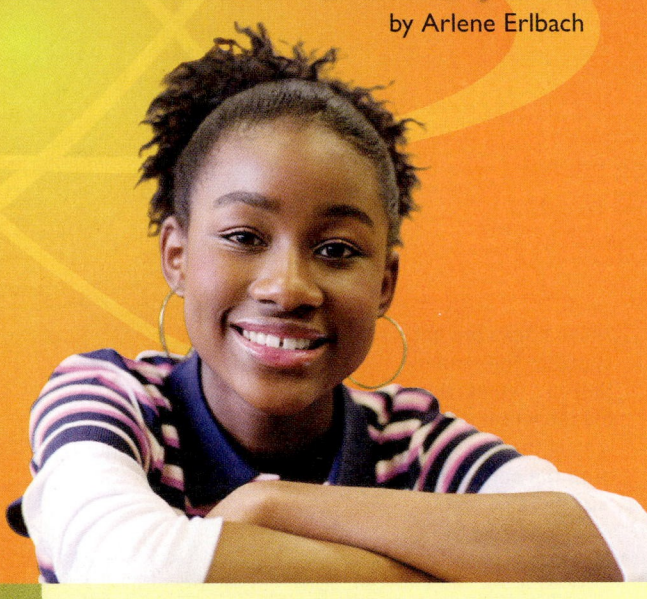

Build Background

See Where Great Ideas Come From

Pair-Share An inventor often invents to solve a problem. They come up with great ideas that help people do things better. Anybody can be an inventor, even kids. All you need is imagination.

Connect

Think–Pair–Share Complete this sentence: A problem I want to solve is _____.

Share your idea with a partner. Brainstorm solutions to the problems.

Digital Library

myNGconnect.com
🌐 View the images.

◀ Young inventor Rikio Kato invented a device that lets kids wheel their backpacks from place to place.

Language & Grammar

Give Information

CD

Look at the photo. What is the student doing? Listen to the student's words. Then listen for more information.

PICTURE PROMPT

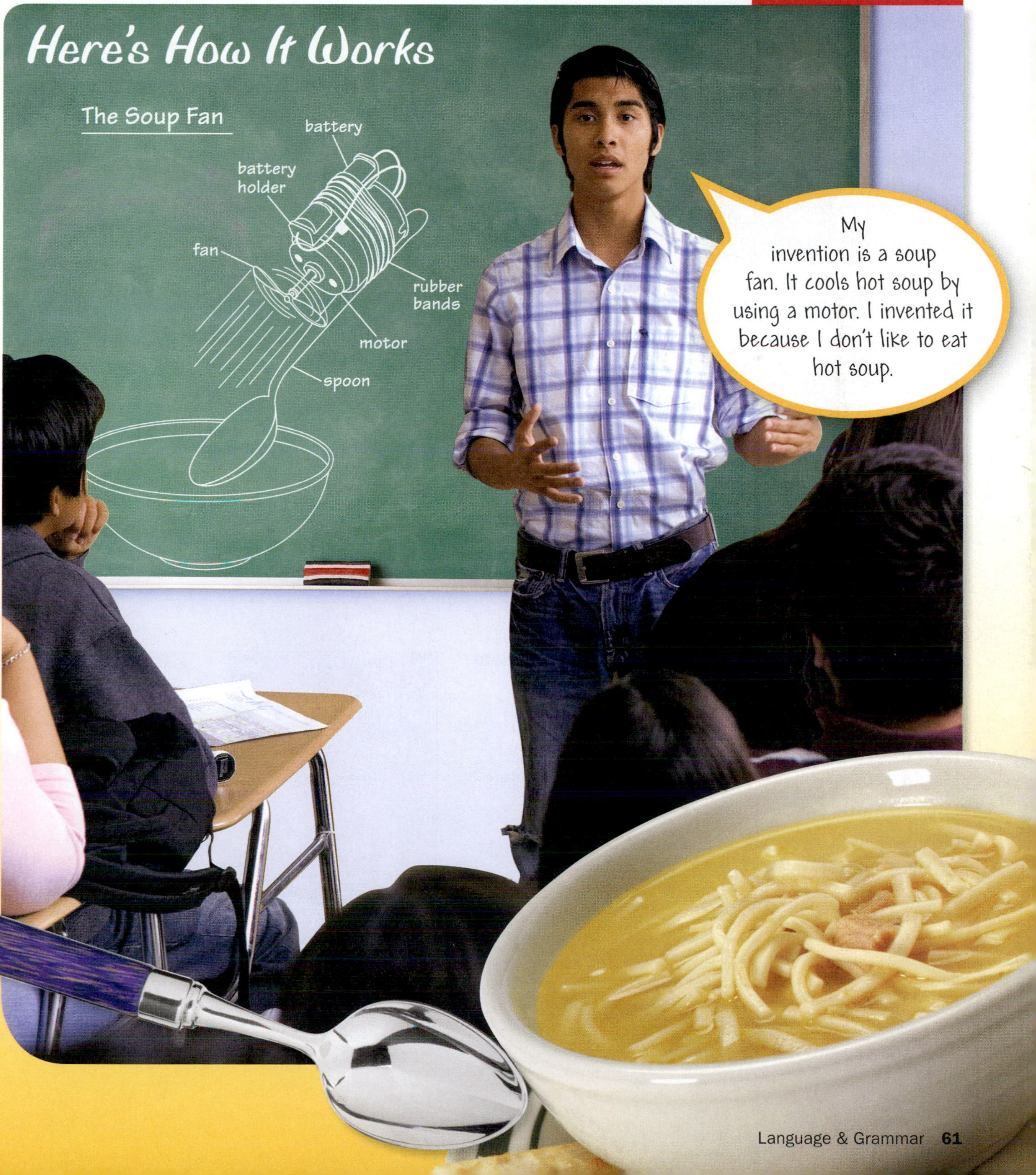

Here's How It Works

The Soup Fan

battery

battery holder

fan

rubber bands

motor

spoon

> My invention is a soup fan. It cools hot soup by using a motor. I invented it because I don't like to eat hot soup.

Use Complete Sentences

A complete sentence expresses a complete thought. It has two parts:
the **subject** and a **predicate**.

| Subject | Predicate |

Inventors solve problems.

To find the parts in most sentences, ask yourself:

1. Whom or what is the sentence about? Your answer is the **subject**.

2. What does the subject do? Your answer is the **predicate**.

Sentence	Whom or What?	What Does the Subject Do?
My friend won first prize at the science fair.	My friend	won first prize.

Incorrect: Won first prize at the science fair!

Correct: My friend won first prize at the science fair!

Practice Together

Match each subject to a predicate. Say the new sentence.

1. My invention   helps students.

2. Students   needs wheels.

3. A textbook   hurt their shoulders.

4. The backpacks   weighs a lot!

5. The backpack   carry a lot of books in their backpacks.

Try It!

Match each subject to a predicate. Write the complete
sentences on a piece of paper.

6. An invention   sketch their ideas.

7. Inventors   solves a problem.

8. A sketch   make people's lives easier!

9. Then the   builds the invention.
    inventor   shows what the invention

10. Inventions   looks like.

▲ The inventor plans her invention.

Tell About an Invention

GIVE INFORMATION

Every object around you was invented. What inventions help you? What inventions are fun? Think of an invention that is important to you, and tell a partner about it.

- To get started, make a list of information about the invention.

> ### Cell Phone
> - can fit in pocket or purse
> - lets families and friends talk in many places
> - can send text messages
> - can sometimes take pictures

- Then come up with your main point.

> Cell phones make our lives easier.

When you tell your partner about the invention, be sure to include facts and details in your description.

HOW TO GIVE INFORMATION

1. Tell your main point.
2. Give facts or details to tell more.

> A cell phone makes life easier. You can always call someone no matter where you are.

USE COMPLETE SENTENCES

Use a **subject** to tell who or what the sentence is about.

EXAMPLES   **A cell phone** fits in my pocket.

My mom can call me.

Use a **predicate** to tell what the invention does.

EXAMPLE   A cell phone **sends text messages**.

Prepare to Read

Learn Key Vocabulary

Study the Words Use the steps below.

1. Pronounce the word. Say it aloud several times. Spell it.
2. Rate your word knowledge.
3. Study the example. Tell more about the word.
4. Practice it. Make the word your own.

Key Words

ability (u-bil-ut-ē) *noun*
▶ page 73

If you have **ability**, you have the skill to do something. This gymnast has the **ability** to balance.
Synonyms: **skill, talent**
Antonym: **inability**

design (di-zīn) *verb*
▶ page 71

When you **design** something, you plan how to make it or do it. People **design** things by making drawings first.

device (di-vīs) *noun*
▶ page 71

A **device** is a tool. A remote control is a **device** that changes channels on a TV.
Synonyms: **gadget, equipment**

exist (ig-zist) *verb*
▶ page 74

To **exist** means to be real. Most people don't believe that ghosts **exist**.
Related Word: **existence**

model (mod-ul) *noun*
▶ page 71

A **model** is a copy of something. He builds **models** of motorcycles as a hobby.

problem (prah-blum) *noun*
▶ page 68

A **problem** is something to be figured out. He thought about the **problem** before he answered it.
Antonym: **solution**

solve (solv) *verb*
▶ page 68

To **solve** a problem means to find the answer. The girl **solved** the math problem on the board.
Synonyms: **answer, explain**

suggestion (sug-jes-chun) *noun* ▶ page 72

A **suggestion** is an opinion or idea. Some restaurants have boxes to leave **suggestions** on paper.
Base Word: **suggest**

Practice the Words Make an Example Chart with each Key Word. Share your chart with a partner.

Word	Definition	Example from My Life
ability	skill to do something	I have the ability to play baseball.

Example Chart

Determine Importance and Synthesize

Determine Importance Look for the author's most important point, or main idea, as you read. You can use the main idea to summarize what the author says. Include details from the text that support the main idea.

Synthesize To synthesize, combine what you read with what you know and learn from other sources to form new ideas. You can then draw conclusions or make generalizations about the information and ideas in the text.

Look Into the Text

Determine Importance: The most important idea is that inventions solve problems.

Chester Greenwood wanted to keep his ears warm, so he invented earmuffs. They solved a problem for him. That's what inventions are supposed to do. Chester's invention made life easier for millions of other people.

Soon Chester's friends wanted earmuffs, too. So he started making earmuffs and selling them. He also applied for a patent.

Synthesize: I generalized that successful inventions solve a problem for many people.

Practice Together

Begin a Reading Strategies Log Use a Reading Strategies Log to show how the strategies help you understand the text. The first row shows how one strategy helped one reader. Reread the passage and add to the Log.

Text I Read	Strategy I Used	How I Used the Strategy
Page: 68 **Text:** They solved a problem for him. That's what inventions are supposed to do.	☑ **Determine Importance** ☐ **Synthesize** ☐ _____	This text helped me to determine the main idea of the passage is inventions solve problems.

Reading Strategies Log

Magazine Article

A magazine article is a type of nonfiction. It usually explains something using facts and information. Sometimes it presents a problem and tells how it was solved.

A magazine article often has **headings**, **photos**, and **captions**. Headings tell you what each part is about. Photos show what is explained in the text. Captions give details about the photos.

Look Into the Text

EARMUFFS — headings

Then and Now

Chester Greenwood's invention is still useful. Many other kinds of ear warmers came from his idea. Today, people even use a type of earmuff to block out all kinds of noise.

photo

▲ This kind of ear warmer came from Chester's idea. — caption

Headings, captions and photos can help you determine which parts of a text are important. You can synthesize, or combine, different ideas from these features to draw conclusions or make generalizations.

Kids ARE INVENTORS, TOO

by Arlene Erlbach

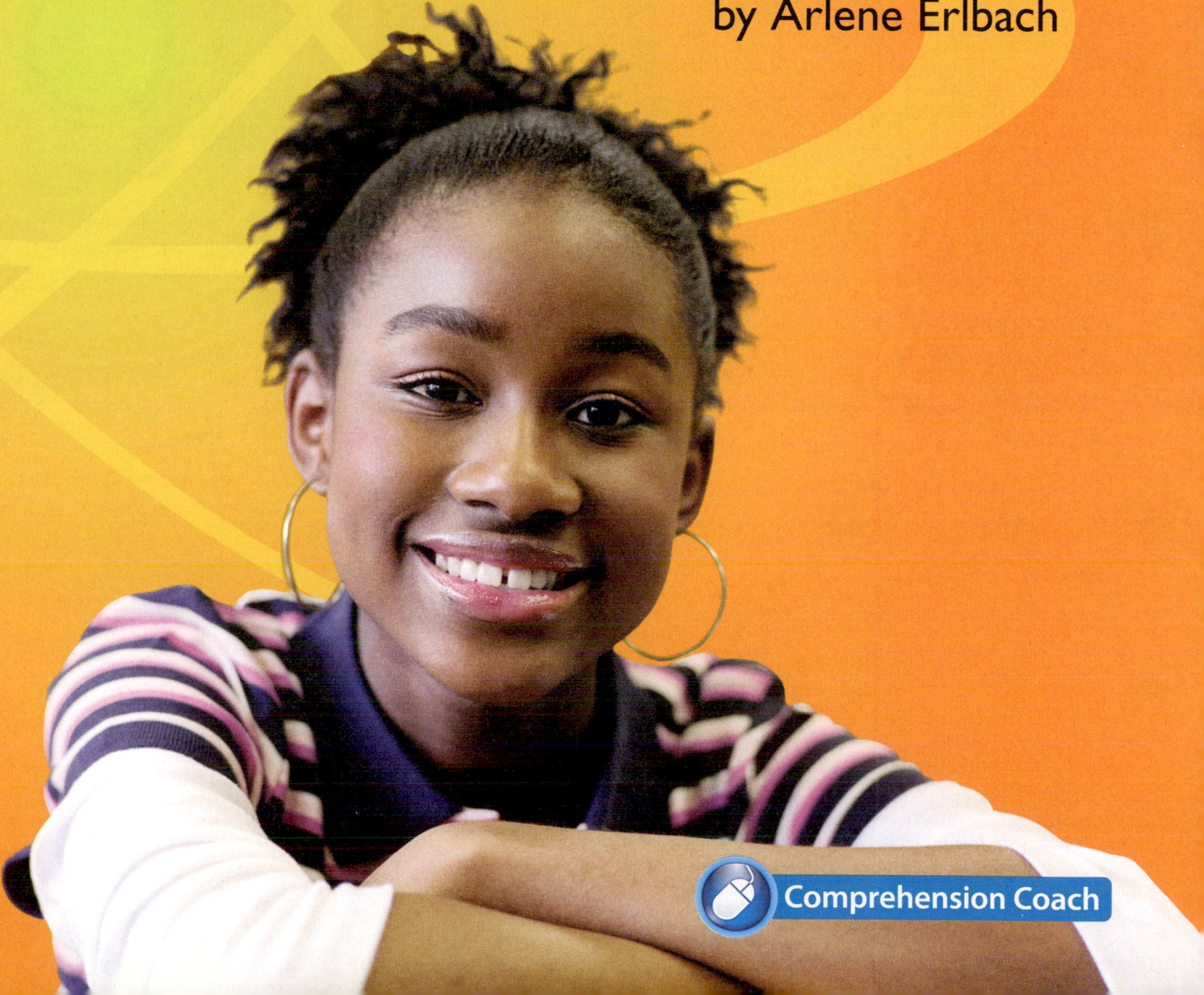

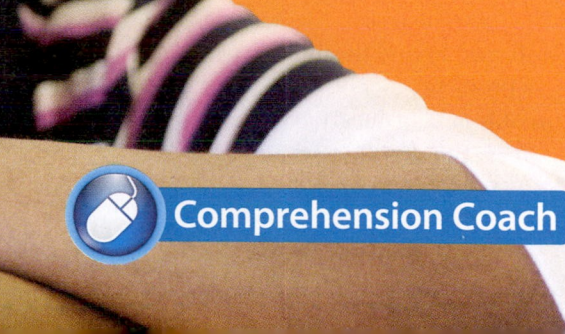
Comprehension Coach

Do you know what's unusual about earmuffs?

They were invented by a kid!

▲ Chester Greenwood, as an adult, still wearing his "Champion Ear Protectors"

Chester Greenwood wanted to keep his ears warm, so he invented earmuffs. They **solved** a **problem** for him. That's what inventions are supposed to do. Chester's invention made life easier for millions of other people.

Chester invented earmuffs in 1873 when he was only fifteen years old. He lived in Farmington, Maine, and he loved to ice skate. Northeastern winters are very cold and can **be hard on your ears**—even when you wear a hat. So Chester took a piece of wire and asked his grandmother to sew cloth pads on the ends.

At first Chester's friends thought his earmuffs looked weird, but they soon **changed their minds**. Chester could stay outside and skate longer than they did. His ears didn't get cold!

Key Vocabulary

solve v., to find the answer to a problem

problem n., a question or an issue that needs a solution

In Other Words

be hard on your ears make your ears hurt

changed their minds thought differently

Soon Chester's friends wanted earmuffs, too. So he started making earmuffs and selling them. He also applied for a patent. A patent is a document **issued by** the U.S. government that protects an inventor's idea so nobody else can make money from it.

Chester began **manufacturing** earmuffs and eventually became rich. He became famous, too. Farmington, Maine, celebrates Chester Greenwood Day each December.

EARMUFFS
Then and Now

Chester Greenwood's invention is still useful. Many other kinds of ear warmers came from his idea. Today, people even use a type of earmuff to block out all kinds of noise.

Then ➡

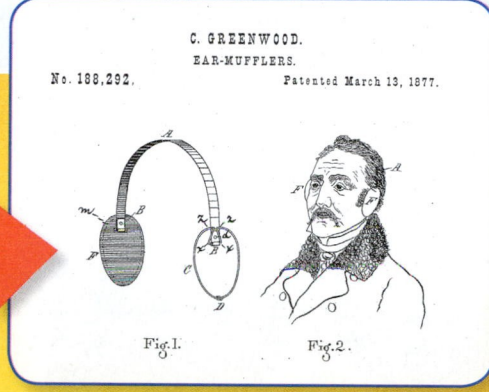

▲ A drawing of Chester's "Champion Ear Protectors" appears on his patent.

⬅ **Now** ➡

▲ This kind of ear warmer came from Chester's idea.

These earphones block out loud noises. ▶

In Other Words
issued by from
manufacturing making

Look Into the Text

1. **Problem and Solution** What **problem** did Greenwood **solve** by inventing earmuffs?
2. **Inference** How did a patent help Greenwood become rich?
3. **Compare and Contrast** How are Greenwood's earmuffs the same as or different from today's ear covers?

The Prosthetic Catch-and-Throw Device

Josh Parsons wanted to help David Potter play baseball. Both of David's arms had been **amputated** below the elbows because of an accident he had when he was two years old. Still, David wanted to be on a **Little League team**. Josh thought he could help David.

Even without hands, David could catch and bat a ball! He caught the ball in a glove he wore at the end of his left arm. To bat, David held the bat between his left upper arm and chest. He used his right arm to push the bat. The only thing David couldn't do was throw a ball. Josh hoped he could change that.

Inventor: Josh Parsons
Hometown: Houston, Texas

David Potter

In Other Words
amputated cut off
Little League team baseball team
for young people

Josh decided to **design** a special glove that would replace David's lower right arm and hand. A **device** that replaces a missing body part is called a prosthesis.

Josh drew pictures of baseball gloves. Finally, he came up with a glove shaped like a scoop.

Josh first made a **model** of the glove out of paper. Next, he sewed a glove from leather. The glove fit onto the end of David's right arm.

Josh hit a ball to David. David caught it in his left glove. Then he **dumped the ball** into the prosthetic glove and threw the ball into the air!

David started playing right field for the Spring Branch Mustangs. They won first place that season.

Josh's invention **drew so much attention** that he and David were interviewed on *Good Morning America* and the Cable News Network. Stories about the glove appeared in newspapers across the United States. Josh received an award from the Easter Seal Society, an organization that helps people with disabilities. He and David even **threw out the first pitch** at a Houston Astros game.

Josh also received a prize from the Houston Inventors' Association—a 291-piece tool kit. He can make plenty of things with that. But, Josh says, "The most important part was that the glove helped David. That's why I invented it."

Key Vocabulary

design *v.*, to draw plans for
device *n.*, a tool that does a special
model *n.*, a small copy of something

In Other Words

dumped the ball let the ball drop
drew so much attention made so many people notice him
threw out the first pitch started the game

Look Into the Text

1. **Steps in a Process** What steps did Parsons take to **design** the special glove?
2. **Summarize** How did Parsons's **device** work?
3. **Inference** What does Parsons's invention tell you about Parsons?

The All-in-One Washer/Dryer

"I wanted to design **an automatic rabbit feeder** for my school invention project," Reeba Daniel said. "But my teacher told me that automatic pet feeders had already been invented."

Then Reeba's mom gave her a **suggestion**. "Invent something everyone could use—something that saves time."

A few days later, while Reeba was folding laundry, she thought about how this common household chore is a two-step job. First, the clothes go into the washer. Then, when they're damp and heavy, somebody needs to lift them into the dryer. Reeba thought about inventing a machine that would wash and dry clothes in one step.

Inventor: Reeba Daniel

Hometown: Palos Park, Illinois

model

REEBA WON!

▲ Reeba standing next to a model of her invention

Key Vocabulary
suggestion *n.*, an idea or a plan

In Other Words
an automatic rabbit feeder
a machine that feeds rabbits without help from a person

The washer could be on top of the dryer and have a **trapdoor** that opens when **the drain cycle is complete**. The clothes would drop into the dryer, making it start. A computerized device could time each of the cycles.

Reeba didn't make a working model of her invention because it would have cost thousands of dollars to build. Instead, she did what many inventors do: Reeba drew a diagram of her invention. Then she made a model of it, from cardboard. From her diagram and model, people could see how her invention would look.

Reeba's invention won a prize at her school's invention fair. She also won a prize from a national organization that included a trip to Washington, DC.

Reeba hopes to become a doctor, engineer, or senator. She believes that the **ability** to keep trying is the **key to anyone's success**. ❖

Key Vocabulary

ability *n.*, the power to do something

In Other Words

trapdoor hidden door at the bottom
the drain cycle is complete all the water has gone out of the washer
key to anyone's success best way to get or do what you want

Look Into the Text

1. **Explain** Daniel's mom made the **suggestion** to invent something that saves time. How does Daniel's invention do this?
2. **Cause and Effect** What causes the dryer to start in Daniel's invention?

INVENTING
to Solve a Problem

When you invent, you create something brand new. An invention can solve a problem, or it can **meet a certain need**.

Some inventions make life easier. **Take** Chester Greenwood's invention, for example. His earmuff invention kept people warm so that they could stay outside longer. Josh Parsons's invention of the prosthetic device made life easier for his friend. Other inventions help people discover new things. People invented telescopes, for example, to learn more about the stars.

People are always trying to make life better. Sometimes they find that they need something that just doesn't **exist**. So they invent it. Let's look more closely at what it takes to invent something.

A telescope is an invention that allows the user to see things that are far away in space. ▶

Key Vocabulary
exist *v.*, to be real

In Other Words
meet a certain need give people something that they need or want
Take Think about

STEP 1

Identify the Need

Need is the **driving force behind** inventing. When people needed lights to help them see in the dark, they invented candles. Then came the lightbulb, followed by the flashlight. The first step in inventing is to **identify the need**.

The Cup Holder Challenge

Imagine that bicycling is something you love to do. And carrying a snack or drink while you're riding makes the experience perfect. The problem? Your bike has a water bottle holder on the frame beneath the seat, but that holder doesn't hold a bag of nuts or a can of lemonade very well.

What you really need is a cup holder on the handlebars. That would keep a drink **upright** or a snack within easy reach. You've never seen a cup holder like that in a bike shop. Guess you'll just have to invent one!

In Other Words
driving force behind reason for
identify the need decide what is needed
upright from falling over

Look Into the Text

1. **Summarize** What are two reasons people invent things?
2. **Steps in a Process** What is the first step of creating an invention? Why is this the first step?

Brainstorm Possible Solutions

What's needed next? Brainpower! Think creatively. **Brainstorm** possible solutions that will meet the need. Sometimes a great idea comes **in a flash**. But more often, it takes time and lots of **mental energy**.

Where Can I Put a Cup Holder on My Bike?

You study the handlebars on your bike. Hmm. . . . You need something like your water bottle holder, but it needs to be smaller and **stubbier**. It could be made out of wire. . . . It has to attach to the handlebars somehow. . . .

You get a paper and a pencil and start to sketch what the cup holder might look like. After a few minutes you come up with a design that you think could work. It's made with things you know you can find around your house.

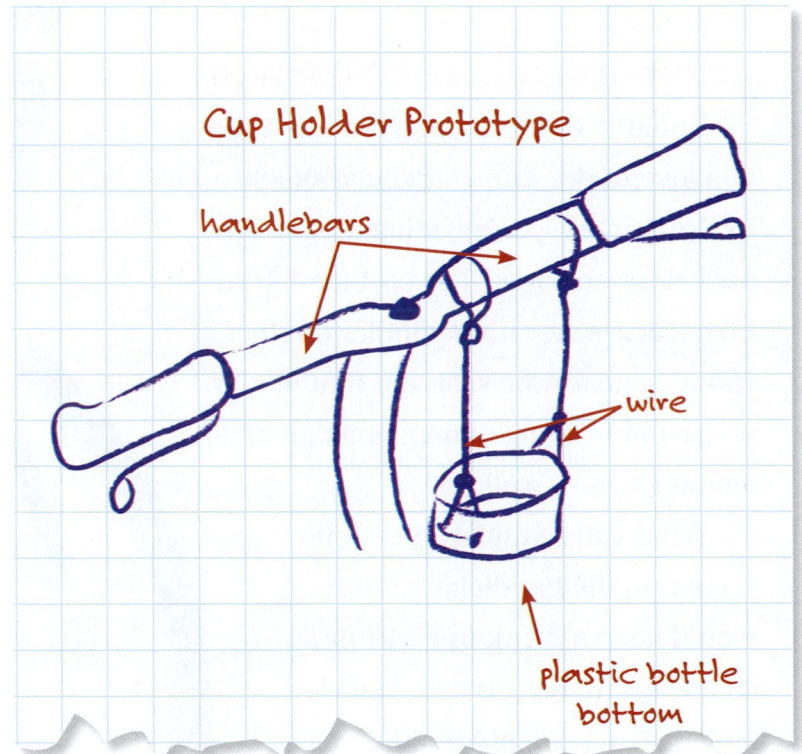

▲ An inventor's sketch

In Other Words
Brainstorm Think of
in a flash very quickly
mental energy thought
stubbier thicker

Build a Prototype

The third step in inventing is to build a prototype. Think of a prototype as a test model of an invention. Building a prototype not only makes an idea real, it also makes problems easier to spot.

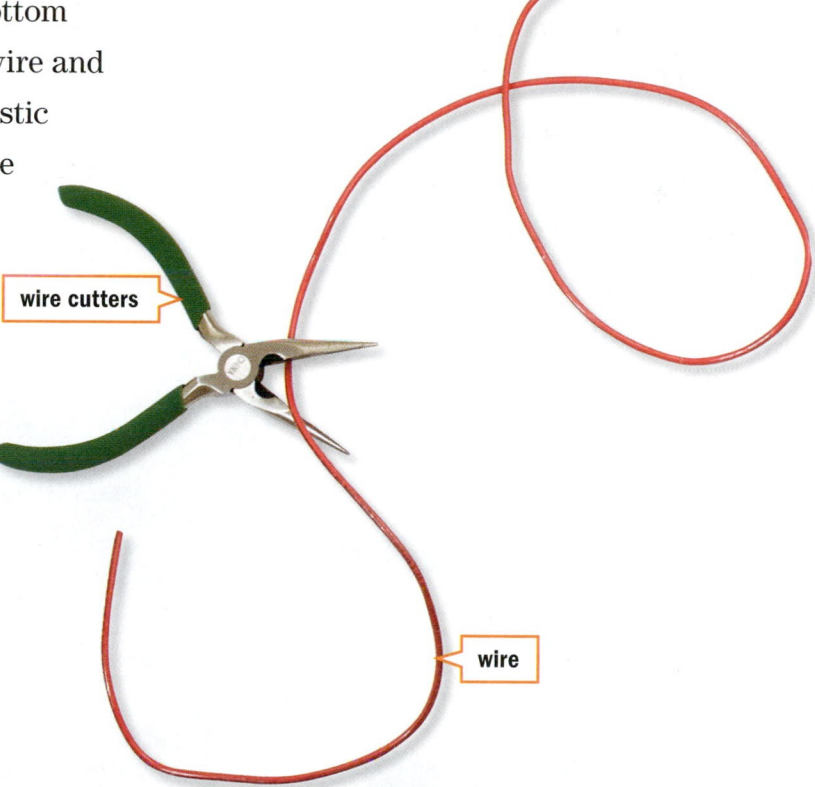

plastic bottle

A Cup Holder Takes Shape

You **rummage** around the house and find what you need. You collect some **sturdy** wire, wire cutters, pliers, and the bottom half of a plastic bottle. You cut the wire and bend it around the bottom of the plastic bottle. Then you twist the ends of the wire onto the handlebars.

wire cutters

pliers

wire

In Other Words
rummage look
sturdy strong

Look Into the Text

1. **Paraphrase** Tell in your own words why the third step of inventing is so important.

2. **Visualize** Describe how the cup holder is attached to the bike.

3. **Compare and Contrast** How are the **model** and the prototype alike? How are they different?

Test and Revise

The final step in inventing is to test and revise. That is, the invention is tested and then **minor** changes are made to "fine tune" it. But expect to revise and test many times. You don't often get it right the first time.

I Did It!

You slip a can of lemonade into your new cup holder. Whoops! The weight of the full can makes the holder slip on the handlebars. The lemonade spills out. You **ponder** this new problem. Just twisting the wire around the handlebars isn't enough. You need to create a tighter grip. What about duct tape?

You find a roll of tape. You use a few strips of tape to strap the wire firmly onto the handlebars.

Then, you test the holder with the can again. This time it stays in place! **Pat yourself on the back**—you've just invented your own bike-handlebar-cup holder!

In Other Words
minor small
ponder think carefully about
Pat yourself on the back
   Be proud of yourself

Look Into the Text

1. **Steps in a Process** What is the final step in creating an invention? Why is this step important?
2. **Cause and Effect** Why does the lemonade spill after the can is put in the cup holder?

Connect Reading and Writing

Vocabulary
ability
design
device
exists
model
problem
solve
suggestion

CRITICAL THINKING

1. SUM IT UP Look back at your Reading Strategy Log. Use it to summarize "Kids Are Inventors, Too" to a partner.

Text I Read	Strategy I Used	How I Used the Strategy
Page: 68 Text: They solved a problem for him. That's what inventions are supposed to do.	☑ Determine Importance ☐ Synthesize ☐ _____	This text helped me to determine the main idea of the passage is inventions solve problems.

Reading Strategies Log

2. Draw Conclusions Could an invention **solve** one problem and cause another? Use an example from the selection.

3. Make Judgments Do you think it really matters if you follow the steps in order when you invent a **device**? Why or why not?

4. Compare Compare the reasons inventors from "Hitching a Ride" and "Kids Are Inventors, Too" **designed** their inventions.

READING FLUENCY

Phrasing Read the passage on page 640 to a partner. Assess your fluency.

1. I did not pause/sometimes paused/ always paused for punctuation.

2. What I did best in my reading was _____ .

READING STRATEGY

What strategy helped you understand this selection? Tell a partner about it.

VOCABULARY REVIEW

Oral Review Read the paragraph aloud. Add the vocabulary words.

> Our math teacher gave us a challenging _____ to _____. We needed to _____ a bridge with the _____ to hold two thousand pounds. I built a small _____ of my bridge. It was my sister's _____ to use Popsicle sticks. My bridge has a _____ that can make it go up and down. I don't think another one like it _____ in the world!

Written Review What could you invent to **solve** the problem from your connect activity on page 60? Write a journal entry about it. Use five vocabulary words.

 **WRITE ABOUT THE GUIDING QUESTION**

Explore the Possibilities
Write about an invention that **solves** a problem for many people. Tell why you think the invention is a good one.

Connect Across the Curriculum

Use Suffixes

> **Academic Vocabulary**
> • **analyze** (a-nu-līz) *verb*
>   To **analyze** something means to study it closely.

If you come to a word you do not know, **analyze** the parts.

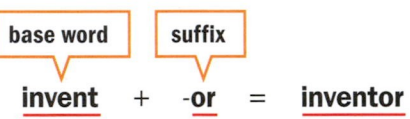

base word	suffix

invent + **-or** = **inventor**

> The base word *invent* means "to make something for the first time." And the suffix *-or* means "the person who does the action." So, an inventor is a person who makes something for the first time.

Analyze Suffixes Work with a partner. Find each word below in the selection. Use the chart to **analyze** the word parts.

1. organization, page 71
2. disabilities, page 71
3. washer, page 72
4. computerized, page 73
5. national, page 73

Suffix	Meaning
-al	relates to
-er / -or	person or thing that does the action
-ity	the quality of
-ize	to make
-less	without
-tion / -ion	the act or state of

Make a Diagram

HEALTH & SCIENCE

> **Academic Vocabulary**
> • **research** (rē-surch) *verb*
>   When you **research** something, you look for information about it.

❶ Use What You Know Josh Parsons invented a catch and throw device.

- How do bones and muscles work together to help your arm move?
- Look at how your arm moves. What do you notice?

❷ Research and Make a Diagram **Research** how your arm works on the Internet and in digital resources.

> **Internet** myNGconnect.com
> Use a search engine to learn how your arm's bones and muscles work. Type the words *arm*, *bone*, and *muscle*.

Use the information to make a diagram. Add visuals and labels. Consider making a diagram online and adding animation.

❸ Give a Presentation Present your diagram to a small group.

Give Information

Share Information Reread "Kids Are Inventors, Too" for information about the invention of earmuffs and the special baseball glove. Share information about the inventions with a friend or family member. Be sure to use complete sentences.

> Chester Greenwood invented earmuffs in 1873. He was 15 years old!

Write Using Effective Sentences

Study the Models When you write, use complete sentences. Complete sentences help readers understand your ideas better. A complete sentence has a **subject** and a **verb**.

NOT OK

> An inventor creates new things. Often, **solves** a problem. Other times, it meets people's needs. Some inventions are very simple, like the wheel. Other **inventions** very complex, like the computer. Still other **seem** silly or even useless. Sometimes, they help an invention later on. **Make** life easier for people. **Inventors** definitely the world a better place.

The writer uses some sentences that are not complete. The reader cannot tell who is doing things or what they are doing.

OK

> An inventor creates new things. Often, the **invention** **solves** a problem. Other times, it meets people's needs. Some inventions are very simple, like the wheel. Other **inventions** **are** very complex, like the computer. Still other **inventions** **seem** silly or even useless. Sometimes, they help an invention later on. **Inventions** **make** life easier for people. **Inventors** definitely **make** the world a better place.

This writer uses a subject and a verb in every sentence. The reader can easily follow the ideas.

Add Sentences Think of two sentences to add to the OK model above. Make sure each sentence has a subject and a verb.

WRITE ON YOUR OWN Write about an invention that you think would help people. Be sure to use complete sentences.

REMEMBER
- Always include a subject and a predicate in the sentences you write.
- The subject is whom or what the sentence is about.
- The predicate is what the subject does.

The Evolution of a Great Idea

BY PETER DIAMANDIS AND STEVEN KOTLER

1   Sir Arthur C. Clarke, inventor of the **geostationary communication satellite** and author of dozens of best-selling science fiction books, knew something about the evolution of great ideas. He described three stages to their development. "In the beginning," says Clarke, "people tell you that's a crazy idea, and it'll never work. Next, people say your idea might work, but it's not worth doing. Finally, eventually, people say, I told you that it was a great idea all along!"

2   When Tony Spear was given the job of landing an unmanned rover on the Martian surface, he **had no inkling** that Clarke's three stages would be precisely his experience. A jovial, white-haired cross between Albert Einstein and Archie Bunker, Spear started his career at NASA's Jet Propulsion Laboratory in 1962. Over the next four decades, he worked on missions from Mariner to Viking, but it was his final assignment, project manager on the Mars Pathfinder, that he describes as his "greatest mission **challenge** ever."

3   The year was 1997, and the United States had not landed a probe on Mars since July 1976. That was Viking, a complex and expensive mission, costing some $3.5 billion (in 1997 dollars). Spear's assignment was to find a way to do everything that the previous mission had done, just "faster, better, cheaper." And when I say cheaper, I mean a *whole lot* cheaper: fifteen times cheaper, to be exact, for a fixed and total development cost of only $150 million. Out the window went the expensive stuff, the traditional stuff, and the proven stuff, including the types of retro-rockets for landing that got the job done on Viking.

4   "To pull this off under these impossible constraints, we had to do everything differently," reflects Spear, "from how I managed, to how we landed. That really scared people. At NASA headquarters, I was assigned six different managers in rapid sequence—each of the first five found a different excuse to get off the project. Finally I was assigned someone about to retire who didn't mind sticking with me

Key Vocabulary
- **challenge** *n.*, a task that is difficult

In Other Words
geostationary communication satellite satellite at a fixed point over Earth
had no inkling could not have imagined

An artist's depiction of the spacecraft descending toward the airbag landing pad on Mars.

at the end of his career. Even the NASA administrator, Daniel Golden, nearly flipped out when he received his initial mission briefing—he couldn't get past how many new things we were trying out."

5   Among the many things Spear tried out, nothing struck people as **zanier** than using airbags to cushion the initial impact, helping

the craft bounce around like a beach ball on the Martian surface, before settling down into a safe landing spot. But airbags were cheap, they wouldn't **contaminate** their landing site with foreign chemicals, and Spear was pretty certain that they would work. The early tests, however, were a disaster, so the experts were summoned.

In Other Words
zanier more unusual
contaminate dirty

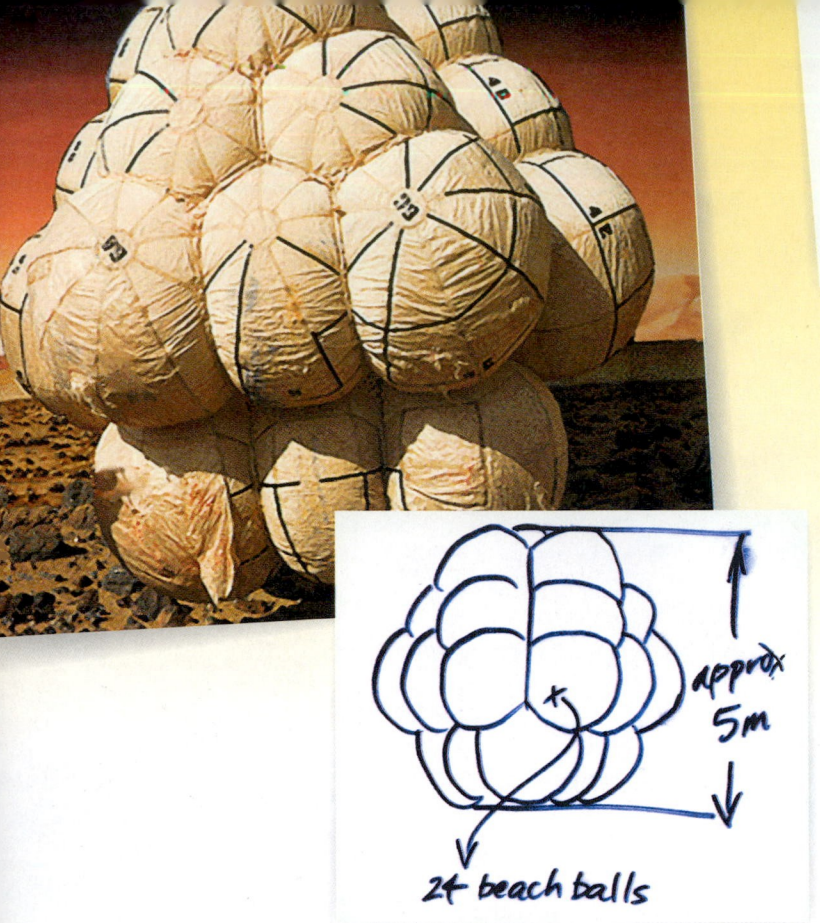

bounce into position

approx 5m

24 beach balls

6   The experts had a pair of opinions. The first was: Don't use airbags. The second was: No, we're totally serious, don't even *consider* using airbags. "Two of them," recounts Spear, "told me flat out that I was wasting government money and should cancel the project. Finally, when they realized I wasn't going to give up, they decided to dig in and help me."

7   Together they tested more than a dozen designs, skidding them along a **faux** rocky Martian surface to see which would survive without shredding to pieces. Finally, just eight months prior to launch, Spear and his team completed qualification testing of a design composed of twenty-four interconnected spheres, loaded it aboard Pathfinder, and launched it into space. But the anxiety didn't end there. The trip to Mars took eight months, during which there was plenty of time to worry about the fate of the mission. "In the weeks just prior to landing," Spear recalls, "everyone was very nervous, **speculating** whether we'd have a big splat when we arrived. Golden himself was wondering what to do: should he come to the JPL control room for the landing or not? Just a few days before our July 4 descent to the surface, the administrator took a **bold tack**, holding a press conference and proclaiming, 'The Pathfinder mission demonstrates a new way of doing business at NASA, and is a success whether or not we survive the landing.' "

In Other Words
faux fake
speculating wondering
bold tack risk

beach balls deflate / Pathfinder opens

8   The landing, though, went exactly as planned. They had spent one-fifteenth the cost of Viking, and everything worked perfectly—especially the airbags. Spear was a hero. Golden was so impressed, he insisted that airbags be used to land the next few Mars missions and was quoted as saying, "Tony Spear was a legendary project manager at JPL and helped make Mars Pathfinder the riveting success that it was."

9   The point here, of course, is that Clarke was right. Demonstrating great ideas involves

"Demonstrating great ideas involves a considerable amount of risk."

a considerable amount of risk. There will always be **naysayers**. People will resist breakthrough ideas until the moment they're accepted as the new norm. Since the road to **abundance** requires significant **innovation**, it also requires significant **tolerance** for risk, for failure, and for ideas that strike most as absolute nonsense. As Burt Rutan puts it, "**Revolutionary** ideas come from nonsense. If an idea is truly a breakthrough, then the day before it was discovered, it must have been considered crazy or nonsense or both— otherwise it wouldn't be a breakthrough."

In Other Words

naysayers people who disagree
abundance many new ideas
innovation trying of new things
tolerance acceptance
Revolutionary Completely new

Compare Across Texts

Compare Writing

"Hitching a Ride," "Kids Are Inventors, Too," and "The Evolution of a Great Idea" tell how different inventions were created. As you reread each selection, <mark>analyze</mark> the text to learn more about why each writer includes certain details.

How It Works

Collect and Organize Information Use a chart to help you compare the articles. First, identify how the articles are similar. Then identify how they are different. Focus on how each author writes about the topic of inventions.

Title	Similarities	Differences
"Hitching a Ride"	Describes how Crittercam was developed.	
"Kids Are Inventors, Too"	Tells how several inventions solve different problems.	
"The Evolution of a Great Idea"		

Comparison Chart

Practice Together

Analyze and Compare Information Use the information in the chart to write a comparison of the selections. Here is the beginning of a comparison.

> "Hitching a Ride," "Kids Are Inventors, Too," and "The Evolution of a Great Idea" all tell about inventions. But they tell about inventions in different way. "Hitching a Ride" and "The Evolution of a Great Idea" each discuss a specific invention, while "Kids Are Inventors, Too" tells about multiple inventions.

Try It!

Study and Compare the Information Think about how each writer addressed the topic. Write a summary comparing the details.

"Hitching a Ride," "Kids Are Inventors, Too," and "The Evolution of a Great Idea" all explain _____. However, each selection tells something different about _____. "Hitching a Ride" tells about _____, while "Kids Are Inventors, Too" tells about _____ and _____ gives information about _____.

Academic Vocabulary
- **analyze** (a-nu-līz) *verb*
  When you **analyze** something, you study it closely.

Imagine
the Possibilities

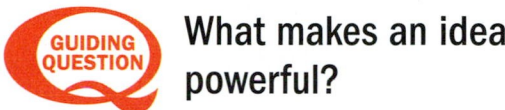 **GUIDING QUESTION** **What makes an idea powerful?**

Content Library

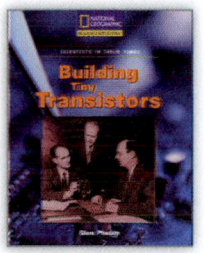

Leveled Library

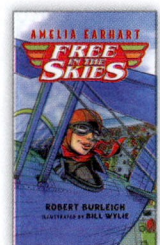  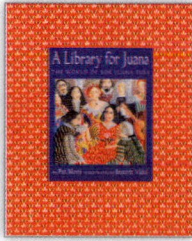

Reflect on Your Reading

Think back on your reading of the unit selections. Discuss what you did to understand what you read.

Reading Strategies

In this unit, you were introduced to eight different reading strategies and how they can be applied to text to make you a better reader. Choose a selection from this unit. Explain to a partner how you applied reading strategies to better understand the text. Tell about at least four different strategies. Then explain how you will plan to use each of the eight reading strategies in the future.

Explore the

Throughout this unit, you have been thinking about the power good ideas have to solve problems. Choose one of these ways to explore the Guiding Question:

- **Discuss** With a group, think of a problem at your school or in your community. Then make a list of ways to solve the problem. Discuss the solutions. As a group, decide the best solution.

- **Draw** Think of something many people find difficult. Draw an invention that could help solve the problem. Share your invention with the class.

- **Write** Write an advertisement for your invention above. Try to convince your audience that your product or service will solve their problem.

Book Talk

Which Unit Library book did you choose? Explain to a partner what it taught you about good ideas that solve problems.

Play
to Your
Strengths

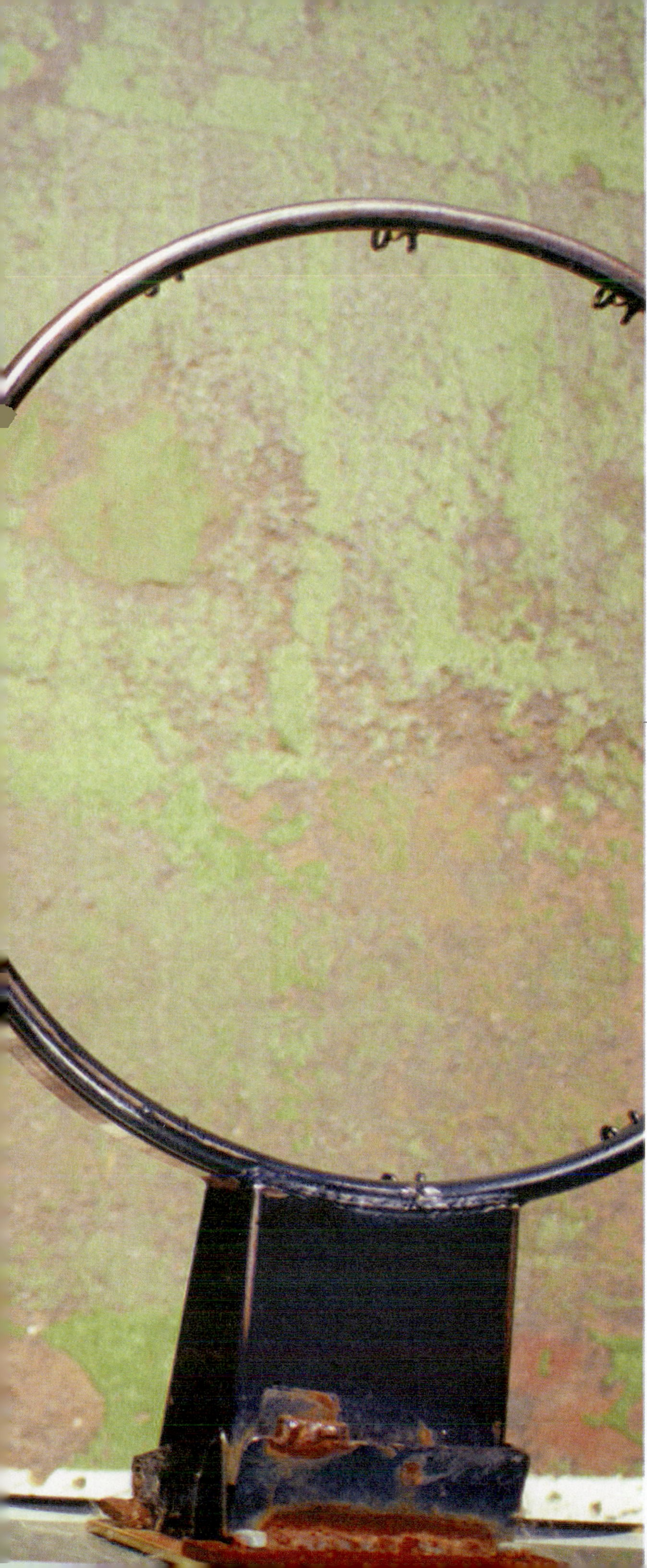

2

 GUIDING QUESTION

How should people use their talents?

READ MORE!

◄ On a sunny day, a basketball player sets up for a winning shot.

Elements of Fiction

▶ **Plot**
▶ **Characters**
▶ **Setting**

Writers create fictional stories to entertain their readers. Writers use key **elements** of fiction—plot, characters, and setting—to build their stories.

Plot: How It Works

The **plot** is the series of events that happen in a story.

- The plot is built around a **conflict**, or problem, that the main character faces.
- During the **rising action**, the plot develops as **complications** occur, and the character tries to solve the problem.
- The **climax** is the turning point, or the most important event of the story.
- **Falling action** leads to the **resolution**, where the problem ends.

Read "The Clever Woman" aloud to understand the stages of the plot.

The Clever Woman

Once upon a time in Korea, there lived a king named Yon-San. Whenever he wanted someone to come live in his castle, he didn't ask. He just took the person away. All the people in the kingdom were afraid that the king would take them away from their families. Nobody wanted to go live in Yon-San's castle!

One day, the king ordered a young woman to come live in the castle. She did not want to go, so she came up with a plan. Before she left for the castle, she took two pieces of smelly fish and hid them in her dress. When the young woman arrived, the king noticed a horrible smell.

"This woman smells terrible!" he cried. "Get out of my castle and never come back!"

The clever and lucky woman left the castle smiling. She would never again need to worry about being taken away to Yon-San's castle.

Setting *Character*
Conflict
Rising Action
Climax, or turning point
Resolution

Academic Vocabulary

- **element** (e-lu-mint) *noun*
  An **element** is a basic part of something.

Plot: Practice Together

Read "The Clever Woman" again, and tell where the events go on this Plot Diagram.

Plot Diagram

Character: How It Works

Characters are the people or animals in the story. Each character's traits , actions, words, and decisions affect what happens in the plot.

Writers tell readers about their characters by:

- saying directly what the character is like
- showing the character's thoughts, words, and actions
- telling what other characters think of him or her.

These writing techniques are called **characterization**. See these techniques in action as the writer characterizes King Yon-San.

> Once upon a time in Korea, there lived a king named Yon-San. Whenever he wanted someone to come live in his castle, he didn't ask. He just took the person away. All the people in the kingdom were afraid that the king would take them away from their families. Nobody wanted to go live in Yon-San's castle!

Tells about the character directly

Shows the character's actions

Use a chart like this one to keep track of what the characters are like in a story.

Character	What the Character Is Like	Effect on Events
Yon-San	selfish	he takes people without asking; they are afraid of him

Character Description Chart

Academic Vocabulary

- **trait** (trāt) *noun*

    A **trait** is a quality or characteristic of something.

Character: Practice Together

Now read the rest of the story aloud with your class. As you read, listen for the ways the writer characterizes the clever woman. After you read, complete the activity and answer the question next to the passage.

> One day, the king ordered a young woman to come live in the castle. She did not want to go, so she came up with a plan. Before she left for the castle, she took two pieces of smelly fish and hid them in her dress. When the young woman arrived, the king noticed a horrible smell.
>
> "This woman smells terrible!" he cried. "Get out of my castle and never come back!"
>
> The clever and lucky woman left the castle smiling.

1. **Make a Character Description Chart for the clever woman.**

2. **How would the plot change if the woman were not clever?**

Setting: How It Works

Setting is the time and place where the story happens.

- In most stories, the setting is one place and one time. In longer fiction, the story can take place in several places and time periods.
- Setting includes the way people live, think, and act at that time and place. It also includes their customs or traditions.
- The time and place affect how the characters think and act.
- Setting also affects the plot. For example, a story set at a time before space travel would not have people taking a spaceship to the moon.

See how the writer uses the setting in "The Clever Woman."

> Once upon a time in Korea, there lived a king named Yon-San. Whenever he wanted someone to come live in his castle, he didn't ask. He just took the person away. All the people in the kingdom were afraid that the king would take them away from their families. Nobody wanted to go live in Yon-San's castle!

Time and place

Customs of the time and place

Setting: Practice Together

Now read a different version of this story aloud with your class. As you read, listen for details about the setting. After you read, complete the activities next to the passage.

> In the year 2245, there lives a king named Yon-San. He lives on the moon. Whenever he wants someone to come to his space tower, he doesn't ask. He just transports the person to the moon on light waves. All the people in the kingdom hope that the king will take them to the moon. Everyone wants to go live in Yon-San's space tower!

1. Describe the time and place and what the people think.
2. Compare the different settings in these two versions of "The Clever Woman."
3. With a partner, predict how the plot of the second story will be different from the plot of the first story.

Try It!

Read the following passage aloud and answer the questions about how the plot, characters, and setting interact.

Anansi, the Story Giver

A long time ago in a faraway place, all the good stories of the world were kept away from the people. Only the gods knew the stories. Anansi, a clever spider, knew that stories were good for people. He wanted to find a way to get the stories from the gods. So Anansi built a spider web that reached up to the gods. He climbed up the web and asked them to give him the stories.

The gods didn't like to share, so they gave Anansi a test. If Anansi caught a jaguar, a stinging hornet, and a falcon, they would give him the stories for the people. The gods thought Anansi wouldn't be able to catch these very dangerous animals. But Anansi was smart. He tricked the three animals and brought them to the gods. The gods were surprised and angry. But they were fair gods, so they gave him their stories to share with the people of the world.

1. What is the setting?
2. Who are the characters, and what are they like?
3. What is the conflict?
4. How does the main character resolve the conflict?
5. How would the plot be different if Anansi was a robot and the setting was in the future?

Remember that the **character**, **setting**, and **plot** are the basic elements of a story. How these elements interact determines what happens in the story.

Focus on Vocabulary

Relate Words

▶ **Synonyms**

Synonyms are words that have nearly the same meaning, or different shades of meaning. For example, one word might create a stronger feeling than its synonym does. Knowing the <mark>exact</mark> meanings of synonyms can help you to better understand what you read.

EXAMPLE   Most of Lee's poems are **funny**, but her newest one is **hilarious**.

> " *Hilarious* is a stronger word than *funny*. I think I'd like the newest poem best. "

A Synonym Scale can help you understand how words are related.

Synonym Scale

amusing   humorous   funny   comical   hilarious

How the Strategy Works

The more words you know about a concept, the better you'll understand what people say and be able to express your own ideas.

1. Whenever you read, take time to learn new words.
2. Put words into groups to see how they are connected.
3. Use a Synonym Scale to rank synonyms in order of their strength.

Use the strategy to figure out the shades of meaning of the underlined words.

The Chess Champion

Marco is a great chess player. Soon after he learned the game, he beat everyone on the school chess team. He was so <u>happy</u>. Then he started playing against a computer. Marco beat the computer three times! Our teachers were <u>delighted</u> to hear that the school was giving him a trophy, but Marco was <u>thrilled</u>!

Strategy in Action

> " *Delighted* and *thrilled* both describe "happy," but *thrilled* is stronger. "

☑ **REMEMBER** Recognize the shades of meanings of synonyms to better understand what you read.

Academic Vocabulary
- **exact** (ig-**zact**) *adjective*
  Something that is **exact** is accurate and specific.

Practice Together

Read this passage aloud. Work with your class to make a Synonym Scale for the underlined words. Discuss how using the scale helps you figure out what each word means and then use that information to better understand the characters' actions.

The Fence

Three friends were walking home from school one day. Suddenly, they found a huge fence blocking the sidewalk and the street that kept them from passing.

Levi grabbed the top of the fence and <u>flipped</u> himself over it. Next Luc took a running start and <u>vaulted</u> over the fence. Jerry looked around and saw a hole in the fence. He <u>crawled</u> through the hole to the other side. Then the friends continued on their way.

Try It!

Read the following passage. Pay attention to the underlined synonyms. Who tells the funniest story? How do you know this?

The Comedy Contest

Our school had a comedy competition to see who could tell the funniest story. The contestant who got the hardest laughs would win a comedy DVD.

First, Shannon got up and told a story about her pet cat. The audience <u>giggled</u> hearing about the cat's tricks. Then, Lorenzo told about the time he fell in the lake at his uncle's wedding. Students <u>howled</u> as he described coming out of the water draped in wet weeds. Ian told about the time he locked himself in the bathroom. Some people <u>chuckled</u> at that. Finally, Sherman described baking a cake without a recipe. The audience <u>laughed</u> when he described trying to eat the rubbery cake that came out of the oven.

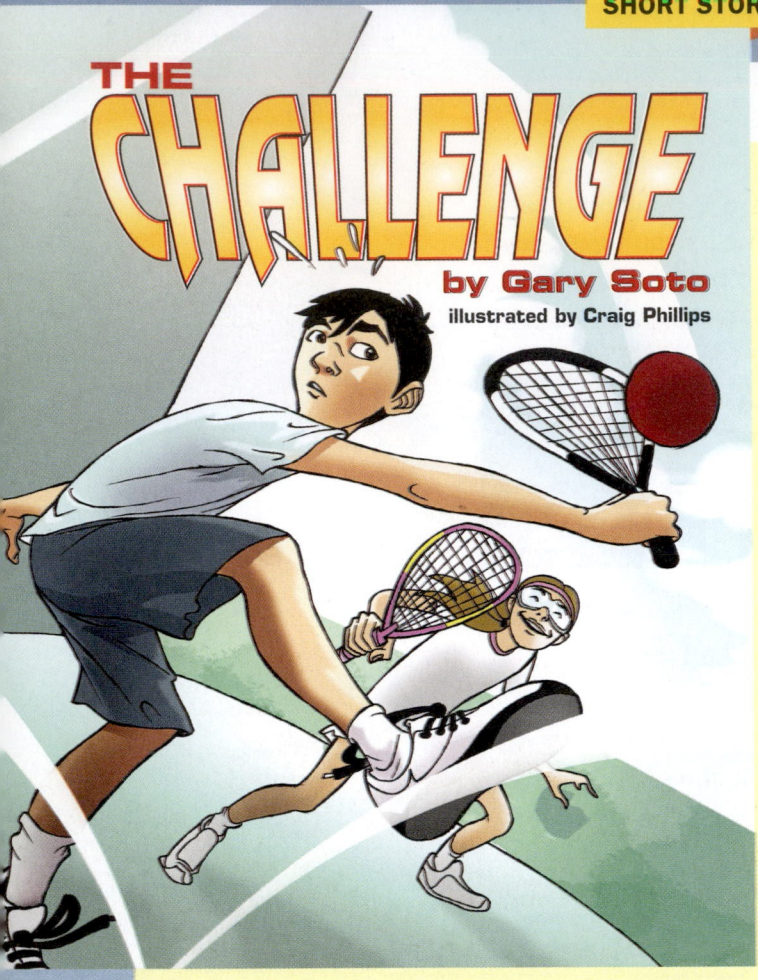

THE CHALLENGE
by Gary Soto
illustrated by Craig Phillips

Build Background

Meet Gary Soto

Award-winning author Gary Soto discusses how he gets ideas for stories and what it's like being a writer.

Digital Library   **myNGconnect.com**
   ⬀ View the video.

◀ Gary Soto started writing when he was 17.

Connect

Anticipation Guide Do you agree or disagree with these statements?

Anticipation Guide

	Agree	Disagree
1. Everything in life is a competition.	_____	_____
2. It is important to face any challenge.	_____	_____
3. It is important to always win.	_____	_____

In groups, discuss your thoughts and opinions about each statement.

Language & Grammar

CD

Engage in Conversation

Listen to the conversation and
chime in. Then role-play the conversation.

STORYBOARD

Are you ready for the big game?

I sure am!

It's the biggest game of the year.

I know! I can't wait!

It will be a hard game.

But Coach Davis thinks we can win!

Look! She's talking to the other coach.

He probably thinks his team will win. I hope they don't.

Well, Coach Davis wants us to cheer our team on.

You mean she really thinks we can win this year?

Yes. She said a team has to play to its strengths. She thinks you're our best player!

Wow! Well, it is a challenge, but I'm up for it!

Good! Here she comes now. Game time!

Language & Grammar   97

1 TRY OUT LANGUAGE
2 LEARN GRAMMAR
3 APPLY ON YOUR OWN

Use Pronouns as Subjects

A **pronoun** refers to a noun. A **subject pronoun** is a pronoun that is the subject of a sentence.

Subject Pronoun	Example
• Use **I** to talk about yourself. • Use **we** to talk about another person and yourself.	• **I** like to play tennis. • My sister and I play in the park. **We** play on Sunday.
• Use **you** to talk to another person. • Use **you** to talk to more than one person.	• **You** are a good baseball player. • **You** are all good baseball players.
• Use **he** to talk about one man or boy. • Use **she** to talk about one woman or girl. • Use **it** to talk about one thing or place. • Use **they** to talk about more than one person, place, or thing.	• Carlos is my friend. **He** is a good football player. • Ana plays tennis. **She** takes lessons every week. • Her tennis racquet is new. **It** is very light. • Carlos and Ana like sports. **They** practice often.

Practice Together

Say each sentence with the correct subject pronoun.

1. _____ go to soccer practice every day.
2. Ms. Rodriguez is our coach. _____ teaches us a lot.
3. We practice in Douglas Park. _____ has a new soccer field.
4. My brother is on my team. _____ is a great player!
5. Our friends are also on the team. _____ make practice fun.
6. The next game is on Saturday. _____ will be a tough one!

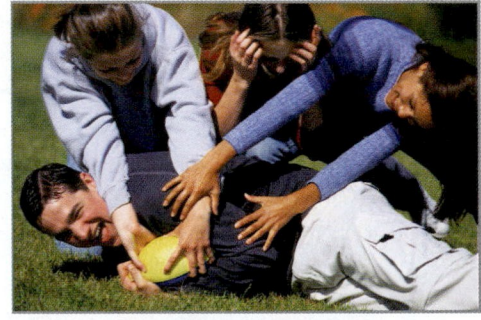

▲ We play sports in a park.

Try It!

Write the correct subject pronoun on a card. Then say the sentence, and add the pronoun.

7. My sister and I play tennis. _____ play twice a week.
8. My sister and her friend play, too. _____ play a lot.
9. You play tennis, too. Why don't _____ join the team?
10. The practice is excellent. _____ is very popular.
11. The coaches are kind. _____ are fair and helpful.
12. The team works hard. _____ is competitive.

Talk to a Friend

ENGAGE IN CONVERSATION

We all have things we like to do with other people. Have a conversation with a partner. Plan what you will talk about. Make a list of things you like to do with other people.

What I Like to Do	Who I Do This With
play baseball	brother
play basketball	friends

Choose one activity from your list. Tell your partner details about your activity. Encourage your partner to ask questions. Show interest in his or her ideas.

HOW TO ENGAGE IN CONVERSATION

1. Say what you want to say about the topic. Give details and examples.
2. Listen to what the other person has to say. Show interest by asking a question.
3. Respect other opinions.

> I play soccer every Saturday.

> You do? Where? My sister plays soccer every Saturday, too. She plays at the park.

USE PRONOUNS AS SUBJECTS

Think about the **pronouns** you will use in your conversation.

- Use *I* to tell about yourself.
- Use *you* for the person or people you are talking to.
- Use *he* or *she* to tell about another person.
- Use *it* to tell about a thing or a place.
- Use *we* to tell about yourself and another person.
- Use *they* to tell about other people, places, or things.

EXAMPLES   My family plays many sports. **We** especially enjoy soccer and tennis.

My dad played tennis in high school. **He** was a state champion!

Prepare to Read

Learn Key Vocabulary

Study the Words Use the steps below.

1. Pronounce the word. Say it aloud several times. Spell it.
2. Rate your word knowledge.
3. Study the example. Tell more about the word.
4. Practice it. Make the word your own.

Key Words

approach (u-prōch) *verb*
▶ page 108

To **approach** means to come toward someone or something. The librarian **approaches** the student to offer help.
Related Word: **approachable**

assume (u-süm) *verb*
▶ page 112

When you **assume**, you guess something is true.
Synonym: **suppose**
Antonym: **doubt**

attention (u-ten-chun) *noun*
▶ page 104

When you give someone your **attention**, you listen to what they say, or watch what they do.

awkward (aw-kwurd) *adjective* ▶ page 110

Someone who is **awkward** feels nervous or clumsy. The boy feels **awkward** at the dance.
Synonym: **uncomfortable**
Antonym: **relaxed**

encourage (in-kur-ij) *verb*
▶ page 112

When you **encourage** people, you give them hope that they can do something. The father **encourages** his son with his homework.
Related Word: **encouragement**

notice (nō-tis) *verb*
▶ page 104

To **notice** something is to see or hear it. You may **notice** the colors in a piece of art.
Antonyms: **miss, ignore**

practice (prak-tis) *verb*
▶ page 112

To **practice** means to do something in order to become better at it. People must **practice** to become good musicians.

weight (wāt) *noun*
▶ page 110

A **weight** is a heavy object used for exercise. People lift **weights** to make their muscles stronger.

Practice the Words Make a Definition Map for each Key Word. Compare your maps to a partner's maps.

WORD: approach
DEFINITION: to come toward
OTHER FORMS: approachable
EXAMPLE: approaching a friend
NON-EXAMPLE: waiting for someone to talk to you
SENTENCE: The baseball player approached the plate.

Definition Map

Analyze Plot

What Happens in a Story? Analyzing how the elements of a story interact, or work together, can help the reader better understand a story. The plot connects the events in the story and moves the story forward. Both characters and setting can influence how the plot develops.

As you read, identify important events and how they relate to the parts of the plot.

Look Into the Text

For three weeks, José tried to get the attention of Estela, the new girl at his middle school....

He thought of tripping in front of her while she was leaving her math class, but he had already tried that with a girl in sixth grade. All he did was rip his pants and bruise his knee, which kept him from playing in the championship soccer game. And that girl had just stepped over him as he lay on the ground, the shame of rejection reddening his face.

"When I reread the second sentence, I see that José has tried before to get a girl's attention."

Practice Together

Begin a Plot Diagram A Plot Diagram can help you analyze the events in a story. The action in a story often starts when a character faces a conflict. Determine the conflict in this story and add it to the Plot Diagram.

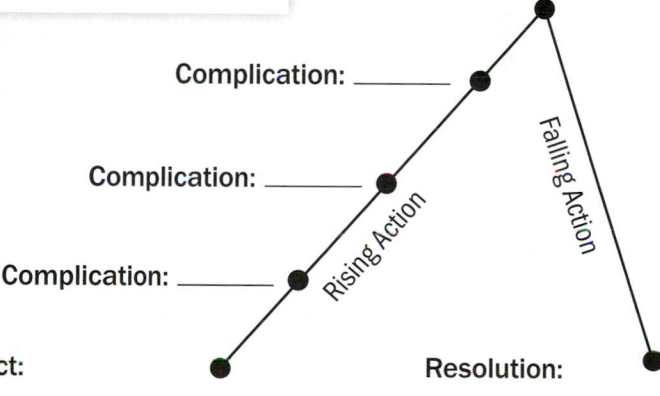

Academic Vocabulary
- **conflict** (**kahn**-flikt) *noun*
  A **conflict** is a problem or disagreement.

Short Story

A short story is a type of fiction. A short story is usually about a main **character** who has a problem, or **conflict**. The events that show how the character solves the problem make up the plot. Analyzing how events are connected to the character's conflict can help you to better understand the story.

Monitor your reading to make sure you understand what José's problem is and how he might solve it. When necessary, reread the text or read further to clarify new ideas.

Look Into the Text

character

For three weeks José tried to get the attention of Estela, the new girl at his middle school. She's cute, he said to himself when he first saw her in the cafeteria . . .

On the way home from school he walked through the alleys of his town, Fresno, kicking cans. He was lost in a dream, **trying to figure out a way to make Estela notice him.**

Conflict

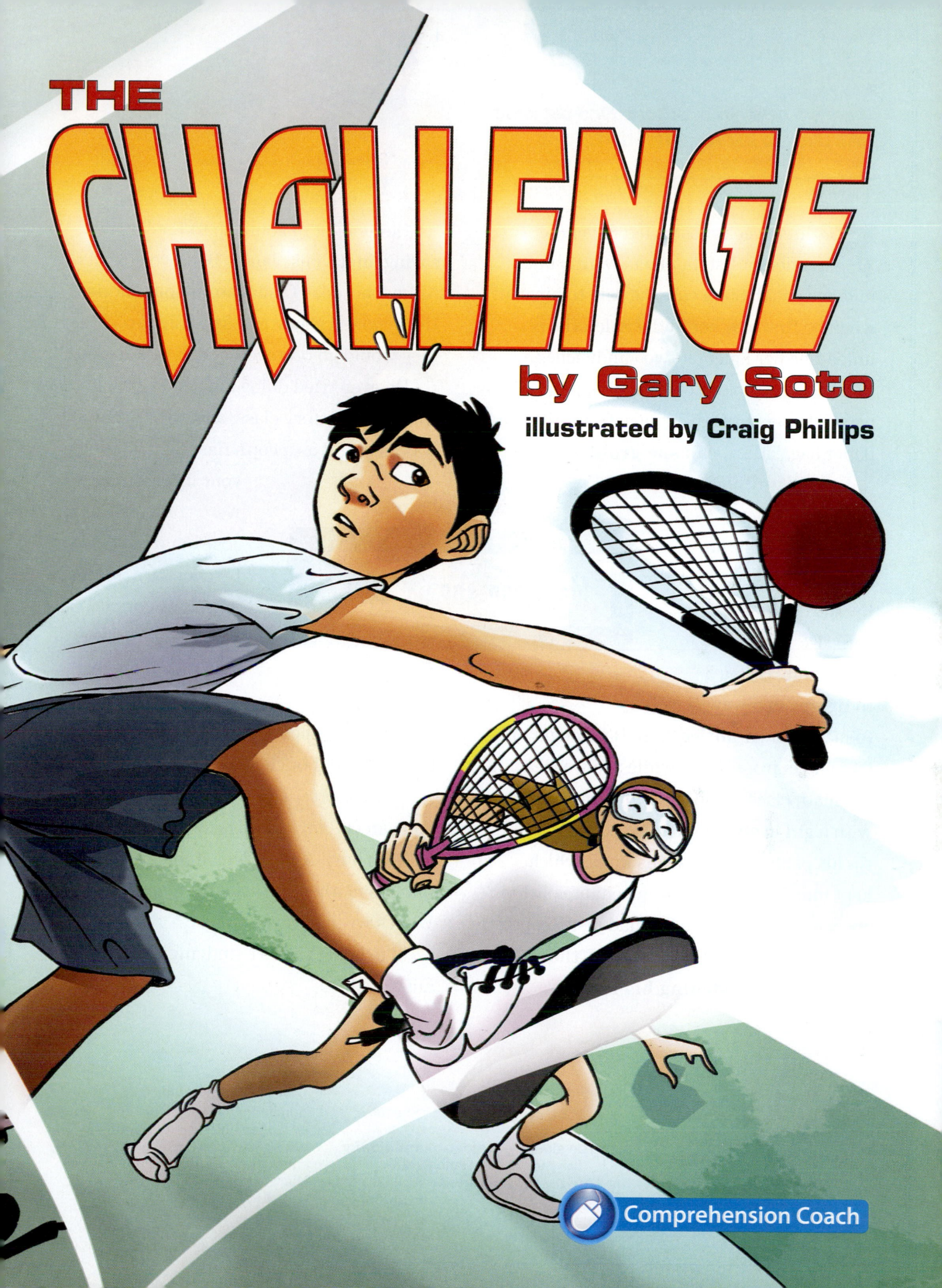

For three weeks José tried to get the attention of Estela, the new girl at his middle school. She's cute, he said to himself when he first saw her in the cafeteria, unloading her lunch of two sandwiches, potato chips, a piece of cake wrapped in waxed paper, and boxed juice from a brown paper bag. **"Man, can she grub!"**

On the way home from school he walked through the alleys of his town, Fresno, kicking cans. He was lost in a dream, trying to figure out a way to make Estela notice him. He thought of tripping in front of her while she was leaving her math class, but he had already tried that with a girl in sixth grade. All he did was rip his pants and bruise his knee, which kept him from playing in the championship soccer game. And that girl had just stepped over him as he lay on the ground, **the shame of rejection reddening his face**.

Man, can she grub!

He thought of going up to Estela and saying, in his best James Bond voice, "Camacho. José Camacho, at your service." He imagined she would say, "Right-o." Then they would go off together and talk in code.

He even tried doing his homework. Estela was in his history class, and so he knew she was as bright as a cop's flashlight shining in your face. While they were studying Egypt, José amazed the teacher, Mrs. Flores, when he scored twenty out of twenty on a quiz. Then he scored eighteen out of twenty when she retested him the same day because she thought that he had cheated.

"Mrs. Flores, I studied hard—*¡de veras!* You can call my mom," he argued, his feelings hurt. And he *had* studied, so much that his mother had asked, "*¿Qué pasó?* What's wrong?"

"I'm going to start studying," he'd answered.

Key Vocabulary
attention *n.*, the act of listening or watching
notice *v.*, to see someone or something

In Other Words
"Man, can she grub!" "She likes to eat a lot!"
the shame of rejection reddening his face feeling embarrassed
¡de veras! It's true! (in Spanish)

Cultural Background
James Bond is a fictional spy created by British author Ian Fleming in the 1950s. Bond is still a popular character in books and movies. His character is well known for being stylish and handsome.

His mother bought him a lamp because she didn't want him to strain his eyes. She even fixed him hot chocolate and watched her son learn about the Egyptian god Osiris, about **papyrus and mummification**. The mummies had scared her so much that she had heated up a second cup of chocolate to soothe herself.

But when the quizzes had been returned and José bragged, "Another A-plus," Estela didn't turn her head and ask, "Who's that brilliant boy?" She just stuffed her quiz into her backpack and left the classroom, leaving José behind to retake the test.

One weekend he had **wiped out** while riding his bike, popping up over curbs with his eyes closed. He somersaulted over his handlebars and saw a flash of shooting stars as he felt the slap of his skin against the **asphalt**. Blood rushed from his nostrils like

In Other Words

papyrus and mummification
  Egyptian paper and the treatment
  of the dead
wiped out fallen, crashed
asphalt street

twin rivers. He bicycled home, his blood-darkened shirt pressed to his nose. When he examined his face in the mirror, he saw that he had **a scrape** on his chin. He liked that. He thought Estela might **pity** him. In history class she would cry, "Oh, what happened?" and then he would talk nonsense about a fight with three *vatos*.

But Estela had been absent the Monday and Tuesday after his **mishap**. By the time she returned on Wednesday his chin had nearly healed.

José figured out another way to get to know her. He had noticed the grimy, sweat-blackened handle of a racket poking out of her backpack. He snapped his fingers and said to himself, "Racquetball. I'll challenge her to a game."

In Other Words
a scrape an injury; a cut
pity feel sorry for
vatos guys (in Spanish)
mishap accident

Look Into the Text

1. **Main Idea and Details** José tries everything to get Estela to **notice** him. Give two details that support this.
2. **Context Clues** How can you tell that Estela plays a lot of racquetball?

The Challenge **107**

He **approached** her during lunch. She was reading from her science book and biting into her second sandwich. It was thick with slabs of meat, cheese, and a blood-red tomato. "Hi," José said, sitting across the table from her. "How do you like our school?"

Estela swallowed, cleared her throat, drank from her milk carton until it **collapsed**, and said, "It's OK. But the hot water doesn't work in the girls' showers."

"It doesn't work in ours either," he remarked. Trying to push the conversation along, he continued, "Where are you from?"

"San Diego," she said. She took another monstrous bite of her sandwich. It amazed José and made him think of his father, a carpenter, who could eat more than anyone José knew.

José, eager to connect, took a deep breath and said, "I see that you play racquetball. You wanna play a game?"

Key Vocabulary
approach *v.*, to come near

In Other Words
collapsed was flat

"Are you good?" Estela asked flatly. She picked up a slice of tomato that had slid out of her sandwich.

"Pretty good," he said without thinking as he **slipped into a lie**. "I won a couple of **tournaments**."

He watched as the tomato slice slithered down Estela's throat. She wiped her mouth and said, "Sure. How about after school on Friday."

"That's tomorrow," José said.

"That's right. Today's Thursday and tomorrow's Friday." She flattened the empty milk carton with her fist and slapped her science book closed. Then she **hurled** the carton and her balled-up lunch bag at the plastic-lined garbage can. "What's your name?"

"Camacho. José Camacho."

"I'm Estela. My friends call me Stinger."

"Stinger?"

"Yeah, Stinger. I'll meet you at the **courts** at 3:45." She got up and **headed** toward the library.

My friends call me STINGER!

After school José pedaled his bike over to his uncle Freddie's house. His uncle was sixteen, only three years older than José. It made José feel **awkward** when someone, usually a girl, asked, "Who's that **hunk**?" and he would have to answer, "My uncle."

"Freddie," José yelled, skidding to a stop in the driveway.

Freddie was in the garage lifting **weights**. He was dressed in sweats and a Raiders sweatshirt. The hem of his T-shirt was sticking out in a fringe. He bench-pressed 180 pounds, then put the weights down and said, "Hey, dude."

"Freddie, I need to borrow your racquetball racket," José said.

Key Vocabulary
awkward *adj.*, uncomfortable
weight *n.*, a heavy object
    lifted to become strong

In Other Words
hunk handsome guy

Freddie rubbed his sweaty face on the sleeve of his sweatshirt. "I didn't know you played."

"I don't. I got a game tomorrow."

"But you don't know how to play."

José had been worrying about this on his bike ride over. He had told Estela that he had won tournaments.

"I'll learn," José said.

"In one day? Get serious."

"It's against a girl."

"So. She'll probably **whip you twenty-one to *nada***."

"No way."

But José's mind twisted with worry. What if she did, he asked himself. What if she **whipped him through and through**. He recalled her crushing the milk carton with one blow of her fist.

He recalled the sandwiches she downed at lunch. Still, he had never encountered a girl who was better than he was at sports, except for Dolores Ramirez. She could hit **homers with the best of them**.

Uncle Freddie pulled his racket from the garage wall. Then he explained to José how to grip the racket. He told him that the game was like handball. The play was off the front, the ceiling, and the side walls. "Whatever you do don't look behind you. The ball comes back—fast. You can get your *ojos* knocked out."

"Yeah, I got it," José said vaguely, feeling the weight of the racket in his hand. He liked how it felt when he pounded the sweet spot of the strings against his palm.

Freddie resumed lifting weights, and José biked home, swinging the racket as he rode.

He recalled her crushing the milk carton with **one blow of her fist.**

In Other Words
whip you twenty-one to *nada* win twenty-one to zero
whipped him through and through won by many points
homers with the best of them homeruns like the best male players

That night after dinner José went outside and asked his father, "Dad, has a girl ever beaten you at anything?"

His father was watering the grass. His pale belly hung over his belt, just slightly, like a deflated ball.

"Only talking," he said. "They can outtalk a man any day of the week."

"No, in sports."

His father thought for a while and then said, "No, I don't think so."

His father's tone of voice didn't **encourage** José. So he took the racket and a tennis ball and began to **practice** against the side of the garage. The ball raced away like a rat. He **retrieved** it and tried again. Every time, he hit it either too softly or too hard. He couldn't **get the rhythm of a rally going**.

"It's hard," he said to himself. But then he remembered that he was playing with a tennis ball, not a racquetball. He **assumed** that he would play better with a real ball.

The next day school was as dull as usual. He took a test in history and returned to his regular score of twelve out of twenty. Mrs. Flores was satisfied.

"I'll see you later," Estela said, hoisting her backpack onto one shoulder, the history quiz crumpled in her fist.

"OK, Estela," he said.

"Stinger," she corrected.

"Yeah, Stinger. 3:45."

José was beginning to wonder whether he really liked her. Now she seemed **abrupt**, not cute. She was starting to look like Dolores "Hit 'n' Spit" Ramirez—tough.

Look Into the Text

1. **Confirm Prediction** Was your prediction correct? Did anything happen that surprised you? Explain.

2. **Character's Viewpoint** Why does José **assume** that he will be able to play well against Estela?

3. **Compare and Contrast** At first, José tries to get Estela's **attention**. How does José feel about her now?

Key Vocabulary

encourage *v.*, to give hope
practice *v.*, to repeat an activity to become better at it
assume *v.*, to guess that something is true

In Other Words

retrieved went to get
get the rhythm of a rally going hit the ball more than once
abrupt rude

Predict

What will happen when José plays racquetball against Estela?

After school José walked slowly to the outdoor three-walled courts. They were empty, except for a **gang of sparrows** pecking at an old hamburger wrapper.

José practiced hitting the tennis ball against the wall. It was too confusing. The ball would hit the front wall, then **ricochet** off the side wall. He spent most of his time running after the ball or cursing himself for bragging that he had won tournaments.

Estela arrived, greeting José with a jerk of her chin and a "Hey, dude." She was dressed in white sweats. A pair of **protective goggles** dangled around her neck like a necklace. She wore sweatbands on both wrists. She opened a can of balls and rolled one out into her palm, squeezing it so tightly that her forearm rippled with muscle. When she smacked the ball against the wall so hard that the echo hurt his ears,

In Other Words
gang of sparrows group of birds
ricochet bounce
protective goggles glasses to
  protect her eyes

José realized that he was in trouble. He felt limp as a dead fish.

"You ready?" she asked, adjusting her goggles over her eyes. "I have to leave at five."

"Almost," he said. He took off his shirt. Then he put it back on when he realized how skinny his chest was. "Yeah, I'm ready. You go first."

Estela, **sizing him up**, said, "No, you go first."

José decided to accept the offer. He figured he needed all the help he could get.

He bounced the ball and **served** it into the ground twice.

"You're out," she said, scooping the ball onto her racket and walking briskly to the **service box**. José wanted to ask why, but he kept quiet. After all, he thought, I am the winner of several tournaments.

"Zero-zero," Estela said, then served the ball, which ricocheted off the front and side walls. José swung wildly and missed by at least a foot. Then he ran after the ball,

In Other Words
sizing him up looking at him very carefully
served hit
service box place where players serve the ball

which had rolled out of the court onto the grass. He returned it to Estela and said, "Nice, Estela."

"Stinger."

"Yeah, Stinger."

Estela called out, "One-nothing." She **wound up again and sizzled the ball** right at José's feet. He swung and hit his kneecap with the racket. The pain jolted him like a shock of electricity as he went down, holding his knee and **grimacing**. Estela chased the ball for him.

"Can you play?" she asked.

He nodded as he rose to his feet.

"Two-nothing," she said, again bouncing the ball off the front wall, this time slower so that José swung before the ball reached his racket. He swung again, the racket spinning

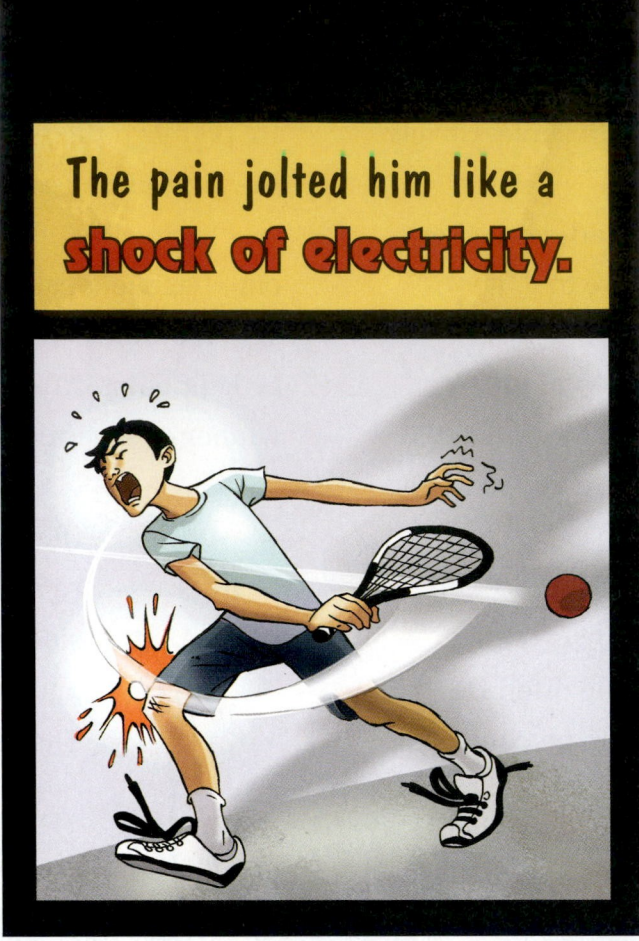

The pain jolted him like a **shock of electricity.**

like a whirlwind. The ball sailed slowly past him. He had to chase it down again.

"I guess that's three to nothing, right?" José said lamely.

"Right." Estela **lobbed the ball**. As it came down, José swung hard. His racket slipped from his fingers and flew out of the court.

"Oops," he said. The racket was caught on the top of the chain-link fence surrounding the courts. For a moment José thought of pulling the racket down and running home. But he had to **stick it out**. Anyway, he thought, my backpack is at the court.

"Four-nothing," Estela called when she saw José running back to the court, his chest heaving. She served again, and José,

In Other Words

wound up again and sizzled the ball swung and hit the ball hard
grimacing frowning in pain
lobbed the ball hit the ball high
stick it out keep playing

closing his eyes, **connected**. The ball hit the wall. For three seconds they had a **rally** going. But then Estela moved in and **killed the ball** with a low corner shot.

"Five-nothing," she said. "It's getting cold. Let me get my sweats back on."

She slipped into her sweats and threw off her sweatbands. José thought about asking to borrow the sweatbands. He had worked up a lather of sweat. But his pride kept him quiet.

In Other Words

connected hit the ball
rally real game
killed the ball won the point

Look Into the Text

1. **Confirm Prediction** Was your prediction about the raquetball game correct?

2. **Character's Motive** During the game, why does Estela insist that José call her Stinger?

3. **Sequence** When did José first know he was "in trouble"?

Estela served again and again until the score was seventeen to nothing and José was **ragged** from running. He wished the game would end. He wished he would score just one point. He took off his shirt and said, "Hey, you're pretty good."

Estela served again, gently this time, and José managed to return the ball to the front wall. Estela didn't go after it, even though she was just a couple of feet from the ball. "Nice corner shot," she lied. "Your serve."

José served the ball and, hunching over with his racket poised, **took crab steps** to the left, waiting for the ball to bounce off the front wall. Instead he heard a thunderous smack and felt himself leap like a trout. The ball had hit him in the back, and it **stung viciously**. He ran off the court and threw himself on the grass, grimacing from the pain. It took him two minutes to recover, time enough for Estela to take a healthy swig from the bottle of Gatorade in her sport bag. Finally, through his teeth, he muttered, "Good shot, Stinger."

"Sorry," Estela said. "You moved into my lane. Serve again."

José served and then cowered out of the way. He held his racket to his face for protection. She fired the ball back, clean and low, and once again she was standing at the service line calling, "Service."

Uncle Freddie was right. He had lost twenty-one to *nada*. After a **bone-jarring** handshake and a pat on his aching back from Estela, he hobbled to his uncle's house. He felt miserable. Only three weeks ago he'd been hoping that Estela—Stinger—might like him. Now he hoped she would stay away from him.

In Other Words
ragged very tired
took crab steps walked sideways
stung viciously hurt a lot
bone-jarring very strong

Uncle Freddie was in the garage lifting weights. Without greeting him, José hung the racket back on the wall. Uncle Freddie lowered the weights, sat up, and asked, "So how did it go?"

José didn't feel like lying. He lifted his T-shirt and showed his uncle the big red mark the ball had raised on his back. "She's bad."

"It could have been your face," Freddie said as he wiped away sweat and lay back down on his bench. "Too bad."

José sat on a pile of bundled newspapers, hands in his lap. When his uncle finished **his "reps,"** José got up slowly. He **peeled the weights down to sixty pounds**. It was his turn to lift. He needed strength to **mend** his broken heart and for the slight chance that Stinger might come back, looking for another victory. ❖

About the Author

Gary Soto

Gary Soto (1952–) was born in Fresno, California. When Soto was five, his father was killed in a factory accident. His mother was left alone to raise her three children with little money. Soto uses his experiences growing up a poor Mexican American in Fresno to create many of his stories and characters. He has written many books, poems, and short stories for young people.

In Other Words
his "reps," lifting weights
peeled the weights down to sixty pounds removed weight from the bar
mend heal, fix

Look Into the Text

1. **Confirm Prediction** Was your prediction about José's feelings toward Estela correct?

2. **Context Clues** What does José mean when he tells his uncle that Estela is "bad"?

3. **Author's Purpose** Why do you think the author chose to end the story with José lifting <mark>weights</mark>?

Connect Reading and Writing

Vocabulary

approached

assumed

attention

awkward

encouraged

notice

practice

weights

CRITICAL THINKING

1. SUM IT UP With a partner, use your completed Plot Diagrams to summarize the most important events in the story. Discuss how you think the characters were affected by these events.

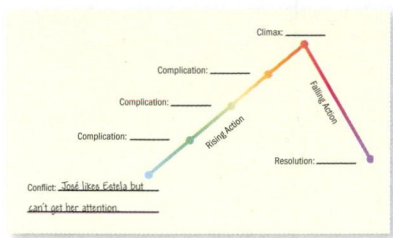

Plot Diagram

2. Analyze In what way does Estela make José feel **awkward**? Use details from the text to support your answer.

3. Make Judgments Think about what José does to get Estela to **notice** him. Do you think this was the best way to get her **attention**? Why or why not?

4. Evaluate Revisit your Anticipation Guide on page 96. Was there something you **assumed**, but no longer think is true? Explain.

READING FLUENCY

Intonation Read the passage on page 641 to a partner. Assess your fluency.

1. My tone never/sometimes/always matched what I read.

2. What I did best in my reading was _____.

READING STRATEGY

What strategy helped you understand this selection? Tell a partner about it.

VOCABULARY REVIEW

Oral Review Read the paragraph aloud. Add the vocabulary words.

I was playing tennis with my older brother. All my _____ was focused on beating him, so I didn't _____ that the coach of the middle school team was watching me play. I felt a little _____ and embarrassed when he asked to speak with me. As I _____ him, I wondered if I had done something wrong. The coach introduced himself and told me that I was a strong player. He _____ I lifted _____, and that I must _____ a lot to be so good. He _____ me to try out for the school team!

Written Review Imagine you have a friend who wants to play on a school sports team but is afraid to try out. Write a letter to **encourage** your friend. Use five vocabulary words.

WRITE ABOUT THE GUIDING QUESTION

Explore Being Yourself

Decide whether or not José would agree or disagree with this statement: "The best way to get **attention** is by being yourself." Reread the selection to find examples that support your ideas.

Connect Across the Curriculum

Vocabulary Study

Use Word Categories

> **Academic Vocabulary**
> • **category** (**ka**-tu-gor-ē) *noun*
>   A **category** is a group of items that have something in common.

One way to relate words is to group them into **categories** .

Use a Word Web In "The Challenge," José challenges Estela to a game of racquetball. From the story, you know that racquetball is a sport in which players use racquets to hit a ball. What are other similar sports? Make a Word Web for the **category** "sports that use racquets."

Build Categories This list shows **categories** of things in "The Challenge." Build a Word Web of related words for each **category** .

1. sports   **2.** clothing   **3.** feelings   **4.** food   **5.** school

Explain to a partner how the words in each **category** belong together.

Media/Viewing

MEDIA & TECHNOLOGY

Compare Sports Reports

> **Academic Vocabulary**
> • **compare** (kum-**pair**) *verb*
>   When you **compare** two things, you think about how they are alike and different.

❶ **Compare Sports Reports** **Compare** a printed news report and a television news report of the same sporting event. Make a T Chart that answers these questions:

• How does each report present the facts?

• What features, such as photographs or video clips, are in each report?

• How does each report use visuals, color, sounds, and motion?

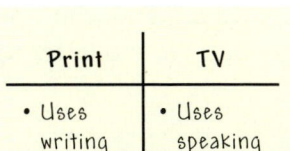

T Chart

❷ **Discuss Opinions** Which report did a better job of informing you? Entertaining you? Discuss your opinions with a partner. Give examples to support your answer.

Engage in Conversation

Role-Play Act out a conversation between two of the characters in "The Challenge" with a partner. Use subject pronouns. Trade roles.

> I need to borrow your racquet.

> I didn't know you played.

Write About a Friend

Study the Models When you write, you want your sentences to be smooth and to flow well. The first time you talk about your friend, use a noun. After that, use a subject pronoun to refer to the same person. Don't repeat the name again and again.

NOT OK

My brother Chris is 18 years old. Chris uses his favorite sport in his job. Chris works for a sporting goods company. Chris tests new snowboards. My sister Ana works for the same company. Ana is 17 years old. Ana tests new skis. My brother and sister board and ski a lot. My brother and sister both use their favorite sport in their jobs.

The reader thinks: "I'm tired of hearing about Chris, and the sentences are choppy."

OK

My brother Chris is 18 years old. He uses his favorite sport in his job. He works for a sporting goods company. He tests new snowboards. My sister Ana works for the same company. She is 17 years old. She tests new skis. My brother and sister board and ski a lot. They both use their favorite sport in their jobs.

The writer thinks: "These sentences flow well—a nice mix of nouns and pronouns."

Add Sentences Think of two more sentences to add to the OK model above. Be sure to use correct subject pronouns.

WRITE ON YOUR OWN Write about someone you know who uses a sport or other ability in his or her job. Use the person's name in the first sentence. Then use the correct subject pronoun after that.

REMEMBER

• Use the correct subject pronoun.

Singular (One)	Plural (More Than One)
I	we
you	you
he, she, it	they

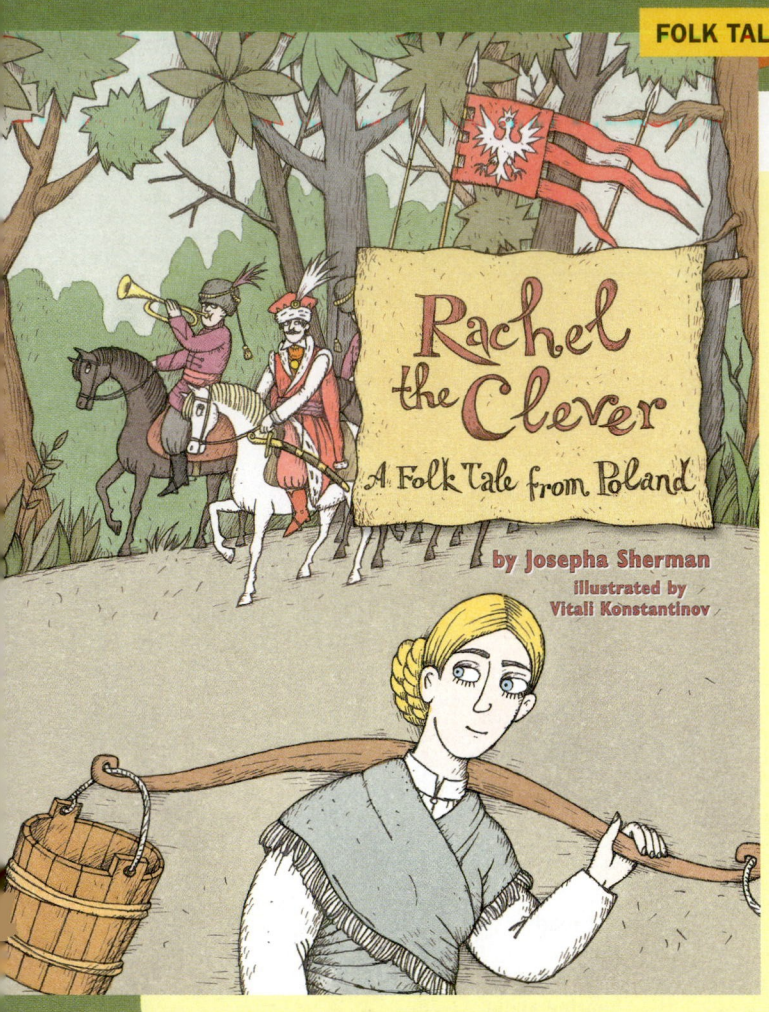

Rachel the Clever
A Folk Tale from Poland

by Josepha Sherman

illustrated by
Vitali Konstantinov

Build Background

Meet Familiar Characters

Literature, movies, and cartoons are often filled with clever characters called "tricksters." Tricksters are a type of character found in folk tales around the world. Meet some other classic characters and think about how they have changed over time.

Connect

Quickwrite Think about a character from a book, movie, TV show, or a person you know who has outsmarted someone else. Write about how this character used his or her intelligence to trick someone.

Digital Library

myNGconnect.com
◐ View the video.

▲ Bugs Bunny is a famous cartoon trickster.

Retell a Story

Listen to a folk tale from Korea. Then look at the pictures and listen to this retelling of the folk tale.

FOLK TALE

The Ungrateful Tiger

Some people in a small village are in danger from tigers in the mountains nearby. The people dig a deep hole outside their village to trap the tigers. They cover the hole with a thin layer of leaves and branches . . .

That night, a tiger falls into the hole. He tries to get out, but he can't.

In the morning, a man passes by. The tiger promises to be grateful if the man will help him get out. So the man puts a branch in the hole and helps the tiger climb out.

Once the tiger is out, he roars at the man, "Now I'm going to eat you!"

Just then, a clever rabbit comes along. He agrees to judge if it is fair for the tiger to eat the man.

The rabbit tricks the tiger back into the hole. Then the rabbit and the man walk away and leave the tiger to his fate.

Use Forms of the Verb *Be*

Use a form of the verb **be** to tell what someone or something is like.

> **Forms of *Be*:** am, is, are

The form of *be* you use depends on your subject. These subjects and verbs go together.

I + am	I **am** a clever rabbit. I like to trick the fox.
he + is	He **is** not very smart. He asks the bird for help.
she + is	She **is** full of ideas! She gives the fox a good idea.
it + is	It **is** funny when the fox tricks the rabbit.
we + are	The bird tells the fox, "We **are** the only animals who can outsmart the rabbit."
you + are	The fox tells the bird, "You **are** the smartest animal in the land!"
they + are	The fox and the bird are friends. They **are** happy to teach the rabbit a lesson.

Practice Together

Read each sentence aloud. Choose the correct form of the verb *be*.

1. It (is / are) a lovely day.
2. The sun is out and the sky (is / are) clear.
3. I (am / is) in the forest.
4. I like to feed carrots to the rabbits. They (is / are) happy to have the delicious carrots.

Try It!

Read each sentence aloud. Write the correct verb on a card. Then say the sentence with the correct verb.

5. Oh, no! I see a fox. It (is / are) over by the rabbits.
6. The rabbits (am / are) scared! They run away.
7. They (is / are) afraid of the horrible smell of the skunk.
8. The clever fox (am / is) happy. Now it can eat all the carrots!

▲ The clever fox outsmarts the rabbit.

Tell a Group a Story

RETELL A STORY

We all like to listen to other people tell stories. You may have heard stories or folk tales from your own family. Think of a folk tale you have heard. Then retell the story to your classmates.

Make a Story Map to name the characters, describe the setting, and outline the events in your story. List important details you want to include.

Story Map

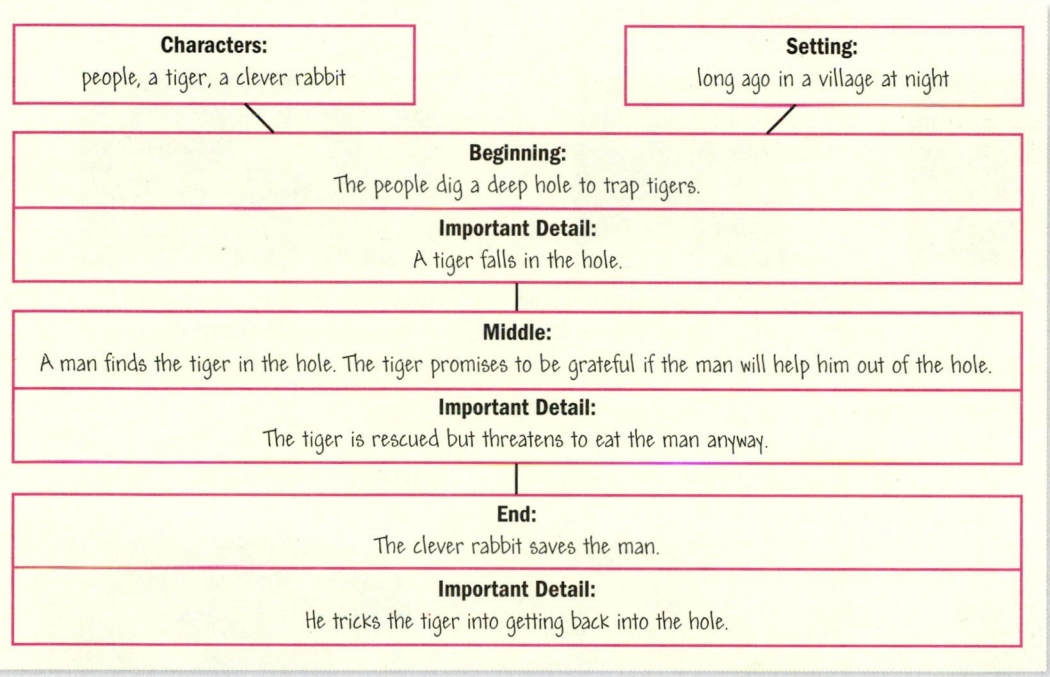

| **Characters:** | **Setting:** |
| people, a tiger, a clever rabbit | long ago in a village at night |

Beginning:
The people dig a deep hole to trap tigers.

Important Detail:
A tiger falls in the hole.

Middle:
A man finds the tiger in the hole. The tiger promises to be grateful if the man will help him out of the hole.

Important Detail:
The tiger is rescued but threatens to eat the man anyway.

End:
The clever rabbit saves the man.

Important Detail:
He tricks the tiger into getting back into the hole.

Now retell your story to a group of classmates. Use your own words to tell about the characters, setting, and events.

HOW TO RETELL A STORY

1. Describe the characters and setting.
2. Describe the main events in each part of the story.
3. Include important details that create a clear picture for the listeners.

> The people of a village make a trap to catch dangerous tigers. One night, a tiger falls in the trap.

USE FORMS OF THE VERB *BE*

When you retell the story, you need to use different forms of the verb **be**. Be sure the form you use matches your subject.

EXAMPLES   The tiger **is** trapped in the hole.
The people in the village **are** happy.

Learn Key Vocabulary

Study the Words Use the steps below.

1. Pronounce the word. Say it aloud several times. Spell it.
2. Rate your word knowledge.
3. Study the example. Tell more about the word.
4. Practice it. Make the word your own.

Key Words

clever (**klev**-ir) *adjective*
▶ page 132

A **clever** person uses intelligence to do something tricky. A magician is **clever**.
Synonym: **smart**

judgment (**juj**-mint) *noun*
▶ page 135

A **judgment** is a decision or ruling. In a court, a judge makes a **judgment** about who is right.

marry (**mair**-ē) *verb*
▶ page 132

To **marry** means to join together. When two people **marry**, they join together to make a family.
Synonym: **wed**
Antonym: **divorce**

obey (ō-**bā**) *verb*
▶ page 136

To **obey** means to do what you are told. The dogs **obey** their owner by sitting.
Related Word: **obedience**

possession (pu-**zesh**-un)
noun ▶ page 136

A **possession** is something that belongs to someone. A toy may be a child's **possession**.
Related Word: **possess**

proud (**prowd**) *adjective*
▶ page 132

To be **proud** means to feel good about yourself. You feel **proud** if you win a trophy.

release (ri-**lēs**) *verb*
▶ page 134

When you **release** something, you let it go. The woman **releases** the balloon.
Synonym: **free**
Antonym: **hold**

riddle (**rid**-ul) *noun*
▶ page 132

A **riddle** is a puzzle or tricky question. A person solves a **riddle** by finding the answer.

Practice the Words Make an Example Chart with each Key Word. Then compare your charts to a partner's charts.

Word	Definition	Example from My Life
obey	to follow the rules	I obey the school rules by not running in the hall.

Example Chart

Analyze Character

How Do Characters Affect the Plot? Most stories focus on a main character who has a problem or a goal. How the character tries to solve the problem or achieve the goal **affects** the plot. To understand how characters **affect** plot, think about the following:

- **character traits**, or qualities, such as pride, cleverness, or courage.
- **character motives**, or the reasons a character does something.
- **character actions**, or what the character does.

Characters usually do things because of their traits or motives. As you read, think about how this character will influence events in the story.

Reading Strategies

- Plan
- **Monitor** Notice confusing parts in the text then reread or read on to make them clear.
- Visualize
- Determine Importance
- Ask Questions
- Make Connections
- Make Inferences
- Synthesize

Look Into the Text

> When I read about the king, I see words like *clever* and *proud*. These give me clues about his traits.

Once, long ago, there lived a king who was very proud of his clever wits. So proud of them was he that he vowed to marry only a woman as clever as he.

Now, one day the king stopped at an inn. There he heard the innkeeper boasting about his daughter, Rachel, who was so clever she could solve any riddle.

Practice Together

Begin a Character Chart A Character Chart can help you analyze a character's behavior in a story. This Character Chart shows one of the king's traits and his motive in the passage above. Reread the passage to determine what the king does. Think about how the king's action might **affect** the plot.

Character: the king

TRAITS	MOTIVES	ACTIONS
proud	wants someone as clever as he is	

Character Chart

Academic Vocabulary

- **affect** (u-**fekt**) *verb* When you **affect** something, you cause a change in a person or thing.

Folk Tale

A folk tale is a story that has been told and retold for many years. The **setting** of a folk tale is usually in the past. The main **character** in a folk tale usually has to overcome a problem as part of the **plot**.

Writers of folk tales include details about the characters to help readers understand what they do and why they do it. As you read, use these story clues and what you already know to understand the characters and clarify new ideas about them.

Look Into the Text

Once, long ago, there lived a king who was very proud of his clever wits. So proud of them was he that he vowed to marry only a | Plot
woman who was as clever as he.

In a folk tale, characters' traits, motives, and actions influence events in the story.

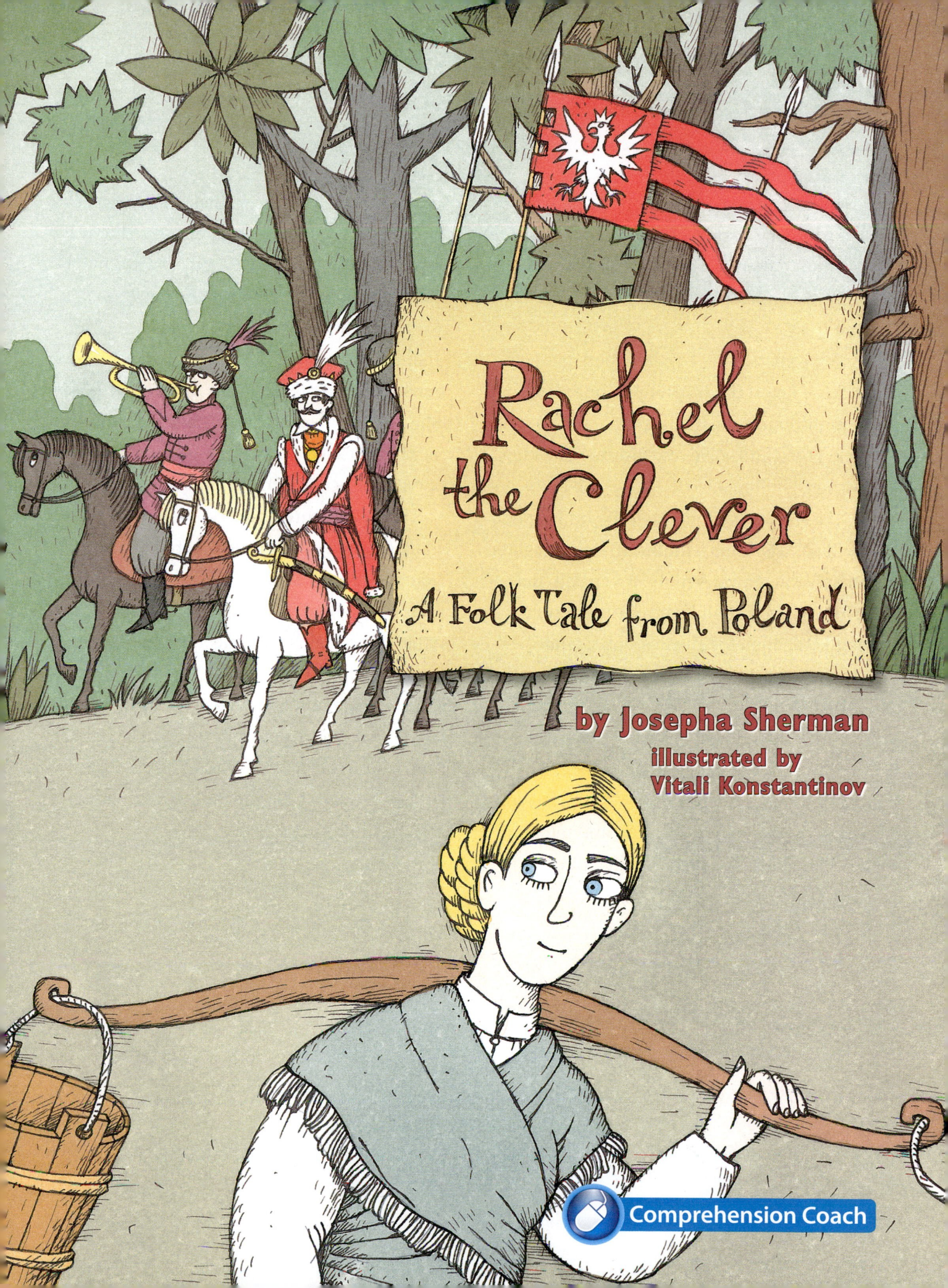

Once, long ago, there lived a king who was very **proud** of his **clever** wits. So proud of them was he that he **vowed** to marry only a woman who was as clever as he.

Now, one day the king stopped at an inn. There he heard the **innkeeper boasting** about his daughter, Rachel, who was so clever she could solve any **riddle**. The king frowned.

"I don't like liars," he told the innkeeper. "I will ask you three riddles. If your daughter can solve them, you will be rewarded. But if she fails, you shall lose your inn. First, what is the fastest thing? Second, what is the richest thing? Third, what is the dearest thing?"

Sadly, the innkeeper went home to his daughter, Rachel, and told her what the king had said. Rachel smiled. "You won't lose the inn, Father. Go to the king and tell him that Thought is the fastest thing. Life-giving Earth is the richest thing. And Love is the dearest thing."

When the king heard these answers, he frowned again. He had vowed to wed only a woman as clever as he. Could that woman be Rachel, a common innkeeper's daughter?

"If Rachel is as clever as she seems," he told the innkeeper, "I wish to meet her. She must come to my palace in three days. But she must come neither walking nor riding, neither dressed nor undressed, and bringing a gift that is not a gift."

Sadly the innkeeper went home, sure that Rachel could never solve this puzzle. But Rachel thought for only a few moments, and then she smiled. "Don't worry, father. I know what to do. Please buy me a goat, a fishnet, and . . . hmm . . . two doves."

Bewildered, the innkeeper did as he was asked. Rachel wrapped herself in the fishnet and sat on the goat so that one leg dragged on the ground. Clutching the doves, she set off for the royal palace.

Key Vocabulary
marry *v.*, to become husband and wife
proud *adj.*, self-important
clever *adj.*, smart and skilled
riddle *n.*, a confusing question

In Other Words
vowed promised
innkeeper boasting owner of the inn bragging
Bewildered Confused

Look Into the Text

1. **Character** What type of woman does the king want to **marry**? What does this show about him?

2. **Character's Motive** Why does the king want Rachel to come to his **palace**?

"I'm Rachel the innkeeper's daughter," she told the king with a grin. "I've come to you neither riding nor walking, as you see. With this fishnet wrapped around me, I'm neither dressed nor undressed."

The king felt himself starting to smile. "And the gift that is not a gift?"

"Here!"

Rachel **released** the two doves. Before the king could catch them, they **fluttered** wildly out the window. The king **burst into laughter**.

"That was most certainly a gift that was not a gift!" he said.

Key Vocabulary
release *v.*, to let go

In Other Words
fluttered flew
burst into laughter laughed loudly

Now, Rachel was as pretty and kind as she was clever. And the king (when he forgot about being proud) was equally handsome and just as kind. They looked at each other once and liked what they saw. They looked at each other twice and forgot he was a king and she was only an innkeeper's daughter. They looked at each other three times and the king said, "I wanted to marry a clever woman. You are surely she. Rachel, will you marry me?"

Rachel happily agreed.

Ah, but all at once the king remembered to be proud. "But you must never disagree with any of the **judgments** I make at court," he warned.

Rachel sighed. **"Very well."**

Key Vocabulary
judgment *n.*, decision, ruling

In Other Words
"Very well." "OK; I agree."

Look Into the Text

1. **Paraphrase** In your own words, tell how Rachel solves the king's second **riddle**.

2. **Conclusion** How does Rachel feel about the promise she makes? How do you know?

So the king and the innkeeper's daughter were married and lived so happily that for a long time the king forgot about his pride. But one day Rachel saw a **peasant** at court with a sad, sad face.

"I own a **mare** that gave birth under my neighbor's wagon," he told her. "The king has ruled that the **foal** belongs to my neighbor."

"Why, that's not right!" cried Rachel. "Go stand under the king's window with a fishing rod and pretend you're catching fish."

The peasant **obeyed**. When the king asked him how he could catch fish on a marble floor, the peasant answered as

Rachel had told him, "If a wagon can give birth to a foal, then I can catch fish on a marble floor."

When the king heard this answer, he knew that only Rachel could have given it. His pride **overpowered** his love.

"Since you have broken our agreement," he told Rachel, "you must leave the palace." Even as he said these harsh words, the king felt his heart break. But his pride was still stronger than his love. "You must leave," he repeated, "but you may take your dearest **possession** with you."

Key Vocabulary
obey *v.*, to do as one is told
possession *n.*, something that a person owns

In Other Words
peasant poor farmer
mare female horse
foal baby horse
overpowered was stronger than

Rachel didn't **weep or wail**. Instead, she slipped a sleeping **potion** into the king's cup. As soon as he was sleeping soundly that evening, Rachel wrapped him in a blanket, **hoisted** him up onto her back, and carried him out into the night. The guards, remembering what the king had said and thinking that Rachel was carrying a golden treasure, never stopped her.

The king woke to the sound of birds and found himself lying under a tree in the middle of a grassy field. Rachel was beside him. "What . . . why . . . ?" the king stammered. "What am I doing here?"

Rachel smiled gently. "I was following your order," she said. "You told me I could take my dearest possession with me. And that, my love, is you."

The king looked into Rachel's warm eyes. And as he looked, he forgot all about his pride, this time forever. "Will you forgive me?" he asked.

"Of course. And will you listen to me before you make your judgments?"

"Of course. Come, my dearest possession," said the king. "Let us go home." ❖

About the Author

Josepha Sherman
and friend

Josepha Sherman (1946–) is a writer of fantasy, science fiction, and folklore. Among her works are many novels based on popular television series, such as *Star Trek*, *Buffy the Vampire Slayer*, *Highlander*, and *Xena: Warrior Princess*. When she isn't writing, Sherman speaks at writers' conferences. She is also a talented storyteller, appearing at schools and libraries.

In Other Words
weep or wail cry
potion drug
hoisted lifted

Look Into the Text

1. **Confirm Prediction** Why does Rachel disagree with the king's **judgment**? Was your prediction correct?
2. **Plot** What is Rachel's dearest **possession**? What does this help the king to realize?

Connect Reading and Writing

Vocabulary

Vocabulary

clever
judgment
marry
obeyed
possession
proud
released
riddle

CRITICAL THINKING

1. SUM IT UP Have students use their completed Character Charts to retell the story of "Rachel the Clever." Discuss how the characters' traits and motives influence their actions.

Character: the king		
TRAITS	MOTIVES	ACTIONS
proud	wants someone as clever as he is	

Character Chart

2. Draw Conclusions Why do you think Rachel does not **obey** the king? Use details from the text and what you already know to support your answer.

3. Make Judgments Look at your Quickwrite from page 124. Is the person you wrote about as **clever** as Rachel? Why or why not?

4. Explain What does Rachel mean when she calls the king her dearest **possession**?

READING FLUENCY

Phrasing Read the passage on page 642 to a partner. Assess your fluency.

1. I did not pause/sometimes paused/ always paused for punctuation.

2. What I did best in my reading was _____.

READING STRATEGY

What strategy helped you understand this selection? Tell a partner about it.

VOCABULARY REVIEW

Oral Review Read the paragraph aloud. Add the vocabulary words.

There once lived a princess whose dearest _____ was a small wooden box. Because the princess never _____ her parents, the king made a _____ that her heart should be locked inside the box. Only the man she was supposed to _____ could open it by solving a _____. Only one young prince was _____ enough to solve it. His answer opened the box and _____ the princess's heart. But he told the princess that he would never make her be his wife. She smiled and took his hand. "I would be _____ to be your wife," she said.

Written Review Imagine you are Rachel and must write a letter to the king defending your decision to help the peasant. What would you say? Use four vocabulary words in your letter.

WRITE ABOUT THE GUIDING QUESTION

Explore Rachel's Strengths

Think about this question: How do Rachel's **clever** wits work for her and against her? Write a paragraph to explain. Support your ideas with examples from the story.

Connect Across the Curriculum

Vocabulary Study

Use Synonyms

Academic Vocabulary
- **similar** (si-mu-lur) *adjective*
  Things that are **similar** are almost the same.

What Are Synonyms? Synonyms are words that have **similar** meanings. You can relate words by finding synonyms for new words. Use a print or online **thesaurus** to help you.

Thesaurus Entry

> **bad** *adj.* of poor quality, not good: That's a really *bad* movie.
>
> **Synonyms** *terrible, awful* very bad: Those stale cookies taste *awful*!
>
> *unsatisfactory* not good enough: I got an *unsatisfactory* grade on my book report.
>
> **Antonyms** *good, great*

Make a Synonym Scale
Use **similar** words by making a Synonym Scale to put synonyms in order from weakest to strongest.

Synonym Scale

smart   clever   intelligent

With a partner, make Synonym Scales for these words from "Rachel the Clever." Use a thesaurus if you need help.

1. proud, p. 132
2. bewildered, p. 132
3. boasting, p. 132
4. harsh, p. 136
5. weep, p. 138
6. hoisted, p. 138

Viewing/Speaking

Illustrate Character Traits

ART

Academic Vocabulary
- **illustrate** (i-lus-trāt) *verb*
  To **illustrate** is to use pictures or examples to make something clear.

1 Plan Your Illustration Plan a drawing or collage that **illustrates** a trait of a character in "Rachel the Clever." Think about these questions:
- How can I show a trait in a picture?
- What details from the story can I use?

2 Create Your Illustration To make your illustration, you can draw, paint, or cut out pictures from magazines to make a collage.

3 Share Your Illustration Ask classmates to guess what character and trait you **illustrated**. Explain your choices.

Retell a Story

Pair Talk Retell "Rachel the Clever" to a partner. Make sure to tell the story in your own words. Use forms of the verbs *be* and *have* in some of your sentences.

> One day, a proud king stops at an inn. He is tired and hungry.

Write About a Folk Tale

Study the Models When you write about a folk tale, use complete and clear sentences so your reader can understand and appreciate what you have to say. A complete sentence has both a subject and a verb. A clear sentence has a subject and a verb that go together.

NOT OK

> Folk tales are made-up stories that often include children and talking animals. Some folk tales <u>is</u> the same in different countries. The theme of "Little Red Riding Hood" <u>is</u> the same in China, France, and Germany. A little girl in red <u>are</u> on her way to visit her grandmother. On her way, she meets a wolf who pretends to be friendly.

The reader thinks: **"Is it one folk tale or more than one folk tale?"** The sentence isn't clear.

OK

> Folk tales are made-up stories that often include children and talking animals. Some folk tales <u>are</u> the same in different countries. The theme of "Little Red Riding Hood" <u>is</u> the same in China, France, and Germany. A little girl in red <u>is</u> on her way to visit her grandmother. On her way, she meets a wolf who pretends to be friendly.

This is clear because the subjects and verbs match.

Add Sentences Think of two sentences to add to the OK model above. Make sure your subjects and verbs agree.

✏ **WRITE ON YOUR OWN**
Write about a folk tale or other story that you know. Check that your subjects and verbs agree.

▲ "Little Red Hat" is the Italian version of "Little Red Riding Hood."

REMEMBER

Use the form of the verb that goes with your subject.

Forms of *Be*	Forms of *Have*
I + am	he she + has it
he she + is it	I you we + have they
we you + are they	

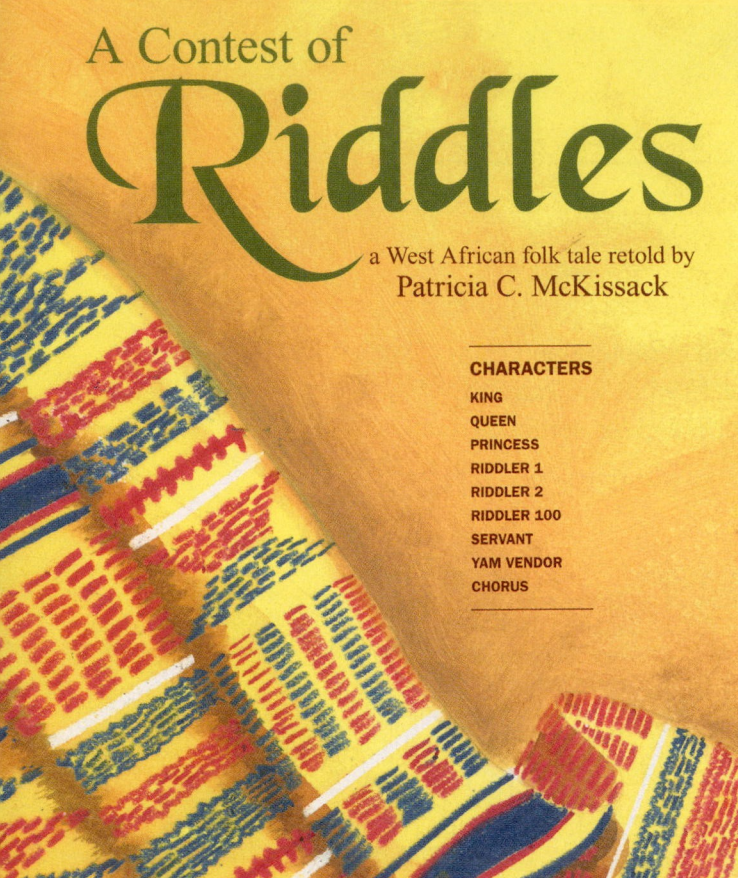

A Contest of Riddles

a West African folk tale retold by
Patricia C. McKissack

CHARACTERS

KING
QUEEN
PRINCESS
RIDDLER 1
RIDDLER 2
RIDDLER 100
SERVANT
YAM VENDOR
CHORUS

SELECTION 3 OVERVIEW

▶ **Build Background**

▶ **Language & Grammar**
Ask for and Give Information
Use Subjects and Verbs

▶ **Prepare to Read**
Learn Key Vocabulary
Analyze Elements of Drama

▶ **Read and Write**
Introduce the Genre
Play
Focus on Reading
Elements of Fiction:
Plot, Character, Setting
Apply the
Focus Strategy
Monitor
Critical Thinking
Reading Fluency
Read with Expression

Vocabulary Review
Write About the
Guiding Question

▶ **Connect Across
the Curriculum**
Vocabulary Study
Use Synonyms and
Antonyms
Listening/Speaking
Act in a Scene
Language and Grammar
Ask for and Give
Information
Writing and Grammar
Write About a Play

Build Background

Connect

Discuss Pros and Cons Should parents make decisions for their children? Make a pro/con list. What is good and bad about parents making the decisions? Discuss with your class. Come up with one statement that reflects what most students think.

Learn About the Abron

"A Contest of Riddles" takes place in a small village in West Africa. It is a retelling of a folk tale from the Abron people, a group with rich cultural traditions.

Digital Library   **myNGconnect.com**
↪ View the images.

▲ The Abron people live in what is now Ghana, West Africa.

Language & Grammar

Ask for and Give Information

CD

Listen to the chant, and chime in.
Role-play the questions and answers.

CHANT and ROLE-PLAY

What Is Drama?

Find out about drama. Do it now.
Ask questions like *Who? What?*
When? Where? Why? and *How?*

What is drama?

It's a play, or story, that people act.

Who are the people?

We call them actors, and that's a fact.

Where do actors put on a play?

They usually perform up on a stage.

How do the actors know what to say?

An author wrote the words, or dialogue, on a page.

How do the actors know what to do?

The pages, or script, give stage directions, too.

Why are the actors important?

Their words and actions bring a story to life for you!

Use Subjects and Verbs

- An **action verb** tells what the subject does. Some action verbs tell about an action that you cannot see.

  EXAMPLES   I **choose** my friends. I **pick** them carefully.

- Make sure an action verb agrees with its subject. Add **-s** if the subject tells about one place, one thing, or one other person.

  EXAMPLES   My friends **help** each other. Amy **helps** me with math. Ben **helps** Amy with music.

- If the verb ends in **sh**, **ch**, **ss**, **s**, **z**, or **x**, add **-es**.

  EXAMPLES   Amy **sings**. She **reaches** high notes. She **misses** her music teacher.

- Some verbs have special forms. The forms of *be* tell what a subject is like.

  EXAMPLES   My friends **are** all different. Ben **is** a storyteller. Amy **is** dramatic. I **am** quiet.

- The forms of *have* tell what a subject owns.

  EXAMPLES   They **have** different interests, too. Each one **has** a special interest.

Practice Together

Say each sentence with the correct verb.

1. My friends all (have/has) special hobbies, too.
2. Ben and I (march/marches) in the marching band.
3. Amy (act/acts) in the drama club at school.
4. She (watch/watches) plays at the theater, too.
5. We (talk/talks) about the plays she sees.

Try It!

Read each sentence. Write the correct verb on a card. Then say the sentence with the correct verb.

6. Chris (relax/relaxes) in the evening.
7. He (find/finds) time to check his e-mail.
8. He (have/has) lots of e-mails to answer.
9. His friends (is/are) happy to hear from him.
10. They (write/writes) him back quickly.

▲ **My friend acts in the school play.**

Talk with a Friend

ASK FOR AND GIVE INFORMATION

Most people can remember a play they saw in school, at a theater, or on TV. Write the name of a play you know about on a sheet of paper. Trade with a partner. Then share ideas. You ask the questions, and your partner gives the information.

Plan your questions. Think about what you could ask your friend. Make a chart.

Question Word	The Answer Will Be	Question
Who?	a person	Who is the star of the play?
What?	a thing or an action	What does the main character do?
When?	a time	
Where?	a place	
Why?	a reason	
How?	an explanation	

Now ask your partner your questions, and listen to the answers. Take notes. Then trade roles.

HOW TO ASK FOR AND GIVE INFORMATION

1. When you want information, ask questions that start with *Who*, *What*, *When*, *Where*, *Why*, or *How*.
2. When you give information, tell the most important idea and give some details.

When did you see the show?

I saw it last summer with my cousin Hector.

USE SUBJECTS AND VERBS

When you give information, the **action verbs** you use need to agree with the subjects of your sentences. Check your verbs. Remember, add **-s** to the verb if the subject is one other person, one place, or one thing.

One person: The actor **acts** in the play.

More than one person: The actors **act** in the play.

Prepare to Read

Learn Key Vocabulary

Study the Words Use the steps below.

1. Pronounce the word. Say it aloud several times. Spell it.
2. Rate your word knowledge.
3. Study the example. Tell more about the word.
4. Practice it. Make the word your own.

Rating Scale

1 = I have never seen this word before.

2 = I am not sure of the word's meaning.

3 = I know this word and can teach the word's meaning to someone else.

Key Words

choice (chois) *noun*
▶ page 150

A **choice** is a decision. You make a **choice** about what to eat each day.
Related Word: **choose**

contest (kahn-test) *noun*
▶ page 150

A **contest** is a game or test to see who is the best at something. The winner of a **contest** often gets a prize.
Related Word: **contestant**

excellent (ek-su-lint)
adjective ▶ page 154

When something is **excellent**, it is very good. The audience thought the play was **excellent**.
Synonyms: **wonderful, terrific**
Antonyms: **terrible, awful**

interpret (in-tur-prit) *verb*
▶ page 152

To **interpret** means to figure out or explain what something means. The woman **interprets** the speech through sign language.
Related Word: **interpreter**

knowledge (nah-lij) *noun*
▶ page 156

Knowledge is what you know. When you learn new things, you add to your **knowledge**.

nonsense (nahn-sens) *noun*
▶ page 156

Nonsense is something that makes no sense. Sometimes riddles are **nonsense**.

outcome (owt-kum) *noun*
▶ page 160

An **outcome** is the result of something. A scoreboard shows the **outcome** of a race.

response (ri-spons) *noun*
▶ page 155

A **response** is an answer or reply. A **response** can be either spoken or written.

Practice the Words Make a Study Card for each Key Word. Compare your cards with a partner's cards.

choice

What it means: a decision

Example: I pick out my clothes.

Not an example: I have to wear a uniform every day.

Study Card

Analyze Elements of Drama

How Is a Play Structured? A play is a story that is written to be acted, or spoken aloud. Special elements help readers understand the story:

- **scenes** how a play is divided; usually a new scene starts when the time or place changes
- **stage directions** descriptions for the crew or instructions for the actors
- **dialogue** the lines, or words, the characters speak
- **narrator or chorus** characters who explain or interpret the action

As you read, notice how each of these dramatic elements helps you understand the meaning of the play.

Reading Strategies

- Plan
- **Monitor** Notice confusing parts in the text then reread or read on to make them clear.
- Visualize
- Determine Importance
- Ask Questions
- Make Connections
- Make Inferences
- Synthesize

Look Into the Text

SCENE 1. *Morning. The private quarters of the* KING *and* QUEEN. *They are in the garden talking about their daughter. The* PRINCESS *approaches them.*

PRINCESS. You sent for me Father? Mother?

QUEEN. Yes, dear. We need to talk to you about your future. It is time for us to choose a husband for you.

PRINCESS. Why do you get to choose the man I will marry?

KING. [*laughs kindly*] That is the way we do things in our kingdom.

"This stage direction helps me understand how the king acts during his line."

Practice Together

Begin a Drama Chart Use a two-column Drama Chart to help you identify what you learn from the play. Reread the passage above. Record your ideas on the chart.

Element of Drama	What I Learn
stage directions	It is morning. The king and queen are talking in the garden when the princess comes in.

Drama Chart

Play

A play is a story that is performed. Characters, dialogue, and stage directions are some of the elements of a play.

As you read, think about what each character's words and actions tell you about the meaning of the play. Reread the dialogue or stage directions to clarify unfamiliar words or phrases.

Look Into the Text

PRINCESS. Why do you get to ◁ dialogue
choose the man I will marry?

character   stage directions

KING. [*laughs kindly*] That is
the way we do things in our
kingdom. The parents always
choose the man their daughter
will marry.

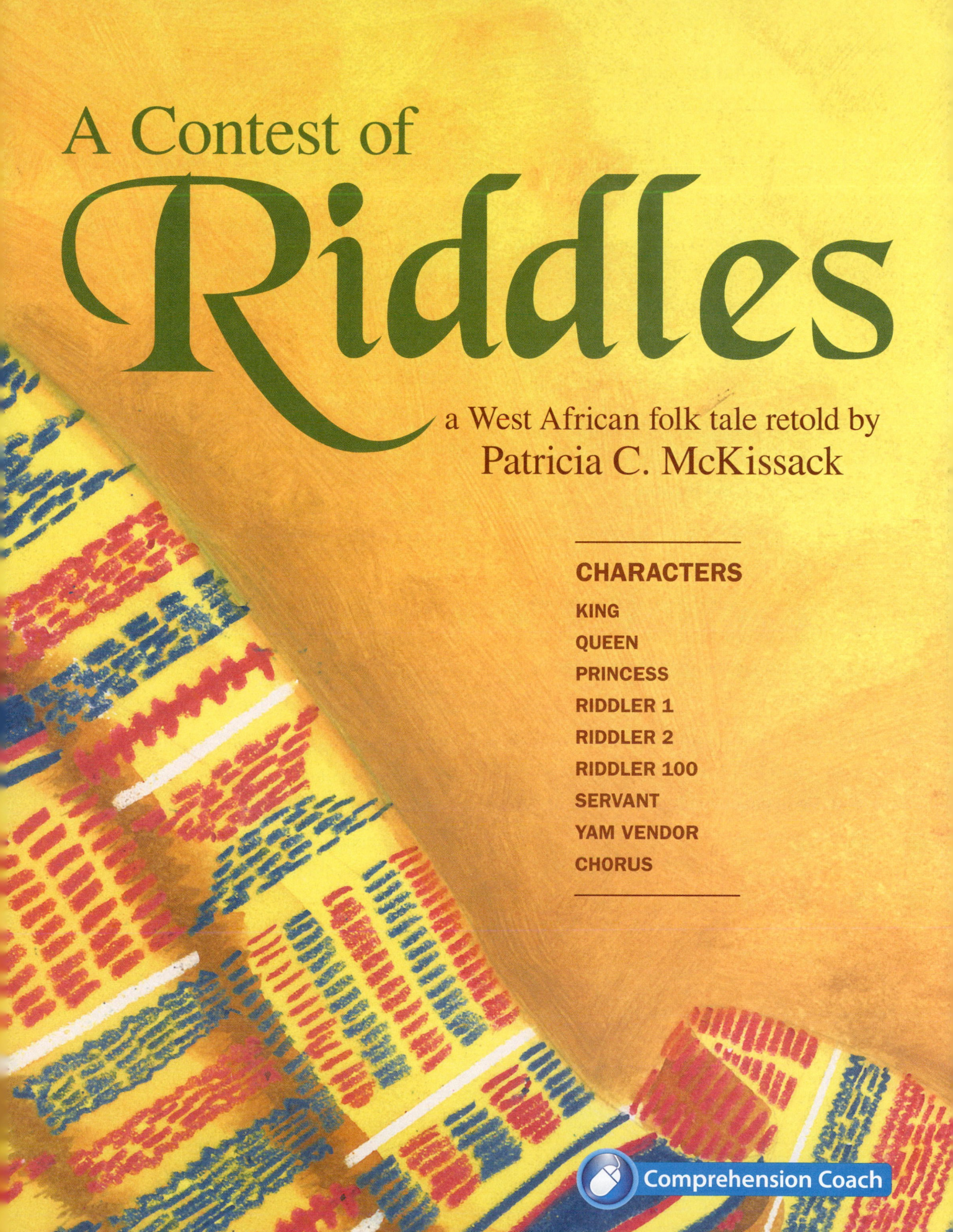

A Contest of
Riddles

a West African folk tale retold by
Patricia C. McKissack

CHARACTERS

KING

QUEEN

PRINCESS

RIDDLER 1

RIDDLER 2

RIDDLER 100

SERVANT

YAM VENDOR

CHORUS

SETTING. *An Abron village in West Africa in the mid-1800s*

SCENE 1. *Morning. The private quarters of the* KING *and* QUEEN. *They are in the garden talking about their daughter. The* PRINCESS *approaches them.*

PRINCESS. You sent for me Father? Mother?

QUEEN. Yes, dear. We need to talk to you about your future. It is time for us to choose a husband for you.

PRINCESS. Why do you get to choose the man I will marry?

KING. [*laughs kindly*] That is the way we do things in our kingdom. The parents always choose the man their daughter will marry.

PRINCESS. What if I am not happy with your **choice**? [*dramatic*] I will be so sad. I will never, ever smile. I will dry up like a flower and fade away. Would you doom your daughter to such a fate?

[*The* QUEEN *looks at her husband and sighs. The* KING *rubs his hands together and paces back and forth. He is thinking.*]

KING. Daughter, your happiness means a lot to us. What if we let you choose your own husband?

QUEEN. [*gasps*] What? No girl in our kingdom has ever been allowed to make her own choice. It is the parents' responsibility to make such an important decision. [**aside**, *with a hint of a smile*] How he spoils that girl!

PRINCESS. Father, I have always wanted to marry someone who enjoys riddles as much as I do. I could marry a man who is as **good a riddler** as I am. That would make me very happy.

KING. [*suddenly claps his hands happily*] I have an idea! We will have a **contest**. You will **match your skills against** young men throughout the kingdom. The one who wins will become your

---

Key Vocabulary

choice *n.*, the person or thing that someone picks or chooses

contest *n.*, a struggle or competition

In Other Words

aside to the audience so none of the other characters can hear
good a riddler clever
match your skills against see if you are better than

husband. [*speaking to the* QUEEN] This is a plan that works for us all. We make the decision, and at the same time, our daughter gets a clever husband.

QUEEN. [*nods*] So let it be done.

[*The* KING, QUEEN, *and* PRINCESS *leave.*]

CHORUS. [*enter **chanting***]

Let the word go out.
Let the word go out.

Let the word go out today.
Bring your riddles.
Bring your riddles.
Bring your riddles today.
I know one. How about you?
I know one. How about you?
I know one. How about you today?

END SCENE 1.

Royal Family, 2007, Kathleen Wilson. Mixed Media, collection of the artist.

▲ **Critical Viewing: Character** How do the three people in this image feel? How can you tell?

In Other Words
chanting singing

Look Into the Text

1. **Summarize** What do the king and queen want for the princess? How will they make their **choice**?
2. **Figurative Language** What does the princess mean when she says "I will dry up like a flower and fade away"?

SCENE 2. *Three months later. The* KING *is on his royal throne. The* QUEEN *is beside him. The* PRINCESS *is seated in a chair below them. Two* RIDDLERS *are standing to the side. The villagers look on.*

CHORUS. [*enter dancing and singing to the* **contestants**]

Let us sing, rejoice, and be glad.

The contest of riddles is about to begin.

Let us sing, rejoice, and be glad.

Here are the rules, so listen, listen.

Let us sing, rejoice, and be glad.

Each contestant gives a riddle.

The princess gives one back.

Giving,

Getting,

Until one wins.

[*The* CHORUS *sits around the* PRINCESS. RIDDLER 1 *stands before the* PRINCESS. *He bows.*]

RIDDLER 1. I asked the wisest men in my village to help me find a riddle that even a princess as smart as you would not be able to **interpret**.

PRINCESS. I am excited to hear it. Please share it with me.

RIDDLER 1. [*begins the riddle*] My life is spent coming and going from left to right and back again, from left to right and back again.

PRINCESS. That is a good riddle, but I know it. It is a **weaver at his loom**. He makes cloth by weaving yarn from left to right. Now here is my riddle for you:

Over water.

Under water.

But it does not touch water.

RIDDLER 1. [*looks at her* **blankly**] I have no idea. [RIDDLER 1 *leaves, disappointed.*]

Key Vocabulary

interpret *v.*, to solve or explain the meaning of something

In Other Words

contestants people in the contest
weaver at his loom person using a special machine to make cloth
blankly with no understanding

▲ **Critical Viewing: Design** Examine the figures and objects in this painting. How does this image provide clues to the princess's riddle?

RIDDLER 2. [*bows*] I know the answer to that last riddle. It is a woman walking with a jug of water on her head. She is under water. Then the woman crosses a bridge. She is over water. Yet, she does not ever touch water.

PRINCESS. Excellent. Now do you have a riddle for me?

RIDDLER 2. I don't have one, but any riddle you put before me, I will be able to interpret it.

PRINCESS. You sound very sure of yourself. Here's one: When we are born, we are given two bottles. One has something sweet inside. One has something **bitter** inside.

RIDDLER 2. Water and . . . [*thinks*] Oh, I don't know the answer. [RIDDLER 2 *walks away, very **disgusted**.*]

KING. [*whispers loudly to the* QUEEN] The sweet bottle is life. The bitter bottle is death. Even I knew that one. I thought these young men would be better at this.

QUEEN. [*raises her eyebrow and smiles*] Our daughter is an excellent riddler. She can create them and interpret them with equal skill. She won't **be defeated** easily.

END SCENE 2.

In Other Words
bitter with a bad taste
disgusted upset
be defeated lose

Look Into the Text

1. **Interpret** Why does Riddler 2 walk away disgusted? Explain the purpose of this stage direction.
2. **Inference** How does the queen feel about her daughter's success? How do you know?

SCENE 3. *Several weeks later. The KING and QUEEN are on their thrones. The PRINCESS is seated below them. They look tired.*

CHORUS. [*enter dancing and singing*]

Come, young men, to the king's
    great palace.
Match your skill with the lovely princess.
Riddle after riddle—one, two, three.
Match your skill with the
    riddling princess.
Young men came to the king's
    great palace.
Matched their skills with the
    clever princess.
Riddle after riddle—one, two, three.
No match for the riddling princess.

KING. [*bored and disgusted*] Whose idea was this? Will it ever end?

QUEEN. Ninety-nine of our strongest and smartest young men have challenged the princess. None of them have been able to win. And here comes another one.

[*RIDDLER 100 enters with a SERVANT. He does not bow.*]

RIDDLER 100. Prepare to be my bride, Princess. You will marry me. And when we **are wed**, there will be no more of these stupid riddles. I've never liked them.

[*The KING and QUEEN look surprised. The PRINCESS frowns. The SERVANT shakes his head sadly. The PRINCESS notices his* **response**, *but says nothing.*]

RIDDLER 100. [*leans toward the SERVANT, the SERVANT whispers in his ear*] Here is my riddle: One is dead, yet it still answers. One is living, but it doesn't answer.

PRINCESS. It is a dead leaf that crunches underfoot. And a green leaf that makes no sound when you walk on it. Here is a riddle for you: It has teeth but cannot bite.

Key Vocabulary
response *n.*, an answer to something that has been done or said

In Other Words
are wed get married

[RIDDLER 100 *leans over to the* SERVANT. *The* SERVANT *whispers the answer in his ear.*]

RIDDLER 100. The answer is a comb—the teeth in a comb can't bite anything. I win!

PRINCESS. You have only won part of the contest. You have answered my riddle, but you haven't given me one that I can't answer. Those are the rules. Do you have another riddle for me?

[RIDDLER 100 *leans again toward the* SERVANT, *who whispers to him.*]

RIDDLER 100. [*sneers*] Can you guess this one? It has eyes but cannot see.

PRINCESS. That's easy. The eyes of a potato can't see. [*hopping to her feet*] I'd like for the servant to enter the contest. He seems to be the one with all the **knowledge**.

You have only won part of the contest.

[*The* SERVANT *looks surprised.*]

RIDDLER 100. [*angrily*] That's **nonsense**. I won't allow it!

PRINCESS. Too bad. This riddle is for you, Servant: It is like a roaring lion, running with his **mane** flying all around him.

SERVANT. [*happily*] That's one of my favorites. The answer is a storm. I can see the dark clouds as they roll in. The thunder **rumbles**, and the lightning flashes all around. I love storms almost as much as I love riddles.

PRINCESS. Give me one!

SERVANT. As you wish:
More valuable than silver or gold,
Yet it cannot be bought or sold.

PRINCESS. [*thinking*] I—I don't know. What is it? [*smiles and winks to let the* SERVANT *know that she really knows the answer*]

Key Vocabulary
knowledge *n.*, information or skills that someone has learned
nonsense *n.*, something that seems to be silly or has no meaning

In Other Words
sneers smiles meanly
mane fur
rumbles makes noise
More valuable Worth more money

SERVANT. [*smiling*] The answer
is love, Princess.

KING. The servant has won the contest.
Oh, my.

QUEEN. Oh my, is right. He's a servant, dear!
It has never been done. Oh, well, times
are changing . . .

KING. I can't choose him unless his master
gives his permission.

RIDDLER 100. And I don't give my
permission! He is my servant, and we
are going home. [*speaking to the*
SERVANT] Get our things ready.
We will leave right away.

[RIDDLER 100 *and the* SERVANT *leave.*
The SERVANT *looks back for one last*
look at the PRINCESS.]

CHORUS. Farewell, true love.
We may never meet again.
Good-bye, dear one.
My heart is filled with pain.

END SCENE 3.

Couple, 2002, Muraina Oyelami. Oil on canvas, collection of the artist.

▲ **Critical Viewing: Mood** How does this painting reflect the
mood of the story at this point?

In Other Words
My heart is filled with pain. I am
very sad and upset.

Look Into the Text

1. **Confirm Prediction** Did the
   princess find love? What happened
   that you did not expect?
2. **Character** What does Riddler
   100's attitude say about him?
3. **Character's Motive** Why does
   the princess pretend she cannot
   <mark>interpret</mark> the servant's riddle?

Predict

The princess is sent a strange riddle from a rich man. Who is it?

SCENE 4. *The next day. The* KING *and* QUEEN *are in the garden.*

QUEEN. The Princess cried all night long. We must think of something. If we had chosen a husband, all of this might have been avoided.

KING. I think you are right.

[*A* **YAM VENDOR** *enters carrying a basket of yams.*]

YAM VENDOR. Great King and Queen. I met a **caravan** along the road. A rich man paid me a lot of money to bring this riddle to the princess. I have no idea what it means, but I promised I would deliver it.

[*The* PRINCESS *enters the garden.*]

PRINCESS. I hear you have something for me. What is it?

YAM VENDOR. [*recites*] A yam tied to a tree will turn sugar into fire.

PRINCESS. [*gasps*] Father, I need two horses. My dearest love has been tied to a tree and left to be stung to death by **fire ants**. I must go rescue him! [*to the* YAM VENDOR] Show me the way back to where you were! [*exits quickly with* YAM VENDOR]

SCENE 5. *A week later. A wedding is taking place in the court. The* KING *and* QUEEN *sit on the throne. The newly-married* PRINCESS *and* SERVANT *are seated together.*

CHORUS. [*enter dancing and singing*]
The princess is here,
And happiness has come.
Her husband is here,
And happiness has come.
They are together,
And happiness is in this place.

In Other Words
YAM VENDOR person who sells a type of vegetable
caravan group of traveling people
fire ants ants with a painful sting

▲ **Critical Viewing: Character** How do the expressions of the man and woman in the artwork reflect the emotions of the princess and the servant?

KING. Seems like we made a good choice for our daughter. Don't you think, dear wife?

QUEEN. We were lucky, my husband. The servant turned out to be a **captive prince, stolen from his homeland**.

KING. That **arrogant** master of his had no idea of how good our daughter is with riddles. If she had not guessed his riddles, the <mark>outcome</mark> would have been different. But all is well that ends well.

QUEEN. Indeed.

CHORUS. The princess is here,
And happiness has come.
Her husband is here,
And happiness has come.
They are together,
And happiness is in this place.

END PLAY. ❖

About the Author

Patricia C. McKissack

Award-winning author **Patricia C. McKissack** (1944–) was a teacher and edited books before she became a full-time writer. She writes many books about the African American experience. She feels strongly that everyone needs good literature about every culture, including her own. McKissack has written almost 100 books. She believes reading "opens up a world beyond where you are in the moment."

Key Vocabulary
<mark>outcome</mark> *n.*, end result

In Other Words
captive prince, stolen from his homeland prince who was taken from his home
arrogant rude

Look Into the Text

1. **Confirm Prediction** Who is the rich man the yam vendor describes? Was your prediction correct?
2. **Inference** Why does the queen feel lucky that the servant was a captive prince?

ATALANTA'S *Race*

In ancient Greece, in the city of Boeotia, there lived a beautiful princess named Atalanta. She was famous for her speed. She loved to run and was faster than anyone in the kingdom.

One day her father, the king, decided that it was time for her to get married. However, Atalanta did not want to marry anyone . . . yet.

"I will only marry a man who can beat me in a race," she told her father. She was sure that no one could outrun her.

Many young men came to race **for her hand in marriage**, but Atalanta beat them all. Then Hippomenes, a prince from a distant kingdom, arrived. He fell in love with Atalanta **at first sight** and decided that he must marry her. He went to speak to the king.

"Let me race against Atalanta," he said. "If I win, I get to marry her. If she wins, she will have the honor of defeating me."

The king accepted Hippomenes's offer, and the date of the race was set. Hippomenes went for a run outside the city. He knew he would have to work hard to win.

Suddenly, a beautiful woman appeared before him. It was Aphrodite, the goddess of love.

"I will help you win the race," she said and held out her hand. "Take these three gold apples and use them wisely."

Hippomenes was not sure how the apples would help him, but he thanked the goddess and put them in his pocket.

In Other Words
for her hand in marriage to be the one who could marry her
at first sight when he first saw her

The morning of the race, Hippomenes lined up at the starting line with Atalanta. At the sound of the trumpets, they were off, running fast.

Atalanta immediately **took the lead** and Hippomenes could not get ahead of her. Then he thought of the gold apples in his pocket. He took one and threw it so it landed in front of her. Atalanta saw the shining apple and decided she could easily pick it up. As she slowed down, Hippomenes ran past her.

But Atalanta wasn't worried. Soon she was beside him again. Hippomenes took out the second apple. Once again, he threw it in front of her and Atalanta slowed to pick it up. Hippomenes passed her for the second time.

Now they were nearing the finish line. Atalanta had caught up to Hippomenes and was about to pass him. Desperately,

Hippomenes took out the third gold apple and flung it toward the side of the path. This time, Atalanta had to **swerve** and stop to pick it up. Hippomenes ran faster and crossed the finish line **a split second** before her.

"I hope you enjoy your apples," Hippomenes said with a smile as Atalanta stopped beside him. Only then did she realize that she had been tricked.

"I shouldn't have been so sure that I would win," she replied. "You're very fast. If I hadn't stopped for the apples, we might have tied for first place."

Atalanta liked the thought of someone running as fast as she could run. She happily agreed to marry Hippomenes, and from then on, the two always ran as equals.

In Other Words
took the lead ran the fastest
swerve run to the side of the path
a split second just

Look Into the Text

1. **Character's Viewpoint** How does Atalanta feel about men who can't beat her? How do you know?
2. **Inference** What is the moral, or lesson, of this story? Cite evidence from the text to support your answer.

Connect Reading and Writing

Vocabulary
choice
contest
excellent
interpret
knowledge
nonsense
outcome
response

CRITICAL THINKING

1. **SUM IT UP** Compare Drama Charts with a partner, explaining what you learned from the different elements in each part of the play. Then work together to summarize the play.

Element of Drama	What I Learn
stage directions	It is morning. The king and queen are talking in the garden when the princess comes in.

Drama Chart

2. **Explain** Think about your **responses** to the pro/con discussion from page 142. Have you changed your ideas since reading the selection? Explain.
3. **Make Judgments** Do you think that a **contest** is a good way to choose a husband or wife? Why or why not?
4. **Compare** Look at "A Contest of Riddles" and "Atalanta's Race." How are the **outcomes** of each story alike? How are they different?

READING FLUENCY

Expression Read the passage on page 643 to a partner. Assess your fluency.

1. My voice never/sometimes/always matched what I read.
2. What I did best in my reading was _____.

READING STRATEGY

What strategy helped you understand this selection? Tell a partner about it.

VOCABULARY REVIEW

Oral Review Read the paragraph aloud. Add the vocabulary words.

Our class saw a play about a dance _____. We must write a _____ to it. Some kids said it was terrible, but that's _____! I loved it. The acting was _____ and the end had a cool _____. Sometimes, it was hard to _____ what the actors were saying. Maybe people would have enjoyed it if they had more _____ about dancing. But we always have a _____ to read about it on our own.

Written Review Imagine you are the princess. Write a letter to the king and queen about why it was important to make your own **choice**. Use four vocabulary words.

 **WRITE ABOUT THE** GUIDING QUESTION

Explore the Strength of Intelligence
How would either the servant in "A Contest of Riddles" or Hippomenes in "Atalanta's Race" respond to this statement: "Sometimes being smart isn't enough." Write a **response** for the character using examples from the text.

Connect Across the Curriculum

Vocabulary Study

Use Synonyms and Antonyms

> **Academic Vocabulary**
> • **similar** (si-mu-lur) *adjective*
>   Things that are **similar** are almost the same.

Most synonyms and antonyms have different shades of meaning. For example, *clever* is a stronger word than *smart*, but *brilliant* is even stronger than *clever*. *Dumb* means the opposite of *smart*, but *stupid* is an even stronger word.

Use a Synonym-Antonym Scale to show the relationship among these words.

Synonym-Antonym Scale

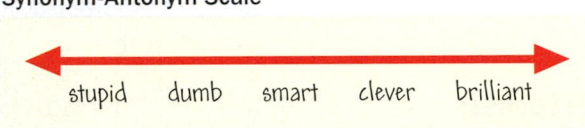

stupid   dumb   smart   clever   brilliant

Make a Synonym-Antonym Scale With a partner, find the words below in "A Contest of Riddles" or "Atalanta's Race." Make a Synonym-Antonym Scale for each word. Use a print or online thesaurus if you need help.

1. rejoice   **2.** arrogant   **3.** bitter   **4.** immediately   **5.** valuable

Listening/Speaking

Act Out a Scene

DRAMA

> **Academic Vocabulary**
> • **role** (rōl) *noun*
>   A **role** is a position someone has in a certain situation.

❶ Determine Characters In a small group, act out Scene 2 of "The Contest of Riddles." Pick **roles** and think about these questions:
- What is my character like?
- How should my character speak and move?

❷ Block the Scene Use Stage Directions to move chairs into place and set up the scene as written.

❸ Act Out the Scene Have characters take their places. Signal the chorus to begin, moving according to the stage directions and ending in a seated circle around the princess. Then have Riddler I continue the scene through p. 154 as written.

❹ Draw Conclusions How is acting out the scene different from just reading it aloud? How did the way actors performed their parts influence your understanding of each character?

Ask for and Give Information

Find out more about a classmate. Take turns. Ask and answer questions about sports, favorite movies, plays, or music. Speak clearly and listen carefully to your partner. Use colorful action verbs.

> What do you do after school?

> I play basketball with my friends. I'm great at it! I run fast, leap high, and slam the ball through the net.

Write About a Play

Study the Models If you want to catch your reader's interest, try using colorful action words when you write. Many words tell what someone does—*talk*, *chat*, *chatter*, *discuss*, *speak*—but some of them are boring. These last four action verbs all mean *talk*, but they are more colorful.

JUST OK

The king and queen <u>sit</u> in their garden. They <u>talk</u> about the future with the princess. She <u>cries</u> when her parents <u>say</u> they will choose her husband. She <u>wants</u> to choose her own husband. She wants to marry someone who is a good riddler. The king <u>has</u> a plan. They will <u>have</u> a contest for riddlers.

> The reader thinks: **"This writing doesn't tell me much about what's happening."**

BETTER

The king and queen <u>relax</u> in their garden. They are <u>discussing</u> the future with the princess. The princess <u>sobs</u> when her parents <u>inform</u> her that they will choose her husband. The princess <u>insists</u>, "I'm the best riddler in the kingdom, and I will only marry a riddler who is as good as me!" The king and queen listen and <u>decide on</u> a new plan. They will <u>sponsor</u> a contest for riddlers to find their daughter's husband.

> The reader thinks: **"This is much better. The word *insists* tells me that the princess has a mind of her own."**

Add Sentences Think of three more sentences to add to the BETTER model above. Try to use colorful verbs from the chart.

Change . . .	to a colorful verb like . . .
cry	weep, whimper, whine, sob, bawl, wail
eat	nibble, munch, gobble, gulp, devour
go	walk, stroll, hurry, rush, race
laugh	grin, giggle, chuckle, cackle, howl
talk	chat, chatter, discuss, speak

WRITE ON YOUR OWN Write about a play or other story you know. Use colorful action words in your sentences. Use words from the chart, or find other specific and colorful verbs in a thesaurus.

REMEMBER

Check your verbs. Do they match your subjects?
Amy **sings**. I **dance**. We all **perform** in the play.

from *The Hobbit*

Riddles in the Dark

by J.R.R Tolkien

1   Deep down here by the dark water lived old Gollum, a small slimy creature. I don't know where he came from, nor who or what he was. He was Gollum—as dark as darkness, except for two big round pale eyes in his thin face. He had a little boat, and he rowed about quite quietly on the lake; for lake it was, wide and deep and deadly cold. He paddled it with large feet dangling over the side, but never a ripple did he make. Not he. He was looking out of his pale lamp-like eyes for blind fish, which he grabbed with his long fingers as quick as thinking. He liked meat too. Goblin he thought good, when he could get it.

2   He was watching Bilbo now from the distance with his pale eyes like telescopes. Bilbo could not see him, but he was wondering a lot about Bilbo, for he could see that he was no goblin at all.

3   Gollum got into his boat and shot off from the island, while Bilbo was sitting on the brink **altogether flummoxed** and at the end of his way and his wits. Suddenly up came Gollum and whispered and hissed:

4   "Bless us and splash us, my precioussss! I guess it's a choice feast; at least a tasty **morsel** it'd make us, gollum!" And when he said *gollum* he made a horrible swallowing noise in his throat. That's how he got his name, though he always called himself 'my precious.'

5   **The hobbit** jumped nearly out of his skin when the hiss came in his ears, and he suddenly saw the pale eyes sticking out at him.

6   "Who are you?" he said, **thrusting** his dagger in front of him.

7   "What iss he, my preciouss?" whispered Gollum (who always spoke to himself through never having anyone else to speak to). This is what he had come to find out, for he was not really very hungry at the moment, only curious; otherwise he would have grabbed first and whispered afterwards.

8   "I am Mr. Bilbo Baggins. I have lost the dwarves and I have lost the wizard, and I don't know where I am; and I don't want to know, if only I can get away."

Cultural Background
Imaginary creatures like goblins are common in fairy tales and traditional stories in many cultures.

In Other Words
altogether flummoxed completely confused
morsel bit of food
The hobbit A small, imaginary creature of the forest; Bilbo
thrusting pushing

9   "What's he got in his handses?" said Gollum, looking at the sword, which he did not quite like.

10   "A sword, a blade which came out of Gondolin!"

11   "Ssss," said Gollum, and became quite polite. "Praps ye sits here and chats with it a bitsy, my preciousss. It like **riddles**, praps it does, does it?" He was anxious to appear friendly, at any rate for the moment, and until he found out more about the sword and the hobbit, whether he was quite alone really, whether he was good to eat, and whether Gollum was really hungry.

12   "Very well," said Bilbo, who was anxious to agree, until he found out more about the creature, whether he was quite alone, whether he was fierce or hungry, and whether he was a friend of the goblins.

13   "You ask first," he said, because he had not had time to think of a riddle.

14   So Gollum hissed:

> *What has roots as nobody sees,*
> *Is taller than trees,*
> *Up, up it goes,*
> *And yet never grows?*

15   "Easy!" said Bilbo. "Mountain, I suppose."

16   "Does it guess easy? It must have a competition with us, my preciouss! If precious asks, and it doesn't answer, we eats it, my preciousss. If it asks us, and we doesn't answer, then we does what it wants, eh? We shows it the way out, yes!"

17   "All right!" said Bilbo, not daring to disagree, and nearly bursting his brain to think of riddles that could save him from being eaten.

> *Thirty white horses on a red hill,*
> *First they champ,*
> *Then they stamp,*
> *Then they stand still.*

18   That was all he could think of to ask—the idea of eating was **rather** on his mind. It was rather an old one, too, and Gollum knew the answer as well as you do.

19   "**Chestnuts, chestnuts**," he hissed. "Teeth! teeth! my preciousss; but we has only six!" Then he asked his second:

> *Voiceless it cries,*
> *Wingless flutters,*
> *Toothless bites,*
> *Mouthless mutters.*

20   "Half a moment!" cried Bilbo, who was still thinking uncomfortably about eating. Fortunately he had once heard something rather like this before, and getting his wits back he thought of the answer. "Wind, wind of course," he said, and he was so pleased that he made up one on the spot.

> *A box without hinges, key, or lid,*
> *Yet golden treasure inside is hid,*

he asked to gain time, until he could think of a really hard one. This he thought a **dreadfully** easy chestnut, though he had not asked it in the usual words. But it proved a **nasty poser** for Gollum. He hissed to himself, and still he did not answer; he whispered and spluttered.

Key Vocabulary
- **riddle** *n.*, a confusing question

In Other Words
rather really
Chestnuts, chestnuts Riddles, riddles
dreadfully very
nasty poser tricky puzzle

"If precious asks, and it doesn't answer, we eats it, my preciousss."

21   But suddenly Gollum remembered **thieving** from nests long ago, and sitting under the river bank teaching his grandmother, teaching his grandmother to suck—"Eggses" he hissed. "Eggses it is!" Then he asked:

> *This thing all things devours:*
> *Birds, beasts, trees, flowers;*
> *Gnaws iron, bites steel;*
> *Grinds hard stones to meal;*
> *Slays king, ruins town,*
> *And beats high mountain down.*

22   Poor Bilbo sat in the dark thinking of all the horrible names of all the giants and ogres he had ever heard told of in tales, but not one of them had done all these things. He had a feeling that the answer was quite different and that he **ought to** know it, but he could not think of it. He began to get frightened, and that is bad for thinking. Gollum began to get out of his boat. He flapped into the water and paddled to the bank; Bilbo could see his eyes coming towards him. His tongue seemed to stick in his mouth; he wanted to shout out: "Give me more time! Give me time!" But all that came out with a sudden squeal was: "Time! Time!"

23   Bilbo was saved by pure luck. For that of course was the answer.

In Other Words
thieving stealing
ought to should

Compare Across Texts

Compare Themes in Literature

"Rachel the Clever," "Atalanta's Race," and "Riddles in the Dark" share a **similar** theme, or main idea. Think about how the different character's motives and actions determine what each story says about pride.

How It Works

Collect and Organize Information Read the information about the king from "Rachel the Clever" in the chart below. Discuss how his actions affect the story. What lesson did he learn?

Theme Chart

Selection	Character Details	Plot Details	Resolution
"Rachel the Clever"	King is proud of his clever wits.	• gives 3 riddles for Rachel to solve • makes Rachel promise never to disagree with his decisions • orders Rachel to leave the palace	• The king realizes that he almost lost his wife.
"Atalanta's Race"	Atalanta		
"Riddles in the Dark"	Gollum		

Practice Together

Compare Complete your own chart about Atalanta. Then **compare** her actions to those of the king from "Rachel the Clever."

> A common theme in literature is that pride often causes people to lose something they want or need. In "Rachel the Clever," the King's pride almost causes him to lose the woman he loves. In "Atalanta's Race," Atalanta's pride causes her to lose the race to Hippomenes.

Try It!

Now add information to your chart about Gollum from "Riddles in the Dark." Write a comparison of the three selections using the frame below.

"Rachel the Clever," "Atalanta's Race," and "Riddles in the Dark" all feature characters who lose something because of their pride. In "Rachel the Clever," _____. In "Atalanta's Race," _____. Finally, in "Riddles in the Dark," _____.

Academic Vocabulary
- **compare** (kum-**pair**) *verb*
  When you **compare** things, you think about how they are alike and different.
- **similar** (**si**-mu-lur) *adjective*
  Things that are **similar** are almost the same.

Play
to Your
Strengths

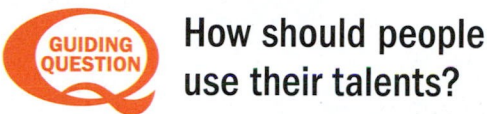

GUIDING QUESTION How should people use their talents?

Content Library

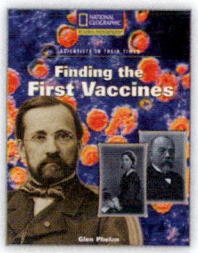

Leveled Library

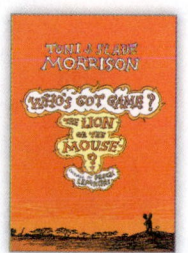 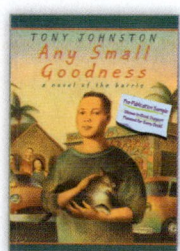 

Reflect on Your Reading

Think back on your reading of the unit selections. Discuss what you did to understand what you read.

Focus on Reading **Elements of Fiction: Plot, Character, Setting**

In this unit, you learned about some elements of fiction. Choose a selection and draw a Character-Setting-Plot Chart. Use your chart to summarize the selection. Share your summary with a partner.

Focus Strategy **Monitor Your Reading**

As you read the selections, you learned to monitor your reading in order to clarify ideas. Explain to a partner how you will use this strategy in the future.

Explore the

Throughout this unit, you have been thinking about how people use their strengths. Choose one of these ways to explore the Guiding Question:

- **Discuss** With a group, discuss movies you've seen or books you've read where people have special talents. What were the characters' talents? Did they always use them wisely? Explain.
- **Role-Play** Imagine you and a partner are each one of the key characters in each selection. Share your talent and how you used it.
- **Interview** Interview a partner about his or her most interesting talent. How could he or she put it to good use? List questions to ask and record the answers. Share your interview with the class.

Book Talk

Which Unit Library book did you choose? Explain to a partner what it taught you about using talent wisely.

A NEW
Chapter

3

How does our past impact our future?

READ MORE!

Content Library
The Struggle for Equality
by Ann M. Rossi

Leveled Library
Necessary Roughness
by Marie G. Lee
The Star Fisher
by Laurence Yep
El Güero
by Elizabeth Borton de Treviño

Web Links
myNGconnect.com

◄ The ruins of the Temple of Apollo stand in contrast to a modern Greek city in the distance.

Focus on Reading

Analyze Interactions

Writers use different ways to show how ideas, individuals, and events in a text are related. You can **analyze** the interaction among these elements to help you better understand the text. An **interaction** is when people, groups, or things communicate or respond to one another.

How It Works

Before you read, preview the text to figure out the topic. Look for clues about individuals, events, and ideas that may be important to understanding the topic.

Cause and Effect One way that a writer can show interactions within the text is to use cause-and-effect relationships. Cause and effect can show how individuals, ideas, and events influence each other. Study the examples of **causes** and effects in the passage. Look for signal words that show the impact individuals had on other individuals and events.

Coming to America

In the 1600s, many people came to North America. Their arrival caused problems for Native Americans who already lived there. Some of the people were sick when they arrived, so the Native Americans also got sick. As a result, many Native Americans died.

Some common signal words and phrases are:

as a result	so
because	therefore
since	thus

Sequence of Events Sometimes **analyzing** the order in which things happen in a text can help you better understand how individuals and ideas influence that order. Watch for **time words** to help you figure out what happens when.

A Traveler's Journal

On January 15, 1645, my youngest sister turned five and was now old enough to make the journey from Europe to North America. We arrived early at the dock to board a huge ship. Families with young children boarded first . The journey was not easy. During our trip, water and food were limited. After sailing many weeks, we were happy to spot land. Finally our journey at sea was over and our new life could begin.

Some common time words are:

after	first
during	later
finally	next

Academic Vocabulary
- **analyze** (a-nu-līz) *verb*
When you **analyze** something, you study it closely.

Read these passages aloud. As you read, listen for clues that show how individuals, ideas, and events interact.

A Different Kind of Summer

Maria reminds me that most kids in California are still sleeping, but I remind her we aren't those kids. As Mexican migrant farmers, our day begins before sunrise. We rumble along in this truck to the field just as dark turns to day. Then we unload baskets and line up for our rows. My family works together. Each day is long, hot, and tiring. I dream while I work, not while I sleep. I dream of Mexico.

The Farm Worker's Plight

Some Mexican citizens come to the U.S. to work on farms. Life for these workers can be hard. Many are separated from their families. As a result, they feel lonely. Also, some do not speak English, or speak very little English. Therefore, they can have trouble communicating with English speakers. The farm workers' lives can also be difficult because of harsh working conditions.

Try It!

Read the following passages aloud. How do ideas and individuals influence events? How do you know?

A Better Life

Alfredo came to the U.S. from Mexico with a dream, to make a better life for his family. Since he spoke little English, the only work Alfredo could get was farm work. He worked long hours for little money and soon realized that he would need to learn English. So he found a better-paying job and started English classes. He worked and studied hard. As a result, he went to medical school. He fulfilled his dream and became a surgeon at the John Hopkins School of Medicine.

Dr. Alfredo Quinones-Hinojosa

In the 1980s, Alfredo Quinones-Hinojosa came to the U.S. from Mexico. He believed in the idea of the American dream, to make a better life for his family. At first, the only work Alfredo could get was on a farm. Alfredo knew that if his dream was to come true, he would need to learn English. He found another job that helped him pay for English classes, and this led to college.

In 1994, Alfredo started medical school. Today, he is a brain surgeon at the John Hopkins School of Medicine.

Focus on Vocabulary

Use Word Parts

Most words are made up of parts, including base words, prefixes, and suffixes. These word parts are usually easy to **identify** . Sometimes, however, the spelling of the base word changes when a suffix is added.

EXAMPLES

The suffix *-able* means "can be done."

move + -able = movable
Movable means "can be moved."

The prefix *un-* means "not." The suffix *-ness* means "state of."

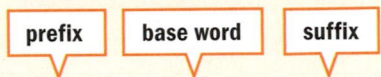

un- + happy + -ness = unhappiness
Unhappiness means "state of being not happy."

How the Strategy Works

When you read, you may come to a word you don't know. **Identify** word parts to help you understand the word's meaning.

1. Look closely at the word to see if you know any of the parts.
2. Cover any prefixes or suffixes. **mov**able
3. Think about the meaning of the base word.
4. Uncover any prefixes or suffixes and determine their meanings.
5. Put the meanings of the word parts together to understand the whole word. Be sure the meaning makes sense in the text.

Use the strategy to figure out the meaning of each underlined word.

From 1892 to 1924, millions of people from Europe sailed past the Statue of Liberty on Liberty Island in New York Harbor. The statue reminded them of their <u>readiness</u> to begin life in a new country. The first stop was Ellis Island.

At Ellis Island, travelers had to have health <u>inspections</u>. It was <u>unavoidable</u>. They also had to answer legal questions. Then, they began their new lives in the U.S.

Strategy in Action

" I see the suffix *-ness* in *readiness*. I'll cover it. What's left is *readi*, which must be the base word *ready*. I know *-ness* means 'state of,' so *readiness* means 'state of being ready.* "

☑ **REMEMBER** Sometimes the spelling of a base word changes when a suffix is added.

Academic Vocabulary
- **identify** (ī-**den**-tu-fī) *verb*
  When you identify something, you recognize, name, or discover it.

Practice Together

Read this passage aloud. Look at each underlined word. Find the word parts. Put their meanings together to figure out the meaning of the underlined word.

Some Word Parts
Prefix: *en-* means "cause to"
Suffix: *-al* means "process of"
Suffix: *-tion* means "act of"
Suffix: *-able* means "can be done"
Suffix: *-ment* means "action or progress"

GRANDFATHER'S STORY

❝Why doesn't Grandpa talk about his <u>arrival</u> in America?"

My mother put a finger to her lips. "Quiet, Mia. Don't let him hear you talk of such things."

"But I don't understand. I thought it would be a great story to tell my friends. Isn't it exciting that he was a Chinese immigrant?"

"Mia, it wasn't the same for the Chinese as it was for most Europeans. In the early 1900s, laws <u>enacted</u> by the government kept many Chinese from entering the United States. Chinese travelers had to pass special health <u>examinations</u>. If they didn't pass, they couldn't enter the country. Your grandfather's brother was not allowed in. It is a very painful memory for him," whispered my mother.

"That's so <u>unfair</u>," I said.

"Times were different back then," answered my mother. "Be grateful for what you have, and be gentle with your grandfather's memories."

Try It!

Read the following passage. What is the meaning of each underlined word? How do you know?

Family History

My great-grandfather came to the U.S. in 1923. He wanted to <u>enrich</u> the lives of his family and find a good job. He traveled by ship from Naples, Italy, and arrived at Ellis Island on October 6. Then he moved near Pittsburgh, Pennsylvania. He found <u>employment</u> at a bakery in a small town. He was a <u>reliable</u> employee. After a few years, he started his own bakery and bought a house. After that, he sent for his wife and children. They arrived in 1928.

THE LOTUS SEED

BY SHERRY GARLAND

ILLUSTRATED BY TATSURO KIUCHI

SELECTION 1 OVERVIEW

▶ **Build Background**

▶ **Language & Grammar**
Describe People, Places, and Things
Use Adjectives That Describe

▶ **Prepare to Read**
Learn Key Vocabulary
Analyze Plot

▶ **Read and Write**
Introduce the Genre
Realistic Fiction
Focus on Reading
Analyze Interactions
Apply the Focus Strategy
Visualize
Critical Thinking
Reading Fluency
Read with Intonation
Vocabulary Review
Write About the Guiding Question

▶ **Connect Across the Curriculum**
Vocabulary Study
Use Prefixes
Literary Analysis
Compare Characters
Language and Grammar
Describe People, Places, and Things
Writing and Grammar
Write About People, Places, and Things

Build Background

Learn About Vietnam's Past

Why do people leave the home they love? Learn what happened in Vietnam and why so many people had to make the hardest decisions of their lives.

Connect to Literature

Quickwrite Suppose you had to leave your home and start a new life in a new place. What one object would you bring with you? Why would you choose that object?

Digital Library **myNGconnect.com**
🌐 View the video.

▲ Many Vietnamese people had to escape the country at the end of the Vietnam War.

Language & Grammar

Describe People, Places, and Things

CD

Look at the photograph and listen to the letter. The letter describes Bao Dai, the last emperor of Vietnam.

PICTURE PROMPT and LETTER

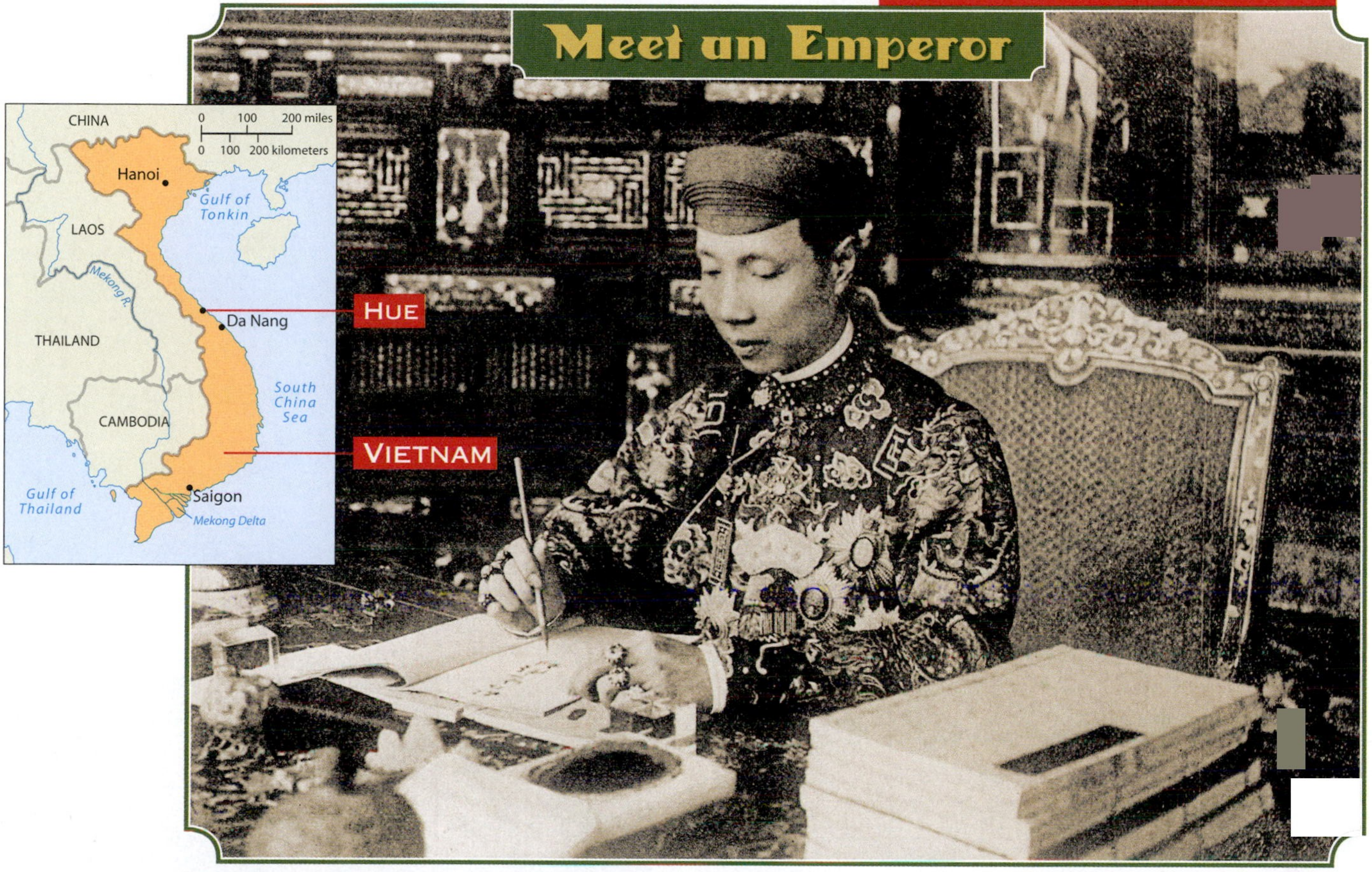

Meet an Emperor

CHINA

Hanoi

Gulf of Tonkin

LAOS

Mekong R.

Da Nang

HUE

THAILAND

South China Sea

CAMBODIA

VIETNAM

Gulf of Thailand

Saigon

Mekong Delta

0   100   200 miles
0   100   200 kilometers

▲ Vietnam's last emperor, Bao Dai

June 12, 1927

Dearest Grandfather,

Father and I had an amazing day. We were invited to the emperor's gigantic palace in the city of Hue. There, we stood before Emperor Bao Dai. He is young to be a leader, Grandfather. Bao Dai took over the Golden Throne of the Sun when he was just 12 years old.

Use Adjectives That Describe

You can describe people, places, or things with **adjectives** . They answer the question: *What is the person, place, or thing like*? Adjectives help the reader see what you are writing about. Use adjectives to describe:

• how something looks or sounds

> EXAMPLES   The emperor sits on a **golden** **throne**.
> I hear a **muffled** **gasp** from the crowd.

• how something feels, tastes, or smells

> EXAMPLE   The emperor wears a **smooth** , **soft** robe.

• someone's mood

> EXAMPLE   The **energetic** **emperor** walks through the crowd.

Adjectives come before nouns they describe or after a form of *be*.

> EXAMPLE   He holds a **golden** **paper** **fan**. The **fan** is **glittery** .

When two adjectives come before a noun, a comma is often placed between them. Both adjectives are equal. If you cannot reverse the order of the adjectives, a comma is not placed between them. The adjectives are not equal.

> EXAMPLES   Serene, melodious bells ring nearby.
> A lovely Vietnamese girl walks beside the emperor.

Practice Together

Say each sentence with an adjective from the box. Use two adjectives in one sentence.

buzzing	fragrant	huge	shady

1. There is a _____ garden at the palace.

2. The garden has many _____ flowers.

3. I hear _____ bees near the flowers.

Try It!

Use an adjective from the box to complete each sentence. Write the sentence on a card. Use two adjectives in two sentences. Use a comma if needed. Then say the sentence.

Asian	colorful	cool	sweet	tall

4. The trees have _____ flowers, too.

5. The blossoms on the trees smell very _____.

6. Birds chirp from high in the _____ trees.

7. Frogs croak from their lily pads in the _____ pond.

▲ The beautiful, well-tended garden is full of colorful exotic flowers.

Create a Symbol

DESCRIBE PEOPLE, PLACES, AND THINGS

Thrones and crowns are symbols of emperors, kings, and queens. Flags are symbols of countries. What object would you choose to represent you? What words would you use to describe this symbol?

Make a list of **adjectives** that describe your symbol and put them in a chart.

Looks	Feels	Tastes	Sounds	Smells
red	smooth			sweet

Describe your symbol to a partner. Can your partner guess your symbol? Tell your partner why you chose that symbol and why it represents you. Trade roles.

HOW TO DESCRIBE A PERSON, PLACE, OR THING

1. Look at or think of the person, place, or thing.
2. Think of descriptive words that help the listener imagine what you are talking about.
3. Use those words to describe the person, place, or thing.

My symbol is a loud animal that has a big mane.

Is it a lion?

USE ADJECTIVES THAT DESCRIBE

When you describe something, you use **adjectives**, so people can understand what it looks like, or visualize it. You can use adjectives to describe how something looks, feels, tastes, sounds, or smells.

The **adjective** often comes before the noun you are describing. If two adjectives both describe the noun equally, use a comma (,) to separate them.

EXAMPLES   I have **smooth red** petals. My **sweet**, **fragrant scent** makes people smile. I am a **beautiful sign** of peace and love. What is my symbol?

Prepare to Read

Learn Key Vocabulary

Study the Words Use the steps below.

1. Pronounce the word. Say it aloud several times. Spell it.
2. Rate your word knowledge.
3. Study the example. Tell more about the word.
4. Practice it. Make the word your own.

Rating Scale

1 = I have never seen this word before.

2 = I am not sure of the word's meaning.

3 = I know this word and can teach the word's meaning to someone else.

Key Words

arrive (u-rīv) *verb*
► page 190

When you **arrive**, you get to a place. Some people like to **arrive** early at a party.
Related Word: **arrival**

bloom (blüm) *verb*
► page 190

To **bloom** means to open up or turn into a flower. Flowers usually **bloom** in spring.

chapter (chap-tur) *noun*
► page 190

A **chapter** is one part of something. A book usually has several **chapters**.

emperor (em-pur-ur) *noun*
► page 186

An **emperor** is a ruler. This **emperor** once ruled Vietnam.
Related Words: **empire, empress**

forget (fur-**get**) *verb*
► page 190

When you **forget** something, you no longer know it. My sister often **forgets** where she puts her keys.
Past Tense: **forgot**
Past Participle: **forgotten**

remember (ri-**mem**-bur) *verb* ► page 186

When you **remember** something, you think of it again. My sister sometimes **remembers** where she puts her keys.
Related Word: **memory**

special (spe-shul) *adjective*
► page 186

When something is **special**, it is different and important. Your birthday is a **special** day.
Related Words: **especially, specialty**

throne (thrōn) *noun*
► page 186

A **throne** is a special chair where a royal person sits. Kings, queens, and emperors sit on **thrones**.

Practice the Words Work with a partner to make a Category Chart. List each Key Word under *Noun, Verb,* or *Adjective.* Write a sentence for each word.

Noun	Verb	Adjective
emperor		
An emperor rules Japan.		

Category Chart

Analyze Plot

How Are Events Related? Elements such as character and setting can influence not only what happens in a story, but also when it happens. Sometimes you can better understand a story if you ==analyze== the order in which things occur and why they happen in this order.

As you read, pay attention to signal words that give you clues about the ==sequence== of events. Then think about how the events are related.

Reading Strategies

- Plan
- Monitor
- **Visualize** Imagine the sights, sounds, smells, tastes, and feel of what the author is describing.
- Determine Importance
- Ask Questions
- Make Connections
- Make Inferences
- Synthesize

Look Into the Text

> My grandmother saw the emperor cry the day he lost his golden dragon throne.
>
> She wanted something to remember him by, so she snuck down to the silent palace, near the River of Perfumes, and plucked a seed from a lotus pod that rattled in the imperial garden. She hid the seed in a special place under the family altar, wrapped in a piece of silk from the *ao dai* she wore that day. Whenever she felt sad or lonely, she took out the seed and thought of the brave young emperor.

Practice Together

Begin a Sequence Chain A Sequence Chain can help you analyze how events in the text are related. By looking at the order of events, you can better understand why events occur in this ==sequence==. The Sequence Chain shows the first event from the passage above. Each oval shows a different event. Reread the passage above, and add to the Sequence Chain.

1. The emperor lost his golden throne.

2.

Academic Vocabulary

- **sequence** (sē-kwents) *noun*
  The **sequence** of events is the order in which the events happen.

Realistic Fiction

Realistic fiction includes stories about people, places, times, and events that could be real but are not.

Writers of realistic fiction often use **sensory images** to help readers feel that they are in the **real place** or time. As you read, use these sensory images to visualize the scene and understand the text better.

Look Into the Text

> She wanted something to remember him by, so she snuck down to the silent palace, near the River of Perfumes, and plucked a seed from a lotus pod that rattled in the imperial garden.

real place

Events in realistic fiction often occur in the order they happen, or in chronological order. Characters and setting can influence how the plot of the story develops.

THE
LOTUS
SEED

BY SHERRY GARLAND

ILLUSTRATED BY TATSURO KIUCHI

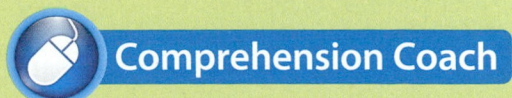
Comprehension Coach

My grandmother saw the **emperor** cry the day he lost his golden dragon **throne**.

She wanted something to **remember** him by, so she snuck down to the silent palace, near the River of Perfumes, and plucked a seed from a lotus pod that rattled in the **imperial** garden. She hid the seed in a **special** place under the family **altar**, wrapped in a piece of silk from the ***ao dai*** she wore that day. Whenever she felt sad or lonely, she took out the seed and thought of the brave young emperor.

And when she married a young man chosen by her parents, she carried the seed inside her pocket for good luck, long life, and many children. When her husband marched off to war, she raised her children alone.

Key Vocabulary

emperor *n.*, a leader
throne *n.*, a royal seat
remember *v.*, to think of again
special *adj.*, unusual or favored

In Other Words

imperial royal
altar religious table
ao dai traditional Vietnamese clothing

Nature Background

Lotus flowers grow in or near water and are popular in Asia. Lotus seeds can last a long time. In the 1980s, one scientist grew a lotus from a 1,200-year-old seed.

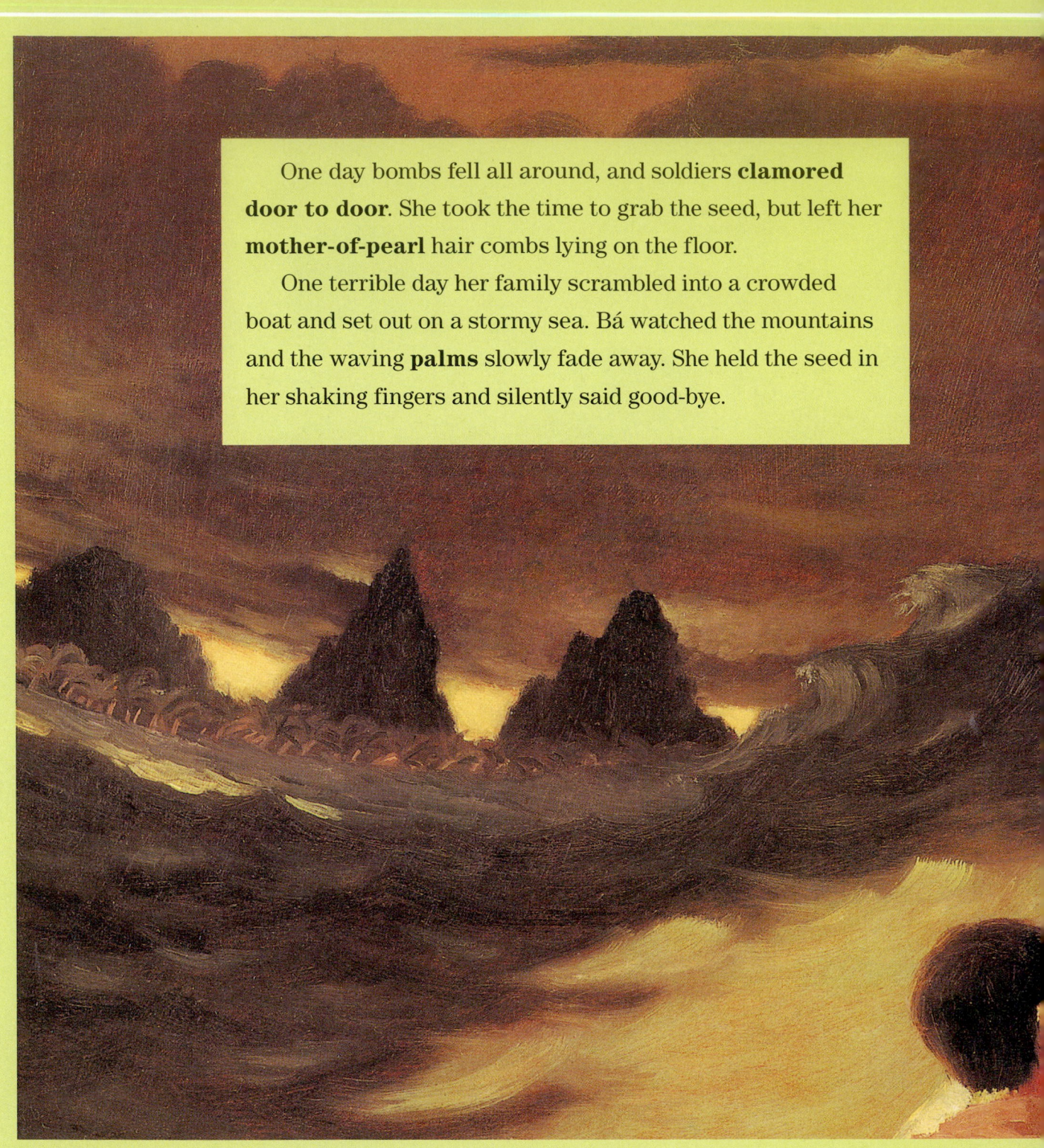

One day bombs fell all around, and soldiers **clamored door to door**. She took the time to grab the seed, but left her **mother-of-pearl** hair combs lying on the floor.

One terrible day her family scrambled into a crowded boat and set out on a stormy sea. Bá watched the mountains and the waving **palms** slowly fade away. She held the seed in her shaking fingers and silently said good-bye.

In Other Words
clamored door to door went to each house
mother-of-pearl expensive, valuable
palms palm trees

Look Into the Text

1. **Cause and Effect** What causes Bá to leave on the boat?

2. **Character** How does Bá feel about the **emperor**?

3. **Inference** Why does the author tell you that Bá left her combs on the floor?

How will Bá feel as she begins a new chapter in her life?

She **arrived** in a strange new land with blinking lights and speeding cars and **towering buildings that scraped the sky** and a language she didn't understand.

She worked many years, day and night, and so did her children and her sisters and her cousins, too, living together in one big house.

Last summer my little brother found the special seed and asked questions again and again. He'd never seen a lotus **bloom** or an emperor on a golden dragon throne.

So one night he stole the seed from beneath the family altar and planted it in a pool of mud somewhere near Bá's onion patch.

Bá cried and cried when she found out the seed was gone. She didn't eat, she didn't sleep, and my silly brother **forgot** what **spot of earth held** the seed.

Key Vocabulary
chapter *n.*, one part of something
arrive *v.*, to reach a place
bloom *v.*, to open up or grow into a flower
forget *v.*, to not remember something

In Other Words
towering buildings that scraped the sky very tall buildings
what spot of earth held where he had planted

Then one day in spring my grandmother shouted, and we all ran to the garden and saw a beautiful pink lotus **unfurling** its petals, so creamy and soft.

"It is the flower of life and hope," my grandmother said. "No matter how ugly the mud or how **long the seed lies dormant**, the bloom will be beautiful. It is the flower of my country." When the lotus **blossom faded** and turned into a pod, Bá gave each of her grandchildren a seed to remember her by, and she kept one for herself to remember the emperor by.

I wrapped my seed in a piece of silk and hid it in a secret place. Someday I will plant it and give the seeds to my own children and tell them about the day my grandmother saw the emperor cry. ❖

In Other Words
unfurling opening
long the seed lies dormant
    old the seed is
blossom faded flower died

Look Into the Text

1. **Confirm Prediction** Was your prediction about Bá correct? Explain.

2. **Character's Viewpoint** Describe how Bá must have felt after she arrived in her new country. Which text tells you this?

About the Author

Sherry Garland

Sherry Garland (1948–) was born in Texas, in the Rio Grande Valley. She is known for writing stories about people of different cultures. She became interested in Vietnam after meeting families who had moved to Texas to escape the Vietnam War. She has written more than twenty-five books. Seven have been inspired by the Vietnamese culture, including *The Lotus Seed*. Garland now lives in central Texas.

About the Illustrator

Tatsuro Kiuchi

Tatsuro Kiuchi (1966–) was born in Tokyo, Japan. *The Lotus Seed* was the first children's book Kiuchi ever illustrated. Having never been to Vietnam, he researched the country through books and photographs. Since then, he has gone on to illustrate over a dozen books and win awards for his art. Today, Kiuchi lives in Tokyo, Japan.

A Suitcase of Seaweed

by Janet Wong

Across the ocean
from Korea
my grandmother,
my Halmoni,
5   has come—
her suitcase
sealed shut
with tape,
packed full
10   of sheets
of shiny black
seaweed
and stacks
of dried squid.
15   We break it open,
this old treasure
chest of hers,
holding
our noses
20   tight
as we release
its ripe
sea smell.

River Maiden, 1997, Wonsook Kim. Acrylic on canvas, collection of the artist.

▲ **Critical Viewing: Effect** Why does the moving water turn into a woman? What kind of mood, or feeling, does the artist create?

In Other Words
Halmoni grandmother (in Korean)
ripe strong

Look Into the Text

1. **Inference** How do the grandchildren feel about the suitcase?
2. **Metaphor** Why does the narrator call the suitcase a "treasure chest"?

Connect Reading and Writing

Vocabulary
arrived
blooming
chapter
emperor
forget
remember
special
throne

CRITICAL THINKING

1. **SUM IT UP** Use your Sequence Chain to describe the events in "The Lotus Seed" and summarize the story to a partner.

1.
The emperor lost his golden throne.

2.

Sequence Chain

2. **Compare** In what ways do Bá from "The Lotus Seed" and Halmoni from "A Suitcase of Seaweed" choose to **remember** their homes? Explain.

3. **Interpret** What does the seed mean to Bá? How do you know?

4. **Inference** Why might the **emperor** have lost his **throne**? Use details from the story to support your ideas.

READING FLUENCY

Intonation Read the passage on page 644 to a partner. Assess your fluency.

1. My tone did/did not change to match what I read.

2. My words correct per minute: _____.

READING STRATEGY

What strategy helped you understand this selection? Tell a partner about it.

VOCABULARY REVIEW

Oral Review Read the paragraph aloud. Add the vocabulary words.

When my family _____ in the United States, it was a new _____ in our lives. Even though I was very young, I will never _____ the day. I _____ that it was spring because all the flowers were _____. When we left the airport, my father carried me on his shoulders. I was sitting so high in the air that I felt like an _____ sitting on a _____. The world looked so new and different. It really was a _____ day.

Written Review Imagine you are Bá and you just **arrived** in Vietnam again after many years. Write a journal entry describing your memories and impressions. Use four vocabulary words.

WRITE ABOUT THE **GUIDING QUESTION**

Explore a New Chapter
Write an opinion paragraph responding to this statement: "It is important to **remember** the past." Use details from the selection to support your ideas.

Connect Across the Curriculum

Vocabulary Study

Use Prefixes

Prefix	Meaning
de-	opposite
en-	cause to
re-	again
un-	not

Academic Vocabulary
- **identify** (ī-**den**-tu-fī) *verb*
  When you **identify** something, you name, recognize, or discover it.

Most English words are made up of word parts. Sometimes, however, letters at the beginning of a word may look like a prefix, but they aren't. If you take away these letters, you are not left with a base word.

Follow these steps to figure out if a word truly has a prefix.
1. Cover up the part of the word that you think is the prefix. un**cle**
2. If you can't **identify** the word part left, it's not a true prefix.

Analyze Prefixes **Identify** the word parts in each word. Not all words have a real prefix. Then write a sentence using each word.

1. desperate **2.** uneasy **3.** review **4.** enemy **5.** encircle

Literary Analysis

Compare Characters

Academic Vocabulary
- **analyze** (a-nu-līz) *verb*
  When you **analyze** something, you study it closely.

All the characters in a story, including the narrator, have opinions and feelings. You can **analyze** how an author develops these viewpoints by looking at the characters' actions, descriptions, and dialogue.

Read this passage from "The Lotus Seed." **Bá's** actions show that she is really upset about losing the seed. The **grandson's** actions show that the seed wasn't that important to him. The **granddaughter's** description shows that she is upset with her brother.

> Bá cried and cried when she found out the seed was gone. She didn't eat, she didn't sleep, and my silly brother forgot what spot of earth held the seed.

Analyze and Compare Look back at "The Lotus Seed" and **analyze** each character's feelings about the lotus seed. Then compare how the different characters feel.

Describe People, Places, and Things

Pair Talk Describe to a partner a familiar person, place, or thing from your life. Have your partner draw what he or she "sees" from your descriptive adjectives. Trade roles.

> My sister Tina is tall. She has brown, curly hair and blue eyes.

Write About People, Places, and Things

Study the Models When you write about people, places, and things, use colorful, descriptive words to bring them to life. Adding descriptive details helps readers see the people, places, and things in their minds.

JUST OK

Mia put on her blue dress and walked out into the small garden. Today her grandson Jamie was coming to visit. Mia cut some flowers and put them into a glass vase and put it on the table. She took her keys from the desk. Then she drove to the airport to get Jamie.

The reader thinks: "I can't really see what Mia and her garden look like."

BETTER

Mia put on her new blue dress and combed her short white hair. She walked into her small garden, where a buzzing, fuzzy, yellow bee zoomed above a fluffy dandelion. Mia hummed a cheerful tune as she cut some colorful, sweet-smelling flowers. Today her youngest grandson Jamie was coming to visit! Mia put the blossoms into a tall glass vase and placed it on the shiny wooden table in the kitchen. She took the keys to her old red truck off the cluttered desk and drove to the airport to get Jamie.

Now the writer uses colorful adjectives. The reader can picture Mia and the places.

Add Sentences Think of two sentences to add to the BETTER model above. Be sure to use descriptive words to help bring the writing to life. Use commas if needed.

WRITE ON YOUR OWN Write about a person, place, or thing. Be sure to use colorful adjectives to help readers see who, where, or what you are writing about.

REMEMBER
- Adjectives usually come before the nouns they describe.
- Use a comma to separate two or more adjectives if you can reverse their order.

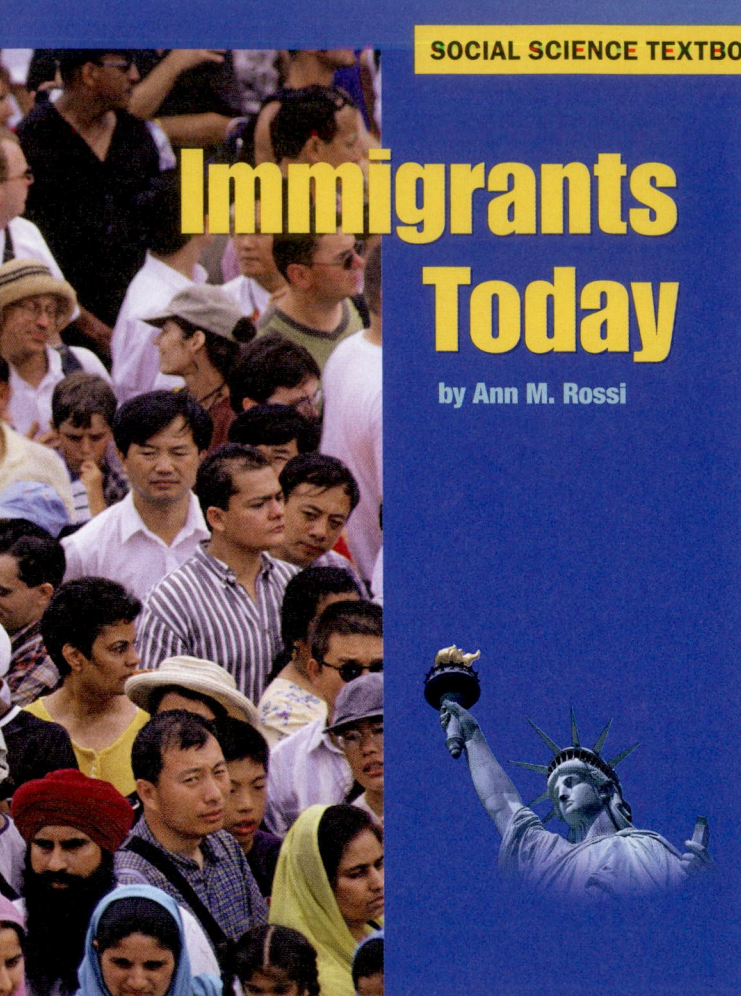

Immigrants Today

by Ann M. Rossi

Build Background

See the Immigrants' Journey

People have been coming to the United States for a long time. See how their journey has changed over the years.

Connect to Literature

Make Your Mark Design a neighborhood with stores, restaurants, and other places of interest. What cultures do you visualize in your neighborhood? Work with a group to sketch your designs. Post them for discussion.

Digital Library myNGconnect.com
View the video.

▲ Italian immigrants wait in line at Ellis Island in New York Harbor, 1905.

Language & Grammar

1 TRY OUT LANGUAGE
2 LEARN GRAMMAR
3 APPLY ON YOUR OWN

Make Comparisons

CD

Study the photographs and listen to the comparisons.
Then find one more way that the photographs are both
alike and different.

PICTURE PROMPT

Celebration!

A Hmong musician plays at
a spring festival in China.

A member of a marching
band makes music at a fall
festival in New Mexico, USA.

Dan: Both of these photos show musicians.

Amy: Yes, but they're in different countries, aren't they?

Dan: That's right. I guess they show that people in all
countries like music!

Language & Grammar **199**

Use Adjectives That Compare

You can use **adjectives** to compare two people, places, or things.

EXAMPLES   Our garden in the U.S. is **smaller** <u>than</u> our garden in China.
My house in the U.S. is **more modern** <u>than</u> my house in China.

There are two ways to turn an adjective into a comparative adjective.

1. If the adjective has one syllable, add **-er**.
   If it ends in **y**, change the **y** to **i** before you add **-er**.

   EXAMPLES   long   long**er**
              tall   tall**er**
              silly   sill**ier**

2. If the adjective has three or more syllables, use **more** before the adjective.

   EXAMPLES   difficult   **more** difficult
              expensive   **more** expensive

If the adjective has two syllables, sometimes you say it either way. Use the form that is easier to say.

   EXAMPLES   friendly   friendl**ier** or **more** friendly
              nervous   **more** nervous

Practice Together

Change the adjective in the box to a comparative adjective. Say it. Then say the sentence with the comparative adjective.

1. | fancy | The festivals in Mexico are _____ than the festivals in the U.S.

2. | colorful | The girls' costumes are _____ than the boys' costumes.

3. | loud | The music is _____ than the crowd.

4. | friendly | The people in the parade are _____ than the crowd.

▲ Some of the girls are shorter than the boy.

Try It!

Change the adjective in the box to a comparative adjective. Write it on a card. Then say the sentence, and add the comparative adjective.

5. | happy | I am _____ at the festival than I am at home.

6. | popular | The music is _____ with teens than with adults.

7. | delicious | Your food is delicious, but my food is _____.

8. | long | Your performance is long, but mine is _____.

Explore Differences

MAKE COMPARISONS

Find two pictures of things that you can compare, such as two types of cars. Cut the pictures from old magazines or download them from the Internet.

Study the two pictures, and make comparisons. How are they alike? How are they different? Complete a T Chart about your pictures.

T Chart

Alike	Different
Both pictures show a car.	The car in this picture is bigger than the one in that picture.
All the cars have black tires.	This car is red, and that one is white.

HOW TO MAKE COMPARISONS

1. Tell how people, places, or things are alike.
2. Tell how people, places, or things are different.
3. Use comparison words.

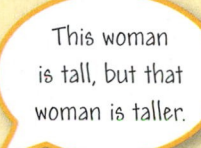
This woman is tall, but that woman is taller.

USE ADJECTIVES THAT COMPARE

When you make comparisons, you describe how things are alike or different. Use comparison adjectives—words that compare nouns.

- Add **-er** to the end of adjectives that have one syllable.

  EXAMPLE   old   old**er**

- If the adjective ends in **y**, change the **y** to **i**, then add **-er**.

  EXAMPLE   early   earl**ier**

- If the adjective has three or more syllables, use **more** before the adjective.

  EXAMPLE   difficult   **more** difficult

Prepare to Read

Learn Key Vocabulary

Study the Words Use the steps below.

1. Pronounce the word. Say it aloud several times. Spell it.
2. Rate your word knowledge.
3. Study the example. Tell more about the word.
4. Practice it. Make the word your own.

Rating Scale

1 = I have never seen this word before.

2 = I am not sure of the word's meaning.

3 = I know this word and can teach the word's meaning to someone else.

Key Words

adjust (ud-**just**) *verb*
▶ page 210

When you **adjust** to something, you become used to it. You can **adjust** to cold weather when you go outside.
Related Word: **adjustment**

community (ku-**myü**-nu-tē) *noun* ▶ page 210

A **community** is a group of people who live in one place. A neighborhood is a kind of **community**.

foreign (**for**-in) *adjective*
▶ page 215

When something is **foreign**, it is from somewhere else. Last summer, my family and I traveled to a **foreign** country.

immigrant (**im**-i-grint) *noun*
▶ page 206

An **immigrant** is someone who moves from one country to another country to live. These **immigrants** came to the U.S. to start new lives.
Related Word: **immigration**

local (**lō**-cul) *adjective*
▶ page 215

Local means nearby. My family goes to the **local** farmers' market every weekend to buy fresh vegetables.

museum (myü-**zē**-um) *noun*
▶ page 211

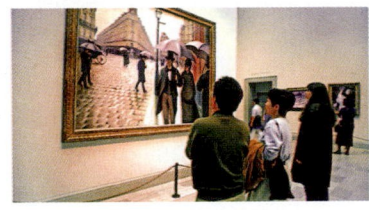

In a **museum**, people can look at art or other valuable objects. Our class saw paintings at the **museum**.

poverty (**pah**-vur-tē) *noun*
▶ page 206

Poverty is the state or condition of being poor. People who live in **poverty** may not have enough food to eat.

preserve (pri-**zurv**) *verb*
▶ page 211

To **preserve** means to keep something from being lost. People celebrate certain holidays to **preserve** their culture.

Practice the Words Make an Idea Web for each Key Word. Write four things the word makes you think of. Share your finished webs with a partner.

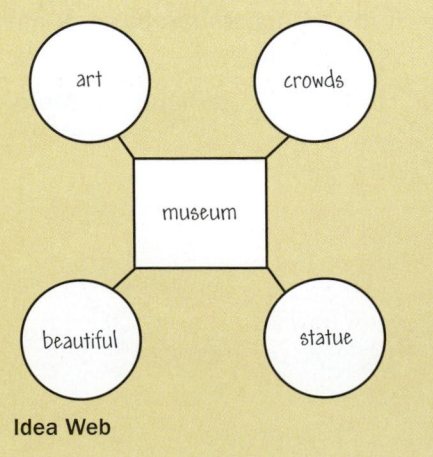

Idea Web

Analyze Interactions Among Ideas

Reading Strategies
- Plan
- Monitor
- ▶ **Visualize** Imagine the sights, sounds, smells, tastes, and feel of what the author is describing.
- Determine Importance
- Ask Questions
- Make Connections
- Make Inferences
- Synthesize

How are Ideas Related? Ideas can influence or be influenced by individuals and events. Analyzing how ideas interact can help a reader better understand a text. Writers often use cause-and-effect relationships to show how ideas, individuals, and events are **connected.**

- A cause is the reason an event happens. An idea can cause an event.

- The effect is the event that happens as a result. Sometimes a cause has more than one effect.

As you read the passage, look for cause-and-effect relationships.

Look Into the Text

> The United States has always been a magnet for immigrants. They have come for religious freedom, for a chance to better their lives, and to escape cruel governments.
>
> Immigrants have come in three great waves. In the mid-1800s, millions of people arrived from northern and western Europe. Most came from Germany and Ireland.
>
> The second wave of immigration was from the late 1800s to the 1920s. These immigrants came mainly from southern and eastern Europe.

Practice Together

Begin a Cause-Effect Chart A Cause-Effect Chart can help you to **connect** ideas with individuals and events. Reread the passage above. Think about how these important ideas influenced immigration to the United States. Record your observations on the Cause-Effect Chart.

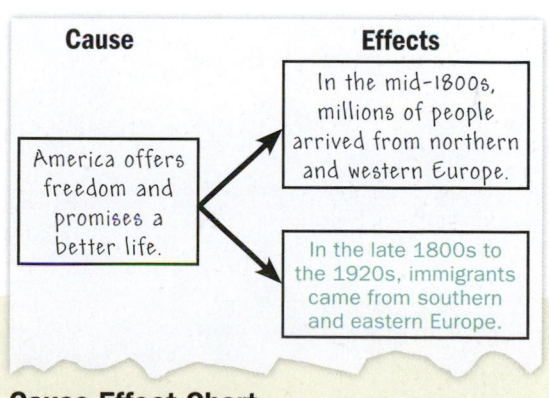

Cause-Effect Chart

Academic Vocabulary
- **connect** (ku-**nekt**) *verb*
  When you **connect** things, you show how they are related.

Social Science Textbook

A social science textbook gives information about real people, places, and events. It often explains how people and events are influenced by ideas.

A social science textbook often uses cause and effect to explain the interaction of ideas. As you read, use information from **graphs** and other visuals to help you make mental pictures of the relationships between ideas, individuals, and events.

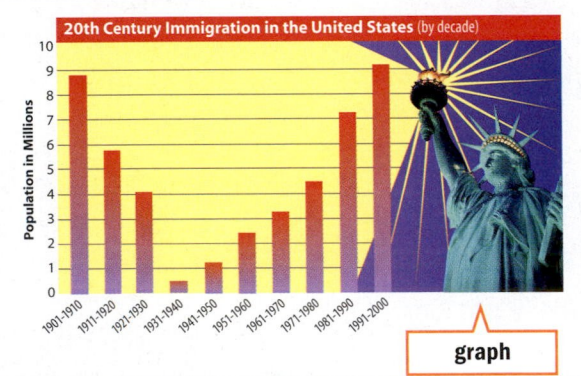

20th Century Immigration in the United States (by decade)

graph

Immigrants Today

by Ann M. Rossi

People come to the United States for many reasons. Why do they come, and how do they build new lives?

◄ The United States is filled with people from many cultures and countries.

Comprehension Coach

Who Are the Immigrants?

The United States has always been a magnet for **immigrants**. They have come for religious freedom, for a chance to better their lives, and to escape from cruel governments.

Immigrants have come in three great waves. In the mid-1800s, millions of people arrived from northern and western Europe. Most came from Germany and Ireland.

The second wave of immigration was from the late 1800s to the 1920s. These immigrants came mainly from southern and eastern Europe. Most of them came from Italy.

Immigration slowed after World War I for two reasons. First, the United States government set limits on the number of immigrants who could enter the country. Second, the American **economy** began to suffer, or slow down, in 1929. Many people struggled with **poverty**, and jobs were hard to find.

After World War II ended in 1945, immigration began to grow again. In 1965, the government made it easier for people to come to the United States. By the 1970s, millions of people were coming. They all came hoping for a better life.

The Three Waves of Immigrants, 1850 to 2000

Alaska (U.S.)

CANADA

UNITED STATES

Hawaii (U.S.)

MEXICO   CUBA   BAHAMAS   DOMI REPU

JAMAICA   HAITI   BELIZE   HONDURAS   GUATEMALA   NICARAGUA   EL SALVADOR

COSTA RICA   PANAMA   VENEZU

COLOMBIA

Galápagos Is. (Ec.)   ECUADOR

PACIFIC OCEAN

SAMOA   Am. Samoa   PERU

TONGA   BO

CHILE   ARG

KEY

The highest percentage of immigrants came from these countries in each time period.

- Mid-1800s to late 1800s
- Late 1800s to 1920s
- Mid-1960s to 2000

▲ **Interpret the Map** From which countries did most immigrants come during each time period? During which time period did immigrants come from the greatest variety of countries?

Key Vocabulary

immigrant *n.*, someone who moves to another country

poverty *n.*, poorness, neediness

In Other Words

economy money system

Look Into the Text

1. **Explain** What does this statement mean: "The United States has always been a magnet for **immigrants**."

2. **Inference** Why would a slow economy affect immigration?

"Give me your tired,
your poor, your **huddled
masses yearning
to breathe free** . . ."
—*"The New Colossus"
Emma Lazarus*

Why Do They Come?

For more than 100 years, the words from "The New Colossus" have welcomed immigrants to the United States from all over the world. The words to this famous poem can be found on the Statue of Liberty, which stands on a small island in New York Harbor. The statue is a symbol of hope and freedom to those who come to the United States in search of a better life.

Immigration has played an important role in American history. The United States

▼ Some immigrants risk their lives trying to get to the U.S. Many people left Cuba by boat in 1994 because of the country's economic and political crisis.

In Other Words
huddled masses yearning to breathe free crowds of people who only want freedom

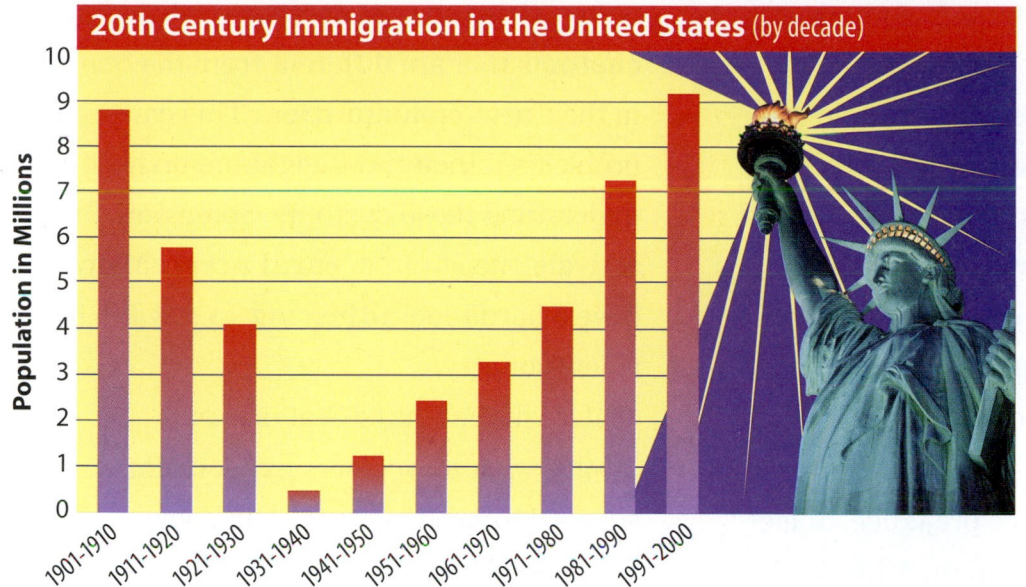

20th Century Immigration in the United States (by decade)

Population in Millions

10
9
8
7
6
5
4
3
2
1
0

1901-1910 | 1911-1920 | 1921-1930 | 1931-1940 | 1941-1950 | 1951-1960 | 1961-1970 | 1971-1980 | 1981-1990 | 1991-2000

◀ **Analyze the Graph** What trend do you notice about immigration over the last century? Has it increased, decreased, or both?

has even been called "the great melting pot" because of the many different cultures that can be found in the United States as a result of immigration.

The reasons that cause people to come to the United States are as varied and unique as the people who come here. Sometimes, people are forced to escape their countries. They are afraid of what might happen to them because of their races or religions. They are afraid they will be punished for their political beliefs. **Refugees** come to the United States in order to live their lives free from these types of prejudice and abuse.

Others come to the United States to escape poverty in their home countries. In the United States, people can find jobs that are not available in their home countries. They can also find jobs that pay them more money. Many immigrants seek to improve the quality of their lives, and their children's futures, too. They leave family, friends, and homes because they want more educational opportunities for themselves and their children.

In Other Words
Refugees Escaping immigrants

Look Into the Text

1. **Cause and Effect** What are some reasons ==immigrants== come to the U.S.?

2. **Explain** Why has America been called "the great melting pot"?

3. **Conclusion** Why would seeing the Statue of Liberty be important to an ==immigrant==?

Becoming Americans

Immigrants face a number of challenges when they arrive in the U.S. Many know little or no English. Even those people who are well-educated are sometimes forced to work at jobs that do not pay well. They continue at these jobs until their English improves or until they can find something better. Sometimes, people are as poor in their new country as they were in their previous one.

Some immigrants face prejudice. Some people do not want them in the United States. Other immigrants have religious **customs** that are different from the ones in their new **communities**. This causes problems if their new neighbors do not understand these customs. Some new arrivals once lived in **rural areas**. Many have a hard time **adjusting** to city life in a new country.

Life in the United States is not always what newcomers expect. Many succeed in their new life right away. Some need help.

▼ Hmong immigrants work at a farmers' market in Minneapolis, Minnesota.

Key Vocabulary

community *n.*, a group of people with common interests

adjust *v.*, to become used to or familiar with something

In Other Words

customs practices, traditions
rural areas small towns; places with few people

Preserving History and Culture

Most immigrants try to keep some of their cultural traditions. A community center can help them do this. A community center is a place for immigrants to spend time together. They can watch movies or listen to music from their homelands. They can share news about their homelands or celebrate **ethnic holidays**.

Many cities have ethnic **museums** or theaters. They give immigrant groups a way to **preserve** and celebrate their cultures and histories. They also give other members of the public a way to learn about other cultures.

Some cities have tours that celebrate the **heritages** of immigrant groups. Miami has tours that help visitors learn about Cuban culture and history. The visitors see museums, art galleries, and **monuments** on Cuban Memorial Boulevard.

Bookstores also help immigrants stay connected to their homelands. A Hmong couple opened a bookstore in St. Paul, Minnesota. Their store sells books about the Hmong culture and history. It also sells Hmong crafts, such as special cloths, dolls, and clothing. The store helps Hmong immigrants to pass their traditions and history to their children.

Many immigrant groups have created Web sites on the Internet. Here, people can find information about cultural events and organizations. They can hear news about what is happening in the countries they left. Young people can learn about the cultures and traditions of their people.

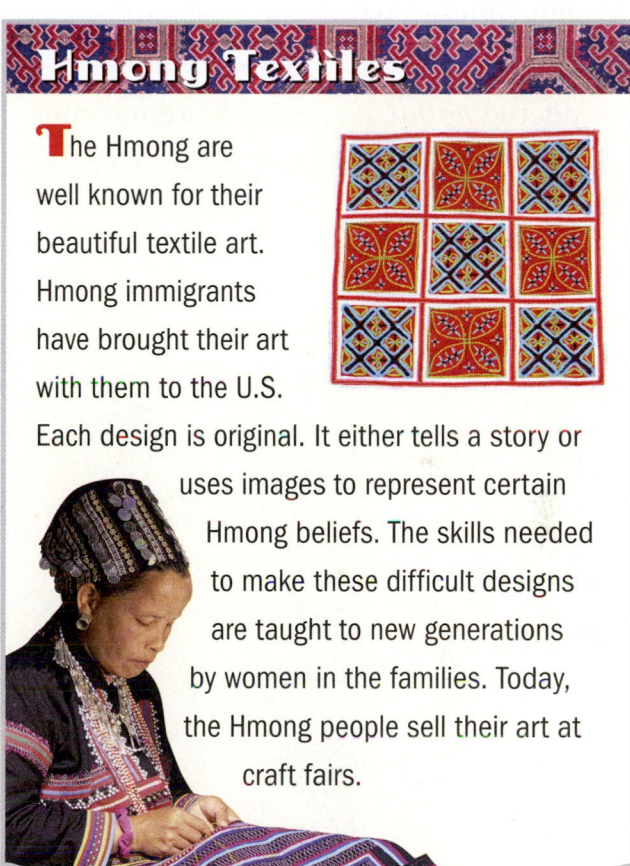

Hmong Textiles

The Hmong are well known for their beautiful textile art. Hmong immigrants have brought their art with them to the U.S. Each design is original. It either tells a story or uses images to represent certain Hmong beliefs. The skills needed to make these difficult designs are taught to new generations by women in the families. Today, the Hmong people sell their art at craft fairs.

Look Into the Text

1. **Inference** What problems do **immigrants** face from members of their new **communities**?
2. **Conclusion and Evidence** Many **immigrants adjust** well to life in the U.S. What evidence supports this?

Special Foods

Most people want to eat the foods they are used to. However, immigrants cannot always find **familiar foods**. So, some open small ethnic grocery stores or restaurants. When enough immigrants from one country move into an area, large ethnic food shops open. These stores often attract customers from far away. They buy foods they remember from their homelands.

Immigrants may avoid certain foods **for religious reasons**. Many Muslims, for example, will eat only food that is considered *hallal*, an Arabic word meaning "permitted." Meat must be prepared a certain way to make it *hallal*. Many Muslim

A restaurant in Chinatown, in New York City, New York

immigrants could not find stores that sold *hallal* meat. So, they opened *hallal* markets in places where they settled.

Almost every immigrant community has its own restaurants. They serve familiar food. Other people enjoy eating there, too. They like to share some of the **tasty traditions** of the immigrant group.

Immigrant families often prepare traditional meals at home. They pass on cultural traditions from one generation to the next.

In Other Words
familiar foods foods they know
for religious reasons because of religious rules or beliefs
tasty traditions good traditional food

Festivals and Holidays

Festivals and holidays are important to most immigrants. They are a way for people to celebrate their cultural traditions. People eat traditional foods, hear familiar music, and display or buy **handicrafts**. Also, people from other cultures can come to enjoy new sights, sounds, and tastes.

Mexican Americans celebrate *Cinco de Mayo* (May 5). This holiday **marks** an important victory of the Mexican Army in 1862. Many Asian Americans celebrate the Chinese New Year with special food and fireworks.

Some festivals are small. A town might **close off a block** for a street festival. Sometimes, these small festivals grow. They become large and well known. Sometimes, people travel long distances to go to them. For example, Boston has a Caribbean festival. It has been held every year since 1973.

▼ Celebrating *Cinco de Mayo* with music and dancing

In Other Words
handicrafts handmade items or crafts
marks celebrates
close off a block close part of a street

Look Into the Text

1. **Summarize** Briefly tell some of the ways that **immigrants preserve** their cultures in their new countries.
2. **Inference** Tell why cultural festivals might be important to a **community**.

Music and Movies

Music and movies are two ways for immigrants to share their cultures among themselves and with others. Ethnic neighborhoods often have music stores. They sell music that is popular in immigrants' homelands. In cities, large music stores **carry** music from many different countries. Also, people can order music through the mail.

Some large immigrant groups have radio stations that play music from their homelands. Radio stations in many states play Hispanic music. There is a Vietnamese radio station in California. Radio stations in New York and Chicago play music from different countries. Some radio stations also **broadcast over** the Internet. People can listen to the music of their homelands online. Immigrants also enjoy the music of their countries by playing in or going to concerts.

In addition to radio, Spanish-speaking immigrants can watch many Spanish-language television programs. These include newscasts, game shows, **soap operas**, and other kinds of programs.

In some cities, it is possible for immigrants to see films made in their homelands. They can often rent these films. Or, they might see movies at film festivals that show Indian, African, Cuban, or Mexican films.

These actors are dancing on a film set in Mumbai, India. "Bollywood" films are becoming more popular in the U.S.

In Other Words
carry sell
broadcast over can be heard on
soap operas dramatic television shows

Newspapers and Magazines

Stores in ethnic communities often sell **foreign** newspapers or magazines. Immigrants like to **keep in touch with** what is happening in their former homelands. They can read about politics or sports teams. They can **keep track of the latest music craze**, or see what movies are popular.

Many ethnic groups have their own **local** newspapers. There are more than 100 Hispanic newspapers in the United States. Some cities have Chinese-language newspapers. These newspapers report about community matters and other important events. They also carry news from their home countries. Some magazines appeal to specific ethnic groups. For example, *Filipinas* is a monthly magazine for people from the Philippines. *Hispanic Magazine* carries features of interest to Hispanics. Several popular magazines, such as *People*, are published in Spanish as well as in English.

One magazine directed to all immigrants is *Immigration Times*. It provides practical advice about living in the United States. It also contains articles about immigrant communities. Today, immigrants can find **a wealth** of information to help them learn about their new country. ❖

A Spanish-language newspaper for sale in Chicago, Illinois

Key Vocabulary
  foreign *adj.*, from another country
  local *adj.*, relating only to a city, town, or other small area

In Other Words
keep in touch with know
keep track of the latest music craze learn about popular music
a wealth a lot

Look Into the Text

1. **Conclusion** Why do people read news from their home countries?
2. **Summarize** What are some ways **immigrants** can experience their cultures in their new **communities**?

The Lemon Story

by Alberto Alvaro Ríos

When I was about four, or maybe five, my parents bought a new house in what would later become a small suburb of Nogales, Arizona, on the border of Mexico, **some** four miles outside town. My father was born in Mexico, on the border of Guatemala, and my mother was born in England. From the very beginning of my life **I had** many languages.

We often drove out to watch the house being built. My mother got to make a number of choices regarding details, among which was the color of various rooms.

My mother was asked by the Mexican workers what color she wanted the kitchen to be painted. They spoke very little English, so she said *limón*. She said it both because

The Soaring Teapot, 2005, Patssi Valdez. Acrylic on canvas, private collection.

▲ **Critical Viewing: Theme** How does the artwork reflect what a person might feel like when learning a new language?

she wanted the kitchen to be yellow and because she wanted to start learning Spanish. The workers nodded yes. But when we came back the next day, the kitchen was painted bright green, like a small jungle. Mexican *limones*, my mother found out, are small and green, that color exactly, no mistake.

The workers, seeing that my mother was upset, offered to paint it again, right away. My mother said, *No, no thank-you. It's fine.*

And that's the color that wall stayed for the next fourteen years. She said it was a reminder to us all that there was a great deal to learn in the world. You might laugh at first, but after fourteen years you start to think about it.

In Other Words
some about, almost
I had I knew how to speak

Connect Reading and Writing

Vocabulary
adjust
community
foreign
immigrant
local
museum
poverty
preserve

CRITICAL THINKING

1. **SUM IT UP** Review the reasons people immigrate and how they build new lives. Use your Cause-Effect Chart to summarize what you learned.

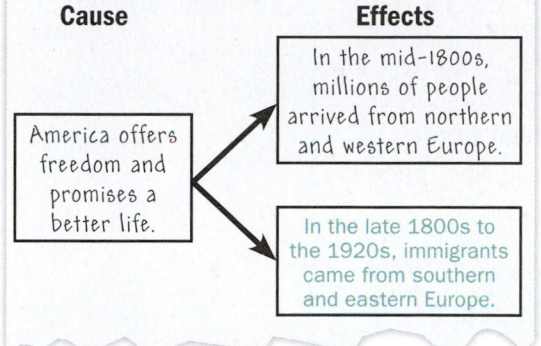

Cause	Effects
America offers freedom and promises a better life.	In the mid-1800s, millions of people arrived from northern and western Europe.
	In the late 1800s to the 1920s, immigrants came from southern and eastern Europe.

Cause-Effect Chart

2. **Make Judgments** What do you think is the hardest part of **adjusting** to a new culture? Why?

3. **Compare** In "The Lemon Story," what difficulties does the mother have in learning a **foreign** language? Compare that to the difficulties **immigrants** face in "Immigrants Today."

4. **Explain** How do **immigrants** **preserve** their cultures?

READING FLUENCY

Phrasing Read the passage on page 645 to a partner. Assess your fluency.

1. I did not pause/sometimes paused/ always paused for punctuation.

2. What I did best in my reading was _____.

READING STRATEGY

What strategy helped you understand this selection? Tell a partner about it.

VOCABULARY REVIEW

Oral Review Read the paragraph aloud. Add the vocabulary words.

My great-grandmother came to the United States as an _____ from Europe after World War II. Because of war, she often did not have enough food to eat. She left to escape _____ . At first, it was hard to _____ to life in a _____ country. But she met wonderful people in her new _____ . Together, they opened a _____ shop nearby that sells arts and crafts from their home countries. She said selling the art helps to _____ her culture. Some of the art is so beautiful that I think it belongs in a _____ .

Written Review Imagine you could donate one object to a **museum** to represent your culture. Write a paragraph to explain what you would choose and why. Use four vocabulary words.

WRITE ABOUT THE GUIDING QUESTION

Explore New Beginnings

Why do people leave their homes to start over in a **foreign** country? How might these reasons affect their new lives? Write your ideas. Give examples from the text and your own life.

Connect Across the Curriculum

Use Prefixes and Suffixes

Word Part	Meaning
im-	into, not
over-	too much; above
-al	process of; having characteristics of
-ful	full of; filling

Academic Vocabulary
- **identify** (ī-**den**-tu-fī) *verb*
  When you **identify** something, you name, recognize, or discover it.

Prefixes and suffixes help you **identify** the meaning of unfamiliar words. But some prefixes and suffixes have more than one meaning. Follow these steps to figure out the meaning of a word with a prefix or suffix.

1. Cover the prefix or suffix. Figure out the meaning of the base word. **re**do
2. Look at the prefix or suffix and decide which meaning works best.
3. Use the meaning in a sentence to see if it makes sense.

Figure Out Word Meanings **Identify** the word parts in each word. If the prefix or suffix has more than one meaning, decide which meaning works best. Then write a sentence using the word to see if it makes sense.

1. immigrate   2. wonderful   3. overeat   4. national   5. arrival

Make an Immigration Graph

MATH

Academic Vocabulary
- **data** (dā-tu) *noun*
  Data is factual information.

Use a visual aid to show **data** on U.S. citizenship.

❶ **Collect and Organize Data** What percentage of people in the United States are U.S. citizens by birth? What percentage are naturalized, or have become citizens since their arrival? Use the Internet to research this **data** between 1900–1999.

> **Internet** myNGconnect.com
> 🔎 Find citizenship data from the U.S. Census Bureau.

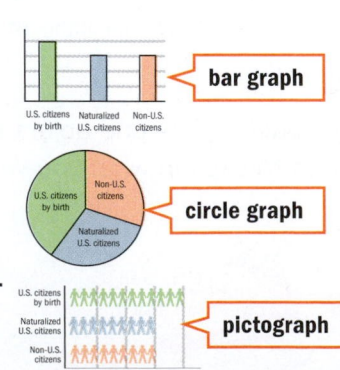

bar graph

circle graph

pictograph

Add the two percentages.

Subtract that number from 100 percent.

This is the percentage who are not U.S. citizens.

❷ **Make Your Graph** Show your **data** in a graph.

❸ **Share Your Graph** Share and explain your graph. Compare your **data** with others.

Make Comparisons

Pair Talk Work with a partner. Compare experiences between groups in the selection or between your families' traditions. Remember to look for ways the experiences or traditions are alike and different. Use comparative adjectives in your discussion.

> We open presents after breakfast on the holidays.

> That's interesting. We always have an earlier celebration. We open gifts right after dinner the night before the holidays.

Write to Compare

Study the Models When you write to compare things or ideas, you want your reader to understand your comparisons. Be sure to use words that show a comparison clearly so that your reader can understand what you have to say.

NOT OK

> This holiday is <u>importanter</u> than any other holiday of the year. We have fireworks and music, so it may be <u>noisyer</u> than usual around here. Some people think the day is <u>interestinger</u> for adults, but the <u>more young</u> citizens have fun, too. They dance and sing and eat delicious foods!

The reader thinks: "What is the writer comparing? It's hard to tell from these words."

OK

> This holiday is <u>more important</u> than any other holiday of the year. We have fireworks and music, so it may be <u>noisier</u> than usual around here. Some people think the day is <u>more interesting</u> for adults, but the <u>younger</u> citizens have fun, too. They dance and sing and eat delicious foods!

The comparative words are correct. Now it is clear what the writer is comparing.

Add Sentences Think of two sentences to add to the OK model above. Look for more ways that the holiday is similar or different.

WRITE ON YOUR OWN Write about a change you have made in your life. How are you different now from before? How are the places and people you have known different from those you know now? Make sure you use the correct forms of the comparison words.

REMEMBER

- Add **-er** to adjectives that have one syllable. If the adjective ends in **y**, change the **y** to **i** before you add **-er**.
  I am **friendlier** than I was before.
- Add **more** before adjectives that have three or more syllables.
  My new school is **more** difficult than my old school.

Brothers in Hope
The Story of the Lost Boys of Sudan

by Mary Williams

Untitled, 1997, Ejai M. Sharif. Oil on canvas, courtesy of Sudan Artists Gallery, Philadelphia.

SELECTION 3 OVERVIEW

▶ **Build Background**

▶ **Language & Grammar**
Describe an Event or Experience
Use Adverbs

▶ **Prepare to Read**
Learn Key Vocabulary
Compare Fiction and Nonfiction

▶ **Read and Write**
Introduce the Genre
Biographical Fiction
Focus on Reading
Analyze Interactions
Apply the Focus Strategy
Visualize
Critical Thinking
Reading Fluency
Read with Expression
Vocabulary Review
Write About the Guiding Question

▶ **Connect Across the Curriculum**
Vocabulary Study
Use Word Parts: Roots
Listening/Speaking
Role-Play a Conversation
Language and Grammar
Describe an Event or Experience
Writing and Grammar
Write About an Event

Build Background

Learn About World Events

In the 1990s, war left thousands of children in Sudan without homes. Learn what happened to them.

Digital Library

myNGconnect.com
🖳 View the video.

Sudan

▲ Sudan is a country in Africa.

Connect

Anticipation Guide Think about families and homes. Tell if you agree or disagree with these statements.

Anticipation Guide

	Agree	Disagree
1. A family should be related by blood.	_____	_____
2. A home is a house or an apartment.	_____	_____
3. Only adults can take care of kids.	_____	_____

Language & Grammar

1 TRY OUT LANGUAGE
2 LEARN GRAMMAR
3 APPLY ON YOUR OWN

Describe an Event or Experience

CD

Look at the illustration and listen to the song about children left homeless from war. Then sing along.

SONG

Song for the Children

Where do they wander
And where can they stay,
These innocent children,
Who have no home today?

Refrain: Where are the families
Who cared for the young?
Why must this lonely and
Sad song be sung?

Dangers left behind them?
Or dangers coming near?
Every day and every night,
They have so much to fear.

Use Adverbs

Adverbs are words that describe verbs, adjectives, or other adverbs. Adverbs can tell *how*, *when*, and *where*.

• Use an adverb to describe a verb. Adverbs often end in **-ly**.

EXAMPLE   The storm came **suddenly**.

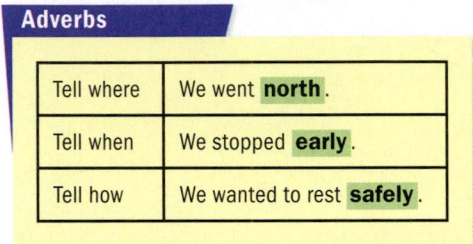

Adverbs

Tell where	We went **north**.
Tell when	We stopped **early**.
Tell how	We wanted to rest **safely**.

• Use an adverb to make an adjective or another adverb stronger.

adjective

EXAMPLES   The trip was **strangely** quiet.
The younger children walked **very** slowly.

adverb

Practice Together

Say each adverb in the box with your class. Choose an adverb from the box to describe the underlined word. Say the sentence with the adverb.

immediately   daily   quickly   often

1. We had to <u>do</u> our chores _____.

2. We tried to <u>complete</u> them _____.

3. We _____ <u>went</u> to the city.

4. We had to <u>leave</u> _____!

Try It!

Choose an adverb from the box to describe the underlined word. Write each sentence with the adverb. Then say the sentence with the adverb.

closer   down   softly   suddenly

5. The children <u>talked</u> _____.

6. We heard a truck <u>coming</u> _____ the road.

7. _____ the truck <u>stopped</u>.

8. The truck <u>took</u> us _____ to the city.

▲ The truck traveled slowly.

Share an Adventure

DESCRIBE AN EVENT OR EXPERIENCE

Have you ever been on a journey? Have you ever wanted to take a journey to someplace special? Make a storyboard about the journey you have taken or want to take. Add details about your journey.

▲ We left early.

▲ The tire was totally flat.

▲ We piled our stuff nearby.

Now use the storyboard to share your experience with a partner. Describe your journey to your partner. Then listen carefully as your partner describes his or her experience.

HOW TO DESCRIBE AN EVENT OR EXPERIENCE

1. Name the event or experience.

2. Tell the most interesting details about the event or experience.

3. Tell *when*, *where*, and *how* events happened.

> We drove to my uncle's farm in the Midwest last summer. Suddenly, we had a flat tire!

USE ADVERBS

When you describe an event or experience, you need to add details that tell *when*, *where*, and *how* things happened. Use **adverbs** to make your description more interesting. Many adverbs that tell *how* end in -**ly**.

Tells *how*:   We waited **patiently** while Dad changed the flat tire.

Tells *when*:   Because of the flat tire, we arrived **late** to my aunt's house.

Tells *where*:   It's a good thing my aunt lives **nearby**!

Prepare to Read

Learn Key Vocabulary

Study the Words Use the steps below.

1. Pronounce the word. Say it aloud several times. Spell it.
2. Rate your word knowledge.
3. Study the example. Tell more about the word.
4. Practice it. Make the word your own.

Key Words

cross (kros) *verb*
▶ page 233

When you **cross** something, you go from one side to another. A hiker **crosses** the bridge.
Related Word: **across**

dangerous (dăn-jur-us)
adjective ▶ page 231

Something **dangerous** is not safe. This sign is warning people that swimming might be **dangerous**.
Base Word: **danger**

education (ej-u-kā-shun)
noun ▶ page 235

Your **education** is everything you learn. **Education** can come from books, people, or experiences.
Base Word: **educate**
Related Words: **educator, educated**

effort (e-furt) *noun*
▶ page 242

When you put **effort** into something, you try harder. A runner puts **effort** into winning a race.

emerge (i-murj) *verb*
▶ page 236

When you **emerge** from a place, you come out of it. A swimmer **emerges** from the water for air.

improve (im-prüv) *verb*
▶ page 240

To **improve** something means to make it better. Painting a house **improves** how it looks.
Related Word: **improvement**

journey (jur-nē) *noun*
▶ page 231

A **journey** is a long trip. People take a **journey** across the ocean in a ship.

tend (tend) *verb*
▶ page 228

When you **tend** something, you take care of it. The man **tends** a plant by watering it.

Practice the Words Make a Frayer Model for each Key Word. Then compare your models with a partner's models.

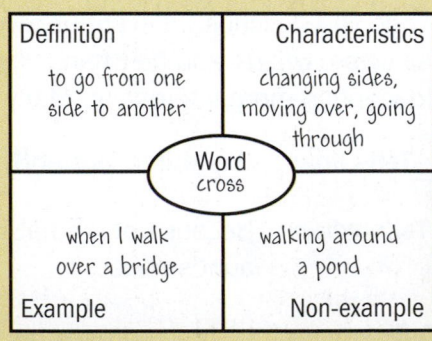

Definition	Characteristics
to go from one side to another	changing sides, moving over, going through
when I walk over a bridge	walking around a pond
Example	Non-example

Word: cross

Frayer Model

Compare Fiction and Nonfiction

Understanding how fiction authors combine facts with literary details can help you **compare** fiction and nonfiction writing. Nonfiction text gives facts. Fiction authors add sensory and other literary details to help you visualize events more clearly. As you read, think about how each author describes the same events.

Reading Strategies

- Plan
- Monitor
- **Visualize** Imagine the sights, sounds, smells, tastes, and feel of what the author is describing.
- Determine Importance
- Ask Questions
- Make Connections
- Make Inferences
- Synthesize

Look Into the Text

"Refugees Find New Lives," page 244

In 1987, soldiers attacked Wal's village while he was away tending his family's herd of cattle. His entire village was killed and Wal, who was only seven years old, found himself completely alone in the world. Wal escaped and soon joined thousands of boys between the ages of four and fourteen who were in the same situation.

"Brothers in Hope," page 228

I was far from home tending my animals when my village was attacked. I could hear bangs like thunder and see flashing lights in the distance . . .

When the **storm of bullets passed**, I ran back to my village to find my family, but everyone was gone. The houses were burning and everything was destroyed.

I began to wander down the road, and soon met other boys who could not find their families...

"Both tell about the same factual event."

Practice Together

Begin a Comparison Chart A Comparison Chart can help you **compare** how two authors describe the same event. Notice the details each author includes. Reread the passages, and add to the Comparison Chart.

"Refugees Find New Lives"	"Brothers in Hope"
• In 1987, soldiers attacked Wal's village while he was away tending his family's herd of cattle.	• I was far from home tending my animals when my village was attacked.

Comparison Chart

Academic Vocabulary

- **compare** (kum-**pair**) *verb*
  When you **compare** two things, you think about how they are alike and different.

Biographical Fiction

Writers of biographical fiction include real people, places, events, and ideas from history as part of the story. As you read, visualize these elements to help you picture the characters and setting and bring the action of the story to life.

Look Into the Text

When I turned eight years old, I began to tend some small calves of my own. I cleaned them, nursed them when they were sick, and led them to the very best pastures and watering holes. I quickly grew to love these animals.

The events in biographical fiction are usually written in chronological order.

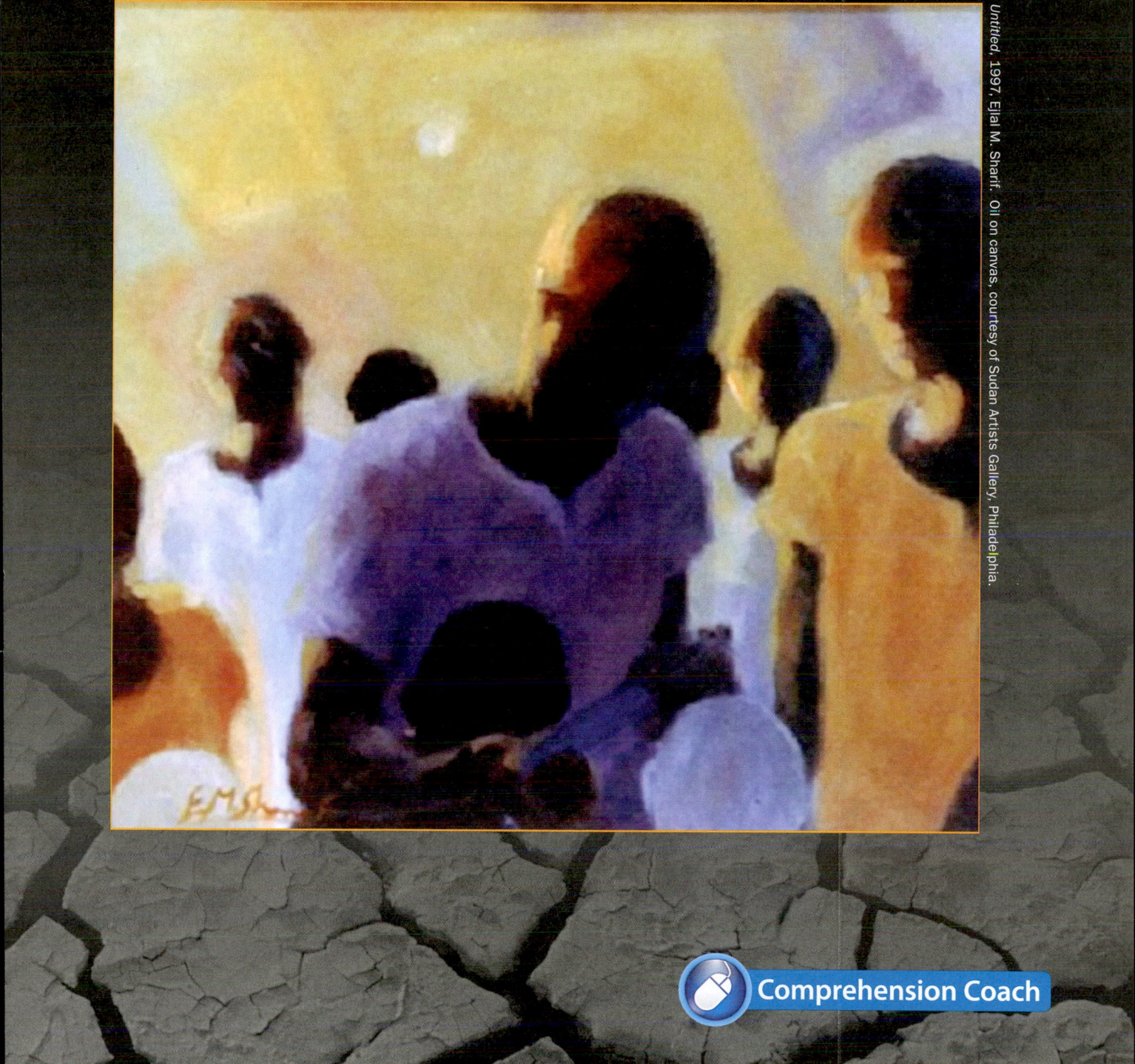

Untitled, 1997, Ejlal M. Sharif. Oil on canvas, courtesy of Sudan Artists Gallery, Philadelphia.

Comprehension Coach

I was born in southern Sudan. I lived with my mother and father, grandparents, and two sisters in a small mud-and-thatch house. We were considered wealthy because my father owned many cattle.

As a young boy, I was frightened of these big animals.

"I am too small to care for such big animals!" I cried when my father told me I would have to learn to **tend** the cattle.

My father just smiled. "Garang, be brave," he said. "Your heart and mind are strong. There is nothing you cannot do."

When I turned eight years old, I began to tend some small calves on my own. I cleaned them, nursed them when they were sick, and led them to the very best **pastures and watering holes**. I quickly grew to love these animals.

Then one day everything in my life changed.

I was far from home tending my animals when my village was attacked. I could hear bangs like thunder and see flashing lights in the distance. Suddenly an airplane was circling above. Clouds of dust rose from the ground and **bullets began to rain down on my herd**. Many of the animals were killed. Others ran away in fear.

My throat and eyes were full of dust, but I found my way to the forest, where I hid in the shadows of the trees.

When the **storm of bullets passed**, I ran back to my village to find my family, but everyone was gone. The houses were burning and everything was destroyed.

I began to wander down the road, and soon I met other boys who could not find their families. We began to search together. As we walked, we met more boys on the road.

At first there was just me—one.
Soon one became many.
Too many to count.

Key Vocabulary
tend *v.*, to take care of someone or something

In Other Words
pastures and watering holes places that had food and water
bullets began to rain down on my herd my cows were shot at
storm of bullets passed shooting stopped

Landscape from "Al-Sababi", 1990, Khalafalla Abboud. Watercolor, courtesy of Sudan Artists Gallery, Philadelphia.

▲ **Critical Viewing: Plot** What connection can you make between the beginning of the story and this image?

Cultural Background

Cattle herding is a way of life in the villages of southern Sudan. People use everything that the cows make, such as their milk. While the cattle are not killed for meat, the people will eat a cow that has died and use its skin to make things.

Before war came, I had never seen so many people in one place. My village had only one hundred people. Now I was in a moving village with thousands of boys.

Like me, the other boys were away from their villages tending their cattle when war came. The adults and girls had **stayed behind**.

Some of the boys were only five years old. The oldest boys were not more than fifteen. We were children, not used to caring for ourselves. Without our parents we **were lost**. We had to learn to take care of one another.

The Return, 1978, Bayo Iribhogbe. Oil on board, private collection.

▲ **Critical Viewing: Perspective** Why might the artist have chosen this view to show a "moving village"?

In Other Words
  stayed behind been left at home
    in the villages
  were lost did not know what
    to do

The older boys decided to have a meeting. "We must work together if we are to survive," one of the boys said. "We will form groups and choose a leader for each group."

"Garang Deng!" someone yelled. My name!

I had been chosen to lead a group of thirty-five boys. I was proud but scared. I knew how to take care of animals, not boys, but I did not want to let my fear keep me from helping **my brothers**. Then I remembered what my father had told me: Garang, be brave. Your heart and mind are strong. There is nothing you cannot do.

I joined the group of leaders, and we decided we would walk to a country called Ethiopia. Before war came to our villages, many of us had heard **our elders** talk of Ethiopia. They had said Ethiopians would **provide** a safe place for Sudanese running from the war.

Some of the older boys knew we must travel east to reach Ethiopia. It was very far and the **journey** would be **dangerous**,

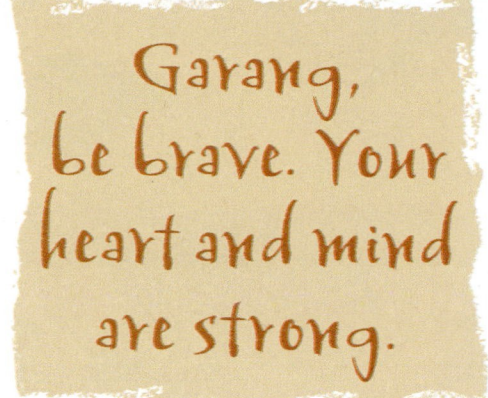

Garang, be brave. Your heart and mind are strong.

but it was our only hope.

We decided it was best to walk at night and sleep in the forest during the day to **avoid** soldiers and the severe heat of the sun. Many argued that it was too dangerous to walk at night because of animals hunting for food. After much talk we agreed that the soldiers and their warplanes were more dangerous than the animals.

We also decided that the older boys would **adopt** younger boys who couldn't care for themselves. I chose a little boy in my group named Chuti Bol. He was only five and cried for his mother.

The next evening we found the road to Ethiopia. We were glad to have a full bright moon, but it was still very dark. To make sure we did not lose anyone, each boy held the hand of the boy in front of him.

Chuti was too small to walk long distances. I often carried him on my back. Everyone was tired and hungry, but no one complained.

Key Vocabulary

journey *n.*, the act of traveling a long distance
dangerous *adj.*, difficult and unsafe

In Other Words

my brothers the other boys
our elders the adults
provide make
avoid stay away from
adopt take care of

Science Background

In southern Sudan, temperatures can reach more than 100 degrees during the day and more than 90 degrees at night. Many animals are nocturnal, which means that they sleep during the hot daytime and hunt for food when it's cool at night.

Disagreement, 1985, Paul Nzalamba. Batik, courtesy of Nzalamba Artworks, Los Angeles.

▲ **Critical Viewing: Character** Which person in this painting reminds you most of Garang? Why?

There were a few boys in my group who knew how to find wild fruits that were good to eat and others who could hunt wild birds. Some days we had food to share, but most days there was no food to be found. We often ate leaves and bark from trees.

Finding food was not the only problem. Many days it was hot and dry and we were very thirsty. Sometimes we had to drink our urine to get **moisture** in our bodies. There were times when we got very sick. We made sure to rest often so the weaker boys could keep up.

We did many things to help us forget our hunger and our **aching** bodies. We played games and told stories. We made animal figures from mud, mostly cattle. I told Chuti how I used to care for calves. He was so **impressed**, he insisted I **sculpt** a herd of cattle for him.

Many days it was hot and dry and we were thirsty.

I was glad Chuti liked the cattle, even if they were just made of mud.

One evening as we were walking on the road, I heard Chuti crying. I picked him up and asked him what was wrong.

"I'm scared you will leave me like my mother and father," Chuti sobbed.

"Chuti, your mother and father did not want to leave you. They loved you very much. They lost you when war came. Don't worry, I will take care of you," I said. "But for now, daylight is coming and we must find a shady place to sleep. We need our strength to **cross** the border into Ethiopia tomorrow."

I put Chuti down under a tree. He was so tired from crying that he fell right to sleep. As I lay down beside him, I thought of my own parents and how much I missed them.

Look Into the Text

1. **Metaphor** What does Garang mean when he says he "was in a moving village"?
2. **Main Idea and Details** The boys' **journey** is difficult. Give details to support this main idea.

Find out what happens to Garang and his group.

The following evening we crossed into Ethiopia. Everyone in my group **made it**. I was proud to be their leader. Other groups were not as lucky. Many boys had died along the way.

The first people we **encountered** were a small group of women washing clothes in a river. They were surprised to see so many boys all alone and scared.

"Who are these lost boys?" an elderly woman asked.

"We are **fleeing** war," said one of our leaders.

"You look hungry and sick," another woman said. "We must show you the way to the refugee camp."

"What is a refugee camp?" I asked.

The women told us a refugee camp is a

Nile Custom, Late 20th century, Khalid Hamid. Oil on canvas, courtesy of Sudan Artists Gallery, Philadelphia.

▲ **Critical Viewing: Setting** How does the scene in this painting compare with the one described in the story?

In Other Words
made it got there safely
encountered met
fleeing running from; escaping

place for people to go when their country is not safe. The kind women stopped their washing and put us on the road to the camp.

In the refugee camp we met a man named Tom who was from the United States. His job was to help refugees like us.

"I will do my best to get you food and **shelter**," Tom said.

Tom was true to his promise. For the first time in a long while, we ate every day. It wasn't much, just lentils and flour, but after months with almost nothing to eat, it seemed like a feast. We were given tools to build our own mud-and-thatch shelters. To me they were palaces!

We also had the chance to go to school. In the beginning we did not want to go. We wanted to play and forget our hard times. The adults tried to **bribe us with cookies**, but still many boys did not go to school. The adults became upset with us.

One day a teacher visited me.

"Garang, you must make sure your group comes to school every day," she said. "**Education** is very important. It can be like your mothers and fathers. It can speak for you in the future, when your parents cannot."

The teacher's words reminded me of how much I missed my parents. I decided to go to school to **honor** them and to feel they were still with me. My group began to go to school, too, even if there were no cookies.

English was my favorite subject. We didn't have pencils and paper, so I practiced writing my lessons in the dirt with a stick.

We also learned to **pray and worship**. Many of us began to go to church every weekend. **Faith** gave us hope and strength. We began to tell people, "I am not lost. God knows where I am."

> Tom was true to his promise.

Just when it seemed things were finally okay for us, we heard war stirring again. In the distance we saw the flashing lights and heard the terrible thunder. Suddenly there were changes in the camp. Many people began to leave. Soon there was not enough food.

The people of Ethiopia began fighting, and we could not stay in their country anymore. We were chased back to the border of Sudan by war.

It was the rainy season and the huge Gilo River was **swollen** with water, blocking us from getting to Sudan on the **opposite bank**. We gathered on the riverbank. Many boys were afraid to enter the river. The **current** was strong and the rushing water roared like an angry lion. I ordered my group to stay together and to help those who were sick or not strong swimmers.

> ...the rushing water roared like an angry lion.

When we fled the refugee camp, I had taken my schoolbooks with me. As I stood at the river's edge, I decided I would not leave them behind. They were my future— my mother and father.

I tied my schoolbooks around my waist, grabbed Chuti, and jumped into the river. I was so afraid, I don't remember being in the water. I only remember hauling Chuti and myself up onto the opposite bank.

I made sure Chuti was okay, and then waited anxiously for the rest of our group. As boys began to **emerge** from the river I prayed and counted.

One . . . 12 . . . 22 . . . 27 . . . 31 . . . 35!

We were **reunited with** everyone in our group—every last one!

We prayed to God to take care of the souls of the brothers we had lost in the river. We also thanked Him for **sparing** us and prayed for a safe end to our journey.

Key Vocabulary
emerge *v.*, to come out of something

In Other Words
swollen filled to the top
opposite bank other side
current flow of water
reunited with joined by
sparing saving

The Storm, 2005, Erik Slutsky mixed media on paper.

▲ **Critical Viewing: Design** What words and phrases in the story could be used to describe the water in this painting?

Later that day, as we prepared for sleep, we saw many big trucks approaching. They were moving very fast, and their rumbling tires sent huge dust clouds into the air. Frightened that there were soldiers in the trucks, we ran to hide.

As the trucks drew closer, my heart began to pound so hard I could hear nothing else. I huddled close to my group, covered my face with my hands, and waited.

After a few minutes I **gathered my courage** and went to peek through the trees. I saw one of the drivers. It was Tom!

"It's safe, it's safe!" I cried. "Tom has come to save us!"

Many of the boys ran out from the forest, and soon the trucks were surrounded by boys. Everyone wanted to be taken to safety.

Tom began to speak. "I'm very sorry,

"It's safe, it's safe!"

but we cannot take all of you. There is not enough room. For now, we will take only the smallest and those who are too sick to walk.

"The rest of you must keep walking to Kenya. We will show you the way. Your worst days will soon be **behind you**."

My group decided that Chuti should go in the truck and the rest of us would walk to Kenya. Chuti wept when I put him in the truck.

"You are leaving me!" Chuti cried.

"No, Chuti," I said, "I am sending you to a safe place. We will join you soon. Until then, you must be strong."

As the trucks drove away, we could see Chuti crying as he watched us through the window. We were sad to see him leave but happy that he would be cared for until we met him in Kenya.

In Other Words
gathered my courage was brave
behind you over, finished

Look Into the Text

1. **Compare and Contrast** How are the events in Ethiopia similar to those in Sudan?
2. **Explain** Why must the group **cross** the river when it's so **dangerous**?
3. **Figurative Language** What does the teacher mean when she says **education** "can speak for you"?

We rejoined the other groups of boys on the road to Kenya. Some parts of the road were well cleared and **marked**. Others were not. We made sure to keep the trail well marked for the groups behind us.

Many weeks later we made it to a refugee camp in Kenya called Kakuma. There were thousands of people in the camp, but I **was determined** to find Chuti.

I asked boys from the other groups if they had seen him. One of the leaders told me Tom was taking care of him. Someone showed me to Tom's house, and there I found Chuti eating candy and drawing a picture.

When he saw me, he ran to me and jumped into my arms.

I thanked Tom for taking such good care of Chuti. Then Tom said he needed my help.

"Although you are safe for now, my work is not done," Tom explained. "The war in

Refugees in the Dark, 1999, Nahla Mahdi. Oil on canvas, courtesy of Sudan Artists Gallery, Philadelphia.

🔺 **Critical Viewing: Effect** Compare this image with Garang's descriptions of the refugee camps. How does the image make you feel?

In Other Words

marked there were signs that told us where to go

was determined knew I must try very hard

Sudan is not over, and you and your brothers need to find a place to **call home**."

"But what can I do?" I asked.

"You must tell me your story—what has happened to you since war came to your country," Tom said. "Your story can help prevent war from **creating** more lost children, and you can help find a home for yourself and your brothers. Your words will **move** caring people to help."

So I shared my story with Tom. I talked all day and all night. Then we cried and prayed. After telling my story, the storm of war no longer seemed as scary. The thunder was not as loud.

A few days after our talk, Tom left the camp. Without Tom around, things began to change. Life in Kenya became very hard. There was not enough food. People were often sick and many died.

"But what can I do?" I asked.

Some boys in my group became so weak from hunger they could no longer attend school. Then we thought of a way for everyone to get food and education. We took turns **foraging** for food and going to school. At night the ones who foraged would share their food and the ones who went to school would share their lessons. This way we were able to feed our bodies and our minds.

As I grew older, I tried to <mark>improve</mark> conditions in the camp. I helped form a drama club and a soccer league so we could have fun things to do. I became a health educator. I taught boys to boil dirty water before drinking it and other ways to prevent sickness.

Chuti was growing older, too. I continued to care for him, and he helped me in my work. He was a very smart boy who often **tutored** other boys in math and English.

Key Vocabulary
improve *v.*, to make something better

In Other Words
call home live safely
creating making
move cause, inspire
foraging looking
tutored helped

Night, Late 20th century, Nasir Bakhiet. Oil on canvas, courtesy of Sudan Artists Gallery, Philadelphia.

▲ **Critical Viewing: Character** How would you describe the young boy in the painting? What details support your description?

I became a young man with **responsibilities**, which made me feel good. But despite my best <mark>efforts</mark>, life continued to be a daily struggle for survival. I often worried about my future and Chuti's.

I was twenty-one years old when Tom returned to Kakuma. When I went out to greet him, I almost did not recognize him. His hair had turned gray. I hugged him very hard.

"You have changed, Tom!" I said.

Tom laughed, "Yes, I am now an old man and you are a young man!"

"Where have you been, Tom? Did you forget about us?" I asked.

"I did not forget you, Garang," Tom said. "Your words have been with me, and I have been sharing them with people in many countries. Now the United States is offering you and your brothers a home."

Tom called a meeting and told us about the United States. He said there would be people coming to teach us about this country **in preparation** for our journey.

Be Free Three, Late 20th century, Kaaria Mucherera. Oil and acrylic on canvas, private collection.

⚠ **Critical Viewing: Symbol** A dove is often recognized as a symbol of peace. How does this symbol relate to Garang's story?

Key Vocabulary
effort *n.*, hard work

In Other Words
responsibilities important jobs in the camp
in preparation to get us ready

I remembered our teachers in Ethiopia telling us that the United States was very far away and life there was very different. I was happy to hear that my brothers and I would have a new place to live, but I was also very afraid. I wondered if people in America would **accept** me, a lost boy with nothing but a few **tattered** schoolbooks. I thought it might be better to stay in Kakuma.

I went to the forest to be alone and think about all the things Tom had told us. I also remembered my father's words: Your heart and mind are strong. There is nothing you cannot do.

When I first heard those words, I did not understand them. Now I knew them to be true. My heart was strong with faith and the love of my brothers, and my mind was filled with wisdom from books and the many changes in my life. I was no longer afraid. I would find the strength to make a new life. I would find a new future. ❖

About the Author

Mary Williams

Ever since **Mary Williams** (1967–) heard about the lost boys of Sudan, she knew she had to help. Williams started an organization called the Lost Boys Foundation. She then wrote a fictional story based on the real events of the lost boys. Located in Atlanta, Georgia, the Lost Boys Foundation helps the Sudanese boys (now young men) receive college educations. Williams says, "I've never met a lost boy not interested in bettering himself and his country."

In Other Words
accept like, want
tattered old and torn

Look Into the Text

1. **Confirm Prediction** Was your prediction about Tom correct? What happened that you did not expect?

2. **Mood** How does the mood change after Garang goes to the forest to be alone?

3. **Summarize** Explain why Garang is no longer afraid at the end of the story. What has he learned?

More than 3,000 "Lost Boys" walked many miles in search of safety.

Refugees Find New Lives

Peter Wal and David Gai landed in Boston, Massachusetts, on a cold March night in 2002, with no money, no coats, and little more than the clothes they were wearing. As refugees from the violence and poverty of Sudan during the late 1980s and 1990s, Wal and Gai had known enough hunger and terror to last a lifetime. Both Wal and Gai looked at their new home and felt no new sense of hope. People were not warm and friendly like the people from their villages, and the lifeless winter landscape was like nothing they had ever experienced. As Gai told a *Time* magazine reporter, "I thought if the trees couldn't survive in this place, how would we?"

In 1987, soldiers attacked Wal's village while he was away tending his family's herd of cattle. His entire village was killed and Wal, who was only seven years old, found himself completely alone in the world. Wal escaped and soon joined thousands of boys between the ages of four and fourteen who were in the same situation. These boys had avoided death because they had been away from their villages at the time of the attacks.

The boys walked for three months. Many died of starvation, disease, or from drowning in the deep rivers of Sudan as they fled to safety. Some were even attacked by wild animals and killed. **Exhausted**, the boys finally found an Ethiopian refugee camp, where aid workers named them the Lost Boys.

But their story does not end here.

A Journey of a Thousand Miles

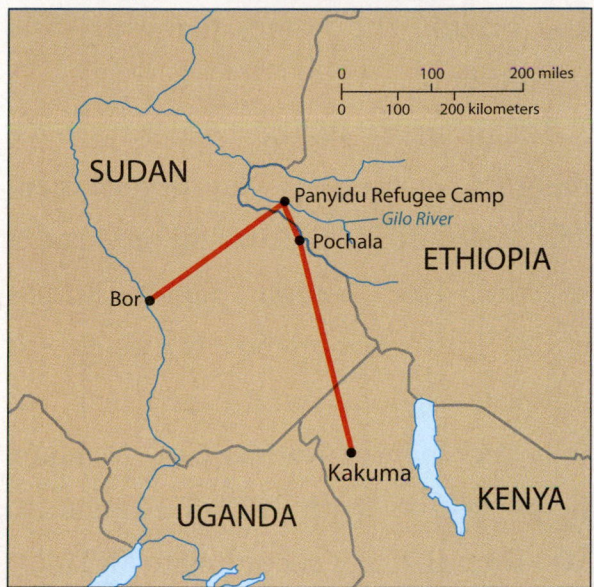

The Lost Boys spent three months walking from Sudan to Ethiopia. It took nearly a year before they finally reached Kenya.

As time passed, the Lost Boys were forced to **seek refuge** in a camp in Kakuma, Kenya. There, United Nations workers provided food, education, and encouragement. By 1999, the United Nations and the United States had agreed to **resettle** close to 4,000 Lost Boys in the U.S., including Wal and Gai. These boys have settled in cities across the U.S. Now college-age and older, they are working hard to receive educations.

Cultural Background
The United Nations is a governmental organization that works for peace and development all over the world.

In Other Words
Exhausted Very tired
seek refuge find safety
resettle find new homes for

Their hope is to one day return to Sudan and rebuild the homes that war stole from them.

Today, many of the Lost Boys have mentors—volunteers who support them and help them receive an education in the U.S. Joseph Taban Rufino is a Lost Boy who is going to medical school with the help of Joey McLiney of Kansas City. McLiney helps Rufino with his adjustment to **Western life**. But according to McLiney, Rufino is the one helping McLiney and his family understand a world outside of their own, a world they will never know **first-hand**.

Rufino works at two jobs to pay bills. He studies for medical school at night. He feels that as long as he can receive an education in the U.S., he can be a doctor. He is determined to succeed. Rufino's story is so inspirational that he and McLiney appeared on *The Oprah Winfrey Show* to tell the story of the Lost Boys.

Even though **civil war** continues in many countries in Africa, the Lost Boys of Sudan remind people that once lost, these boys continue to find their way.

In Other Words
Western life life in the United States
first-hand from experience
civil war war among people within one country

1. **Summarize** Describe the boys' **journey** from Sudan to the United States.
2. **Compare and Contrast** How was life in Sudan different from life in the U.S. for the boys?

Connect Reading and Writing

Vocabulary
cross
dangerous
education
effort
emerged
improve
journey
tended

CRITICAL THINKING

1. **SUM IT UP** Start with your Comparison Chart and summarize the key events in the story as you compare fictional details with nonfiction facts.

"Refugees Find New Lives"	"Brothers in Hope"
• In 1987, soldiers attacked Wal's village while he was away tending his family's herd of cattle.	• I was far from home tending my animals when my village was attacked.

Comparison Chart

2. **Compare** How do Rufino's views about **education** in "Refugees Find New Lives" and Garang's views in "Brothers in Hope" compare? Are they similar or different? Why?

3. **Conclusion** How does Garang **emerge** from his situation a stronger person? Use details from the text to support your answer.

4. **Evaluate** Revisit your Anticipation Guide. Do you still agree with your answers? Why or why not? Discuss your ideas with your classmates.

READING FLUENCY

Expression Read the passage on page 646 to a partner. Assess your fluency.

1. My voice never/sometimes/always matched what I read.

2. What I did best in my reading was _____.

READING STRATEGY

What strategy helped you understand this selection? Tell a partner about it.

VOCABULARY REVIEW

Oral Review Read the paragraph to a partner. Add the vocabulary words.

I just read about African boys on a _____ to freedom. They had to _____ a river and walk on roads that were very _____. It took a lot of _____ to continue walking. The older boys _____ the younger ones. When they finally _____ from the desert, they were weak and hungry. One boy discovered the value of a good _____. He used his knowledge to _____ the lives of others.

Written Review Imagine one of the Lost Boys will continue his **education** at your school. Write him a letter about what to expect. Use four vocabulary words.

WRITE ABOUT THE **GUIDING QUESTION**

Explore the Past

How did the boys' experiences on their **journey** help them find new lives in the United States? Write your opinion. Reread the selection to find examples to support your opinion.

Connect Across the Curriculum

Use Word Parts: Roots

Academic Vocabulary
- **connect** (ku-**nekt**) *verb*
  When you **connect** things, you show how they are related.

What Is a Root? A **root** is a word part that needs to have a prefix and/or suffix added to it. If you know the meaning of a root, you can figure out the meaning of words that contain it.

Root	Meaning
cept	to take; hold; grasp
civ	citizen
cog	to know
famil	family
fin	to end
frig	cool
par	arrange; prepare; get ready; set
port	to carry
simil	together, likeness
viv	life

The root *anim* means "life." Look at some words that are formed when you **connect** prefixes or suffixes to this root. What are their meanings?

anim + al = animal   anim + ate = animate

Find Word Meanings Identify the root in each word below, and figure out the meaning of the word. Then brainstorm with a partner to find other words that have the same root. Use a dictionary or online reference to help you.

1. final
2. survive
3. accept
4. family
5. frigid
6. civil
7. compare
8. recognize

Role-Play a Conversation

DRAMA

Academic Vocabulary
- **role** (rōl) *noun*
  A **role** is a position someone has in a certain situation. In a play, the **role** is the character, or part, played by the actor.

Think about how Garang must feel when he first arrives in the United States. What questions might he have?

1 **Write Questions and Answers** With a partner, make a list of questions that Garang might ask. Then answer each question as someone would who has lived in the U.S. for a long time.

2 **Act Out Your Conversation** Decide who will play each **role**. Use your list of questions and answers as you role-play a conversation between the two people. Perform your role-play for the class.

Describe an Event or Experience

Pair Share Sometimes one event can cause things to change in the future. Describe to a partner an event from your past that had a big effect on you. Use adverbs to add details. Trade roles.

> Yesterday, my aunt came from Canada to live with us. Now I don't have my own room anymore. I had to move in with my noisy little sister. I'm glad my aunt's here, but I really miss my privacy!

Write About an Event

Study the Models When you write about events, you want to keep your readers' interest. One way to do that is to give your readers interesting, descriptive details about *when*, *where*, and *how* the events happen. You may also want to compare details about the events.

NOT OK

The Lost Boys walked <u>more fast</u> to get to safety. Some days they could hardly find any food or water. But finding food <u>not</u> was their only problem. They weren't sleeping either. Life got more dangerous every day. "What would happen to them?" they wondered. The boys heard a truck. Was it a friend or an enemy?

The reader thinks: **"This writing isn't clear. I don't understand what problems they had."**

OK

The Lost Boys walked <u>faster</u> to get to safety. Some days they could hardly find any food or water. But finding food was <u>not</u> their only problem. They weren't sleeping <u>well</u> either. Life became more dangerous every day. "What would happen to them?" they wondered. <u>Suddenly</u>, the boys heard a truck. Was it a friend or an enemy?

The reader thinks: **"This is much better. Now I can understand what problems they had."**

Add Sentences Think of two sentences to add to the OK model above. Make the sentences tell about when, where, or how the event ended.

✏️ **WRITE ON YOUR OWN** Write about an event from the selection that was especially interesting to you. Use adverbs to add details about *when*, *where*, and *how* the event happened.

REMEMBER

- Many adverbs end in **-ly**.
- Add **-er** to an adverb that has one syllable, or use **more** with an adverb that has three or more syllables to compare two actions.
- Some adverbs are irregular:

  | well | better |
  | least | worse |

The New Colossus

by Emma Lazarus

Not like the brazen giant of Greek fame,
With conquering limbs astride from land to land;
Here at our sea-washed, sunset gates shall stand
A mighty woman with a torch, whose flame
5   Is the imprisoned lightning, and her name
Mother of Exiles. From her beacon-hand
Glows world-wide welcome; her mild eyes command
The air-bridged harbor that twin cities frame.

"Keep, ancient lands, your storied pomp!" cries she
10 With silent lips. "Give me your tired, your poor,
Your huddled masses yearning to breathe free,
The wretched refuse of your teeming shore.
Send these, the homeless, tempest-tost to me,
I lift my lamp beside the golden door!"

Historical Background

The Colossus of Rhodes was an ancient statue of a Greek giant. The statue was destroyed in 226 BC.

In Other Words

beacon-hand hand that holds the guiding light
storied pomp extravagant ceremonies
yearning desiring
wretched refuse of your teeming shore hopeless and unwanted citizens from crowded countries
tempest-tost the people affected by hard times

The poem, "The New Colossus" was written about the Statue of Liberty in New York Harbor. ▶

Compare Across Texts

Compare Writing on the Same Topic

"Brothers in Hope" and "Refugees Find New Lives" both tell about boys who lose their homes and families but find new lives elsewhere. Compare how the fiction author uses or alters facts on the same topic in order to tell a story.

How It Works

Organize Information You can use a Venn Diagram to collect information about two selections on the same topic. Compare the facts about the real event to the fictional details from the story. On your paper, write what is different under each title. Write what is the same in the middle part.

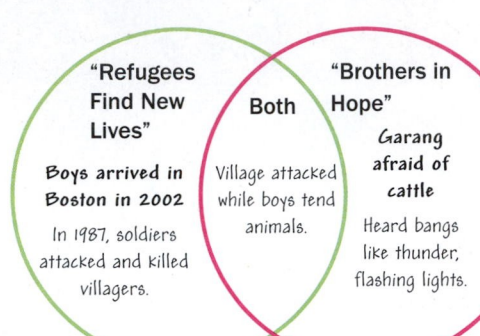

Venn Diagram

"Refugees Find New Lives"

Boys arrived in Boston in 2002

In 1987, soldiers attacked and killed villagers.

Both

Village attacked while boys tend animals.

"Brothers in Hope"

Garang afraid of cattle

Heard bangs like thunder, flashing lights.

Practice Together

Compare Information <mark>Analyze</mark> the information in the Venn Diagram. Compare how each selection addresses the same topic: the experiences of the Lost Boys of Sudan. Write about the details that are the same first. Then write about the details that are different. Here is the beginning of a comparison between the two selections.

Comparison

> "Brothers in Hope" and "Refugees Find New Lives" are both about the Lost Boys of Sudan. These boys were able to escape death because they were away when their villages were attacked.

Try It!

Use a Venn diagram to show events that are the same and details that are different in the two stories. <mark>Analyze</mark> these details to understand how a fiction author bases a story on real events. You may want to use this frame to help you express your ideas.

Even though both selections are about the same topic, the details that each writer uses are different. In "Refugees Find New Lives," the writer tells about how _____ find new lives in _____. This writer provides facts about _____. The writer of "Brothers in Hope" tells a story about _____. The fiction author uses literary details such as _____ to describe _____.

Academic Vocabulary

- **analyze** (a-nu-līz) *verb*
  When you **analyze** something, you study it closely.

A NEW Chapter

 How does our past impact our future?

Content Library

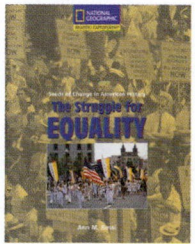

Leveled Library

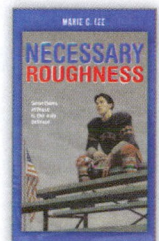 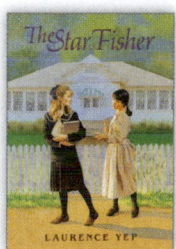 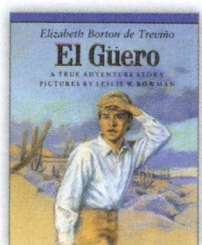

Reflect on Your Reading

Think back on your reading of the unit selections. Discuss what you did to understand what you read.

Focus on Reading **Analyze Interactions**

In this unit, you learned about some ways that writers show interactions among individuals, events, and ideas. Choose a selection from the unit and draw a diagram or other graphic to analyze some of these relationships; for example, a Cause-and-Effect Chart or a Sequence Chain. Use your graphic to explain the relationships to a partner.

Focus Strategy **Visualize**

As you read the selections, you learned to visualize. Explain to a partner how you will use this strategy in the future.

Explore the GUIDING QUESTION

Throughout this unit, you have been thinking about new chapters in life. Choose one of these ways to explore the Guiding Question:

- **Discuss** With a group, discuss new chapters in your lives. Ask questions with *Why, What, When, Where,* or *How.* Share what you learned about one classmate with the class.
- **Write** Think about one experience the characters in either "Brothers in Hope" or "Refugees Find New Lives" had after arriving in the United States. Write a journal entry about it.
- **Draw** Think about a television show or movie where someone had to start over. Create a visual that shows the experience. Describe it to a partner.

Book Talk

Which Unit Library book did you choose? Explain to a partner what it taught you about starting a new chapter in life.

Every Body Is a Winner

4

GUIDING
QUESTION

Why is the human body so amazing?

READ MORE!

Content Library
The Science of You
by Kate Boehm Jerome

Leveled Library
Of Sound Mind
by Jean Ferris
Emako Blue
by Brenda Woods
Ties That Bind, Ties That Break
by Lensey Namioka

Web Links
myNGconnect.com

◄ A group of students practice forms, or
movements, of the ancient martial art of kung fu.

Focus on Reading

Text Structure: Main Idea and Chronological Order

Writers choose a structure that best fits their purpose. Analyzing text structure, or how text is organized, can help you understand the meaning of the text.

How It Works

Expository nonfiction is used to explain topics . It includes articles, reports, and other informational texts. Writers often organize this type of writing using main ideas and supporting details. They often divide text into sections with headings . Read the following passage to analyze how this type of structure works.

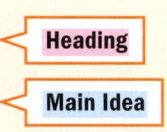

Food Labels

Nutrition labels on food packaging provide important information. A list of ingredients helps people find healthy foods and avoid those that trigger allergies. The serving size shows portion and the servings per container show how many are in the package. Information about calories per serving helps people eat the right amount of food. The daily values list shows the percentage of important nutrients in each serving.

Poems also have different forms and structures. Lyric poetry, such as odes and sonnets, expresses a poet's feelings or emotions. Read the following poem to see how the structure supports the meaning.

A December Day by Sara Teasdale

Dawn turned on her purple pillow,
    And late, late, came the winter day;
Snow was curved to the boughs of the willow,
    The sunless world was white and grey.

At noon we heard a blue-jay scolding,
    At five the last cold light was lost.
From blackened windows faintly holding
    The feathery filigree of frost.

Academic Vocabulary
- **topic** (**tah**-pik) *noun*
   A **topic** is something that you talk or write about.

Practice Together

Read the following passages aloud. As you read, listen for clues that tell you what kind of structure is used.

Reasons to Run

Fitness experts agree that running is good for most people. Research shows that running

- burns more calories than most other kinds of exercise
- helps prevent and fight diseases, such as stroke, high blood pressure, and diabetes
- improves levels of HDL, the cholesterol that is not harmful to people
- promotes better lung function.

Running for Good Health

Two years ago, neighbors in the 300 block of Main Street decided to start running for their health. Three mornings each week, they met at the corner at 6:30 to run together.

Now, two years later, all the runners report feeling stronger and healthier. In addition, most say they feel happier and sleep better at night. These neighbors all agree that running is a great way to stay healthy!

Try It!

Read the following passages aloud.
How is each passage organized? How does the structure help you understand the meaning of each passage?

Fog

by Carl Sandburg

The fog comes
on little cat feet.

It sits looking
over harbor and city
on silent haunches
and then moves on.

Proper Weight Training

Lifting weights is good exercise, but it is important to do it correctly to avoid injuries. Use movements that are slow and controlled, not fast and jerky. A set of 12 repetitions for each exercise is enough to be effective. Choose weights that are just heavy enough that muscles are tired after 10 or 12 repetitions. Your workout needs to be no more than 30 minutes long.

Focus on Vocabulary

Use Context Clues

When you see a word you don't know, it helps to look at how it is written in context. These are called context clues. There are several types of context clues. Signal words can help you recognize them.

A **restatement** repeats the same idea in different words.

> EXAMPLE   A sports physician, **or doctor**, helps athletes stay healthy.

A **definition** defines the new word.

> EXAMPLE   A nutritionist **is someone** who studies how food helps people stay healthy.

An **example** names things that explain the new words.

> EXAMPLE   Aerobic exercises, **such as** swimming and biking, are good ways to stay healthy.

Helpful Signal Words
is called
is someone
like
or
such as

How the Strategy Works

When you come to a word you don't know, use these steps to figure out its meaning.

1. Notice how the word is used in a sentence.
2. Look for signal words to help identify clues.
3. Decide if the clue is a restatement, a definition, or an example.
4. If you cannot find any clues, look up the word in the dictionary.
5. Determine the meaning that best fits the sentence.

Use the strategy to figure out the meaning of the underlined words.

Suppose you are a sports fan interested in <u>medical issues</u>, such as pain relief and injuries. What <u>occupation</u>, or job, might you choose?

You might want to be a <u>physical therapist</u>. This is a person who treats sports injuries and keeps athletes healthy.

Strategy in Action

" I don't know what *medical issues* means. I see the signal words *such as*. Medical issues must be topics about medicine, like pain relief and injuries. "

☑ **REMEMBER** You can use context clues to help you figure out the meaning of an unknown word.

Academic Vocabulary

● **context** (kon-tekst) *noun, adjective*
  1. Context is the surrounding text near a word or phrase that helps explain its meaning. **2.** A **context** clue helps you figure out a word's meaning.

Practice Together

Read this passage aloud. Pay attention to the underlined words. Use context clues to help you figure out the meaning of each underlined word.

The Exerciser's Diet

If you exercise, you need to eat certain foods to give your body the nutrients, or healthy ingredients, it needs. Here are some rules for healthy eating:

1. Before you exercise, eat some carbohydrates, such as fruit or bagels. The sugars in these foods will give your body energy for exercising.

2. Before and during exercise, drink plenty of water to avoid dehydration. This is the loss of too much water, which can cause your muscles to become sore.

3. After exercise, continue drinking water and eat a balanced mix of healthy foods. This will help you replenish, or replace, energy.

Try It!

Read this passage aloud. What is the meaning of each underlined word? How do you know?

Why Sports Are Good for You

Do you play a sport such as baseball, volleyball, or football? If so, you are doing something good for your body and mind. Sports help you stay in shape, which means you're less likely to become obese, or overweight. Engaging in sports can also influence how you think and feel. For example, playing a sport can help you feel less tense and more in control. Finally,

▲ Playing a sport has many benefits.

sports can teach you about teamwork. This means thinking more about what is good for the team than just about yourself. All of these skills will benefit, or help you, as you move into adulthood.

The Human Machine
by Catherine Stephens

SELECTION 1 OVERVIEW

▶ **Build Background**

▶ **Language & Grammar**
Define and Explain
Use Possessive Nouns

▶ **Prepare to Read**
Learn Key Vocabulary
Text Structure:
Main Idea and Details

▶ **Read and Write**
Introduce the Genre
Science Article
Focus on Reading
Text Structure: Main Idea
and Chronological Order
**Apply the
Focus Strategy**
Determine Importance
Critical Thinking
Reading Fluency
Read with Appropriate
Phrasing
Vocabulary Review
**Write About the
Guiding Question**

▶ **Connect Across
the Curriculum**
Vocabulary Study
Use Context Clues:
Definition and
Restatement
Listening/Speaking
Deliver an Informative
Presentation
Language and Grammar
Define and Explain
Writing and Grammar
Write About Athletes

Build Background

See the Body in Action

The human body is an amazing machine with many parts that work together. These parts help us walk, run, swim, and perform our best.

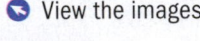
Digital Library   **myNGconnect.com**
                              ◉ View the images.

◀ The human
body in action

Connect

Idea Web Think about how the parts of your body work as you swim. In a group, make an Idea Web. Share your web with the class.

Idea Web

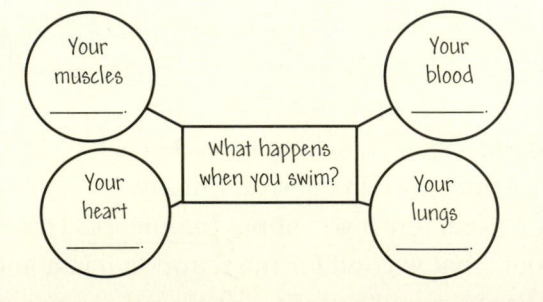

Language & Grammar

1 TRY OUT LANGUAGE
2 LEARN GRAMMAR
3 APPLY ON YOUR OWN

Define and Explain

CD

Look at the picture. How would you define and explain the lungs? Listen to the chant, and then chime in.

CHANT

The Mighty Lungs

The lungs are two organs
That keep the air flowing.
The right and the left keep your body going.
They work every second, every hour of the day.
24/7, they are working away.

Your lungs keep you breathing.
There's one on each side.
You breathe air through your nose and also your mouth.
The trachea takes the air and pulls it on through
To your diaphragm that helps push it in and then out.

So the next time you are taking
A deep breath or a sigh,
Running a race, or sleeping at night,
Know that your lungs are working
From morning until night.

Use Possessive Nouns

You know that a **noun** names a person, place, or thing. Use a **possessive noun** to show who owns, or possesses, something.

	Action	Examples
One Owner	Add **'s**.	**Juan's** lungs worked hard as he crossed the finish line. Each **racer's** face was red.
More Than One Owner	Add **'** if the noun already ends in **-s**.	The **girls'** team did warm-up exercises. The **runners'** feet pounded the track.
	Add **'s** if the noun does not end in **-s**.	Some **people's** lungs don't work well. **Children's** organs are different from those of adults.

Practice Together

Change each set of underlined words into a possessive noun. Then say each sentence.

1. The lungs that belong to John are strong.
2. The eyes of the twins are brown.
3. A doctor listens to the heart that belongs to Chico.
4. The athletes accept the advice of the coaches.
5. The coaches care about the health of their players.

Try It!

Change each set of underlined words into a possessive noun. Write the possessive noun on a card. Then say each sentence.

6. The research of the scientist tells about keeping your lungs healthy.
7. The hearts of the children beat fast when they skate.
8. The mom of Marissa wants her to eat healthy foods.
9. The exercises make the legs of the runner tired.
10. The girls exercise in the gym of their school.

▲ The swimmer's arms are strong.

Explore the Human Body

DEFINE AND EXPLAIN

The chant on page 261 defines and explains the lungs. How would you define and explain the brain or stomach in a chant?

Work with a group to write a chant about one of these body parts: brain, nose, knee, elbow, feet, heart, stomach, or arms. Make a list of interesting facts or uses for the body part. Use your list as you define and explain the body part in a chant. Share your chant with the class.

Knee
connects the two long leg bones
is called a joint
can bend
helps me walk

HOW TO DEFINE AND EXPLAIN

1. Define, or give the meaning of, the word or topic.
2. Explain what it does or how it is used.
3. Give details or examples of what it does.

> This is my elbow, where my arm bones meet. It bends to wave at people as they walk down the street.

USE POSSESSIVE NOUNS

When you define and explain something, you may need to use possessive nouns. Remember to use the apostrophe (') correctly.

	Action	Example
One Owner	Add 's.	A **person's** fingers can bend.
More Than One Owner	Add ' if the noun ends in -s.	Those **musicians'** fingers are strong.
	Add 's if the noun does not end in -s.	Some **people's** fingers are short.

Prepare to Read

Learn Key Vocabulary

Study the Words Use the steps below.

1. Pronounce the word. Say it aloud several times. Spell it.
2. Rate your word knowledge.
3. Study the example. Tell more about the word.
4. Practice it. Make the word your own.

Key Words

cell (sel) *noun*
▶ page 269

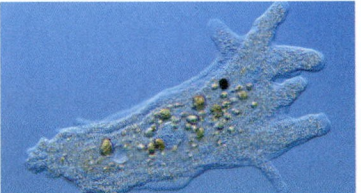

A **cell** is the smallest working part of a living thing. People are made up of millions of **cells**.
Related Word: **cellular**

circulate (sur-kū-lāt) *verb*
▶ page 275

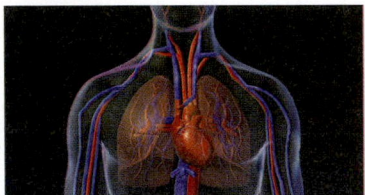

When something **circulates**, it moves along a path that returns to the place it started. Blood **circulates** throughout your body.
Related Words: **circle, circuit**

examine (ig-**zam**-un) *verb*
▶ page 269

When you **examine** something, you look at it very closely. A doctor **examines** you to make sure you are healthy.
Related Words: **examination, exam**

involve (in-**vahlv**) *verb*
▶ page 272

To be **involved** means to be part of something. A team **involves** people working together.
Synonym: **include**
Related Word: **involvement**

organ (**or**-gun) *noun*
▶ page 269

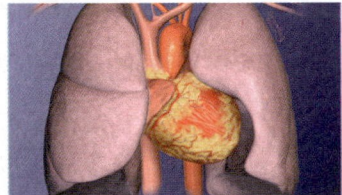

An **organ** is a body part that has a certain job to do. Your heart and lungs are important **organs**.

oxygen (**ahk**-si-jun) *noun*
▶ page 272

Oxygen is the air we breathe. We use extra **oxygen** to exercise.

system (**sis**-tum) *noun*
▶ page 268

A **system** is a group of parts that work together to do a job. People use a **system** of roads to drive to places more quickly.

vessel (**ves**-ul) *noun*
▶ page 275

A **vessel** is a tube through which liquid travels in a living thing. The **vessels** in a plant deliver water to the leaves.

Practice the Words Make an Example Chart with each Key Word. Share your chart with a partner.

Word	Definition	Example from My Life
organ	A body part with a certain job	My stomach is an organ.

Example Chart

Text Structure: Main Idea and Details

How Is Writing Organized? Some nonfiction writing is <mark>organized</mark> in sections. The main idea of each section supports the main idea of the whole text. Readers can determine the main idea of the whole text by identifying the most important point the author makes about the topic.

As you read, look for clues that help you identify the main idea and details in each section.

Reading Strategies
- Plan
- Monitor
- Visualize
- **Determine Importance**
  Focus your attention on the author's most significant ideas and information.
- Ask Questions
- Make Connections
- Make Inferences
- Synthesize

Look Into the Text

This text is about the body—the human machine. It's about Megan's body, your body, and every human body on the planet. Because on the inside, our bodies all work pretty much the same way.

What Is Inside?

Imagine you could peek inside your body. . . . A beating heart? Yes. But there is more. Much more! Long ago, people could only guess at the inner workings of the human body. The invention of the microscope helped change that. It allowed scientists to examine bits of the body in detail. One of the first things they discovered was that our bodies are made up of tiny parts called cells.

"This sentence gives the <mark>main idea</mark> of the whole text: how the human body works."

"The heading tells me this section is about what is inside the human body."

Practice Together

Begin a Main Idea Chart A Main Idea Chart can help you see how a text is organized. This Main Idea Chart shows the main idea of the second section in the passage. Reread the second section, and add details to the Main Idea Chart.

Main Idea:
Our bodies are made up of tiny parts called cells.

Detail:

Detail:

Academic Vocabulary
- **organize** (or-gu-nīz) *verb*
  To **organize** means to arrange things in a certain order.

Science Article

Science articles are expository nonfiction. They often include headings to identify main sections of information. Many include **diagrams** that explain details and **technical terms** in each section. As you read, identify the main idea and details to help you develop an understanding of how all the systems of the body work together.

Look Into the Text

How You Breathe

In a single day, you will take close to 20,000 breaths of air. When you breathe in, air travels into your mouth or nose, down your trachea, or windpipe, and into your lungs.

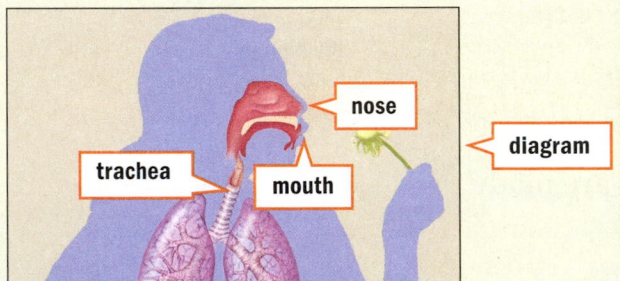

trachea | nose | mouth | diagram

The Human Machine

by Catherine Stephens

The seconds were flying by . . . 30 seconds . . . then 45 . . . Megan Quann was swimming as fast as she could. Would it be fast enough? Would she reach the finish line?

Comprehension Coach

◀ Megan Quann wins the gold medal at the 2000 Summer Olympics.

The Olympic aquatic center **buzzed** with noise. The fans were cheering, but Megan focused on **her form**—stroke, stroke, breathe, stroke. This 100-meter breaststroke race was her best event.

At the 50-meter mark, Megan was in third place. But she swam **a furious final lap**, and then it was over. The race was so close that Megan didn't know the results until she looked up at the scoreboard. It read: *1. Megan Quann, U.S.A.* She had won the gold medal! Megan, a teenager from Puyallup, Washington, had traveled to the 2000 Olympic Games to win a gold medal. She had trained hard, and her body met the challenge.

Whether you're winning Olympic medals, riding your bike, or simply sitting on the couch, your body is at work. Like a complex machine, your body parts work together in **systems** to keep you breathing and moving.

This text is about the body—the human machine. It's about Megan's body, your body, and every human body on the planet. Because on the inside, our bodies all work pretty much the same way.

Key Vocabulary

system *n.*, a group of things that work together to make one working unit

In Other Words

buzzed was loud
her form how well she swam
a furious final lap very hard

What Is Inside?

Imagine you could peek inside your body. What would you see? Bones and blood? A beating heart? Yes. But there is more. Much more! Long ago, people could only guess at the inner workings of the human body. The invention of the microscope helped to change that. It allowed scientists to **examine** bits of the body in detail. One of the first things they discovered was that our bodies are made of tiny parts called **cells**.

Millions of Cells

The **microscopic amoeba that oozes along the pond floor** has only one cell. Bigger creatures, such as beetles, have tens of thousands of cells. All plants and animals are made of many cells.

Your body has millions and millions of cells, but they're not all the same. There are bone cells, blood cells, brain cells, and cells for every part of your body. Each kind of cell has a certain job to do. Groups of different kinds of cells that work together to perform a specific job are called **organs**. Your stomach and your heart, for example, are two organs in your body.

Organs that work together form a system. Your body has many systems. Each system performs one major job, such as breathing or moving. The systems in your body work to keep your body active and strong.

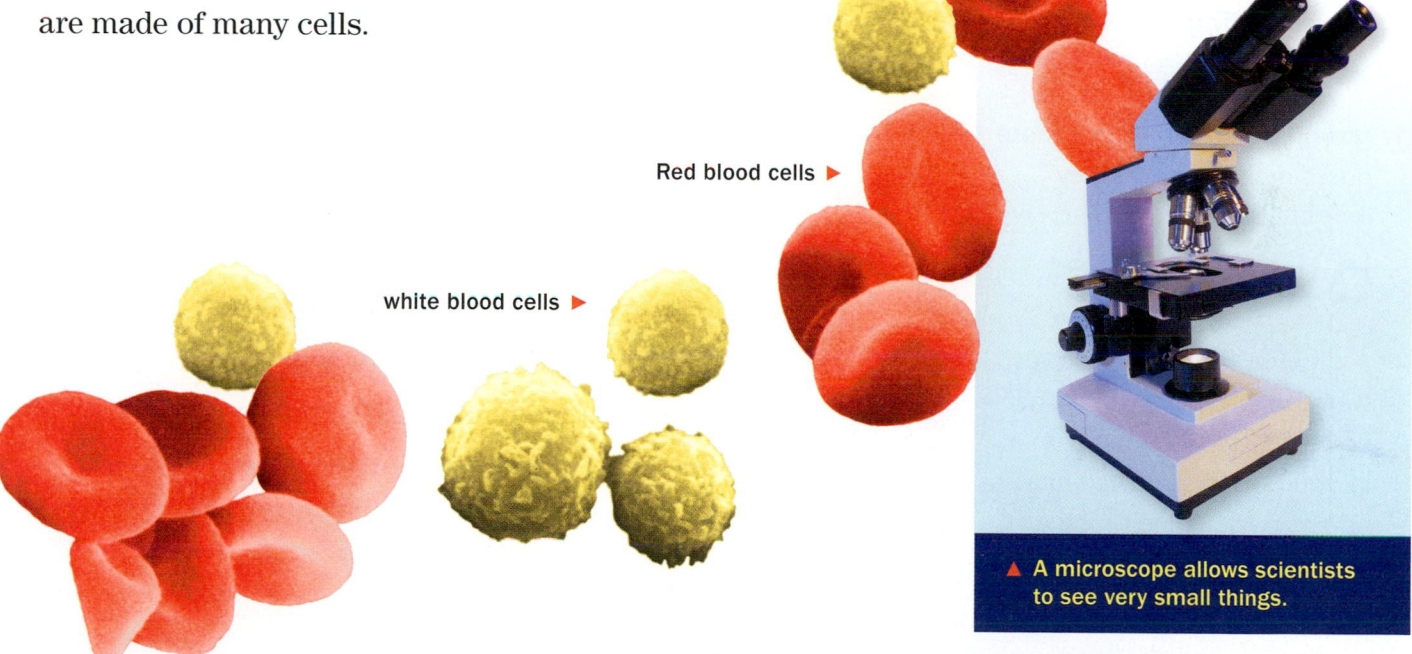

Red blood cells ▶

white blood cells ▶

▲ A microscope allows scientists to see very small things.

In Other Words

microscopic amoeba that oozes along the pond floor smallest living thing

Look Into the Text

1. **Conclusion** How would our understanding of the body be different without the microscope?

2. **Paraphrase** In your own words, explain the importance of your body's **systems**.

Q When I think about food, my mouth waters. Why?

A Your brain is "telling" your salivary glands to make extra saliva. In your lifetime, you'll make enough saliva to fill about 200 bathtubs.

Q My stomach makes a lot of noise. What's all the rumbling?

A Before and after you eat, gases can be produced. These gases make noise as they gurgle along.

Q Why do I burp?

A Gases from digesting, as well as the air that you swallow while you eat, can build up in your stomach. When there's no room left, some of the gas can come back up in the form of a burp.

Where Does It Go?

You're sitting at lunch, finishing that last bit of sandwich and chomping on your apple. Then you go outside. In a few minutes, you're probably talking with friends and not thinking about the food you just ate. While you've moved on to other things, your body's digestive system is hard at work.

Digestion starts in the mouth, where your teeth cut and grind food into small pieces. Saliva, made by the salivary glands, wets and softens food. When you swallow, the food squeezes down a long tube, called the esophagus, into your stomach. The stomach churns your food and adds a digestive juice that turns the food into a soupy liquid. Muscles move the liquid into the small intestine.

In the small intestine, more digestive juices break food into tiny **particles** called nutrients. These digestive juices are made by organs, such as the liver and pancreas, and delivered to the small intestine. Lining the small intestine are millions of **fingerlike structures** called villi. Villi capture nutrients that are eventually carried away to feed the cells in your body. Any undigested food moves on to the large intestine where water is **absorbed**. The remaining material leaves the body as waste.

In Other Words

particles pieces
fingerlike structures long, thin tissues
absorbed taken in; sucked up

Look Into the Text

1. **Steps in a Process** What is the first step of digestion? What happens next?
2. **Summarize** What does your body do with nutrients?
3. **Viewing** Look at the diagram on page 271. How does it help you understand how organs are used for digestion?

Digestive System

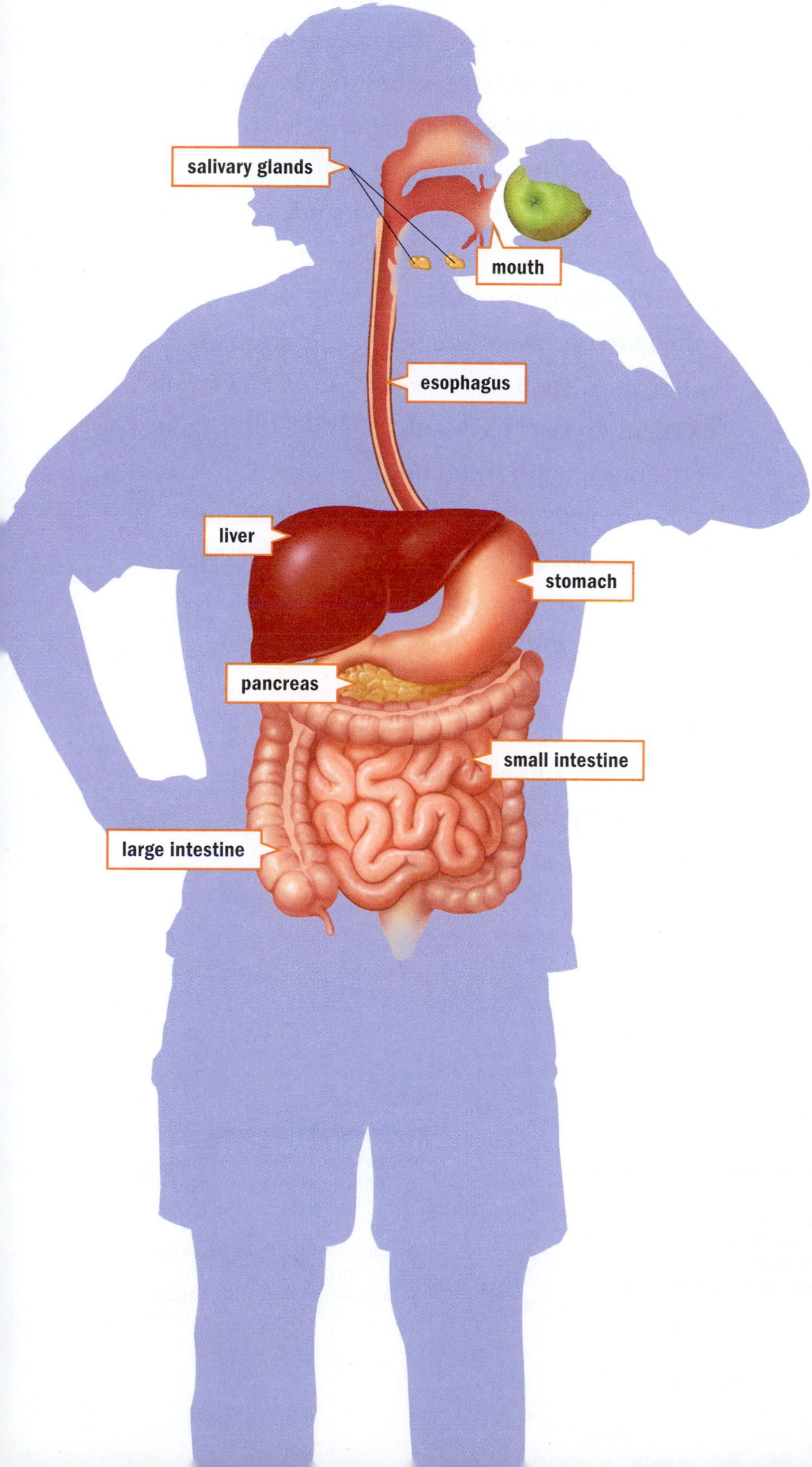

salivary glands

mouth

esophagus

liver

stomach

pancreas

small intestine

large intestine

▲ Digestion starts in the mouth.

▲ Teeth cut and grind food into tiny pieces.

▲ Healthy foods provide nutrients for the body.

Scientists ask questions and then collect **data**. Then they examine the data to find answers. You can also collect and examine data to answer questions about your body.

For example, what is your breathing rate, or number of breaths you take in a minute? To find out, count the number of times you exhale, or breathe out, during one minute. This is your breathing rate. How does your breathing rate compare with the rates of other animals in the chart?

Breathing Rates of Animals While at Rest

Animal	Breathing Rate (breaths per minute)
Blue Whale	4
Cat	26
Chipmunk	65
Guinea Pig	90
Horse	10
Mouse	135

Key Vocabulary

oxygen *n.*, a a colorless gas that humans and animals breathe

involve *v.*, to include

In Other Words

data information
sheet large area
get rid of release; let out
respiratory breathing

How You Breathe

In a single day, you will take close to 20,000 breaths of air. When you breathe in, air travels into your mouth or nose, down your trachea, or windpipe, to your lungs. You have two lungs—one on the right side of your body and one on the left. Beneath your lungs is a **sheet** of muscle called the diaphragm. When this muscle moves down, air moves into your lungs. When the diaphragm moves up, air leaves your lungs.

Inside each lung are millions of air sacs called alveoli. When you breathe in, fresh air enters the alveoli. This air contains a lot of **oxygen**. Oxygen passes through the thin walls of the alveoli into your body.

As the cells in your body use oxygen, they release a gas called carbon dioxide. Red blood cells return to your alveoli carrying carbon dioxide. You **get rid of** this carbon dioxide when you breathe out. Working together, the trachea, lungs, alveoli, and other body parts **involved** in breathing make up your **respiratory** system.

Look Into the Text

1. **Main Idea and Details** What does the respiratory **system** do? Name three body parts that are **involved**.
2. **Cause and Effect** How does the diaphragm affect air movement into and out of your lungs?

Respiratory System

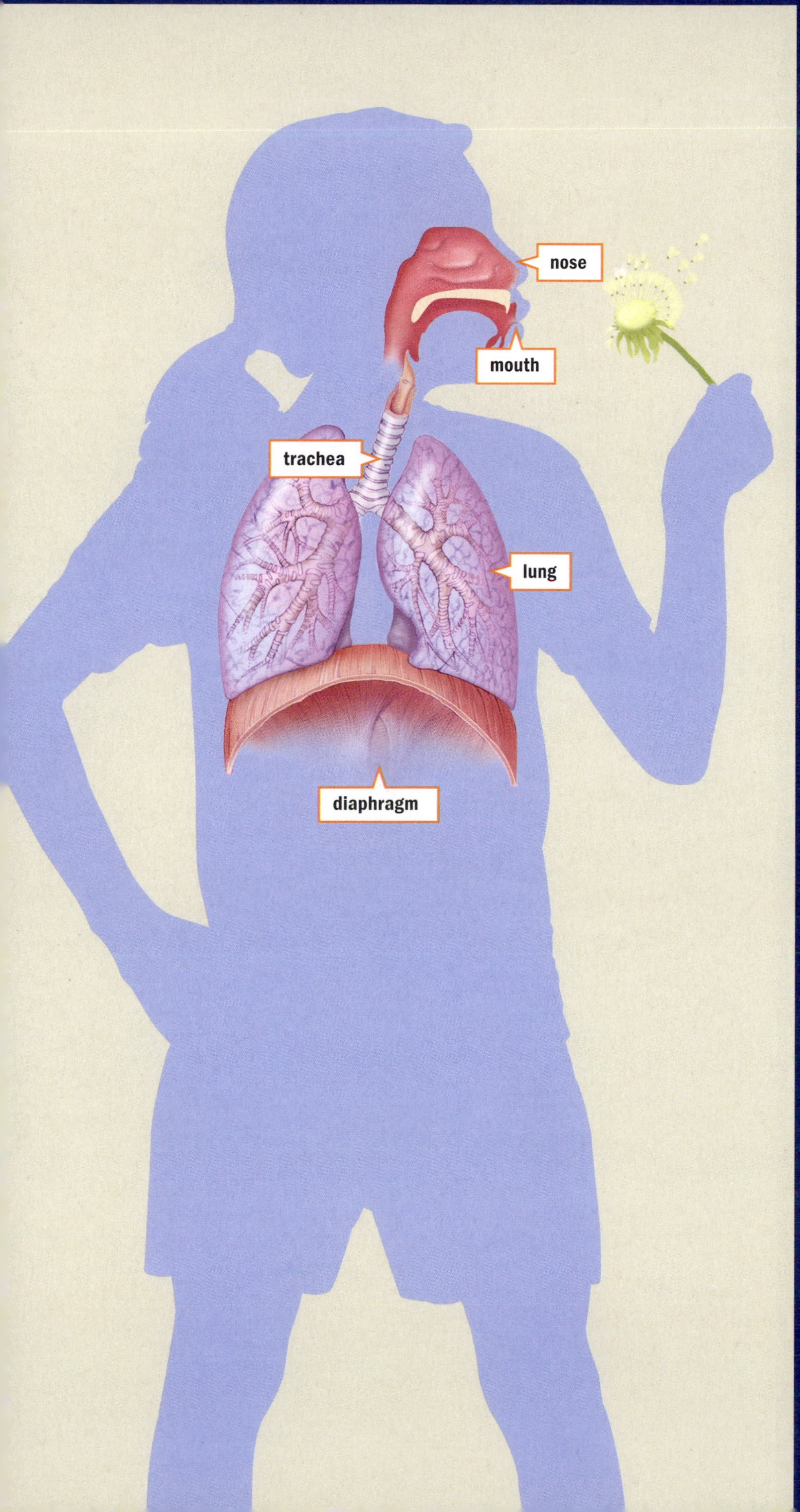

nose

mouth

trachea

lung

diaphragm

▲ Air leaves your lungs when you breathe out.

▲ Air enters your lungs when you breathe in.

▲ You take nearly 20,000 breaths of air a day.

Circulatory System

▲ Blood circulates faster when
▼ you exercise.

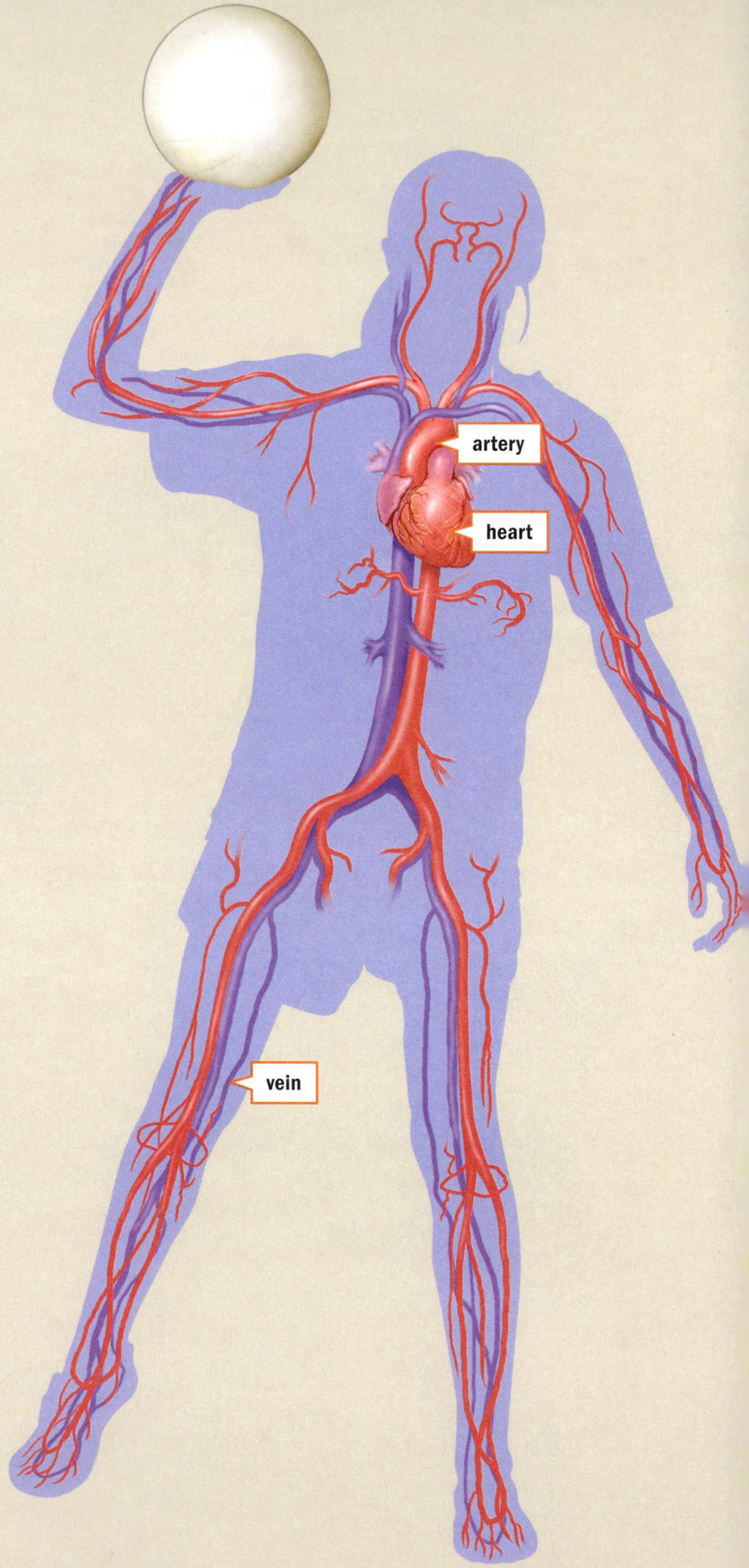

artery

heart

vein

Your Beating Heart

Make a fist with your hand. This is about the size of your heart. Now tighten your fist and let go. Do this about twenty times. This action is similar to the way a heart beats. Is your hand tired? The good thing about a healthy heart is that it doesn't get tired. Day in and day out, your heart keeps beating.

How Blood Circulates

Your heart **pumps** blood throughout your body. With every heartbeat, blood surges out of your heart and into tubes called blood **vessels**. When blood leaves the heart, it enters **blood vessels called arteries**. The arteries divide into smaller and smaller blood vessels that carry blood to all parts of the body. The smallest kind of blood vessel in your body is the capillary. Capillaries are so small that you need a microscope to examine them. **Blood vessels called veins** carry blood back to your heart.

Blood always **circulates** around your body in the same direction. Blood leaves the heart, travels to each of the cells in your body, and returns to the heart with much less oxygen. The heart then pumps this blood to the lungs to get more oxygen. The oxygen-rich blood travels back to the heart, and the cycle begins all over again. Your heart and blood vessels make up your circulatory system. ❖

What Is in Blood, and Why Is It Red?

About half your blood is water that contains dissolved sugar, salt, and other chemicals. The rest is made up mostly of disease-fighting white blood cells, sticky pieces of cells called platelets, and many millions of red blood cells.

Iron in red blood cells gives human blood its red color. But not every animal has red blood. Examine a lobster's blood, and you'll see that it's blue. That's because it doesn't have iron in it.

Lobster ▶

My Fabulous Footprint

My body can
do so many things.
Before, I never really
thought about it. My legs
5 walked without my knowing.
One foot in front of the
other. Step, step, step.
Now that I am older,
I've learned to be
10 more deliberate.

I know where
I'm going. I've
even learned how
to leave my
15 footprint.

In Other Words
my knowing me realizing it
deliberate exact, sure

Look Into the Text

1. **Metaphor** What does the speaker mean by leaving "my footprint"?
2. **Author's Style** How does the shape of the poem help you to better understand its meaning?

Connect Reading and Writing

Vocabulary
cell
circulates
examine
involved
organs
oxygen
systems
vessels

CRITICAL THINKING

1. **SUM IT UP** With a partner, use your Main Idea Chart to summarize what you learned about one body system.

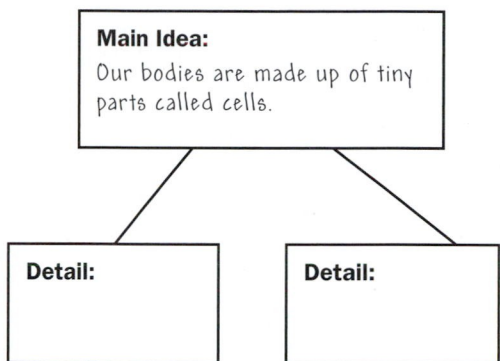

Main Idea:
Our bodies are made up of tiny parts called cells.

Detail:

Detail:

2. **Make Judgments** Examine the Idea Web you made on page 260. Do you or your teammates want to make any changes or additions? Explain.

3. **Infer** Blood circulates faster when we exercise. Given what you know about how the heart beats, why do you think this is true?

4. **Compare** Explain how "The Human Machine" and "My Fabulous Footprint" each examine what the human body does.

READING FLUENCY

Phrasing Read the passage on page 647 to a partner. Assess your fluency.

1. I did not pause/sometimes paused/ always paused for punctuation.

2. What I did best in my reading was _____.

READING STRATEGY

What strategy helped you understand this selection? Tell a partner about it.

VOCABULARY REVIEW

Oral Review Read the paragraph aloud. Add the vocabulary words.

Do you know what's _____ in keeping you alive? The human body is organized into many different _____. Let's _____ how your lungs work. Your lungs take in _____ from the air you breathe. That oxygen _____ to every tiny _____ in your body. Your blood carries it through the _____ to and from your heart. This makes your heart one of the most important _____ in your body.

Written Review Imagine you were small enough to take a trip through the circulatory system. Write a journal entry about what you would see, touch, and hear on your trip. Use four vocabulary words.

WRITE ABOUT THE GUIDING QUESTION

Explore the Amazing Human Body
What is the most amazing thing about how your body's systems work? Write your opinion. Reread the selection to find details that support your opinion.

Connect Across the Curriculum

Use Context Clues: Definition and Restatement

> **Academic Vocabulary**
> • **context** (**kon**-tekst) *noun, adjective*
>   **1 Context** is the surrounding text near a word or phrase that helps explain its meaning.
>   **2** A **context** clue helps you figure out a word's meaning.

- A **definition clue** defines the word in the text.

  EXAMPLE   **Veins** <u>are</u> blood vessels that carry blood back to your heart.

- A **restatement clue** says the same thing in a different way.

  EXAMPLE   Use a microscope to **examine**, <u>or</u> study, cells.

Use the **context** clues to figure out the meaning of each underlined word.

1. <u>Villi</u> are fingerlike structures that line the small intestine.
2. Digestive juices break food into sources of nourishment, or <u>nutrients</u>.
3. Inside each lung are millions of air sacs called <u>alveoli</u>.

Deliver an Informative Presentation

HEALTH & SCIENCE

> **Academic Vocabulary**
> • **topic** (**tah**-pik) *noun*
>   A **topic** is something that you talk or write about.

In "The Human Machine," you learned about several body processes. Deliver a presentation on one of these processes.

1. **Possible topics** include ear wax or hiccup.
2. **Research the Topic** Write questions that you have about your **topic**. Use online or library resources to find answers.
3. **Prepare Your Presentation** Organize your presentation by using your questions as main points and the answers as supporting details. Add visuals.
4. **Practice and Deliver Your Presentation** Practice in front of another classmate or a mirror. Then deliver your presentation.

Define and Explain

Role-Play Work with a partner. Pretend you have to explain how the human body works to someone from another planet. Use information from the selection to explain the respiratory system. Use possessive nouns and technical terms.

> Lungs pull in oxygen from the air and push out carbon dioxide. Below the lungs is a muscle called a diaphragm. It helps move air in and out of the lungs.

Write About Athletes

Study the Models When you write about people and actions, you want readers to understand whether you are talking about one person or more than one person. Make sure you communicate the right meaning to your readers.

NOT OK

> Many Americans hopes were high. The nations Olympic swimming team looked good. All the swimmers bodies were strong. Each swimmers suit was designed with the red, white, and blue of Americas flag. The teams coach thought Megan Quann might win a medal. He was right. He and Megans' fans cheered as she won the Olympic gold medal.

The reader thinks: **"I can't tell whether the writer means one or more than one."**

OK

> Many Americans' hopes were high. The nation's Olympic swimming team looked good. All the swimmers' bodies were strong. Each swimmer's suit was designed with the red, white, and blue of America's flag. The team's coach thought Megan Quann might win a medal. He was right. He and Megan's fans cheered as she won the Olympic gold medal.

Now it is clear who the writer is talking about.

Add Sentences Think of two sentences to add to the OK model above. Use possessive nouns correctly.

✏ **WRITE ON YOUR OWN** Write about how a runner's arms and legs move as he or she runs. Pay attention to your possessive nouns. Check them for correct spelling.

Spelling Rules

1. If there's one owner, add **'s**.
   Kim's stomach is upset.

2. If there's more than one owner and the noun ends in **-s**, just add **'**.
   All the **doctors'** offices were closed.

3. If there's more than one owner and the noun does not end in **-s**, add **'s**.
   The **children's** lunches were full of healthy foods.

REMEMBER
- Possessive nouns tell readers who owns or has something.
- All possessive nouns have an apostrophe (**'**).

The BEAT Goes On

by Nancy Finton

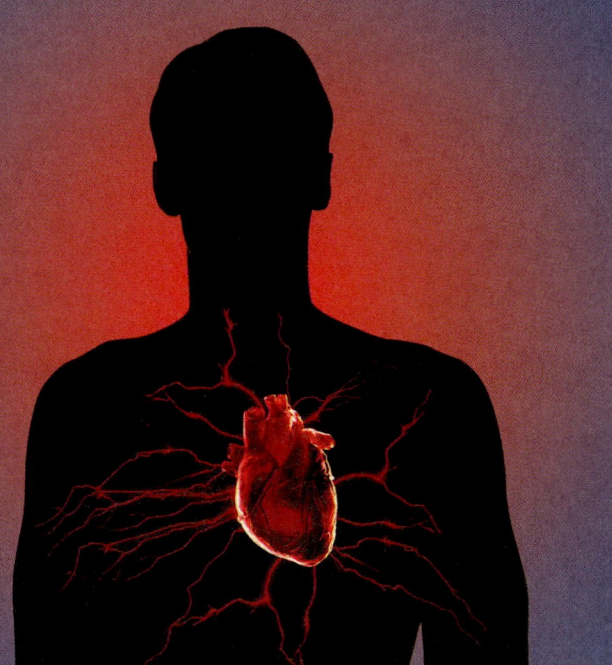

Build Background

See the Heart at Work

Your heart is hard at work every second. It keeps your body running smoothly. But what happens when it doesn't work well? Can it be fixed?

Digital Library

myNGconnect.com

View the video.

◀ Doctors can learn a lot about a person's heart using medical technology.

Connect

KWL Chart Discuss, and then write what you know about the human heart in the K column of the KWL chart. In the W column, write what you want to know. Use the L column to list what you learned after reading the article.

KWL Chart

WHAT I KNOW	WHAT I WANT TO KNOW	WHAT I LEARNED
The heart is an organ.	I want to know how fast a heart beats.	

Give and Follow Directions CD

Listen to the song and to the instructions.
Join in with the song. Follow the directions.

SONG and DIRECTIONS

Exercise to Energize

We give our bodies
Exercise.

We exercise
To energize!

First, step to the right.
One, two!
Then step to the left.
Three, four!
Do it again.
One, two, three, four!
One, two, three, four!

To keep your heart
And body strong,

Give them lots
Of oxygen!

Next, step to the front!
One, two!
Then step to the back!
Three, four!
Do it again.
One, two, three, four!
One, two, three, four!

Use Possessive Adjectives

A **possessive adjective** tells who someone or something belongs to.

- **My**, **your**, **his**, **her**, **its**, **our**, and **their** are possessive adjectives.
- The possessive adjective always comes before a **noun**.
- Match the possessive adjective to the **noun** or **pronoun** that it goes with.

I ➔ **my**	I have a healthy heart. Dr. Lee listens to **my** heart once a year.
you ➔ **your**	Do **you** go to Dr. Lee? Yes. Is Dr. Lee **your** doctor, too?
he ➔ **his**	**Tom** bikes everyday. **He** rides to school. Is that **his** bike?
she ➔ **her**	**My sister** is a swimmer. **She** is good. You should see **her** exercise program!
it ➔ **its**	**My sister's program** is tough. **Its** goal is to decrease her heart rate.
we ➔ **our**	**We** got a new exercise machine. **Our** old machine is broken.
they ➔ **their**	**Dr. Lee and the nurse** advised us to eat healthy food. Try **their** healthy snacks.

Practice Together

Say each sentence and add the correct form.

1. Is that (he/his) basketball?
2. No, it is (you/my) ball.
3. (They/Their) team is not very fit.
4. (We/Our) players are faster.
5. Should I play on their team or (you/your) team?

Try It!

Say each sentence. Write the correct form on a card. Then say each sentence, and add the correct form.

6. You can play on (I/my) team if you want.
7. Our team won all (it/its) games last year!
8. What about your sister? Will she play on (they/their) team?
9. No, she'll play on (we/our) team.
10. (She/Her) strong skills will help us win!

▲ **Exercise is good for our hearts!**

Explore Exercise

GIVE AND FOLLOW DIRECTIONS

Exercise is good for the heart. What exercises do you know how to do? Could you teach one to your classmates?

Work with a group to write directions for an exercise you all know. Make a list of directions like the one below.

Jumping Jacks

1. Stand straight with your arms at your sides and your feet together.
2. Jump out, swinging your arms up and your feet out.
3. Jump back, bringing your arms down and your feet together.

Give directions to another group for doing your exercise. Then follow the other group's directions for their exercise.

HOW TO GIVE AND FOLLOW DIRECTIONS

1. Speak clearly and loudly enough for everyone to hear.
2. Tell how, where, and in what order to move as you explain how to do your activity.
3. Repeat the step-by-step directions so your classmates can join in and do the activity.
4. Listen to and follow your classmates' directions.

My knees are bent, but your legs are straight. You need to bend your knees. Remember to relax!

Try to keep your arms up like this. Take a deep breath.

USE POSSESSIVE ADJECTIVES

When you give directions, you may need to use **possessive adjectives**. You may also hear possessive adjectives when you follow directions. Be sure they match the **noun** or **pronoun** that they go with.

EXAMPLES   Watch how **I** move **my** arms. **You** move **your** arms like that.

Some **people** are not lifting **their** knees high enough.

Prepare to Read

Learn Key Vocabulary

Study the Words Use the steps below.
1. Pronounce the word. Say it aloud several times. Spell it.
2. Rate your knowledge.
3. Study the example. Tell more about the word.
4. Practice it. Make the word your own.

Key Words

artery (art-u-rē) *noun*
▶ page 288

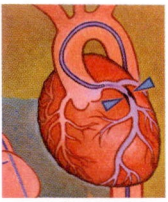

An **artery** is a type of blood vessel. **Arteries** carry blood away from the heart.

healthy (hel-thē) *adjective*
▶ page 290

Someone who is **healthy** is not sick. It is important to eat **healthy** food.
Synonyms: **fit, well**
Antonyms: **ill, sick**

muscle (mus-ul) *noun*
▶ page 289

A **muscle** is an organ that gives you strength to move. You can see and feel the **muscles** in your arm.
Related Word: **muscular**

pump (pump) *verb, noun*
▶ page 288

1 *verb* To **pump** something is to push liquid from one place to another. In some places, people **pump** water from wells. **2** *noun* People also use **pumps** to deliver water.

section (sek-shun) *noun*
▶ page 290

A **section** is one part of something. I cut the sandwich into equal **sections**.
Synonym: **part**
Antonym: **whole**

transplant (trans-plant) *noun, verb* ▶ page 291

1 *noun* A **transplant** is something taken from one place to another. Heart **transplants** are common. **2** *verb* Trees are sometimes **transplanted** from a forest to a park.

vein (vān) *noun*
▶ page 288

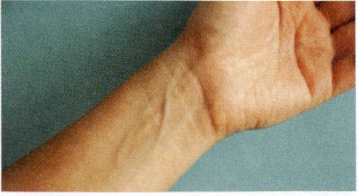

A **vein** is a blood vessel that carries blood to the heart. You can see **veins** through your skin.

ventricle (ven-tri-kul) *noun*
▶ page 289

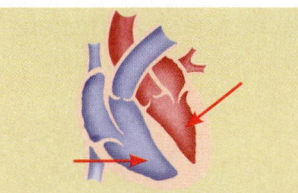

A **ventricle** is a lower area of the heart. The **ventricles** pump blood out of your heart.

Practice the Words Work with a partner to make a Category Chart. List each Key Word under *Noun*, *Verb*, or *Adjective*. Write a sentence for each word.

Noun	Verb	Adjective
	donate I donate my old clothes to charity.	

Category Chart

Text Structure: Main Idea and Details

How Text Is Organized One way to understand how ideas are developed throughout a text is to analyze how the author organizes information. Identify the most important information in each section and summarize it. Then think about how the author uses each section to develop the main idea of the whole text.

As you read, identify and summarize the most important information in each section.

Reading Strategies

- Plan
- Monitor
- **Determine Importance** Focus your attention on the author's most significant ideas and information.
- Ask Questions
- Visualize
- Make Connections
- Make Inferences
- Synthesize

Look Into the Text

MIGHTY MUSCLE

Your heart works hard. It beats around ninety times a minute. Each minute, in fact, this powerhouse pumps your body's entire supply of blood. That's roughly 100,000 beats a day and 2.5 billion over a lifetime. Each beat sends oxygen and disease-fighting cells throughout your body.

> This is an important idea.

Practice Together

Begin a Summary Chart A Summary Chart can help you identify main ideas and details in the text and analyze how the author organized information to develop the ideas. Reread the passage above. Record other important ideas in the Summary Chart.

Main Idea and Details	Summary
The heart works hard pumping blood.	The heart works hard pumping blood to keep the body healthy.

Summary Chart

Science Article

Many science articles are **expository text** and include information on how to do something. The "how to," or **procedural text**, gives readers numbered steps to follow. Analyzing the steps in the procedure can help you accomplish the task described and also better understand how this procedure supports the main idea of the text.

Look Into the Text

Breathe. Within seconds, the oxygen you took in is cruising throughout your body.

Oxygen is carried by fast-flowing rivers of blood.

expository text

1 Place two fingers on your wrist. Find a spot where you feel a thump. That's your pulse. Each thump represents a heartbeat.

procedural text

Summarizing the steps can help you to determine what information is most important.

The BEAT Goes On

by Nancy Finton

Your heart beats **100,000** times a day. Each beat gives your body the oxygen it needs to survive. But what happens when the heart cannot do its job?

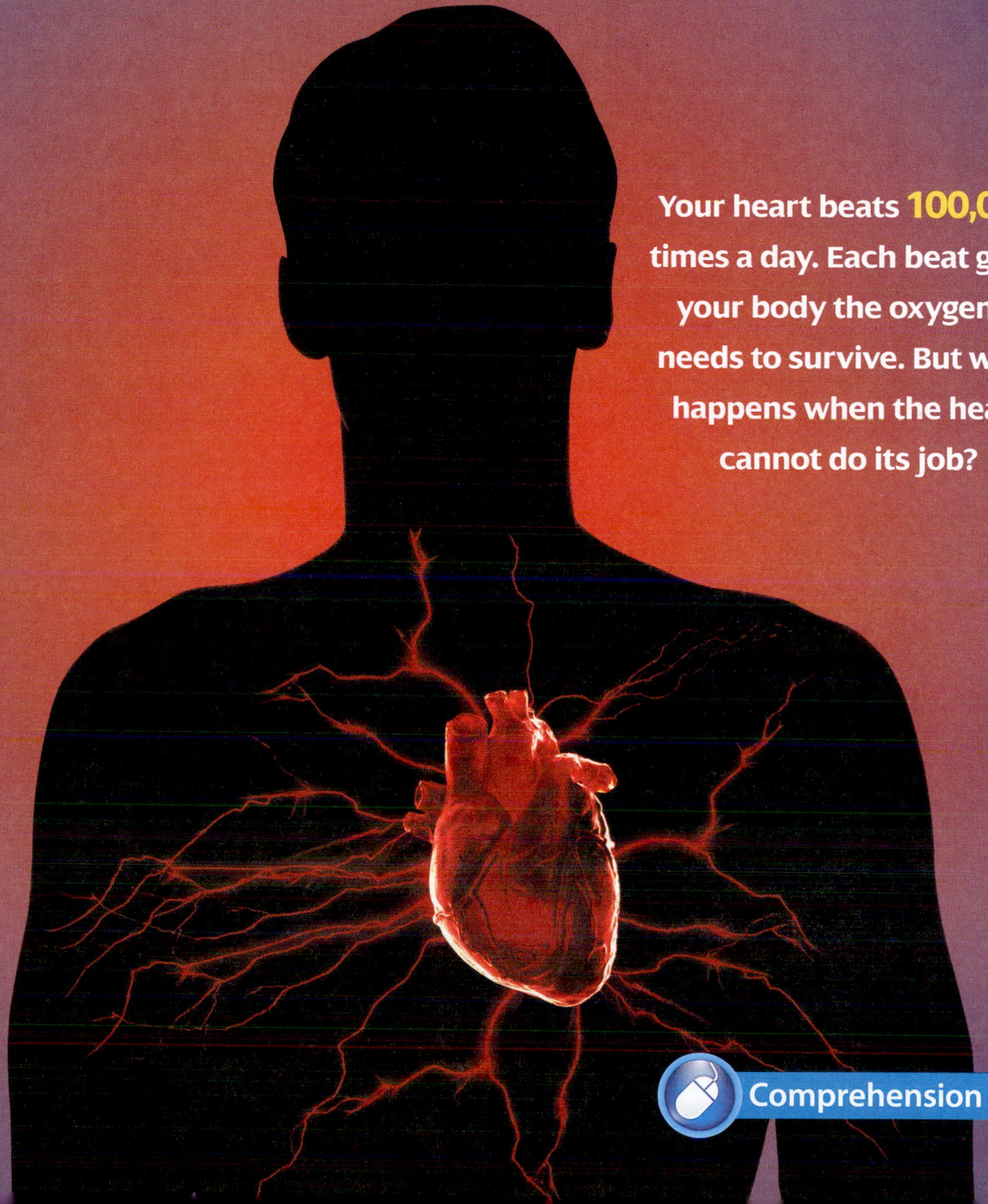

Comprehension Coach

MIGHTY MUSCLE

Your heart works hard. It beats around ninety times a minute. Each minute, in fact, this powerhouse **pumps** your body's entire supply of blood. That's roughly 100,000 beats a day and 2.5 billion over a lifetime. Each beat sends oxygen and disease-fighting cells throughout your body.

How does it happen? The next time you're in a swimming pool, squeeze your hands together. Watch the water shoot up. The heart does basically the same thing. Each time it contracts, or squeezes, blood squirts through tubes called blood vessels.

Blood vessels come in three main types. **Arteries** carry blood away from the heart. They branch off into smaller and smaller tubes. The smallest are called capillaries.

Capillaries have thin walls, so oxygen and other materials can travel from the blood and into cells where they're needed. **Veins** bring "used" blood back to the heart.

BROKEN HEARTS

Most kids have healthy hearts. Trouble usually comes years later, when parts of this pumping "machine" wear out or **get clogged with fat**.

But there are hearts that need help sooner. Some babies are born with heart problems. Sometimes there's a hole that blood leaks through. At other times, parts of the heart are incorrectly formed—or missing. Like life-saving mechanics, doctors **step in to tune up** and repair failing hearts.

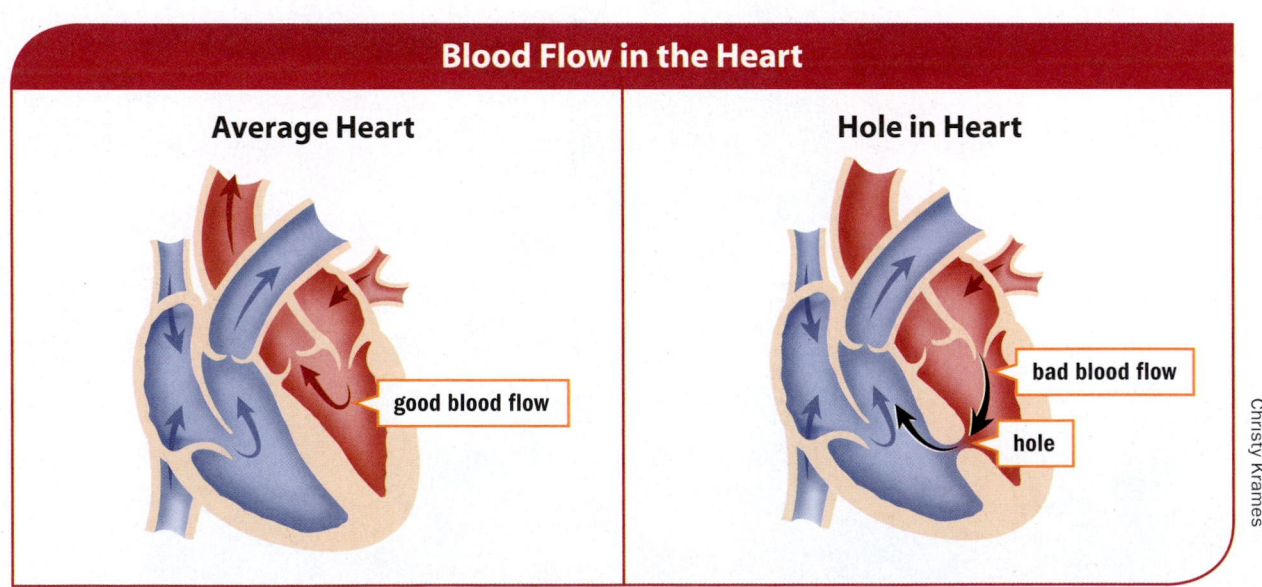

Blood Flow in the Heart

Average Heart

good blood flow

Hole in Heart

bad blood flow

hole

Christy Krames

Key Vocabulary

pump *v.*, to move
artery *n.*, a vessel that carries blood from the heart
vein *n.*, a vessel that carries blood to the heart

In Other Words

get clogged with fat become blocked because of an unhealthy diet
step in to tune up work to fix

Breathe. Within seconds, the oxygen you took in is **cruising** throughout your body.

Oxygen is carried by **fast-flowing rivers of blood**. **What powers that bloodstream?** Feel the answer for yourself. Just put your hand on your chest. Beneath the skin and bone lies a thumping, pumping **muscle**—your heart.

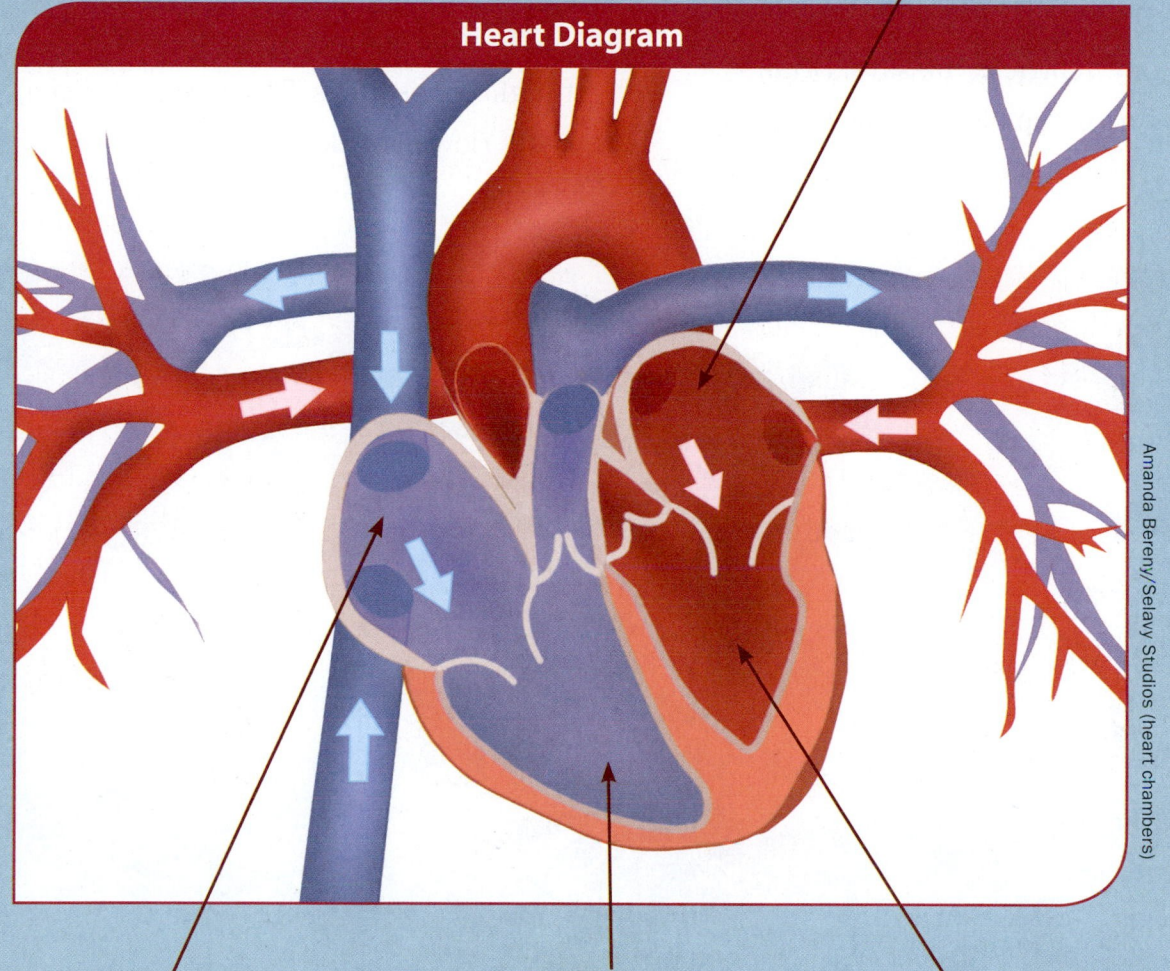

Heart Diagram

Left Atrium
Receives oxygen-rich blood from the lungs

Amanda Bereny/Selavy Studios (heart chambers)

Right Atrium
Receives "used" blood from throughout the body

Right Ventricle
Pumps blood to the lungs to pick up oxygen

Left Ventricle
Pumps oxygen-rich blood throughout the body

Key Vocabulary
muscle *n.*, a body tissue that produces movement
ventricle *n.*, an area of the heart

In Other Words
cruising moving easily
fast-flowing rivers of blood blood that moves quickly in your body
What powers that bloodstream? What helps the blood move?

Look Into the Text

1. **Explain** Name the three types of blood vessels. Explain how the heart **pumps** blood through them.
2. **Main Idea and Details** What are two reasons that a heart may have to be repaired?
3. **Paraphrase** Tell in your own words how **arteries** help the body.

SOMETHING'S MISSING!

Healthy hearts have four chambers, or **sections**. The two upper chambers, called atria, receive blood from veins. The ventricles, or lower sections, pump blood into arteries.

That's **the plan anyway**. But Brian Whitlow's life began differently. "I was born with only one ventricle," he says. Brian's heart couldn't pump blood to his lungs to get oxygen.

But Whitlow's mother didn't give up. Nor did his doctors. When Brian was just a few weeks old, surgeons operated on him.

"We can't rebuild chambers that haven't grown," says Dr. Daniel Bernstein, one of Whitlow's childhood doctors. Instead, the surgeons rearranged his blood vessels to **bypass** the missing chamber.

After the operation, Whitlow's blood ran straight to his lungs. There it got oxygen, then it flowed back to his heart. Whitlow's

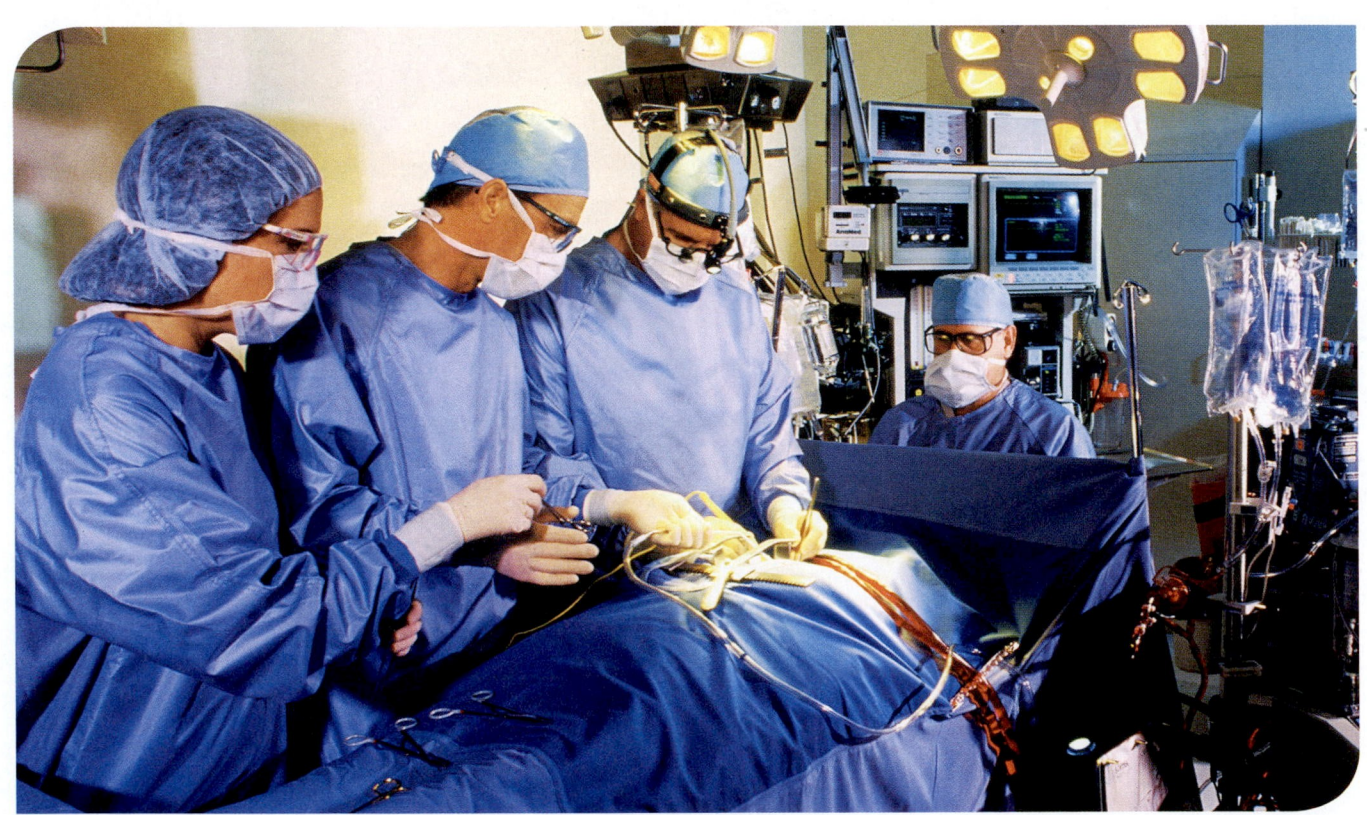

▲ Doctors use special tools to operate on this patient's heart. New tools and medicines have greatly reduced the **risks** of heart surgery.

Key Vocabulary
healthy *adj.*, well; without illness
section *n.*, a part that is separated

In Other Words
the plan anyway how the heart should work
bypass go around

single ventricle then sent oxygen-rich blood **gushing** throughout his body.

That worked pretty well, Whitlow says. "I did all the normal things, including playing Little League baseball." Then things changed.

THE GIFT OF LIFE

By the time Whitlow turned fourteen, his patched-up heart was pretty tired. It was too weak to keep his body strong. "I had trouble running and had to nap all the time," he remembers.

Doctors recommended a heart **transplant**. That's when a damaged body part gets replaced. "New" hearts come from people who agreed to **donate** their hearts to others before they died. "It's a difficult thing when someone has to die in order for you to live," says Whitlow. "But giving someone the **gift of life** is just plain wonderful."

That gift took a while to arrive. Each year about 35,000 people in this country need heart transplants. There are only a small number of replacements available. So Whitlow waited a month, then another, then another.

Heart Transplants in the United States

- In 2005, 2,125 heart transplants were performed.

- 72.4 % of heart transplants are for males.

- In 2006, the one-year or longer survival rate for heart transplant patients was 86.1% for males and 83.9% for females.

- People who need new hearts often have to wait. The wait for a new heart can be as little as a few days, or as long as a year.

Source: American Heart Association, 2007

Key Vocabulary
transplant *n.*, the act of moving an organ from one body to another

In Other Words
gushing flowing quickly
donate give
gift of life chance to keep living

Look Into the Text

1. **Compare and Contrast** Compare how Brian Whitlow's heart was different from a **healthy** heart.

2. **Cause and Effect** What caused Whitlow to need a heart **transplant**?

HAVING TO WAIT

Jessica Melore knows just how Brian Whitlow felt. She had a heart attack at sixteen. Her left ventricle was destroyed. Melore needed a new heart. But would she get one in time?

Luckily, scientists have invented machines that can help patients like Melore lead normal lives during the long wait. Surgeons attached a **doughnut-sized device** to Melore's heart. Powered by batteries, it did the pumping her left ventricle would have done.

The artificial pump allowed Melore to finish high school and get into college. Four days before graduation, she **got word** that doctors had found a new heart for her. Melore missed graduating with the class but says, "The heart was a good graduation gift."

NEW HEARTS

Back to Brian Whitlow. Altogether, he waited thirteen months for a new heart. Finally, doctors called with good news. There was a heart available for him. Because hearts can't live long outside the body, Whitlow hurried to the hospital.

In the operating room, doctors **hooked Whitlow** to a machine that adds oxygen to blood while the heart isn't working. Then surgeons removed his damaged heart and put the new heart in its place.

Whitlow recovered quickly. "I had my surgery and started practice for high school basketball the following October," he says. But the recovery wasn't easy.

"I moved to a new high school after the transplant," Whitlow recalls. "I was taking medicine and gained seventy pounds. Other students made fun of me, and that was hard. I had to keep telling myself they didn't know my story."

Anti-Rejection Drugs

Many organ transplant patients need to take medicine for the rest of their lives. This is because their bodies can reject the new organ. The human body works hard to stay healthy, and it may decide to fight against a new heart or liver. Doctors work closely with their patients to be sure the medications are working properly. Like most medications, these drugs may cause side effects, or problems.

In Other Words

doughnut-sized device small, round machine
got word heard; was told
hooked Whitlow attached Whitlow's body

Today Whitlow is on his college lacrosse team. "My teammates tease me that I'm slow, because it takes me a little longer to **warm up**," he says. But now he knows that they're only teasing. "Last year, they voted me the Most Inspirational Player. That felt good."

TELLING THEIR STORIES

Today Brian Whitlow and Jessica Melore are healthy college students. They have received a lot of attention. They've appeared on talk shows and given interviews. Newspapers and magazines have written about them.

Both students hope their extraordinary stories will inspire others. They'd like to see more people arrange to have their organs donated to others after death. "We really need more organ donors," Melore says. "It's a little-known issue."

Whitlow and Melore also want to help other kids who face obstacles. "Focus on the positive things in your life," Jessica tells young audiences. "You can't change what's in the past, so **make the most of the future**." ❖

In Other Words
warm up get ready to play the game
make the most of the future think about the years ahead

A HELPING HEART

Some people are not healthy enough to wait for a heart transplant. Machines can help people while they wait. This machine can replace a human heart.

Tube
A large tube carries the blood into and out of each pump.

Pump
This machine has two pumps. Each has a motor that pushes blood out of the heart and into the body.

Valve
Four valves control the flow of blood through the heart and into the body.

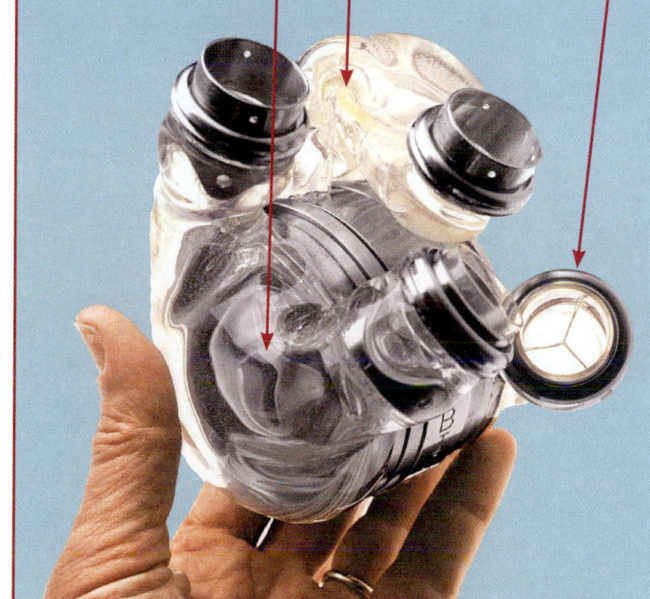

Look Into the Text

1. **Cause and Effect** What did Melore's artificial heart device allow her to do?
2. **Conclusion** How are Whitlow and Melore helping others who need new hearts?
3. **Summarize** How do anti-rejection drugs keep patients who have had transplants healthy?

Your Circulatory System

Your body needs oxygen to survive. Getting oxygen to all parts of your body is the job of the circulatory system. It includes your heart, several quarts of blood, and more than 60,000 miles of blood vessels.

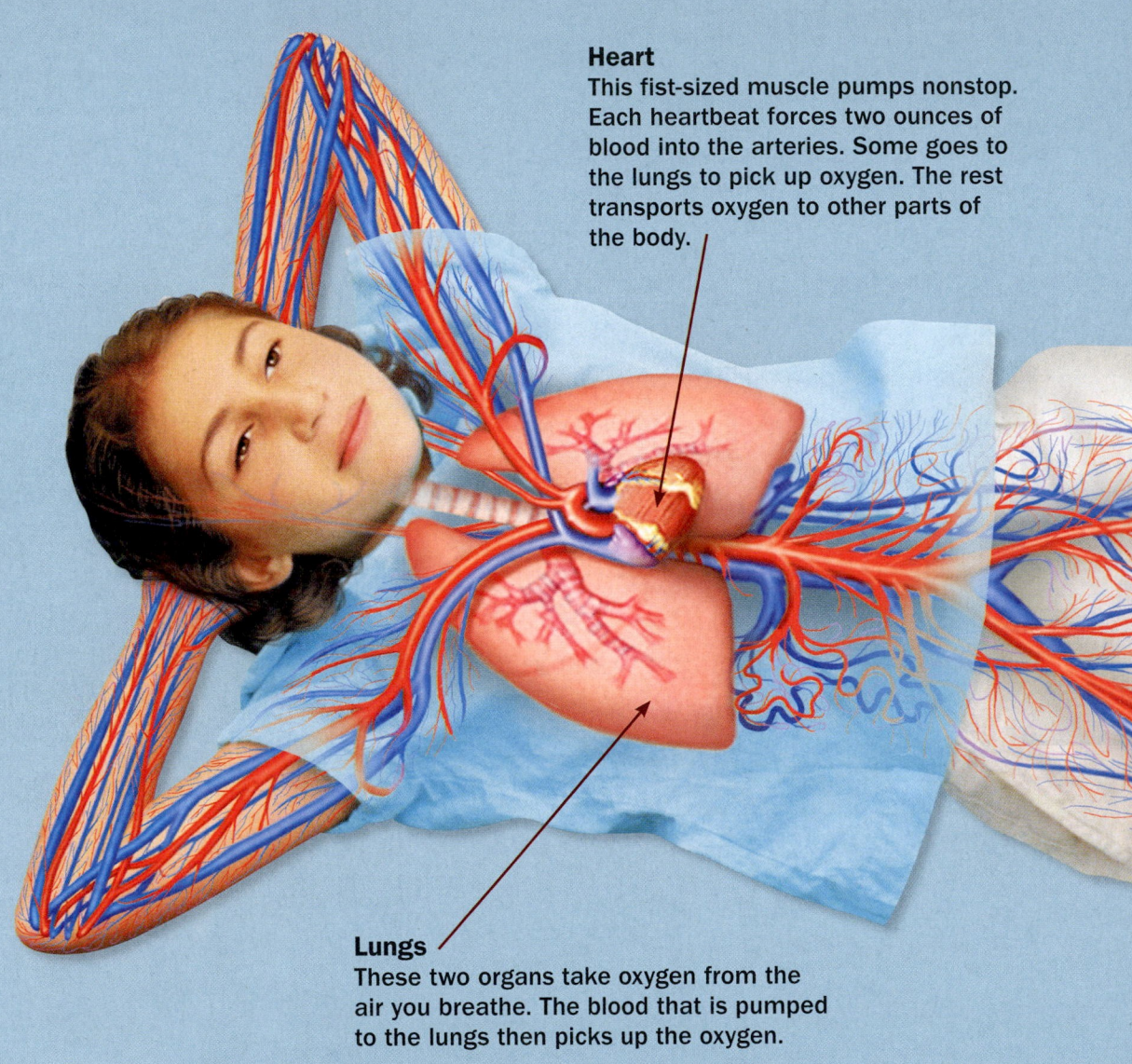

Heart
This fist-sized muscle pumps nonstop. Each heartbeat forces two ounces of blood into the arteries. Some goes to the lungs to pick up oxygen. The rest transports oxygen to other parts of the body.

Lungs
These two organs take oxygen from the air you breathe. The blood that is pumped to the lungs then picks up the oxygen.

Artery
Blood flows away from the heart through blood vessels called arteries. They generally carry oxygen-rich blood, which is bright red.

Vein
Blood flows back to the heart through blood vessels called veins. "Used" blood has a darker color.

Look Into the Text

1. **Inference** Why do you think "used" blood is darker than "fresh" blood?

2. **Viewing** How does this picture help you understand how **veins** and **arteries** transport blood throughout the body?

ALL PUMPED UP

Each beat of your heart pumps blood through your body. That blood is packed with oxygen. When you exercise, your body needs more of this oxygen-rich blood to keep going. So when you're active, your heart **really gets pumping**.

How does exercise affect your heartbeat? You can find out by doing this easy experiment. You may want to work with a partner.

MAKE A PREDICTION

- Exercise will make my heart beat faster.

GATHER YOUR MATERIALS

- watch or other timepiece that has a second hand
- notebook paper; pencil

CONDUCT YOUR INVESTIGATION

Use the following steps to help determine if your prediction is correct.

1 Place two fingers on your wrist. Find a spot where you feel a **thump**. That's your pulse. Each thump represents a heartbeat.

2 Count how many thumps you feel in thirty seconds. Write down the number.

3 Now run **in place** as fast as you can for two minutes.

4 As soon as you finish, count your pulse again. How many thumps do you feel in thirty seconds now?

CONCLUSIONS

- Did your heart beat more or less after you exercised?
- Why did your heartbeat change when you exercised?

In Other Words
really gets pumping works very hard
thump beat
in place without moving forward

Look Into the Text
1. **Cause and Effect** Why does exercise affect your heart rate?
2. **Explain** How does this experiment help you better understand the article?

Connect Reading and Writing

Vocabulary
arteries
healthy
muscle
pumping
section
transplant
veins
ventricle

CRITICAL THINKING

1. SUM IT UP Use your Summary Chart for "The Beat Goes On" to summarize the whole article.

Main Idea and Details	Summary
The heart works hard pumping blood.	The heart works hard pumping blood to keep the body healthy.

Summary Chart

2. Describe Tell a partner what happens during a heart **transplant**. Use details from the text to give a clear picture.

3. Explain Look at the KWL Chart you made on page 280. In the L column, write what you learned about the heart **muscle**. Discuss your completed chart with a group.

4. Speculate Why might Brian Whitlow's story be inspiring to others?

READING FLUENCY

Intonation Read the passage on page 648 to a partner. Assess your fluency.

1. My tone never/sometimes/always matched what I read.

2. What I did best in my reading was _____.

READING STRATEGY

What strategy helped you understand this selection? Tell a partner about it.

VOCABULARY REVIEW

Oral Review Read the paragraph aloud. Add the vocabulary words.

> Last year, my grandpa needed a heart _____. His left _____ stopped _____ blood. So when his _____ returned blood to his heart, his weak heart _____ wasn't strong enough to pump the blood back into his _____, which carry blood to the rest of his body. My family visited him in the _____ of the hospital for people recovering from surgery. We were all happy to learn that Grandpa now has a _____ new heart.

Written Review Imagine a friend needs a heart **transplant**. Write an editorial about why it is important for people to donate organs to those who need them. Use four vocabulary words.

 **WRITE ABOUT THE** **GUIDING QUESTION**

Explore the Human Heart

Why is a **healthy** heart so amazing? Write your opinion. Reread the selection to find details that support your opinion.

Connect Across the Curriculum

Vocabulary Study

Use Context Clues: Synonyms and Antonyms

Academic Vocabulary
- **context** (**kon**-tekst) *noun, adjective*
  1 **Context** is the surrounding text near a word or phrase that helps explain its meaning.
  2 A **context** clue helps you find a word's meaning.

Sometimes writers provide synonyms and antonyms as **context** clues.

- **Synonyms** are words with similar meanings.

  EXAMPLE   Each time the heart contracts, or squeezes, blood squirts through blood vessels.

- **Antonyms** are words with opposite meanings.

  EXAMPLE   Many bodies accept a transplanted organ. However, others can reject it.

Use Context Clues Work with a partner. Read each sentence. Use **context** clues to figure out the meaning of each underlined word.

1. His heart was too weak to keep his body strong.
2. Healthy hearts have four chambers, or sections.
3. Anti-rejection drugs may cause side effects, or problems.

Research/Technology

Make a Public Service Announcement

HEALTH & SCIENCE

A Public Service Announcement (PSA) is an advertisement to inform people about important **topics**. Create a PSA about the human heart.

1 **Choose a Topic** Search the Internet, newspapers, and magazines to learn about a heart-related **topic**.

2 **Research Your Topic** Decide what you want people to know about your **topic**. Use the Internet or library to find information.

3 **Make Your PSA** Use graphic software, colored pencils or markers, or a recording device to make your PSA. Be sure the information in the announcement supports your claims and is easy to read or hear.

4 **Present Your PSA** Display or play your PSA for classmates. Use eye contact and speak clearly. Ask your classmates to evaluate how well your evidence supports your message.

Give and Follow Directions

Pair Share Work with a partner. Talk about how activities, like dancing, can help the heart. Then show and tell your partner how to do your favorite activity. Give the steps in order. Use possessive adjectives as you give directions. Trade roles.

> How do I start? Do I take two steps to my right?

> No, I go right. First, you take two steps to your left! Here. Follow along. It's easy.

Write Directions to a Place

Study the Models When you write directions to a place, you may need to use possessive words. Be sure to use words that show the relationship clearly so your reader can understand you.

NOT OK

It is easy to get to the Recreation Center from our school. As you leave school, turn right. Then turn right again at Elm Street. Go three blocks until you get to Main Street. You will see a hospital on their right. Turn right on Main Street and walk two more blocks to First Avenue. You will see the library on your left. Turn left on First Avenue. The Recreation Center is on First Avenue on his left. You can't miss it.

The reader thinks: "Whose right? I can't tell where the hospital is."

OK

It is easy to get to the Recreation Center from our school. As you leave school, turn right. Then turn right again at Elm Street. Go three blocks until you get to Main Street. You will see a hospital on your right. Turn right on Main Street and walk two more blocks to First Avenue. You will see the library on your left. Turn left on First Avenue. The Recreation Center is on First Avenue on your left. You can't miss it!

This writer uses correct possessive words to make the meaning clear.

Add Sentences Think of two sentences to add to the OK model above. Use at least one possessive word. Be sure that it goes with the noun or pronoun you are talking about.

WRITE ON YOUR OWN Write directions to the library or another place in your community. Check your possessive words. Make sure they match the noun or pronoun.

REMEMBER

- Use possessive words to show who owns or has something.
- Use the form that matches the noun or pronoun.
- Use an apostrophe in a possessive noun:
  the boy**'s** heart   *(one boy)*
  the boys**'** hearts   *(more than one boy)*

Subject Pronoun	I	you	he	she	it	we	they
Possessive Adjective	my	your	his	her	its	our	their
Possessive Pronoun	mine	yours	his	hers		ours	theirs

Two Left Feet, Two Left Hands,
and Too Left on the Bench

by David Lubar

Build Background

See What Drives Us

Athletes must work to be good at their sport, but some athletes only become successful after failing first.

Digital Library
myNGconnect.com
🔗 View the images.

◀ Basketball great Michael Jordan failed to make his high school basketball team.

Connect

Anticipation Guide Tell whether you agree or disagree with the statements in the guide.

Anticipation Guide

	Agree	Disagree
1. If you're not good at something, you should not do it.	_____	_____
2. If you practice something long enough, you will be good at it.	_____	_____
3. People should find what they do well and do only that.	_____	_____

Language & Grammar

Engage in Discussion CD

Look at the photograph and listen to the discussion.

PICTURE PROMPT

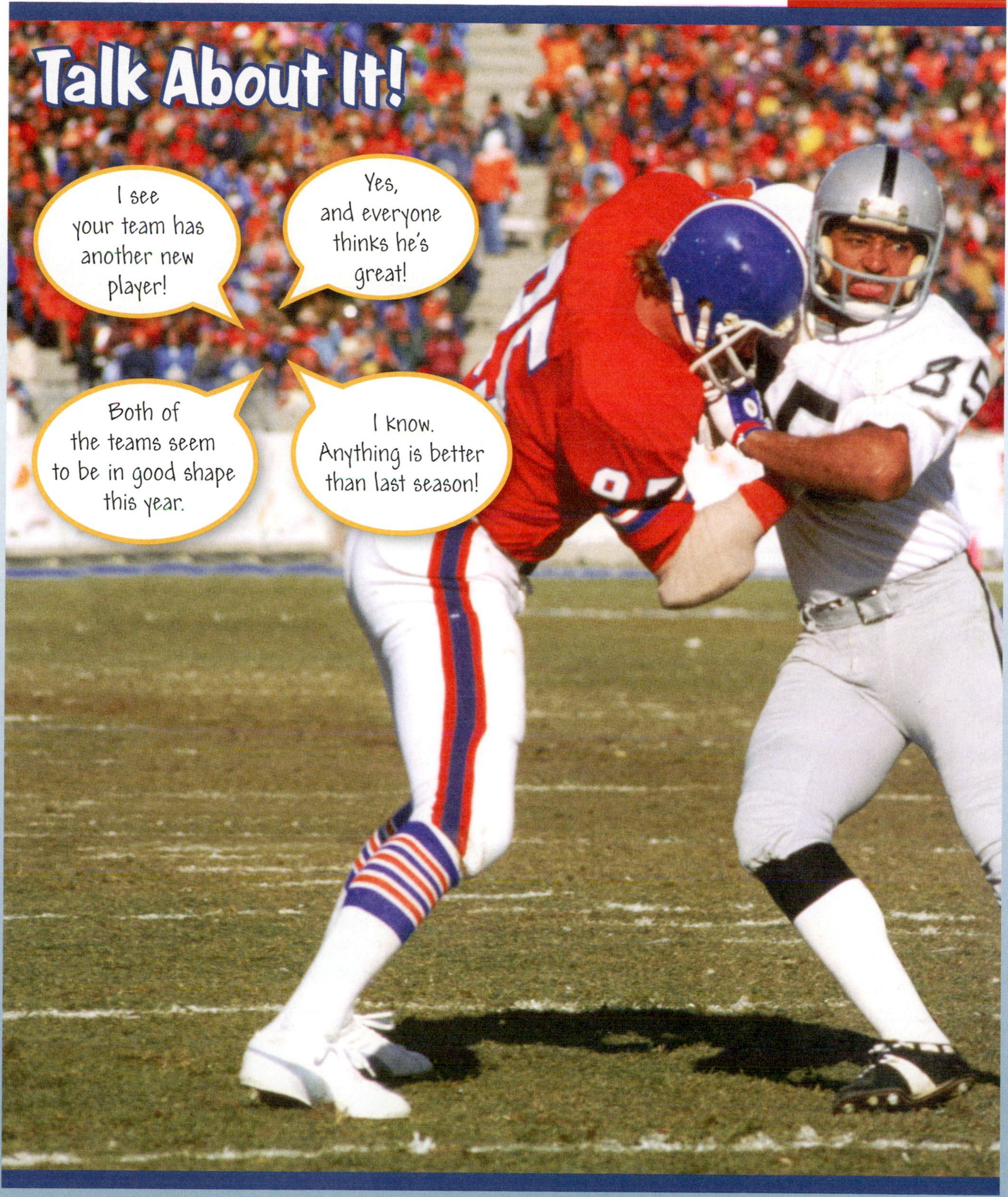

Use Indefinite Pronouns

When you are not talking about a specific person or thing, you can use an **indefinite pronoun**.

> EXAMPLE **Everyone** is good at **something**!

- Some **indefinite pronouns** are always singular. They always need a **singular verb** that ends in **-s**.

> EXAMPLES **Everybody knows** that the soccer game is tonight.
> **Nobody wins** more games than Roy's team does.

Singular Indefinite Pronouns

another	each	everything	nothing
anybody	either	neither	somebody
anyone	everybody	no one	someone
anything	everyone	nobody	something

- Some **indefinite pronouns** are always plural. They need a **plural verb** that does not end in **-s**.

> EXAMPLES **Many** of my friends **play** on the school soccer team.
> **Both** of my cousins **hope** to be on the team next year!

Plural Indefinite Pronouns

both	many	several
few	others	

Practice Together

Say each sentence. Use the correct form of the verb.

1. Several of my friends (play/plays) soccer.
2. Everyone (think/thinks) about how to win.
3. Many (cheer/cheers) when our team scores a goal!
4. Everybody (know/knows) that Carmen is our best player.

Try It!

Read each sentence. Write the correct form of the verb on a card. Then say the sentence and add the correct verb.

5. Each of us (work/works) hard, and that's what counts.
6. Everybody (want/wants) to play on our team.
7. Few (give/gives) up easily.
8. Nobody (forget/forgets) to come to practice.

▲ Everyone on the team works hard.

Explore Sports Shots

ENGAGE IN DISCUSSION

Sports are exciting to watch and play. What sport do you find exciting? Find a sports photo in a magazine, newspaper, or on the Internet. Or, if you play sports, bring in a photo of yourself in action.

Make a list of things you might say to start a discussion about the photo with your classmates.

> **Discussion Prompts**
> Look at the diver twisting in the air!
> Isn't it amazing how high she can go?
> You can almost hear everyone cheering!

Work with a group. Take turns sharing the sports photos each of you found. Tell about your photo, and discuss the others.

How To ENGAGE IN DISCUSSION

1. Give your ideas.
2. Take turns speaking.
3. Listen while others speak and show respect for their ideas.
4. Use words and gestures to show that you are listening.
5. Focus on the topic of discussion.

> Last year, someone gave my cousin tickets to this hockey game.

> Did both of you go? What was it like?

USE INDEFINITE PRONOUNS

When you engage in a discussion, you may use **indefinite pronouns** if you are not talking about a specific person or thing. Make sure your subjects and **verbs** agree.

Singular indefinite pronouns:
Joy and Jan like baseball. **Neither thinks** softball is quite as exciting as baseball. I think **nothing is** better than a friendly softball game.

Plural indefinite pronouns:
Many hope this team will make it to the finals this year. **Others believe** this team is struggling.

Prepare to Read

Learn Key Vocabulary

Study the Words Use the steps below.

1. Pronounce the word. Say it aloud several times. Spell it.
2. Rate your word knowledge.
3. Study the example. Tell more about the word.
4. Practice it. Make the word your own.

Key Words

accept (ak-**sept**) *verb*
▶ page 314

When you **accept** something, you admit that it is true. The team **accepted** that they had lost.
Related Words: **acceptance, acceptable**

assignment (u-**sin**-mint)
noun ▶ page 309

An **assignment** is a task or job given to someone. An **assignment** is often more fun to do in pairs.
Base Word: **assign**

clueless (**klü**-lis) *adjective*
▶ page 311

To be **clueless** means to be confused or to not know something. The girl was **clueless** about how to answer the question.
Base Word: **clue**

determined (di-**tur**-mind)
adjective ▶ page 317

When you are **determined**, you try very hard to do something. Each runner is **determined** to win.

disaster (diz-**as**-tur) *noun*
▶ page 308

A **disaster** is a very bad event. Weather can sometimes cause a terrible **disaster**.

glory (**glor**-ē) *noun*
▶ page 314

Glory is a moment of great success. Winning the science award was my greatest moment of **glory**.
Related Words: **glorious, glorify**

realize (**rē**-u-līz) *verb*
▶ page 310
To **realize** means to understand something. I **realized** the correct answer too late.
Related Words: **reality, real**

survive (sur-**vīv**) *verb*
▶ page 315
To **survive** means to get through something difficult. Surgery wasn't fun, but I **survived**.
Synonym: **live**

Practice the Words Make an Idea Web for each Key Word. Write four things the word makes you think of. Share your finished webs with a partner.

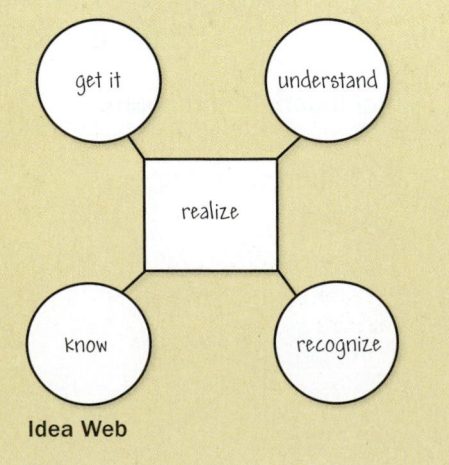

get it   understand   realize   know   recognize

Idea Web

Text Structure: Chronological Order

How Is Text Organized? Writers of narrative nonfiction, such as biographies and histories, describe real people, places, and events. They often use chronological order to organize events and actions in the **sequence** that they happened.

As you read, look for time words to help you determine the **sequence** of events.

Reading Strategies
- Plan
- Monitor
- **Determine Importance:** Focus your attention on the author's most significant ideas and information.
- Ask Questions
- Visualize
- Make Connections
- Make Inferences
- Synthesize

Look Into the Text

> I'm not even sure what grade I was in when I decided to join the after-school football program. Second grade sounds about right. I don't remember the gym teacher's name, either. So let's just call him Mr. Growler. The first fact about sports that caught my attention as I wandered toward the field behind the school was that everyone else seemed to have been born knowing not only the rules to the game, but also exactly what to do.

"The phrase 'Second grade' places the event in a specific time period."

Practice Together

Begin a Sequence Chain A Sequence Chain can help you organize important events in chronological order. Reread the passage above. Determine the important events and add them to your Sequence Chain.

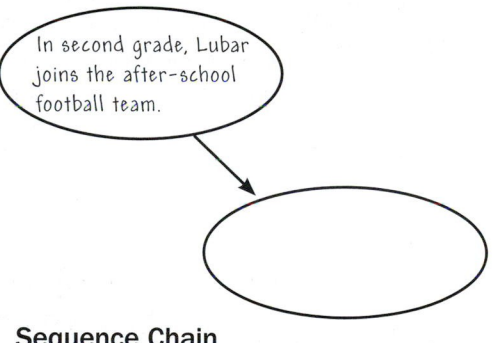

In second grade, Lubar joins the after-school football team.

Sequence Chain

Academic Vocabulary
- **sequence** (sē-kwents) *noun*,
  The sequence of events is the order in which the events happen.

Autobiography

An autobiography is narrative nonfiction in which the writer tells the story of his or her own life. Autobiographies are written in **first-person point of view**. Events in a story may be written in chronological order, but the author may shift between past and present to comment on these events. **Time words** show the order of events.

As you read, think about how putting the events of an autobiography, or other nonfiction, in chronological order helps you determine importance.

Look Into the Text

You could hear the laughter six blocks away. In the glorious tradition of guys everywhere, I was severely mocked for having something that wasn't exactly like everyone else's.

Today, small basketballs are cute. They're hot. You can win them at carnivals. Sadly, that wasn't the case back then. . . .

Two Left Feet, Two Left Hands,

and Too Left on the Bench

by David Lubar

Comprehension Coach

Inauspicious. Isn't that a great word? **Let it roll off the tongue**: in-awe-spish-us. I love words, which—as you'll soon see—is a very good thing. There are all sorts of definitions for this particular word. If you check the dictionary, you'll learn it means "suggesting that the future is **unpromising**." So, an inauspicious event is a **disaster** that points toward a whole lot more disasters down the road. Think of it as a bad start. Better yet, let's define it by example. My first **encounter** with organized sports was definitely "inauspicious."

I'm not even sure what grade I was in when I decided to join the after-school football program. Second grade sounds about right. I don't remember the gym teacher's name, either. So let's just call him Mr. Growler. The first fact about sports that caught my attention as

▲ Lubar (left) with his older brother Jon

I wandered toward the field behind the school was that everyone else seemed to have been born knowing not only the rules to the game, but also exactly what to do.

I followed my teammates to one end of the field. "Lubar!" Mr. Growler shouted at me.

Key Vocabulary
disaster *n.*, a terrible event

In Other Words
Let it roll off the tongue Listen to how it sounds
unpromising probably going to be bad
encounter experience

"What?" Wow. I'd already been **singled out** for attention. I decided I loved football.

"You wanna guard?"

Wow again. He was asking me if I wanted to be a guard. Ten seconds into my sporting career, and I was being given an important **assignment**. Knowing absolutely nothing about the position of a guard in football, and being **a total nerd at heart**, I figured I should do the one thing I was good at: seek out information. "Where do I stand?" I asked.

"What?" Mr. Growler seemed **puzzled**.

"Where does a guard stand?" I asked.

Key Vocabulary
assignment *n.*, a task that is given to a person to do

In Other Words
singled out specially chosen
a total nerd at heart better at school than at sports
puzzled confused

He sighed and stared at me as if **I'd just arrived from Pluto**. Around me, I could hear kids **snickering**. Mr. Growler pointed at my head. "Would you like a guard for your glasses?"

"Oh…" I ==realized== a manly battle like football could **be hard on glasses, though, in truth,** I had the world's most unbreakable pair. My uncle was an optometrist, and he gave our family free glasses. While that was great for my parents' budget, it meant I ended up with the ugliest, thickest, most unwanted frames on the planet. I could have clubbed an ogre with my glasses. Or hammered together a house. "Yeah, sure, thanks," I mumbled.

And so I started my first game with a padded head guard and no clue whatsoever. Someone on our team kicked the ball.

I could have clubbed an ogre with my glasses.

Everyone else ran down the field shouting. I ran down the field shouting. Everyone stopped running. I wasn't sure why, but I was more than happy to stop, too. We lined up. The other team snapped the ball. (At the time, I had no idea it was called a "snap," but if I limited myself to the sports vocabulary I had back then, this would be a really ugly little passage.) I noticed people all around me were bumping into each other with their arms crossed. A guy from the other team ran toward me. I crossed my arms and ran into him as hard as I could.

He was way bigger than I was. I bounced off to the side. He kept running. But I figured I'd done well. As my moment of sports heroism played through my mind, it occurred to me that this guy was different

Key Vocabulary
==realize== *v.*, to understand

In Other Words
I'd just arrived from Pluto I was from another planet
snickering quietly laughing
be hard on glasses, though, in truth, break my glasses, but

from the rest of the players. He was clutching a football. Wow—I'd actually bumped the guy who had the ball. **Score one for me.**

Or so I thought.

After the guy ran the ball into the end zone, my teammates began to question me. "Why didn't you tag him?" "You had him." "What are you doing?" "Don't you know *anything*?"

Did I mention that this was touch football? If I'd had a clue what I was doing, I could have ended the play and been a hero in my very first game **merely** by uncrossing my arms and touching the guy with the ball. Instead, I'd been **clueless**.

Key Vocabulary

clueless *adj.*, having no understanding or knowledge about what is happening

In Other Words

Score one for me. I had done well.
merely simply

Look Into the Text

1. **Summarize** What are some clues that suggest Lubar's first game will be a **disaster**?
2. **Word Choice** Why does Lubar begin by defining the word *inauspicious*?

Eventually, I realized that football wasn't my best sport. I discovered basketball. I hung around the playground after school, shooting baskets with anyone who'd let me play. Since it wasn't always easy to convince others to allow me to join their game, what I really wanted was my own basketball. I begged my parents to get me one. I pleaded. But we didn't have a lot of money, and sports equipment was far down the list of things to buy.

Finally, my mom told me she'd seen a special offer from StarKist. If she sent in a bunch of tuna labels and a couple of dollars, she could get me a Charlie the Tuna basketball. (I need to pause here and assure the readers that I am dead serious about this. There **honest-to-goodness** really was an offer for a Charlie the Tuna basketball. I have no clue what tuna and basketballs have in common, other than the fact that I'd rather not eat either of them raw. And,

to tell the truth, as I dredge up these memories, I myself have a hard time believing this. But I swear all of it is true.)

So Mom sent away for it, and eventually my basketball arrived. It was round. It was rubber. It was brownish orange. And it was about two-thirds the size of every other basketball on the planet. Once again clueless, I dribbled it to the playground.

You could hear the laughter six blocks away. In the **glorious** tradition of guys everywhere, I was severely mocked for having something that wasn't exactly like everyone else's.

Today, small basketballs are cute. They're **hot**. You can win them at carnivals. Sadly, that wasn't the case back then. I guess I can't blame Charlie the Tuna for keeping me out of the NBA. I'm 5'8" and can only make a shot when I'm not jumping. But still, every time I see a can of tuna, I **shudder just a little**.

In Other Words
honest-to-goodness actually
glorious wonderful
hot popular
shudder just a little remember
  being embarrassed

Cultural Background
StarKist is a popular brand of canned tuna fish. A cartoon tuna fish named Charlie often appears on the can. Food companies during this time frequently offered free gifts to people in exchange for purchasing their products.

▲ **Critical Viewing: Mood** How does this image express the mood of the selection?

As elementary school progressed, I pretty much **accepted** the fact that I was bad at sports and would always be picked last. But even the least likely kid on a team can have a moment of greatness.

It was a rainy day. We were inside for gym class, playing kickball. When my turn came, I gave the ball a good, hard kick. Which didn't mean anything. My hard kicks could end up dribbling a couple of feet with the wobble of a wounded woodchuck, or flying **far foul** at frightening angles, or occasionally actually going somewhere useful before being scooped up by an infielder and **hurled** back at me with terrifying force as I huffed toward first base.

But this one went somewhere. Oh, boy, did it go somewhere. It sailed straight over second base. But that wasn't the end of its glorious trip. It arced all the way across the gym—and then dropped through the basketball hoop on the other side. *Swish.* **Nothing but net.**

"Automatic home run," Mr. Growler said.

I had no clue about this rule, either. But I rounded the bases, which was something I had never done before (and would never do again).

"That's the first time anyone did that," Mr. Growler told me.

Wow. I'd done something nobody else had ever done. And, finally, after **countless humiliating** experiences, I'd had my one small moment of **glory** in the totally meaningless but unbelievably important world of elementary school sports.

> ## Even the least likely kid on a team can have a moment of greatness.

Key Vocabulary

accept *v.*, to take; to understand

glory *n.*, a moment that brings praise and happiness

In Other Words

far foul the wrong way
hurled thrown
Nothing but net. It was perfect.
countless humiliating many embarrassing

Look Into the Text

1. **Confirm Prediction** Was your prediction about Lubar correct? Explain.
2. **Summarize** What was Lubar's "moment of greatness"?
3. **Main Idea and Details** Lubar is **clueless** about sports. Give details to support this main idea.

If this were a work of fiction, that would be the end of the story. But in real life, the moment of glory rarely comes at the right time. After the basket, things returned to normal. In other words, I was hopelessly bad at sports and was often ridiculed. But I **survived**. Middle school brought moments so awful that I'm not going to even try to put them on paper.

In high school, I **went out for fencing**. The team was new, and none of us had a clue what we were doing, so I was in good company. It was fun. When the season ended, I wanted to keep in shape, so I signed up for a karate class. Much to my surprise—years after my first **disastrous** encounter with touch football—I found my sport. Let me say that again. I found my sport. I was

Key Vocabulary

survive *v.*, to live through a difficult situation

In Other Words

went out for fencing tried sword fighting

disastrous awful

▲ Lubar practicing karate, years ago.

actually good at karate. I eventually earned a black belt and even taught classes to others.

It turned out that I'd learned more than I realized. One day, when I was in college, I was with some friends at a local softball field. Someone had brought a bat and ball. Just for fun, I tossed the ball in the air and **took a swing**.

The ball went right over the fence.

After I **bent down and picked up my jaw from where it had dropped on the ground**, I realized what had happened.

All of the karate practice had helped teach me to focus my power. We had a fun time while I hit flies into the outfield for everyone to catch.

Imagine that. Me—hitting balls far into the outfield. If someone had told me back in elementary school that I could put one over the fence with ease, I would have laughed.

So I grew up, discovered I was a lot better with words than with bats, became a writer, and became a father. Hoping to give my daughter a better start than I had,

I signed her up for T-ball when she was in first grade. She seemed to have **inherited** my skills. After T-ball, she played softball for a couple of years, but didn't like it. I signed her up for basketball. She didn't like that either.

Finally, one day during the summer before seventh grade, she asked if she could take karate lessons. She was so **determined** that she actually started looking through ads in the paper to find a school. To my delight, the school she picked taught a style similar to the one I'd learned. I signed her up. And she was good at it. Really good. She'd found her sport. She won tournaments. She **dazzled** everyone. She made me proud.

So, what does all of this mean? I guess it means you can survive being a clueless player surrounded by kids who know the rules, and you can survive **showing up with** a Charlie the Tuna basketball. Really, my friends, you can survive anything. And sometimes, magically, when all you're hoping for is to make it to first base, the ball flies across the gym and **swishes** through the basket. And sometimes, after looking hard and nearly giving up, you find your sport. ❖

About the Author

David Lubar

David Lubar (1954–) has written at least a dozen books for young adults. Lubar worked for many years as a video game designer. That job was exciting, but Lubar loved writing more. The first piece of writing he ever sold was a joke to a comedian—for 75 cents. Lubar lives in Pennsylvania with his wife, daughter, and three cats.

Look Into the Text

1. **Summarize** How do Lubar's skills change after he learns karate?
2. **Compare and Contrast** How are Lubar and his daughter alike?
3. **Metaphor** What does Lubar mean when he says "I picked up my jaw from where it dropped on the ground"?

How Coach Told Me I Didn't Make the Cut

by Gary Soto

So Coach said, "Go out for a pass,"
And me, I took off, running hard
Because here was my one chance.
Coach yelled, "Farther! Farther!"
His arm cocked and ready to throw the football.   [5]
My legs were like pinwheels, a blur.
I ran with my hands out,
My fingers wiggling for the touch
Of a ball. Once it was in my arms,
I wouldn't fumble.   [10]
No, I would carry it in for a touchdown.
"Deeper, deeper," I heard him yell.
I outpaced a barking dog and an old man
On a rusty bicycle.
Coach got smaller and smaller,   [15]
Until he was just a fleck of dust on my eyelids.
I slowed down, caught my breath,
And rubbed my eyes. Was that Coach so far away?
I walked home. The living room was empty.
When I turned on the TV, crowds were cheering   [20]
Those who had made the team.

In Other Words
cocked pulled back
pinwheels spinning toys
fumble drop it
deeper farther
outpaced ran faster than

Look Into the Text
1. **Simile** How were the narrator's legs "like pinwheels"?
2. **Mood** How does the poem make you feel? What words does the speaker use to make you feel this way?

Connect Reading and Writing

Vocabulary
accepted
assignment
clueless
determined
disaster
glory
realized
survived

CRITICAL THINKING

1. **SUM IT UP** Have students use their Sequence Chains to summarize the story.

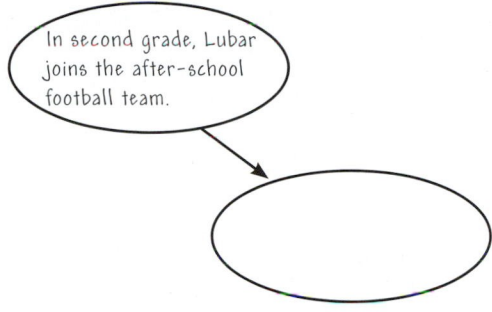

In second grade, Lubar joins the after-school football team.

Sequence Chain

2. **Paraphrase** In your own words, explain to a partner why the author thinks of himself as **clueless**. Use examples from the text to support your ideas.

3. **Evaluate** Revisit your Anticipation Guide. Do you still agree with your answers? If not, what did the selection help you **realize**?

4. **Compare** Explain why both Lubar and the speaker of the poem might call their sports experiences **disasters**.

READING FLUENCY

Expression Read the passage on page 649 to a partner. Assess your fluency.

1. My voice never/sometimes/always matched what I read.

2. What I did best in my reading was _____.

READING STRATEGY

What strategy helped you understand this selection? Tell a partner about it.

VOCABULARY REVIEW

Oral Review Read the paragraph aloud. Add the vocabulary words.

My first _____ for the school newspaper was to write a story about our first football game. Unfortunately, I was _____ about football. I didn't want this story to be a _____, so I was _____ to learn about the sport. Eventually, I _____ that I would have to ask my brother for help. I have now _____ the fact that he knows a lot about football. With his help, I wrote a great article about our school's moment of _____ when we scored a winning touchdown. Without my brother's help, I don't think I would have _____ the experience!

Written Review Think about things you are proud of. Write a paragraph about your greatest moment of **glory**. Use four vocabulary words.

WRITE ABOUT THE GUIDING QUESTION

Explore Being a Winner
Can we make our bodies do what we want if we are **determined** enough? Or does it take more than desire to be good at something? Write your ideas. Reread the selection to find support for your opinion.

Connect Across the Curriculum

Use Context Clues: Examples

> **Academic Vocabulary**
> • **context** (kon-tekst) *noun, adjective*
>   **1 Context** is the surrounding text near a word
>   or phrase that helps explain its meaning.
>   **2** A **context** clue helps you find a word's meaning.

Sometimes, writers include **examples** to help explain unfamiliar words and phrases.

> EXAMPLE I experienced many <u>disasters</u> playing sports. **For example**, I broke my arm trying the high jump.

Use Context Clues Work with a partner. Read each sentence. Use **context** clues to figure out the meaning of each underlined word.

1. I didn't have sports <u>equipment</u> like basketballs, footballs, and hockey sticks when I was growing up.
2. I chose <u>individual</u> sports, such as hiking and bicycle riding.
3. An amazing <u>feat</u>, such as kicking the football through the basketball hoop, was talked about for days.

Analyze Structure of a Poem

> **Academic Vocabulary**
> • **element** (e-lu-mint) *noun*
>   An element is a basic part of something.

Poets often use **elements** of structure to support a poem's meaning. Sentences and phrases, line length and where lines break, and repetition and rhyme are all **elements** of poetry.

Analyze Structure Reread lines 1–10 of the poem on page 318. The chart shows examples of **elements** the poet used.

Elements	Example	How Affects Meaning
Short Lines	And me, I took off, running hard Because here was my one chance.	Short lines and phrases build the action as the poem heads toward its climax.
Repetition	Coach yelled, "Farther! Farther!"	Repetition emphasizes words that are important to the meaning.
Sentences		

Work with a partner to identify other examples from the poem. Tell how each **element** contributes to the poem's meaning.

Engage in Discussion

Group Talk With a group, discuss favorite sports or teams. Be sure to involve everyone in the discussion. Use indefinite pronouns as subjects of some sentences.

Do any of your friends snowboard?

Yes, several do. Everyone got excited about the sport after seeing it on TV.

Writing and Grammar

Write About a School Sports Team

Study the Models When you write about a school sports team, you want your reader to understand what you have to say. Be sure your sentences make sense and the subjects and verbs match, so your reader won't be confused.

NOT OK

> Everyone <u>love</u> a winner! But how many teams actually win every game? Few <u>wins</u> all the time. Just being on the team is a great experience. Both of my cousins <u>plays</u> on our basketball team. Most of the players practice every day. No one wants to miss a practice.

The reader thinks: **"Few wins? What does that mean?"**

OK

> Everyone <u>loves</u> a winner! But how many teams actually win every game? Few <u>win</u> all the time. Just being on the team is a great experience. Both of my cousins <u>play</u> on our basketball team. Most of the players practice every day. No one wants to miss a practice.

Now the subjects and verbs match. The meaning is clear.

Add Sentences Think of two sentences to add to the OK model above. Be sure that your sentences are clear and make sense.

WRITE ON YOUR OWN Write about one of your school's sports teams. What is good about it? What could be better? Write clear sentences for your reader to follow.

REMEMBER

These **indefinite pronouns** use a singular verb:

another	each	everything	nothing
anybody	either	neither	somebody
anyone	everybody	no one	someone
anything	everyone	nobody	something

These **indefinite pronouns** use a plural verb:

both	few	many
others	several	

These **indefinite pronouns** use either a singular or a plural verb:

all	most	some
any	none	

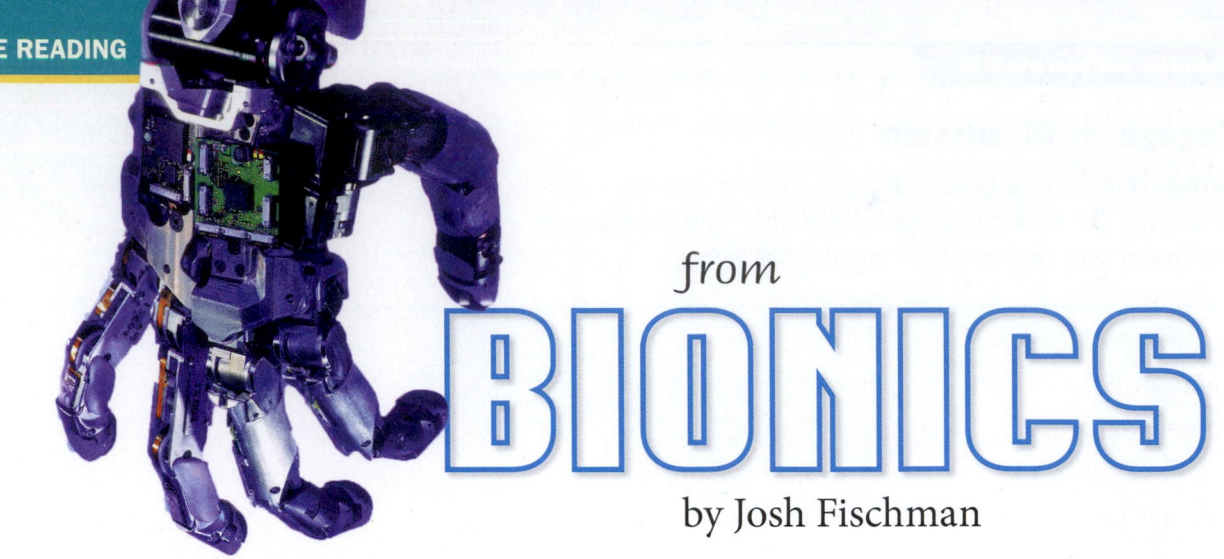

from BIONICS

by Josh Fischman

1   Amanda Kitts crouches down to talk to a small girl, putting her hands on her knees.

2   "The robot arm!" several kids cry.

3   A boy reaches out, hesitantly, to touch her fingers. What he brushes against is flesh-colored plastic, fingers curved slightly inward. Underneath are three motors, a metal frame, and a network of sophisticated electronics. The **assembly** is topped by a white plastic cup midway up Kitts's biceps. It encircles a stump that is almost all that remains from the arm she lost in a car accident in 2006.

4   "I don't really think about it. I just move it," says the 40-year-old.

5   Kitts is **living proof** that, even though the flesh and bone may be damaged or gone, the nerves and parts of the brain that once controlled it live on. In many patients, the nerves sit there waiting to communicate—dangling telephone wires, separated from a handset. With **microscopic electrodes and surgical wizardry**, doctors have begun to connect these parts in other patients to devices such as cameras and microphones and motors.

As a result, the blind can see, the deaf can hear, and Amanda Kitts can fold her shirts.

6   Kitts is one of "Tomorrow's People," a group whose missing or ruined body parts are being replaced by devices embedded in their nervous **systems**. These devices respond to commands from their brains. The machines they use are called neural prostheses or—as scientists have become more comfortable with a term made popular by science fiction writers—bionics.

7   As scientists have learned that it's possible to link machine and mind, they have also learned how difficult it is to maintain that connection. If the cup atop Kitts's arm shifts just slightly, for instance, she might not be able to close her fingers. Still, bionics represents a big leap forward, helping researchers to give people back much more of what they've lost than was ever possible before.

8   Todd Kuiken, a physician and **biomedical engineer**, was the person responsible for the "bionic arm." He knew that nerves in an amputee's stump could still carry signals from

---

Key Vocabulary
• **system** *n.*, a group of things that work together to make one working unit

In Other Words
assembly device; machine
living proof a human example
microscopic electrodes and surgical wizardry highly advanced materials and methods
biomedical engineer person who designs artificial body parts

the brain. He also knew that a computer in a **prosthesis** could direct electric motors to move the limb. The problem was making the connection. Nerves **conduct** electricity, but they can't be spliced together with a computer cable. (Nerve fibers and metal wires don't get along well. And an open wound where a wire enters the body could lead to infections.)

9   Kuiken needed **an amplifier to boost the** signals from the nerves to avoid the need for a direct splice. He found one in <mark>muscles</mark>. When muscles contract they give off an electrical burst strong enough to be detected by an electrode placed on the skin. He developed a technique to reroute **severed** nerves from their old, damaged spots to other muscles. Those muscles could give their signals the proper boost.

10   In October 2006 Kuiken set about rewiring Amanda Kitts. The first step was to save major nerves that once went all the way down her arm. A surgeon rerouted those nerves to different areas of her upper-arm muscles. For months, the nerves grew into their new homes.

11   Then Kitts was fitted with her first bionic arm. Now the challenge was to change signals from her muscles into commands to move the elbow and hand. A microprocessor in the prosthesis had to be programmed to find the right signal and send it to the right motor.

12   "It wasn't easy at first," Kitts says. "I would try to move it, and it wouldn't always go where I wanted." But she worked at it, and the more she used the arm, the more lifelike the motions felt. What Kitts would really like now is sensation. That could come next.

"... it's possible to link machine and mind, ..."

Key Vocabulary
• <mark>muscle</mark> *n.*, a body tissue that produces movement

In Other Words
prosthesis machine-made body part
conduct help move
an amplifier to boost the something to make louder or stronger
severed cut

Closing In On a Lifelike Limb

The abilities of today's Proto 1 Bionic Arm will triple in the next prototype.

Human Arm
22+ Movements

From the shoulder to a finger's last joint, an arm has at least 22 points of movement. Nerves carry the brain's instructions from the spinal cord to the muscles.

Traditional Prosthesis
3 Movements

The pincer-hand prosthesis has cables that move when the chin or other arm presses levers on a harness. It is the only device available to most amputees.

Proto 1
7 Movements

Nerves that once reached the lower arm are rerouted into other muscles. Electrodes placed on those muscles capture the brain's commands and send them by wires in the prosthesis.

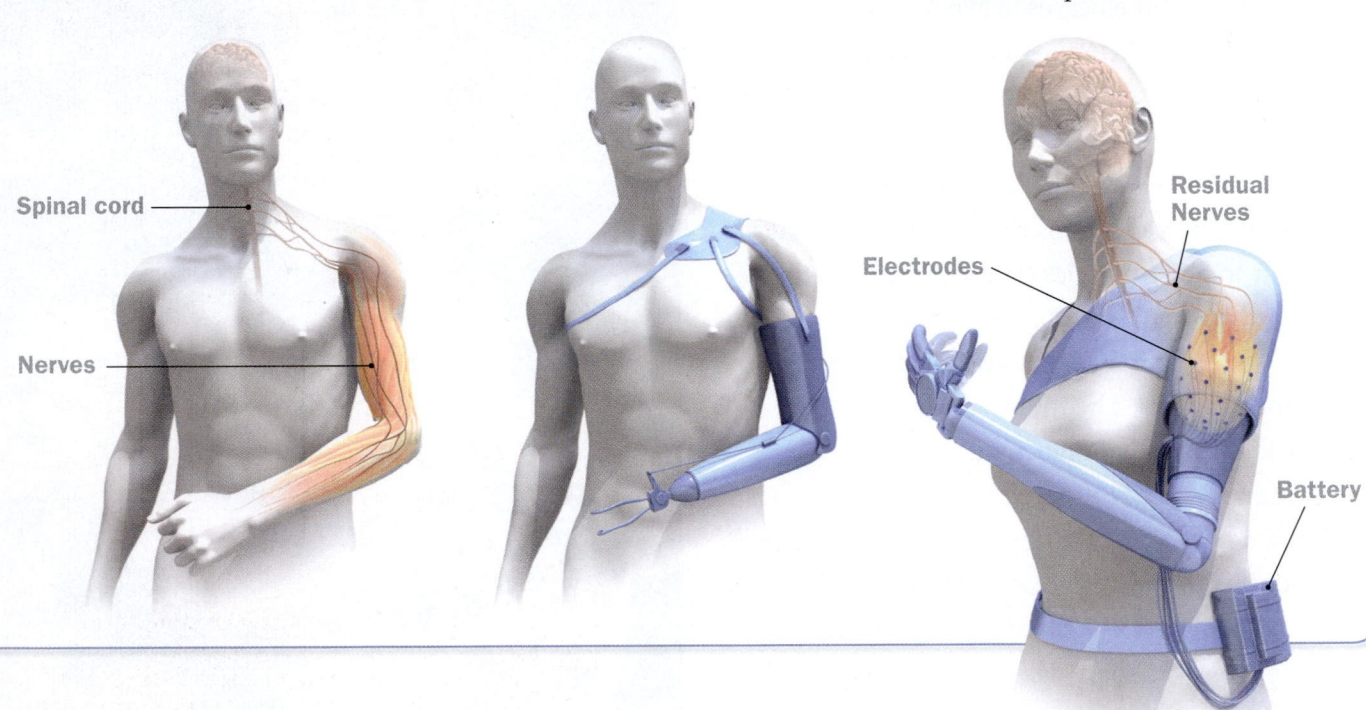

Spinal cord

Nerves

Electrodes

Residual Nerves

Battery

Modular Design Placing the controller in the palm lets the prosthesis work for both full and partial amputations.

Sensory Data Fingertip nodes will detect pressure, vibration, and temperature. The data will be sent to the brain.

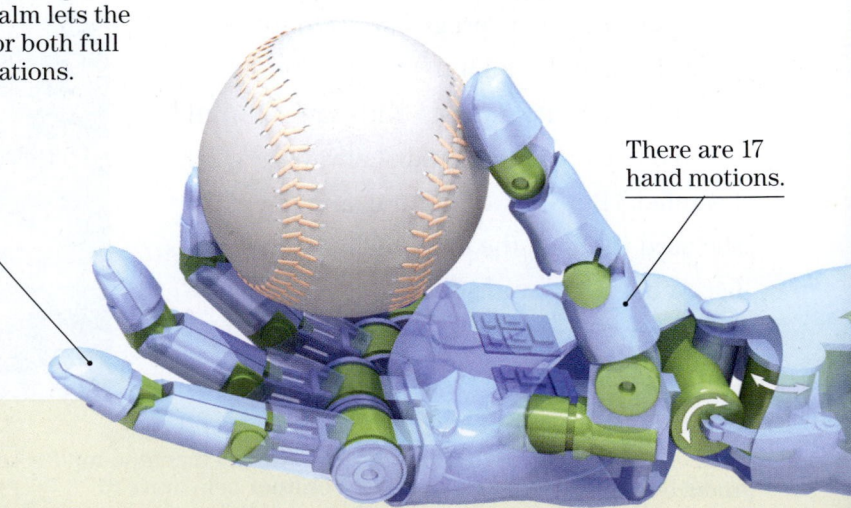

There are 17 hand motions.

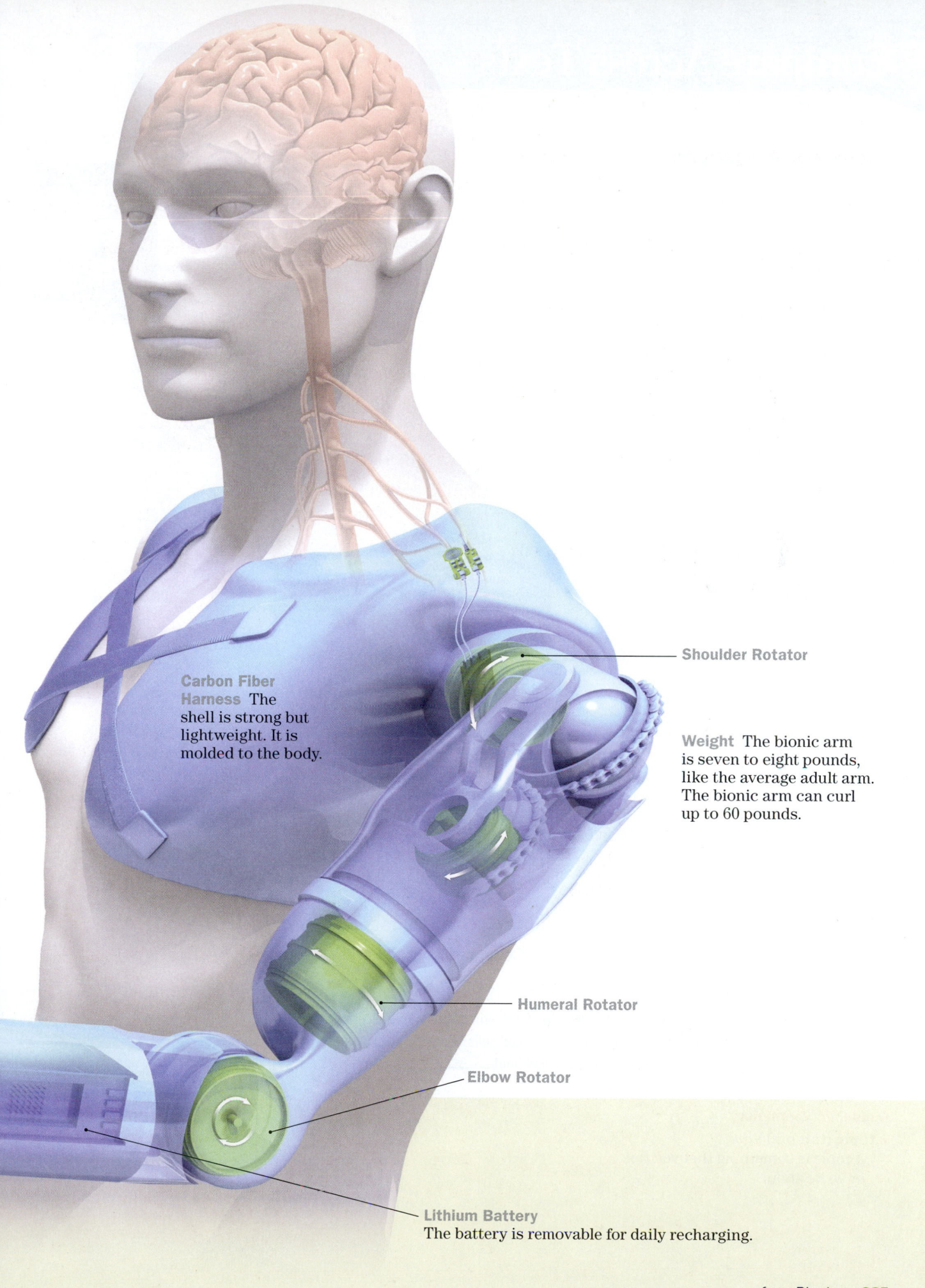

Shoulder Rotator

Carbon Fiber Harness The shell is strong but lightweight. It is molded to the body.

Weight The bionic arm is seven to eight pounds, like the average adult arm. The bionic arm can curl up to 60 pounds.

Humeral Rotator

Elbow Rotator

Lithium Battery
The battery is removable for daily recharging.

Compare Across Texts

Compare Topics

"The Human Machine," "The Beat Goes On," and "Bionics" all explain how systems of the human body work. However, each author approaches the **topic** in a different way. Compare how the authors present information about similar **topics**.

How It Works

Collect and Organize Information Use a chart to compare the **topic** of each article. First, identify how the articles are similar. Then identify how they are different.

Comparison Chart

Selection	Topic	Similarities	Differences
"The Human Machine"	How the human body works	Describes how systems in the body work	Tells about more than one system
"The Beat Goes On"	How the human heart works	Describes how the circulatory system works	
"Bionics"			

Practice Together

Compare Topics Use your chart to make a comparison of the how each selection addresses the same topic. Here is a sample.

Comparison

> "The Human Machine" and "The Beat Goes On" are science articles about systems in the human body. They each describe how the body works.

Try It!

Think about how the selections are different. Copy and fill in the chart. Write a comparison of the differences.

"The Human Machine," "The Beat Goes On," and "Bionics" are science articles about the same topic, the human body. However, "The Human Machine" tells about _____ while "The Beat Goes On" tells about _____, and "Bionics" tells about _____.

Academic Vocabulary
- **topic** (tah-pik) *noun*
  A topic is something that you talk or write about.

Every **Body** Is a Winner

Why is the human body so amazing?

Reflect on Your Reading

Think back on your reading of the unit selections. Discuss what you did to understand what you read.

Text Structure: Main Idea and Chronological Order

In this unit, you learned how analyzing the structure of a text can help you to understand its meaning. Choose a selection from the unit and draw a diagram to show the kind of text structure the writer used. Use your diagram to explain the text structure to a partner.

Determine Importance

As you read the selections, you learned to determine importance. Explain to a partner how you will use this strategy in the future.

UNIT LIBRARY

Content Library

Leveled Library

Explore the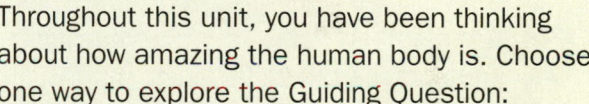

Throughout this unit, you have been thinking about how amazing the human body is. Choose one way to explore the Guiding Question:

- **Discuss** With a group, discuss a movie, television show, or sporting event that helped you understand how amazing the human body is.

- **Draw** Create a visual of an athlete competing in an event. Tell a partner what the athlete needs to be able to do to win the event. Include details from the selections.

- **Write** Based on what you read in the selections, write a routine a person could follow to stay healthy. Include food and exercise and explain why each is important.

Book Talk

Which Unit Library book did you choose? Explain to a partner what it taught you about the human body.

Close
Encounters

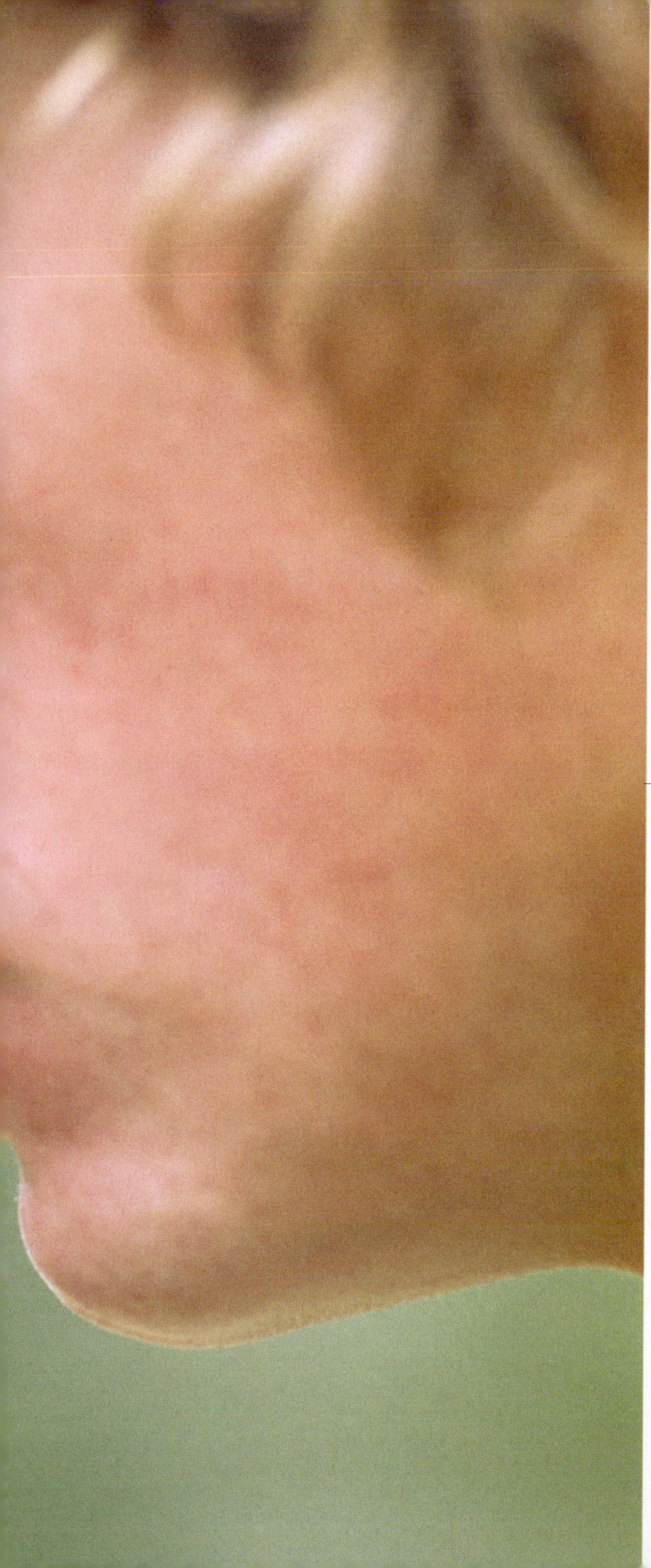

5

What happens when cultures cross paths?

READ MORE!

Content Library
Mexico
by Kevin Supples

Leveled Library
The Trojan Horse
by Justine and Ron Fontes
Monster
by Walter Dean Myers
The Color of My Words
by Lynn Joseph

Web Links
myNGconnect.com

◀ How does understanding cultural differences
help us avoid conflict?

Focus on Reading

Compare Fiction and Nonfiction

Nonfiction texts give information about real events, people, and places to inform or explain. However, writers may emphasize or interpret information differently. Readers can compare authors' work on a topic by **contrasting** the facts they use and how they present similar information.

Fiction writers use their imaginations to create characters, settings, and events to entertain readers. Fictional texts may include real people, places, and events. Accurate details in setting or clothing provide historical background. However, fiction writers sometimes alter facts, such as making up dialogue between real people.

How It Works

When comparing and **contrasting** two nonfiction selections on the same topic, consider the following:

- What kind of information does each author emphasize? For example, if two authors write about the growth of cities, one might include statistics about the number of projects. The second might include details about the effects of this growth.

- How does each author interpret the information? The first author might focus on the benefits of development. The other might focus on the negatives, highlighting crime statistics and environmental issues.

Study the example below to see the kinds of facts the author emphasized.

European Explorers

Christopher Columbus

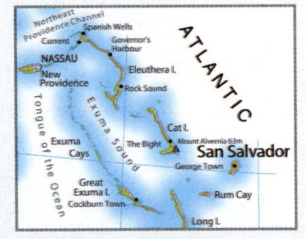

Christopher Columbus was a European explorer and **colonizer**. His journey across the Atlantic Ocean in 1492 eventually caused European settlers to come to the Americas to live. The first place he landed was on an island in the Bahamas called *San Salvador*. He mistakenly called the people there "Indians" because he thought he had found a trade route to India. While his discovery opened new opportunities for Europe, it had a negative impact on the native people.

◁ **Fact**

Academic Vocabulary

- **contrast** (kun-**trast**) *verb*
  When you **contrast** things, you tell how they are different.

How It Works

Study the nonfiction article below to analyze the information this author gives about Columbus. Compare this article with the previous nonfiction text on Columbus.

The Columbus Effect

Christopher Columbus is known for his contributions to exploration. But there is another side to the story of his journey in 1492. Columbus and his men encountered many native people in the New World. He used the term "Indians" to identify them because he thought that he had landed in India. However, the natives suffered far worse injustices than being wrongly named.

Like other European explorers, Columbus hoped to find great riches. Unfortunately, this focus led to poor treatment of the people he and his men encountered. The sailors used violence to take the riches they desired and even made slaves of the native inhabitants. Natives were also exposed to new diseases carried by the explorers. As a result, sickness spread and many died. When we celebrate Columbus's discovery, we should also remember that Europe's expansion was achieved at a cost to the native populations.

> **Fact**

Now read the fiction passage below. Compare and **contrast** this story of Columbus's journey with the nonfiction account above. How does the fiction author use or alter the facts?

I hid until the group of men from the big boats went past. Papa had been here a moment ago. Now I could not find him. I ran to where I knew my sister would be grinding cassava for our meal.

"Is Papa here?" I asked, knowing the answer before she spoke.

"No," my sister muttered, refusing to look at me.

"They took him, didn't they?"

She nodded, looking away.

"Why? Papa is a medicine man. He cannot help them find gold." I did not speak my greater fear that Papa, like so many younger men in our village, would be forced to work for Columbus's men.

> **Fictional Detail**

"Go play, child. Our village, our yacayeque, has suffered much. We must be strong. We must ask our zemis for guidance."

"For guidance!" I scoffed. "They couldn't stop the dying! First these pale-skinned men give us a strange sickness. Now they take those of us left and make us slaves. When will they leave?"

> **Factual Detail**

Practice Together

Read the following nonfiction passages aloud with your class. As you read, analyze the information given in each. Then compare how each author chose to write about a similar topic.

Music: A Universal Language

U2 is a rock band from Ireland. The band formed in 1976, when the band members were teenagers. By the 1980s, the band was known all over the world. U2 spoke a language everyone understood—music.

The Success of U2

U2 has sold more than 170 million albums and has won 22 Grammy Awards. The band was named to the Rock and Roll Hall of Fame in 2005. The most recognized band member is Bono, known not only for his song writing and singing, but also for helping millions of people around the world. The success of bands like U2 gives people like Bono the chance to speak out about world hunger and problems in poor countries. He has spoken before the United Nations, the U.S. Congress, and to world leaders everywhere.

Bono: Activist, Leader, Musician

On June 18, 2012, Bono, lead singer of the rock band U2, presented the Ambassador of Conscience award to Aung San Suu Kyi, leader of the National League for Democracy in Burma. The presentation marked another example of Bono's work for peace and justice in the world.

▲ Bono is known for helping others as well as for his music.

Bono is more than just a celebrity musician. He has worked closely with leaders of the United States and other countries to make a difference for people in need. In 2002, Bono co-founded DATA (Debt, AIDS, Trade, Africa), which led to the creation of ONE: The Fight to End Extreme Poverty. This group's mission is to end hunger and disease worldwide. Bono has found a way to use his music and fame to be a force of change in the world.

Try It!

Read the following passages aloud. Then answer the questions on the right.

1. **Compare the similarities between the two passages.**
2. **How does the fiction passage differ from the nonfiction passage?**

Show Time!

Every year, kids from different cultures show off their musical and artistic abilities for delighted audiences at the Los Angeles Children's Festival. The shows are free and open to the public, so everyone can enjoy the fun.

▲ Traditional folk dancers

A recent line-up at the event featured a middle school concert band, Latino dancers, puppet shows, karate demonstrations, and a group of kids who write and perform their own original comedy routines. The L.A. Children's Festival is run in partnership with the yearly *Feria De Los Niños*, or Children's Fair. The event celebrates kids' differences and honors cultures living together.

My Turn to Dance

Moving toward the stage, Juanita caught sight of what looked like a brightly colored painting. It took a moment for her to realize the painting was her own reflection in the mirror. This year she had finally been selected to perform with a group of Latino dancers in the Los Angeles Children's Festival. Her traditional costume looked amazing.

Juanita's grandmother had come all the way from Mexico to see her dance and sing. She and Juanita's parents were waiting in special seats reserved for VIPs. Juanita put her hands on her stomach to calm the butterflies. Just then the first sounds of the mariachi band played out. Juanita smiled and was swept into the crowd of dancers.

Focus on Vocabulary

Go Beyond the Literal Meaning

Words and phrases that have meanings beyond their literal **definitions** are called **figurative language**. Here are some common types:

- A **simile** compares two things using *like, as,* or *than*.
  > EXAMPLES   She is *as* lovely *as* a summer day. Her eyes are *like* diamonds.

- A **metaphor** compares two things by suggesting one thing *is* the other.
  > EXAMPLE   His face was a wall of stone.

- **Personification** gives human qualities to things that are not human.
  > EXAMPLE   The wind whispered through the trees.

- In an **idiom**, the words together mean something different than the words by themselves. In the example below, *cut it out* means "stop doing that."
  > EXAMPLE   I was bouncing a ball inside, and Mom asked me to *cut it out*.

How the Strategy Works

When you come across figurative language, follow these steps to help you figure out what the words and phrases mean.

1. For metaphors and similes, ask yourself what two things are being compared. How are they alike?

2. When a writer uses personification, picture what the writer is saying. Ask yourself: *How can wind sound like it is whispering?*

3. You can often guess what an idiom means by looking at the other words around it. If you can't figure it out, ask someone or check the dictionary.

Use the strategy to figure out the figurative language below.

The Caribbean is made up of a mix of cultures. These islands are <u>as colorful as a quilt</u>. People from many places settle there. <u>Let the lazy breezes invite you</u> to just <u>kick back</u> and relax. <u>The islands are a hidden treasure waiting to be discovered</u>.

Strategy in Action

" This is a simile because it compares using *as*. "

" Breezes can't invite or be lazy. These are human actions and qualities, so it's personification. "

" I see the phrase *kick back*. This must mean 'relax' because it relates to being lazy. "

Academic Vocabulary
- **definition** (def-u-**nish**-un) *noun*
  The meaning of a word is its **definition**.

Practice Together

Read the passage aloud. Look at each underlined phrase. Identify the phrase as a simile, a metaphor, personification, or an idiom. Then figure out the meaning of each phrase.

Caribbean Dreams

Sarah lay wrapped in a towel under her beach umbrella, looking as peaceful <u>as a sleeping baby</u>. She was <u>wiped out</u>. Her mother suggested she take a nap before she <u>came down with something</u>. All the swimming and sun had exhausted her.

Sarah had never been anywhere this amazing. The Caribbean Islands were <u>a rainbow of flavors, sounds, and sights</u> that filled her mind each time she closed her eyes. The water was her favorite. It was <u>as warm as a bath</u> and <u>as blue as sapphires</u>. Breathing in its salty scent, she <u>let the waves sing to her</u> as she <u>drifted off to sleep</u>.

Try It!

Read the following passage aloud. Look at each underlined phrase. Is it a simile, a metaphor, personification, or an idiom? How do you know? What does it mean?

MUSIC OF THE CARIBBEAN

Caribbean music is <u>as varied as its people</u>. European instruments swing to African rhythms. Folk tunes blend with jazzy harmonies. The <u>sound is a sunny smile</u>. The music of the Caribbean <u>grabs you and won't let go</u>. If you're feeling <u>down in the dumps</u>, listen to Caribbean music. Soon you'll feel <u>as right as rain</u> again.

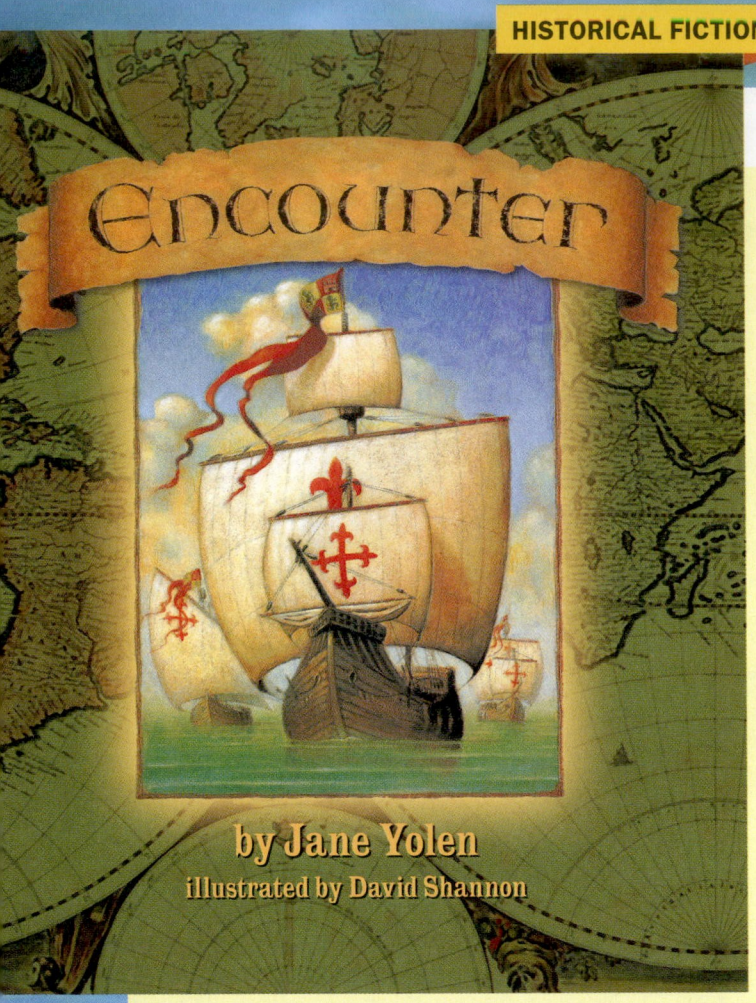

Encounter

by Jane Yolen

illustrated by David Shannon

SELECTION 1 OVERVIEW

▶ **Build Background**

▶ **Language & Grammar**
Make Comparisons
Use Verbs in the Present Tense

▶ **Prepare to Read**
Learn Key Vocabulary
Analyze Plot, Characters, and Setting

▶ **Read and Write**
Introduce the Genre
Historical Fiction
Focus on Reading
Compare Fiction and Nonfiction
Apply the Focus Strategy
Ask Questions
Critical Thinking
Reading Fluency
Read with Expression
Vocabulary Review
Write About the Guiding Question

▶ **Connect Across the Curriculum**
Vocabulary Study
Analyze Personification
Listening/Speaking
Give an Oral Response to Literature
Language and Grammar
Make Comparisons
Writing and Grammar
Write About Events

Build Background

Meet the Taino People

In 1492, Columbus landed on the island of Hispaniola and claimed it for Spain. Spanish explorers brought disease and death to the Taino people who lived there.

Connect

Quickwrite What would you do if people from another planet arrived in your community? How would it make you feel? Write about how you think you would react to their arrival.

Digital Library
myNGconnect.com
🌐 View the images.

▲ The Taino people lived in the Caribbean regions about 1,000 years before Columbus arrived in 1492.

Language & Grammar

Make Comparisons

CD

Look at the photo, and listen to the comparisons. Role-play the comparisons below. Can you think of another way to compare the beings?

PICTURE PROMPT and ROLE-PLAY

Are You Human?

Ken: That robot looks almost like a human!

Tom: Well, not quite. It doesn't have hands like a human.

Ken: That's true, but they both walk and talk.

Tom: But the human uses a brain, not a computer!

Ken: Do you think all robots will look like this one someday?

Tom: I'm not sure. But I would like that because this one looks very friendly.

Ken: Friendly? You make her sound almost human!

Tom: So do you. You call it a "her" like a real person!

1 TRY OUT LANGUAGE
2 LEARN GRAMMAR
3 APPLY ON YOUR OWN

Use Verbs in the Present Tense

An action **verb** tells what the subject of a sentence does. The tense of a verb shows when the action happens.

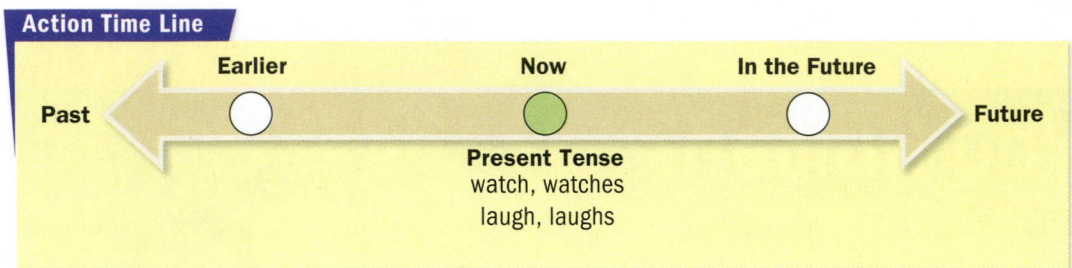

Action Time Line

Earlier	Now	In the Future

Past ← → Future

Present Tense
watch, watches
laugh, laughs

- Use the **present tense** to talk about an action that happens now or that happens often.

  EXAMPLES   We **watch** a new action movie every week.
  I **rent** movies that have robots as the characters.

- Add **-s** to the verb if the subject tells about one place, one thing, or one other person.

  EXAMPLES   My friend William **rents** a movie and **invites** me over.
  William's uncle **lives** with his family.

- Add **-es** if the verb ends in **sh**, **ch**, **ss**, **s**, **x**, or **z**.

  EXAMPLE   William **watches** adventure and action movies with his uncle.

- Do not add **-s** or **-es** to the verb if the subject is **I**, **you**, **we**, **they**, or a plural noun.

  EXAMPLES   We **watch** movies together.

Practice Together

Say each sentence. Choose the correct form of the verb.

1. William (watch/watches) many movies.
2. His uncle (laugh/laughs) with us.
3. William (rent/rents) a different movie each week.
4. We (learn/learns) a lot about film.

Try It!

Say each sentence. Write the correct form of the verb. Then say the sentence using the correct verb.

5. My friend William (tell/tells) me about different movies.
6. He (describe/describes) the scenes in the movie.
7. I (smile/smiles) as he describes a funny robot.
8. The movie (remind/reminds) me of another movie.

▲ We all enjoy the movie together.

Explore Likenesses and Differences

MAKE COMPARISONS

How are people alike? How are they different? You can find out by asking questions of two people.

Make a chart like the one below. Plan your own questions. Write each person's answers in your chart.

Question	Person 1 Answers	Person 2 Answers
When is your birthday?		
How tall are you?		
What color are your eyes?		
What are your hobbies?		
Who's your favorite singer?		
What's your favorite food?		

Share the answers you collect with your classmates. Use the information to make comparisons.

HOW TO MAKE COMPARISONS

1. Tell how people are alike. Use words like *both*, *and*, and *too*.
2. Tell how people are different. Use words like *but* or *different*. Use comparison words like *taller* and *more musical*.

> Both Ali and Joe have brown eyes, but Ali is taller than Joe. Both like to play basketball. Ali likes spicy food, but Joe doesn't. They both enjoy rap music.

USE VERBS IN THE PRESENT TENSE

Use verbs in the **present tense** when you make comparisons between people, places, or things the way they are now. Be sure your subjects and verbs agree.

Add -s   if the subject is *he*, *she*, *it*, or a singular noun:
Kim **celebrates** her birthday in May, but Tina **celebrates** hers in June.

Add -es   if the verb ends in *sh*, *ch*, *ss*, *s*, *x*, or *z*:
Maria **fishes** for fun, but Rob **fixes** old bikes.

Do not add -s or -es   if the subject is *I*, *you*, *we*, *they*, or a plural noun:
Max and Diana **play** guitar in the band. I am different because I **play** drums.

Prepare to Read

Learn Key Vocabulary

Study the Words Use the steps below.

1. Pronounce the word. Say it aloud several times. Spell it.
2. Rate your word knowledge.
3. Study the example. Tell more about the word.
4. Practice it. Make the word your own.

Key Words

custom (kus-tum) *noun*
▶ page 345

A **custom** is something that a certain group of people usually do. In the U.S., it is a **custom** to shake hands when meeting someone.
Synonyms: **tradition, habit**

desire (di-zī-ur) *verb*
▶ page 349

When you **desire** something, you really want it. This boy **desires** the bike in the store window.

dream (drēm) *noun*
▶ page 344

A **dream** is a thought or an image in your mind when you sleep. This girl is having a good **dream**.

encounter (en-kown-tur)
noun ▶ page 344

An **encounter** is a meeting. The photographer took pictures of his **encounter** with a bear.

shore (shor) *noun*
▶ page 344

A **shore** is the land beside a large body of water. A **shore** can be rocky or made of sand.
Synonym: **beach**

stranger (strānj-ur) *noun*
▶ page 345

A **stranger** is someone you do not know. Everyone at the party was a **stranger** to her.
Base Word: **strange**

warning (wor-ning) *noun*
▶ page 344

A **warning** lets you know that there is danger ahead. Traffic signs are **warnings** to drive carefully.
Base Word: **warn**

welcome (wel-kum) *verb*
▶ page 344

When you **welcome** someone, you greet that person kindly. We all **welcome** our relatives.

Practice the Words Make a Study Card for each Key Word. Compare your cards with a partner's cards.

> **welcome**
>
> **What it means:** to greet kindly
>
> **Example:** I welcome my grandma when she visits.
>
> **Not an example:** I welcome someone I don't like.

Study Card

Analyze Plot, Characters, and Setting

How do these elements work together? Writers of historical fiction base their stories on actual people and events. They often include factual details about the clothing and customs of a certain people or time period to make the story more realistic. Fictional details, such as dialogue, help develop their plot and characters.

As you read the following passage, <mark>analyze</mark> how the writer's use of historical and fictional details affects the characters, setting, and plot.

Reading Strategies

- Plan
- Monitor
- Visualize
- Determine Importance
- **Ask Questions** Think actively by asking and answering questions about the text.
- Make Connections
- Make Inferences
- Synthesize

Look Into the Text

All dreams are not true dreams, my mother says. But in my dream that night, three great-winged birds with voices like thunder rode wild waves in our bay. They were not like any birds I had ever seen, for sharp, white teeth filled their mouths.

I left my hammock and walked to the beach. There were my dream birds. Only now they were real—three great-sailed canoes floating in the bay. I stared at them all through the night.

When the sun rose, each great canoe gave birth to many little ones that swam awkwardly to our shore.

The writer created the dream part of the story. The sensory details help me imagine the event through the boy's eyes.

This historical detail refers to the actual arrival of Columbus's ships.

Practice Together

Begin a Details Chart A Details Chart can help you compare historical and fictional details in a story. Use the information to <mark>analyze</mark> why the writer included these details and how they develop the story. Reread the passage and add details to the Details Chart.

Historical Details	Fictional Details
	Three great-winged birds with voices like thunder rode wild waves into our bay.

Details Chart

Academic Vocabulary

- **analyze** (a-nu-līz) *verb*
  When you **analyze** something, you study it closely.

Historical Fiction

Historical fiction takes place in a historical setting. While some characters and events are made up by the author, other details, such as clothing and locations, are accurate. This background information can help you figure out how the setting influences the events and characters.

As you read, ask questions about details you do not understand or would like to learn more about.

Look Into the Text

We did not know them as human beings, for they hid their bodies in colors, like parrots. Their feet were hidden, also.

And many of them had hair growing like bushes on their chins. Three of them knelt before their chief and pushed sticks into the sand.

Accurate details give background about the time period.

Illustrations and details provide more background information about the time period.

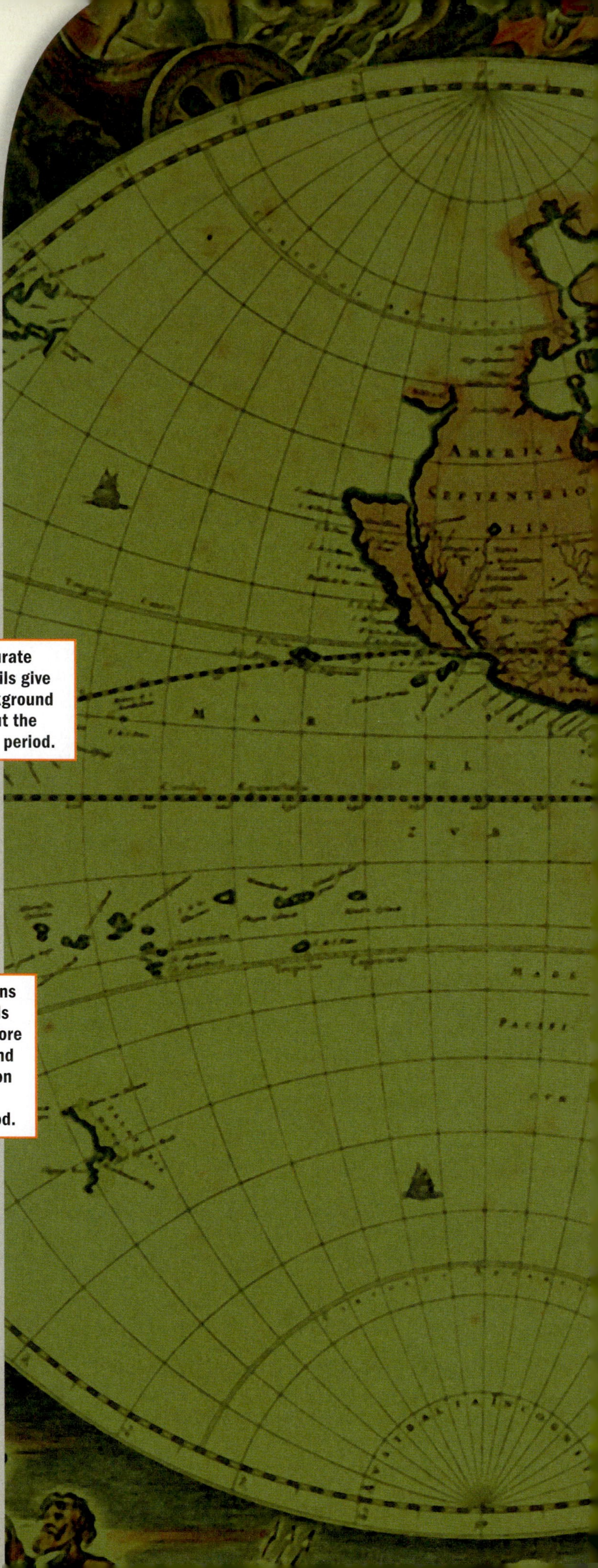

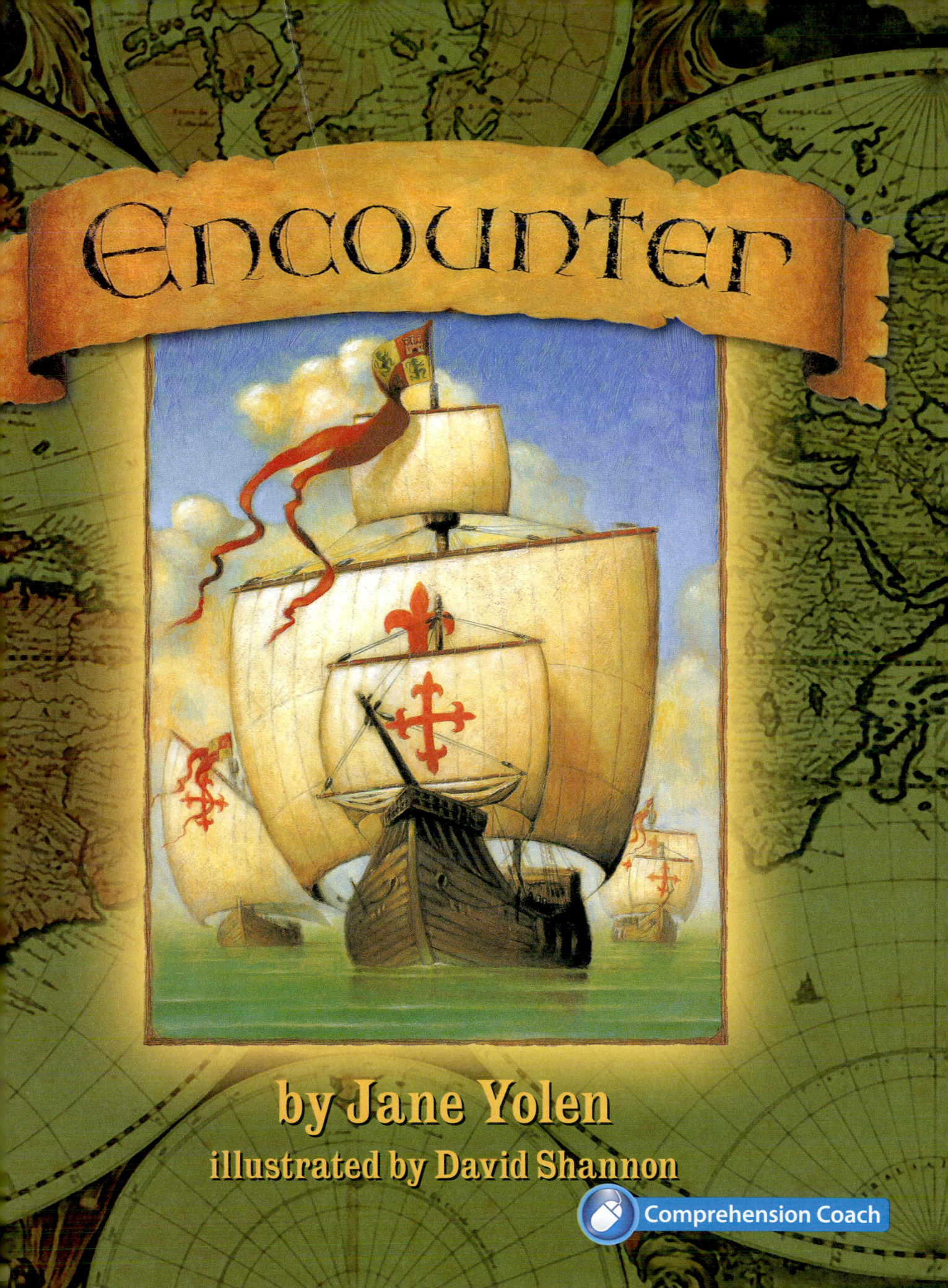

Encounter

by Jane Yolen

illustrated by David Shannon

Comprehension Coach

The moon was well overhead, and our great fire had burned low. A loud clap of thunder woke me from my **dream**.

All dreams are not true dreams, my mother says. But in my dream that night, three great-winged birds with voices like thunder rode wild waves in our bay. They were not like any birds I had ever seen, for sharp, white teeth filled their mouths.

I left my hammock and walked to the beach. There were my dream birds again. Only now they were real—three **great-sailed canoes** floating in the bay. I stared at them all through the night.

When the sun rose, each great canoe **gave birth to many little ones that swam awkwardly** to our **shore**.

I ran then and found our chief still sleeping in his hammock.

"Do not **welcome** them," I begged him. "My dream is a **warning**."

Key Vocabulary
encounter *n.*, a meeting
dream *n.*, thoughts and pictures during sleep
shore *n.*, the place where land and water meet
welcome *v.*, to kindly greet
warning *n.*, advice to be careful about something

In Other Words
great-sailed canoes boats with very large sails
gave birth to many little ones that swam awkwardly released little boats that moved in an odd way

But it is our **custom** to welcome **strangers**, to give them the tobacco leaf, to **feast** them with the pepper pot, and to trade gifts.

"You are but a child," our chief said to me. "All children have bad dreams."

The baby canoes **spat out** many strange creatures, men but not men. We did not know them as human beings, for they hid their bodies in colors, like parrots. Their feet were hidden, also.

And many of them had hair growing like bushes on their chins. Three of them **knelt** before their chief and pushed sticks into the sand.

Then I was even more afraid.

Key Vocabulary
custom *n.*, a usual way
stranger *n.*, an unknown person

In Other Words
feast feed
spat out released; let out
knelt bent down on their knees

Look Into the Text

1. **Compare and Contrast** How are the canoes like the birds in the boy's **dream**?
2. **Character's Motive** Why does the boy ask the chief to not **welcome** the visitors?
3. **Describe** What are the visitors like?

Our young men left the shelter of the trees. I—who was not yet a man—followed, crying, "Do not welcome them. Do not call them friends."

No one listened to me, for I was but a child.

Our chief said, "We must see if they are **true** men." So I took one by the hand and pinched it. The hand felt like flesh and blood, but the skin was moon to my sun.

The stranger made a funny noise with his mouth, not like talking but like the barking of a yellow dog.

Our chief said to us, "See how pale they are. No one can be that color who comes from the earth. Surely they come from the sky."

Then he leaped before them and put his hands up, pointing to the sky, to show he understood how far they had flown.

"Perhaps they have tails," said my older brother. "Perhaps they have no feet."

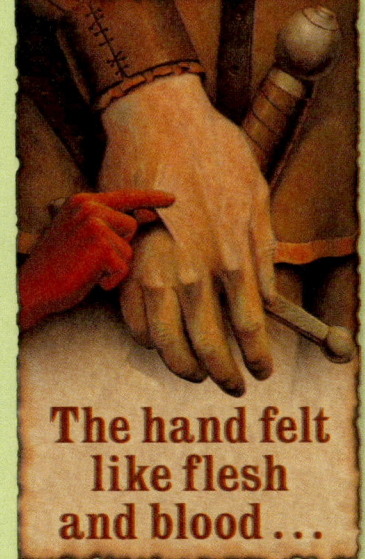

The hand felt like flesh and blood . . .

Our young men **smiled, but behind their hands** so the guests would not feel bad. Then they turned around to show that *they* had no tails.

Our chief gave the strangers balls of cotton thread to **bind them to us in friendship**. He gave them spears that they might fish and not starve. He gave them gum-rubber balls for sport. He gave them parrots, too—which made our young men laugh behind their hands all over again, knowing it was our chief's little joke, that the strangers looked like parrots.

But the strangers behaved almost like human beings, for they laughed, too, and gave in return tiny smooth balls, the color of sand and sea and sun, strung upon a thread. And they gave **hollow shells with tongues** that sang *chunga-chunga*. And they gave woven things that fit upon a man's head and could cover a boy's ears.

In Other Words
true real
smiled, but behind their hands hid their smiles
bind them to us in friendship make them our friends
hollow shells with tongues bells

Historical Background

People have been making and trading beads made from shells, bones, stones, and glass for more than 30,000 years. Native Americans made beads from shells long before the Europeans arrived. People around the world use beads to decorate their hair, clothing, and household items.

For a while I forgot my dream.

For a while I was not afraid.

So we built a great feasting fire and readied the pepper pot and yams and cassava bread and fresh fish. For though the strangers were not quite human beings, we would still treat them as such.

Our chief rolled tobacco leaves and showed them how to smoke, but they coughed and snorted and clearly did not know about these simple things.

Then I leaned forward and stared into their chief's eyes. They were blue and gray like the shifting sea.

Suddenly, I remembered my dream and stared at each of the strangers **in turn**. Even those with dark human eyes looked away, like dogs before they are driven from the fire.

So I **drew back** from the feast, which is not what one should do, and I watched how the sky strangers touched our golden nose rings and our golden armbands but not the

flesh of our faces or arms. I watched their chief smile. It was the serpent's smile—no lips and all teeth.

I jumped up, crying, "Do not welcome them."

But the welcome had already been given.

In Other Words
in turn individually; one at a time
drew back moved away

Look Into the Text

1. **Confirm Prediction** How does the boy feel about the **strangers** now? Why? Was your prediction correct?
2. **Inference** Why does the boy forget his **dream** for a while?
3. **Cause and Effect** What causes the chief to think the **strangers** came from the sky?

Find out how the strangers treat the people.

I ran back under the trees, back to the place where my *zemis* stood. I fed it little pieces of cassava, and fish and yam from the feast. Then I prayed.

"Let the pale strangers from the sky go away from us."

My *zemis* stared back at me with unblinking wood eyes. I gave it the smooth balls a stranger had dropped in my hand.

"Take these eyes and see into the hearts of the strangers from the sky. If it must be, let something happen to me to show our people what they should know."

My *zemis* was silent. It spoke only in dreams. Indeed, it had spoken to me already.

When I returned to the feast, one of the strangers let me touch his **sharp silver stick**. To show I was not afraid, I grasped it firmly, as one would a spear. It **bit my palm** so hard the blood cried out. But still no one understood; no one heard.

My zemis stared back at me.

They did not hear because they did not want to listen. They **desired** all that the strangers had brought: the sharp silver spear; **round pools to hold in the hand that gave a man back his face**; darts that sprang from sticks with a sound like thunder that could kill a parrot many paces away.

We were given none of these—only singing shells and tiny balls on strings. We were patted upon the head as a child pats a yellow dog. We were smiled at with many white teeth, a serpent's smile.

The next day the strangers returned to their great canoes. They took five of our young men and many parrots with them. They took me.

I knew then it was a sign from my *zemis*, a sign for my people. So I was brave and did not cry out. But I *was* afraid.

Key Vocabulary
desire *v.*, to want

In Other Words
sharp silver stick sword
bit my palm cut my hand
round pools to hold in the hand that gave a man back his face mirrors

Cultural Background
A *zemis* is a carved stone that represents a spirit. It is used in the religion of the Tainos. According to Taino legend, a *zemis* warned the Taino of the arrival of the Spanish.

That night, while my people slept on shore, the great-sailed canoes left our bay, going farther and farther than even our strongest men could go. Soon the beach and trees and everything I knew **slipped away**, until my world was only a thin, dark line stretched between sky and sea.

What else was there to do?

In the early morning, **another land lay close enough to see**. Silently, I let myself over the side of the great canoe. I fell down

In Other Words
slipped away disappeared
another land lay close enough to see I could see a different shore

and down and down into the cold water.
Then I swam to that strange shore.

Many days I walked, following the sun.
Many nights I swam. And many times the
sky was full with the moon and stars.

All along the way I told the people of
how I had sailed in the great canoes. I told
of the pale strangers from the sky. I said **our
blood would cry out in the sand**. I spoke
of my dream of the white teeth.

But even those who saw the great canoes
did not listen, for I was a child.

In Other Words
**our blood would cry out in the
sand** our people would be killed

So it was we lost our lands to the strangers from the sky. We **gave our souls to their gods**. We **took their speech into our mouths**, forgetting our own. Our sons and daughters became *their* sons and daughters, no longer true humans, no longer ours.

That is why I, an old man now, dream no more dreams. That is why I sit here wrapped in a stranger's cloak, counting the stranger's bells on a string, telling my story. May it be a warning to all the children and all the people in every land. ❖

About the Author

Jane Yolen

Jane Yolen (1939–) has always loved writing. When she was a teenager, she started a newspaper for her neighbors. She interviewed them and wrote articles about them. As an adult, Yolen has written almost 300 books. Because she likes to study birds, Yolen often includes them in her stories, such as the dream birds in *Encounter*.

About the Illustrator

David Shannon

David Shannon (1959–) grew up wanting to be an artist. After graduating from college, he illustrated his first picture book. Shannon says: "I was amazed at the quality and variety of children's stories, and more and more I found myself drawing things I drew as a boy—baseball players, pirates and knights. I realized that children's books were what I had been working toward my whole life."

In Other Words
gave our souls to their gods changed to their religion
took their speech into our mouths spoke their language

Look Into the Text

1. **Conclusion and Evidence** The <mark>strangers</mark> treat the people badly. How do you know this?
2. **Narrator's Viewpoint** How does the boy feel about his life now? How do you know?

Connect Reading and Writing

Vocabulary
custom
desired
dream
encounter
shore
strangers
warning
welcome

CRITICAL THINKING

1. **SUM IT UP** Use your Details Chart to analyze the historical and fictional details in "Encounter," and then summarize the story to a partner.

Historical Details	Fictional Details
	Three great-winged birds with voices like thunder rode wild waves into our bay.

Details Chart

2. **Discuss** Review your Quickwrite from page 336. Explain to a partner why you would or would not **welcome** the **stranger**.

3. **Judgment** The narrator escaped from the boat and swam to the **shore**. Do you think he did the right thing? Why or why not?

4. **Explain** What **warning** might have told the people that the strangers were not friendly?

READING FLUENCY

Expression Read the passage on page 650 to a partner. Assess your fluency.

1. My voice never/sometimes/always matched what I read.

2. What I did best in my reading was _____ .

READING STRATEGY

What strategy helped you understand this selection? Tell a partner about it.

VOCABULARY REVIEW

Oral Review Read the paragraph aloud. Add the vocabulary words.

Every summer, my family takes a vacation at the _____ . It is our _____ to stay at the same house every year. This year, we had some new neighbors. We decided to _____ the _____ by having a party for them. We ate as much as we _____ . My mother gave me a _____ not to eat too much, or I would be sick. Our neighbors had never had an _____ with anyone who could eat as much as me. That night, I had a _____ about hamburgers and chocolate cake!

Written Review How would you feel if you had to give a **warning** to people, but they didn't believe you? Write a journal entry. Use five vocabulary words.

 **WRITE ABOUT THE** **GUIDING QUESTION**

Explore Encounters

When people from different cultures have an **encounter** with one another for the first time, how should they act? Find examples in the text to support your opinion.

Connect Across the Curriculum

Analyze Personification

Academic Vocabulary
- **image** (**im**-ij) *noun*
  An **image** is a mental picture of something.

When writers use **personification**, they give human qualities to nonhuman things. Read the example below.

> EXAMPLE   The lonely tree reached toward the sun for friendship.

A tree cannot feel lonely or seek out a friend—these are human abilities. Compare the example to a sentence without personification, such as: "There was one tree." Personification creates a stronger **image** .

Analyze Personification With a group, read each example from "Encounter." Tell what **image** you picture. Then discuss what the sentence means.

1. A loud clap of thunder woke me from my dream.
2. The baby canoes spat out many strange creatures . . .
3. They gave hollow shells with tongues that sang . . .
4. The spear bit my palm so hard the blood cried out.

Give an Oral Response to Literature

Academic Vocabulary
- **response** (ri-**spons**) *noun*
  A **response** is an answer or reply to something that has happened or been said.

What did you like and dislike about "Encounter"? Give a **response** to the story by telling what you think and why.

1 Plan Your Oral Response After reading the story several times, think about your reaction to it. How did it make you feel? What do you think the story means? Write some notes about your **response** .

2 Practice Your Oral Response Briefly summarize the story. Tell how you feel about it. Practice in front of another person who knows the story. Ask your listener how you can make your **response** better.

3 Present Your Oral Response Use your tone, facial expressions, and gestures to express your feelings about the story. Make eye contact and speak clearly and loudly.

Make Comparisons

Pair Comparisons With a partner, talk about your school-day habits or routines. Use present tense verbs. Trade roles. Then compare your habits or routines.

> On school days, I get up at 6:00 A.M., but you get up at 7:30. I eat cereal for breakfast, but you eat eggs and toast. We both start school at 8:30.

Write About Events

Study the Models When you write about events that happen regularly or events that happen in the present, use action words that make it clear when things are taking place.

NOT OK

> Every day I walk to the beach to watch the fishing boats. I am watching them at the beach now. The boats come in one by one. One boat <u>move</u> very quickly. It doesn't look familiar to me. There are strange creatures in it. One creature <u>wave</u> at me. Another <u>smile</u>. This is scary, so I run home to warn my family.

This writer doesn't use action words correctly. The reader thinks: "**Is it one boat or more than one boat?**"

OK

> Every day I walk to the beach to watch the fishing boats. I am watching them at the beach now. The boats come in one by one. One boat <u>moves</u> very quickly. It doesn't look familiar to me. There are strange creatures in it. One creature <u>waves</u> at me. Another <u>smiles</u>. This is scary, so I run home to warn my family.

This writer makes the action clearer.

Add Sentences Think of two sentences to add to the OK model above. Be sure that the action takes place now.

✎ **WRITE ON YOUR OWN** Write about your school-day routine and how it compares to your partner's routine from the Make Comparisons activity above. Choose words that make it clear that your routine happens on a regular basis. Check that your subjects and verbs match.

REMEMBER

Make sure your subjects and verbs agree:
- Add **-s** to the verb if the subject is *he, she, it,* or a singular noun.

  My partner **wakes** up at 6:30 A.M. Then she **eats** breakfast.
- Add **-es** if the verb ends in *sh, ch, ss, s, x,* or *z*.

  She **washes** her hair.
- Do not add **-s** or **-es** if the subject is *I, you, we, they,* or a plural noun.

  I wake up at 7:00 A.M.

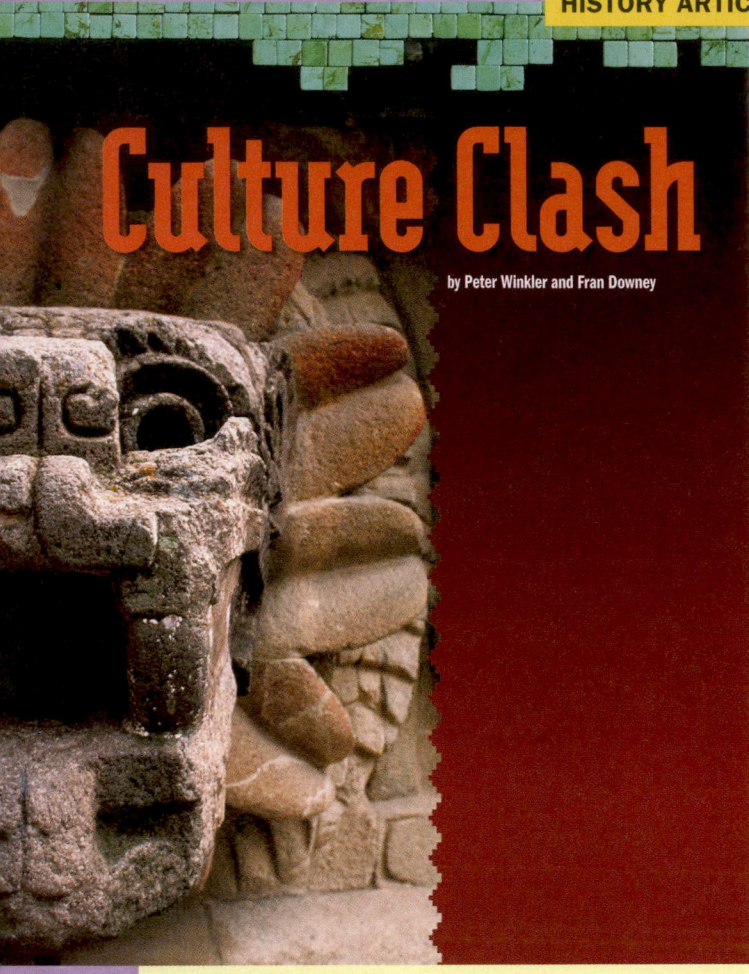

Culture Clash

by Peter Winkler and Fran Downey

SELECTION 2 OVERVIEW

▶ **Build Background**

▶ **Language & Grammar**
Make Comparisons
Use Verbs in the Past Tense

▶ **Prepare to Read**
Learn Key Vocabulary
Compare a Topic

▶ **Read and Write**
Introduce the Genre
History Article
Focus on Reading
Compare Fiction and Nonfiction
Apply the Focus Strategy
Ask Questions
Critical Thinking
Reading Fluency
Read with Intonation
Vocabulary Review
Write About the Guiding Question

▶ **Connect Across the Curriculum**
Vocabulary Study
Understand Idioms
Literary Analysis
Compare Fiction and Nonfiction
Language and Grammar
Make Comparisons
Writing and Grammar
Write About Past Events

Build Background

Connect

Anticipation Guide Tell if you agree or disagree with these statements.

Anticipation Guide

	Agree	Disagree
1. When two cultures meet, one loses everything.	_____	_____
2. A new culture that forms from two cultures is better than the original cultures.	_____	_____
3. People from different cultures cannot live together peacefully.	_____	_____

See Aztec Ruins

In 1519, Hernán Cortés took the Aztec Empire for Spain and changed the future of Mexico.

Digital Library   myNGconnect.com
🔵 View the video.

▲ Today, Aztec ruins can be found around Mexico City.

Language & Grammar

Make Comparisons

CD

Listen to the chant, and study the picture about the Aztec and Spanish cultures of long ago. Join in on the chant, and think about the comparison.

CHANT and DISCUSSION

Mix of Cultures

Two different cultures in just one land,

Could they walk together, hand in hand?

In some ways they were different,

And in some ways the same,

The Aztec and Spanish—we know them by name.

The Aztec were there when the Spanish arrived.

With different traditions, both cultures survived.

Then slowly the two cultures

Started to blend,

And Mexico had a new culture in the end.

Use Verbs in the Past Tense

The tense of a **verb** shows when an action happens.

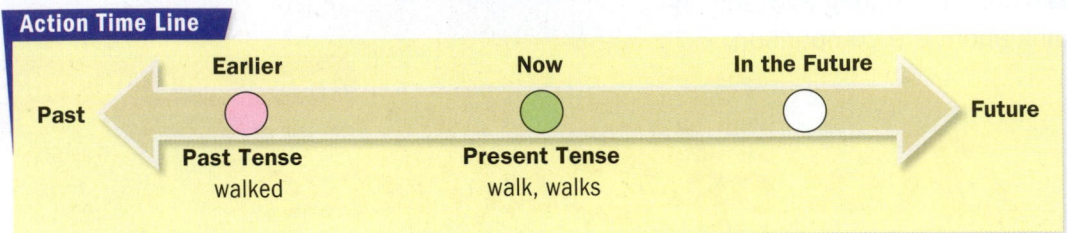

Action Time Line

Earlier	Now	In the Future
Past		Future
Past Tense	**Present Tense**	
walked	walk, walks	

- Use the **present tense** to tell about an action that happens now or often.

  EXAMPLE   Grandpa and I often **camp** in the mountains.

- Use the **past tense** to tell about an action that already happened.

  EXAMPLE   Last year, Grandpa and I **camped** in a state park.

- Add **-ed** to most verbs when you talk about a past action.

  EXAMPLE   Grandpa and I **walked** for three hours.

Practice Together

Change the verb in the box to the past tense and say it. Then add the past tense verb and say the sentence.

1. | fish | My grandpa _____ in the stream.
2. | slip | I _____ on a rock by the shore.
3. | dry | Grandpa _____ my jacket by the campfire.
4. | help | Grandpa _____ me with the tent.

Try It!

Change the verb in the box to the past tense. Write the past tense verb on a card. Then say the sentence, and add the past tense verb.

5. | arrive | Some other campers _____.
6. | join | They _____ us for dinner.
7. | stay | Grandpa and I _____ a week at the park.
8. | enjoy | We really _____ the trip.

Spelling Rules

Sometimes you need to change the spelling of a **verb** before you add **-ed**.

- If a verb ends in silent **e**, drop the **e**. Then add **-ed**.
  live + -ed = lived
      Long ago, Grandpa **lived** on a farm.

- If a one-syllable verb ends in one vowel and one consonant, double the consonant. Then add **-ed**.
  stop + p + -ed = stopped
      We **stopped** in a town.

- If a verb ends in a consonant plus **y**, change the **y** to **i** before you add **-ed**.
  try + -ed = tried
      The people **tried** to make us feel at home.

- If a verb ends in a vowel plus **y**, just add **-ed**.
  stay + -ed = stayed
      They **stayed** to help us.

Explore Changes Over Time

MAKE COMPARISONS

Lots of things change over time, like our hair styles and clothing fashions. Look at the photos. How are the teens from the past and present alike? How are they different?

With a partner, use an Idea Web to list some ways you might compare the teens.

Idea Web

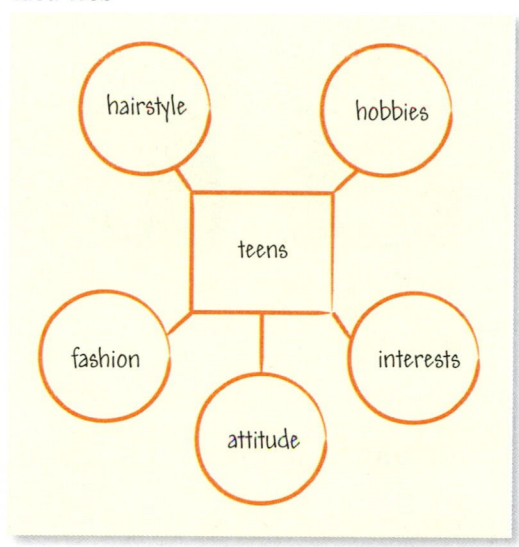

▲ Female athletes in the past   ▲ Female athletes today

Now take turns telling each other how you would compare the teens.

HOW TO MAKE COMPARISONS

1. Tell how things are alike. Use words like *and*, *also*, *too*, *alike*, or *same*.
2. Tell how things are different. Use words like *but* and *different*.
3. Use comparison words like *longer*, *more*, and *less*.

> In the past, girls played basketball in long dresses. Today, girls wear shorts.

> The long dresses of the past were more formal. Shorts are more casual.

USE PRESENT AND PAST TENSE VERBS

When you make comparisons, you might tell about how styles and customs are right now. If so, use a **present tense** verb. Or you may tell about customs and styles from the past. If so, use a **past tense** verb.

In the Present: Athletes **dress** more comfortably today than they did in the past.

In the Past: Female athletes **dressed** in long skirts in the past.

Language & Grammar   **359**

Prepare to Read

Learn Key Vocabulary

Study the Words Use the steps below.

1. Pronounce the word. Say it aloud several times. Spell it.
2. Rate your word knowledge.
3. Study the example. Tell more about the word.
4. Practice it. Make the word your own.

Rating Scale

1 = I have never seen this word before.

2 = I am not sure of the word's meaning.

3 = I know this word and can teach the word's meaning to someone else.

Key Words

blend (blend) *verb*
▶ page 369

When you **blend** things, you mix them together. In cooking, you **blend** the ingredients.
Synonyms: **mix, combine**
Antonym: **separate**

capital (kap-ut-ul) *noun*
▶ page 364

A **capital** is the city where a government is located. Washington, D.C., is the **capital** of the United States.

conflict (kahn-flikt) *noun*
▶ page 368

A **conflict** is a problem or a disagreement. A **conflict** often leads to anger.

conquer (kahn-kur) *verb*
▶ page 365

To **conquer** means to win control of people through force. Adolf Hitler tried to **conquer** all of Europe in World War II.
Related Word: **conqueror**

culture (kul-chur) *noun*
▶ page 369

A **culture** is the way of life for a group of people. Dance is part of one's **culture**.
Related Word: **cultural**

defeat (di-fēt) *noun*
▶ page 369

A **defeat** is a loss. He felt responsible for his team's **defeat**.
Antonyms: **win, victory**

empire (em-pī-ur) *noun*
▶ page 364

An **empire** is a large group of areas ruled by one person. The Romans had an **empire** that included lands from Europe to Africa.
Related Word: **emperor**

ruler (rü-lur) *noun*
▶ page 365

A **ruler** is a person who runs a country. Elizabeth I is known by many as England's greatest **ruler**.
Related Words: **rule, ruling**

Practice the Words Make an Example Chart for each Key Word. Share your chart with a partner.

Noun	Definition	Example from My Life
capital	The city where a government is located.	Sacramento is the capital of California.

Example Chart

Compare a Topic

How Do Different Authors Treat the Same Topic? When authors write about the same topic, their work may differ based on their <mark>sources</mark> , the information they include, and which facts they emphasize. You can better understand a topic by comparing details in multiple texts and analyzing how writers interpret similar facts and information.

As you read, compare the details each author included about the Aztecs.

Reading Strategies

· Plan
· Monitor
· Visualize
· Determine Importance
· **Ask Questions** Think actively by asking and answering questions about the text.
· Make Connections
· Make Inferences
· Synthesize

Look Into the Text

❝This passage uses sensory details and figurative language to describe the city in detail.❞

"Culture Clash," page 364

In the sunlight, the place seemed to float on a shimmering lake. No wonder. The city stood on an island with long, thin roads that linked it to the shore.

Rising above the skyline was a stone pyramid— twenty stories high. Two temples perched on top of it, one bright red and the other deep blue.

"Mexico City," page 371

The Aztec didn't build an ordinary city, either. They created one that had temples filled with riches. It had a palace with lush gardens, an aquarium, and two zoos. The Aztec called their city Tenochtitlán. It showed the success and power of the Aztec.

❝This passage gives basic facts about the city.❞

Practice Together

Begin a Compare Texts Diagram A Compare Texts Diagram can help you understand how two authors interpret a similar topic. Reread the passages above. Compare the kinds of details each author used to tell about the Aztecs and add to the chart.

"Culture Clash" Includes sensory details about the ancient city.	"Mexico City" Lists places in the city.
Compare Texts	

Compare Texts Diagram

Academic Vocabulary
· **source** (sors) *noun*
  A **source** is something that you get information from.

History Article

A history article is nonfiction that tells about **real people** and real events from the past. History writers often include evidence such as **realia**, maps, and primary source text. Primary sources are actual documents or items that have survived from the past.

Look Into the Text

Meanwhile, the Spanish grabbed as much gold as they could. . . . They melted down the statues . . .

real people

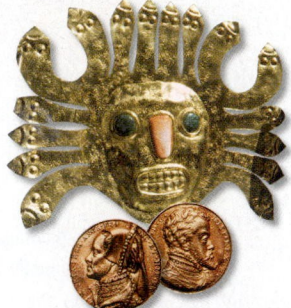

Realia are objects that are real.

▲ The Spaniards melted Aztec treasures to make coins like these.

Asking questions about the meaning and purpose of these items can help readers understand what life was like in the past.

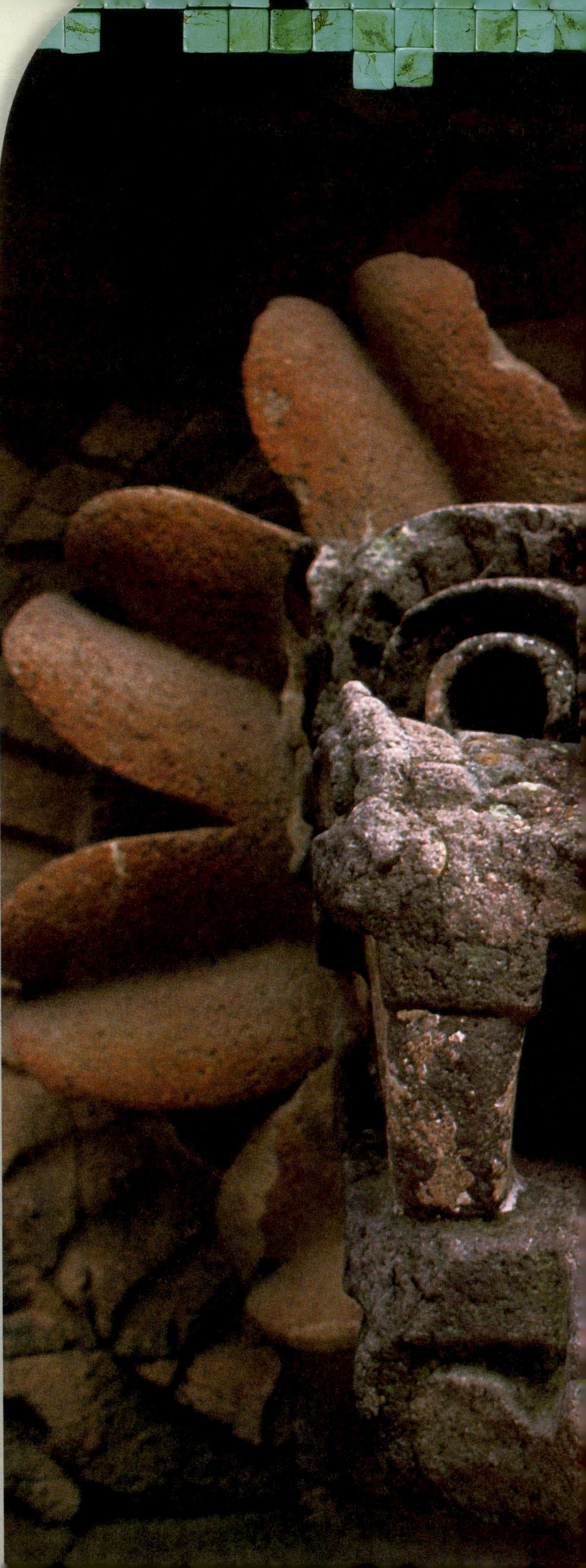

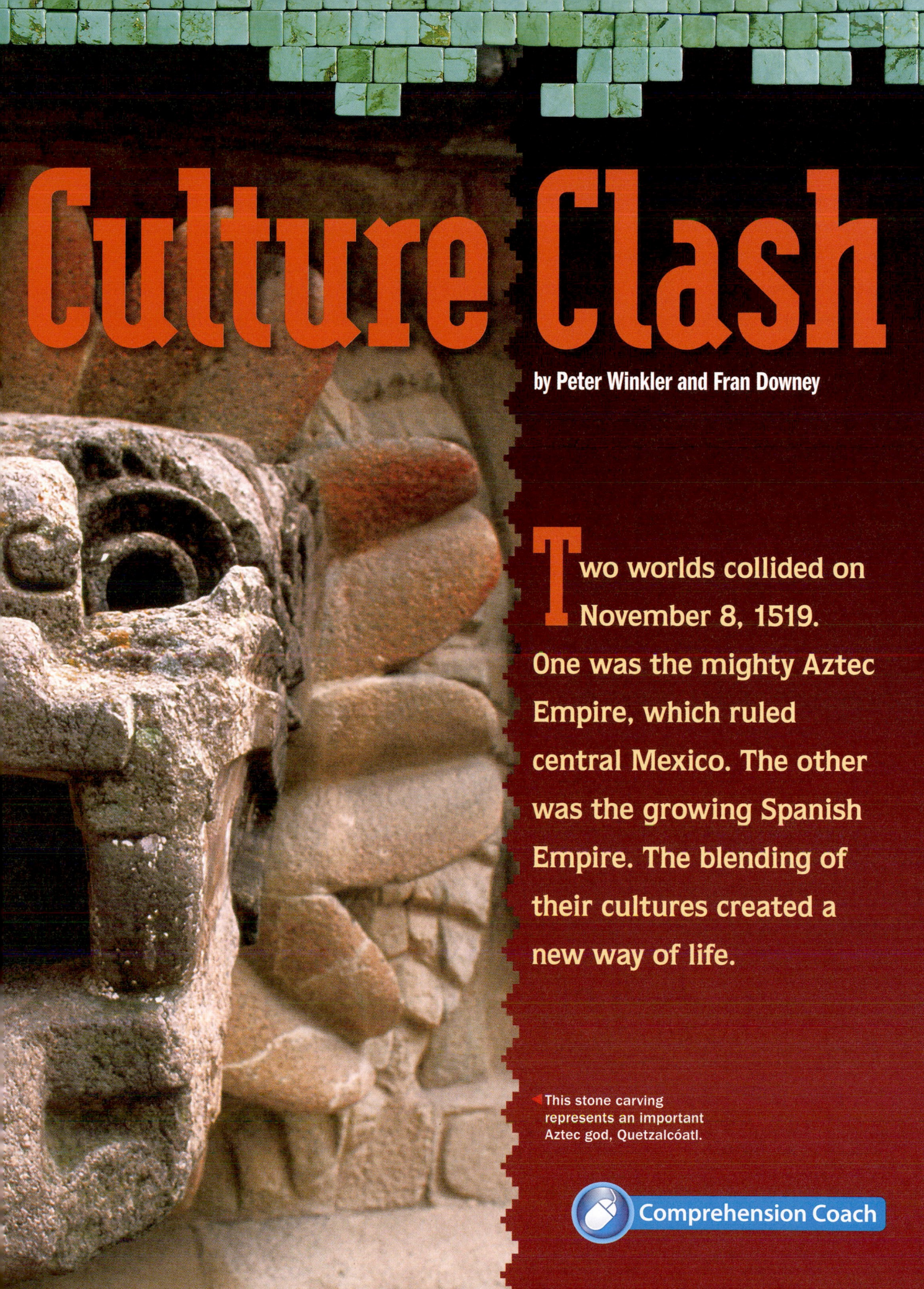

Culture Clash

by Peter Winkler and Fran Downey

Two worlds collided on November 8, 1519. One was the mighty Aztec Empire, which ruled central Mexico. The other was the growing Spanish Empire. The blending of their cultures created a new way of life.

◄ This stone carving represents an important Aztec god, Quetzalcóatl.

Comprehension Coach

"Is This a Dream?"

That's what Spanish explorers wondered as they entered an amazing city. In the sunlight, the place seemed to float on a shimmering lake. **No wonder.** The city stood on an island with long, thin roads that linked it to the shore.

Rising above the skyline was a stone pyramid—twenty stories high. Two temples perched on top of it, one bright red and the other deep blue. Dozens of buildings stood around the pyramid. Circling them were thousands of tidy houses and shops. Roads and **canals tied** everything together.

Awestruck, the Spaniards eyed the city hungrily. They had never seen anything like it.

Proud City, Simple Beginning

What was this **eye-popping** place? Its name was Tenochtitlán and almost 200,000 Aztec lived there. Tenochtitlán, the largest city in the Americas (North, Central, and South America), was the ==capital== of the powerful Aztec ==Empire==. The gleaming city was designed to **impress** visitors, and it did.

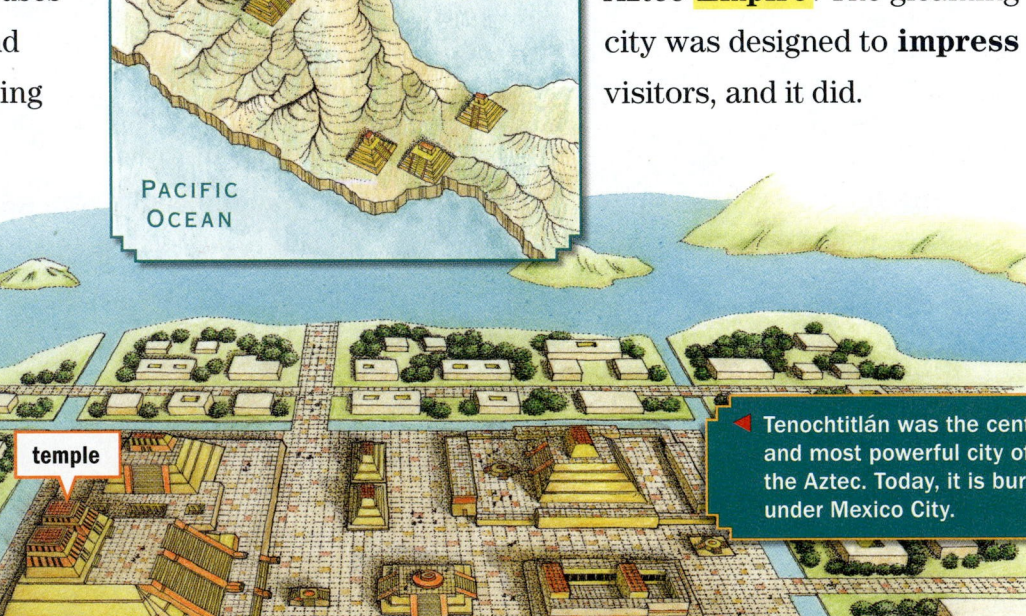

Aztec Empire, 1500

GULF OF MEXICO

PACIFIC OCEAN

Lake Texcoco

temple

pyramid

canal

◀ Tenochtitlán was the central and most powerful city of the Aztec. Today, it is buried under Mexico City.

Looking at Tenochtitlán, you'd never guess that the Aztec were once a small, weak group. Their **ancestors** lived in what is now the southwestern United States. They hunted animals and gathered wild plants. To find food, the group moved from place to place.

Over the years, the Aztec migrated, or moved, south and eventually **wound up** near Lake Texcoco in what is now central Mexico. It seemed like a good place to live, but there was just one problem. People already lived there.

The Unexpected Empire

The people living near Lake Texcoco didn't want to give up their land. They forced the Aztec onto a few small islands. They figured that would keep the newcomers out of the way.

The plan did not quite work the way they thought it would. On the islands, the Aztec learned how to farm. Freed from the need to move around, they began building towns. They built something else, too—a strong army.

Soon the Aztec started to **conquer** their neighbors. By the time the Spaniards arrived in 1519, the Aztec ruled a **wealthy** empire that covered most of central Mexico.

The Aztec were tough **rulers**. They forced the people they had conquered to give them food, gold, and other valuable things. Not surprisingly, many of these people hated the Aztec.

Key Vocabulary
conquer *v.*, to take something, such as land, by force; to win in war
ruler *n.*, a person who has power over a group of people

In Other Words
ancestors relatives from long ago
wound up stopped
wealthy rich

Look Into the Text
1. **Conclusion** Why were the Spanish so surprised when they saw Tenochtitlán?
2. **Paraphrase** In your own words, explain how the Aztec **Empire** became so powerful.

Cortés Arrives

Spanish explorers heard all about the Aztec. The Aztec had just what the Spanish leader, Hernán Cortés, wanted—land and gold.

Cortés wasn't just an explorer. He was a *conquistador. Conquistadors* conquered land for Spain, a country in Europe. Cortés wanted to add Mexico to the Spanish Empire.

He wanted Aztec gold as well. Many Mexicans promised to help Cortés fight the Aztec. So Cortés decided to lead his army into the center of the Aztec Empire.

CORTÉS'S ROUTE TO MEXICO

▲ **Interpret the Map** What bodies of water did Cortés cross to get to Tenochtitlán? What directions did he travel?

Wonder and Welcome

The Spaniards reached the Aztec capital on November 8, 1519. They found themselves facing thousands of curious eyes. The Aztec examined the Spanish explorers closely. To them, the explorers seemed very different.

For example, the strange visitors appeared to be made of glowing metal. That's because sunlight reflected off their **armor**.

The Aztec stared especially hard at the visitors' horses. These animals were new to the Aztec. Some even wondered if horse and rider were a single, giant monster.

Despite their confusion, the Aztec welcomed the Spanish. The Aztec king, Moctezuma, even **swapped** gifts with Cortés. To the Aztec that meant the two men were friends.

What Moctezuma didn't know was that Cortés was **a wolf in sheep's clothing**. He wanted more than gifts.

In Other Words
armor metal suits
swapped traded
a wolf in sheep's clothing not his friend, but his enemy

Historical Background
Conquistadors were Spanish soldiers and explorers. During the 1400s–1500s, they conquered much of the Americas. These areas mostly remained under Spanish control until the 1800s.

Not Good Guests

Just days after arriving in Tenochtitlán, Cortés kidnapped Moctezuma and made him a Spanish prisoner. King Moctezuma still officially ruled Mexico, but he was forced to follow the Spaniards' orders.

Meanwhile, the Spanish grabbed as much gold as they could. They robbed Moctezuma's treasury, and plucked golden statues from temples. They melted down the statues and made gold bars, which were easier to ship home.

Gold Aztec treasure

Spanish coins

▲ The Spaniards melted Aztec treasures to make coins like these.

Montezuma II (1466–1520) watching a comet, 1579. Vellum, Biblioteca Nacional, Madrid, Spain, The Bridgeman Art Library.

DID THE AZTEC KNOW THE SPANISH WERE COMING?

After the fall of the Aztec Empire, a **friar** named Bernardino de Sahagún listened to the Aztec stories. He wrote these stories in a book called *The Florentine Codex*. According to his **account**, the Aztec saw and heard things which they believed were signs that something bad was going to happen.

Bad Luck Signs Before the Spanish Arrived

- A flame went across the sky each night for almost a year. The Aztec feared this flame would hurt the sun, so that it would not rise anymore.
- Lake Texcoco began to boil one afternoon, even though there was no wind or extra heat. Many houses flooded near the lake.
- An unseen wailing woman was heard at night. She warned people that they were all going to die.

Look Into the Text

1. **Sequence** What events followed Cortés's arrival at the Aztec **capital**?
2. **Conclusion and Evidence** The Aztec trusted the Spanish. What evidence supports this?

A Time of Conflict

The Aztec soon grew sick of their guests. **Conflict** between the two groups **erupted into bitter warfare** that lasted two years.

Each side had its strengths. The Aztec hugely outnumbered the Spanish and were fighting on familiar ground. But Cortés's soldiers had steel swords, cannons, and guns—weapons unknown to the Aztec. And they had **an accidental ally**. Soon, the Aztec Empire would be **up for grabs**.

△ **Critical Viewing: Mood** How does this image reflect the mood of the conflict between the Aztec and the Spanish?

Aztec Weaponry

▲ An Aztec shield

▲ A macuahuitl, an Aztec weapon

Key Vocabulary
conflict *n.*, fighting between people or groups of people

In Other Words
erupted into bitter warfare caused a fight
an accidental ally unplanned help
up for grabs available to take

Biological Battle

Without realizing it, the Spaniards brought a germ to Mexico. It caused smallpox, a deadly disease. The germ soon infected the Aztec.

Smallpox hadn't existed in Mexico. That meant the Aztec had no immunity, or resistance, to it. The disease spread quickly through the population, killing tens of thousands of Aztec.

Weakened by illness, the Aztec couldn't **harvest their crops**. So even more people died of hunger. Sick, hungry, and unable to defend themselves, the Aztec finally lost to the Spaniards in 1521.

That **defeat** ended the Aztec Empire, and Mexico became part of New Spain. Yet **the Aztec influence** lived on.

The Mexican Mix

After 1521, Mexico slowly developed a new **culture**. This new culture was neither Aztec nor Spanish. It was both!

For example, most Spanish were Catholic and celebrated the holidays of All Saints' Day and All Souls' Day in November. At about the same time of year, the Aztec performed special **rituals** for their ancestors.

▲ Mexicans celebrating the Day of the Dead today

Before long, a new Mexican holiday formed. It was called *Día de los Muertos*, or Day of the Dead. This holiday honors ancestors and the spirits of loved ones. Today, the Day of the Dead is a national holiday in Mexico.

You can also taste that mixed culture in the food we eat today. A good example is the taco. The shell is made of corn, an Aztec crop. Inside you might find beef and cheese, products that came to the Americas with the Spaniards.

Of course, a taco is just a small example of how cultures can **blend**. Each situation is different. Mexico's culture clash **sparked** warfare. Sometimes, though, cultures meet and mix peacefully. Whatever happens between cultures, the result will be both challenging and interesting. ❖

Key Vocabulary

defeat *n.*, a loss of something to someone else

culture *n.*, the language, art, and beliefs of a group

blend *v.*, to mix

In Other Words

harvest their crops get food

the Aztec influence part of Aztec society

rituals ceremonies

sparked caused

Look Into the Text

1. **Cause and Effect** How did smallpox help cause the Aztec **defeat**?

2. **Conclusion** How was the **blending** of the Aztec and Spanish **cultures** good and bad? Give examples.

CITY PROFILE

Mexico City

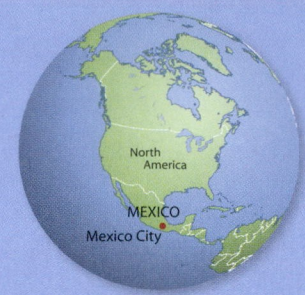

▼ Dancers perform an Aztec ceremony in front of the Basilica of the Virgin of Guadalupe in Mexico City.

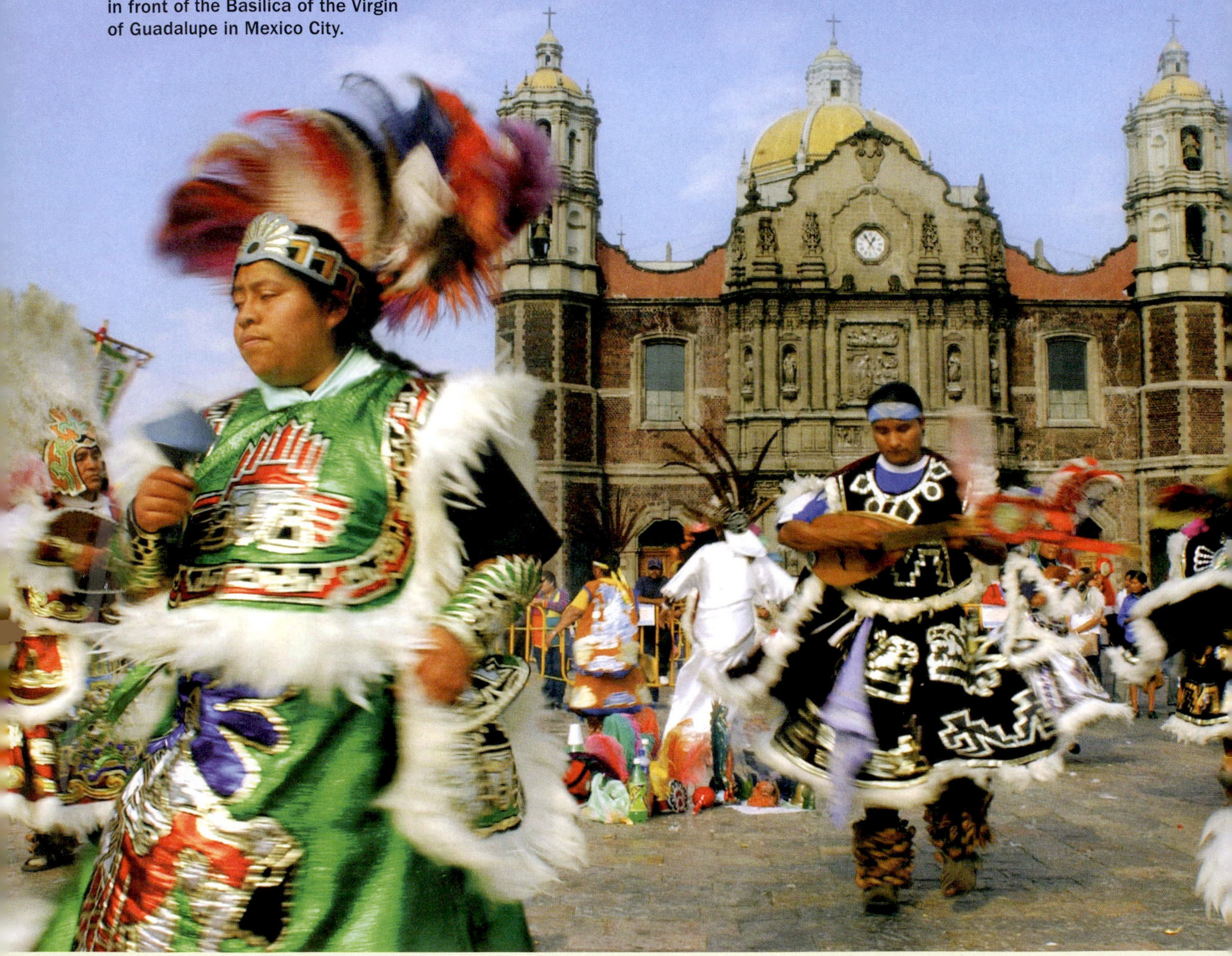

Ancient Beginnings

Mexico City is the capital of Mexico. It is also the oldest city in the Americas. People have lived there nonstop since the time of the Aztec.

The city's long history begins with an Aztec legend. According to the story, a god spoke to the Aztec. He told them to look for an eagle eating a snake on top of a cactus. The Aztec were to build a **sacred** city on the spot where the eagle stood. They did just that.

The Aztec didn't build an ordinary city, either. They created one that had temples filled with riches. It had a palace with lush gardens, an aquarium, and two zoos. The Aztec called their city Tenochtitlán. It showed the success and power of the Aztec.

A Spanish City in Mexico

Today, almost nothing remains of this ancient city. What happened to its pyramids and temples? The *conquistador* Hernán Cortés tore most of them down. In their place, he built a new city. This city reflected his own Spanish culture.

Catholic churches replaced Aztec temples. Spanish-style buildings soon stood where Aztec communities once **thrived**. Many people moved from Spain to this new city, and it soon became one of the most important cities in North America.

A Mix of Past and Present

In 1810, Mexico **declared its independence** from Spain. Mexico soon became its own country with its own flag. The eagle on the flag honors the long history of the Aztec. The flag's colors—green, white, and red—were chosen at independence. So the Mexican flag, like the country's capital, is a mix of old and new.

▲ The Mexican flag shows an eagle eating a snake on top of a cactus.

In Other Words

sacred holy; very important
thrived lived and grew
declared its independence separated

You can see this mix of cultures in Mexico's architecture. Throughout the country, old and modern buildings sit side by side. Some Spanish-style buildings are hundreds of years old. Other buildings and homes were built just a few years ago.

That's the case in an area of Mexico City. It's known as the *Plaza de las Tres Culturas*, or the Plaza of Three Cultures. This area has Aztec **ruins** and a Spanish church from the 1600s. These historical sites are right beside modern office buildings.

Mexico City Today

Today, Mexico City is one of the largest urban areas in the world. The city is full of businesses and cultural centers. Each neighborhood is filled with beautiful parks and gardens. The people who live there are surrounded by reminders of their rich cultural heritage. They continue to grow and build one of the world's greatest cities.

The Plaza of Three Cultures ▶

In Other Words
ruins remains of old buildings

Look Into the Text

1. **Compare and Contrast** How is the city different from when the Spanish **conquered** the Aztec?
2. **Conclusion** Why is there an eagle, a snake, and a cactus on the Mexican flag?
3. **Main Idea and Details** Mexico today is a **blend** of **cultures**. What details support this main idea?

Connect Reading and Writing

Vocabulary

blend

capital

conflict

conquered

cultures

defeat

empire

ruler

CRITICAL THINKING

1. **SUM IT UP** Use your Compare Texts Diagram to summarize to a partner the kinds of information presented in "Culture Clash" and "Mexico City."

"Culture Clash"	"Mexico City"
Includes sensory details about the ancient city.	Lists places in the city.
Compare Texts	

Compare Texts Diagram

2. **Describe** Tell what the Aztec **capital** looked like. Use details from text features in your description.

3. **Evaluate** Revisit your Anticipation Guide. Do you still agree with your opinions about **blending** two **cultures**? Discuss with a partner.

4. **Interpret** The Spanish were able to **conquer** the Aztec. List the reasons for their **defeat** .

READING FLUENCY

Intonation Read the passage on page 651 to a partner. Assess your fluency.

1. My tone never/sometimes/always matched what I read.

2. What I did best in my reading was _____ .

READING STRATEGY

> What strategy helped you understand this selection? Tell a partner about it.

VOCABULARY REVIEW

Oral Review Read the paragraph aloud. Add the vocabulary words.

> I want to write stories about the great _____ of the world. I also want to write about famous people, like Moctezuma, the Aztec _____ . His people built a really cool city. It was the _____ of the Aztec _____ . When the Spanish explorers came, there was _____ for many years. The Spanish _____ the Aztec with their powerful weapons. Disease also caused the Aztec's _____ . Today, Mexico is a _____ of Aztec and Spanish heritage.

Written Review Imagine you are the Aztec **ruler** and have been **conquered** in a great **conflict** . Write a short speech to tell about it. Use five vocabulary words.

WRITE ABOUT THE GUIDING QUESTION

Explore the Aztec-Spanish Conflict
What might the Aztec people have done differently to prevent **conflict** with the Spanish when they met? Reread the selection to find examples to support your judgment.

Connect Across the Curriculum

Understand Idioms

> **Academic Vocabulary**
> • **image** (im-ij) *noun*
>   An **image** is a picture of something.

An **idiom** is a group of words that, when used together, has a different meaning than each of the individual words.

Visualize Idioms Creating a mental **image** of the idiom can help you understand what it means and apply it to a situation. For example, when you tie two pieces of string, you connect them. By visualizing how roads connect neighborhoods, you can understand the meaning of *tie together*.

▲ Roads tie a city together.

Analyze Idioms With a partner, discuss each underlined idiom.
1. What was this <u>eye-popping</u> place?
2. So Cortés decided to lead his army into <u>the heart of</u> the Aztec Empire.
3. Your culture <u>shapes your life</u>.

Compare Fiction and Nonfiction

Both writers of fiction and nonfiction may choose similar topics for their work. By comparing a fictional account of an event with a factual account, you can see how a fictional author uses this information. You can also determine if an author has altered the facts to tell a story.

Compare how gift giving is described in each of these passages.

> Our chief gave the strangers balls of cotton thread to bind them to us in friendship. He gave them spears that they might fish and not starve. He gave them gum-rubber balls for sport.

> Despite their confusion, the Aztec welcomed the Spanish. The Aztec king, Moctezuma, even swapped gifts with Cortes.

Analyze and Compare Find other places the author of "Encounter" used or altered history in the story. Analyze the examples and compare them to details in "Culture Clash."

Make Comparisons

Role-Play With a partner, act out a news interview with Moctezuma or Cortés. Ask questions as a reporter for your partner to answer. Compare each man's life before and after the *conquistadors* arrived. Use past tense verbs. Trade roles.

> Moctezuma, is it true that you have a lot of gold?

> No, I don't have much gold now, but I had a lot before Cortés arrived!

Write About Past Events

Study the Models When you write about events that happened in the past, you need to be consistent about when the events took place. Be sure to choose words that tell about the past.

NOT OK

> Long ago, the Aztec had a lot of land and gold. Moctezuma **is** the Aztec King. Then Cortés and the other Spanish explorers **arrived**. They **have** horses and guns. The Spanish invaders wanted the Aztec land and gold. The two cultures **collide** and the Spanish eventually **defeat** the Aztec.

This writer confuses the reader by switching between the past and the present.

OK

> Long ago, the Aztec had a lot of land and gold. Moctezuma **was** the Aztec King. Then Cortés and the other Spanish explorers **arrived**. They **had** horses and guns. The Spanish invaders wanted the Aztec land and gold. The two cultures **collided** and the Spanish eventually **defeated** the Aztec.

This writer talks about the past in a consistent way.

Add Sentences Think of two sentences to add to the OK model above. Be consistent when you write about the past.

WRITE ON YOUR OWN Think about an event that happened in your town. Write about how the event changed the town or people's lives. Tell what life was like before and after the event. Use past tense words.

	Forms of *be*			Forms of *have*		
Present Tense	I **am**	he, she, it **is**	we, you, they **are**	I, you, we, they **have**	he, she, or it **has**	
Past Tense	I **was**	he, she, it **was**	we, you, they **were**	I, you, we, they **had**	he, she, or it **had**	

REMEMBER

- If a verb ends in silent **e**, drop the **e**, then add **-ed**. **save + -ed = saved**
- If a one-syllable verb ends in one vowel and one consonant, double the consonant. Then add **-ed**. **step + p + -ed = stepped**
- If a verb ends in a consonant plus **y**, change the **y** to **i**. Then add **-ed**. **try + -ed = tried**

When Cultures Meet

by Ann Rossi

Build Background

Connect

KWL Chart Create a KWL Chart for what you know about the early European settlers in America. List what you already know and what you want to know. Later, you will list what you learn from the selection.

WHAT I KNOW	WHAT I WANT TO KNOW	WHAT I LEARNED
People came from Spain and England.	Why did they come?	

KWL Chart

Discover the Past

Christopher Columbus thought he had discovered a new world in 1492. Find out which other cultures had existed there for thousands of years.

Digital Library   **myNGconnect.com**
🔄 View the video.

▲ Columbus landing on the island of Guanahani, West Indies

Language & Grammar

Summarize

CD

Look at the illustration, and listen to the speech.
Then listen to a summary of the speech.

SUMMARY

An Explorer's Point of View

▲ Illustration of Native Americans greeting French explorers.

SUMMARY

The speaker described his recent experience in the New World to some of his countrymen and women. He proudly claimed new land for his country. He realized that there were people already there, and he felt he made friends with them. The native people showed the explorers how to grow new crops. Unfortunately, the explorers brought illness to these people that killed many of them. Also, the explorers took some of the natives' land, but the speaker felt that there was lots of land to share. He planned to return to this new land with his family.

Use Verbs in the Past Tense

A past tense **verb** shows an action that already happened. For most verbs, add **-ed** to show past tense.

> EXAMPLE   I **traveled** to the fishing village yesterday.

Use special past tense forms with **irregular verbs**.

In the Present: I **find** good places to fish.

In the Past: I **found** the best place yesterday.

Some Irregular Verbs

Present	Past	Example in the Past
bring	brought	We **brought** gifts to them.
eat	ate	We **ate** dinner together.
go, goes	went	Then we **went** to sleep.
know	knew	The strangers **knew** where we wanted to go.
make	made	One of the men **made** a map for us to follow.
meet	met	We **met** some villagers by the big river.
see	saw	We **saw** their canoes on the shore.
take	took	The villagers **took** us to their village.

Practice Together

Say each sentence. Then say it again, and change the <u>verb</u> to the past tense.

1. I <u>see</u> someone in a canoe.
2. I <u>ask</u> for a ride.
3. The man <u>takes</u> me to his village.
4. I <u>make</u> a new friend.

Try It!

Say each sentence. Write the past tense of the <u>verb</u> on a card. Then say the sentence, and add the past tense verb.

5. The next day, we <u>go</u> to fish in the river.
6. I <u>find</u> the perfect place to fish.
7. We <u>bring</u> the fish back to the village.
8. The villagers <u>cook</u> corn bread to share with us.

▲ **We rented canoes on our vacation.**

Explore Different Points of View

SUMMARIZE

Imagine you are a guest at the dinner where the explorer that you learned about on page 377 spoke. You just listened to the explorer give his speech about the New World. What do you think of his speech? Do you agree with his point of view?

Share your point of view about the explorer's speech with a partner. Take notes as you listen to your partner give his or her point of view.

Next, summarize your partner's point of view. Decide on the most important information to include in your summary. Leave out unnecessary details. Your summary should be shorter than the original telling.

HOW TO SUMMARIZE

1. Identify the main ideas and the most important details.
2. Tell the facts in just a few sentences. A summary is always shorter than the original text.
3. Use your own words to summarize the information.

> My Partner's Point of View: She thinks it was wrong to take the native people's land, even in the name of "progress." It was also wrong to bring new illnesses, even if the explorers didn't know they had sick people in their group.

> Summary of My Partner's Point of View: The explorers made many mistakes when they came to the New World.

USE PRESENT AND PAST TENSE VERBS

When you summarize, you might tell about events that happened in the past. If so, you need to use verbs in the **past tense**. Or you may need to tell about something that is true in the present. If so, use verbs in the **present tense**.

In the Past: The natives **shared** their land and food with the explorers. But soon more people **arrived**. They **brought** gifts and diseases with them.

In the Present: The explorers **think** the native people **are** happy to be part of the changes and progress in the world.

Prepare to Read

Learn Key Vocabulary

Study the Words Use the steps below.

1. Pronounce the word. Say it aloud several times. Spell it.
2. Rate your word knowledge.
3. Study the example. Tell more about the word.
4. Practice it. Make the word your own.

Key Words

contact (**kahn**-takt) *noun*
▶ page 384

Contact is the act of meeting or communicating. Friends stay in **contact** over the phone.

crop (**krop**) *noun*
▶ page 387

A **crop** is a type of plant grown in large amounts to eat or use. The farmer has a good **crop** of corn this year.

forever (for-**e**-vur) *adverb*
▶ page 390

Forever means for a time without end. This road looks like it goes on **forever**.
Related Words: **ever, never**

route (rowt) *noun*
▶ page 384

A **route** is a path that leads somewhere. The bridge is the quickest **route** to the other side of the river.

settler (set-lur) *noun*
▶ page 386

Settlers are people who move to a new area to live. American **settlers** worked hard to survive in their new homes.
Related Words: **settle, settling**

spread (spred) *verb*
▶ page 386

When something **spreads**, it moves across a larger area. Milk **spreads** all over the floor when spilled.

starve (starv) *verb*
▶ page 386

To **starve** means to not have enough food to live. If you do not eat for a long time, you will **starve**.

tool (tül) *noun*
▶ page 384

A **tool** is something that makes work easier. A saw is a **tool** used to cut wood.

Practice the Words Make an Idea Web for each Key Word. Write the word in the center of the web. Write four things the word makes you think of in the circles. Share your webs with a partner.

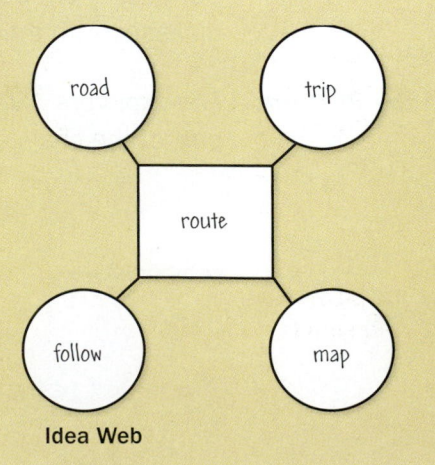

road

trip

route

follow

map

Idea Web

Analyze Text Features

How Do Text Features Add Meaning? The visuals that appear in fiction or nonfiction texts can be just as important as the words. Illustrations, photographs, diagrams, graphs, and maps are all visual <mark>features</mark> that support or add meaning to a text. These visuals can clarify details in the text that are difficult to describe or understand. They can also provide new information about the topic or answer questions that readers may have as they read.

As you read, use the <mark>features</mark> to further your understanding of the text.

Reading Strategies

- Plan
- Monitor
- Visualize
- Determine Importance
- **Ask Questions** Think actively by asking and answering questions about the text.
- Make Connections
- Make Inferences
- Synthesize

Look Into the Text

Native Americans had been living in the lands Europeans thought were "new" for more than 10,000 years. By the time the Europeans arrived in the late 1400s , there were already many Native American cultures in the Americas.

These cultures spoke different languages and lived in different ways. Some Native Americans lived in large cities. Others were farmers who lived in small villages. Still others were hunters and gatherers. They moved when they needed more food.

Interpret the Map According to the map, what did Columbus find in the New World?

Practice Together

Begin a Comparison Chart A Comparison Chart will help you organize and compare information. Reread the passage above and study the map. Use the Comparison Chart to compare and contrast information found in the text with that found in the map. Continue to add information to the Comparison Chart as you read the selection.

Text	Both	Text Features
page 384 Each culture had its own language and way of life.	There were many different Native American cultures in the Americas.	page 385

Comparison Chart

Academic Vocabulary

- **feature** (fē-chur) *noun*
  A **feature** is a part of something that stands out or is noticeable.

History Textbook

You use a history textbook in your history or social science class. It teaches **facts** about historical events and people from the past.

Most history textbooks have text features such as **historical photographs,** maps, and charts. Many also include primary sources, first-hand accounts of events told by the people who were really there.

historical photograph

facts

▲ This historical photograph shows a Lakota Native American camp in South Dakota, around 1890. As more people traveled westward through Native American land, contact between Native Americans and settlers became more unfriendly.

As you read, ask questions about the information in the text features. Understanding how these features support and add to the written text will help you better understand the selection.

► This historical photograph shows a Lakota Native American camp in South Dakota, around 1890. As more people traveled westward through Native American land, contact between Native Americans and settlers became more unfriendly.

When Cultures Meet

by Ann Rossi

Seeds of Change

Nearly 500 years ago, Christopher Columbus sailed from Spain in search of a trade **route** to the riches of Asia. He landed instead **in the Americas**. European explorers who followed thought that they had discovered a new world, but what they had really discovered was a world that was new to *them*.

Native Americans had been living in the lands Europeans thought were "new" for more than 10,000 years. By the time the Europeans arrived in the late 1400s, there were already many Native American cultures in the Americas. These cultures spoke different languages and lived in different ways. Some Native Americans lived in large cities. Others were farmers who lived in small villages. Still others were hunters and gatherers. They moved when they needed more food. Many of the **tools** and **resources** the explorers brought with them from Europe were **unfamiliar** to Native Americans. Likewise, many Native American resources and tools were new to Europeans. **Contact** between these two cultures would change life in the Americas.

Untitled, Date Unknown, Artist Unknown. Hand-colored woodcut. North Wind Picture Archives.

▲ Columbus and his ships along the northern shore of Cuba

Key Vocabulary
route *n.*, a course or path used for travel
tool *n.*, an item used to make or fix something
contact *n.*, the act of meeting

In Other Words
in the Americas on the American continent
resources items that made life easier
unfamiliar new and different

Native American
Cultural Regions
North America, 1500

⚠ **Interpret the Map** According to the map, what did Columbus find in the New World?

Historical Background
The 1500s–1700s are often called the "Age of Discovery." European explorers traveled in search of new items to trade, such as spices, silver, and gold.

Look Into the Text

1. **Paraphrase** Tell in your own words what Columbus found instead of a trade **route** to Asia.
2. **Compare and Contrast** Explain the differences among some of the Native American cultures.

Breaking Bread

In spite of the conflicts between Native Americans and Europeans, the two cultures learned many things from one another. They learned about new foods. Europeans brought seeds for many of their favorite foods to the Americas, but many **settlers** could not wait for the seeds to grow. They had to eat new foods or they would **starve** to death. The Native Americans introduced the settlers to many new foods.

One of these foods was corn, or maize. In fact, it was the most important food grown by Native Americans. Scientists think corn was first grown in South and Central America. It **spread** through other parts of North and South America.

Corn could be eaten, boiled, or roasted on the cob. It could be dried and ground into cornmeal. Like we do today, Native Americans even made popcorn!

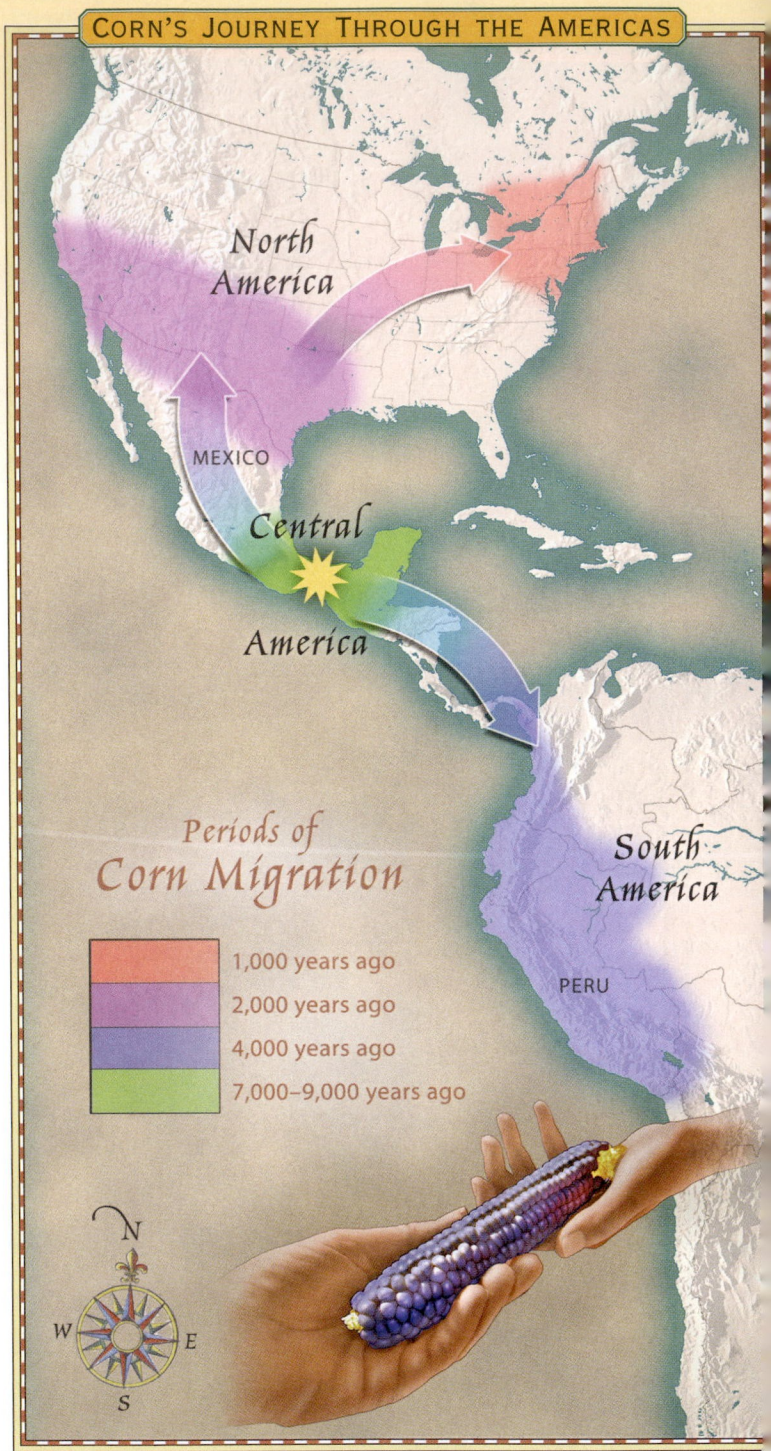

CORN'S JOURNEY THROUGH THE AMERICAS

North America

MEXICO

Central America

South America

PERU

Periods of Corn Migration

1,000 years ago
2,000 years ago
4,000 years ago
7,000–9,000 years ago

▶ **Analyze the Map** Describe corn's journey through the Americas. What may have caused corn's spread to the eastern part of North America?

FOODS GROWN IN NORTH AMERICA

Corn

Beans

Pumpkins

Potatoes

Tomatoes

Corn also became one of the most important **crops** grown by the European settlers. Native Americans in the Northeast taught the settlers how to plant corn. They used a system called hilling. They formed small hills of dirt in rows, and then they planted a corn **kernel** in each hill. Planting corn this way was much better than the European way. Europeans threw seeds onto the ground. Birds and other animals saw the seeds and quickly ate them. By covering seeds with dirt, crops had a better chance to grow.

Many Native Americans planted squash, beans, and corn together. They called the plants the Three Sisters. Planting the crops together took up less space in a garden, and the plants helped each other grow better. Beans **twisted up** the cornstalks. The squash **choked** weeds and kept the soil moist.

Look Into the Text

1. **Paraphrase** Tell in your own words why hilling was a good way to plant corn.
2. **Main Idea and Details** What three **crops** were known as the Three Sisters? How did they get this name?

Running Wild

Native Animals

Europeans saw some animals they did not recognize when they reached North America. These animals included wild turkeys and buffalo. Wild turkeys lived in most of America. Early Spanish explorers had brought some turkeys back to Spain. People liked the tasty birds. Soon, turkeys became a popular food throughout much of Europe.

The American elk, a type of deer, **roamed** much of the United States and southern Canada. Native Americans hunted them. Soon, Europeans began hunting elk, too. They hunted thousands of elk. After a time, elk could only be found west of the Rocky Mountains.

About 50 million buffalo once roamed the North American Plains. The Plains Indians used the buffalo for food, clothing, shelter, tools, fuel, and medicine. European settlers hunted the buffalo, too. Often they hunted **for sport** or they took the skins and left the meat to **rot** in the sun. Settlers killed millions of buffalo. By 1889, there were only about 1,000 buffalo in the United States. Soon, the Plains Indians had to change their way of life because too few buffalo remained to support them.

WILD ANIMALS FOUND IN NORTH AMERICA

	ELK	BUFFALO	WILD TURKEY
Native American Uses	• used large antlers to make farming tools • used skins for clothing • used meat for food	• used meat for food • used skins to make shelter, such as teepees, bedding, and clothing • used bones and horns as tools	• used feathers for ceremonial clothing • used meat for food • helped keep insects and small animals from eating crops
European Settler Uses	• hunted for sport • used meat for food	• hunted for sport • used meat for food	• used meat for food • sold in markets for money

In Other Words

roamed lived and moved around in
for sport for fun
rot go bad; spoil

Science Background

The American buffalo is also known as the bison. These huge animals usually live in groups called "herds" for protection. For this reason, the buffalo have few enemies besides humans. Thanks to people who wanted to save the buffalo, there are about 200,000 of them in the U.S. today.

ANIMALS BROUGHT BY EUROPEANS

	GOAT	COW	SHEEP	PIG
Native American Uses	• used wool to make blankets	• raised to trade with Europeans	• used wool to make blankets	• raised to trade with Europeans
European Settler Uses	• used meat and milk for food	• used as work animals on farms • used milk for food	• used meat for food • used wool and skins for clothing	• used meat for food

Nonnative Animals

Europeans brought different kinds of animals to the Americas, including pigs, cattle, goats, and sheep.

Pigs became a good food for Native Americans, as well as settlers. However, pigs destroyed many plants and animals that were native to the Americas. Pigs **trampled** grasses. And **how they ate**! They dug roots and vegetables out of the ground. They **gobbled up** baby birds, eggs, fruits, and vegetables. They even ate shellfish!

Nothing seemed to stop them. If the sun was too hot, the pigs crawled under bushes or into holes. One Spanish explorer reported that in sixteen years his herd of pigs had increased from 24 to 30,000! Pigs were soon running wild.

In 1598, Spanish settlers came to New Mexico along with their herds of cattle, sheep, and goats. These settlers forced the Pueblo Indians to work for them. The work included taking care of the animals.

In Other Words
trampled stepped on and killed
how they ate they ate so much
gobbled up ate

Look Into the Text

1. **Cause and Effect** What caused the buffalo population to shrink? How did this affect Native Americans?
2. **Paraphrase** In your own words, tell how pigs caused problems for Native Americans and **settlers**.

Raising Animals

The Spanish taught the Pueblo how to raise animals. The Pueblo passed these valuable skills on to many Navajo. Sheep, goats, and cattle became a new part of the Native American diet. Goats produced milk to be made into cheese and butter.

The Pueblo and Navajo also used the wool from sheep. They spun the wool and **dyed** it with plants. Then they wove it into clothing and blankets. Raising animals and weaving became important work for many Native Americans.

Sheep and goats **were especially suited to the climate** of the Southwest. They could eat the dry, tough plants that grew there. Cattle did well in the **rich pastures** of the grasslands.

One animal, however, would change **forever** how the Native Americans lived. It was the horse.

▲ A Navajo woman in the American Southwest cuts wool from sheep. Sheep are still an important part of Navajo life.

In Other Words
dyed colored
were especially suited to the climate did well in the weather
rich pastures green fields

Cultural Background
The Navajo learned how to dye wool from the Pueblo. They weaved wool into rugs using roots, herbs, and soil. Navajo blankets and rugs were made of solid, dark colors until they began to weave brighter Spanish threads into their designs.

Hold Your Horses

Some Native Americans living in the Southeast first saw horses when Spanish explorers came to Florida and the Carolinas in the 1500s. Most Native Americans in North America, however, did not see a horse until 1598. That was the year a band of Spanish settlers arrived in New Mexico. Among the animals they brought to New Mexico were horses.

Some Native Americans called the horse "big dog." Others called it "sky dog." They thought it was a **monster**. Still others called the horse "elk dog" because it was the same size as an elk. This confusing animal changed the way of life for many Native Americans. It changed the way they traveled, hunted, and fought.

Over time, the Native Americans watched how the Spaniards treated their animals. They learned how to care for the horses. They also learned how to ride. The Spaniards had **bridles and saddles** for their horses, but many Native Americans learned to ride without either. They soon became

Hernando de Soto at the Mississippi River, 1920, E. Boyd Smith. © Corbis.

▲ Native Americans had never seen an animal like the horse.

skilled riders. Warriors rode their horses in battle. They could hide themselves by slipping to one side of the animal. That way, the horse was similar to a galloping shield!

In 1680, the Pueblo **revolted** against the settlers in New Mexico. Many of the settlers fled. They left their animals behind. Native Americans kept some horses. Other horses ran wild. They formed herds that spread north into the Plains. Soon, other Native Americans would be riding, too.

In Other Words

monster scary animal
bridles and saddles riding equipment
revolted fought back

Look Into the Text

1. **Conclusion and Evidence** Raising animals was a useful skill to the Pueblo. How do you know?
2. **Paraphrase** In your own words, describe how horses **spread** across the Plains.
3. **Metaphor** How were horses "galloping shields" to Native Americans?

The Navajo and the Horse

Before the Navajo had horses, they traveled, fought, and hunted **on foot**. Once they had horses, they could do all these things on horseback. It became important for men and boys, who did the hunting, to ride well.

Horses could travel faster and farther than people. Now, the Navajo could go farther to trade because their horses could carry heavy bundles of goods. It became important to have many horses. More horses could carry more goods.

With horses, the Navajo had more choices about where to live. They could live farther away from water and their farms. Their horses could carry heavy water bags to their homes.

Horses also changed the way Navajo warriors fought. On horseback, the Navajo could **strike swiftly** and leave quickly. Thanks to the horse, few Spanish settlers wanted to live on Navajo land.

▼ Navajo Native Americans riding horses, about 1905

In Other Words
on foot by walking or running
strike swiftly attack quickly

The Plains Indians and the Horse

The horse also changed the Plains Indians' way of life. Before they had horses, many Plains Indian families lived in villages along rivers. Their houses were **earth lodges**. In the summer, the men lived on the Plains to hunt buffalo. Their summer homes were teepees made of animal skins.

Hunting buffalo on foot was hard and dangerous work. Sometimes, hunters covered themselves with animal skins. Slowly, they crept up to the grazing buffalo. Then they **hurled their spears**. Others forced buffalo off a cliff, so they would be easier to kill. A third way to hunt buffalo was to light a circle of fire around a grazing herd. The animals would trample each other, or they might **suffocate** from the smoke. This approach was dangerous because a hunter could be injured by the hooves or horns of **stampeding** buffalo.

By the end of the 1600s, horses were living on the northern Plains.

▲ A herd of stampeding buffalo

In Other Words

earth lodges homes made of dirt
hurled their spears threw their
weapons
suffocate choke and die
stampeding running

Look Into the Text

1. **Explain** Explain why few Spanish settlers lived on Navajo land.
2. **Main Idea and Details** Horses changed how the Plains Indians lived. List three details that support this idea.

Native Americans of the eastern Plains still lived in earth lodges. The horse made it easy for the Plains hunters to reach the buffalo herds quickly. Their horses could pull dead buffalo back to the village.

Groups living on the western Plains no longer lived in earth lodges. These Native Americans became year-round buffalo hunters. Large teepees became their homes. Horses pulled the teepees from camp to camp.

Now that buffalo were so much easier to hunt, buffalo skins became the main material for clothing. Buffalo **hides** were also used for bedding and teepees. Buffalo meat became the main food. Native Americans dried buffalo meat in the sun to **preserve it**. It tasted good and lasted a long time. They made tools from the horns and bones.

They used dried buffalo manure, called buffalo chips, as fuel.

▲ A Native American camp, early 1900s. Many groups moved frequently because camps could be moved more easily with the help of horses.

In Other Words
hides skins
preserve it make it last longer;
   stop it from spoiling

With a horse, hunting took much less time. As a result, Plains Indians had more time to do other things. Women spent more time sewing costumes for **ceremonial** dances. Some men spent time **raiding** other groups for horses and supplies. They also protected their families and homes from attacks by settlers or other Native Americans.

Some groups were pushed farther west as settlers took their land. As one group moved, it pushed other groups off their hunting grounds. Many of these **relocated** groups, such as the Sioux and Comanche, began to use the horse.

Some Native Americans continued to farm. Often, they were attacked by warring, horse-riding Native Americans who stole their crops. Soon, even some farming groups, such as the Cheyenne, **adopted** the horse.

The horse brought other changes, too. It made trade easier. Horses could carry heavy loads and travel long distances. Native American groups who had never before met were now trading.

The horse, brought to the New World by the Europeans, became a major part of Native American life and legends. It changed the way Native Americans lived forever. ❖

▲ A Plains Indian (Assiniboine) warrior's shirt made from buffalo hide and beads. Warriors believed the beadwork gave them special powers.

In Other Words
ceremonial special
raiding attacking
relocated moved
adopted started using

Look Into the Text

1. **Cause and Effect** How did the horse make **contact** easier between groups of Native Americans?

2. **Opinion** Was the horse helpful or harmful to Native Americans? Why?

Old World New World

by John Agard

Spices and gold once cast a spell
on bearded men in caravels.

New World New World cried history
Old World Old World sighed every tree.

5   But Indian tribes long long ago
had sailed this archipelago.

They who were used to flutes of bone
translated talk of wind on stone.

Yet their feathered tongues were drowned
10 when Discovery beat its drum.

New World New World—spices and gold
Old World Old World—the legends told.

New World New World—cried history
Old World Old World—sighed every tree.

Vasco Nuzez de Balboa Discovering the Pacific Ocean, 1931, J. L. Kraemer

▲ **Critical Viewing: Theme** Balboa "discovered" the Pacific Ocean in 1513. How would the local Native Americans have viewed this "discovery"?

In Other Words
caravels Spanish ships
archipelago group of islands

Look Into the Text

1. **Context Clues** Who lives in the "New World"? Who lives in the "Old World"?

2. **Figurative Language** Why does history cry, "New World"? Why do the trees sigh for the "Old World"?

Connect Reading and Writing

Vocabulary
contact
crops
forever
route
settlers
spread
starve
tools

CRITICAL THINKING

1. **SUM IT UP** Use your Comparison Chart to summarize what you learned from both the text and text features of "When Cultures Meet."

Text	Both	Text Features
page 384 Each culture had its own language and way of life.	There were many different Native American cultures in the Americas.	page 385

Comparison Chart

2. **Compare** Both "When Cultures Meet" and "Old World New World" are about **settlers** in the New World. How does each selection suggest that life changed in the Americas **forever**?

3. **Explain** Revisit the KWL Chart you made on page 376. In the L column, write what you learned from the selection.

4. **Make Judgments** Do you think **contact** between Europeans and Native Americans was positive or negative? Explain.

READING FLUENCY

Phrasing Read the passage on page 652 to a partner. Assess your fluency.

1. I did not pause/sometimes paused/ always paused for punctuation.

2. What I did best in my reading was _____.

READING STRATEGY

What strategy helped you understand this selection? Tell a partner about it.

VOCABULARY REVIEW

Oral Review Read the paragraph aloud. Add the vocabulary words.

On our field trip, we walked down a very old path. It was a _____ used by early _____ to travel back and forth to their fields. They grew _____ of corn and beans so that they would have food and would not _____. It wasn't easy to grow them. They did not have machines or modern _____ to help them. They had to _____ seeds by hand. Sometimes, they came in _____ with birds that ate the seeds. It must have taken _____ to plant an entire field!

Written Review Imagine you are a Native American living one hundred years ago and European **settlers** have come to live near you. Write a journal entry about the encounter. Use four vocabulary words.

 **WRITE ABOUT THE** GUIDING QUESTION

Explore the New World
What would the world be like if Columbus had taken a different **route**? Write your opinion. Use examples to support your ideas.

Connect Across the Curriculum

Analyze Idioms

> **Academic Vocabulary**
> • **context** (kon-tekst) *noun, adjective*
>   1. **Context** is the surrounding text near a word or phrase that helps explain its meaning.
>   2. A **context** clue helps you figure out a word's meaning.

An **idiom** is a group of words that, when used together, has a different connotation or suggested meaning than the individual words.

> EXAMPLE   The Europeans were all ears. They listened carefully to learn everything they could from Native Americans.

Use Clues to Interpret Idioms You can often use the **context** as clues to figure out idioms. In the example above, *listened carefully* is a clue. After you use the **context** to guess the meaning, try it in the sentence.

Identify Idioms The heading "Seeds of Change" on p. 384 is an idiom. The **context** in this section is about the changes happening at the time. The changes were like seeds because they grew into bigger changes.

Analyze Idioms Analyze the meaning of the idioms "cross paths" (p. 329), "a force of change" (page 332), "calm the butterflies" (page 333), and "swept into the crowd" (page 333).

Analyze Personification

> **Academic Vocabulary**
> • **analyze** (a-nu-līz) *verb*
>   When you **analyze** something, you study it closely.

What Is Personification? When writers use **personification**, they give human qualities to nonhuman things. They make word choices to create a specific tone or add meaning to the text. Look at the personification in the lines below. How does the author's word choice add to the meaning of "Old World New World" on page 396?

> New World New World—cried history
> Old World Old World—sighed every tree.

Analyze Personification With a partner, find other examples of personification in "Old World New World."

Summarize

Pair Share With a partner, summarize how lives of the Plains Indians changed after horses came. Use past tense verbs. Share your summary with the class.

> Before they had horses, the Plains Indians hunted on foot.

> Horses made travel and hunting much easier.

Writing and Grammar

Write About Past Events

Study the Models When you write about past events, use words that clearly tell about the past. Avoid confusing your reader by changing back and forth between the past and the present.

NOT OK

> Settlers brought farm animals from Europe. Native Americans <u>show</u> the settlers how to grow corn. Soon settlers <u>eat</u> a lot of corn. It was a very important crop. Some settlers <u>take</u> corn back to Europe with them.

The reader thinks: "I'm not sure when this happened."

OK

> Settlers brought farm animals from Europe. Native Americans <u>showed</u> the settlers how to grow corn. Soon settlers <u>ate</u> a lot of corn. It was a very important crop. Some settlers <u>took</u> corn back to Europe with them.

This writer is clearly talking about the past.

Add Sentences Think of two sentences to add to the OK model above. Be consistent when you write about the past.

WRITE ON YOUR OWN Think about an event that happened in your community. What were the most important details? Write a summary of the event. Be consistent in telling about the past.

Spelling Rules

Sometimes you need to change the spelling of a verb before you add **-ed**.

- If a verb ends in silent **e**, drop the **e** before you add **-ed**.
  live + -ed = lived
  EXAMPLE   Long ago, Grandpa **lived** in another country.

- If a one-syllable verb ends in one vowel and one consonant, double the consonant before you add **-ed**.
  stop + p + -ed = stopped
  EXAMPLE   On our last vacation, we **stopped** by his old house.

- If a verb ends in **y**, change the **y** to **i** before you add **-ed**.
  try + -ed = tried
  EXAMPLE   We **tried** to understand what his life was like there.

REMEMBER

- Use past tense verbs to tell about events that already happened.
- Many past tense verbs end in **-ed**.
  learn**ed**   walk**ed**
- Many past tense verbs are irregular.
  ate   **took**

FROM

The Log of Christopher Columbus--•

BY CHRISTOPHER COLUMBUS

translated by Robert Fuson

Saturday, 13 October 1492

1 After sunrise people from San Salvador again began to come to our ships in boats fashioned in one piece from the trunks of trees. These boats are wonderfully made, considering the country we are in, and every bit as fine as those I have seen in Guinea. They come in all sizes. Some can carry 40 or 50 men; some are so small that only one man rides in it. The men move very swiftly over the water, rowing with a blade that looks like a **baker's peel**. They do not use **oarlocks**, but dip the peel in the water and push themselves forward. If a boat capsizes they all begin to swim, and they rock the boat until about half of the water is splashed out. Then they bail out the rest of the water with gourds that they carry for that purpose.

2 The people brought more balls of spun cotton, spears, and parrots. Other than the parrots, I have seen no beast of any kind on this island.

3 I have been very attentive and have tried very hard to find out if there is any gold here.

I have seen a few natives who wear a little piece of gold hanging from a hole made in the nose. By signs, if I interpret them correctly, I have learned that by going to the south, or rounding the island to the south, I can find a king who possesses a lot of gold and has great containers of it. I have tried to find some natives who will take me to this great king, but none seems **inclined** to make the journey.

4 Tomorrow afternoon I intend to **go to the SW**. The natives have indicated to me that not only is there land to the south and SW, but also to the NW. I shall go to the SW and look for gold and precious stones. Furthermore, if I understand correctly, it is from the NW that **strangers** come to fight and capture the people here.

5 This island is fairly large and very flat. It is green, with many trees and several bodies of water. There is a very large lagoon in the middle of the island and there are no mountains. It is a pleasure to gaze upon this place because it is all so green, and the weather

---

Key Vocabulary
- **stranger** *n.*, an unknown person

In Other Words
baker's peel wooden board with a long handle
oarlocks brackets to hold the oars in place
inclined to want
go to the SW explore the sea to the southwest

baker's peel

is delightful. In fact, since we left the Canaries, God has not failed to provide one perfect day after another.

6   I cannot get over the fact of how **docile** these people are. They have so little to give but will give it all for whatever we give them, if only broken pieces of glass and **crockery**. One seaman gave three Portuguese *ceitis* (not even worth a penny!) for about 25 pounds of spun cotton. I probably should have forbidden this exchange, but I wanted to take the cotton to Your Highnesses, and it seems to be in abundance. I think the cotton is grown on San Salvador, but I cannot say for sure because I have not been here that long. Also, the gold they wear hanging from their noses comes from here, but in order not to lose time I want to go to see if I can find the island of Japan.

"I have tried very hard to find out if there is any gold here."

Critical Viewing Compare how the artist shows the two groups. What can you infer from what he chose to paint? ▼

The Landing of Christopher Columbus in the New World, 1821, Frederick Kemmelmeyer, oil on canvas

Geographical Background

Canary Islands
San Salvador
Guinea
Africa
Atlantic Ocean
South America

In Other Words
docile calm, agreeable
crockery pottery; dishes

Compare Across Texts

Analyze Word Choice and Tone

"Encounter" and "When Cultures Meet" both describe how two different cultures can affect one another. Think about each author's purpose for writing and why an author might choose specific words. **Compare** the language and **analyze** how each affects the tone, or writer's feeling about the topic.

How It Works

Collect and Organize Language A Comparison Chart can help you tell how an author's language affects the tone of each selection.

Selection	Word Choice	Impact on Tone
"Encounter"	The baby canoes spat out many strange **creatures**, men but not men.	Suggests the boy's feelings of fear or wonder in response to the strangers
"When Cultures Meet"		

Comparison Chart

Practice Together

Analyze Language Identify specific words and phrases used in "Encounter." Then **analyze** how the language helps you understand the tone of the text. Give examples to support your ideas.

> The authors of "Encounter" and "When Cultures Meet" both choose words to create a specific tone. In "Encounter," the author uses the word *creatures* to show how different the Europeans appeared to the native people ...

Try It!

Make a chart and find more examples of each author's word choices. Then analyze why the author chose these words and how they affect the tone in each selection.

In "Encounter," the author uses words such as _____. These words create a tone that is _____. In "When Cultures Meet," the author uses words such as _____. The tone is _____.

Academic Vocabulary
- **compare** (kum-**pair**) *verb*
  When you **compare** things, you tell how they are alike and different.
- **analyze** (**a**-nu-līz) *verb*
  When you **analyze** something, you study it closely.

Close Encounters

GUIDING QUESTION

What happens when cultures cross paths?

Content Library

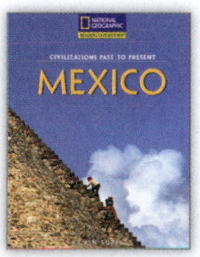

Leveled Library

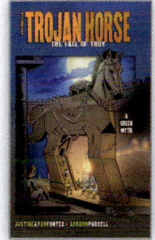  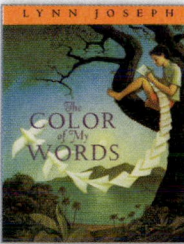

Reflect on Your Reading

Think back on your reading of the unit selections. Discuss what you did to understand what you read.

Focus on Reading **Compare Fiction and Nonfiction**

In this unit, you learned how to compare fiction and nonfiction selections on the same topic. Compare the fiction selection "Encounter" with Columbus's actual log in the close reading. Make notes about which information was accurate and which was made up. Then discuss with a partner how the fiction author used or altered history.

Focus Strategy **Ask Questions**

As you read the selections, you learned to ask questions. Explain to a partner how you will use this strategy in the future.

Explore the **GUIDING QUESTION**

Throughout this unit, you have been thinking about what happens when cultures cross paths. Choose one of these ways to explore the Guiding Question:

- **Discuss** With a group, discuss a time when you met someone from a different cultural background than your own. What did you learn about the other person that you didn't know before?
- **Role-Play** With a partner, role-play an interview with a European settler. Decide which role each person will play. Plan the questions and answers. Then conduct the interview.
- **Draw** Make a visual representation of the poem "Old World New World." Explain your artwork.

Book Talk

Which Unit Library book did you choose? Explain to a partner what it taught you about close encounters.

TO THE
RESCUE

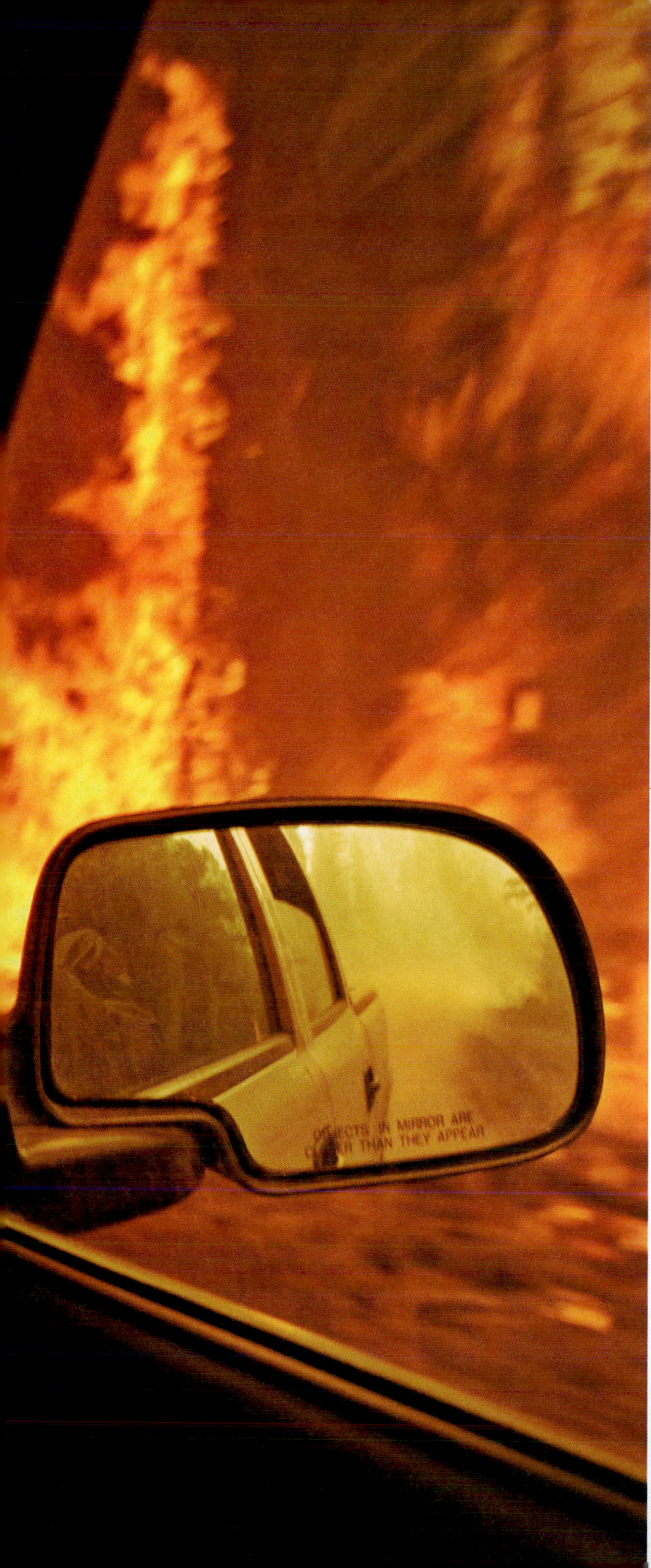

6

GUIDING
QUESTION

How do we come to the aid of one another?

◀ While others move to safety, firefighters prepare to battle a wildfire in Montana.

Determine Viewpoints

An author's viewpoint is the author's opinion or belief about a topic or issue. Fiction authors develop characters' viewpoints through words, thoughts, and actions. These details **aid** readers not only in understanding what each character thinks but also in distinguishing, or contrasting, among viewpoints.

Nonfiction authors reveal their own viewpoints through their word choice and the facts and opinions they include. Analyzing the kinds of information and words an author emphasizes can help a reader distinguish the author's viewpoint from other viewpoints.

How It Works

Viewpoint in Fiction Look for words and actions that show each character's viewpoint. Analyze these details to determine how the author distinguishes the viewpoints of different characters.

> ### A Helping Hand
>
> I desperately wanted to play hockey on the frozen pond. I was determined. It was cold, but the day was warming up. My friend Greg warned, "Let's not risk playing today. I have a bad feeling about this." Then I heard a CRACK! "Look out!" Greg called. The ice split under me, and I fell into the water! "Grab my hockey stick!" Greg called. I did, and he pulled me to safety.

The author's word choice and details distinguish each character's feelings about the situation.

Author's Viewpoint in Nonfiction Analyze the author's choice of words, facts, and opinions to determine the author's viewpoint.

> ### Citizens Help Katrina Victims
>
> Hurricane Katrina came ashore in Louisiana, bringing with it widespread damage from wind and flood waters. Many people lost their homes. People all over the world sent aid. Some donated money. Other individuals took time from their busy lives to travel to the site and offer their talents in the recovery effort.

The author's word choice emphasizes the value of service in the relief effort.

Academic Vocabulary
- **aid** (ād) *verb*
  To **aid** someone is to help or give support.

Read the following passages aloud with your class. As you read, listen for clues to help you determine viewpoints.

Not Just a Number

On any given night, over 630,000 people in the United States are homeless. This is a sad fact, but what does this number really mean? 630,000 people is more than the entire population of Milwaukee, Wisconsin. The homeless on a given night could fill the seats of approximately nine NFL football stadiums.

These numbers mean people. The next time you hear the number of homeless in America, give it a second thought.

A Coat for Mim

Mim pulled the coat tighter. "Oh, this is nice," she said to Sasha. "Thank you for the coat!"

"We have to help each other," replied Sasha. "The weather is too cold to have no coat, especially when I have two."

Mim looked a bit embarrassed. "I've never had to worry about being cold before. I'm sure things will be better once my dad finds a new job."

"We all need a helping hand sometimes. You have mine," Sasha said, reaching to shake Mim's.

Try It!

Read these passages. What viewpoints are expressed? How do you know?

The Cookout

"I'm sorry you're sick," said Maria. "Dad caught some great fish for the cookout!"

Rosine hung up the phone sadly. She hated to miss the best cookout of the year. Finally, she fell asleep. She awoke to see Maria's family. "What are you doing here?" asked Rosine.

"Since you can't come to the cook*out*, we'll make it a cook*in*!" laughed Maria's dad.

Soup's On

Many students volunteer in their communities. Some prefer to work one-on-one tutoring younger children and visiting senior citizens.

Other students choose inspiring activities that make a big impact on their community, such as cleaning up a local playground. Another popular volunteer activity is serving hundreds a day in a soup kitchen. Most students agree that volunteering is very rewarding.

Focus on Vocabulary

Use Word Origins

Many English words are based on words that come from older languages such as Greek, Latin, and an early form of English called Anglo-Saxon.

Roots are word parts that have meaning but cannot stand on their own as a word. Knowing common roots can help you figure out new words.

> **EXAMPLE**   The Greek root *phys* means "nature," so *physical* means "having to do with nature."

Borrowed words come from other languages. They keep the meaning and sounds from their **original** language. *Pizza*, *elephant*, and *tsunami* are borrowed words.

How the Strategy Works

When you come to a word you don't know, look for the root to help you figure out the meaning.

1. Break the word into meaningful parts. If you cannot break the word into parts, it may be a borrowed word.

   EXAMPLE

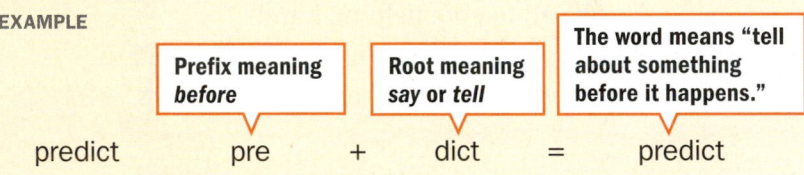

| | Prefix meaning *before* | | Root meaning *say* or *tell* | | The word means "tell about something before it happens." |

predict   pre   +   dict   =   predict

2. Focus on the root. Think of other words that have the same root or use a dictionary to find its meaning.

3. Put the meanings of all the word parts together. See if the meaning makes sense in the sentence.

Use the strategy to figure out the meaning of each underlined word.

> Did elephants predict a tsunami that struck the Indian Ocean? Elephants can hear sounds that are not <u>audible</u> to the human ear. Some scientists think the elephants heard the sound of the tsunami coming and fled to higher <u>territory</u>.

Strategy in Action

" I see the root *aud* and the suffix *ible* in the word *audible*. The root *aud* is also in *audio*. *Audible* must mean 'can be heard'. "

✓ **REMEMBER** You can use the meanings of word parts to figure out the meaning of an unknown word.

Academic Vocabulary

- **original** (u-**rij**-un-ul) *adjective*
  Something that is **original** is the first of its kind.

Read the passage aloud. Look at each underlined word. Use the Roots Chart to figure out what each word means.

Service Horse

Would you want a horse in your <u>apartment</u>? Patty Cooper does. Patty has a disease that makes her bones very weak. Four years ago, Patty <u>fractured</u> her back. She now needs a wheelchair. She has asked for permission to use a horse for things she can't do on her own.

Patty's landlords usually have no problem with service animals. The <u>physiology</u> of a service horse raised some questions, though. Is keeping a horse in such a small space <u>logical</u>?

Patty is sure that all the questions will be answered, and she and her service horse will be happy together.

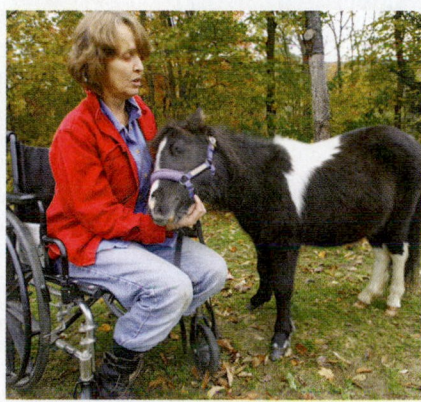
▲ **Patty Cooper and her service horse**

Roots Chart

Root	Origin	Meaning
aud	Latin	to hear
dict	Latin	to say or tell
fit	Anglo-Saxon	having the right shape
fract	Latin	to break
log	Greek	reason, study
part, pars	Latin	portion, part
phys	Greek	nature
poli	Greek	city
port	Latin	to carry
psych	Greek	mind
sci	Latin	to know
terra	Latin	earth

Try It!

Read this passage aloud. What is the meaning of each underlined word? How do you know? Use the Roots Chart to figure out what each word means.

Patty's Supporters

Patty's situation has become a <u>political</u> cause. City newspapers print articles about her. Supporters say that Patty's horse makes a <u>fitting</u> helper. He <u>transports</u> her bags. More importantly, he keeps her in good <u>psychological</u> health.

DOGS AT WORK

BY TERRELL SMITH

Build Background

Connect

KWL Chart Create a KWL Chart about working dogs. In the K column, list what you already know. In the W column, list what you want to know. Use the L column to list what you learn from the selection.

KWL Chart

WHAT I KNOW	WHAT I WANT TO KNOW	WHAT I LEARNED
Some dogs dig through snow to find people.	What kinds of dogs are used?	

See Dogs at Work

Dogs are known for being great pets, but there are some that live to help and work for others.

Digital Library   myNGconnect.com
🔵 View the video.

▲ A guide dog helps a person cross the street.

Language & Grammar

1 TRY OUT LANGUAGE
2 LEARN GRAMMAR
3 APPLY ON YOUR OWN

Summarize

CD

Look at the photograph, and listen to the interview.
Then read and listen to the summary of the interview.

INTERVIEW and SUMMARY

Interview with a Musher

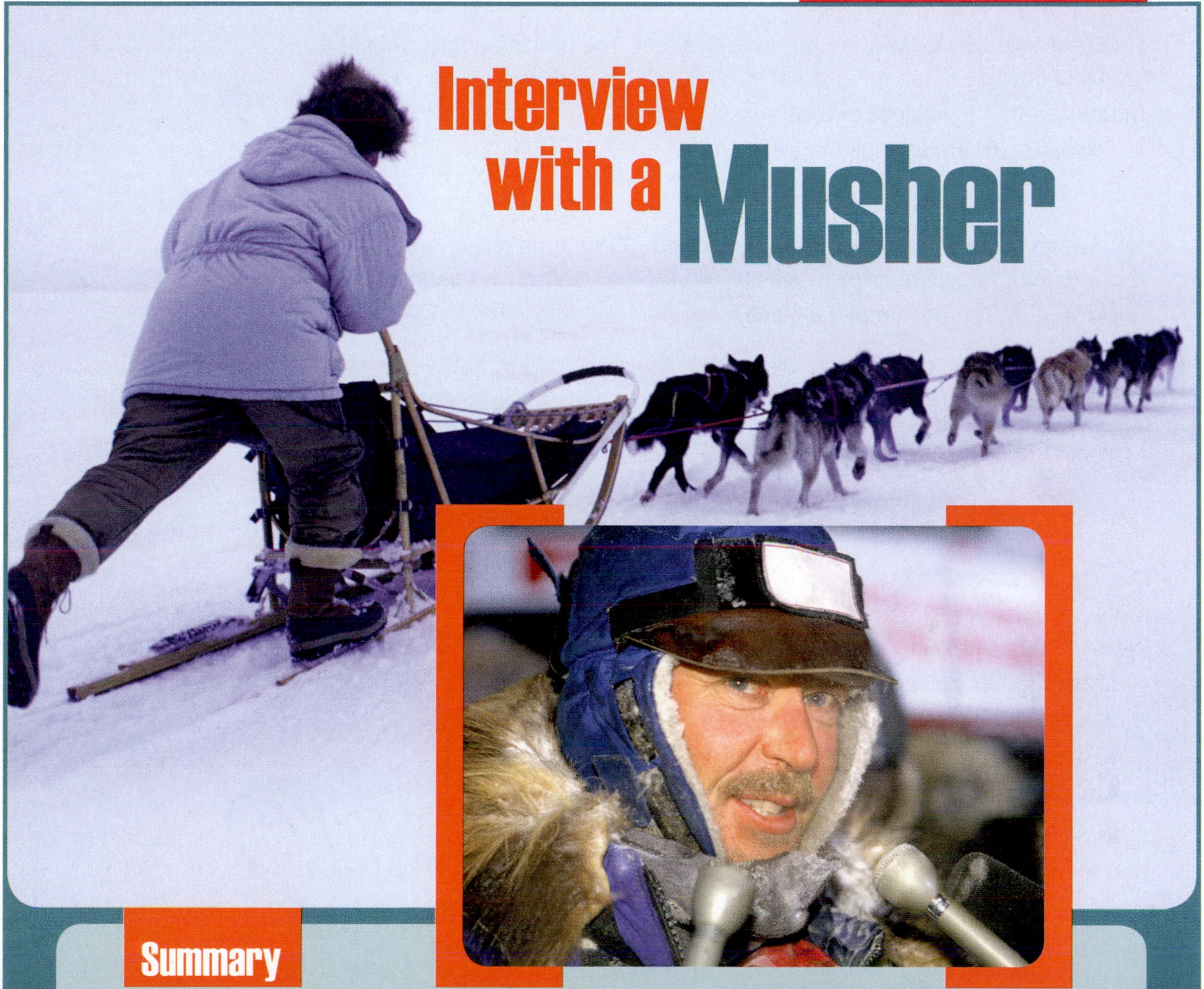

Summary

The sports reporter interviewed one of the mushers, or sled guides, who finished well in the Iditarod, the world-famous sled dog race in Alaska. The musher explained that he used teams of 12 to 16 dogs to travel over 1,000 miles over extremely cold and rugged terrain. In order to finish the difficult race, the musher and his dogs depended on each other during the race. The musher added that his dogs were brave and willing to work hard, and, in return, he cared for and respected them like family. As the musher and his dogs left the finish line, the reporter wished them well.

Use Nouns in the Subject and Predicate

A complete sentence has two parts: the **subject** and the **predicate** .

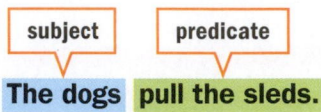

subject — The dogs
predicate — pull the sleds.

The subject tells who or what you are talking about. The predicate tells what the subject does.

- Nouns can be the **subject** of a sentence.

  EXAMPLE   The **dogs** pull the sleds.

  subject

- Nouns can also be the **object** of an action verb. To find the object, turn the verb into a question like: "Dogs pull what?" Your answer is the object.

  EXAMPLE   The dogs **pull** the **sleds**.

  verb   object

- Many English sentences follow this pattern: subject ➔ verb ➔ object.

  EXAMPLE   **Chris interviewed mushers**.

  subject   verb   object

Practice Together

Say each sentence and tell the job of the <u>noun</u>. Is it a subject or an object?

1. My <u>brother</u> trained our dog, Chase.
2. The Iditarod trail crosses <u>Alaska</u>.
3. We have a <u>trail</u>, but it's much shorter than the Iditarod.
4. <u>Chase</u> likes treats a lot.
5. Chase pulls our <u>sled</u> easily!

Try It!

Say each sentence. Write the job of the <u>noun</u> on a card. Is it a subject or an object?

6. My friend Steven has a <u>dog</u> named Rufus.
7. <u>Steven</u> thinks Rufus is faster than Chase.
8. Steven asked my <u>brother</u> to train Rufus.
9. Today the dogs had a <u>race</u>.
10. <u>Chase</u> beat Rufus by a mile!

▲ Our dog can do tricks.

Explore Information

SUMMARIZE

Summarize what you hear, see, and read to share the information with others. If you see a great ball game, you may want to tell your friends about it. But they don't need to hear every detail. So you tell only the most important things, or summarize.

Work with a partner. Plan your own summary of the interview with a musher on page 411. Brainstorm a few important facts in an Idea Web.

Idea Web

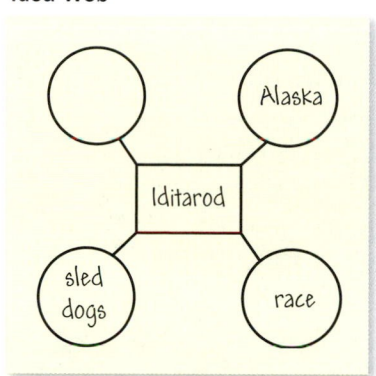

Now use the facts to write a summary with your partner. Share your summary with the class.

HOW TO SUMMARIZE

1. Identify the topic and the main ideas about it.
2. Write a few key details that support the main ideas.
3. Leave out unimportant or repeated information.
4. Summarize in just a few sentences. A summary is always shorter than the original text.

> The Iditarod is a sled dog race in Alaska. The dogs pull the sleds and drivers, called mushers, over 1,000 miles of snow and ice for 10 days or more.

USE NOUNS IN THE SUBJECT AND PREDICATE

Use complete sentences when you summarize. A complete sentence has a subject and a predicate. Many English sentences follow this pattern: subject ➔ verb ➔ object.

EXAMPLES   The **dogs pull** the **mushers**.

Reporters ask questions.

subject	verb	object

Prepare to Read

Learn Key Vocabulary

Study the Words Use the steps below.

1. Pronounce the word. Say it aloud several times. Spell it.
2. Rate your word knowledge.
3. Study the example. Tell more about the word.
4. Practice it. Make the word your own.

Key Words

dependable (di-**pen**-du-bul)
adjective ▶ page 418

A **dependable** person can be trusted to do the right thing. Parents want **dependable** babysitters.
Related Words: **depend, dependent**

employee (im-**ploi**-ē) *noun*
▶ page 418

An **employee** is a person who works for someone else. This person is an **employee** at the store.
Related Words: **employer, employment, unemployment**

job (job) *noun*
▶ page 418

A **job** is work you do. This person has a **job** in a restaurant.
Synonyms: **employment, profession, occupation**

obedient (ō-**bē**-dē-int)
adjective ▶ page 420

When you're **obedient**, you do what you are told to do. This **obedient** dog listens to commands.
Related Word: **obey**

odor (**ō**-dur) *noun*
▶ page 420

An **odor** is a smell. Not all **odors** are good ones. The trash can has a strong **odor**.
Synonym: **scent**

search (surch) *verb, noun, adjective* ▶ page 420

1 *verb* To **search** for something means to look for it. **2** *adjective* This **search** team is looking for something. **3** *noun* They are on a **search** to find a missing person.

service (**sur**-vis) *noun, adjective* ▶ page 419
A **service** is something done to help someone else. Free gift-wrapping is a **service** some stores provide.
Related Words: **serve, server**

train (trān) *verb*
▶ page 419
When you **train** someone, you teach that person how to do something correctly. A coach **trains** athletes.
Related Words: **training, trainer**

Practice the Words Make an Idea Web for each Key Word. Write four things the word makes you think of. Share your finished webs with a partner.

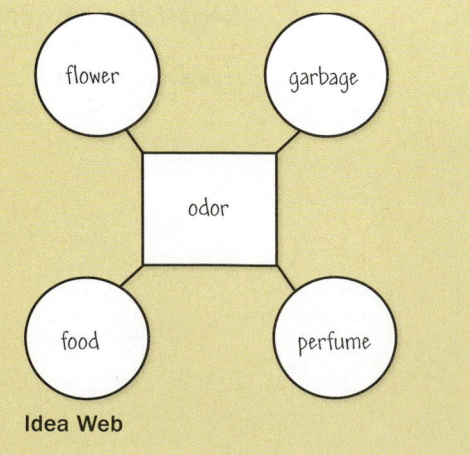

Idea Web

Analyze Author's Purpose and Tone

How Does an Author's Purpose Affect Tone? Every author has a ==purpose,== or reason for writing: to inform, to persuade, or to entertain. Sometimes an author has more than one purpose. To figure out the author's ==purpose,== the reader must recognize the author's tone, or attitude, toward the topic. Tone is reflected in the author's choice of words and details.

- To entertain, the author might use simple language and an informal or emotional tone.
- To inform or to explain, the author might use formal language and a serious tone.

As you read, analyze word choice and tone to determine the author's ==purpose== .

Reading Strategies
- Plan
- Monitor
- Visualize
- Determine Importance
- Ask Questions
- **Make Connections**
  Combine your knowledge and experiences with the author's ideas and information.
- Make Inferences
- Synthesize

Look Into the Text

> Some of the best workers in America don't get paid. But these employees aren't quitting or even complaining. Why? They're dogs! Professional pooches do a variety of tasks. Dogs can be "eyes" for the blind and "ears" for the deaf. And they sometimes bring joy to nursing home residents.
>
> Dogs do many other jobs, too. That's because they are doggone dependable! They pull sleds and help solve crimes. They inspect luggage for illegal drugs and food items.

Humorous phrases such as this give a lighthearted tone.

Words like *inspect luggage* and *illegal drugs* are <u>formal</u>.

Practice Together

Begin a Tone and Purpose Chart A Tone and Purpose Chart can help you analyze how word choice reflects an author's ==purpose== and tone. Reread the passage. Add other examples of word choices to the Tone and Purpose Chart.

Word Choice	Tone	Purpose
Professional pooches	informal: funny, lighthearted	to entertain

Tone and Purpose Chart

Academic Vocabulary
- ==purpose== (**pur**-pus) *noun*
  A **purpose** is a reason for doing something.

Magazine Article

Magazine articles are nonfiction texts that give information. The author's purpose is mainly to **inform**, so articles also include photos and captions that add information.

Some writers also hope to **entertain** so that readers enjoy the magazine article. The tone of the article will vary according to the author's purpose and choice of words.

As you read, think about any personal connections you can make to the words and ideas in the text. What experiences have you had or seen with dogs as workers?

Imagine if you couldn't turn on a light or open the refrigerator. Life might be pretty frustrating. You'd have to have dependable people around you all the time. Or would you?

> **Authors write to entertain.**

Some people with physical disabilities rely on special dogs. These animals provide a service and give their owners a welcome sense of independence. They do this by helping with daily activities.

> **Facts are given to inform.**

DOGS AT WORK

BY TERRELL SMITH

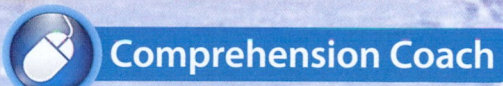

Some of the best workers in America don't get paid. But these **employees** aren't quitting or even complaining. Why? They're dogs! Professional pooches do **a variety** of tasks. Dogs **can be "eyes" for the blind and "ears" for the deaf**. And they sometimes bring joy to nursing home residents.

Dogs do many other **jobs**, too. That's because they are doggone **dependable**! They pull sleds and help solve crimes. They inspect luggage for illegal drugs or food items. They hunt for missing persons. They even help with cattle herds.

Key Vocabulary

employee *n.*, a worker who works for another person, usually for money

job *n.*, a set of tasks

dependable *adj.*, helpful

In Other Words

a variety many different types

can be "eyes" for the blind and "ears" for the deaf help people who are blind or deaf

How Dogs Help

Imagine if you couldn't turn on a light or open the refrigerator. Life might be **pretty frustrating**. You'd have to have dependable people around you all the time. Or would you?

Some people with physical disabilities **rely on** special dogs. These animals provide a <mark>service</mark> and give their owners a welcome sense of independence. They do this by helping with daily activities.

The best known service dogs are guides for the visually impaired. But four-legged friends perform other roles, too. One group called Canine Companions for Independence <mark>trains</mark> dogs to open and close doors. They also train them to **switch** lights on and off and pick up dropped objects. They can even train dogs to pull wheelchairs.

▲ Andrew Brenes has cerebral palsy. He uses his service dog, Tonka, to regain balance.

Making Life Better

Service dogs can also help others to better understand people with disabilities. That's what happened for a girl named Megan. Megan is seven. She has a medical condition called Angelman syndrome. She can't speak or walk. People felt uncomfortable around Megan when she was younger. Megan was lonely.

Things changed when Gabri came along. The two-year-old Labrador retriever became Megan's furry friend. "Gabri is the perfect **icebreaker**," says her mother. "People who didn't know what to say before come right up and ask about Megan's dog."

Megan gets help to feed and brush Gabri. "If this dog makes Megan's life a tiny bit more fun, then it's worth it."

Look Into the Text

1. **Main Idea and Details** Name three <mark>jobs</mark> that dogs can be <mark>trained</mark> to do.
2. **Explain** Tell how Gabri changed Megan's life.

USING THEIR NOSES

Some canine careers are focused on scent, or smelling. A dog's nose has twenty times more sniffing cells than a human's. Dogs may learn to smell bombs or drugs. They are even trained to find money or food.

Fruits, vegetables, meat, and other food items sometimes carry insects and diseases. Food from foreign countries could infect crops or animals in the United States. To prevent that, the U.S. Department of Agriculture created the Beagle Brigade. Furry, four-legged baggage inspectors sniff purses and bags at international airports. The beagle calmly sits down next to anything that smells **suspicious**. The hound's human partner then checks for illegal items.

Why beagles? They're friendly and cute. They don't scare people as they sniff through the crowds. Beagles have amazing noses. They can sense **odors** better than many high-tech machines.

Beagles can work for six to ten years. A Beagle Brigade dog can remember up to fifty different odors by the end of its career. Sometimes harmless products, such as lemon-scented shaving cream, fool the dogs.

But not often. The Beagle Brigade **sniffs out the truth** 84 percent of the time.

CANINE DETECTIVES

Dogs also use their mighty noses to go on **searches** to find people who are alive or dead. Dogs use their powerful snouts to smell tiny clues that people leave behind wherever they go. These clues include dead skin cells and bacteria. The clues could also be clothing fragments or hairs. Odors can lead a dog to a hidden person. This person is known as a "find."

Search-and-rescue (SAR) dogs have **tracked missing hikers** in Yosemite Park. They've searched through piles of rubble after earthquakes and other disasters. SAR dogs aided rescue workers in New York City after the September 11, 2001, terrorist attacks. Animals hunted for survivors buried under concrete and steel.

German shepherds, Labrador retrievers, and border collies make good SAR dogs. But so do many other breeds, or types. The dog's personality is more important than its breed.

SAR dogs must be strong and **obedient**. They must be very athletic and smart. Most of all, they must love to play. Trainers

---

Key Vocabulary

odor *n.*, a smell; a scent
search *n.*, the act of carefully looking for something or someone
obedient *adj.*, willing to do what people ask

In Other Words

suspicious illegal or wrong
sniffs out the truth finds a real problem
tracked missing hikers found people who were missing

look for dogs that **go bonkers over** a favorite toy, such as a tennis ball. Those dogs will give any job a Herculean effort as long as the reward is playtime when they're done.

For SAR dogs, a mission may just be a big game of hide-and-seek. But people could die if the dogs don't find them. That's why SAR dogs are so important. No machine—not even a robot or a **motion detector**—can **match the performance of** a canine detective.

▲ A German shepherd rescue dog searches through the rubble of a building after an earthquake.

▲ A beagle working for the Beagle Brigade in Miami, Florida

In Other Words
go bonkers over get excited about
motion detector machine that can tell when something is moving
match the performance of do the job as well as

Look Into the Text

1. **Paraphrase** Tell in your own words why, in addition to being **obedient**, it is important for SAR dogs to like to play.
2. **Conclusion** Why do certain types of dogs make good SAR dogs?

Dogs at Work **421**

POOCH PAYCHECKS

No matter what the job, **countless** dogs do great work. What do they get in return? They do not get money.

But a working dog's "salary" includes some valuable things. They get love and food. They also get a place to live and good care. Dogs have become so dependent on people that they couldn't live without us. And, for millions of dog lovers, the feeling is mutual.

WHAT IS A SERVICE DOG?

Service dogs help people in many ways, but it takes a lot of training to get a pooch ready for its full-time job. Dogs and other service animals must pass some tough tests before beginning work.

The training **serves them well**. When they finish, service animals have the skills and the confidence they need to do their jobs.

How exactly are service animals trained? It depends on the kind of job the animal will do. To see how some service animals are trained, let's look at dogs that help the visually impaired.

▲ A service dog named Kayla assists others by answering telephones, picking up items, and providing companionship.

A beagle from the Beagle Brigade sniffs agricultural goods at the El Paso, TX airport ▶

In Other Words
countless many
serves them well is very useful to the dogs

How to Train a
GUIDE DOG

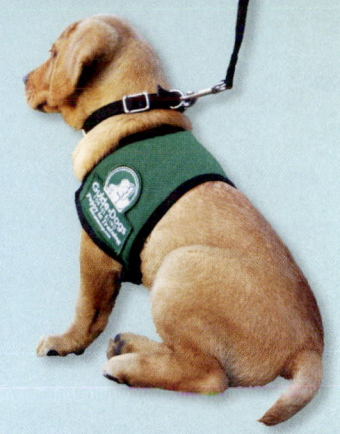

STEP 1

Guide dogs start their training when they are just eight weeks old. What can a puppy learn at such a young age? That's simple. It learns to love people.

As it gets older, the puppy learns basic skills. The pooch is taught to sit and stay. It learns to walk beside someone and not to pull on its leash. The puppy learns to be a well-behaved dog!

STEP 2

When the dog is a year and a half old, its training really **takes off**. An instructor works with the dog every day. The dog learns voice commands. So if a person says, "Halt," the dog knows to stop.

The pooch also learns other important **tricks of the trade**. The instructor teaches the dog to look both ways before crossing a street. The dog is also taught to **tune out** distractions. Why? A guide dog must not chase animals or follow tempting smells. Its owner's safety is more important than anything else.

STEP 3

Soon the service dog has mastered the basics. Now it must learn to lead. The pooch is taught to guide an instructor onto buses. It learns to lead a person safely around town.

The guide dog must also learn to disobey. Why? If a car is speeding down a street, the dog should not cross—no matter what the instructor asks it to do. So the dog learns to use its own judgment.

STEP 4

The dog must first pass a few tests before it can go to work. The instructor wears a **blindfold**. Then the dog shows off its skills.

The dog guides the instructor up stairs and along crowded sidewalks. It goes across busy streets. It leads the way through office buildings and malls. The dog even goes onto escalators and elevators.

The tests are tough. But the training is tougher. The pooch can go to work as soon as it passes its tests. The dog will "see" for someone who is visually impaired. ❖

In Other Words
takes off begins to get serious
tricks of the trade job skills
tune out ignore
blindfold cover over the eyes

Look Into the Text

1. **Main Idea and Details** What do service dogs do? What do they get in return for their work?
2. **Steps in a Process** Describe the steps for <mark>training</mark> a dog to help the visually impaired.

In 1925, diphtheria threatened the lives of many children in Alaska. Sled dogs carried medicine more than 674 frozen miles. Togo, a husky, was one of them.

The Wonder Dog
by J. Patrick Lewis

Togo
Alaska, 1925

Oh, when Togo took off running
With that plucky sled and cunning,
That brave Wonder Dog was stunning—
It was 52° below!
5   And I'll tell you what he did, he
Relayed his sled dog committee
Many miles towards the city
Through the frozen wastes of snow.

Togo showed 'em how to roam
10   To save sickly kids at home,
Mushing medicine from Anchorage
Across the ice to Nome.

It's a shaggy-doggy story—
Togo running west to glory,
15   And it ended hunky-dory
For those children long ago.

▲ Dogsled racer Leonard Seppala, and his lead dog, Togo, in the 1920s

In Other Words
plucky fearless
cunning smartness
Mushing Running
hunky-dory happily, well

Look Into the Text

1. **Mood** What is the mood of this poem? What words from the poem tell you this?
2. **Conclusion and Evidence** Togo's journey was difficult. What evidence supports this conclusion?
3. **Author's Purpose** Why do you think the poet wrote about Togo?

Connect Reading and Writing

Vocabulary
dependable
employees
job
obedient
odors
searched
services
train

CRITICAL THINKING

1. **SUM IT UP** Compare your Tone and Purpose Chart to with a partner. Then make a list of the headings in the article and work together to summarize the article.

Word Choice	Tone	Purpose
Professional pooches	informal: lighthearted	to entertain

Tone and Purpose Chart

2. **Make Judgments** Tell a friend which of the working-dog **jobs** in the selection you think is most important. Use details from the text to support your ideas.

3. **Explain** Revisit the KWL Chart you made on page 410. In the L column, write what you learned about the **services** that working dogs provide. Discuss your completed chart with your classmates.

4. **Compare** Both "Dogs at Work" and "The Wonder Dog" are about **dependable** dogs. How were the dogs' situations different? How were they the same?

READING FLUENCY

Intonation Read the passage on page 653 to a partner. Assess your fluency.

1. My tone never/sometimes/always matched what I read.

2. What I did best in my reading was _____ .

READING STRATEGY

What strategy helped you understand this selection? Tell a partner about it.

VOCABULARY REVIEW

Oral Review Read the paragraph aloud. Add the vocabulary words.

I _____ for weeks then found a summer _____ working with guide dogs. The manager said they needed _____, who were _____, to teach dogs to provide helpful _____ to people who are visually impaired. It's important work. The dogs are very smart. They can smell _____ better than humans. They are also _____, so it is not hard to _____ them.

Written Review Imagine you **train** dogs to **search** for missing people. Write a summary of your **job**. Use five vocabulary words.

WRITE ABOUT THE GUIDING QUESTION

Explore Dogs and Rescue
Why are dogs so good at **searching** for missing people? Write your opinion. Find examples in the selection to support your ideas.

Connect Across the Curriculum

Use Words and Phrases from Mythology

> **Academic Vocabulary**
> - **refer** (ri-**fur**) *verb*
>   **Refer** means to relate to something that came before.

Learn About Mythology Myths are ancient stories of gods, heroes, and great deeds. Sometimes an author **refers** to mythology to express an idea.

Those dogs will give any job a **Herculean effort** as long as the reward is playtime when they're done.

Hercules, a Greek hero, had to perform twelve difficult tasks. So, *to make a Herculean effort* is to try extremely hard.

Use Words and Phrases from Mythology Work with a partner. Read each sentence and its mythological connection. Then explain each sentence.

Sentence	Mythological Connection	What the Sentence Means
Video games were Mark's <u>Achilles' heel</u>.	The Greek hero Achilles's only weakness was his heel.	
When she saw him, Carmen was <u>struck by Cupid's arrow</u>.	Cupid was the Roman god of love. He shot people with an arrow to make them fall in love.	

Analyze Poetry

> **Academic Vocabulary**
> - **characteristic** (kair-ik-tu-**ris**-tik) *noun*
>   A **characteristic** is a quality of something.

One **characteristic** of poetry is a **rhyme scheme.** The pattern of rhyme in a poem can add to the poem's meaning. Read aloud the first stanza of the poem on p. 424. Point out that the rhyming words *running*, *cunning*, and *stunning* add to the meaning by creating a feeling of movement.

Analyze a Poem Reread "The Wonder Dog" on page 424. Find another example of the poet's use of rhyme. How does this rhyme add to the poem's meaning?

Summarize

Pair Share With a partner, summarize how working dogs help people and how people help the dogs. Remember to tell the main idea and just the most important details. Use nouns as subjects and objects in your summary.

> Dogs help people with disabilities do things that they can't do for themselves. People give dogs a home, food, respect, and love.

Write About People, Places, and Things

Study the Models When you write about people, places, and things, help your reader understand what you have to say by using words correctly and precisely. Use complete sentences.

NOT OK

> Service dogs use their noses in helpful ways. The dogs can follow the scent of a missing person. Also help them locate illegal or dangerous items. In return, the police reward they. With some serious playtime and a lot of love.

The reader thinks: **"Who helps whom locate illegal or dangerous items?"**

OK

> Service dogs use their noses in helpful ways. The dogs can follow the scent of a missing person. They also help the police locate illegal or dangerous items. In return, the police reward the dogs with some serious playtime and a lot of love.

Now the writer completes each idea and uses words precisely.

Add Sentences Think of two sentences to add to the OK model above. Be sure to write in complete sentences using correct pronouns.

WRITE ON YOUR OWN Write about a time when you helped someone. Use sentences that express complete ideas.

REMEMBER

- A noun or pronoun used as a **subject** tells whom or what the sentence is about.
- A noun or pronoun used as an **object** tells who or what receives the action of the sentence.

Subject Pronouns	I	you	he	she	it	we	you	they
Object Pronouns	me	you	him	her	it	us	you	them

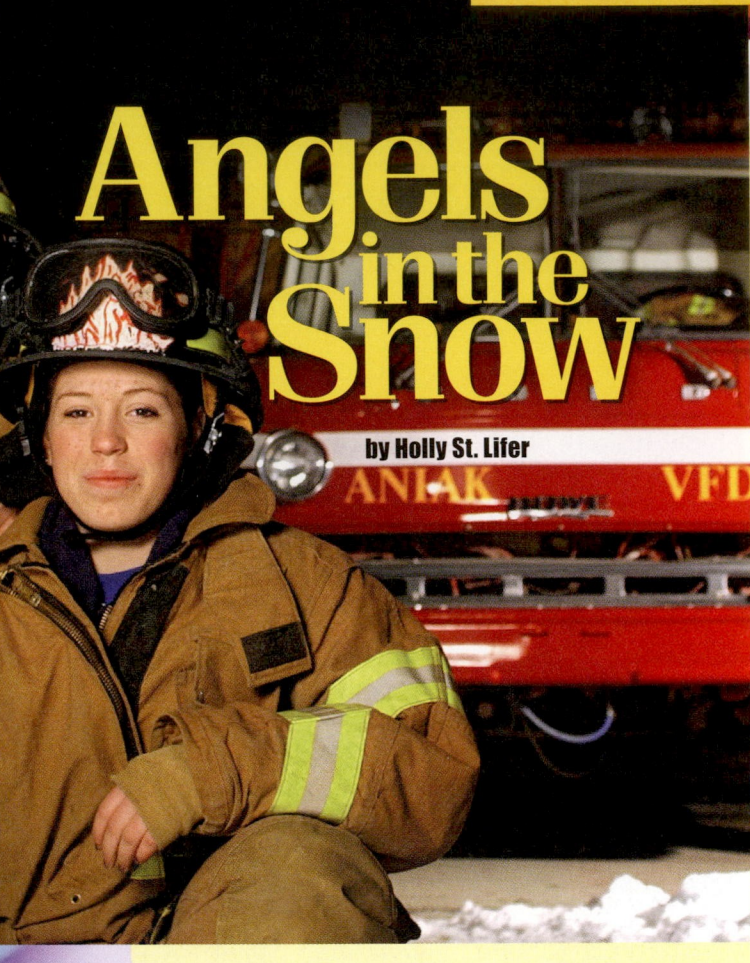

Angels in the Snow

by Holly St. Lifer

Build Background

Connect

Anticipation Guide Think about how people help one another. Decide if you agree or disagree with these statements.

Anticipation Guide

		Agree	Disagree
1.	We have a duty to help our family.	_____	_____
2.	We have a duty to help others in our community.	_____	_____
3.	We have a duty to help others in the world.	_____	_____

See Rescue in Action

For rescue workers, saving others in dangerous situations is all in a day's work.

Digital Library
myNGconnect.com
View the images.

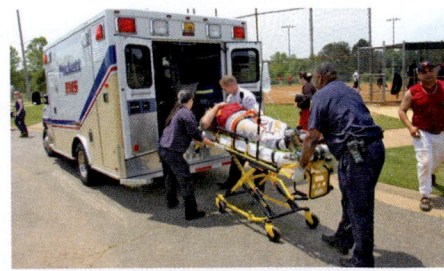

▲ Emergency workers come to the aid of people on a daily basis.

Language & Grammar

Clarify and Verify
CD

Look at the photos, and listen to the emergency call. What information does the caller verify? What information does the operator clarify? Role-play the call.

A Call for Help

PICTURE PROMPT and ROLE-PLAY

911 Operator: 911 emergency. What are you reporting?

Caller: I think there's someone outside my house. I'm all alone because my mom had to go to the store to get some medicine.

911 Operator: OK. Can you give me your name?

Caller: Rachel Garcia.

911 Operator: How do you spell your last name?

Caller: G-A-R-C-I-A. I called my mom's cell phone, but she didn't answer!

911 Operator: OK, Rachel. Now what is your address?

Caller: 123 East Street.

911 Operator: What is the cross street?

Caller: Oh . . . I just know we're right off Main Street!

911 Operator: So you are at 123 East Street near Main Street, and your phone number is 555-8919, correct?

Caller: Yes, that's right. Please help. I hear footsteps outside the front door!

Use Prepositions

Prepositions are words that help show location, direction, and time.

Prepositions That Show Location

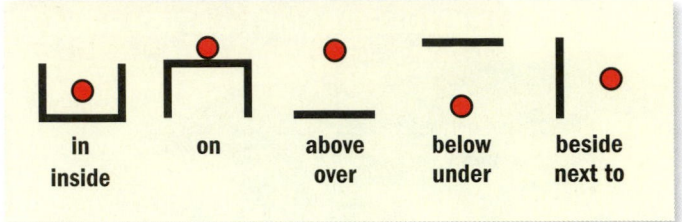

in
inside   on   above
over   below
under   beside
next to

- Use location prepositions to tell where someone is.

    EXAMPLES   Rachel lives **on** East Street **in** the city.

Prepositions That Show Direction

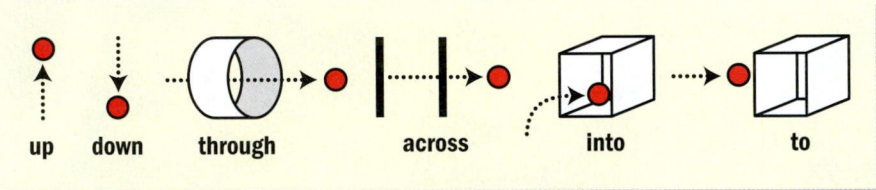

up   down   through   across   into   to

- Use direction prepositions to tell where someone goes.

    EXAMPLES   The police drove **into** her neighborhood. They went **up** the stairs **to** her front door.

Prepositions That Show Time
- Use prepositions of time to tell when something happens.

    EXAMPLES   Rachel called **at** 9 p.m. The police arrived **in** five minutes. They stayed **until** 10 p.m. **After** 10 p.m., Rachel went to bed. She fell asleep **before** 11 p.m.

Practice Together

Say each sentence with the correct preposition.

    1. Just (at/on) midnight, the rain started.

    2. (After/until) an hour, it began to pour. It rained hard.

    3. When the thunder started, the cat ran (into/over) the bedroom.

Try It!

Read each sentence. Write the correct preposition on a card. Then say the sentence with the correct preposition.

    4. Water dripped (down/up) the window.

    5. The cat hid (above/under) the bed.

    6. The rain continued (before/until) 6 a.m.

Explore Details

CLARIFY AND VERIFY

Imagine you are having an emergency and you need to call for help. What information would you need to provide? What questions might the 911 operator ask you?

Work with a partner to plan a 911 call script like the one on page 429. Think of an emergency, such as an accident. Make a list of the information you would need to provide a 911 operator. Add questions to the list that the 911 operator might ask.

Information to Provide	Questions Operator Might Ask
A car just crashed into the house across the street.	Where do you live?

Now take turns being the caller and the 911 operator. Clarify and verify information.

HOW TO CLARIFY AND VERIFY

1. Ask questions about what is unclear. Make sure you understand exactly what the speaker is saying.
2. Restate what you heard in your own words.

> I picked up a pot with hot oil in it. I didn't know it was hot. My hands really hurt.

> So you weren't wearing anything on your hands?

USE PREPOSITIONS

When you clarify and verify information, you may need to use **prepositions** to add important details about locations, directions, and time.

EXAMPLES   I see smoke coming **under** the door.
My brother fell **down** the steps.
The fire started **at** ten o'clock.

Prepare to Read

Learn Key Vocabulary

Study the Words Use the steps below.

1. Pronounce the word. Say it aloud several times. Spell it.
2. Rate your word knowledge.
3. Study the example. Tell more about the word.
4. Practice it. Make the word your own.

Key Words

accident (ak-su-dent) *noun*
▶ page 437

An **accident** is a sudden event that causes damage to people or things. These cars were in an **accident**.
Related Word: **accidental**

career (ku-rēr) *noun*
▶ page 439

A **career** is the type of work a person does. This woman has a **career** as an architect.
Synonym: **profession**

department (di-part-mint) *noun* ▶ page 437

A **department** is a part of a larger group or business. You get a driver's license at a motor vehicle **department**.
Related Word: **depart**

difficult (dif-i-kult) *adjective*
▶ page 439

Something that is **difficult** is hard to do. Gymnastics is very **difficult**.
Synonyms: **hard, tricky, tough**
Antonyms: **easy, simple**

emergency (i-mur-jen-sē) *adjective, noun* ▶ page 436

1 *adjective* An **emergency** service helps people in serious situations. The **emergency** medical team rides in an ambulance. **2** *noun* An **emergency** is a sudden, serious situation.

experience (ik-spēr-ē-uns) *noun* ▶ page 437

Experience is knowledge or skill that comes from having already done something. A chef has a lot of cooking **experience**.

region (rē-jun) *noun*
▶ page 439

A **region** is a specific area. The Arctic **region** is covered in snow and ice.

team (tēm) *noun*
▶ page 436

A **team** is a group that works together. This **team** practices together in order to improve.

Practice the Words Make a Study Card for each Key Word. Then compare your cards with a partner.

> **difficult**
>
> **What it means:** something that is hard
> **Example:** I run a marathon.
> **Not an example:** I watch a movie.

Study Card

Analyze Author's Viewpoint

How can I determine an author's viewpoint? Authors write about things they know and care about. Their writing reflects their ==perspectives==, or viewpoints, about topics. To recognize an author's ==perspective==:

- Look closely at the details and words the author chooses.
- Determine how the author distinguishes his viewpoint from that of others.

As you read, look for clues in the text that help you determine the author's viewpoint.

Reading Strategies

- Plan
- Monitor
- Visualize
- Determine Importance
- Ask Questions
- **Make Connections**
  Combine your knowledge and experiences with the author's ideas and information.
- Make Inferences
- Synthesize

> **Look Into the Text**
>
> By that time the walls, ceilings, and carpets were in flames. "I knew to drop to my knees and follow the wall," Marteney says. "I couldn't see a foot in front of my face and it hurt to breathe." Marteney stayed brave. She found the boy huddled behind the bathroom door. She grabbed him and rushed him out to safety.
>
> Most teens would not want to run into a burning building. But Marteney is a member of the Dragon Slayers. They are a teenage emergency medical team.

Marteney's actions support the author's viewpoint.

Practice Together

Begin a Two-Column Chart A Two-Column Chart can help you record clues about the author's viewpoint. The first entry shows the author's opinion of Marteney's actions. Reread the second paragraph above. Identify other words and phrases that reflect the author's ==perspective== and add them to the Two-Column Chart.

Words and Phrases	What I Learn About the Author's Viewpoint
Marteney stayed brave.	The author believes Marteney's actions show she is brave.

Two-Column Chart

Academic Vocabulary
- **perspective** (pur-**spek**-tiv) *noun*
  A **perspective** is a way of thinking about something.

Online News Article

An online news article is a nonfiction text on the Internet. The article gives information about real news events. Authors of online news articles inform readers while also giving their own viewpoints about a topic. By looking at the details they include and their word choice, you can determine what they think is important and how they feel about the topic.

Online articles often include an **introduction** and a **menu**, or list, of links to related stories that aid and add to a reader's understanding. The introduction and links can connect the information in the article with what you know about the world around you. For example, you could find a fire station near your home or learn how you might be able to volunteer.

Look Into the Text

About the Article

When the emergency alarm sounds in the cold, dark night, the Dragon Slayers are here to help.

An introduction helps you decide if you want to read the article.

>> Links

>> Fire Safety

>> Find a Fire Station

>> Volunteer

A menu of links leads to more information.

Angels in the Snow

by Holly St. Lifer

FIRE FIGHTER PROFILES

FIRE FIGHTERS   FIRE NEWS

Angels
in the
Snow

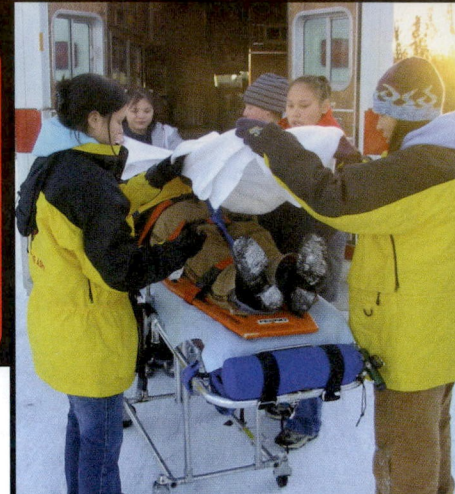

▲ Dragon Slayers practice the correct way to rescue someone with a spinal injury.

About the Article
When the emergency alarm sounds in the cold, dark night, the Dragon Slayers are there to help.

» Links

» Fire Safety

» Find a Fire Station

» Volunteer

The Dragon Slayers

On Christmas Day 2002, fourteen-year-old Erinn Marteney was at her best friend's house when she smelled smoke. Marteney and the friend gathered up the friend's four younger siblings. They ran outside. Marteney stood barefoot in the snow and watched smoke pour out of the windows. Then she noticed a two-year-old child was missing. She ran back into the house.

By that time the walls, ceilings, and carpets were in flames. "I knew to drop to my knees and follow the wall," Marteney says. "I couldn't see a foot in front of my face and it hurt to breathe." Marteney stayed brave. She found the boy huddled behind the bathroom door. She grabbed him and rushed him out to safety.

Most teens would not want to run into a burning building. But Marteney is a member of the Dragon Slayers. They are a teenage **emergency** medical **team**. They live and work in Aniak, Alaska.

The Dragon Slayers have about 160 hours of combined emergency **trauma** and firefighting training, and they respond to about 400 calls a year. They **service** an area of fourteen villages with 3,000 residents.

 Page 1 of 5 ▶

Go to page: [　] **Go**

Key Vocabulary
emergency *adj.*, for use in a sudden, dangerous event
team *n.*, a group of people who work together

In Other Words
trauma injury
service help people in

FIRE FIGHTERS   FIRE NEWS

Angels in the Snow

▲ Aniak fire chief Pete Brown trains the girls how to fight fires.

Team members have rescued survivors of plane crashes and snowmobile **accidents**. They have revived grandmothers **in cardiac arrest**. Just this past December, they began a search to find the body of a fifteen-year-old boy. He fell through the ice and drowned. They are still looking for him.

Creating the Team

The idea of recruiting teenagers was the brainchild of Aniak fire chief Pete Brown. He is a retired Vietnam medic. According to Brown, everyone knew there was a tremendous need for an expanded Emergency Medical Services (EMS) team.

The eight adults in the **department** couldn't handle all of the work. Brown started recruiting high school kids. Most of them were girls.

Team members have to make 90 percent of the meetings. The meetings are ongoing training. They take place twice a week for two hours. Tobacco, alcohol, and drugs are prohibited. And although these high school heroines **are on call 24/7**, they have to maintain passing grades.

Brown is proud of the girls. He says their level of training and competency is **on par with** adults. He goes out on every call with the Dragon Slayers. He is selective about what each girl actually does on each call based on **experience** and age. Still, it's obviously a job with risks.

◀ Page 2 of 5 ▶   Go to page: [   ] Go

Key Vocabulary

accident *n.*, an unexpected event that causes injury

department *n.*, a part of a larger group or business

experience *n.*, knowledge gained by doing something

In Other Words

in cardiac arrest who are having heart attacks

are on call 24/7 have to be available every day and night

on par with equal to

Look Into the Text

1. **Cause and Effect** How did Marteney's **experience** help her during the fire?

2. **Conclusion** Is it easy or hard to be a Dragon Slayer? How do you know?

3. **Context Clues** What does "brainchild" mean? How do you know?

FIRE FIGHTER PROFILES

FIRE FIGHTERS   **FIRE NEWS**

Angels in the Snow

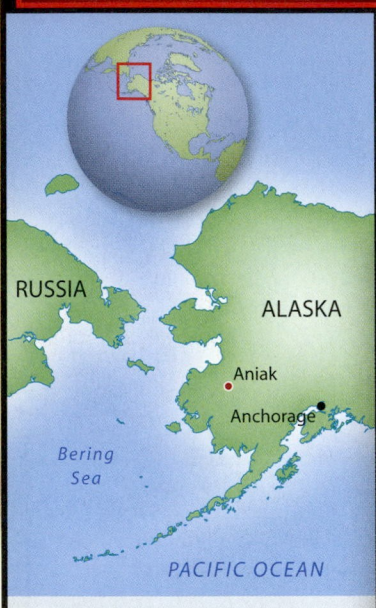

RUSSIA

ALASKA

Aniak

Anchorage

Bering Sea

PACIFIC OCEAN

▲ Aniak is in central Alaska. Even though Alaska is part of the United States, it is located on the northwest side of Canada.

Are the girls ever scared? "The only thing that scares you is the sound of the pager startling you at three in the morning," says seventeen-year-old Erica Kameroff. She joined the crew as a sophomore. **"But the adrenalin takes over.** You don't think about anything but doing whatever has to be done, whether it's medical or fire."

▲ It is important to work together as a team to handle emergencies.

A Unique Rescue Mission

Lydia Hess is a seventeen-year-old firefighter from Boulder, Colorado. She came to Aniak last year to become a Dragon Slayer. "I read about them, and I wanted to work alongside kids my own age," Hess says. She finds the quality of care and the level of professionalism equal to that of a big city department. But there are two **significant** differences.

Getting to the victims in arctic Aniak is far more challenging than in an average city. The Dragon Slayers can't just drive an ambulance to the scene of an emergency. Most of the people they help are Yupik Eskimos and Athabascan Indians, like the Dragon Slayers. Aniak is a landlocked village of 600 people. It is surrounded by rivers. The nearest major city is Anchorage.

◀ Page 3 of 5 ▶

Go to page: [ ] Go

In Other Words
But the adrenalin takes over. You become alert and ready.
significant big; very important

FIRE FIGHTERS   FIRE NEWS

Angels in the Snow

▲ Mariah Brown practices answering a fire call.

It is 350 miles west. The team uses frozen waterways as roads through early May. They travel in snowmobiles and **four-wheelers**. They have to rely on boats when the ice melts. "And here, members of the team almost always know the person who's injured or sick. So it's very personal. There's an emotional aspect to knowing the victim your whole life that you don't have in a larger city," Hess says.

▲ Dragon Slayer Agnes Nicoli

Marteney has had to deal with her share of **difficult** and emotional calls. "After we have a really hard call, we all meet at the fire station. We talk about the person we may have lost, what happened on the call, what we did right," says Marteney. "Then we do a group hug and go for a walk. It really helps."

A World of Opportunities

Brown's team provides vital services to **an indigent**, isolated **region**. It also opens up a world of opportunities for its members that would never be available to them otherwise. "Unless you want a job unloading and loading planes, there's not much to strive for here," says Brown. All of the Dragon Slayers who have left Aniak have gone on to related **careers**. Three **alumni**, one of them Brown's daughter, Mariah, are now medic rescue swimmers.

◀ Page 4 of 5 ▶   Go to page: [   ] Go

Key Vocabulary

difficult *adj.*, very hard
region *n.*, a specific geographical area
career *n.*, a job or a series of jobs

In Other Words

four-wheelers small vehicles
an indigent a poor
alumni people who have left the group

Look Into the Text

1. **Compare and Contrast** How are the Dragon Slayers like EMS **teams** in big cities? How are they different?
2. **Explain** Tell why the Dragon Slayers are so important to a **region** like Aniak.

FIRE FIGHTER PROFILES

▲ Erica Kameroff cleans up after a training fire.

▲ Members of the Dragon Slayers practice an emergency call.

FIRE FIGHTERS   **FIRE NEWS**

Angels in the Snow

▲ Members of the Dragon Slayers practice an emergency call.

They work for the Navy. Four others attend universities around the country studying medicine.

"This experience gave me the confidence to try my best," says Kameroff. She was **granted** a full four-year academic scholarship to the University of Alaska Fairbanks.

Marteney plans to stay in emergency medicine. Another team member is applying to the Coast Guard Academy. The four other Dragon Slayers all plan to pursue careers in medicine. When they do move on they will be replaced by a younger group. This new group has four girls and one boy. They are already in training and are known as the Lizard Killers. "Girls graduate from this program and feel like they're ready to **take on the world**," says Brown. "And they do." ❖

▲ Erica Kameroff cleans up after a training fire.

▲ Four-wheelers allow the teams access to places cars and trucks cannot go.

◀ Page 5 of 5 ▶   Go to page: [   ] [Go]

In Other Words

granted given money for
take on the world try many
new adventures

Look Into the Text

1. **Tone** What is the tone of this article? Give examples of words and language that set the tone.
2. **Cause and Effect** How does being a Dragon Slayer help teenagers with their future **careers**?

▲ Four-wheelers allow the teams access to places cars and trucks cannot go.

Connect Reading and Writing

Vocabulary

accidents

career

departments

difficult

emergencies

experience

region

teams

CRITICAL THINKING

1. SUM IT UP Compare your Two-Column Charts with a partner. Then work together to summarize "Angels in the Snow."

Words and Phrases	What I Learn About the Author's Viewpoint
Marteney stayed brave.	The author believes Marteney's actions show she is brave.

Two-Column Chart

2. Paraphrase In your own words, explain to a partner how a teenager becomes a member of the Dragon Slayers **team**. Use details from the text to support your ideas.

3. Evaluate Revisit your Anticipation Guide. Do you want to change your answers? Why or why not? Discuss your ideas with your classmates.

4. Infer Why do you think the Aniak Fire **Department** named their young **team** of emergency workers the Dragon Slayers? Explain.

READING FLUENCY

Phrasing Read the passage on page 654 to a partner. Assess your fluency.

1. I did not pause/sometimes paused/ always paused for punctuation.

2. What I did best in my reading was _____.

READING STRATEGY

What strategy helped you understand this selection? Tell a partner about it.

VOCABULARY REVIEW

Oral Review Read the paragraph aloud. Add the vocabulary words.

California is a _____ of the country where the fire and police _____ handle many _____. There are many wildfires and car _____. Thank goodness these _____ of workers have the _____ to do their _____ jobs well! Maybe I'll choose to have a _____ helping people, too.

Written Review Imagine you are a member of the Dragon Slayers **team**. Write a journal entry about an **emergency** you handled. What was **difficult** about it? Use five vocabulary words.

WRITE ABOUT THE **GUIDING QUESTION**

Explore Why People Help

Is "Angels in the Snow" a good title for this article? Write your opinion. Reread the selection to find examples to support your ideas.

Connect Across the Curriculum

Vocabulary Study

Use Greek, Latin, and Anglo-Saxon Roots

Academic Vocabulary
- **original** (u-**rij**-un-ul) *adjective*
  Something that is **original** is the first of its kind.

Learn About Roots When you know a word's **original** root, you can figure out its meaning.

Root	Original Language	Meaning
bi	Latin	two
cardia	Greek	heart
medic	Latin	physician; to heal
sib	Anglo-Saxon	kinship, relationship
sophos	Greek	wise

Apply What You Know With a team, find the roots in each of these words below. Use their meanings to figure out the meaning of each English word. Compare your findings with another team.

1. cardiac   **2.** combined   **3.** medical   **4.** siblings   **5.** sophomore

Media/Viewing

Analyze Media

MEDIA &
TECHNOLOGY

Academic Vocabulary
- **communicate** (ku-**myū**-nu-kāt) *verb*
  When you **communicate**, you give and get information.

Media organizations give news and other information to the public. Some examples are magazines, newspapers, television networks, radio stations, and the Internet. Each kind of media **communicates** information differently.

❶ Compare Different Media Choose an event in the news, and find three different kinds of media that talk about it. Make a chart to compare how each type **communicates** information and clarifies the main idea of the event.

❷ Discuss Media Which kind of media does the best job of **communicating** information about the event you chose? Why? Discuss your opinion with your class.

Clarify and Verify

Pair Talk Work with a partner. Give your partner directions for doing something, like playing a video game. Your partner will ask questions to clarify and verify the information you give. Use prepositions to add details. Trade roles.

> Go through the forest and look in each cave to find the treasure chest.

> In other words, I have to look inside each cave for the treasure chest. Is that correct?

Write to Add Important Details

Study the Models When you write, you want to make your writing interesting for the reader. To do that, add important details and information.

JUST OK

The Dragon Slayers are teenage girls. They are in Alaska. The girls help save lives. They make life better for the communities they serve. There are 14 villages that have 3,000 people. The girls go where they are needed. No matter what the weather is like, the Dragon Slayers come to the rescue.

> The reader thinks: **"This writer doesn't give many details about this group. I wonder what they do."**

BETTER

The Dragon Slayers are a group of teenage girls who live in Alaska. They are part of an emergency team that services 14 different villages with a population of 3,000 people. The girls fight fires and bring medical help and other emergency assistance to the people who live in those communities. At any time of day or night and in any weather, people know that the Dragon Slayers will come to their rescue. Through deep snow and over flooded rivers, the Dragon Slayers are on their way with assistance!

> The writer added a lot of interesting details and phrases to tell more about the Dragon Slayers' work.

Add Sentences Think of two sentences to add to the BETTER model above. Be sure to use details that add interest and meaning to your writing.

WRITE ON YOUR OWN Would you like to see an organization like the Dragon Slayers in your town? Write a letter to the local fire department. Explain what such a group might do to help your community. Use interesting details to make the writing more engaging.

> **REMEMBER**
>
> Prepositional phrases can tell:
> - location
> - direction
> - time

Zlateh the Goat

by Isaac Bashevis Singer

SELECTION 3 OVERVIEW

▶ **Build Background**

▶ **Language & Grammar**
Tell an Original Story
Use Pronouns in the Subject and Predicate

▶ **Prepare to Read**
Learn Key Vocabulary
Analyze Plot and Theme

▶ **Read and Write**
Introduce the Genre
Classic Short Story
Focus on Reading
Determine Viewpoints
Apply the Focus Strategy
Make Connections
Critical Thinking
Reading Fluency
Read with Expression
Vocabulary Review
Write About the Guiding Question

▶ **Connect Across the Curriculum**
Vocabulary Study
Use Borrowed Words
Listening/Speaking
Respond to Literature
Language and Grammar
Tell an Original Story
Writing and Grammar
Write an Original Story

Build Background

Learn How People Rely on Animals

Before automobiles, supermarkets, and modern machinery, people relied on animals for survival. Throughout the world today, people still rely on animals.

Connect

Quickwrite Write about the ways animals are important in your life. How are they important in the lives of people you know? What would life be like without them?

Digital Library
myNGconnect.com
🔍 View the images.

▲ In many parts of the world, people need animals to survive.

Language & Grammar

1 TRY OUT LANGUAGE
2 LEARN GRAMMAR
3 APPLY ON YOUR OWN

Tell an Original Story CD

Listen to the song and join in.
Then listen to an original story.

SONG and STORY

Stories

A story's not a story if it hasn't got a plot.
Characters and setting, too, will really add a lot.
A single voice must tell the tale to add a point of view.
That someone could be you.

A story's not a story if it doesn't have a theme.
With a valued message that is never too extreme:
Love and courage, loss and hope, to mention just a few.
The message must be true.

A story's not a story if it doesn't have an end,
All the questions answered, nothing left to comprehend.
When characters have changed a bit and solved their problems, too,
The tale is finally through.

1 TRY OUT LANGUAGE
2 LEARN GRAMMAR
3 APPLY ON YOUR OWN

Use Pronouns in the Subject and Predicate

A noun can be the **subject** of a sentence or the **object** of a verb in the predicate.

A **pronoun** refers to a noun. Like a noun, it can also be the **subject** of a sentence or the **object** of a verb. Study the chart. Which pronouns are the same for subject and object?

Subject Pronouns	I	you	he	she	it	we	you	they
Object Pronouns	me	you	him	her	it	us	you	them

- Use a **subject pronoun** as the subject of a sentence.

  EXAMPLES **Misty** is our cat. **She** likes milk.

  The milk is fresh. **It** came from the store.

- Use an **object pronoun** as the object of the verb.

  EXAMPLES Misty drinks the **milk**. She drinks **it** from a dish.

  Misty catches **mice**. She leaves **them** by the door.

Remember, most English statements follow this pattern:
subject ➜ verb ➜ object.

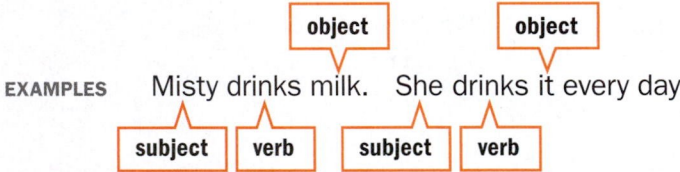

EXAMPLES   Misty drinks milk.   She drinks it every day.

Practice Together

Say each sentence. Choose the correct pronoun.

1. I got a kitten for my birthday. My parents surprised (I/me).
2. We named (her/them) Princess.
3. (She/Her) is really cute with black and white fur.
4. Princess loves to watch butterflies. She often chases (they/them).

Try It!

Say each sentence. Write the correct pronoun on a card. Then say the sentence with the pronoun.

5. My brother has a new pet, too. (He/Him) got a dog.
6. He plays with his dog, Eddie, every day. Eddie follows (he/him) everywhere.
7. Eddie loves stuffed toys. He carries (they/them) everywhere.
8. Sometimes (we/us) play with our cat and dog together.

▲ Our dog loves toys. He plays tug-of-war with them.

Explore Storytelling

TELL AN ORIGINAL STORY

Everyone can be a storyteller. What story do you want to tell? Make up a tale that includes both people and animals and how they help one another.

List a few ideas for the characters, setting, and plot in a story chart like this one.

Story Chart

Characters	Setting	Plot
a dog—name is Gremlin	on a farm in mid-winter	dog helps farmer
a fox		
a farmer		

Work with a partner and take turns telling your stories using the information in your charts. Practice together several times until you can tell the tales easily. Then share your stories with the class.

HOW TO TELL AN ORIGINAL STORY

1. Introduce your characters.
2. Tell when and where your story takes place.
3. Tell about the problem your character faces.
4. Tell how the problem is solved and how the story ends.

> It was a stormy night. The wind howled as it blew my hat out over the frozen lake. I pulled my coat close around me and wondered how I would find my hat.

USE PRONOUNS IN THE SUBJECT AND PREDICATE

When you tell your story, you don't want to bore your listeners by repeating the same nouns over and over. Instead, use **subject** and **object** pronouns to keep your story interesting.

EXAMPLE   Rob and Lou went skiing. **They** had a surprising adventure. Pedro and Rosa are their friends. They invited **them** to go skiing, too.

EXAMPLE   Lucas is hungry. **He** wants to get pizza.
Trey and Henry are his friends. He invites **them** to go, too.

Prepare to Read

Learn Key Vocabulary

Study the Words Use the steps below.

1. Pronounce the word. Say it aloud several times. Spell it.
2. Rate your word knowledge.
3. Study the example. Tell more about the word.
4. Practice it. Make the word your own.

Key Words

blizzard (bli-zurd) *noun*
▶ page 454

A **blizzard** is a strong snowstorm. It's hard to see where you are going in a **blizzard**.

confidence (kahn-fu-dints) *noun* ▶ page 454

When you have **confidence**, you believe you can do something. He has **confidence** that he will win the game.
Related Word: **confident**

continue (kun-**tin**-yū) *verb*
▶ page 454

To **continue** means to keep doing something. This runner **continues** the race for his team.
Related Word: **continuation**

decide (di-sīd) *verb*
▶ page 452

When you **decide**, you make a choice about something. He cannot **decide** what to wear.
Related Word: **decision**

patiently (pā-shint-lē) *adverb*
▶ page 452

When you do something **patiently**, you do not get upset. My dog waits **patiently** for me to finish shopping.
Related Words: **patient, patience**

peasant (pe-zint) *noun*
▶ page 452

A **peasant** is a European small farm worker. **Peasants** worked hard for the things they had.

shelter (shel-tur) *noun*
▶ page 454

A **shelter** is something that covers and protects you. A bus **shelter** can protect you from the weather.
Related Word: **sheltered**

trust (trust) *verb*
▶ page 452

To **trust** someone means to believe that they will do what is best for you. This girl **trusts** her friend to catch her.
Related Words: **mistrust, trusting, trustworthy**

Practice the Words Work with a partner. Write a question using two Key Words. Answer your partner's question, using at least one Key Word in your answer. Ask and answer questions until you have each used all of the Key Words.

Questions	Answers
Do you trust me to continue my work?	Yes, I have confidence in you.

Analyze Plot and Theme

Plot is not just what happens in a story. It is the series of events that characters go through to solve a problem or achieve a goal. A writer uses plot to develop the theme, or main message. Analyzing important events such as conflict, complications, climax, and resolution will help you to understand how plot **affects** the theme.

As you read, identify key events that **affect** the theme.

Look Into the Text

> For Reuven the furrier it was a bad year, and after long hesitation he decided to sell Zlateh the goat. She was old and gave little milk. Feivel the town butcher had offered eight gulden for her. … Reuven told his oldest boy Aaron to take the goat to town.
>
> Aaron understood what taking the goat meant, but had to obey his father. Leah, his mother, wiped the tears from her eyes when she heard the news.

Practice Together

Begin a Plot Diagram A Plot Diagram can help you identify key events that develop a theme. This Plot Diagram reveals the theme. Reread the passage above and add to the Plot Diagram.

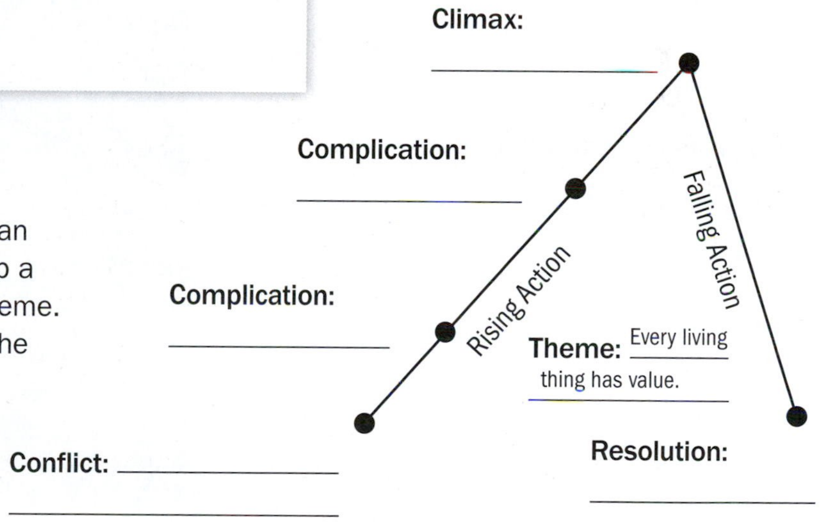

Climax: _____

Complication: _____

Complication: _____

Rising Action

Falling Action

Theme: Every living thing has value.

Conflict: _____

Resolution: _____

Academic Vocabulary
- **affect** (u-**fekt**) *noun*
  When you affect someone or something, you cause a change.

Classic Short Story

A classic short story is fiction. The story has few characters and simple settings. The plot focuses on a single event, and the characters face one main **conflict**, or problem.

The details of how the conflict develops can also provide you with clues about the theme. Changes in setting and character can create complications in the plot.

Making connections to other texts can help you understand the plot and theme better. As you read, think about stories you have read with a similar theme and how the theme was developed.

Look Into the Text

In his twelve years Aaron had seen all kinds of weather, but he had never experienced a snow like this one. It was so dense it shut out the light of day. In a short time their path was completely covered. The wind became as cold as ice.

The character faces a problem.

Zlateh the Goat

by Isaac Bashevis Singer

At Hanukkah time the road from the village to the town is usually covered with snow, but this year the winter had been a mild one. Hanukkah had almost come, yet little snow had fallen. The sun shone most of the time. The **peasants** complained that because of the dry weather there would be a poor harvest of winter grain. New grass sprouted, and the peasants sent their cattle **out to pasture**.

For Reuven the **furrier** it was a bad year, and after long hesitation he decided to sell Zlateh the goat. She was old and gave little milk. Feivel the town **butcher** had offered eight gulden for her. Such a sum would buy Hanukkah candles, potatoes and oil for pancakes, gifts for the children, and other holiday necessaries for the house. Reuven told his oldest boy Aaron to take the goat to town.

Aaron understood what taking the goat to Feivel meant, but had to obey his father. Leah, his mother, wiped the tears from her eyes when she heard the news. Aaron's younger sisters, Anna and Miriam, cried loudly. Aaron put on his quilted jacket and a cap with earmuffs, bound a rope around Zlateh's neck, and took along two slices of bread with cheese to eat **on the road**. Aaron was supposed to deliver the goat by evening, spend the night at the butcher's, and return the next day with the money.

While the family said goodbye to the goat, and Aaron placed the rope around the neck, Zlateh stood as **patiently** and good-naturedly as ever. She licked Reuven's hand. She shook her small white beard. Zlateh **trusted** human beings. She knew that they always fed her and never did her any harm.

When Aaron brought Zlateh out on the road to town, she seemed somewhat astonished. She'd never been led in that direction before. She looked back at him questioningly, as if to say, "Where are you taking me?" But after a while she seemed to come to the conclusion that a goat **shouldn't ask questions**. Still, the road was different. They passed new fields, pastures, and huts with thatched roofs. Here and there a dog barked and came running after them, but

---

Key Vocabulary

decide v., to make a choice
peasant n., a poor farmer
patiently adv., calmly, kindly
trust v., to believe

In Other Words

out to pasture to eat the grass
furrier coat maker
butcher meat seller
on the road while he walked
shouldn't ask questions should trust its owner

Cultural Background

Hanukkah is a Jewish festival that lasts eight days in November or December. Families celebrate by lighting candles on each night and by giving gifts.

Aaron chased it away with his stick.

The sun was shining when Aaron left the village. Suddenly the weather changed. A large black cloud with a bluish center appeared in the east and spread itself rapidly over the sky. A cold wind blew in with it. The crows flew low, croaking. At first it looked as if it would rain, but instead it began to hail as in summer. It was early in the day, but it became dark as dusk. After a while the hail turned to snow.

In his twelve years Aaron had seen all kinds of weather, but he had never experienced a snow like this one. It was so dense it shut out the light of the day. In a short time their path was completely covered. The wind became as cold as ice. The road to town was narrow and winding. Aaron no longer knew where he was. He could not see through the snow. The cold soon penetrated his quilted jacket.

At first Zlateh didn't seem to **mind** the change in weather. She, too, was twelve years old and knew what winter meant.

But when her legs sank deeper and deeper into the snow, she began to turn her head and look at Aaron **in wonderment**. Her mild eyes seemed to ask, "Why are we out in such a storm?" Aaron hoped that a peasant would come along with his cart, but no one passed by.

The snow grew thicker, falling to the ground in large, whirling flakes. Beneath it Aaron's boots touched the softness of a plowed field. He realized that he was no longer on the road. He had gone astray. He could no longer figure out which was east or west, which way was the village, the town. The wind whistled, howled, whirled the snow about in **eddies**. It looked as if white **imps** were playing tag on the fields. A white dust rose above the ground. Zlateh stopped. She could walk no longer. Stubbornly she **anchored her cleft hooves** in the earth and bleated as if pleading to be taken home. Icicles hung from her white beard, and her horns were glazed with frost.

In Other Words

mind care about
in wonderment with confusion
eddies circles
imps elves, children
anchored her cleft hooves stuck her feet

Look Into the Text

1. **Character's Motive** Why does the family **decide** to sell Zlateh?
2. **Inference** How can you tell that the family loves Zlateh and does not want to sell her?
3. **Plot** How does the author show that Aaron and Zlateh might be in danger?

Aaron did not want to admit the danger, but he knew just the same that if they did not find **shelter** they would freeze to death. This was no ordinary storm. It was a mighty **blizzard**. The snowfall had reached his knees. His hands were numb, and he could no longer feel his toes. He choked when he breathed. His nose felt like wood, and he rubbed it with snow. Zlateh's bleating began to sound like crying. Those humans in whom she had so much **confidence** had dragged her into a trap. Aaron began to pray to God for himself and for the innocent animal.

Suddenly he made out the shape of a hill. He wondered what it could be. Who had piled snow onto such a huge heap? He moved toward it, dragging Zlateh after him. When he came near it, he realized that it was a large haystack which the snow had **blanketed**.

Aaron realized immediately that they were saved. With great effort he dug his way through the snow. He was a village boy and knew what to do. When he reached the hay, he **hollowed out a nest** for himself and the goat. No matter how cold it may be outside, in the hay it is always warm. And the hay was food for Zlateh. The moment she smelled it she became contented and began to eat. Outside, the snow **continued** to fall. It quickly covered the passageway Aaron had dug. But a boy and an animal need to breathe, and there was hardly any air in their hideout. Aaron bored a kind of a window through the hay and snow and carefully kept the passage clear.

Zlateh, having eaten her fill, sat down on her hind legs and seemed to **have regained her confidence in man**. Aaron ate his two slices of bread and cheese, but after the difficult journey he was still hungry. He looked at Zlateh and noticed her udders were full. He lay down next to her, placing himself so that when he milked her he could squirt the milk into his mouth. It was rich and sweet. Zlateh was not accustomed to being milked that way,

---

Key Vocabulary

shelter *n.*, something that covers or gives protection; a safe place

blizzard *n.*, a bad snowstorm

confidence *n.*, a belief or trust in something or someone

continue *v.*, to keep happening

In Other Words

blanketed covered
hollowed out a nest dug a hole
have regained her confidence in man believe in people again

but she did not resist. On the contrary, she seemed eager to reward Aaron for bringing her to a shelter whose very walls, floor, and ceiling were made of food.

Through the window Aaron could **catch a glimpse of the chaos** outside. The wind carried before it whole drifts of snow. It was completely dark, and he did not know whether night had already come or whether it was the darkness of the storm. Thank God that in the hay it was not cold. The dried hay, grass, and field flowers **exuded** the warmth of the summer sun. Zlateh ate frequently; she nibbled from above, below, from the left and right. Her body gave forth an animal warmth, and Aaron cuddled up to her. He had always loved Zlateh, but now she was like a sister. He was alone, cut off from his family, and wanted to talk. He began to talk to Zlateh. "Zlateh, what do you think about what has happened to us?" he asked.

"Maaaa," Zlateh answered.

"If we hadn't found this stack of hay, we would both be **frozen stiff** by now," Aaron said.

"Maaaa," was the goat's reply.

"If the snow keeps on falling like this, we may have to stay here for days," Aaron explained.

"Maaaa," Zlateh bleated.

"What does 'maaaa' mean?" Aaron asked. "You'd better speak up clearly."

"Maaaa, maaaa," Zlateh tried.

"Well, let it be 'maaaa' then," Aaron said patiently.

"You can't speak, but I know you understand. I need you and you need me. Isn't that right?"

"Maaaa."

Aaron became sleepy. He made a pillow out of some hay, leaned his head on it, and dozed off. Zlateh, too, fell asleep.

When Aaron opened his eyes, he didn't know whether it was morning or night. The snow had blocked up his window. He tried to clear it, but when he had bored through to the length of his arm, he still hadn't reached the outside. Luckily he had his stick with him and was able to break through to the open air.

In Other Words

catch a glimpse of the chaos view the trouble
exuded gave off
frozen stiff dead from the cold

It was still dark outside. The snow continued to fall and the wind wailed, **first with one voice and then with many**. Sometimes it had the sound of devilish laughter. Zlateh, too, awoke, and when Aaron greeted her, she answered, "Maaaa."

Yes, Zlateh's language consisted of only one word, but it meant many things. Now she was saying, "We must accept all that God gives us—heat, cold, hunger, satisfaction, light, and darkness."

Aaron had awakened hungry. He had eaten up his food, but Zlateh had plenty of milk.

For three days Aaron and Zlateh stayed in the haystack. Aaron had always loved Zlateh, but in these three days he loved her more and more. She fed him with her milk and helped him keep warm. She comforted him with her patience. He told her many stories, and she always **cocked** her ears and listened. When he patted her, she licked his hand and his face. Then she said, "Maaaa," and he knew it meant, I love you, too.

The snow fell for three days, though after the first day it was not as thick, and the wind quieted down. Sometimes Aaron felt that there could never have been a summer, that the snow had always fallen, ever since he could remember. He, Aaron, never had a father or mother or sisters. He was a snow child, **born of** the snow, and so was Zlateh. It was so quiet in the hay that his ears rang in the stillness. Aaron and Zlateh slept all night and a good part of the day. As for Aaron's dreams, they were all about warm weather. He dreamed of green fields, trees covered with blossoms, clear brooks, and singing birds. By the third night the snow had stopped, but Aaron **did not dare** to find his way home in the darkness. The sky became clear and the moon shone, casting silvery nets on the snow. Aaron dug his way out and looked at the world. It was all white, quiet, dreaming dreams of **heavenly splendor**. The stars were large and close. The moon swam in the sky as in a sea.

On the morning of the fourth day Aaron heard the ringing of sleigh bells. The haystack was not far from the road. The peasant who drove the sleigh pointed out the way to him—not to the town and Feivel the

---

In Other Words

first with one voice and then with many loudly and with many sounds
cocked turned
born of used to
did not dare knew he shouldn't try
heavenly splendor happiness

butcher, but home to the village. Aaron had decided in the haystack that he would never **part with** Zlateh.

Aaron's family and their neighbors had searched for the boy and the goat but had found **no trace of them** during the storm. They feared they were lost. Aaron's mother and sisters cried for him; his father remained silent and gloomy. Suddenly one of the neighbors came running to their house with the news that Aaron and Zlateh were coming up the road.

There was great joy in the family. Aaron told them how he had found the stack of hay and how Zlateh had fed him with her milk. Aaron's sisters kissed and hugged Zlateh and gave her a special treat of chopped carrots and potato peels, which Zlateh gobbled up hungrily.

Nobody ever again thought of selling Zlateh, and now that the cold weather had finally set in, the villagers needed the services of Reuven the furrier once more. When Hanukkah came, Aaron's mother was able to fry pancakes every evening, and Zlateh got her portion, too. Even though Zlateh had her own pen, she often came to the kitchen, knocking on the door with her horns to indicate that she was ready to visit, and she was always **admitted**. In the evening Aaron, Miriam, and Anna played dreidel. Zlateh sat near the stove watching the children and flickering of the Hanukkah candles.

Once in a while Aaron would ask her, "Zlateh, do you remember the three days we spent together?"

And Zlateh would scratch her neck with a horn, shake her white bearded head, and **come out with** a single sound which expressed all her thoughts, and all her love. ❖

In Other Words
part with leave, sell
no trace of them no clues to show where they could be
admitted let inside
come out with make

Cultural Background
A dreidel is a four-sided top. A top is a children's toy that spins on the ground or a surface. The dreidel game is often played during Hanukkah as part of the celebration.

Look Into the Text

1. **Confirm Prediction** Was your prediction correct about Aaron and Zlateh? Explain.
2. **Details** How did Zlateh keep Aaron alive? Give examples from the text.
3. **Character's Viewpoint** How have the family's feelings for Zlateh changed? How do you know?

About the Author

Isaac Bashevis Singer (1904–1991) was best known for his use of folklore, legend, and magical elements in his writing. In 1978, he won the Nobel Prize for Literature for his novel, *Shosha*. Singer knew that writing wasn't always easy. He famously said, "The wastebasket is the writer's best friend." Singer died in 1991.

Isaac Bashevis
Singer

No camel route is long with good company.

– Turkish proverb

The Story of Mzee and Owen

Mzee, a giant tortoise, and Owen, a baby hippo, made global headlines after they met in 2004.

▲ Mzee and Owen in 2005. Then Owen weighed just 660 pounds.

On December 26, 2004, a powerful earthquake hit the floor of the Indian Ocean, sending a **tsunami** as far away as the coast of Kenya. The wave washed away a **pod** of hippos into the sea. Only one hippo survived, a baby that would one day be known as "Owen." Residents of the coastal town of Malindi, Kenya, worked to rescue Owen. Today, he lives happily in a wildlife **sanctuary** called Haller Park, near Mombasa. But what is really remarkable is the story of Owen and his best friend, a 130-year-old tortoise named Mzee. Mzee (whose name means "wise old man") **took the hippo under his wing** after the hippo's arrival. Mzee protected Owen and taught him to survive.

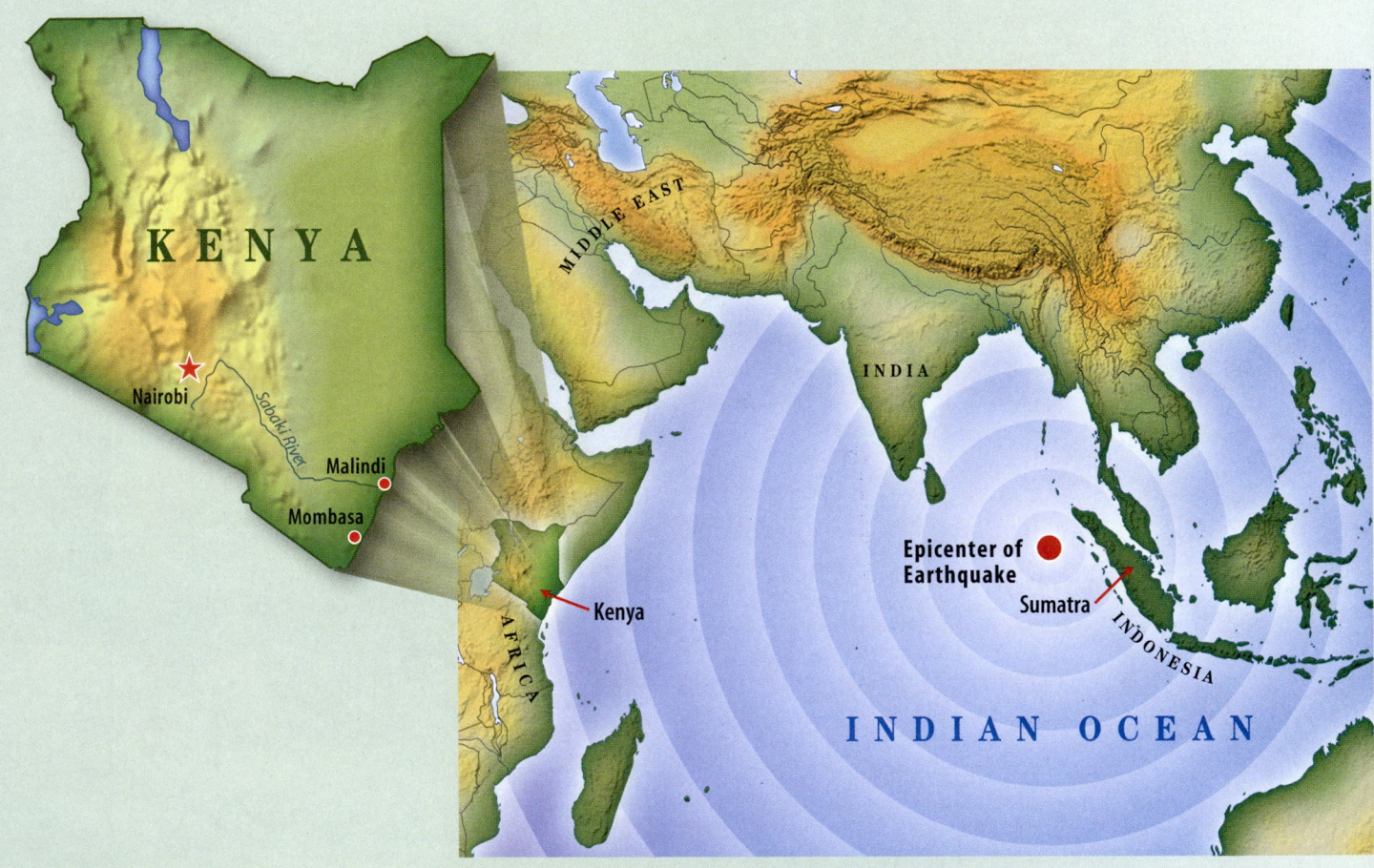

In Other Words
tsunami great ocean wave
pod group
sanctuary shelter
took the hippo under his wing took care of Owen

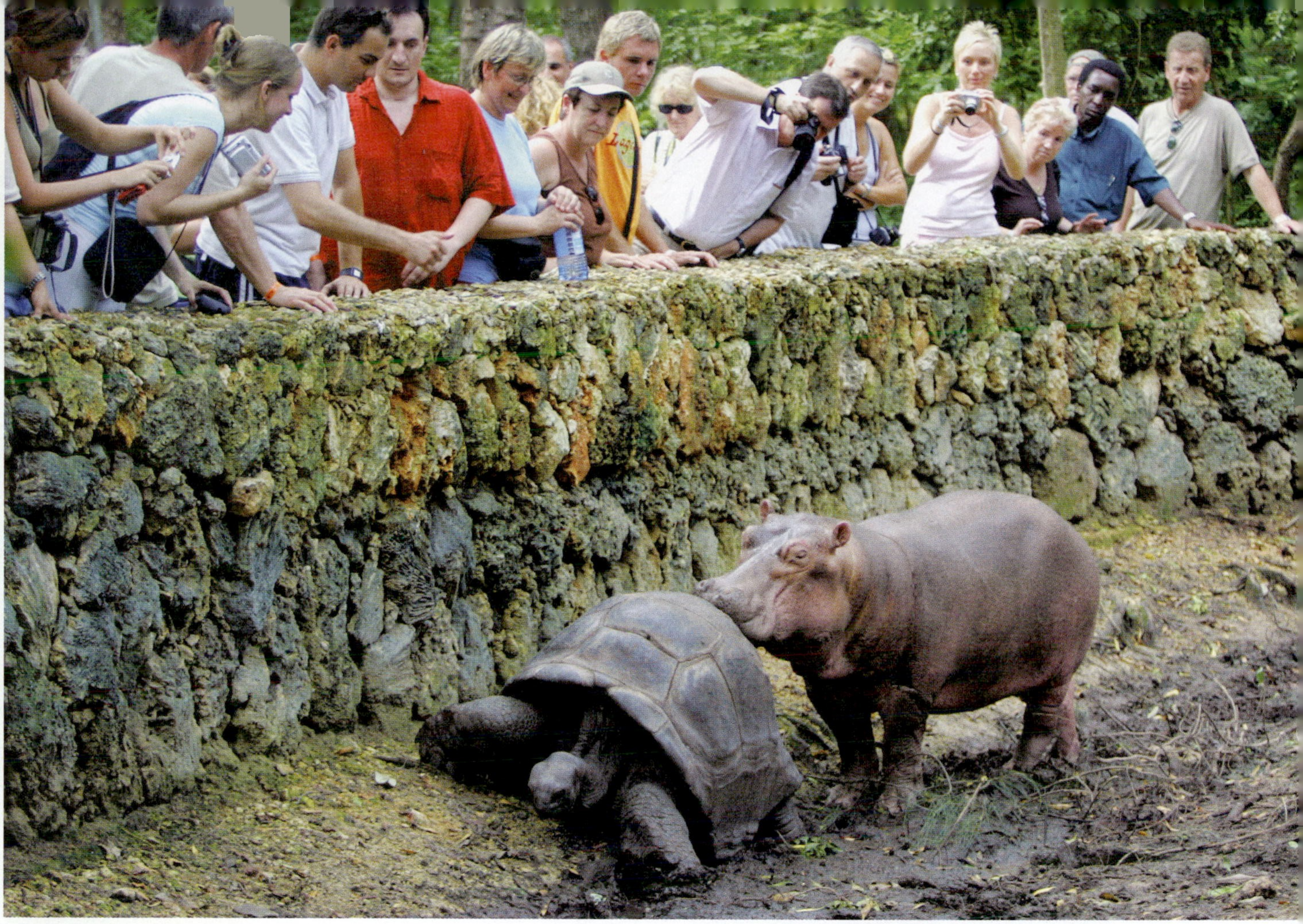

▲ Owen follows Mzee wherever he goes. Visitors to Haller Park gather to watch feeding time every afternoon.

When Owen was first introduced to his new home at Haller Park, he hid behind Mzee for safety. He was frightened and alone. Then, to everyone's surprise, Owen began to follow Mzee wherever he went.

Park officials say that Mzee liked to be alone until Owen came along. Mzee wasn't sure about Owen at first. Gradually, Mzee began to accept his new **companion**.

▲ The two friends take in the sights.

In Other Words
companion friend

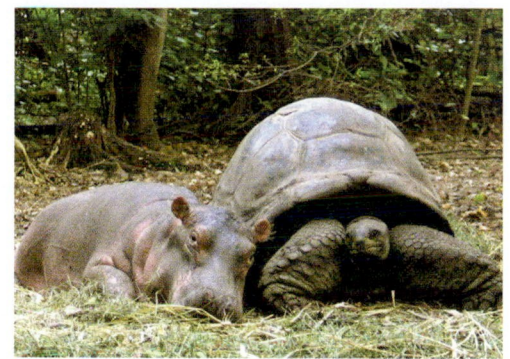

▲ Sharing a snack

Owen began to do everything Mzee did, too. Mzee taught Owen how to eat, so Owen ate when Mzee ate. Mzee taught Owen how to find leaves. When Mzee drank, Owen did, too.

Lately, the scientists who study the pair have noticed that the two share a strange, new language. They have heard low, growl-like sounds coming from both of them. These sounds aren't sounds hippos or tortoises usually make. Owen and Mzee have found a special way to communicate. Sometimes they talk like this for hours.

▲ Mzee talks to Owen in their own special language.

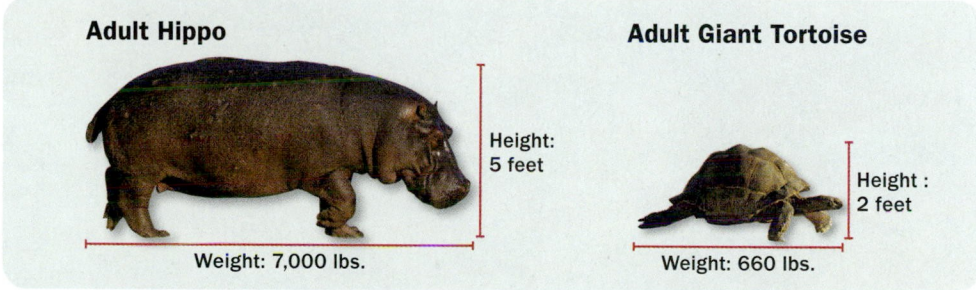

A herd of hippos rest on the edge of the water in Africa.

Hippos are social animals and depend on a group to be happy. Although Mzee is Owen's friend, scientists have worried that Owen may need the company of other hippos as he grows older. Scientists have also worried that he would hurt Mzee **unintentionally**. A full-grown hippo could crush a tortoise with one blow of its foot.

Size Comparison Diagram

Adult Hippo	**Adult Giant Tortoise**
Height: 5 feet	Height: 2 feet
Weight: 7,000 lbs.	Weight: 660 lbs.

In Other Words
unintentionally without meaning to

It is likely that Owen and Mzee will be separated. But park officials do not want them to lose their special bond, so Owen will always be close by. This special pair have taught the world that there is still a lot to learn about the relationships between animals, and that sometimes the unlikeliest friendships are the best of all.

▼ Mzee and Owen in 2006, two years after Owen's arrival.

Look Into the Text

1. **Cause and Effect** What caused Owen and Mzee to meet?
2. **Explain** What did Mzee do for Owen?
3. **Inference** For what reasons might Owen be attached to Mzee?

Connect Reading and Writing

Vocabulary
- blizzard
- confidence
- continued
- decided
- patiently
- peasants
- shelter
- trust

CRITICAL THINKING

1. SUM IT UP Use your Plot Diagram to summarize the story with a partner. Think about what happened before, during, and after the **blizzard** .

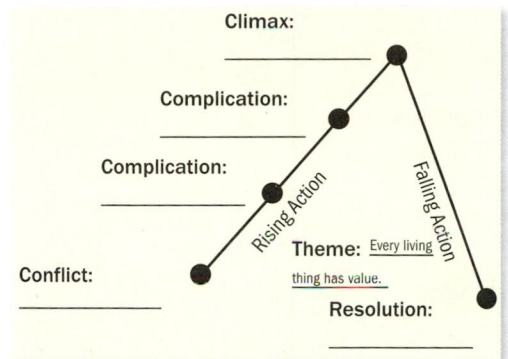

Plot Diagram

2. Paraphrase In your own words, tell a partner how Aaron knew he needed **shelter** . Use details from the text.

3. Compare Compare the relationships between Zlateh and Aaron and Owen and Mzee. What is similar about the two relationships?

4. Discuss Share your Quickwrite with a partner. How did you **decide** that animals were important? Explain.

READING FLUENCY

Expression Read the passage on page 655 to a partner. Assess your fluency.

1. My voice never/sometimes/always matched what I read.

2. What I did best in my reading was _____ .

READING STRATEGY

What strategy helped you understand this selection? Tell a partner about it.

VOCABULARY REVIEW

Oral Review Read the paragraph aloud. Add the vocabulary words.

After a big _____ , the snow was so high that it covered my dog's house. It was his only _____ . I _____ to bring the dog inside, but Grandpa refused. He grew up in a village of _____ and farmers. Animals never came inside. I didn't have much _____ that I could change his mind. But I _____ explained why it was important. I _____ to tell Grandpa that he could _____ me.

Written Review Imagine you are a reporter interviewing Aaron about the **blizzard** . Write a short article. Use five vocabulary words.

WRITE ABOUT THE GUIDING QUESTION

Explore Our Bond with Animals
Why do we **trust** animals? Why do they **trust** us? Write your ideas. Reread the selection to find examples to support your ideas.

Connect Across the Curriculum

Borrowed Words

Academic Vocabulary
- **original** (u-**rij**-un-ul) *adjective*
  Something that is **original** is the first of its kind.

A **borrowed word** is a word that we use in English in almost the same way it is used in its **original** language. For example, the word *dreidel* is a borrowed word from the Hebrew language. A dreidel is a toy you play a game with.

Study Borrowed Words Work with a partner to find each word in a dictionary or online source. Study the entry to figure out the **original** language from which the word was borrowed.

1. Hanukkah   **2.** monsoon   **3.** poodle   **4.** hurricane

Respond to Literature

Academic Vocabulary
- **response** (ri-**spons**) *noun*
  A **response** is an answer or reply to something that has happened or has been said.

Every person's **response** to literature is different. Share your ideas by presenting your **response** to "Zlateh the Goat."

❶ Prepare Your Response Study the story closely.
- Think about your reaction to the story. How did it make you feel?
- Decide what part or parts you liked best.
- Write down some notes about what you are going to say.

❷ Practice Giving Your Response Practice speaking in front of another person.
- Briefly summarize the story and its message.
- Describe your reaction and what you learned from the story.
- Give examples from the story to support your views.
- Ask your listener what you could do to make your **response** better.

❸ Deliver Your Response Keep your **response** focused and clear.
- Make eye contact with your audience. Don't stare down at your notes.
- Speak clearly and answer any questions.

Tell an Original Story

Teamwork Tale Work with a group to create a story. First, brainstorm an overall topic for the tale. Then, one person starts the story with a sentence or two. Each time someone stops, the next person continues the story to tell what happens next. Continue around the group several times until the story is finished. Use pronouns correctly.

> The farmer had no idea how he would pay the rent.

> Then he remembered the box he had hidden away so long ago!

Write an Original Story

Study the Models When you write a story, make sure you talk about events in the order that they happened. Don't confuse your reader by using the wrong form of words.

NOT OK

> One day at the lake, my dog started acting strange. He kept nudging me with his nose and barking. Then <u>him</u> would run to the lake. <u>Him</u> did this over and over. Finally, <u>me</u> looked out in the water and saw a woman waving her arms. <u>Her</u> needed help. <u>Us</u> called 911 on my dad's cell phone, and an emergency crew came immediately. <u>Them</u> saved her. Actually, my dog was the real hero that day!

This writer confuses the reader by not using the correct words.

OK

> One day at the lake, my dog started acting strange. He kept nudging me with his nose and barking. Then <u>he</u> would run to the lake. <u>He</u> did this over and over. Finally, <u>I</u> looked out in the water and saw a woman waving her arms. <u>She</u> needed help. <u>I</u> called 911 on my dad's cell phone, and an emergency crew came immediately. <u>They</u> saved her. Actually, my dog was the real hero that day!

The writer uses the correct forms of words. The reader gets a clear idea.

Add Sentences Think of two sentences to add to the OK model above. Be sure to use the correct forms of words.

WRITE ON YOUR OWN Write about the story you helped to create in your group. Make sure the events are in order and that you use words correctly to avoid confusing your reader.

REMEMBER

Use subject and object pronouns to make your writing more interesting, but make sure the meaning is clear.

- Use *I, you, he, she, it, we,* and *they* as the **subject** of a sentence.
- Use *me, you, him, her, it, us,* and *them* as the **object** of the verb.
- Note that *you* and *it* are the same in both forms.

A Conflict Close to Home

by Aziz Abu Sarah

1   A disaster can strike your nation, your state, or even the house of your next-door neighbor, but as long as it strikes someone else, it is still a distance away. Like many in Jerusalem, I grew up seeing many people die because of a "worthless conflict." I felt sad for them, but I **continued** to live my life just as before. My reaction was the same as others who see an **accident** on the side of the road, think "how sad," and drive on. However, my life changed forever the moment the disaster struck my house and my family, and the casualty was my brother.

2   In the spring of 1990, I shared a room with four of my brothers. One ordinary day I was woken at 5:00 a.m., as Israeli soldiers **burst** into my room. They asked us for our identity cards, and questioned the five of us. "Where were you yesterday? Did you throw stones?" They demanded the answers, and when they received none, they took my 18-year-old brother with them. My mother pleaded desperately with the soldiers but in the end they took Tayseer with them. She would not hold him again until eleven months later, when he was released from prison.

3   Tayseer was kept without trial. He was **interrogated** and beaten for fifteen days until he admitted that he had thrown stones at Israeli cars. During the eleven months he was imprisoned, we met him three times. Although we spoke with him through two fences, it was obvious that with each visit his health was **deteriorating** from the beatings. Finally, in the late days of March, he was released from prison. His condition was critical, and he was throwing up blood. We rushed him to the hospital.

4   Tayseer held on for about three weeks, before dying after surgery. I was 10 years old at that time, and Tayseer had been closest to me in age and closest to me as a friend and brother. I could not accept his death. He had helped me with homework. He **had accompanied** me on my first day of school.

5   I became extremely bitter and angry. Even at ten I understood that his death was not natural, and someone was responsible. I grew up with anger burning in my heart. I wanted justice. I wanted revenge.

6   In my high school years I started writing for a youth magazine. I was a consistent writer

Key Vocabulary
- **continue** *v.*, to keep happening
- **accident** *n.*, an unexpected event that causes injury

In Other Words
burst came quickly
interrogated questioned
deteriorating getting worse
had accompanied came with

and wrote about two articles a week. I wrote with anger and bitterness, and used my anger to spread hatred against the other side. My success soon earned me the position of editor at the magazine. However, the more I wrote the more empty and angry I became. Eventually I grew tired of the anger, so I quit the magazine and tried to move out of the country.

7   I failed to get anywhere. After graduating from high school I found myself stuck in Jerusalem. I had refused to learn Hebrew growing up: it was the "enemy's" language. Now, to attend university or get a good job I would have to compromise. I started studying in a Hebrew Ulpan, an institute for Jewish newcomers to Israel. It was the hardest

"Eventually I grew tired of the anger."

experience I had faced yet, but its results were the best I have encountered. It was the first time I had sat in a room of Jews who were not superior to me. It was the first time I had seen faces different from the soldiers at the checkpoints. Those soldiers had taken my brother; these students were the same as me. My understanding of the Jewish people started to collapse after just a few weeks of the Ulpan. I found myself confused, thinking, "How can they be normal human beings, just like me?" I was amazed that I could build friendships with these students and share their struggles. We went out for coffee together. We studied together. Sometimes we even found that we shared the same interests. For me, this was a turning point in my life.

8   I came to understand that unfortunate things happen in our lives which are out of our control. A ten-year-old could not control the soldiers who took his brother. But now as an adult, I could control my response to these hurts. **They** had acted unjustly and murdered Tayseer, but I had the choice, and I still have the choice, of whether to follow in the same direction.

9   Each day I live I refuse to become like those soldiers fifteen years ago, and I choose to put aside the rage I worshipped as a teenager. I will always have this choice. It is a hard decision to abandon revenge, and an easy road to follow your feelings. Yet hatred **begets** hatred, and the same tools you use on the others will be used on you. As a result, each day I must choose again to love and forgive those around me.

10   As humans, we try to rationalize our hatred. In our minds we demonize the enemy, and discredit their humanity. This is the lie that fires the conflict between Israel and Palestine.

11   Maybe I will never see the world restored to perfect humanity, but I still feel obligated to believe that the tools for peace are not tools of violence and hatred. More than this, I feel obligated to use my pain to spread peace, rather than using it to fuel a hatred that would have eventually **consumed me**. I believe we are all obligated to do our best to create peace, and not wait until it **hits home**. After all, there is no good war or bad peace.

In Other Words
They The Israeli soldiers who captured my brother
begets creates more
consumed me taken over my life
hits home directly affects our families

Compare Across Texts

Compare Characters and Setting

"The Challenge" on page 103 and "Zlateh the Goat" both tell about a character who faces a conflict, or problem. Compare how the conflicts in these texts are **affected** by the characters and setting.

How It Works

Collect and Organize Story Elements To compare conflicts, organize information from the story in a chart. Think about how the settings **affect** the conflicts. Also note how characters' actions influence the conflict and resolution of the problem.

Selection	Conflict	How Setting Affects Conflict	How Characters Affect Conflict
"The Challenge"	José is trying to get Estela's attention.	In school, Jose has many chances to try to make Estela notice him.	
"Zlateh the Goat"	Aaron must sell the family's goat.	The blizzard stops him from getting to town.	

Comparison Chart

Practice Together

Compare the Effect of Setting and Characters Compare the information from the chart. State each conflict and then show how the setting **affects** it. Here is the beginning of a comparison between two texts.

Comparison

> Both José in "The Challenge" and Aaron in "Zlateh the Goat" have conflicts they want to resolve. José can't get the attention of a girl he likes, and Aaron has to sell his goat to the butcher. In each story, the setting affects the conflict . . .

Try It!

Copy and complete the chart. Compare how the characters **affect** the conflict in each selection. Use this frame to help you.

The characters in "The Challenge" and in "Zlateh the Goat" affect the conflict through their actions and desires. In "The Challenge," _____ . In "Zlateh the Goat," _____ .

Academic Vocabulary
● **affect** (u-fekt) *verb*
   When you **affect** someone or something, you cause a change.

TO THE
RESCUE

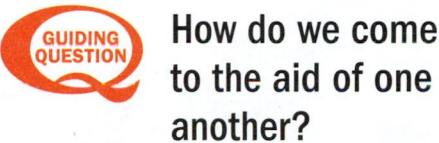 **How do we come to the aid of one another?**

Content Library

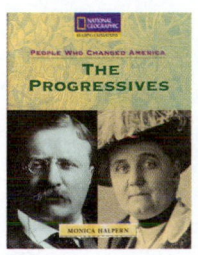

Leveled Library

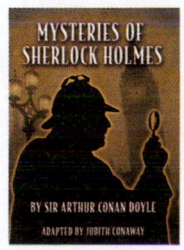  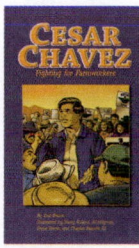

Reflect on Your Reading

Think back on your reading of the unit selections. Discuss what you did to understand what you read.

Focus on Reading **Determine Viewpoints** In this unit, you learned how authors use word choice and details to reveal their viewpoints in nonfiction or that of their characters in fiction. Choose a selection from the unit and draw a diagram or other graphic that shows the viewpoint of the author or a character. Use your graphic to explain your ideas to a partner.

Focus Strategy **Make Connections** As you read the selections, you learned to make connections. Explain to a partner how you will use this strategy in the future.

Explore the

Throughout this unit, you have been thinking about how we come to the aid of others. Choose one of these ways to explore the Guiding Question:

- **Discuss** With a group, discuss a time when you came to someone's rescue or someone came to yours. Explain what happened and how the experience affected you.
- **Role-Play** Imagine that you and a partner are Aaron from "Zlateh the Goat" and one of the Alaskan children described in "The Wonder Dog." Describe to each other how an animal or animals saved your life. Talk about your problems, how you tried to solve them, and whether you were successful.
- **Draw** Draw a comic strip showing all the different ways dogs come to the aid of people. Share your comic strip with a partner.

Book Talk

Which Unit Library book did you choose? Explain to a partner what it taught you about how people try to help others.

MORE THAN A GAME

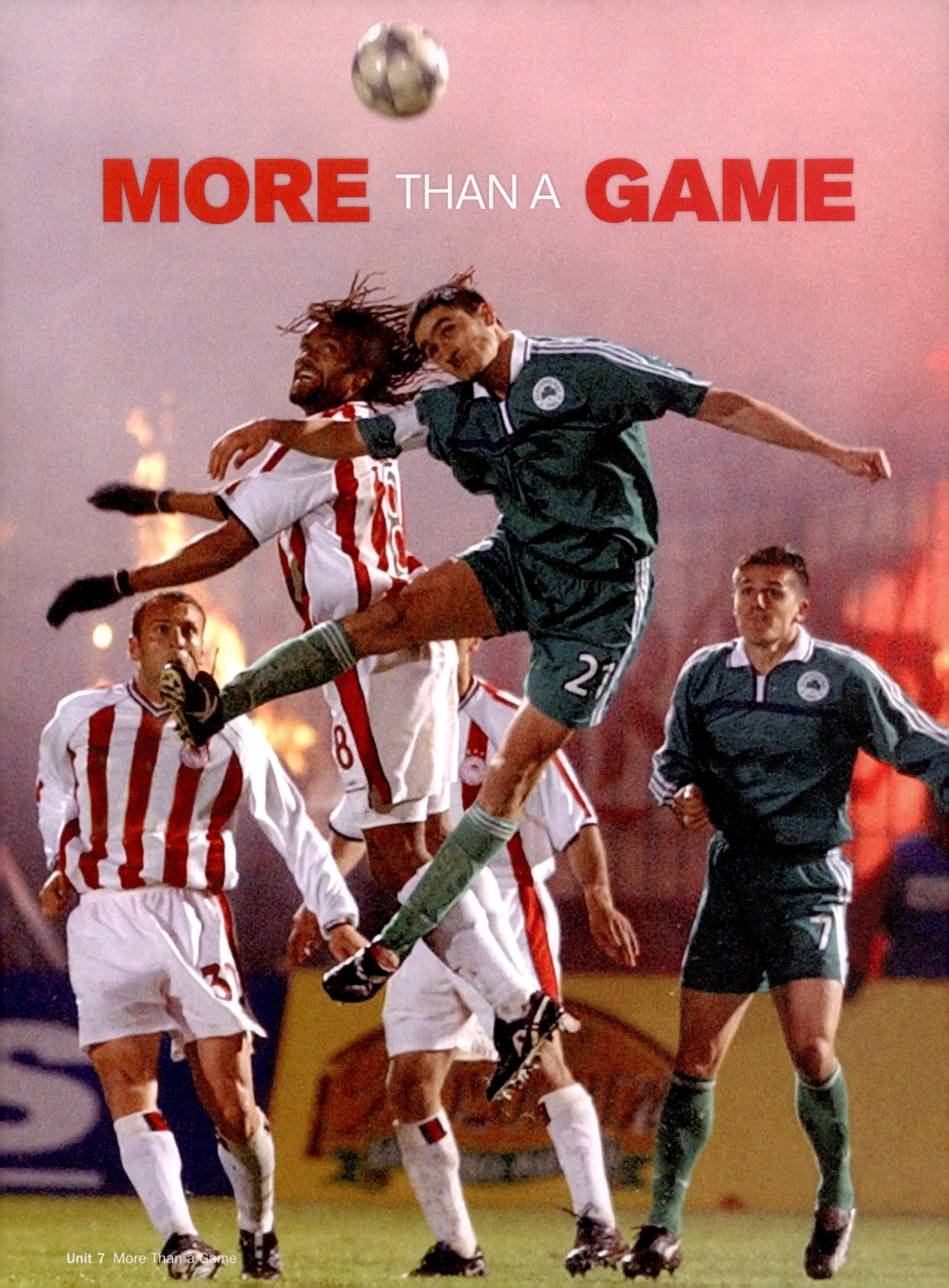

7

GUIDING QUESTION

How do sports bring people together?

READ MORE!

Content Library
Bones and Muscles
by Rebecca L. Johnson

Leveled Library
Keeper
by Mal Peet
A Strong Right Arm
by Michelle Y. Green
from **First Crossing**
by Donald R. Gallo

Web Links
myNGconnect.com

◄ Players jump for a high ball as fans hold flares in the stands during a soccer game in Athens, Greece.

Focus on Reading

Text Structure: Chronological Order

The **goal** of **narrative nonfiction** is to tell about the life of a real person or about something that really happened. Events are usually told in the order that they happened, or in **chronological order**.

How It Works

When you read biographies, histories, and other nonfiction narratives, the chronological order helps you keep track of events and ideas.

- Like other nonfiction, **narrative nonfiction** may include elements such as facts, statistics, and references to experts and other reliable sources.
- Some **narrative nonfiction** is as entertaining as a fictional story. The difference is that nonfiction is about real people, places, and events.
- Authors who write in **chronological order** use dates and **time words** to organize events in sequence.

Study this example of narrative nonfiction and watch for clues to help you follow the chronological order.

Roberto Clemente

A Natural Athlete

Roberto Clemente was born in Puerto Rico in 1934. As a child, he excelled in many sports, but baseball was his favorite. He was only 14 when he began playing for amateur baseball leagues. By the time he was 18, he had a contract to play professional baseball in Puerto Rico.

Facts, dates, and real people

Playing in the Big Leagues

In 1954, Roberto signed with the Brooklyn Dodgers, but he spent little time on the field. The Dodgers didn't want other teams to find out how good he was, but Roberto was becoming frustrated. Luckily, a year later, he was chosen to play for the Pittsburg Pirates. Roberto was finally able to show his talents as a ballplayer. In his first game with the Pirates, he hit a single—against the Dodgers! For the next 17 years, until his death in 1972, Roberto demonstrated his mastery of baseball for the world to see.

"Clemente could field the ball in New York and throw out a guy in Pennsylvania," broadcaster Vin Scully commented.

Reliable source

Academic Vocabulary

- **goal** (gōl) *noun*
  A **goal** is a purpose or what you want to happen.

Practice Together

Read this passage aloud. As you read, listen for clues that show elements of narrative nonfiction.

A Sudden Quiet

On June 10, 1944, Joe Nuxhall became the youngest person to play in a modern Major League Baseball game. He was just a skinny, 15-year-old ninth grader. On his first day, the young left-handed pitcher threw two-thirds of an inning for the Cincinnati Reds.

After that game, Nuxhall played in the minor leagues and finished high school. Finally, in 1952, he returned to the Cincinnati Reds and spent most of his major league career with them.

Nuxhall retired from baseball in 1966. He later became a famous sports announcer who ended each show by saying, "This is the ol' left-hander, rounding third and heading for home."

Try It!

Read this passage aloud. How is it organized? What clues tell you this?

The World of Auto Racing

How It Began

Organized stock-car racing began in 1939, but it wasn't until 1947 that NASCAR (National Association for Stock Car Auto Racing) was formed. NASCAR soon turned car racing into a serious business and a national passion.

The first NASCAR race was in 1948. The cars were "stock," or ordinary cars that drove on regular streets. Back then, the first NASCAR champion's car averaged a speed of 97 to 100 miles per hour (mph).

NASCAR Today

Now, cars race around the track at speeds over 175 mph! In 2007, experts estimated there were more than 75 million NASCAR fans. That makes car racing America's second most popular sport.

Focus on Vocabulary

Use Context Clues: Multiple-Meaning Words

Many English words have multiple, or more than one, meaning. The meaning depends upon the ==situation==, or how the word is used in a sentence.

> **EXAMPLE** Please put the glass on the **table**. (*table* = furniture)
> This **table** shows the state capitals. (*table* = chart)

When you see a word that doesn't make sense in the ==situation==, it probably has more than one meaning.

How the Strategy Works

When you read a word that has more than one possible meaning, use context clues to help you figure out which meaning fits best in that ==situation==. Use a dictionary to help you check meanings and also verify pronunciation and part of speech. Some words are pronounced more than one way depending on their meaning.

> **EXAMPLE** Every baseball season, Tomas anticipates that moment when the pitcher **winds** up and throws the first ball of the game.

1. Think about the topic of the text where the word appears.
2. Look in the same sentence for clues to the word's meaning.
3. Next, look for clues in the sentences that come before and after.
4. Check a dictionary to find the meaning that makes the most sense.

Use the strategy to figure out the meaning of each underlined word.

> **M**y mother loves baseball. She always <u>roots</u> for the same team and hates it when they lose. She goes to every game and sits in the same place in the <u>stands</u>. She even goes early to watch the groundskeepers prepare the <u>diamond</u> and the players warm up. She likes to watch the <u>pitchers</u> best. I have gone to many games with my mother. I share her love of baseball and probably always will.

☑ **REMEMBER** You can use both context clues and a dictionary to figure out the meanings of **multiple-meaning words**.

---

wind (wĭnd)

1. *n.* moving air. *The wind blew through the night.*
2. *v.* to make short of breath. *Climbing this long flight of stairs tends to wind me.*

wind (wīnd)

1. *v.* to wrap or turn in circles *I wind the loose thread around the spool.*

Strategy in Action

❝ I think roots are parts of plants. But that makes no sense. The topic is baseball. The context says the mother always roots for the same team and hates it when they lose. *Roots* must mean something like hoping a team will win. ❞

Academic Vocabulary

● **situation** (si-chū-wā-shun) *noun*
   Situation is the context in which a word is used.

Practice Together

Read this passage aloud. Look at each underlined word. Use context clues to figure out the word's meaning.

HOW ATHLETES PREPARE

TRAINING

Whether you want to be a track star or a great baseball player, it is important to train hard. A true athlete knows the right kinds of exercises to build muscles.

STRETCHING

It is very important to stretch both sides of your body before every game or race. Even if you throw with your right arm, you need to stretch your left side, too.

TRACKING

It is helpful to track your progress as you work out. This helps you see how much you've improved. It also helps you focus on your goal like a train speeding toward the station.

RESULTS

If you have worked hard, your body will still have strength left in the final stretch of the race or game. Your strength will last through the entire game, even if you come in last.

Try It!

Read this passage aloud. What is the meaning of each underlined word? How do you know?

The Excitement of Baseball

A high school baseball game is an exciting event. Of course the players are excited, but so are the fans. The beats of the drums in the band increase the mood. Then suddenly a batter sends a ball sailing over the fence and the team scores two runs! That's when the excitement reaches its highest pitch. It's the most exciting night of the spring.

▲ The batter slides into home plate.

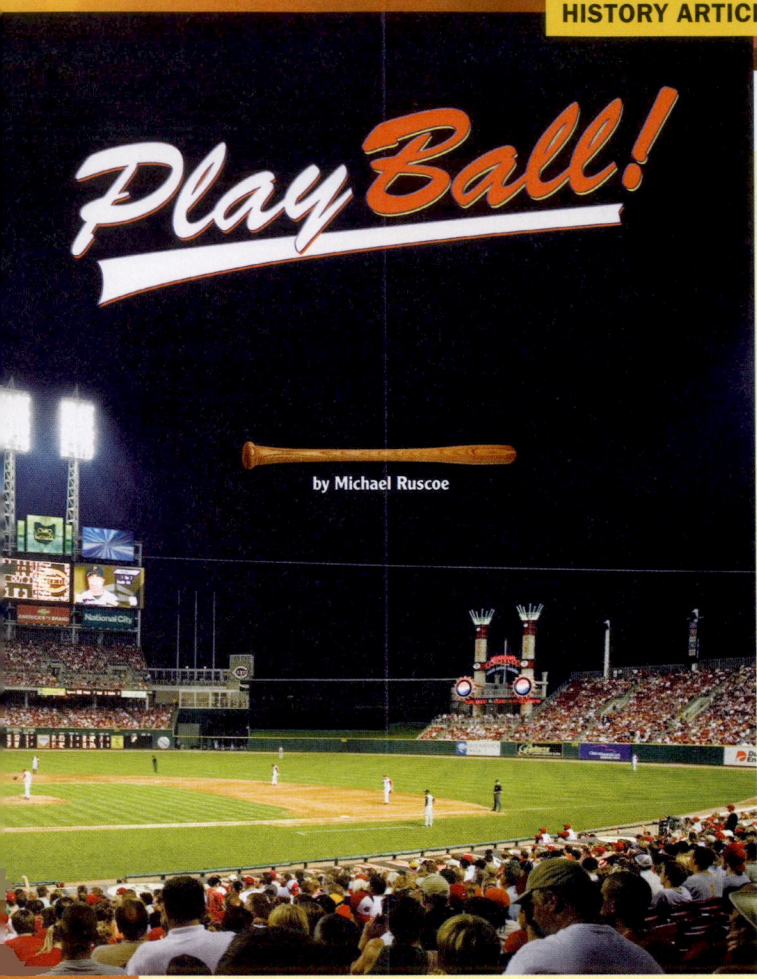

Play Ball!

by Michael Ruscoe

Build Background

Connect

KWL Chart What do you know about the history of baseball? What do you want to know? Create a KWL Chart. In the K column, list what you know. In the W column, list what you want to know. You'll use the L column to write what you learned from the selection.

KWL Chart

WHAT I KNOW	WHAT I WANT TO KNOW	WHAT I LEARNED
Baseball has been a popular sport in the United States for a long time.	When was baseball invented?	

See Baseball Today

Baseball is one of the most watched and played sports in the United States. It reflects the history of America—in both good and bad times.

Digital Library   **myNGconnect.com**
🔄 View the video.

▲ People support their team by attending a baseball game.

Language & Grammar

1 TRY OUT LANGUAGE
2 LEARN GRAMMAR
3 APPLY ON YOUR OWN

Express Opinions

CD

Look at the photograph and listen to the announcers.
What do they have to say?

PICTURE PROMPT

SPORTS TALK

FIRST ANNOUNCER: Hello, sports fans. Welcome to today's important game. In case you're just joining us, the score is tied at 3–3.

SECOND ANNOUNCER: And what a game it's been! But we're still waiting for Ron Dasher, the talented left-hander from Center City, to amaze us. He's 0 for 3! I don't think he is as good as people say he is, Pat.

FIRST ANNOUNCER: In my opinion, this game is quite a surprise. The home team was expected to win easily, but I believe they may lose. Their hitting is weak. That could keep them out of the championship.

Language & Grammar **479**

Use Complete Sentences

A **complete sentence** expresses a complete thought. It has a <mark>subject</mark> and a <mark>predicate</mark>.

- The subject is whom or what the sentence is about. Often the subject is a **noun**.

  EXAMPLES   The <mark>pitcher</mark> winds up and throws the ball toward first base.

  The <mark>ball</mark> bounces past first base and rolls into the outfield.

- The predicate often tells what the subject does. The most important word in the predicate is the **verb**.

  EXAMPLES   The coach <mark>**walks** out to the pitcher's mound</mark>.

  The umpire <mark>**dusts the plate**</mark>.

A **simple sentence** has one <mark>subject</mark> and one <mark>predicate</mark>. In most statements, the subject comes before the verb.

- Mixing short, but complete, simple sentences with longer sentences is very effective. Short sentences speed reading. They also help with comprehension.

  EXAMPLES   <mark>The next batter</mark> <mark>**misses the ball**</mark>.

  <mark>The umpire</mark> <mark>**yells,"Strike one!"**</mark>

Practice Together

Put the words in order to make a complete thought.
Say the complete sentence.

1. play / we / baseball / every Saturday / .
2. comes / my Dad / to / every game / .
3. into / many pieces / my bat / broke / .
4. had to use / I / a different bat / .

Try It!

Put the words in order to make a complete thought. Write the sentence on a card.
Say the complete sentence.

5. plays / Marco / my team / on / .
6. won / our team / last year / the championship / .
7. after school / practice / we / .
8. a lot / have / we / of fun / .

▲ The players always do their best.

Explore Views

EXPRESS OPINIONS

Everyone has opinions. The sportscasters had some. Those opinions were about a baseball team and its players. We know that baseball is a popular sport, but is it the most popular sport with students your age? What's your opinion?

To get started, gather your opinions and reasons for them in a list like this one.

My Opinions	Reasons
In my opinion, soccer is more popular than baseball.	The reason I think that is because every school in town has a soccer team, but not all have a baseball team.

Now express your opinions to a group about what sport is the most popular with students your age. Take turns.

HOW TO EXPRESS OPINIONS

1. Tell what you think about something. Use words like *I think*, *I believe*, and *In my opinion*.

2. Give reasons for your opinion or details to explain why you feel as you do about the subject.

3. If you share an opinion with someone else, say, *I agree with _____ about _____*. If you have a different opinion, say, *I disagree with _____ because _____*.

> In my opinion, surfing is the most popular sport with kids our age.

> I disagree with you because lots of kids our age don't live anywhere near the ocean!

USE COMPLETE SENTENCES

When you express your opinions, you need to put your thoughts and ideas into complete sentences. This helps others better understand what you want them to know. Make sure each sentence has a subject and a predicate.

EXAMPLE

In my opinion, basketball **is the most important sport**

subject   predicate

Prepare to Read

Learn Key Vocabulary

Study the Words Use the steps below.

1. Pronounce the word. Say it aloud several times. Spell it.
2. Rate your word knowledge.
3. Study the example. Tell more about the word.
4. Practice it. Make the word your own.

Key Words

champion (cham-pē-un)
noun ▶ page 488

A **champion** is a winner. This person became **champion** by winning first place in a contest.

compete (kum-pēt) *verb*
▶ page 490

When you **compete**, you take part in a contest. The athletes **compete** to win the race.
Related Word: **competition**

fan (fan) *noun*
▶ page 486

A **fan** is someone who supports a particular team or person. **Fans** go to games to cheer for their team.

league (lēg) *noun*
▶ page 488

A **league** is a group of teams that play the same sport. My friends and I all play in our neighborhood baseball **league**.

pastime (pas-tīm) *noun*
▶ page 488

A **pastime** is an activity that you often do for fun. What's this family's favorite **pastime**?

popular (pop-yu-lur)
adjective ▶ page 490

To be **popular** means to be liked by many people. Popcorn is a **popular** snack eaten at the movies.
Related Word: **popularity**

professional (pru-fesh-un-ul)
adjective ▶ page 486

A **professional** is someone who does a job for money. My aunt is a **professional** dancer.
Related Word: **profession**

segregate (se-gri-gāt) *verb*
▶ page 487

Segregate means to separate or keep apart. Gym classes usually **segregate** the boys and girls.
Related Word: **segregation**
Antonym: **integrate**

Practice the Words Make an Example Chart for each Key Word. Share you chart with a partner.

Noun	Definition	Example from My Life
league	a group of teams	My dad is in a bowling league.

Example Chart

Text Structure: Chronological Order

How Is Writing Organized? Most writing about events in history is organized by **chronological order**, the order in which events happened.

History articles and texts are often divided into sections. Each section gives information about specific events or time periods and shows how they relate to other events or to history as a whole. Dates and time order words help to organize this **sequence**.

As you read the passage, look for time order words to help you identify the **sequence** of events.

Reading Strategies

· Plan
· Monitor
· Visualize
· Determine Importance
· Ask Questions
· Make Connections
· **Make Inferences**
  When the author does not say something directly, use what you know to figure out what the author means.
· Synthesize

Look Into the Text

War Games

In 1861, the United States went to war against itself. ... The two sides fought the Civil War.

Soldiers on both sides played baseball whenever they could. The game helped prisoners of war fight boredom. Sometimes prisoners even played against their captors. ...

A World Championship

A few years after the Civil War ended, the first professional baseball league was created. In 1876, the first group of teams officially became the National League.

Practice Together

Make a Time Line A Time Line shows the most important events by date. It also provides an overview of history. This Time Line shows an event from "Play Ball!" Reread the passage above, and add to the Time Line.

Time Line

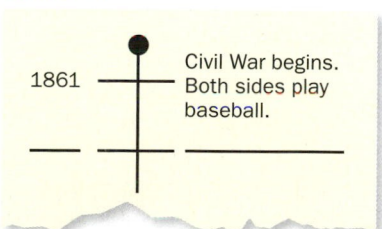

1861 — Civil War begins. Both sides play baseball.

Academic Vocabulary

· **sequence** (sē-kwents) *noun*
  The **sequence** of events is the order in which the events happen.

History Article

A history article is nonfiction. It tells about real events that happened in the past. Many history articles present information in chronological, or time, order. As you read, look for **time words** and dates that tell you the order in which the events happened. Use this information to help you make inferences about the relationships between events.

Look Into the Text

A World Championship

A few years after the Civil War ended, the first professional baseball league was created. In 1876, the first group of teams officially became the National League.

In 1901, the American League was created.

> I can infer that by 1901 there were enough baseball teams to form two leagues.

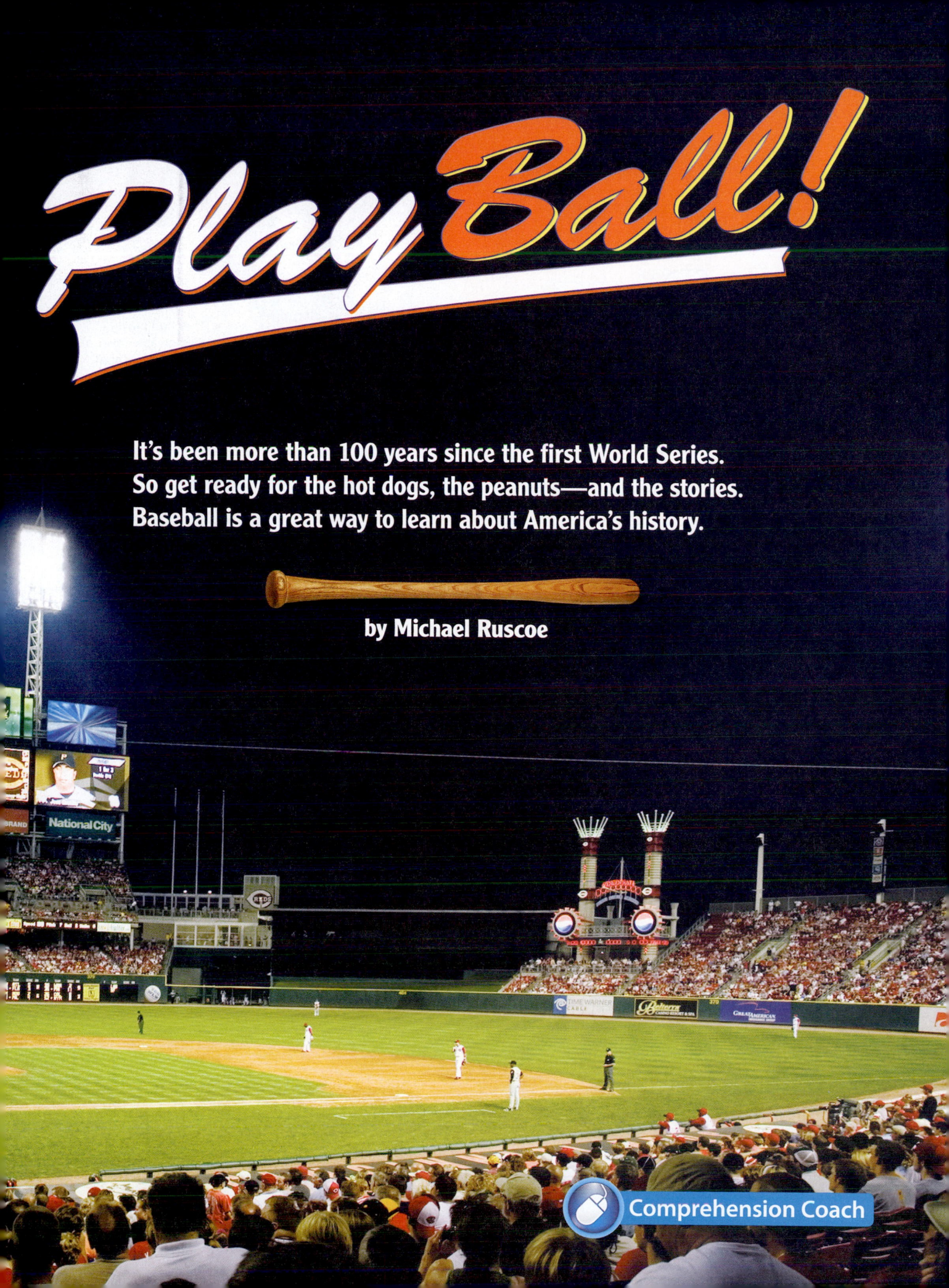

Play Ball!

It's been more than 100 years since the first World Series.
So get ready for the hot dogs, the peanuts—and the stories.
Baseball is a great way to learn about America's history.

by Michael Ruscoe

Comprehension Coach

A REFLECTION OF OUR PAST

Almost 70 million people go to **professional** baseball games each summer. What do they see? They see athletes, of course, and maybe some action. But that's not all.

They may not know it, but those **fans** also see American history. Since the 1800s, baseball has grown with the United States. Changes in the sport reflect those in the nation.

◄ This ball player was on the cover of an 1890 baseball guidebook.

War Games

In 1861, the United States went to war against itself. Thirteen states seceded. This means they broke away from the nation. They formed a new country called the Confederate States of America. President Abraham Lincoln **was determined** to bring the country together again. He sent **troops** to take back the states. To **resist** Lincoln, the Confederacy created its own army. The two sides fought the Civil War.

Key Vocabulary

professional *adj.*, done as a job instead of as a hobby

fan *n.*, a person who likes and watches a certain sport

In Other Words

was determined worked hard
troops soldiers
resist show they did not agree with

▲ This illustration shows Union prisoners of war playing ball in Salisbury, North Carolina. Confederate guards watch the game—and the prisoners.

Library of Congress

Soldiers on both sides played baseball whenever they could. The game helped prisoners of war **fight boredom**. Sometimes prisoners even played against their **captors**.

Perhaps the biggest Civil War game took place on December 25, 1862. Nearly 40,000 Union soldiers gathered at Hilton Head, South Carolina, to watch.

The war ended in 1865. Returning soldiers **spread** baseball across the United States. Some cities had two teams. One was for blacks; another for whites. Baseball was **segregated**, or divided by race. So was the country.

Many Civil War soldiers ate peanuts during baseball games because they were easy to grow and not expensive. ▶

Key Vocabulary
segregate *v.*, to keep apart or to separate

In Other Words
fight boredom entertain themselves
captors guards, enemies
spread took

Look Into the Text

1. **Cause and Effect** Why did people play baseball even during times of war?
2. **Compare and Contrast** How did **segregated** baseball reflect what the nation was like in the 1800s?

A World Championship

A few years after the Civil War ended, the first professional baseball **league** was created. In 1876, the first group of teams officially became the National League.

In 1901, the American League was created. Other leagues had formed throughout the years, but only these two leagues survived. These are the same two leagues that play today.

For a few years, the National League and the American League never played baseball against each other. But, in 1903, things changed. Baseball officials decided to hold a series of games at the end of that year's baseball season. They would call the event the World Series.

The best teams from the National League and the American League would play against each other. They would play nine games. The team who won the most games out of nine would win the series. Today, there are only seven games in the World Series.

The first World Series **pitted** the Boston Pilgrims (later the Red Sox) against the Pittsburgh Pirates. Pittsburgh won the first game; Boston the second.

Pittsburgh won the next two. Just two more wins, and Pittsburgh would be the "world **champion**."

Then things changed. Boston won the next four games in a row. On October 13, 1903, the Pilgrims became baseball's first World Series winner.

There was no World Series in 1904. The New York Giants refused to play the Pilgrims. But after that, the two leagues agreed to hold the World Series every year.

A National Sport

Over the next **two decades**, people's interest in baseball **soared**. The game truly became, as it's often called, "the national **pastime**."

It helped that baseball fans included several presidents. On opening day in 1910, William H. Taft threw the first pitch at a Washington Senators game. Doing so became a presidential tradition.

Woodrow Wilson was the first president to attend a World Series. He watched Boston beat Philadelphia in 1915. Calvin Coolidge went to several World Series games in 1924.

Key Vocabulary

league *n.*, a group of sports teams who play each other
champion *n.*, a first-place winner
pastime *n.*, something that is done as a hobby or for fun

In Other Words

pitted matched
two decades twenty years
soared became greater

President Taft throwing the first pitch at a baseball game in 1910

He became the first president to throw a World Series Game 1 pitch.

Baseball's early decades also witnessed the start of another tradition. The United States entered World War I in 1917. The conflict deepened many Americans' **patriotism**. During the war, fans started singing "The Star-Spangled Banner" at the beginning of baseball games.

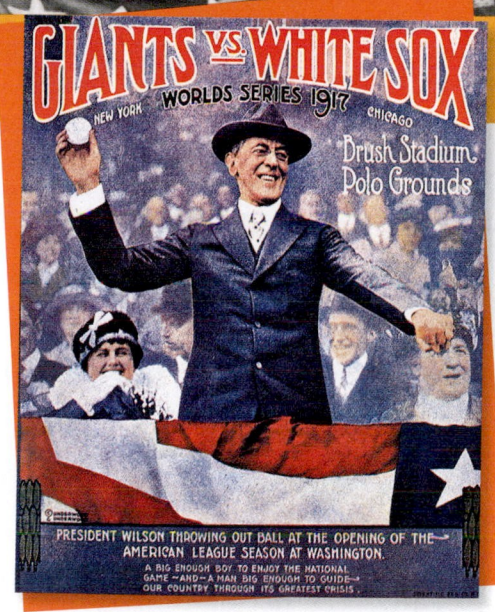

GIANTS VS WHITE SOX
NEW YORK WORLDS SERIES 1917 CHICAGO
Brush Stadium Polo Grounds

PRESIDENT WILSON THROWING OUT BALL AT THE OPENING OF THE AMERICAN LEAGUE SEASON AT WASHINGTON.

A BIG ENOUGH BOY TO ENJOY THE NATIONAL GAME — AND — A MAN BIG ENOUGH TO GUIDE — OUR COUNTRY THROUGH ITS GREATEST CRISIS.

President Wilson on a poster for the 1917 World Series

In Other Words
patriotism love of their country

Historical Background
"The Star-Spangled Banner" is the national anthem, or song, of the United States. The song was written in 1814 by Francis Scott Key. It was made into the national anthem in 1931.

Look Into the Text

1. **Sequence** How did the World Series begin? What happened next?

2. **Conclusion** Why is baseball called "the national **pastime**"?

3. **Summarize** How does a baseball team become the World Series **champion**?

A New League

World War II **erupted** just twenty years after World War I. The U.S. entered the conflict several years later, in 1941. Baseball officials offered to stop playing the game for as long as the war lasted. They felt this would help support the country.

But President Franklin D. Roosevelt didn't want the national pastime to stop. In a letter to baseball officials, he wrote, "I honestly feel that it would be best for the country to keep baseball going." The games continued.

Many players did go from ball fields to battlefields. Their absence gave women a chance to play ball professionally. Many other women went to work, too. They filled the jobs men left to fight in the war.

The All-American Girls Professional Baseball League formed in 1943. Talented young women came from all over the U.S. and Canada to play in the new league. Some of its players were as good as the men they replaced.

The league proved so **popular** that it continued after the war. It didn't **fold** until 1954. By then, more than 600 women had played professional baseball.

◀ During the 1940s, ten All-American Girls teams had about 1 million fans a year.

Ending Segregation

Even after World War II, black and white players could not **compete** together. Baseball and America were still segregated. But baseball players, managers, and others soon **moved** to end segregation.

In 1947, Jackie Robinson became the first African American player in the modern big leagues. He helped lead the Brooklyn Dodgers to the World Series that year. (They lost to the New York Yankees.)

Key Vocabulary
popular *adj.*, liked by many people
compete *v.*, to play against one another

In Other Words
erupted began
fold end
moved started; took action

Robinson showed that African Americans could succeed—when given a chance. African Americans were beginning to fight for equal treatment. Only a few years later, the Supreme Court decided that segregation of blacks and whites in public schools was **unconstitutional**. Black and white students would now be allowed by law to attend the same schools.

▲ Jackie Robinson joined the majors in 1947. Two years later, he was named Most Valuable Player in the National League.

International Pastime

America's pastime has won global popularity. Athletes from around the world come to the United States to play baseball. Of course, they're just a **sliver** of the millions of people who have immigrated to the United States throughout its history.

As a result, the World Series has really begun to live up to its name. Recent games have featured players from Japan, the Dominican Republic, Nicaragua, Cuba, Australia, South Korea, and Curaçao. And, in 1992, the Toronto Blue Jays were the first non-U.S. team to become world champions.

More teams will compete in the World Series in the future. **Countless** people will follow the games. Playing and watching, they'll all be part of America's **still unfolding** history.

In Other Words

unconstitutional not legal
sliver small number
Countless Many
still unfolding continuing, changing

Look Into the Text

1. **Cause and Effect** How did Jackie Robinson affect the country by playing professional baseball?

2. **Relate Ideas** How did world events lead to the formation of the All-American Girls Professional Baseball League?

3. **Context Clues** How is the World Series starting to "live up to its name"?

The Color of Baseball

Jackie Robinson wasn't the first black man to play professional baseball. **That honor actually goes to** Bud Fowler.

Fowler joined a white professional team in 1878. He was the only black player in the league. By the late 1800s, as many as fifty blacks played on white teams.

Yet by 1900, these players were **banned from** white teams. Segregation kept them from playing baseball with whites. Where did the players go? They played on all-black teams.

Andrew "Rube" Foster founded the Negro National League in 1920. It had eight teams. Soon other black leagues formed.

Life in the Leagues

The Negro leagues were a big success. Black teams barnstormed. This means they traveled around the country in buses and on trains. The players were heroes in many black communities. People **dropped everything** to see a famous team play when they came to town.

Andrew "Rube" Foster founded the first black baseball league in 1920. ▶

In Other Words
That honor actually goes to The first African American player was
banned from not allowed to play on
dropped everything stopped whatever they were doing

Beginning in 1933, the best players in the leagues competed in an all-star game at Chicago's Comiskey Park. Crowds of people came to see their favorite players. Between 20,000 and 50,000 fans attended the games.

Black baseball stars were popular. But, they faced the same **hardships** as other blacks in the United States. Players weren't welcome in many restaurants or hotels. They often had to sleep in their buses. Sometimes they slept along the roadside. Segregation still affected their lives.

Combining Teams

The major leagues **opened to black players** in 1947. Soon the black teams began to shut down. All of their best players were leaving. By the early 1960s, no all-black teams were left in the United States.

SATCHEL PAIGE

▲ Satchel Paige helped the Cleveland Indians win the World Series in 1948. In 1971, he was elected into the Baseball Hall of Fame.

▲ Black teams often rode buses on barnstorming trips.

In Other Words
hardships problems
opened to black players allowed black players to join their teams

Look Into the Text

1. **Paraphrase** Describe in your own words the hardships black baseball players faced.
2. **Theme** How does this section relate to the theme "More Than a Game"?
3. **Inference** Why did the Negro league shut down?

BASEBALL HISTORY TIME LINE

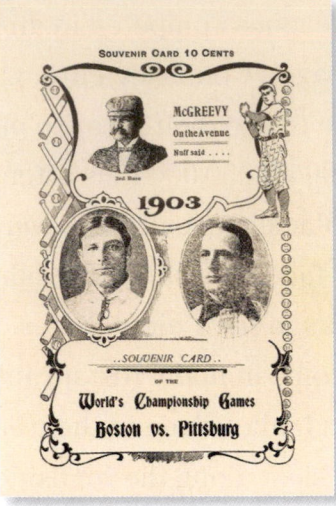

1903

The Boston Pilgrims win the first official baseball World Series against the Pittsburgh Pirates.

1845

Alexander J. Cartwright creates a set of official rules for baseball. He also creates the New York Knickerbockers Base Ball Club.

1884

Seventeen-year-old John A. "Bud" Hillerich invents the most popular baseball bat, the Louisville Slugger.

1935

Babe Ruth, who is considered to be the best baseball player in history, retires with 714 home runs.

FUN FACT

Today, more than 60% of major league baseball players use the Louisville Slugger.

1947

Major league teams allow African American players. Segregation in baseball ends.

2004

The Boston Red Sox win the World Series and become champions for the first time since 1918!

1943

The All-American Girls Professional Baseball League is formed during World War II. Dorothy "Dottie" Schroeder becomes one of the most famous players.

1973

Roberto Clemente becomes the first player born in Latin America to be **inducted into** the Baseball Hall of Fame.

In Other Words
inducted into chosen for

Look Into the Text

1. **Sequence** When was the first World Series? What happened just before that event on the time line?

2. **Conclusions** What do the events listed on the time line tell you about how **professional** baseball has changed?

Play Ball! **495**

Analysis of BASEBALL

by May Swenson

Strike, 1949, Jacob Lawrence. Tempera on hardboard, Howard University Gallery of Art, Washington, DC, USA.

▲ **Critical Viewing: Details** Which details in the painting remind you of the words in the poem?

It's about
the ball,
the bat,
and the mitt.
Ball hits
bat, or it
hits mitt.
Bat doesn't
hit ball, bat
meets it.
Ball bounces
off bat, flies
air, or thuds
ground (dud)
or it
fits mitt.

Bat waits
for ball
to mate.
Ball hates
to take bat's
bait. Ball
flirts, bat's
late, don't
keep the date.
Ball goes in
(thwack) to mitt,
and goes out
(thwack) back
to mitt.

Ball fits
mitt, but
not all
the time.
Sometimes
ball gets hit
(pow) when bat
meets it,
and sails
to a place
where mitt
has to quit
in disgrace.
That's about
the bases
loaded,
about 40,000
fans exploded.

It's about
the ball,
the bat,
the mitt,
the bases
and the fans.
It's done
on a diamond,
and for fun.
It's about
home, and it's
about run.

In Other Words

mate meet
flirts comes close
bat's late the batter doesn't swing fast enough
mitt has to quit in disgrace a player can't catch it

Look Into the Text

1. **Figurative Language** What does the speaker mean by saying the bat does not "keep the date"?
2. **Tone** What is the tone of this poem? What words or phrases help create the tone?

SINGING AND STRETCHING

Many baseball games have something known as the "seventh-inning stretch." Fans get up to stretch their legs and move around in the middle of the seventh inning of the baseball game.

During the seventh-inning stretch, the crowd will often sing "Take Me Out to the Ball Game." This song was written in 1908. Jack Norworth wrote the words to the song but had never been to a baseball game!

DID YOU KNOW?
Many fans like to sing the name of their own team instead of "home team." For example, in San Diego, California, Padres fans would sing, "Let me root, root, root for the Padres . . ."

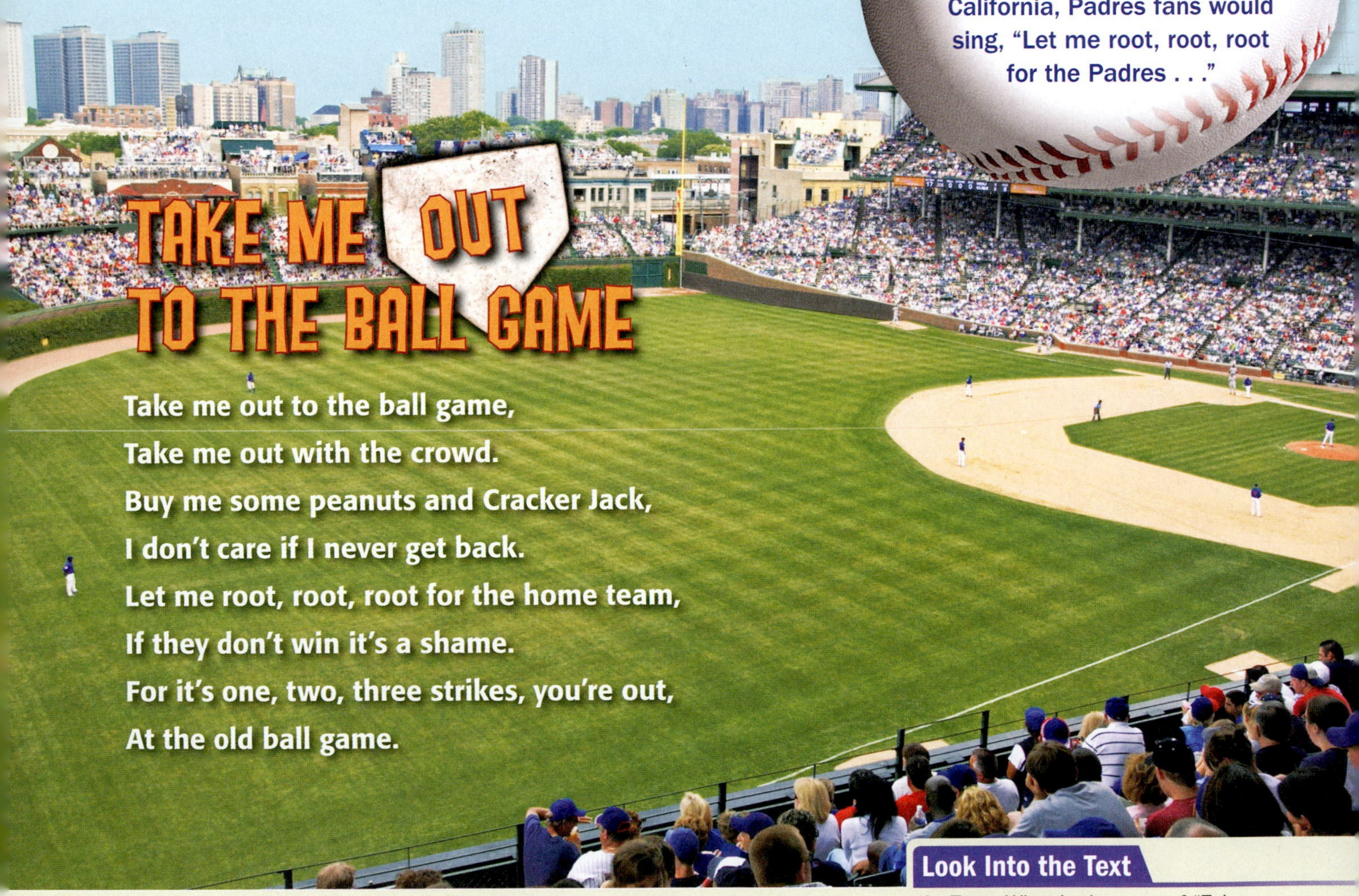

TAKE ME OUT TO THE BALL GAME

Take me out to the ball game,
Take me out with the crowd.
Buy me some peanuts and Cracker Jack,
I don't care if I never get back.
Let me root, root, root for the home team,
If they don't win it's a shame.
For it's one, two, three strikes, you're out,
At the old ball game.

In Other Words
get back go home
root cheer, yell
it's a shame it will be sad

Look Into the Text

1. **Tone** What is the tone of "Take Me Out to the Ball Game"? What words and language help create this tone?
2. **Conclusion** What do seventh-inning stretches tell you about baseball games?

Connect Reading and Writing

Vocabulary
champions
compete
fans
league
pastime
popular
professional
segregate

CRITICAL THINKING

1. SUM IT UP Compare Time Lines with a partner and then use them to summarize the article.

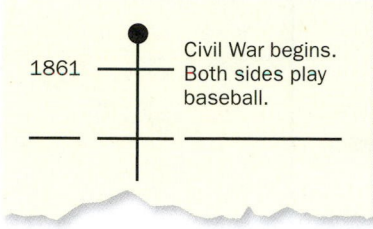

1861 — Civil War begins. Both sides play baseball.

Time Line

2. Make Judgments Explain to a partner which change in the history of **professional** baseball you think is the most important. Use details from the text to support your ideas.

3. Explain Revisit your KWL Chart. In the L column, write what you learned about the history of baseball. Discuss your completed chart with your classmates.

4. Compare Compare how "Play Ball!" and "Analysis of Baseball" both suggest that **fans** are important to the sport and to the players.

READING FLUENCY

Phrasing Read the passage on page 656 to a partner. Assess your fluency.

1. I did not pause/sometimes paused/ always paused for punctuation.

2. What I did best in my reading was _____.

READING STRATEGY

What strategy helped you understand this selection? Tell a partner about it.

VOCABULARY REVIEW

Oral Review Read the paragraph to a partner. Add the vocabulary words.

Our baseball team had to _____ against last year's state _____. Although they were better players, our team was more _____ with the _____ because we had girls on our team. Some people wanted to _____ the girls from the boys. We want them to play because they are serious players! Baseball is not just a _____ for them. Our coach found out that the _____ has a rule that says everyone is allowed to play. Now I think that women should be allowed to play _____ baseball with male players, too.

Written Review Pretend you are a black or female player in the early days of baseball. Write a letter to a baseball official that explains why it is wrong to **segregate** baseball. Use five vocabulary words.

WRITE ABOUT THE **GUIDING QUESTION**

Explore the Game
How does baseball bring people together? Write your opinion. Reread the selection to find examples that support your ideas.

Connect Across the Curriculum

Vocabulary Study

Use Multiple-Meaning Words Across Content Areas

Academic Vocabulary
- **situation** (si-chu-**wā**-shun) *noun*
  Situation is the context in which a word is used.

When you come across a word with different meanings, use **context clues** and a dictionary to figure out which meaning fits that **situation** .

1. Think about the topic of the text where the word appears.

2. Look for context clues to the meaning and part of speech.

3. Check a print or online dictionary, to clarify the precise meaning.

Figure Out Word Meanings Look through the selection to find the words below. Follow the steps above to figure out each word's meaning.

1. race, p. 487   **3.** row, p. 488   **5.** diamond, p. 497

2. pitch, p. 488   **4.** lead, p. 490   **6.** root, p. 498

Literary Analysis

Analyze Language

Academic Vocabulary
- **reflect** (ri-**flekt**) *verb*
  To **reflect** means to be a sign of something.

An author often chooses language to **reflect** the time period of the text. This word choice gives clues about that time.

Compare Ideas Reread "Analysis of Baseball" (written in 1971) and "Take Me Out to the Ball Game" (written in 1908). Copy the chart and add examples of language that **reflect** the time in which each poem was written. Explain what ideas the language reflects. Then compare each time to the present.

Selection	Language Example	What It Says About the Time	Comparison to Today
"Take Me Out to the Ball Game"	Take me out with the crowd.	People liked to sit with other fans.	People watch games on TV.
"Analysis of Baseball"	It's about the ball, the bat, and the mitt.	Baseball was about playing the sport. Nothing else was important.	Now it's also about making lots of money.

Express Opinions

Group Share With a group, think about this: Although some women played professional baseball during World War II, there are no women players on major league teams today. What opinion do you have about women playing baseball in the major leagues? Give reasons for your opinions. Use complete sentences.

> In my opinion, women should be able to try out for major league baseball teams.

> I don't agree because most women are not as strong and fast as men.

Write Complete Sentences

Study the Models When you write, you want your readers to understand what you are telling them. If you leave out important words, your readers may be confused. If you don't include enough details, readers won't be interested.

NOT OK

In baseball, the pitcher throws the ball. **Hits** the ball with a bat. I think that baseball is more than just a game. **Teaches** people about teamwork. Every **is** important. Every hit counts. A successful **team** always together.

> The reader thinks: **"Every what on a team is important? The writer left something out."**

OK

In baseball, the pitcher throws the ball. **The batter** **hits** the ball with a bat, usually made of wood. I think that baseball is more than just a game. **It** **teaches** people about the value of teamwork. Every **player** **is** important. Every hit that a batter makes counts. A successful **team** always **works** together as a group. In my opinion, that's hard to beat!

> Now each sentence is complete, and the writer varies the sentence structure. The writer also includes additional details.

Add Sentences Think of two sentences to add to the OK model above. Be sure to write complete sentences and to include phrases that add details.

✏ **WRITE ON YOUR OWN** What is it like to be part of a team? Write about an experience you've had and tell why it was meaningful to you. Write in complete sentences that provide reasons for your thinking and details to keep your readers interested.

REMEMBER

Make sure your sentences express complete thoughts.
- A complete sentence has a subject and predicate.
- The subject is who or what the sentence is about.
- The predicate tells what the subject does, has, or is.

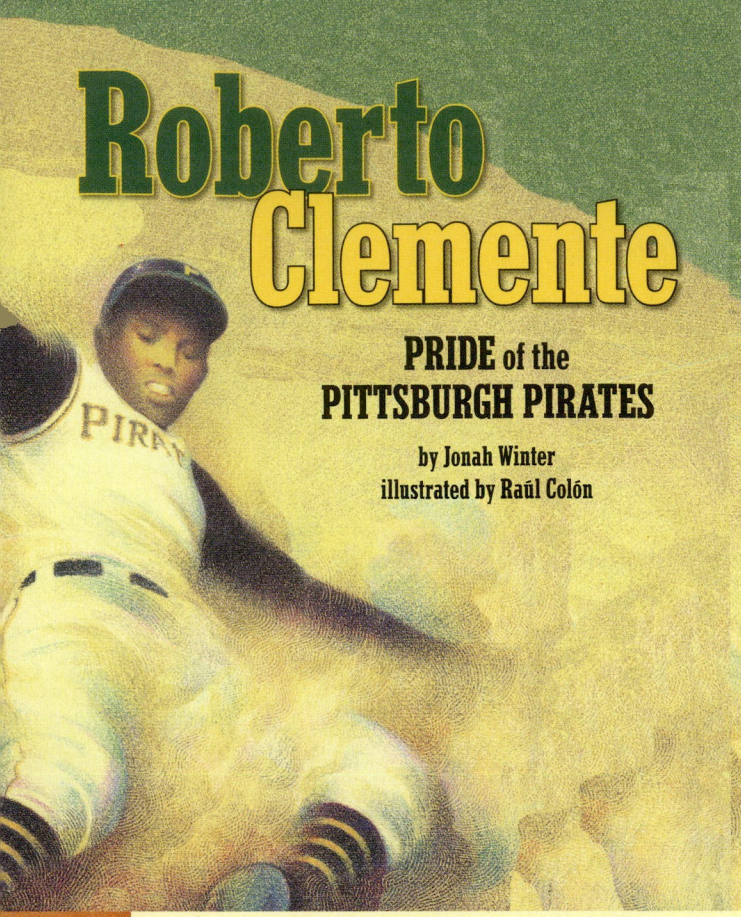

Roberto Clemente

PRIDE of the PITTSBURGH PIRATES

by Jonah Winter
illustrated by Raúl Colón

SELECTION 2 OVERVIEW

▶ **Build Background**

▶ **Language & Grammar**
Justify
Use Compound Sentences

▶ **Prepare to Read**
Learn Key Vocabulary
Compare Media

▶ **Read and Write**
Introduce the Genre
Biography
Focus on Reading
Text Structure:
Chronological Order
Apply the
Focus Strategy
Make Inferences
Critical Thinking
Reading Fluency
Read with Intonation
Vocabulary Review
Write About the
Guiding Question

▶ **Connect Across the Curriculum**
Vocabulary Study
Interpret Jargon
Literary Analysis
Infer the Main Idea
Language and Grammar
Justify
Writing and Grammar
Combine Your Ideas

Build Background

Meet Athletes Who Made History

People do amazing things every day in sports. But some athletes change the sport forever. Learn about athletes who did what nobody said they could do.

Connect

Quickwrite Write about an athlete who plays sports today who you think of as a hero. What makes this person a hero? Is it his or her athletic talent, or is it something else?

Digital Library myNGconnect.com
View the video.

▲ Jesse Owens won four gold medals in track and field in the 1936 Summer Olympics.

Justify CD

Look at the photo and listen to the discussion. Think about what reasons the teens give to explain, or justify, their views on heroes.

PICTURE PROMPT

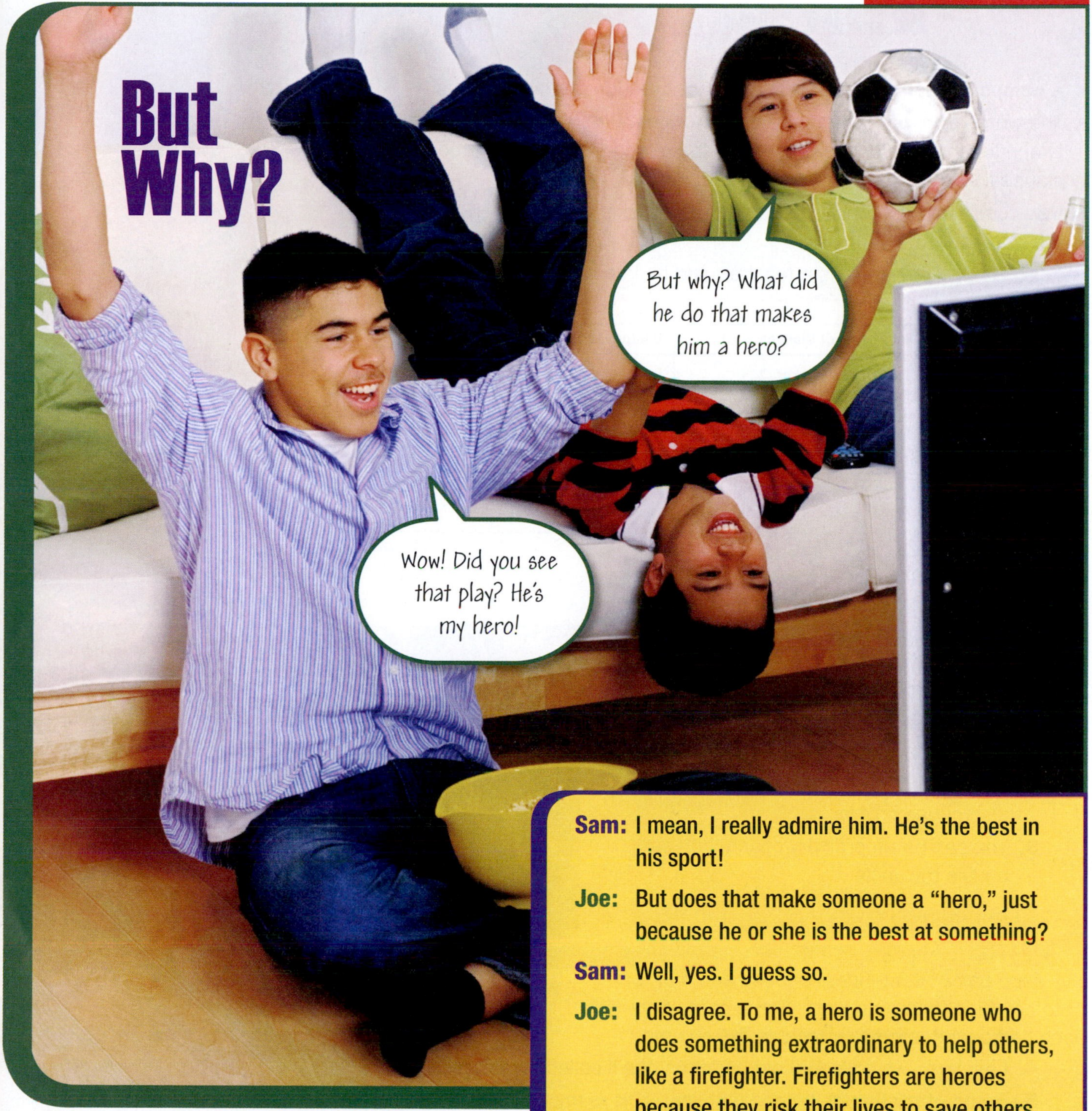

But Why?

> But why? What did he do that makes him a hero?

> Wow! Did you see that play? He's my hero!

Sam: I mean, I really admire him. He's the best in his sport!

Joe: But does that make someone a "hero," just because he or she is the best at something?

Sam: Well, yes. I guess so.

Joe: I disagree. To me, a hero is someone who does something extraordinary to help others, like a firefighter. Firefighters are heroes because they risk their lives to save others.

Use Compound Sentences

- A **clause** contains a **subject** and a **verb**. An **independent clause** contains a subject and a verb and can stand alone as a sentence.

  EXAMPLES   **My uncle** **is** a soccer coach.
  independent clause

  He **teaches** young players.
  independent clause

- A **compound sentence** contains at least two independent clauses.

- The words **and**, **but**, and **or** are **conjunctions**. When they are used to join two independent clauses, they show the relationship between the two clauses. Add a comma before *and, but,* and *or*.

- Use compound sentences to add sentence variety and show how ideas are related.

  EXAMPLE   My uncle is a teacher, **and** he is a soccer coach.
  independent clause   independent clause

Conjunction	Independent Clauses	Compound Sentence
Use **and** to join similar ideas.	I went to the corner. I waited for the bus.	I went to the corner, **and** I waited for the bus.
Use **but** to join different ideas.	I arrived a bit late. The game had not begun.	I arrived a bit late, **but** the game had not begun.
Use **or** to show a choice.	I could watch from the sidelines. I could watch from the stands.	I could watch from the sidelines, **or** I could watch from the stands.

Practice Together

Say each pair of sentences. Tell how the ideas are related. Choose *and*, *but*, or *or* to combine them. Say each new compound sentence.

1. My uncle is a great role model. He is a hero to many.
2. A sport can bring people together. It can also cause problems.
3. You can be an ordinary coach. You can be like my uncle.

Try It!

Say each pair of sentences. Choose *and*, *but*, or *or* to combine them and write it on a card. Write each compound sentence. Include the comma.

▲ We collect sports equipment, and we give it to teams in need.

4. Last year, we collected old uniforms. We'll collect again this year.
5. Some of my friends helped last year. This is my first year helping.
6. We could collect toys next year. We could collect sports equipment.

Explore Reasons

JUSTIFY

Does playing a team sport build friendships and teach teamwork? Not everyone thinks the same way about it. People may take different sides for different reasons on an issue. Someone may say that playing a team sport is better than playing an individual sport because team sports help create good relationships with others. Someone else may have a different view. What's your position? Can you justify your views?

List some of your ideas in a chart like this one:

Opinion or Position	Justifications or Reasons
Team sports are better for everyone.	• The players learn teamwork, and that is a lifelong skill. • Teammates help each other, but they work individually, too.

Now justify your position to a group. Be sure to listen carefully as other people justify their positions.

HOW TO JUSTIFY

1. State an opinion or idea.

2. Give logical reasons for your idea.

3. Combine your ideas to make the logic clear.

My mom is my hero. She works two jobs to provide for our family, and she volunteers in our community.

USE COMPOUND SENTENCES

Compound sentences can help you justify a position on an issue. When you use conjunctions to point out similar ideas, show a contrast, or offer a choice, you clarify your position.

Simple Sentences: People can learn a lot about themselves through sports. They can also learn about others.

Compound Sentence: People can learn a lot about themselves through sports, **and** they can also learn about others.

▲ Playing a team sport can build friendships, and it can teach teamwork.

Prepare to Read

Learn Key Vocabulary

Study the Words Use the steps below.

1. Pronounce the word. Say it aloud several times. Spell it.
2. Rate your word knowledge.
3. Study the example. Tell more about the word.
4. Practice it. Make the word your own.

Key Words

celebrate (**sel**-u-brāt) *verb*
▶ page 512

To **celebrate** means to do something fun because of an important event. Every year you **celebrate** your birthday.
Related Word: **celebration**

credit (**kred**-ut) *noun*
▶ page 514

When you are given **credit**, you are noticed for something you have done well. You want **credit** from your parents for a good grade.

honor (**ahn**-ur) *noun*
▶ page 510

An **honor** is a symbol of high praise from others. It is an **honor** to be given an award.
Related Word: **honorary**

introduce (in-tru-**düs**) *verb*
▶ page 510

To **introduce** means to present someone by name. You may **introduce** one friend to another.
Related Words: **introduction, introductory**

invitation (in-vu-**tā**-shun) *noun* ▶ page 510

An **invitation** is a request for you to do something. People getting married send wedding **invitations**.
Related Word: **invite**

mighty (**mī**-tē) *adjective*
▶ page 512

To be **mighty** means to be powerful and strong. Crocodiles have **mighty** jaws.

respect (ri-**spekt**) *noun*
▶ page 512
When you have **respect** for someone, you have a good opinion of that person. You show **respect** by being polite.
Related Word: **respectable**

spirit (**spir**-ut) *noun*
▶ page 516
Your **spirit** is the kind of person you are. Everyone likes my brother for his fun-loving **spirit**.

Practice the Words Make an Idea Web for each Key Word. Write four things the word makes you think of. Share your finished webs with a partner.

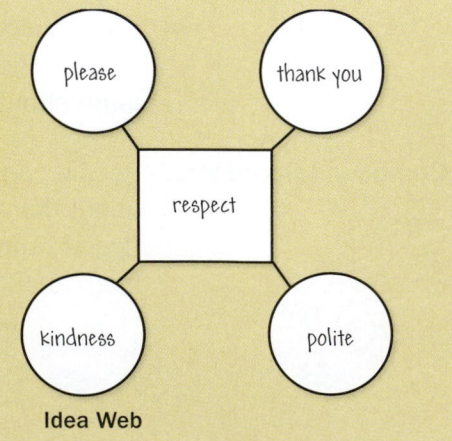

Idea Web

Compare Media

How Do Different Media Affect Comprehension? Reading a text silently and hearing the same text read aloud can influence your understanding of the content. When you read a text, you notice typographical elements such as punctuation, italics, and capital letters. When you hear a text read aloud, you listen for auditory cues such as pace, phrasing, intonation, and expression.

As you read the following excerpt and then listen to it being read aloud, compare how each medium influences how you interpret the text.

Reading Strategies
- Plan
- Monitor
- Visualize
- Determine Importance
- Ask Questions
- Make Connections
- **Make Inferences**
  When the author does not say something directly, use what you know to figure out what the author means.
- Synthesize

Look Into the Text

His first time at bat, he heard the announcer stumble through his Spanish name:

"ROB, uh, ROE . . . BURRT, um let's see, TOE CLUH-MAINT?" It echoed in the near-empty stands. Roberto Clemente was his name, and this is pronounced "Roe-BEAR-toe Cleh-MEN-tay."

As if to introduce himself, Roberto *smacked* the very first pitch. …

The Pittsburgh fans checked their scorecards. Who was this guy, "Roberto Clemente?"

[margin note:] n I hear eone read text, I feel I'm at the ium.

Practice Together

Make a Two-Column Chart One way to compare reading and listening to a text is to record your reactions in a Two-Column Chart. This chart shows one listener's response to reading the passage and hearing it read aloud. Reread the passage above, and add to your Two-Column Chart.

Experience Reading the Text	Experience Listening to the Text Read
As I read the text, the capital letters stood out. They show me how hard the announcer struggled to pronounce his name.	Listening to my partner read the text, I can imagine how this sounded over a loudspeaker.

Two-Column Chart

Biography

A biography is narrative nonfiction about a real person's life. The author writes about events in the person's life using chronological, or time, order. Biographies can be both entertaining and informative.

Reading the text and then hearing the text read aloud may also help you better understand the meaning of events. You can use this information to make inferences about the person's life that the author does not directly explain.

Look Into the Text

Playing right field, he had no equal. He was always leaping, diving, crashing, rolling. Once, trying to catch a pop fly, running full speed, he SLAMMED into the right field wall. . . . At last, slowly, he lifted his glove. The ball was inside.

> **Strong action words** help make the biography entertaining.

> By noticing the way the word *SLAMMED* is written, you can infer that Roberto made a strong effort.

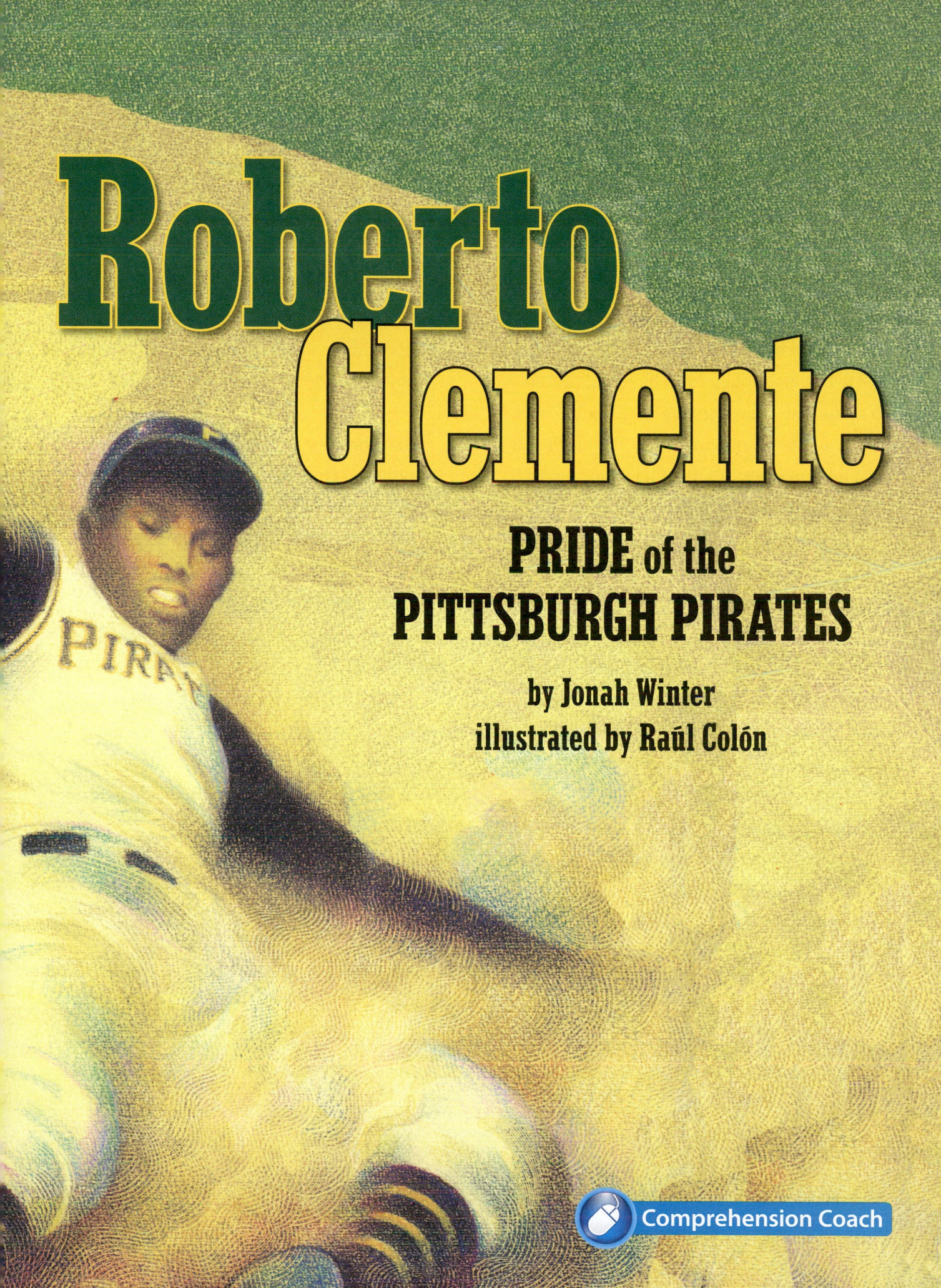

Roberto Clemente

PRIDE of the PITTSBURGH PIRATES

by Jonah Winter

illustrated by Raúl Colón

Comprehension Coach

On an island called Puerto Rico, where baseball players are as plentiful as tropical flowers in a rain forest, there was a boy who had very little but a **fever** to play and win at baseball.

He had no money for a baseball bat, so he made one from a guava tree branch. His first glove he also made, from the cloth of a coffee-bean sack. His first baseball field was muddy and crowded with palm trees.

For batting practice he used empty soup cans and hit them farther than anyone else. Soup cans turned into softballs. Softballs turned into baseballs.

Little League turned into minor league turned into winter league: professional baseball in Puerto Rico. He played so well he received an **invitation** to play in the major leagues in America!

What an **honor**!

But the young man was sent to a steel-mill town called Pittsburgh, Pennsylvania, where his new team, the Pittsburgh Pirates, was in *last place*.

Now this was something very strange, being on a losing team. For the young Puerto Rican, everything was strange. Instead of palm trees, he saw **smokestacks**. Instead of Spanish, he heard English.

Instead of being *somebody*, he was nobody.

His first time at bat, he heard the announcer **stumble through** his Spanish name:

"ROB, uh, ROE . . . BURRT, um let's see, TOE CLUH-MAINT?" It echoed in the near-empty stands. Roberto Clemente was his name, and this is pronounced "Roe-BEAR-toe Cleh-MEN-tay."

As if to **introduce** himself, Roberto *smacked* the very first pitch. But it went right up the infield and into the shortstop's glove. Still, Roberto ran like lightning—and **beat the throw** to first base.

The Pittsburgh fans checked their scorecards. Who was this guy, "Roberto Clemente"?

Key Vocabulary

invitation *n.*, an offer to come somewhere

honor *n.*, a way to show respect

introduce *v.*, to present a person to others

In Other Words

fever desire, need
smokestacks factory chimneys
stumble through have trouble with
beat the throw got

To his new fans in Pittsburgh, Roberto was like a jolt of *electricity*. He could score from first base on a single. He could hit line drives, bunts, towering home runs, sacrifice flies—whatever was needed. Once he even scored an inside-the-park GRAND SLAM!

Playing right field, he had no equal. He was always leaping, diving, crashing, rolling. Once, trying to catch a pop fly, running full speed, he SLAMMED into the right-field wall—and fell to the ground. At last, slowly, he lifted his glove. The ball was inside.

But it wasn't just how he played. He had *style*. He was *cool*. He had this move he did with his neck before each at bat, creaking it one way, then the other.

Soon kids who wanted to be just like Roberto were doing it, too, twisting their necks this way and that.

Roberto did it to **ease** the pain he felt from playing **his heart out** in every game.

"If you don't try as hard as you can," he said, "you are wasting your life."

He had *style.*
He was *cool.*

Roberto tried so hard, he helped the last-place Pirates make it all the way to the World Series where they beat the **mighty** NEW YORK YANKEES!

After the series, down in the streets of Pittsburgh, Roberto walked alone among his fans, who were so busy **celebrating**, they didn't even notice him. That didn't bother Roberto.

He was happy to feel lost in the crowd of a party he had helped create. But there was something that would have made Roberto's joy a little sweeter. As much as fans loved him, the newspaper writers did not.

When Roberto was in such pain he couldn't play, they called him "lazy." They mocked his Spanish accent, and when Roberto got angry, the mainly white newsmen **called him a Latino "hothead."**

Roberto swore he would be so good, he would *have* to get the **respect** he deserved. He would become the greatest all-around baseball player there ever was.

Key Vocabulary

mighty *adj.*, powerful, strong
celebrate *v.*, to show joy or happiness because of an event
respect *n.*, admiration

In Other Words

ease end, lessen
his heart out as hard as he could
called him a Latino "hothead" said he had an angry temper because he was Latino

Look Into the Text

1. **Summarize** What happened when Clemente joined the Pirates?

2. **Conclusion and Evidence** Clemente did not always get the **respect** he deserved. Give two examples that support this.

3. **Paraphrase** Tell in your own words how Clemente planned to get **respect**.

At home that Christmas, Roberto went back to the same muddy field he'd played on as a boy. In his pocket was a bag full of bottle caps that he emptied into the hands of some kids. They threw him the caps, and he hit each one again and again.

When he returned to Pittsburgh **come** spring, baseballs looked HUGE, and he **clobbered them as never before**. That season, he hit .351, the highest batting average in the National League. And still he did not get the **credit** he deserved for being so great.

"It's because I'm black, isn't it?" he asked the **sneering** reporters. "It's because I am Puerto Rican. It's because I am proud."

Key Vocabulary
credit *n.*, acknowledgment; opinion that builds a reputation

In Other Words
come in the
clobbered them as never before hit them harder than he ever had before
sneering rude, hateful

Sports Background
In baseball, a batting average is a statistic, or type of measurement, that shows how often a player hits the ball. Today, a batting average higher than .300 is considered excellent. Clemente's season average of .351 was amazing!

It was starting to seem as if Roberto might never be respected in the big world outside of Pittsburgh and Puerto Rico. And then something happened.

The year was 1971. The Pirates were in the World Series again, playing against the Baltimore Orioles, who were favored to win.

All around America and Puerto Rico, people sat watching on TV as Roberto **put on a one-man show**. Stealing bases, hitting home runs, playing right field with **a *fire*** most fans had never seen before.

Finally, *finally*, it could not be denied: Roberto was the greatest all-around baseball player of his time, maybe of all time.

The very next year, he did something that few have ever done: During the last game of the season, Roberto walked to the plate, creaked his neck, dug in his stance, stuck his chin toward the pitcher, and **walloped a line drive** off the center-field wall—his *three thousandth* hit!

The crowd cheered, and they wouldn't stop cheering. For many minutes the players stopped playing and Roberto stood on second base, amazed. How far he had come.

And yet, when the season was over, the hero returned to the place where his story began, to the land of muddy fields and soup cans and bottle caps, to his homeland of Puerto Rico, where he was **worshipped**.

But did he sit around and polish his trophies? No. That rainy New Year's Eve, Roberto sat in the San Juan airport and waited for mechanics to fix the tired old airplane that would take him to Central America.

In Other Words
put on a one-man show played better than anyone else
a *fire* an effort; a passion
walloped a line drive hit a ball
worshipped loved, admired

There had been a terrible earthquake, and he wanted to help the victims. The plane would carry food and supplies that Roberto had paid for.

Right before midnight, he **boarded**. The rain was really coming down. One of the propellers buzzed loudly. As the plane took off, the engines failed and the plane fell into the ocean. Just like that, it was over. Roberto was gone. How could his story end this way, so suddenly, and with such sadness? The story doesn't end here.

When someone like Roberto dies, his <mark>spirit</mark> lives on in the hearts of all he touched.

And Roberto's spirit is still growing. It grows in the bats and gloves and arms and legs of all the Latino baseball players who have **flooded into** the major leagues.

His spirit grows in the **charities** he started for poor people in Puerto Rico.

And his spirit is still growing in Pittsburgh, where people who saw him play

tell their children and grandchildren of how **he used to sparkle**—running, diving, firing game-saving throws from deep right field all the way to home plate—SMACK—right into the catcher's glove. ❖

Key Vocabulary
spirit *n*., the memory of a person

In Other Words
boarded got on the plane
flooded into played in
charities helpful organizations
he used to sparkle great he was

Look Into the Text

1. **Confirm Prediction** What did Clemente do to finally earn **respect** from reporters? Was your prediction correct?
2. **Summarize** What happened to Clemente on his way to Central America?

Connect Reading and Writing

Vocabulary
- celebrate
- credit
- honor
- introduced
- invitation
- mighty
- respect
- spirit

CRITICAL THINKING

1. **SUM IT UP** Make a list of Roberto Clemente's **honors** and achievements throughout his lifetime. Use your list to summarize the selection.

   > Clemente's Achievements
   > 1. Clemente plays Little League, then professional ball in Puerto Rico.
   > 2. He signs with the Pittsburgh Pirates.

2. **Speculate** Roberto Clemente died in 1972, but people still **respect** his talent. Do you think that in the future your kids will hear or read about him in school? Why or why not?

3. **Evaluate** Do you agree that reporters did not give Roberto Clemente the **credit** he deserved because he was Puerto Rican? Use examples from the text to support your opinion.

4. **Discuss** Share your Quickwrite from page 502. Explain why you think your athlete deserves this **honor**.

READING FLUENCY

Intonation Read the passage on page 657 to a partner. Assess your fluency.

1. My tone never/sometimes/always matched what I read.

2. What I did best in my reading was _____.

READING STRATEGY

> What strategy helped you understand this selection? Tell a partner about it.

VOCABULARY REVIEW

Oral Review Read the paragraph aloud. Add the vocabulary words.

> Every year, each of our school athletes receives an _____ in the mail to _____ our achievements at a ceremony. The auditorium is decorated in our school colors, and the band plays music. The whole room is filled with school _____. Then the principal gives out awards in _____ of the best players. I won a soccer award. In my speech, I gave all the _____ to my coach. He was the person who _____ me to the game of soccer. My _____ for his opinions and his _____ talent as a soccer player helped me become the best I could be.

Written Review Your town has just declared today Roberto Clemente Day. How would you **celebrate** it? Write a paragraph. Use five vocabulary words.

 **WRITE ABOUT THE** **GUIDING QUESTION**

Explore the Sports Connection

Can a sport bring people from different cultures together? Write your opinion. Reread the selection to find examples that support your ideas.

Connect Across the Curriculum

Vocabulary Study

Interpret Jargon

> **Academic Vocabulary**
> • **interpret** (in-**tur**-pret) *verb*
>   When you **interpret** something, you tell what you think it means.

Every field of study or work uses familiar words in special ways. These words are called **jargon**. What comes to mind when you hear *diamond*? A jeweler pictures one thing while a baseball player sees another.

Use context clues to help you **interpret** the meaning of jargon.

1. Look for words or phrases that may be clues to the word's meaning.

2. Test the meaning in the sentence to see if it makes sense.

3. If you still can't figure it out, check a print or online dictionary.

Figure Out Word Meanings Look through the selection to find the baseball jargon listed below. Use context clues to figure out their meaning.

1. infield, p. 510   **3.** grand slam, p. 512   **5.** hit .351, p. 514

2. a single, p. 512   **4.** a pop fly, p. 512   **6.** stealing bases, p. 515

Literary Analysis

Infer the Main Idea

> **Academic Vocabulary**
> • **evidence** (e-vu-dents) *noun*
>   Evidence is facts or information that show that something is true.

The **main idea** of a text is the most important point. Often, it is not directly stated. You have to **make inferences** to figure it out:

1. Read the text. Pay attention to facts and ideas about the topic.

2. Think of what you already know about the topic.

3. Combine **evidence** in the text with what you already know to figure out what the author has not told you directly.

Make an Inference Chart

Reread "Roberto Clemente" with a partner. Use the Inference Chart to infer the main idea.

I Read	I Know	And So . . .
Roberto practiced hitting bottle caps and then went on to get the highest batting average in the National League.	Bottle caps are smaller than baseballs and harder to hit.	I think he got a high batting average because after hitting bottle caps, balls were easier to hit.

Justify

Group Talk Was Roberto Clemente right to get on that plane? With a group, take turns justifying your opinion about Clemente's decision. Use compound sentences when you present some of your ideas. Listen respectfully to everyone's position.

> I think he was right. People needed his help, and he knew how to help them!

> I don't think he was right. The plane was old, and the weather was bad! When I read that, I knew there was trouble ahead.

Combine Your Ideas

Study the Models You can make your writing more interesting if you use different kinds of sentences. For example, include some simple sentences and combine others into longer sentences. Be careful not to run too many sentences together!

NOT OK

> Roberto Clemente heard about the terrible earthquake. He wanted to help. He bought food and supplies, and went to the airport and hired a plane and packed the things on the plane and waited while mechanics checked the engine. Then the plane took off. It crashed. Roberto died. His spirit lives on in the charities he started to help the needy.

This writing is not smooth. One sentence uses _and_ to connect too many ideas. The sentence is hard to follow. The writing also has too many simple, choppy sentences.

OK

> Roberto Clemente heard about the terrible earthquake, and he wanted to help. He bought food and supplies, and he hired a plane. He went to the airport, packed the things on the plane, and waited for mechanics to check the engine. Then the plane took off, but it crashed. Roberto died, but his spirit lives on in the charities he started to help the needy.

This passage flows better. It has a mix of simple and compound sentences and no run-on sentences.

Add Sentences Think of two sentences to add to the OK model above. Use one simple sentence and one compound sentence.

✏️ **WRITE ON YOUR OWN** Write a paragraph about something you or someone you know did that might cause people to say, "What a heroic thing to do!" Use a variety of sentences.

REMEMBER

- In compound sentences, use **and** to join similar ideas. Use **but** to join different ideas. Use **or** to show when there is a choice.
- Insert a comma before the **and**, **but**, or **or**.
- Don't string together too many ideas with commas or **and**.

Raymond's Run

adapted from a story by **Toni Cade Bambara**

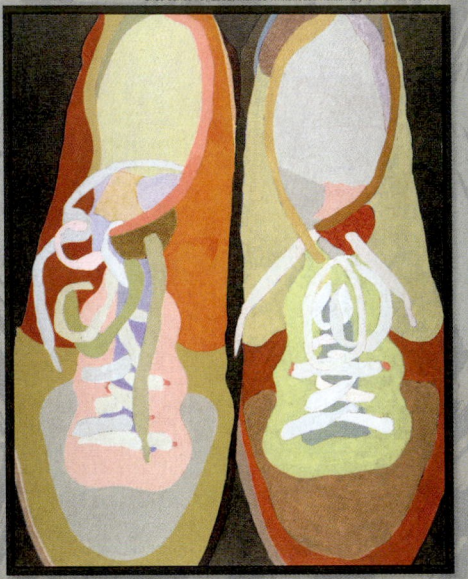

Shoe Series #9, 1982, Marilee Whitehouse-Holm. Acrylic. Private collection.

Build Background

Connect

Anticipation Guide Think about what is important when it comes to competition. Tell if you agree or disagree with these statements.

Anticipation Guide

	Agree	Disagree
1. Winning is the most important thing in a competition.	_____	_____
2. Losing can teach you something.	_____	_____
3. Sometimes, you should let someone else win.	_____	_____

Meet Athletes with Drive

Athletes from all over the world train hard for years in order to compete in the Special Olympics. Meet serious athletes who overcame big challenges in order to succeed.

Digital Library   **myNGconnect.com**
                            ↘ View the video.

▲ Athletes train hard to compete.

Language & Grammar

1 TRY OUT LANGUAGE
2 LEARN GRAMMAR
3 APPLY ON YOUR OWN

Elaborate

CD

Listen to the chant about running. Then, listen again and chime in. Listen to the people elaborate on, or tell more about, the kinds of running they do.

CHANT

Do You Run?

Steve: Have you ever run a marathon?

Laura: No, never. What's a marathon?

Steve: It's a great big race that's really long.

Laura: How long is long in a marathon?

Steve: Over twenty-six miles from start to stop.

Laura: Running six miles would make me drop.

Steve: Well, you don't need to run *six* miles or *twenty*. Walking or jogging even *two* miles is plenty.

Use Complex Sentences

- A clause has a **subject** and a **verb**. An **independent clause** has a subject and a verb, and it can stand alone as a sentence.

  EXAMPLE **We jog** every day.

independent clause

- A **dependent clause** also has a subject and a verb. However, it cannot stand alone because it isn't a complete thought.

  EXAMPLE **unless it rains**

dependent clause

- When you connect a dependent clause to an independent clause, the new sentence is complete, and it is called a **complex sentence**. The dependent clause can function as a noun, an adjective, or an adverb in the sentence.

  EXAMPLE We jog every day **unless** it rains.

adverb clause

  The boys **who** jog every day are fit.

adjective clause

  I believe **that** it is good to jog.

noun clause

Some Words Used to Form Complex Sentences	
after	that
although	unless
as	when
because	whenever
before	wherever
if	while
since	who

Practice Together

Match each independent clause on the left to a dependent clause on the right. Say the new complex sentence. Then tell how it functions in the sentence.

1. I feel the happiest   although I can't win them all
2. I enter a lot of races   who run beside me
3. I think   after the race is over
4. I don't watch the boys   when I compete in a race
5. We all celebrate   that races are exciting

▲ We run every day because the race is next week.

Try It!

Match each independent clause on the left to a dependent clause. Write the dependent clause on a card. Say the new complex sentence. How does the dependent clause function?

6. We do warm-up exercises   because he was the fastest
7. My friend Alex won the race   if it rains on the day of the race
8. I am proud   that go up and down hills
9. I don't know what I'll do   before we run a race
10. I like races   that I ran a good race

Describe an Experience

ELABORATE

Tell a partner about a race or other sports event that you participated in or would like to participate in.

Start by writing down ideas that you would like to share. Then think of ways you would like to elaborate, or tell more about them. Add examples, details, and explanations to elaborate.

Ideas	Elaborate
I trained for the race.	I ran three miles each day for two months before the race. I also jumped rope for 10 minutes every day.
I didn't give up.	During the race, I got very tired. But I didn't give up because I wanted to finish the race well. I stayed focused, and I just kept on running!

Now share information about the race or competition with your partner. Trade roles.

HOW TO ELABORATE

1. Tell the main idea or point that you want to make.
2. Add details. Give background information, examples, or explanations.
3. When you give more information, you need to use complete sentences with a subject and a predicate.

I ran in a race.

I ran the race on May Day—May 1—in my home town. I was happy because I finished with my best time ever!

USE COMPLEX SENTENCES

When you describe an experience, you can use complex sentences to combine some of your ideas. Complex sentences help to show relationships between your ideas. A word like *because* will "hook" a reason to your idea.

Simple Sentences: I almost missed the whole race. I overslept.
Complex Sentence: I almost missed the whole race **because** I overslept.

▲ My sister runs fast because she loves to win!

Prepare to Read

Learn Key Vocabulary

Study the Words Use the steps below.

1. Pronounce the word. Say it aloud several times. Spell it.
2. Rate your word knowledge.
3. Study the example. Tell more about the word.
4. Practice it. Make the word your own.

Rating Scale

1 = I have never seen this word before.

2 = I am not sure of the word's meaning.

3 = I know this word and can teach the word's meaning to someone else.

Key Words

congratulate (kun-**grach**-u-lāt) *verb* ▶ page 536

When you **congratulate** someone, you let that person know you are happy for something they have achieved. This woman is **congratulated** for finishing school.

energy (**e**-nur-jē) *noun* ▶ page 534

Energy is the power or force to do things. Young children have lots of **energy**.
Related Words: **energize, energetic**

exercise (**ek**-sur-sīz) *noun* ▶ page 530

Exercise is an activity you do to stay fit and healthy. Many people ride bicycles for **exercise**.

gesture (**jes**-chur) *noun* ▶ page 532

A **gesture** is an action done to show how you feel. Our neighbor made us dinner as a friendly **gesture**.

honest (**ahn**-ust) *adjective* ▶ page 536

An **honest** person tells the truth. Abe Lincoln was known as **Honest** Abe because of his truthfulness.
Related Word: **honestly**
Antonym: **dishonest**

interrupt (int-u-**rupt**) *verb* ▶ page 530

To **interrupt** means to break into a conversation or activity. It is impolite to **interrupt** a conversation.
Related Word: **interruption**

serious (**sir**-ē-us) *adjective* ▶ page 530
When you are **serious** about something, you feel that it is important. Many people are **serious** about their work.
Related Word: **seriously**

squeaky (**skwē**-kē) *adjective* ▶ page 528
A **squeaky** noise is a high-pitched sound. Mice make **squeaky** noises.

Practice the Words Make a Definition Map for each Key Word. Compare your maps to a partner's maps.

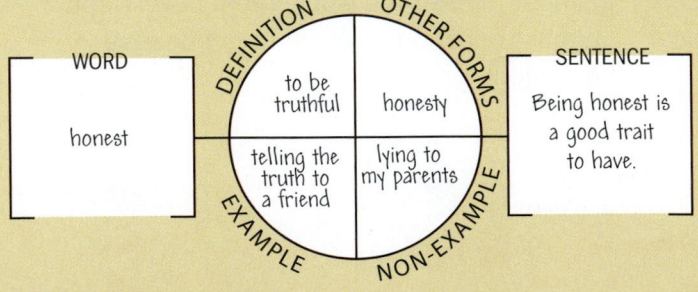

Definition Map

Determine Viewpoint

How Does the Author Distinguish Viewpoints? A viewpoint is what a person thinks about a topic. A fiction author develops characters' viewpoints through their actions, dialogue, and thoughts. Each character may have a different viewpoint. To <mark>distinguish</mark> between two or more characters' viewpoints, you can analyze and compare these details.

As you read, look for details that show a character's viewpoint.

Reading Strategies

- Plan
- Monitor
- Visualize
- Determine Importance
- Ask Questions
- Make Connections
- **Make Inferences**
  When the author does not say something directly, use what you know to figure out what the author means.
- Synthesize

Look Into the Text

> I don't have much work to do around the house like some girls. My mother does all that. All I have to do in life is mind my brother Raymond, which is enough.
>
> Sometimes I slip and say my little brother Raymond. But as any fool can see he's much bigger and he's older, too. He needs looking after cause he's not quite right. If anybody has anything to say to Raymond, they have to come by me.

Practice Together

Begin a Viewpoint Chart A Viewpoint Chart can help you organize information about characters' viewpoints. It also helps <mark>distinguish</mark> viewpoints among characters. The first entry in this chart shows how Squeaky feels about her brother. Reread the passage above, and add to your Viewpoint Chart.

Character's Words and Actions	Character's Viewpoint
Minding Raymond is enough work.	Taking care of Raymond is a full-time job.

Viewpoint Chart

Academic Vocabulary

- **distinguish** (di-**sting**-wish) *verb*
  To **distinguish** is to recognize and understand the difference between two or more things.

Short Story

A short story is fiction. Short stories usually have characters who have problems, or conflicts. The settings and plot events are often simple and uncomplicated.

In a short story, authors use the characters' viewpoints to let you experience a topic or event through their eyes. In a first-person narrative, events are seen through one character's eyes. You can use details from the story and knowledge from your own experiences to make inferences about different characters' viewpoints.

Look Into the Text

I'm about to take a stroll down Broadway so I can practice my breathing exercises. I've got Raymond ◁ **character's actions** walking on the inside close to the buildings, cause he's subject to fits of fantasy and starts thinking he's a circus performer and that the curb is a tightrope. This is OK by me so long ◁ **character's thoughts** as he doesn't run me over or interrupt my breathing exercises. I'm serious about my running and I don't care who knows it.

Raymond's *Run*

adapted from a story by **Toni Cade Bambara**

Shoe Series #9, 1982, Marilee Whitehouse-Holm. Acrylic. Private collection.

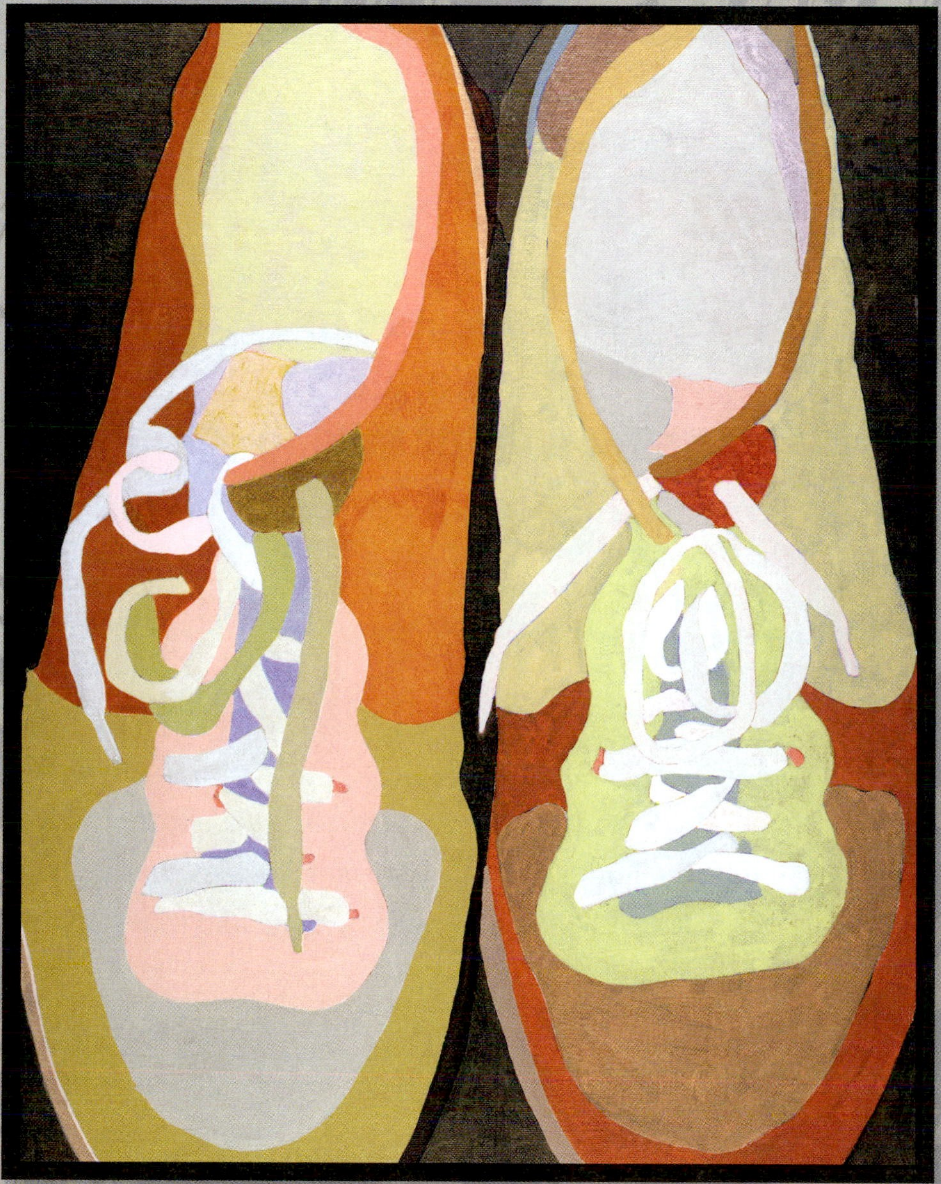

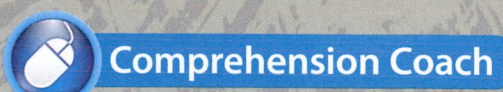

Comprehension Coach

I don't have much work to do around the house like some girls. My mother does that. All I have to do in life is **mind** my brother Raymond, which is enough.

Sometimes I slip and say my little brother Raymond. But as any fool can see he's much bigger and he's older, too. He needs **looking after** cause he's not quite right. If anybody has anything to say to Raymond, they have to **come by me**. I don't believe in standing around doing a lot of talking. I'd much rather just knock you down and take my chances even if I am a little girl with skinny arms and a **squeaky** voice, which is how I got the name Squeaky. And if things get too rough, I run. And as anybody can tell you, I'm the fastest thing on two feet.

I don't believe in standing around doing a lot of talking.

There is no track meet that I don't win the first place medal. The big kids call me Mercury cause I'm the swiftest thing in the neighborhood. Everybody knows that—except two people who know better, my father and me. He can beat me to Amsterdam Avenue with me **having a two fire-hydrant head-start** and him running with his hands in his pockets and whistling.

But that's private information. So as far as everyone's concerned, I'm the fastest. That goes for Gretchen, too, who has **put out the tale** that she is going to win the first-place medal this year. Ridiculous. In the second place, she's got short legs. In the third place, she's got freckles. In the first place, no one can beat me and that's all there is to it.

Key Vocabulary
squeaky *adj.*, high-sounding

In Other Words
mind take care of
looking after to be taken care of
come by me ask me first
**having a two fire-hydrant head-
    start** getting a start ahead of him
put out the tale told everyone

FlyGirl2, 2002, Iana Amauba. Oil on canvas. Private collection.

▲ **Critical Viewing: Character** How does the girl's facial expression in this photograph remind you of Squeaky? Why?

Language Background

Mercury was the messenger god in Roman mythology. He was known for his amazing speed. Mercury was often pictured wearing a hat and sandals with wings.

1. **Inference** Why does Squeaky spend so much time with Raymond?
2. **Character's Viewpoint** How does Squeaky feel about Gretchen? Give two examples to support your answer.
3. **Fact and Opinion** Squeaky says Gretchen's tale is ridiculous. Is this a fact or an opinion? Why?

I'm about to take a **stroll** down Broadway so I can practice my breathing **exercises**. I've got Raymond walking on the inside close to the buildings, cause **he's subject to fits of fantasy** and starts thinking he's a circus performer and that the curb is a tightrope. This is OK by me so long as he doesn't run me over or **interrupt** my breathing exercises. I'm **serious** about my running, and I don't care who knows it.

So I'm strolling down Broadway breathing out and breathing in on counts of seven, which is my lucky number. I see Gretchen and her sidekicks Mary Louise and Rosie steady coming up Broadway.

"You signing up for the May Day races?" smiles Mary Louise, only it's not a smile at all.

"I don't think you're going to win this time," says Rosie.

"I always win cause I'm the best," I say straight at Gretchen who is, as far as I'm concerned, the only one talking in this **ventriloquist-dummy routine**. Gretchen smiles, but it's not a smile. Then they all look at Raymond and they're about to see what trouble they can get into through him.

"What grade you in now, Raymond?"

"You got anything to say to my brother, you say it to me, Mary Louise Williams."

"What are you, his mother?" sasses Rosie.

"That's right. And the next word out of anybody and I'll be *their* mother, too." Then Gretchen puts her hand on her hip and is about to say something with her freckle-face self but doesn't. So me and Raymond smile at each other. I continue with my breathing exercises, strolling down Broadway with not a care in the world cause I am Miss Quicksilver herself.

I take my time getting to the park on May Day because the track meet is the last thing on the program. The biggest thing on the program is the May Pole dancing. I can do without this, thank you, even if my mother thinks **it's a shame I don't take part** and act like a girl for a change. You'd think she'd be glad her daughter ain't out there prancing

Key Vocabulary
exercise *n.*, a physical action
interrupt *v.*, to break in an action
serious *adj.*, not joking

In Other Words
stroll walk
he's subject to fits of fantasy he likes to pretend
ventriloquist-dummy routine conversation
it's a shame I don't take part I should join the dance

Cultural Background
May Day (May 1) celebrates the beginning of spring. Some people celebrate this day by "dancing around the May Pole." The May Pole is a tall pole decorated with ribbons and flowers. People twist or weave the ribbons together as they dance.

around a May Pole. Instead of trying to act like a fairy or a flower you should be trying to be yourself.

I put Raymond in the little swings, which is a tight squeeze this year and will be impossible next year. Then I look around for Mr. Pearson, who pins the numbers on. I'm really looking for Gretchen if you want to know the truth, but she's not around. The park is **jam-packed**.

Then here comes Mr. Pearson. He sticks out in a crowd because he's **on stilts**. We used to call him Jack and the Beanstalk to get him mad. But I'm the only one that

Ices 1, 1960, Jacob Lawrence. Egg tempera on hardboard. Private collection.

▲ **Critical Viewing: Mood** What is the mood of this painting? How is it like the mood of the park?

In Other Words
jam-packed full of people
on stilts very tall

can outrun him and I'm too grown for that silliness now.

"Well, Squeaky," he says, checking my name off the list and handing me number seven and two pins. And I'm thinking he's got no right to call me Squeaky, if I can't call him Beanstalk.

"Hazel Elizabeth Deborah Parker," I correct him and tell him to write it down on his board.

"Well, Hazel Elizabeth Deborah Parker, going to give someone else **a break** this year?" I **squint** at him real hard to see if he is seriously thinking I should lose the race on purpose just to give someone else a break. He looks around the park for Gretchen like a periscope in a submarine movie. "Wouldn't it be a nice <mark>gesture</mark> if you were . . . to ahhh . . ."

I give him such a look he couldn't finish putting that idea into words. Grownups **got a lot of nerve** sometimes. I pin number seven to myself and stomp away. I'm so **burnt**, I go straight for the track.

Key Vocabulary
  <mark>gesture</mark> *n.*, any action done to show how a person feels

In Other Words
  a break a chance to win
  squint stare; narrow my eyes
  got a lot of nerve can say mean things
  burnt angry, mad

Joggers, 1982, Graham Dean.

▲ **Critical Viewing: Design** What does the artist's use of shadow and light show about the relationship of runners in this art?

Look Into the Text

1. **Conclusion** Why don't Squeaky and Gretchen like each other?

2. **Character** Squeaky thinks its important to be herself. What does this show about her?

3. **Inference** Why does Mr. Pearson say it would be a nice **gesture** to let someone else win the race?

Raymond's Run **533**

Predict
Will Squeaky change her mind about Gretchen?

Raymond is hollering from the swings. He knows I'm about to do my thing cause the man on the loudspeaker has just announced the fifty-yard dash. Then as I get into place I see that ole Raymond is on line on the other side of the fence, bending down with his fingers on the ground just like he knew what he was doing. I was going to yell at him but then I didn't. It burns up your **energy** to holler.

I spread my fingers in the dirt and **crouch over the Get on Your Mark**.

Key Vocabulary
energy *n.*, the available power to do active things

In Other Words
crouch over the Get on Your Mark lean over the start line

I am telling myself, Squeaky you must win. **The pistol shot explodes in my blood and I am off**, flying past the other runners. My arms pump up and down, and the whole world is quiet except for the crunch of gravel in the track. On the other side of the fence is Raymond with his arms down to his side and the palms tucked up behind him, running in his very own style. It's the first time I ever saw that and I almost stop to watch my brother on his first run. But the white ribbon is bouncing toward me. I tear past it, racing into the distance till my feet start digging up footfuls of dirt and brake me short. Then all the kids standing on the side pile on me, banging me on the back and slapping my head with their May Day programs, for I have won again.

"In the first place . . ." the man on the loudspeaker pauses and the loudspeaker starts to whine. **Then static.** Here comes Gretchen walking back, for she's overshot the finish line, too. Huffing and puffing with her hands on her hips, breathing in steady time like a real pro. I sort of like her a little for the first time. "In first place . . ." Then I hear Raymond yanking at the fence to call me and I wave to shush him. He keeps rattling the fence like a gorilla in a cage. But then like a dancer he starts climbing up nice and easy but very fast. And it occurs to me that Raymond would make a very fine runner. Doesn't he always keep up with me on my trots? And he surely knows how to breathe in counts of seven. He's always doing it at the dinner table. And I'm smiling to beat the band cause I can always retire as a runner and begin a whole new career as a coach with Raymond as my champion.

I am off, flying past the other runners.

In Other Words

The pistol shot explodes in my blood and I am off I hear the sound to start, and I run

Then static. Then the man is hard to hear.

So I stand there **with my plans**, laughing out loud by this time as Raymond jumps down from the fence and runs over. I'm jumping up and down so glad to see him—my brother Raymond. But of course everyone thinks I'm jumping up and down because the men on the loudspeaker are announcing, "In first place—Miss Hazel Elizabeth Deborah Parker." **(Dig that.)** "In second place—Miss Gretchen P. Lewis." And I look over at Gretchen wondering what the "P" stands for. And I smile. Cause she's good, no doubt about it. Maybe she'd like to help me coach Raymond. And she nods to **congratulate** me and then she smiles. And I smile. We stand there with this big smile of respect between us. It's about as real a smile as girls can do for each other. We don't practice real smiling every day, you know, cause maybe we too busy being flowers or fairies instead of something **honest** and worthy of respect . . . you know . . . like being people. ❖

About the Author

Toni Cade Bambara (1939–1995) lived the first ten years of her life in the New York City neighborhood of Harlem, near Amsterdam Avenue, the setting of "Raymond's Run." Bambara was influenced by the Harlem community, especially the street corner poets. She gave credit to the popular jazz musicians of that time for helping to give her writing a special rhythm and beat.

Key Vocabulary
congratulate *v.*, to let someone know you are happy for them
honest *adj.*, truthful, real

In Other Words
with my plans and think about coaching Raymond
(Dig that.) (Isn't that great?)

Look Into the Text
1. **Confirm Prediction** Squeaky and Gretchen **congratulate** each other. How do they feel about each other now? Was your prediction correct?
2. **Conclusions** Why would Squeaky retire from running?
3. **Main Ideas and Details** Raymond wants to be like Squeaky. List three details to support this.

Connect Reading and Writing

Vocabulary
congratulated
energy
exercise
gesture
honest
interrupt
serious
squeaky

CRITICAL THINKING

1. **SUM IT UP** Use your Viewpoint Chart to summarize the events that led to Squeaky's decision to **interrupt** her training to coach Raymond.

Character's Words and Actions	Character's Viewpoint
Minding Raymond is enough work.	Taking care of Raymond is a full-time job.

Viewpoint Chart

2. **Evaluate** Revisit your Anticipation Guide. Are these still your **honest** opinions? Discuss your ideas with your classmates.

3. **Infer** Tell a partner why you think Squeaky is so **serious** about winning.

4. **Interpret** What does Squeaky mean when she says girls are too busy "being flowers or fairies instead of something **honest**"?

READING FLUENCY

Expression Read the passage on page 658 to a partner. Assess your fluency.

1. My voice never/sometimes/always matched what I read.

2. What I did best in my reading was _____.

READING STRATEGY

What strategy helped you understand this selection? Tell a partner about it.

VOCABULARY REVIEW

Oral Review Read the paragraph aloud. Add the vocabulary words.

The _____ truth is most kids our age don't get enough _____. It's a _____ problem. If we do not exercise, we won't have any _____. I decided to start a running club. I thought it would be a nice _____ to show students we have the power to change. My gym coach _____ me on getting kids to _____ their usual routines and do something healthy. Most afternoons, you can hear us running laps on the _____ gym floor!

Written Review Imagine you are running a race. Write a letter about why you should be **serious** about the training. Use five vocabulary words.

WRITE ABOUT THE **GUIDING QUESTION**

Explore the Power of Sports
How did sports and **exercise** bring Squeaky closer to both Raymond and Gretchen? Write your opinion. Reread the selection to find examples that support it.

Connect Across the Curriculum

Use Context Clues: Multiple-Meaning Words

Academic Vocabulary
- **situation** (si-chu-**wā**-shun) *noun*
  Situation is the context in which a word is used.

Some English words are spelled the same but have different meanings in different **situations** . Use context clues to help you figure out the correct meaning and pronunciation of a word. If you are still unsure, look up the word in a print or online dictionary.

Figure Out Word Meanings Work with a partner. Find each word listed below in the selection. Follow the steps above to figure out its meaning.

1. subject, p. 530
2. meet, p. 530
3. board, p. 532
4. break, p. 532
5. watch, p. 535
6. tear, p. 535

Evaluate Information

Academic Vocabulary
- **evaluate** (i-**val**-yu-wāt) *verb*
  To **evaluate** is to decide how good or useful something is.

When you research a topic, you need to **evaluate** the information you find to decide if it is useful to you. One part of evaluating information is recognizing how writers present their viewpoints. A writer will often include facts, opinions, and inferences that support the main idea of the text.

Practice Together

Analyze Author's Point of View Read the passage. Analyze how the author uses facts and opinions to support her viewpoint.

> Girls on the Run is a national organization designed to foster young girls to be healthy, independent, and confident through running, conversation, and games. The truth of its success is in the numbers: Girls on the Run began in 1996 with 13 girls; by 2000, the program served 200 cities nationwide.

Elaborate

Role-Play With a partner, act out an interview with an athlete who has just won a big sports competition. One partner plays the role of a news reporter and the other partner answers as the athlete. The athlete elaborates with details and examples. Use complex sentences to combine some of your ideas. Trade roles.

> I hoped to win, but I wasn't sure I could. Before I knew it, it was time to go to the rink. I was a little scared because it was my first big race. As I watched the other skaters warm up, I was nervous. This was not going to be easy!

Use a Variety of Sentences

Study the Models You can make your writing more interesting by using a variety of sentences and by combining related ideas. Be careful not to join too many ideas with commas or the word *and* because this creates confusing sentences.

NOT OK — not a complete sentence

Because Raymond needs looking after. Squeaky watches him. She takes him with her when she trains for the race, and she lets him stay outside the fence, and then she sees him run alongside her when she wins. Squeaky and Gretchen might become friends. If they get to know each other better and maybe even work together to train Raymond.

This selection does not read smoothly. The writer has short and incomplete sentences and one run-on sentence.

OK

Because Raymond needs looking after, Squeaky watches him. She takes him with her when she trains for the race. She lets him stay outside the fence, and then she sees him run alongside her when she wins. Squeaky and Gretchen might become friends if they get to know each other better. Maybe they will even work together to train Raymond.

This passage reads better. The sentences are more varied, and none go on and on!

Add Sentences Add two or three sentences to the OK model. Use sentences that are complete and varied to keep your reader's interest.

✎ **WRITE ON YOUR OWN** Write about how you would feel and what you would do if anyone made fun of someone close to you. Use a variety of sentences and combine related ideas when appropriate.

REMEMBER
- In a **compound** sentence, use the conjunctions and, but, and or to combine ideas.
- In a **complex** sentence, use a conjunction to join an independent and a dependent clause.
- Don't string together too many ideas with commas or and.

from PRESSURE

Is a Privilege

BY CHRISTINE BRENNAN

1　September 20, 1973. I was just starting my sophomore year in high school in the suburbs of Toledo, Ohio, when Billie Jean King played tennis hustler and **self-declared male chauvinist** Bobby Riggs in the "Battle of the Sexes." That was a very different time in our world. There were only three or four channels to pick from on the television dial, so when a big event was **aired**, the audience was huge and the impact was immediate.

2　Billie Jean's win was an historic moment witnessed by millions of people at the same time. We all watched as history was made. In the course of just a few hours, the perception of women in the United States changed forever.

3　Billie Jean ruled women's tennis in the late 1960s and early 1970s with a demeanor on court that was a startling departure from that of the more **demure** women who preceded her. It was great to see a female athlete who was so aggressive. As a young player myself, I wore a tennis dress that looked like the kind King wore, sleeveless with a zipper up the middle and a big striped collar. I was so enthusiastic about the sport that my family took a small black-and-white television set on vacation to northern Michigan every year so I wouldn't miss Wimbledon.

4　Women's and girls' sports were very different in those days. Although I was **the "tomboy" of** the neighborhood, playing and watching sports with the boys for weeks on end, there were no organized teams for me to join until my freshman year of high school. When I did get to play on a team, my experience was quite different from the boys'. Before field hockey games, we sometimes had to dash out and mow the grass on our field, then add the white lines. (Of course, the football field was in pristine condition three days before the next game.) We didn't have buses for our games and had to cancel softball games if we didn't have enough parents to drive us. And the cheerleaders for the boys' teams had better uniforms than we did.

5　This was the world of girls' and women's sports the day Billie Jean played Bobby. Our gym teacher and the coach of most of our girls' sports teams, Sandy Osterman, had us all worked up in the days leading to the match.

In Other Words
self-declared male chauvinist
　someone who said he was better
　than women
aired　shown on TV
demure　quiet, calm
the "tomboy" of　a girl who
　behaved more like the boys in

Historical Background
Wimbledon is an international tennis tournament near London. It is one of the four major international tennis tournaments played each year. Champions at Wimbledon earn great prestige in the sport of tennis.

In gym class and at our practices, if a boy came by, Miss O yelled out, "We know who's going to win the big match!" There were side bets worth all of a few dollars between Miss O and her male coaching counterparts. "We'll see who wins," she'd say with a mischievous laugh.

6   I finished my homework early to watch the match that night. It was **a carnival atmosphere** when Billie Jean and Bobby came on the court. Years later, when I got to know Billie, she told me that she had been extremely nervous. But I never knew. On television, she looked calm and confident. Before the match started, my father and mother pointed out the subtlety behind Riggs's over-the-top bravado; while he was a blatant male chauvinist, they said he didn't seem to be a terrible guy. "He's acting bad, but in some ways, he's just playing along," my Dad said. "He's the perfect opponent for Billie Jean. He makes you want her to win even more."

"On television, she looked calm and confident."

7   As it was, I already wanted her to win very badly. Billie Jean was one of the very few female sports heroes I had. But there was no reason for me to worry that night. Billie Jean **routed** Bobby, 6-4, 6-3, 6-3, throwing her wood racket into the air as we cheered in the family room. It was the first time I had ever seen a woman beat a man at anything.

8   The next day at our lockers in the high school hallway, I spotted one of the star boy athletes in my grade, an athletic rival of mine who also was a good friend.

9   "We won," I said to him. "The girls won."

10   "Yeah, I know," he said, grimacing and walking away.

11   In the many years since, a few men have told me they thought it was one of the most **over-hyped** sports events of all time. I always disagree. "For you, maybe, but not for me," I tell them. I have talked to Billie Jean quite a few times in interviews, at dinners, at Wimbledon, even at a White House dinner, where, nearly two decades into my career, she pulled me aside to get my thoughts on the women's sports movement. I smiled about that later: there was Billie Jean King asking me for my opinion on the topic that she pioneered and forever changed for the better.

12   No matter when or where we talk, I always make sure to thank Billie Jean for what she did that night in Houston. It is surely overkill by now, but I cannot help it.

13   "What you meant to a fifteen-year-old girl in Toledo, Ohio . . . " I tell her.

14   I never complete the sentence. She knows.

In Other Words

a carnival atmosphere festive and thrilling
routed easily overpowered
over-hyped sensationalized

Compare Across Texts

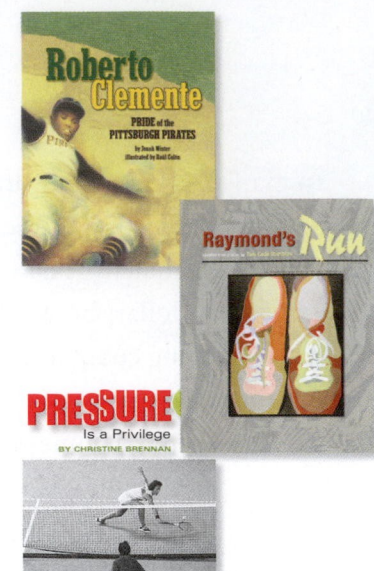

Compare Authors' Styles

Even though "Roberto Clemente" and "Pressure Is a Privilege" are nonfiction and "Raymond's Run" is fiction, they have a similar **goal**: to tell about athletes who work hard to be the best. Compare how the style of each selection fits the author's purpose.

How It Works

Organize Elements of Style Use a Comparison Chart to record style elements. List the author's purpose and then analyze how the point of view and tone contribute to the author's style.

Selection	Purpose	Point of View and Tone
"Roberto Clemente"	to show that Clemente was a great baseball player and person	third-person sympathetic tone—tells how Clemente deserved more respect than he got at first
"Raymond's Run"		

Comparison Chart

Practice Together

Compare Authors' Styles Take the information in the chart and compare the authors' styles. Here is the beginning of a comparison.

Comparison

> "Roberto Clemente," "Raymond's Run," and "Pressure Is a Privilege" are all about athletes who work hard to be the best. In "Roberto Clemente," the author uses chronological order and third-person perspective to tell the reader about Clemente's remarkable career...

Try It!

Complete the chart. Use this frame to compare authors' styles.

The author of "Raymond's Run" wants the reader to know _____. She uses a _____ for this purpose. She also uses a _____ point of view and a _____ tone. However, the author of "Pressure is a Privilege" uses _____ and _____ to tell about _____.

Academic Vocabulary
• **goal** (gōl) *noun*
  A **goal** is a purpose or what you want to happen.

MORE THAN A GAME

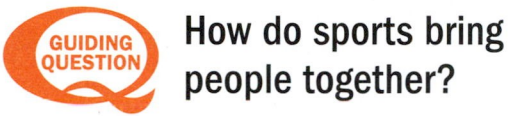

GUIDING QUESTION How do sports bring people together?

Content Library

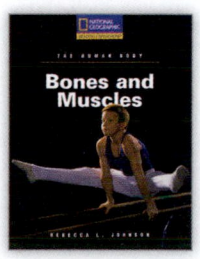

Leveled Library

 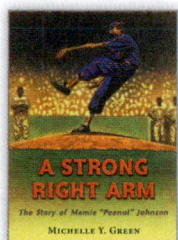 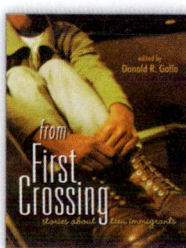

Reflect on Your Reading

Think back on your reading of the unit selections. Discuss what you did to understand what you read.

Focus on Reading Text Structure: **Chronological Order**

In this unit, you learned about some ways writers organize their ideas. Choose a selection from the unit and draw a diagram or other graphic that shows how the text is organized in chronological order. Use your graphic to explain the organization to a partner.

Focus Strategy Make Inferences

As you read, you learned to make inferences. Tell a partner how you will use this strategy in the future.

Explore the

Throughout this unit, you have been thinking about how people bond over sports. Choose one of these ways to explore the Guiding Question:

- **Discuss** With a group, think of a problem at your school or in your community. Then make a list of ways to solve the problem. Discuss the solutions. As a group, decide the best solution.
- **Role-play** With a partner, role-play an interview with one of the people mentioned in "Play Ball!" Include a question about how playing the sport brought certain people together. Then conduct the interview. Perform your role-play for the class.
- **Draw** Draw a sporting event. Include details that show people connecting because of the sport. Describe your visual to a partner.

Book Talk

Which Unit Library book did you choose? Explain to a partner what it taught you about people coming together.

GLOBAL
WARNINGS

8

How can changing our ways benefit the Earth?

READ MORE!

Content Library
Sylvia Earle: Protecting the Seas
by Rebecca L. Johnson

Leveled Library
Matthew Henson
by Maryann N. Weidt

A Walk in the Tundra
by Rebecca L. Johnson

Julie of the Wolves
by Jean Craighead George

Web Links
☐ **myNGconnect.com**

◄ A high-emitting coal-fired power plant in Germany sits in contrast to the calm waters of a nearby lake.

Focus on Reading

Analyze Argument

Writers of **persuasive writing** try to convince readers to agree with their <mark>position</mark> or viewpoint on an issue. They make **claims** expressing what they believe to be true about their <mark>position</mark>. By analyzing a piece of persuasive writing, you can decide whether or not you agree with it, and form your own opinions about the topic.

How It Works

Persuasive writers often state their claim, or **argument**, and follow it up with **support**, or reasons and evidence, as to why readers should agree with them. Readers need to decide if they think the author's reasoning, or way of thinking about things, makes sense and then evaluate the support before making a decision.

- Think about whether the author's argument is based on sound reasoning. Ask yourself: *Does this argument make good sense?*
- Look for support you can trust. Evidence should be relevant information that includes facts, statistics, opinions of experts, and details from personal experience.
- Watch out for reasons that don't help prove the writer's <mark>position</mark>, such as facts that are not relevant, or related, to the issue, unsupported inferences, or personal details intended to sway the reader.

Study this passage to learn more about argument and support.

Rescue the Rain Forest

The Amazon rain forest is in big trouble. — **The writer's argument**

Since the 1960s, people have cut down millions of trees to build farms, roads, and airports. The result is that the rain forest once covered almost 2.7 million square miles, but today covers only about 1.5 million square miles.

> **The writer's support: statistics and facts**

"Any changes that happen here have a great influence on whether the Earth gets warmer," says Professor Philip Fernside of Brazil's National Institute for Amazon Research.

> **Expert opinion**

I've just come back from Brazil, and I now know that we need to protect the animals and plants that live there. So if you really care about the environment, join me in giving to the Rescue the Rain Forest fund!

> **Personal experience and inference**

Academic Vocabulary

- **position** (pu-**zish**-un) *noun*
  Your **position** on an issue is what you think or believe about it.

Practice Together

Read the following passage aloud. As you read, listen for the author's argument. Look for the kinds of evidence the author uses to support his position. Assess if the argument is reasonable.

A POWER-ful Product

This is the best cereal ever! No kidding! Once, just the thought of science class made me want to stay in bed. Now, I don't mind getting up, as long as I start my day with MUNCH-OHS.

▲ The goal of commercials is to persuade you to buy things.

I read on the box that this famous scientist Dr. Knowsit said just one bowl provides 40 percent more vitamins and energy than any other food! All I know is that MUNCH-OHS give me energy to survive until lunchtime. Do the right thing for your growing body! Try MUNCH-OHS.

Try It!

Read the following passage. What kinds of evidence does the author use to support the argument? Do you think the author's reasoning makes sense?

Helpers, Indeed, for Pets in Need

Massive floods, earthquakes, and wildfires this year have forced thousands of people to leave their homes. Sadly, some have to leave their pets behind.

▲ During Hurricane Katrina, about 250,000 pets were abandoned.

Some of the animals find a way to escape. Rescue groups take the frightened animals to shelters. Then the real work begins. Shelter workers have to find new homes for the pets. Volunteers play with the animals and make them feel loved.

How about you? Will you give up a few hours a week to make some furry friends feel wanted? Only you can help these helpless victims.

Focus on Vocabulary

Use Context Clues: Specialized Vocabulary and Language

Writers of persuasive texts use technical words, figurative language, and words with strong connotations to support their arguments. Context clues can help you figure out the meanings of special kinds of words.

- **Technical words** are <mark>associated</mark> with science, trade, the arts, and other fields. Often, the meaning depends on the field where it is used. For example, *pitch* refers not only to throwing in baseball, but also to sounds in music.
- **Figurative language**, such as simile and idiom, can also be used in nonfiction. It goes beyond the literal meaning to create a mental image. For example, *pulling the wool over someone's eyes* means to fool them.
- **Connotation** refers to the feelings <mark>associated</mark> with a word, rather than its denotation, or dictionary meaning. For example, you might call someone who saves money "frugal" or "cheap." Both words have similar meanings, but "frugal" is more positive than "cheap."

How the Strategy Works

When you see a word that is confusing, use the context to figure out the meaning that makes the most sense.

1. Think about the topic of the text.
2. Reread the sentence and look for clues in the other words.
3. Read the sentences before and after to find more clues.
4. Check the word in a dictionary to compare its denotation with its connotation or to check the definition against the meaning you determined from the context.

Follow the Strategy in Action to figure out the meaning of each underlined word. Identify technical terms, figurative language, and connotation.

> Is there a <u>link</u> between environmental education and teens' behaviors? Scientific studies have established just such a connection. They show that the more teens know about environmental issues, the more likely they are to care about them. Some of these teens have <u>turned the tables</u> on their <u>elders</u>. The young have become the leaders; older people have begun to follow.

Strategy in Action

" I know that links in a chain connect to each other. I see *connection* in the next sentence about scientific studies. This tells me that the word *link* is figurative language for a scientific connection. "

☑ **REMEMBER** You can use the context of a word to figure out the meaning that fits in the situation.

Academic Vocabulary

- **associate** (u-sō-shē-āt) *verb*
  When you **associate** two things, you connect, or relate, them in your mind.

Practice Together

Read the passage. Use context to figure out the meaning of each underlined word. Identify technical terms and figurative language.

Poisonous Air and Water

Industrial activities are major causes of air pollution. Factories that build cars, make leather items, or process foods often give off chemicals. Poisonous fumes belch from tall smokestacks. Toxic rivers flow through the countryside, past cities, and into the oceans. These emissions can kill animal and plant life.

Factory activities also disturb aquatic environments. Many factories use water to cool their machines. Water intake structures can pull fish and their eggs into the factories like giant vacuum cleaners. Inside the factories, the organisms may be killed by the heat or chemicals used to clean the cooling system.

Clearly, it is time to find new ways to make some products. Plants and animals, including humans, deserve cleaner environments.

Try It!

Read the passage aloud. What do the underlined words mean in this context? How do you know?

The Costs of Our Comforts

Many things that elevate our standard of living have hidden costs. Modern homes and offices are safe and warm, but materials the construction industry uses can pollute our air and water. Plastic shopping bags are handy, but factories that produce them give off harmful byproducts. Tape and self-stick notes are useful, too, but when we throw them away, plants and animals can absorb the

▲ Common items can hurt our environment.

adhesives from them. When we eat those plants and animals, do we really want this sticky residue in our food? Scientists are always looking for ways to keep producing modern products without damaging our environment.

Handle with Care

by Kate Boehm Jerome

Build Background

Learn to Make a Difference

People don't always do what's best for the planet. The good news is that we can change that. People just like you are making a difference every day.

Connect

Team Brainstorm Work with a small group. Brainstorm what your school could do to be more "green," or take better care of our environment. Share your group's ideas with the rest of the class.

Digital Library

myNGconnect.com
◀ View the images.

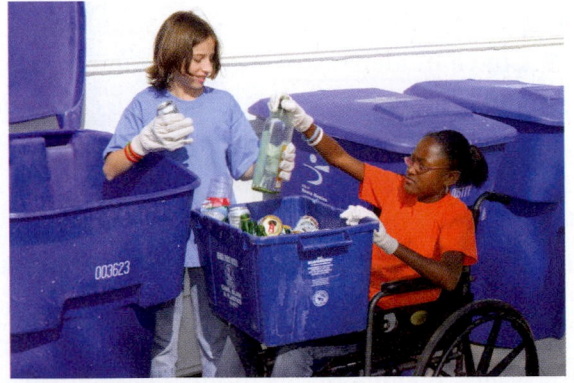

▲ Recycling is one way to help the environment.

Language & Grammar

1 TRY OUT LANGUAGE
2 LEARN GRAMMAR
3 APPLY ON YOUR OWN

Persuade

CD

When you try to persuade someone, you try to convince that person to do something. Look at the photo and listen to the speech. What does the speaker try to persuade people to do?

SPEECH

Show You Care

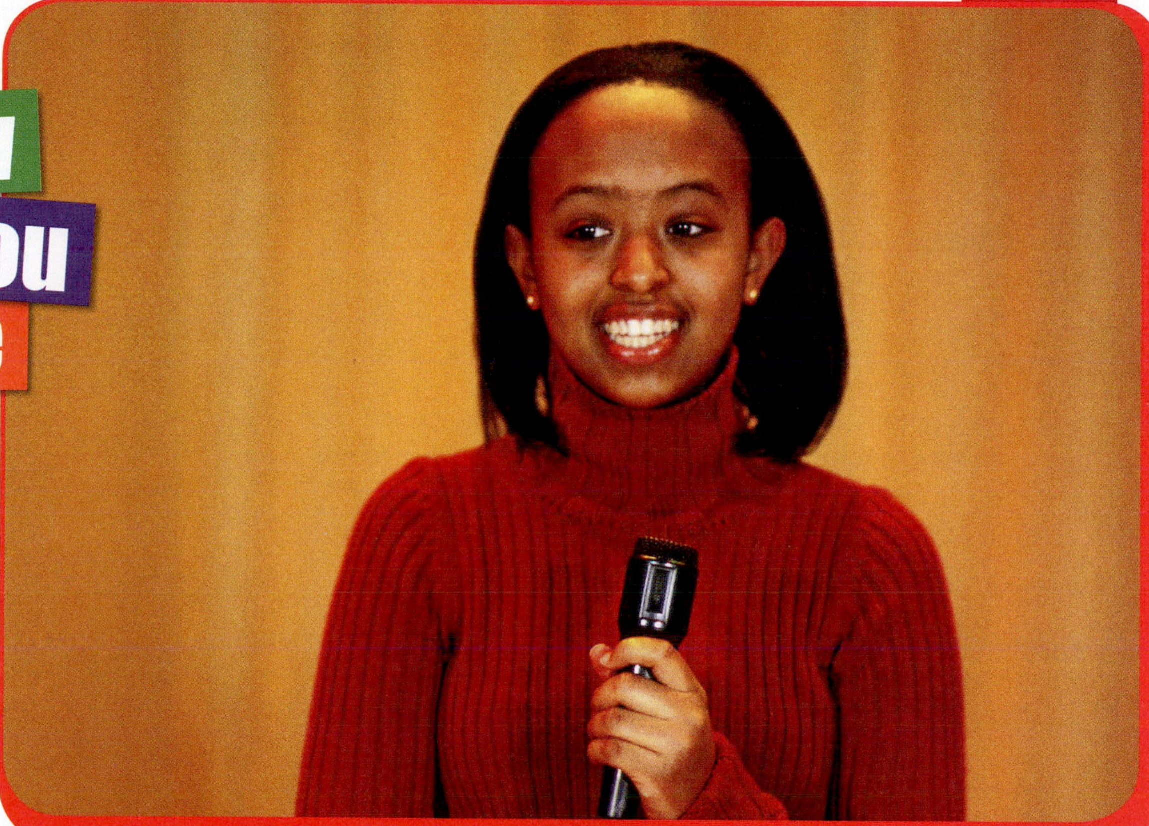

First of all, I'd like to thank Principal Rogan for letting me speak to you today. I'll take just a few minutes of your time to talk about a problem we have in our community and how, together, we can solve it!

The park down the street, where many little kids in town play, is a disaster area! A group of students went to the park yesterday and found litter all over the ground—and even broken glass. The playground equipment needs to be repaired and repainted. The park needs new trash cans and recycling bins. The wooden fence is falling over, so it can't keep the little kids safely inside. Finally, the water fountain isn't working, so kids can't get a drink of water anymore.

I know this all sounds like a lot of work. And it is! But, with your help, we can make the park a better place for everyone. All we're asking is for you to donate a few hours of your time next Saturday.

Use Verbs in the Present, Past, and Future Tense

The tense, or time, of a **verb** shows when an action happens.

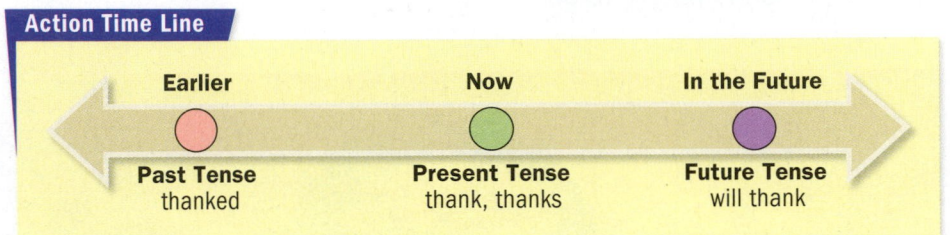

Action Time Line

Earlier	Now	In the Future
Past Tense thanked	**Present Tense** thank, thanks	**Future Tense** will thank

- **Present tense** verbs tell about actions that happen now or often. The verb ends in **-s** only when it tells about one other person, one place, or one thing.

  EXAMPLE   The speaker **donates** his time to persuade people.

- **Past tense** verbs tell about actions that already happened. Add **-ed** to most verbs to form the past tense. Or use the correct form of an irregular verb.

  EXAMPLES   The students **found** litter all over the ground.
  They **contacted** the local hardware stores.

- **Future tense** verbs tell about actions that have not yet happened. Use **will** before the main verb to form the future tense.

  EXAMPLES   The local store **will donate** giant trash bags.
  The kids **will thank** you.

Practice Together

Say each sentence. Change the <u>verb</u> to the past tense and the future tense. Say both new sentences.

1. The playground <u>is</u> not safe.
2. Some swings <u>need</u> new seats.
3. We <u>sort</u> the litter into trash and recycled items.

Try It!

Say each sentence. Write the past tense and the future tense of each <u>verb</u> on a card. Then say both new sentences.

4. My dad <u>fixes</u> the fence.
5. I <u>paint</u> the fence white.
6. The city workers <u>take</u> away the trash.

▲ Teens sort trash and recycled items.

Help Your Community

PERSUADE

What problems do you know of in your community? Maybe there is litter that needs to be collected. Maybe some children need tutors to help them in school. How can you persuade people to take action?

Work with a small group. Brainstorm a problem to solve. State why people should take action. Then list evidence or reasons to support your argument. Use persuasive language that would convince others to do what you want.

Argument: Each of us has something we can teach a younger child. If we each give two hours a week reading to first graders, we can help those kids be more successful in school by the time they reach our age.

Support
1. You don't have to be the smartest person in the world to help a child learn.
2. If we read to younger kids, we help them find success and believe in themselves.
3.

Present your argument and support to another group. Then trade roles. Which group was more successful at convincing the other? Why?

HOW TO PERSUADE

1. Present your argument.
2. Give evidence and reasons to support your argument.
3. Use persuasive language to convince others to agree with your argument and to take action.

I love math, and I'm pretty good at it.

Then tutor a student who has trouble with math. You can help him or her succeed!

USE VERBS IN THE PRESENT, PAST, AND FUTURE TENSE

When you make a persuasive argument, you need to use verbs. Use the correct verb tense to show when an action happens. If it happens often or now, use the **present tense**. If it already happened, use the **past tense**. If it hasn't happened yet, use the **future tense**.

In the Present: Some kids **need** help with their school work.

In the Past: We **learned** the same things when we **were** their age.

In the Future: We **will help** kids do better in school.

Prepare to Read

Learn Key Vocabulary

Study the Words Rate how well you know each word. Then:

1. Pronounce the word. Use the steps below.
2. Rate your word knowledge.
3. Study the example. Tell more about the word.
4. Practice it. Make the word your own.

Rating Scale

1 = I have never seen this word before.

2 = I am not sure of the word's meaning.

3 = I know this word and can teach the word's meaning to someone else.

Key Words

damage (dam-ij) *verb*
▶ page 560

To **damage** means to cause harm. Wind and water from a storm can **damage** a building.

issue (ish-ü) *noun*
▶ page 558

An **issue** is a problem or concern. Taking care of the environment has become an important **issue**.

prevent (pri-**vent**) *verb*
▶ page 558

To **prevent** something means to keep it from happening. Airbags can **prevent** injuries in a car crash.
Related Word: **prevention**

protect (prō-tekt) *verb*
▶ page 558

To **protect** means to keep safe. Penguin fathers **protect** their young from the cold.
Related Word: **protection**

recycle (rē-sī-kul) *verb*
▶ page 561

To **recycle** means to use again, usually in a different way. People usually **recycle** glass, paper, and plastic.
Related Word: **recycling**

resource (rē-sors) *noun*
▶ page 558

A **resource** is something you can use. Trees are a natural **resource** for wood used in house building.
Related Word: **resourceful**

source (sors) *noun*
▶ page 562

A **source** is where something comes from. Lakes are the **source** for much of our drinking water.

waste (wāst) *noun*
▶ page 561

Waste is something that is left over or thrown away. People put their **waste** outside to be picked up each week.
Related Words: **wasteful, wasted**

Practice the Words Make a Study Card for each Key Word. Then compare your cards with a partner's cards.

> **recycle**
>
> **What it means:** to use again
>
> **Example:** I refill a plastic water bottle.
>
> **Not an example:** I throw out paper when I could use the other side.

Study Card

Analyze Argument and Reasons

What are Persuasive Appeals? To state their arguments, persuasive writers often make claims in the form of appeals intended to get a certain response. Good readers must evaluate if the appeal is based on **sound reasoning**. There are three main kinds of appeals.

- An **appeal to logic** shows why something makes sense.
- An **appeal to ethics** suggests the right way to behave or think.
- An **appeal to emotions** tries to make you feel strongly about an issue.

As you read, look for the appeals and reasoning the writer uses to convince you.

Reading Strategies
- Plan
- Monitor
- Visualize
- Determine Importance
- Ask Questions
- Make Connections
- Make Inferences
- **Synthesize** Bring together ideas gained from texts and blend them into a new understanding.

Look Into the Text

Human activities such as plowing fields, mining, and building highways can destroy the land. … Soil erosion and overgrazing by animals eventually can turn rich farmland into a desert wasteland. So does this mean we shouldn't build a highway or plow a field? Of course not. But it does mean we should consider Earth-friendly ways of doing those things.

"Destroy" is a strong word. It makes me feel concerned.

Practice Together

Begin a Three-Column Chart A Three-Column Chart can help you record different kinds of appeals you find in the text. Use the chart to review the writer's reasoning and decide if the writer's claims are supported. Reread the passage above and add to the Three-Column Chart.

Kind of Appeal	Example	My Evaluation
appeal to emotions and logic	Human activities such as plowing fields, mining, and building highways can destroy the land.	The word "destroy" worries me. There is evidence in the text to support this statement.

Three-Column Chart

Academic Vocabulary
- **appeal** (u-pēl) *noun*
  An **appeal** is a strong request for something.

Persuasive Essay

A persuasive essay is nonfiction text that states an **argument**. The author's purpose is to persuade, or convince, readers to agree with that argument. To do that, the author presents reasons and **evidence** that support the author's opinion. Evidence may include facts, statistics, quotes from experts, personal remarks, or words that appeal to the emotions.

Identify important ideas as you read in order to draw conclusions about the author's reasoning and evidence.

Look Into the Text

Another human activity that hurts ◄ argument
the land is deforestation. This is the
removal of large numbers of trees
from a forest. Millions of acres of ◄ evidence
the tropical rain forest biome are
cleared away each year. When this
happens, many plants and animals
lose their habitat. They may die out,
or become extinct.

Handle with Care

by Kate Boehm Jerome

Save energy! Don't litter! Reduce air pollution!

Bumper stickers and environmental slogans are everywhere. But do they make a difference in protecting the environment?

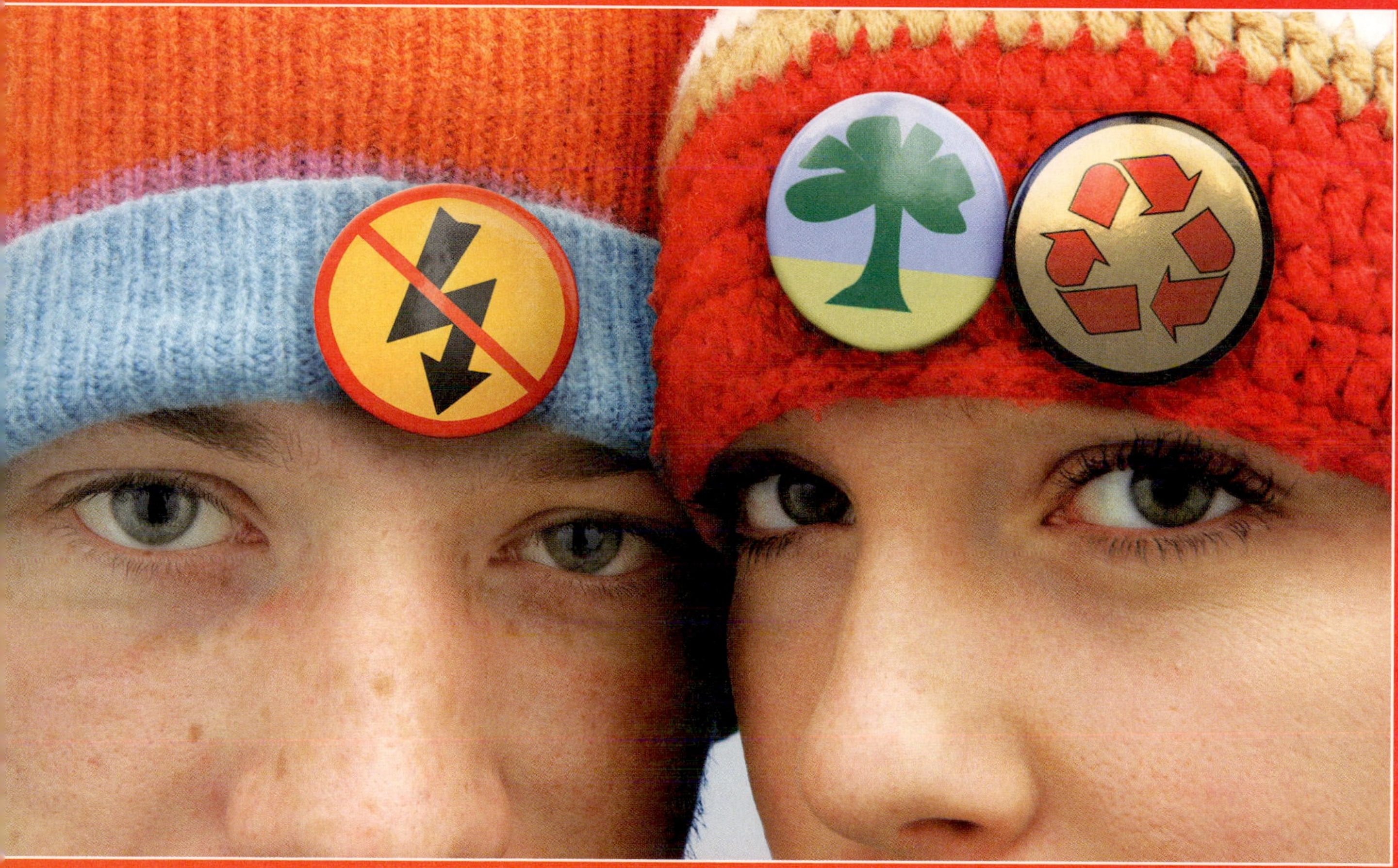

Comprehension Coach

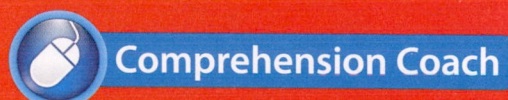

The answer is yes. Even the efforts of one person can help **protect** our planet. The **issues** may be easier to understand if you know not only what you should do but also why you should do it.

Consider the basics. Plants and animals, including humans, need food and water to survive. These needs are met by the natural **resources** found in the **biosphere** of Earth. To protect these resources, we need to keep the air clean and the water drinkable. How do we do that?

Protect the Land

The soil that covers fields and farms provides much of the food we eat. Human activities such as plowing fields, mining, and building highways can destroy the land. Erosion occurs when wind and water wear away the soil. Soil erosion and overgrazing by animals eventually can turn rich farmland into a **desert wasteland**. So does this mean we shouldn't build a highway or plow a field? Of course not. But it does mean we should consider Earth-friendly ways of doing those things.

Today, farmers plow their fields in a variety of ways designed to **prevent** erosion. They try to limit the amount of water they use for their crops. They keep animals from grazing in just one area. Farmers also plant trees to prevent soil from blowing or washing away.

Save the Trees

Another human activity that hurts the land is deforestation. This is the removal of large numbers of trees from a forest. Millions of acres of the **tropical rain forest biome** are cleared away each year. When this happens, many plants and animals lose their habitat. They may die out, or become extinct. Scientists haven't even discovered all the organisms living in the tropical rain forest. We may be losing **species** without even knowing they exist.

According to scientists, every day an estimated one hundred plant and animal species are lost to deforestation. Some scientists predict that about 50 percent of the Earth's species will vanish within the next one hundred years.

Key Vocabulary
protect *v.*, to keep safe from harm
issue *n.*, something that is a problem or causes disagreements
resource *n.*, something that can be used for support or help
prevent *v.*, to stop

In Other Words
biosphere land and water
desert wasteland place where nothing can grow
tropical rain forest biome jungle
species types of plants and animals

The Effects of Deforestation

▲ Forests like these cover the Earth and keep it cool. They provide habitats for plant and animal life.

▲ Widespread deforestation like this can cause Earth to become too hot. When the Earth is too hot, animals, plants, and even humans are affected by the rising temperatures.

Look Into the Text

1. **Cause and Effect** What causes soil erosion? What can help **prevent** it?
2. **Paraphrase** In your own words, tell what this means: "We may be losing species without even knowing they exist."
3. **Viewing** How do the photos help explain deforestation?

Trees absorb carbon dioxide and use it when they make food. Increased deforestation means fewer trees. This adds to the buildup of carbon dioxide in the air and contributes to the greenhouse effect. As certain gases in Earth's atmosphere increase, Earth may get too warm.

Environmentalists encourage careful management of the forests so people do not **damage** them. They call for replanting after forests are cut down. They support creation of national parks to protect the forests and the animals that live there.

The Greenhouse Effect

When trees are cut down, they can't absorb carbon dioxide.
Carbon dioxide can keep heat from escaping Earth's atmosphere.

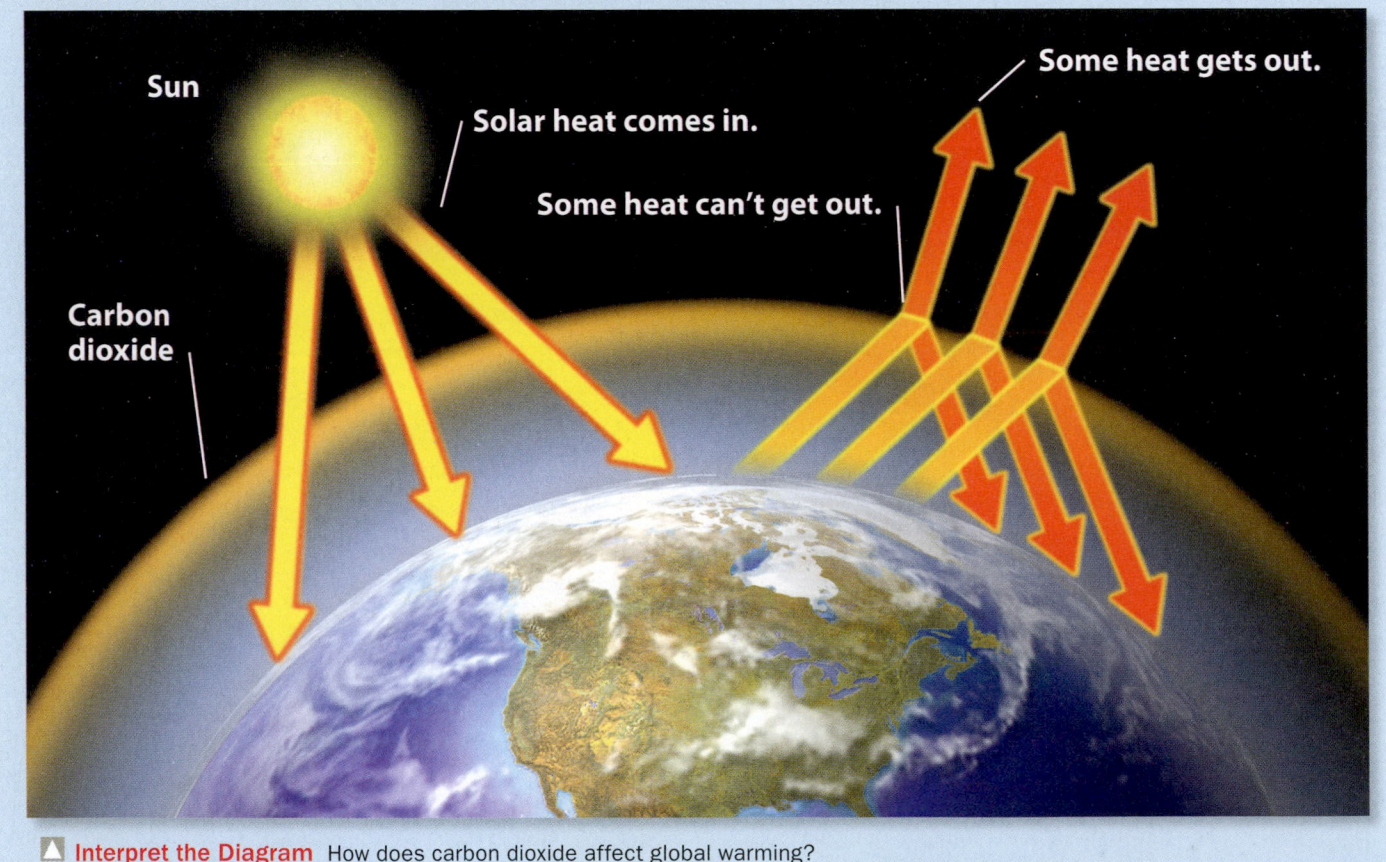

Sun

Solar heat comes in.

Some heat gets out.

Some heat can't get out.

Carbon dioxide

▲ **Interpret the Diagram** How does carbon dioxide affect global warming?

Key Vocabulary
damage *v.*, to cause harm to or to ruin something

In Other Words
Environmentalists People who work to help the environment

Reduce, Reuse, Recycle

You wad up a piece of paper, take aim, and toss the paper into the wastebasket. It doesn't seem terribly wasteful—but it adds up. The average American makes about ten tons of trash in thirteen years.

Where does that trash go next? Much of our trash ends up in **landfills**. Landfills take up valuable land and sometimes make the water, air, and land around them dirty. More than a third of the trash in landfills is paper. Reusing and reducing what you throw away can cut down on the need for more landfills. In fact, about 80 percent of household trash can be ==recycled==.

==**Wastes**== from certain jobs or activities can also cause problems. Wastes are especially harmful if they are hazardous, or dangerous, to humans and other species. The United States has passed laws to control both **the disposal and the storage of** hazardous wastes that may be poisonous or cause diseases.

From TRASH to Treasure

A simple way to protect Earth is to reduce the amount of trash we throw away. Just what's in our trash? There is paper and glass. There are plastics and metals. How much of that trash can be reused? How much can be turned into something useful?

Kids around the world have found some clever ways to reuse trash. They've turned their trash into toys.

▲ Wheeled coconut-shell boat (Indonesia)

▲ Soccer ball made of twine and plastic (Kenya)

◄ Sailboat made of a broken rubber sandal and a piece of a plastic bag (Kenya)

Key Vocabulary

==**recycle**== *v.*, to use something again

==**waste**== *n.*, an unwanted product that is left over from human activities

In Other Words

landfills garbage dumps
the disposal and the storage of where to throw away and where to keep

Look Into the Text

1. **Summarize** What is the greenhouse effect?
2. **Problem and Solution** Recycling is one way to create less ==waste==. What are two other ways?

Every Drop Counts

Think of all the ways we use water. Water power is a **source** of electricity for some homes and businesses. We drink water and wash with it. Farmers use water for their land. Much of the food we eat is either grown with it or caught from it. We use water for **recreation**. Clean water is **essential** to our lives.

But water sometimes becomes polluted. Brush your teeth or flush the toilet. The water you used isn't clean any more. In some places polluted water is released directly back into streams and lakes. This allows the growth of certain harmful bacteria, which can cause disease.

We tackle this problem in several ways. We send polluted water to water treatment plants before releasing it back into the environment. We are trying to use less water in our cities, homes, and businesses and on our farms. If we use water only when we need it, there is less polluted water to clean up.

How Much Water Do We Need?

▲ Approximately 50 percent of the water used every year in very dry states such as Texas goes to watering lawns.

▲ People who own homes in desert regions can lower their water usage by 50 percent if they plant trees and bushes that grow naturally in the area.

Key Vocabulary
source *n.*, where something comes from

In Other Words
recreation fun activities
essential very important

Protect the Water Supply

Surprisingly, one of the biggest sources of water pollution is the erosion of land. Sediment, or bits of soil, washing into streams and oceans can kill organisms. So by **preserving** plants that grow naturally, we can prevent soil erosion and also protect the water. This helps the planet.

Toxic chemicals also threaten our water supply. Sometimes fertilizers wash off the land. They end up in the rivers, lakes, streams, and groundwater. Groundwater in springs and wells is the main source of drinking water for many people. Chemicals in the fertilizers that kill weeds and insects also can kill fish. They also pollute drinking water. Some poisons remain in the sediment for many years.

Action is being taken, however, to protect our water supply. Farmers are using less fertilizer or fertilizing their crops less often. **Industries** are being forced to pay large fines when they pollute. Some have **reduced their output of** hazardous waste and made other improvements to obey the Clean Water Act.

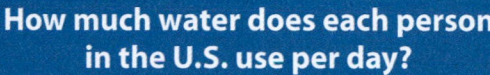

A farmer sprays pesticides on a field. Pesticides eventually "run off" into streams and groundwater, polluting the water we drink.

How much water does each person in the U.S. use per day?	
It is estimated that a person in the United States uses about 379 liters (100 gallons) of water each day. What is this water used for?	
Bathing	76 liters (20 gallons)
Running a dishwasher	15 liters (4 gallons)
Flushing a toilet	91 liters (24 gallons)
Drinking and cooking	8 liters (2 gallons)

In Other Words
preserving protecting, saving
Toxic chemicals also threaten Dangerous liquids also enter
Industries Large businesses
reduced their output of made less

Legal Background
The Clean Water Act is a set of U.S. laws passed in 1972 to stop water pollution. The goal of the act is to make all lakes and rivers in the country safe.

Look Into the Text

1. **Explain** Explain how water is important to our lives. What can we do to use less of it?

2. **Cause and Effect** How do toxic chemicals affect people and animals?

Reduce Air Pollution

The main source of air pollution is the burning of fossil fuels. Fossil fuels, including oil, coal, and natural gas, are our main sources of energy. When energy sources are burned, sulfur and nitrogen compounds are **produced**. When these gases mix with moisture, they form sulfuric acid and nitric acid.

Sulfuric and nitric acids in rainwater and snow fall to the planet as acid rain. When acid rain falls into rivers and lakes, many organisms in these habitats cannot survive. Acid rain damages forests and crops. It also **eats away at** buildings, bridges, and statues.

Cars and trucks cause almost a third of the air pollution in the United States.

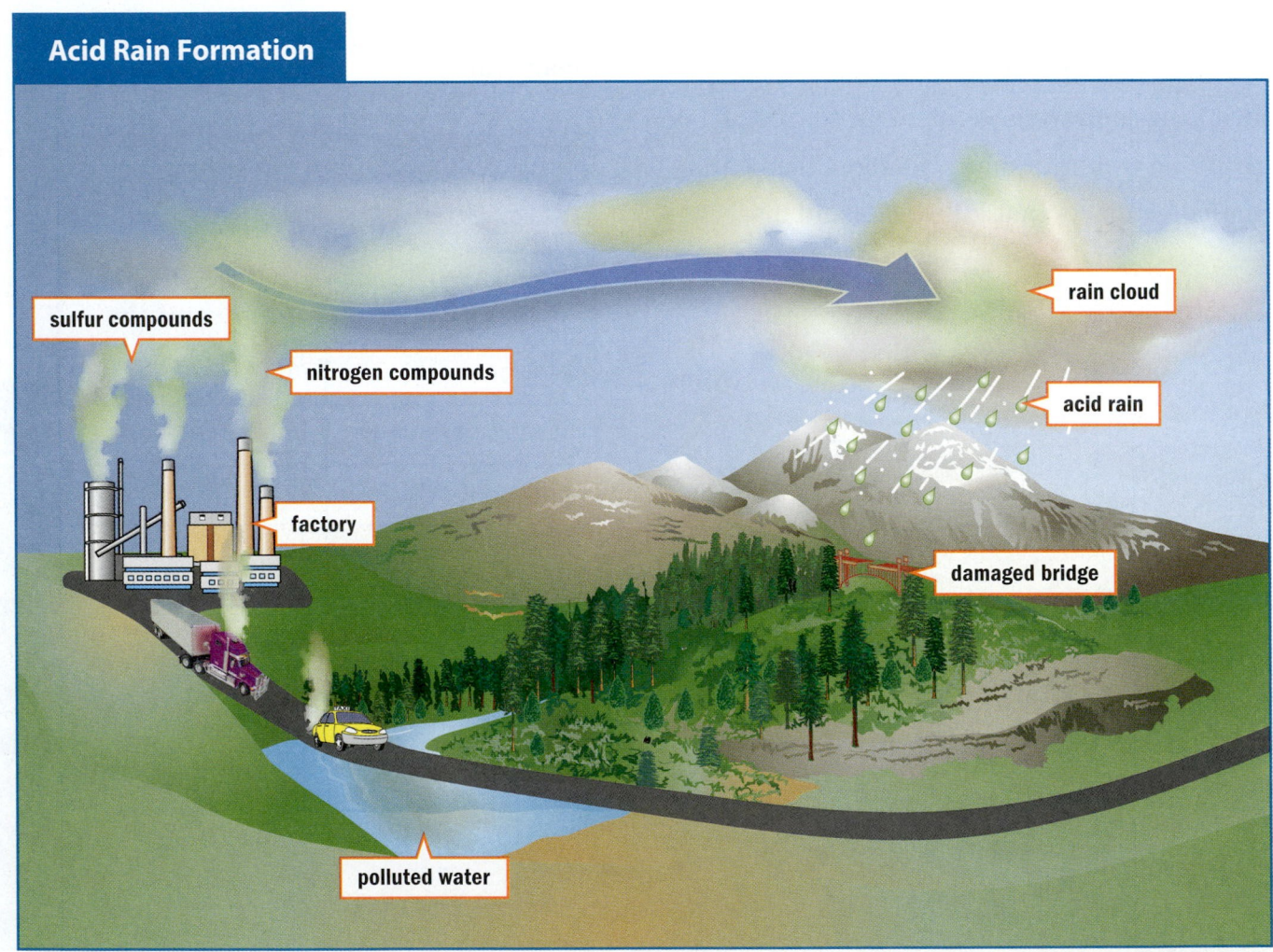

Acid Rain Formation

sulfur compounds

nitrogen compounds

factory

polluted water

rain cloud

acid rain

damaged bridge

In Other Words
produced made
eats away at slowly destroys

So walking, biking, and using public transportation are ways to reduce the amount of air pollution. The **buildup** of pollution also comes from power plants and other industrial sources, particularly in cities in the eastern United States. To fight the problem, industries can use pollution-control devices called scrubbers on their smokestacks.

Handle Everything with Care

As you can see, humans affect the biosphere in many different ways. We all need to consider our actions and their effect on Earth's natural riches. To protect our planet in the future, we must make responsible decisions today. ❖

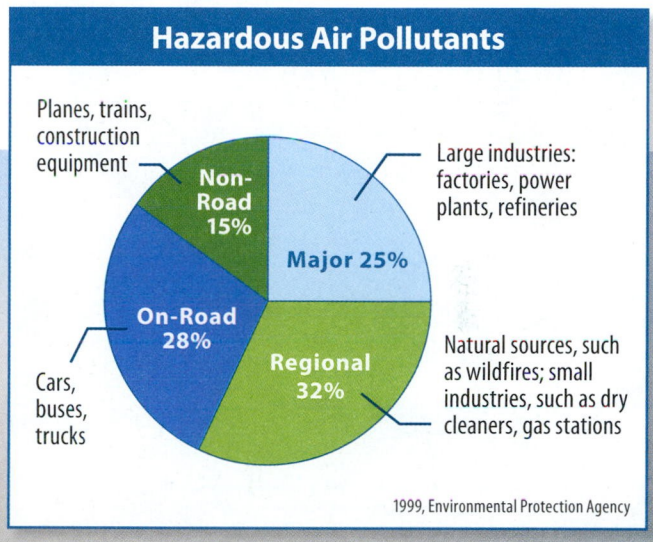

Hazardous Air Pollutants

Planes, trains, construction equipment — Non-Road 15%

Large industries: factories, power plants, refineries — Major 25%

On-Road 28% — Cars, buses, trucks

Regional 32% — Natural sources, such as wildfires; small industries, such as dry cleaners, gas stations

1999, Environmental Protection Agency

▼ Shanghai's large population and many factories have caused its air pollution. Recently, Shanghai has spent billions of dollars to clean up its air and waterways.

In Other Words
buildup large amount

Look Into the Text

1. **Problem and Solution** What are the **sources** of air pollution? How can people help stop it?
2. **Text Features** According to the pie chart, what causes the highest percentage of air pollution?

GOING GREEN
with Cameron Diaz

I'm Cameron Diaz. You may know me as Princess Fiona. But did you know I'm also an environmentalist? We can't keep Earth healthy without your help, so I wanted to **speak out** about protecting the planet. I want to talk about **eco-friendly tips**, the power of kids, and recycling stinky **sneakers**.

In Other Words
speak out share information
eco-friendly tips ways to help Earth
sneakers shoes

Why do you care so much about protecting the Earth?

Think about the planet as your house. If you don't take care of it, it falls apart, and you can't live in it. Earth is the same way. We don't have another planet, and we can't live without clean air and water. We have to take care of them right now.

What are you doing to help the environment?

I love driving my **hybrid car**. The gas mileage is fantastic, and the low **emissions** mean less carbon dioxide, a gas that may contribute to global warming.

What else are you doing?

I'm careful how long I let the water run. I try not to turn on my lights until it gets dark and use compact fluorescent lightbulbs. I can go a year on just one roll of plastic wrap.

Really?

Yep. I wash the plastic wrap after I use it, but I also do things like put a plate over the bowl instead of plastic wrap. I just try to figure out how to do things differently so it's better for the environment.

You're just one person, though. Why is it important for everyone to pitch in?

I like to snowboard, but I have friends who don't, so we don't **connect on that**. But there's one thing that we can all connect on: We all need the Earth's resources. There's not one person who can say, "I don't need clean water or air." So everybody has to do their part.

Even kids?

Especially kids! Think about it: All the great inventors were kids once. So how are today's kids going to make the world a better place? They're the ones who will figure out how to make a car more efficient, or how to purify water.

▲ Bumper stickers that go on vehicles often show people's opinions.

In Other Words

hybrid car car that produces less pollution

emissions amounts of harmful fumes or gases

connect on that have that in common

But a lot of our readers may think, "I'm just a kid and can't make a difference."

They're so wrong. Businesses **bend over backward** to find out what kids want. If kids demand green products, then we will have green products. That's a huge power.

Are there other things that kids can do?

Think about how you can reuse things. Like, when I buy something, I save all the packaging—the little boxes, the plastic wrapping, the twist ties. To me it's like a puzzle figuring out how to reuse them.

Any other advice?

Be selfish—it's OK to want the best. You already want the best pair of sneakers, the best video game, the best bike. Why not the best oxygen, the best water, the best soil? You deserve it!

We have another idea how kids can help. We're asking them to recycle their used sneakers, which will be recycled into athletic surfaces.

That's a great idea! Instead of letting your shoes sit in a dump, you're making them into something that kids all over the country can enjoy. You get to take all the fun and energy that those shoes gave you and put them back into the world. Can I ask a question?

Sure!

Can I be the first to donate my sneakers?

In Other Words
bend over backward try
  very hard

Economic Background
Many businesses are now offering "green" products as a way to help the environment. These products are called "green" because they may be made out of recycled material or are easily recycled.

Look Into the Text

1. **Evaluating Sources** Do you think Diaz is the right person to offer advice on taking care of Earth? Why or why not?

2. **Opinion** Diaz believes kids have the power to make a difference. Do you agree with her? Why or why not? Use examples from the text to support your answer.

Connect Reading and Writing

Vocabulary
damages
issue
prevent
protect
recycle
resources
source
waste

CRITICAL THINKING

1. SUM IT UP Use your Three-Column Chart to evaluate with a partner the author's claims and reasoning in "Handle with Care." Then summarize the selection.

Kind of Appeal	Example	My Evaluation
appeal to emotions and logic	Human activities such as plowing fields, mining, and building highways can destroy the land.	The word "destroy" worries me. There is evidence in the text to support this statement.

Three-Column Chart

2. Analyze Think back to the Team Brainstorm you had about ways for your school to go "green." Was the selection a **source** for more ideas? Discuss your additions with the team.

3. Make Judgments Which **issue** mentioned in the essay is the biggest threat to our environment? Why do you think so?

4. Compare "Handle with Care" and "Going Green" are both about caring for natural **resources**. How do both suggest that humans are responsible for **protecting** Earth's environment?

READING FLUENCY

Intonation Read the passage on page 659 to a partner. Assess your fluency.

1. My tone never/sometimes/always matched what I read.

2. What I did best in my reading was _____.

READING STRATEGY

What strategy helped you understand this selection? Tell a partner about it.

VOCABULARY REVIEW

Oral Review Read the paragraph aloud. Add the vocabulary words.

Our garbage _____ the environment. One problem, or _____, is that we dump too much of our _____ into landfills. We can _____ this from happening if we _____. We need to find new _____ for making paper before we cut down too many trees. Humans may be the _____ of the problem, but we can _____ the planet if we work together.

Written Review Imagine you are the planet Earth. Write a speech to persuade people to **protect** your natural **resources**. Use five vocabulary words.

WRITE ABOUT THE GUIDING QUESTION

Explore How We Can Help Earth
What's one thing that everyone could do to **protect** our planet? Write your opinion. Reread the selection to find support for your opinion.

Connect Across the Curriculum

Vocabulary Study

Understand Denotation and Connotation

Academic Vocabulary
- **associate** (u-**sō**-shē-āt) *verb*
  When you **associate** two things you connect or relate them in your mind.

A word's **denotation** is its dictionary definition. **Connotation** is the feeling you **associate** with a word. For example, try the word *hurt* and then *destroy* in this sentence: Our actions _____ the Earth.

You probably **associate** *hurt* with the idea of harm or injury. But you probably **associate** the word *destroy* with danger or death.

Analyze Words Read the sentences. Look up the denotations of the underlined words in a print or online dictionary. Use the context to identify their connotations. Compare the denotation and the connotation.

1. Soil erosion can turn rich farmland into a <u>desert wasteland</u>.
2. Clean water is <u>essential</u> to our lives.
3. Acid rain <u>eats away at</u> buildings, bridges, and statues.

Media/Viewing

Analyze Propaganda in the Media

MEDIA & TECHNOLOGY

Academic Vocabulary
- **logical** (**lah**-ji-kul) *adjective*
  Something that is **logical** seems believable or reasonable.

Propaganda is information that is either false or partially true. Even though it seems believable, it is not **logical** . Propaganda techniques include testimonials, bandwagon, transfer, and name calling. Look at some ads and decide whether they use propaganda or **logical** evidence.

1 **Collect Advertisements** With a partner, look at newspapers, magazines, and the Internet to find ads for common products.

2 **Analyze Persuasive Techniques** Think about how each ad is trying to persuade you. Does it contain propaganda?

3 **Share and Discuss Your Advertisements** Present the ads. Point out examples of propaganda or **logical** evidence. Discuss: Are people easily convinced by propaganda? Why could this be dangerous?

Persuade

Role-Play Work with a group. Half the group role-plays citizens who are against building houses in a popular wilderness area. The other half role-plays the business people who want to build more houses in that area. One person acts as the judge. The citizens try to persuade the judge to help save the land. The business people try to persuade the judge that they will bring new jobs, services, and money into the community. The judge decides. Use verbs in the correct tense. Trade roles.

> We will create about 800 new jobs!

> New jobs cannot make up for the damage to the environment and loss of animal homes.

Write About Community Action

Study the Models When you write, you want your readers to understand when things happen. Decide whether the events are happening now, or if they happened in the past, or will happen in the future. Don't switch back and forth or your writing may not be clear.

NOT OK

Earth has a problem. There is too much trash and we created more each day. We used too many things. So follow the 3Rs—reduce, reuse, and recycle. You can recycle paper, metal, and glass into new objects. You can reduce the amount of trash. How? Buy things that will be made from recycled materials. You can reuse stuff and create art from trash. And you will give away old clothes. Don't throw them out!

> The reader thinks: " **This is confusing. It's about the present, but the writer switches between present, past, and future!** "

OK

Earth has a problem. There is too much trash and we create more each day. We use too many things. So follow the 3Rs—reduce, reuse, and recycle. You can recycle paper, metal, and glass into new objects. You can reduce the amount of trash. How? Buy things that are made from recycled materials. You can reuse stuff and create art from trash. And you can give away old clothes. Don't throw them out!

> **This is better because the writer sticks to the present.**

Add Sentences Think of two more sentences to add to the OK model. Be sure to write about events that are happening in the present.

✎ **WRITE ON YOUR OWN** Do people in your school recycle? Write about an action you or your classmates took to recycle at school or improve the environment in another way.

> **REMEMBER**
> - **Present tense** verbs tell about actions that happen now or often.
> - **Past tense** verbs tell about actions that already happened.
> - **Future tense** verbs tell about actions that haven't yet happened.

Melting Away

by Glen Phelan

Build Background

Connect

KWL Chart Create a KWL Chart about global warming. In the K column, list what you already know. In the W column, list what you want to know about it. You'll use the L column to list what you learned after reading.

KWL Chart

WHAT I KNOW	WHAT I WANT TO KNOW	WHAT I LEARNED
Earth is getting hotter. Weather patterns have changed.	Why is Earth getting hotter? How can there be global warming if winters are colder?	

Stay Cool

Glaciers and ice caps aren't just homes for polar bears. They provide a habitat for many living things. So what will happen if global warming melts them away?

Digital Library
myNGconnect.com
◐ View the video.

▲ Greenland's ice cap is melting at an alarming speed.

Use Appropriate Language

Listen to the chant and chime in. Then listen to a formal presentation and an informal conversation.

CHANT

Choosing Your Words

Use appropriate language
Carefully choose your words,
When you want to express your thoughts,
When you want your ideas heard.

Match words to the occasion
At school or social events,
Always speak politely,
With respect and intelligence!

Use appropriate tone and volume
With words you want to stress.
Along with body gestures,
This guarantees success.

Ladies and gentlemen, thank you for coming to our presentation about global warming. Today, you will hear from speakers about how Earth is changing. We will explore the reasons why Earth is warmer. We will examine if warmer temperatures mean changes in weather and changes in our lives.

Use Verbs in the Present Perfect Tense

- If you know when an action happened in the past, use a **past tense** verb.

    EXAMPLE   Last month, scientists **attended** a global warming conference.

- If you're not sure exactly when a past action happened, use a verb in the **present perfect tense**.

    EXAMPLE   They **have attended** many conferences.

- You can also use the present perfect tense to show that an action started in the past and may still be going on.

    EXAMPLES   Scientists **have studied** the temperature of ocean water for a long time. (And they are probably still studying it.)

                    The temperature **has increased** over time. (And it is probably still increasing.)

- To form the **present perfect**, use the helping verb **have** or **has** plus the past participle of the main verb. For regular verbs, the past participle ends in **-ed**.

Verb	Past Tense	Past Participle
melt	melted	melted
increase	increased	increased
study	studied	studied

Practice Together

Say each sentence. Choose the correct form of the verb.

1. Melting glaciers (added/have added) more water into Earth's oceans over the years.
2. Last year, this glacier (melted/has melted) a lot.
3. During my vacation, we (traveled/have traveled) far by ship to study the glacier.

Try It!

Choose the correct verb to complete each sentence. Read the new sentence aloud.

4. I (wanted/have wanted) to take a trip like this for a long time.
5. Yesterday, I (watched/have watched) some ice fall.
6. My friend (tried/has tried) very hard today to take pictures of it, and she is still trying.

▲ We have watched the ice fall for several hours.

Present a Plan

USE APPROPRIATE LANGUAGE

The language you use and the way you speak will vary depending on your audience and your purpose. For example, use formal language for presentations and interviews. Use informal, or relaxed, language when you talk with family and friends.

With a partner, role-play how you would talk to a friend about setting up a school recycling program. Then role-play how you would talk to a teacher about setting it up. Trade roles.

> Formal: We would like to discuss the possibility of starting a recycling program with you.
>
> Informal: Hey, what do you think about starting a recycling program? Good idea?

Perform your role-plays for a small group. Let them decide if your language is appropriate for each situation.

HOW TO USE APPROPRIATE LANGUAGE

1. Use words that match the audience and the occasion.
   - Use formal language in school.
   - Use informal language with friends and family.
2. Use proper body language, tone, and volume.
   - Formal situation: stand up straight, make eye contact, look serious, and speak loudly and clearly so everyone can hear you.
   - Informal situation: be more relaxed.

> Formal:
> Good morning, Mrs. Rutan. Thank you very much for inviting me.

> Informal:
> Man, am I glad you came over!

USE VERBS IN THE PRESENT PERFECT TENSE

Be sure to use the correct tense. If you know when in the past an event happened, use the **past tense**.

EXAMPLE   Last year, we **talked** about starting a recycling center.

If you're not sure when an event happened in the past or if the event is still happening now, use the **present perfect tense**.

EXAMPLES   Mom **has volunteered** to help start a recycling center.
We **have talked** about starting a recycling program for a long time.

Prepare to Read

Learn Key Vocabulary

Study the Words Use the steps below.

1. Pronounce the word. Say it aloud several times. Spell it.
2. Rate your word knowledge.
3. Study the example. Tell more about the word.
4. Practice it. Make the word your own.

Key Words

area (air-ē-u) *noun*
▶ page 582

An **area** is a section of a place often set aside for special use. Fences are often used to mark **areas** where people are not allowed to go.
Synonym: **section**

atmosphere (at-mu-sfir) *noun* ▶ page 585

The **atmosphere** is the air that surrounds Earth. Airplanes fly through the **atmosphere**.

feature (fē-chur) *noun*
▶ page 582

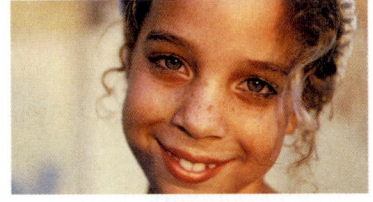

A **feature** is a part of something that stands out. My sister's eyes are her best **feature**.

glacier (glā-shur) *noun*
▶ page 580

A **glacier** is a huge body of moving ice. Many mountains are formed by moving **glaciers**.

melt (melt) *verb*
▶ page 580

To **melt** means to change from a solid to a liquid. When the sun is out, the snow begins to **melt**.
Antonym: **freeze**

reef (rēf) *noun*
▶ page 584

A **reef** is a series of rocks or coral near the surface of the ocean. This **reef** is home to many ocean animals.

soil (soi-ul) *noun*
▶ page 580

Soil is the dirt that covers the ground. Most trees and plants need rich, wet **soil** to help them grow.

temperature (tem-pur-u-chur) *noun* ▶ page 581

The **temperature** is how hot or cold something is. The **temperature** in the United States is usually at its highest during the summer.

Practice the Words Make an Example Chart for each Key Word. Share your chart with a partner.

Noun	Definition	Example from My Life
soil	dirt	We water the soil to help the plants grow.

Example Chart

Analyze Argument and Evidence

How Do Writers Use Evidence? To make a convincing argument, writers include <mark>evidence</mark> to support their claims. Analyzing the amount and kind of information can help you to evaluate the strength of the writer's argument. To analyze <mark>evidence</mark>, ask the following questions:

1. Is there enough, or sufficient, <mark>evidence</mark> to support the claim?
2. Is the information reliable? Are these facts or opinions?
3. Is the information relevant, meaning is it clearly related to the topic?

As you read, evaluate the kind of <mark>evidence</mark> the writer uses and how well it supports the writer's claims.

Reading Strategies
- Plan
- Monitor
- Visualize
- Determine Importance
- Ask Questions
- Make Connections
- Make Inferences
- **Synthesize** Bring together ideas gained from texts and blend them into a new understanding.

Look Into the Text

The park's glaciers, however, are in danger of melting away. Take Grinnell Glacier, for instance. It's the most famous one in the park.

The glacier has melted a lot throughout the years. It is much smaller now than it was in 1938. Water from the glacier has formed a new lake in the park.

At this rate, the once mighty Grinnell Glacier could soon vanish completely. So could the park's twenty-five other glaciers.

[evidence]

Practice Together

Make an Evidence Chart An Evidence Chart can help you evaluate information. This Evidence Chart shows an example of how to analyze text <mark>evidence</mark>. Reread the passage above and look at the photos on page 581. Then add to the Evidence Chart.

Claim: The once mighty Grinnell Glacier could soon vanish completely.

Text Evidence	My Evaluation
It is much smaller now than it was in 1938.	This fact can be checked and is supported by photos from a reliable source.

Evidence Chart

Academic Vocabulary
- <mark>evidence</mark> (e-vu-dents) *noun*
  Evidence is facts or information that shows that something is true.

Environmental Report

A report gives information about a topic. An environmental report tells what is going on in Earth's environment. The author's purpose might be to provide information or to persuade readers.

A good report includes **evidence** , such as facts, statistics, and **expert opinions** to support claims made by the writer. A writer can also use visuals, such as photos, **maps**, and diagrams. Analyzing the amount and kind of evidence can help you evaluate the writer's argument.

As you read other texts on similar topics, you can compare and evaluate the evidence that different writers include in order to achieve their purposes or make their claims.

2005

Russia

North Pole

Greenland

Alaska (U.S.)

Canada

map

The map provides relevant information to support that the ice is melting.

▲ By 2005, large amounts of ice had melted. The outside red line shows where solid ice used to be. Now there is only ocean water. Many scientists say the ice in the area will continue to melt.

expert opinion

Melting Away

by Glen Phelan

Temperatures are rising worldwide.
That's causing weather to change.
It is also affecting wildlife.

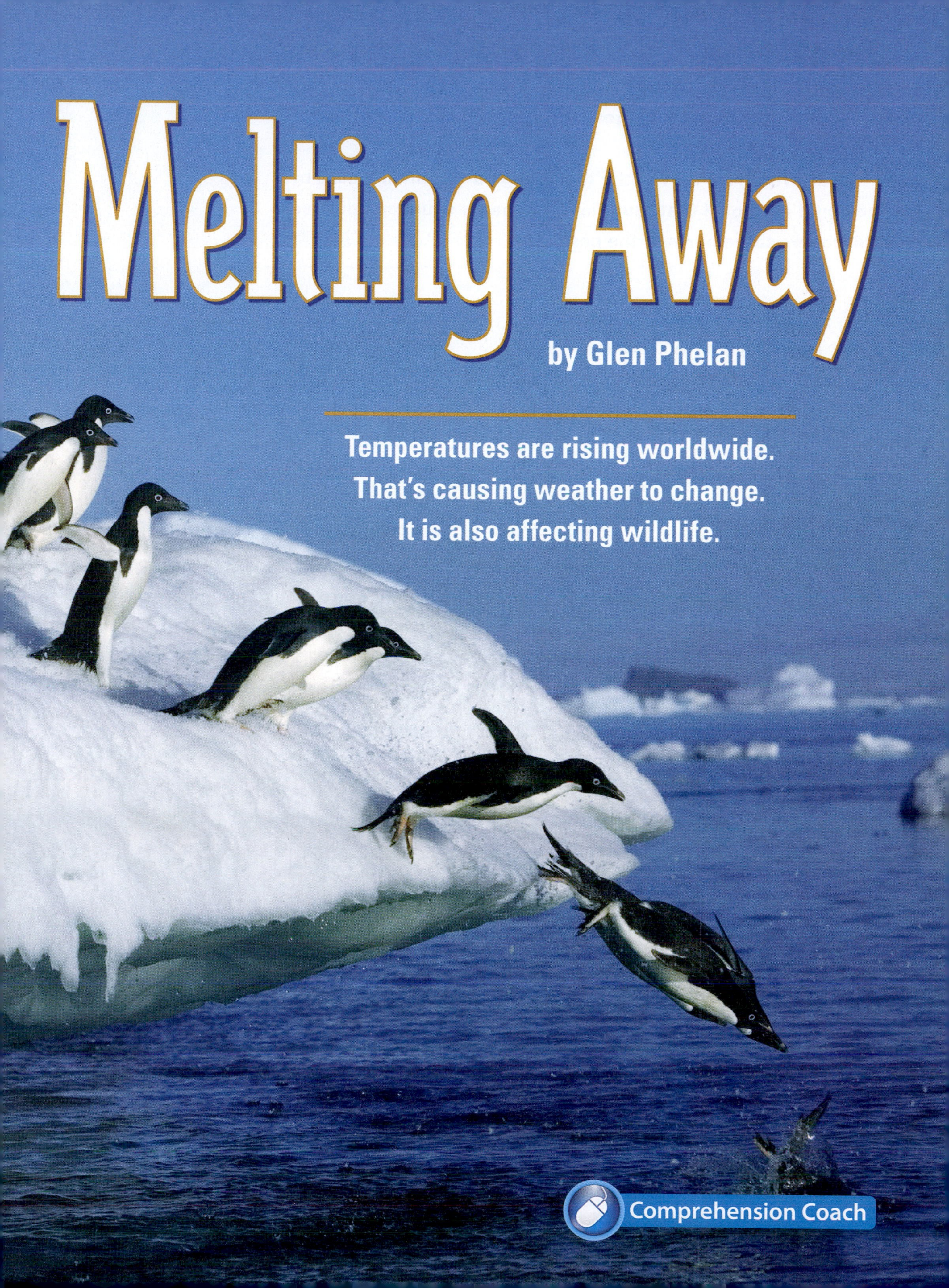

Comprehension Coach

Glacier National Park in Montana is a place of beauty. It has towering cliffs, **jagged ridges**, and deep valleys. All of these were made by ice.

That's right: Ice carved the rocks. Of course, small pieces of ice could not do all that. But giant ice sheets could and did. Ice still covers some parts of the park.

Ice at Work

Ice sheets form when more snow falls in winter than can **melt** in summer. The snow never completely melts, so, year after year, the snow piles up, and huge mounds cover the land. The bottom layers of snow slowly turn into ice.

When the ice grows heavy enough, it starts to move downhill. That's when a sheet of ice becomes a **glacier**. People often describe glaciers as "rivers of ice." Some glaciers were once more than a mile thick. Only the highest mountains poked through the giant ice sheets.

This has been happening at Glacier National Park for millions of years. Glaciers have slowly moved across the land, changing the landscape. They plowed away the **soil**, **ground down** mountains, and carved out valleys.

Glaciers don't last forever, though. If the weather heats up, they melt. That happened at Glacier National Park about 10,000 years ago. And it is happening again today.

Today, twenty-six glaciers cover parts of the park. Those glaciers are still changing the land.

◄ Melting snow and ice formed this lake in Glacier National Park.

Key Vocabulary

melt *v.*, to turn to liquid because of heat

glacier *n.*, a moving body of ice

soil *n.*, the dirt in which plants grow

In Other Words

jagged ridges sharp hills
ground down cut away parts of

The park's glaciers, however, are in danger of melting away. **Take** Grinnell Glacier, for instance. It's the most famous one in the park.

The glacier has melted a lot throughout the years. It is much smaller now than it was in 1938. Water from the glacier has formed a new lake in the park.

At this rate, the once mighty Grinnell Glacier could soon vanish completely. So could the park's twenty-five other glaciers.

Turning Up the Heat

Why is Grinnell Glacier **wasting away**? It's simple: The park is getting warmer. Since 1910, the average summer **temperature** there has risen more than three degrees Fahrenheit (F).

The park isn't the only place that's warming up. Most scientists agree that the rest of Earth is slowly warming up, too.

The rising surface temperature is called global warming. Since 1850, Earth has warmed by about one degree Fahrenheit. Some places, such as Glacier National Park, have warmed up more, and some have warmed up less.

Grinnell Glacier 1938–2006

The red lines show the glacier getting smaller.

1938   1981

1998   2006

U.S. Geological Survey

Look Into the Text

1. **Summarize** How do **glaciers** form? What do they do to the landscape?
2. **Paraphrase** In your own words, tell why some **glaciers** are **melting**.
3. **Viewing** Look at the photos. About how much has Grinnell Glacier melted since 1938?

The Meltdown

If the warming continues, glaciers in Glacier National Park will continue to melt. Of course, other **features** of the **area** will still be there, but the glaciers will be gone.

The melting glaciers could push wildlife out of the area. Grizzly bears are one example. They often move into the park's **meadows** to eat berries and other favorite snack foods.

Huge avalanches make the meadows. An avalanche happens when lots of snow suddenly crashes down a mountainside.

The crashing snow tears down trees, giving berry bushes a place to grow. Without avalanches, there will be fewer berries. That means fewer bears. And bears are just one of the many animals affected by global warming.

The warming trend could affect many plants and animals because it is happening very fast. Some plants and animals might have to find new homes. Others might die out, or become extinct. To survive, they will all have to find ways to **beat the heat**.

▲ Grizzly bear feeding grounds in national parks are becoming smaller due to the effects of global warming.

Key Vocabulary
feature *n.*, a part or detail that stands out
area *n.*, an amount of space or land

In Other Words
meadows fields
beat the heat stay cool in warm weather

Worldwide Warming

One degree may seem small, but it is causing big changes worldwide. In the Antarctic and Arctic, sea ice is melting. The meltdown forms clouds that can make more snowfall than usual. More snow can harm wildlife.

Penguins in Antarctica are having a hard time finding a place to lay eggs. They normally lay eggs on dry ground in the spring. But more snow is falling now. The penguins have to lay their eggs in the snow. When the snow melts, the water rots many of the eggs. That's causing the number of penguins to **drop**.

▲ Because of global warming, some penguins cannot find dry places to lay eggs.

In Other Words
drop get smaller

Arctic Sea Ice Coverage

Rising temperatures have affected the huge sheets of ice surrounding the North Pole. These images show how.

1979

Russia

• North Pole

Greenland

Alaska (U.S.)

Canada

▲ In 1979, ice covered much of the Arctic throughout the year.

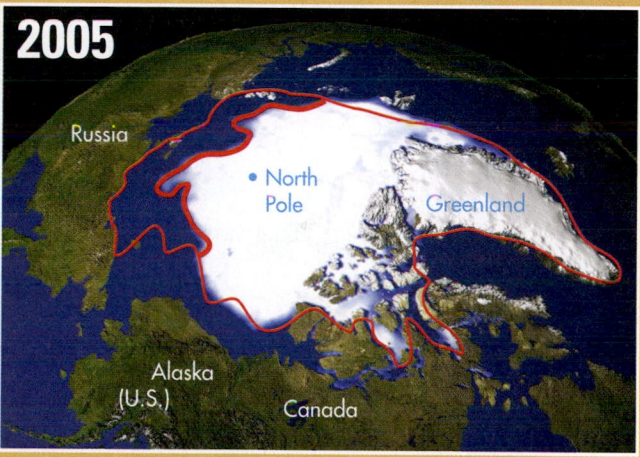

2005

Russia

• North Pole

Greenland

Alaska (U.S.)

Canada

▲ By 2005, large amounts of ice had melted. The outside red line shows where solid ice used to be. Now there is only ocean water. Many scientists say the ice in the area will continue to melt.

Look Into the Text

1. **Sequence** Describe how the grizzly bears' food source is affected by melting glaciers.
2. **Viewing** Look at the sea ice pictures above. What do you think a photo of the area will show in twenty more years?

Trouble in the Tropics

Earth's warmer areas are also affected by rising temperatures. Tiny animals called coral polyps build huge **reefs** in warm ocean water. Reefs come in many different colors. Fish **dart** around the reefs, and a lot of other ocean animals call coral reefs home. But many coral reefs are in trouble.

Because of global warming, ocean water is heating up. If the water near a reef gets too warm, the polyps die. Then the once colorful reef turns white. When a reef dies, fish have to find new homes, or they will die, too.

▲ A live reef

▲ A dead reef

What's Happening?

No one is sure what is causing the worldwide warm-up. Most scientists blame some gases in Earth's **atmosphere**. They point to one gas in particular—carbon dioxide.

Most people depend on oil, coal, and natural gas. These fuels help run cars, heat homes, and power factories. But they also give off carbon dioxide. Carbon dioxide heats the atmosphere and makes Earth warmer.

Over time, cars and factories have changed the atmosphere. Today, the air has about 30 percent more carbon dioxide than in the days before cars and factories. Other heat-trapping gases have also **skyrocketed**.

Each year, people cut down a lot of trees for paper and wood, and this is a problem because forests actually help lower carbon dioxide levels. Trees use carbon dioxide to make their own food.

When people cut down forests, more carbon dioxide **hangs around** in the atmosphere. That drives temperatures even higher.

People also produce a lot of trash, and most of it gets dumped into landfills. These are areas filled with trash and then covered with dirt.

As trash sits in landfills, it makes methane gas. The methane rises into the air and traps heat. More trash means more methane, and more methane means a warmer Earth.

The message, scientists say, is clear. People need to change their ways—beginning now, not next year. The future of Earth is **at stake**. ❖

Methane gas from landfills can make Earth warmer. ▶

Look Into the Text

1. **Cause and Effect** What causes a **reef** to die? Why is this bad for ocean life?
2. **Main Idea and Details** Humans do things to cause global warming. List three details to support this.

Global Warnings

Most scientists say Earth is heating up. That means changes all over the world. This map shows you a bit of what's happening.

Virgin Islands
Warmer weather is causing problems for sea turtles. Many more females are **hatching** than males. Scientists don't know how that will affect sea turtle populations. ▶

Hudson Bay

NORTH AMERICA

NORTH ATLANTIC OCEAN

● Virgin Islands

SOUTH AMERICA

SO
ATLA
OC

SOUTH PACIFIC OCEAN

● Argentina

Argentina
Rising temperatures and **water shortages** have **sparked massive** wildfires in recent years. ▶

Antarctic Peninsula ●

In Other Words
hatching being born
water shortages too little water
sparked massive started large

Hudson Bay
Winter ice melts two to three weeks earlier than before. That makes it harder for polar bears to find food.

Kenya and Tanzania
Malaria, a deadly disease, is spreading. It's carried by mosquitoes. And they love warmer weather.

TIC OCEAN

ROPE

ASIA

NORTH PACIFIC OCEAN

ICA

● Kenya and Tanzania

INDIAN OCEAN

● Great Barrier Reef

AUSTRALIA

Great Barrier Reef
Ocean water is slowly growing warmer. The heat is hurting and even killing big pieces of the world's largest coral reef.

TARCTICA

Antarctic Peninsula
Winter temperatures are nine degrees higher than in 1950. Sea ice has shrunk by one fifth. These changes make it much tougher for Adélie penguins to survive. Bird populations are **sinking**.

In Other Words
sinking getting smaller

Look Into the Text

1. **Summarize** What do all the changes tell you about what is happening to Earth?
2. **Details** Which animals are in danger because of melting sea ice?

Plant a Tree

One way you can help slow global warming is to plant a tree. Trees absorb, or take in, carbon dioxide, while giving off life-giving oxygen. That's natural air pollution control. Trees can help save energy, too. For example, trees cool the air around a house by providing shade. This means that people use air conditioners less often.

Materials:
- tree
- shovel
- **compost**
- garden hose (for watering)
- **wooden stakes** and nylon socks (optional)

Planting Steps

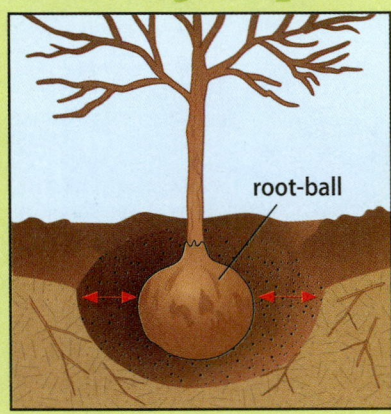

root-ball

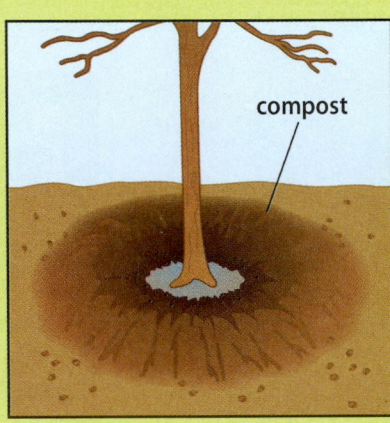

compost

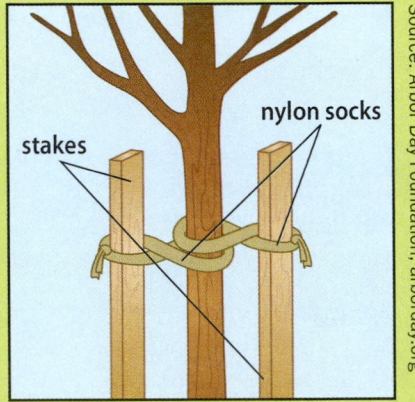

stakes

nylon socks

Source: Arbor Day Foundation, arborday.org

1. Select an area appropriate for planting your tree. Consult an adult about what to plant and where.

2. Dig a hole twice the size of the root-ball.

3. Put the tree into the hole and cover the roots with dirt.

4. **Mulch** the surrounding area with approximately 4 inches of compost.

5. Water the tree in order to settle the dirt around the roots.

6. Support the tree trunk, if necessary, with wooden stakes and nylon socks.

In Other Words

compost rich, healthy dirt
wooden stakes tall, thin pieces of wood for support
Mulch Fill, Cover

Look Into the Text

1. **Main Idea and Details** Planting trees helps to slow global warming. Provide two details to support this.

2. **Steps in a Process** Do you mulch the <mark>area</mark> before or after you water?

Connect Reading and Writing

Vocabulary
areas
atmosphere
feature
glaciers
melting
reefs
soil
temperature

CRITICAL THINKING

1. **SUM IT UP** Use your Evidence Chart to evaluate text evidence in "Melting Away" and summarize the selection to a partner.

   Claim: The once mighty Grinnell Glacier could soon vanish completely.

Text Evidence	My Evaluation
It is much smaller now than it was in 1938.	This fact can be checked and is supported by photos from a reliable source.

   Evidence Chart

2. **Explain** Revisit the KWL Chart you made on page 572. Write what you learned about global warming in the L column. How are Earth's **features** affected? Discuss your completed chart with classmates.

3. **Speculate** If the **glaciers** continue to melt, how might this affect the Earth's **atmosphere** in the future? What might happen to living things?

4. **Paraphrase** In your own words, explain to a partner how a change in **temperature** can affect a **reef**. Use the text to support your ideas.

READING FLUENCY

Phrasing Read the passage on page 660 to a partner. Assess your fluency.

1. I did not pause/sometimes paused/always paused for punctuation.

2. What I did best in my reading was _____.

READING STRATEGY

What strategy helped you understand this selection? Tell a partner about it.

VOCABULARY REVIEW

Oral Review Read the paragraph aloud. Add the vocabulary words.

People are worried that Earth's _____ is rising. Gases in the _____ aren't protecting us like they used to. Large _____ covered by ice sheets, or _____, are _____ and becoming smaller. Coral _____ are dying because of the heat. They are an important _____ of the ocean. If the ocean is heating up, that means the _____ is getting warmer, too.

Written Review Imagine you live in a future in which the **glaciers** have all **melted**. Write a letter to the people of the past. Tell them about your world and how they need to change their actions. Use five vocabulary words.

WRITE ABOUT THE GUIDING QUESTION

Explore Why Earth Is Changing

Why are **melting glaciers** and dying **reefs** warnings? Write your opinion. Reread the selection to find support for your opinion.

Connect Across the Curriculum

Vocabulary Study

Understand Technical Language

Academic Vocabulary
- **unique** (yu-nēk) *adjective*
  Something that is **unique** is unusual or one of a kind.

Every field of work or study uses words that are **unique** to that field. These kinds of words are called **technical language**. When you come across technical language, use context clues to help you figure out the meaning.

1. Look for clues to the meaning in the same paragraph.
2. Look for any photos or graphics that give more information.
3. If you need more information, check a print or online dictionary.

Figure Out Word Meanings Follow the steps above to figure out the meaning of each technical term below.

1. global warming, p. 581
2. degrees Fahrenheit, p. 581
3. coral polyps, p. 584
4. carbon dioxide, p. 585
5. methane gas, p. 585
6. compost, p. 588

Listening/Speaking

Give a Persuasive Speech

HEALTH & SCIENCE

Academic Vocabulary
- **logical** (lah-ji-kul) *adjective*
  Something that is **logical** seems believable or reasonable.

Look around your school for ways to help the environment. Write a speech to persuade the school to take action.

❶ **Choose a Topic and Gather Evidence** Choose a topic that people at your school can relate to. Find out everything about it. Make a list of reasons people should take action. Support those reasons with **logical** evidence.

❷ **Make Visual Aids** Use a computer for photographs, drawings, or diagrams that will help support your claims.

❸ **Deliver Your Speech** Speak loudly, slowly, and clearly enough so your audience can understand you. Make eye contact and use gestures.

❹ **Ask for Feedback** Ask your audience if your argument was strong and if you included enough **logical** evidence to support your claim.

Use Appropriate Language

Act It Out With a partner, role-play a conversation telling a young family member how to plant a tree. Use information from page 588 to guide your directions. Then role-play as if you were giving a formal presentation to the class on how to plant a tree. Use language appropriate to the situation. Be sure to use verb tenses correctly. Trade roles.

> Informal:
> Pick a good place for the tree. Think about how big it will grow.

> Formal:
> Always choose an appropriate place to plant a tree. Ask for advice, if needed.

Write About Actions

Study the Models When you write, make sure a reader can follow the action without getting confused. Remember that the wording will change depending on when the action happens.

NOT OK

> Julia wanted to help the community. So she has volunteered last week to plant a tree. Yesterday, she has received a box with a tiny tree and directions for planting it. First, she has read the directions carefully. Now she has prepared the ground by her house, and she started to plant the tree. The directions helped her a lot. The tree is growing nicely, and now Julia decided to plant another tree!

It's not clear when things happened. This writer goes back and forth between things happening now and things that happened in the past.

OK

> Julia wanted to help the community. So she volunteered last week to plant a tree. Yesterday, she received a box with a tiny tree and directions for planting it. First, she read the directions carefully. Now she has prepared the ground by her house, and she has started to plant the tree. The directions helped her a lot. The tree is growing nicely, and now Julia has decided to plant another tree!

This writer makes it clear when events already happened and what is happening now.

Add Sentences Think of two sentences to add to the OK model. Think about when the action happened.

✏ **WRITE ON YOUR OWN** Write about something you have done in the past to help the environment. Be sure to use verbs correctly so readers know when the action happens.

REMEMBER
- Use the past tense if you know when an action happened.
- Use the present perfect tense to tell about a past action that may still be going on.

The Legend of the Yakwawiak

by Joseph and James Bruchac

illustrated by Stefano Vitale

SELECTION 3 OVERVIEW

▶ **Build Background**

▶ **Language & Grammar**
Negotiate
Use Participles as Adjectives

▶ **Prepare to Read**
Learn Key Vocabulary
Analyze Theme

▶ **Read and Write**
Introduce the Genre
Legend
Focus on Reading
Analyze Argument
Apply the Focus Strategy
Synthesize
Critical Thinking
Reading Fluency
Read with Expression
Vocabulary Review
Write About the Guiding Question

▶ **Connect Across the Curriculum**
Vocabulary Study
Understand Figurative Language
Literary Analysis
Analyze Changes in the English Language
Language and Grammar
Negotiate
Writing and Grammar
Write About a Story

Build Background

Discover Myths and Legends

Like many cultures, Native Americans have used myths and legends to tell the history of the world and to teach valuable lessons.

Connect

Quickwrite Make a list of natural events you would like explained. For example, you may wonder: Why does it thunder? Why do leaves change colors? What causes earthquakes?

Digital Library myNGconnect.com
🔊 View the video.

▲ Many Native American myths are passed down by storytellers.

Negotiate CD

When we negotiate, we try to reach an agreement with each other. Listen to the story about why leaves change color. In the story, what do Snow and Tree negotiate?

STORY

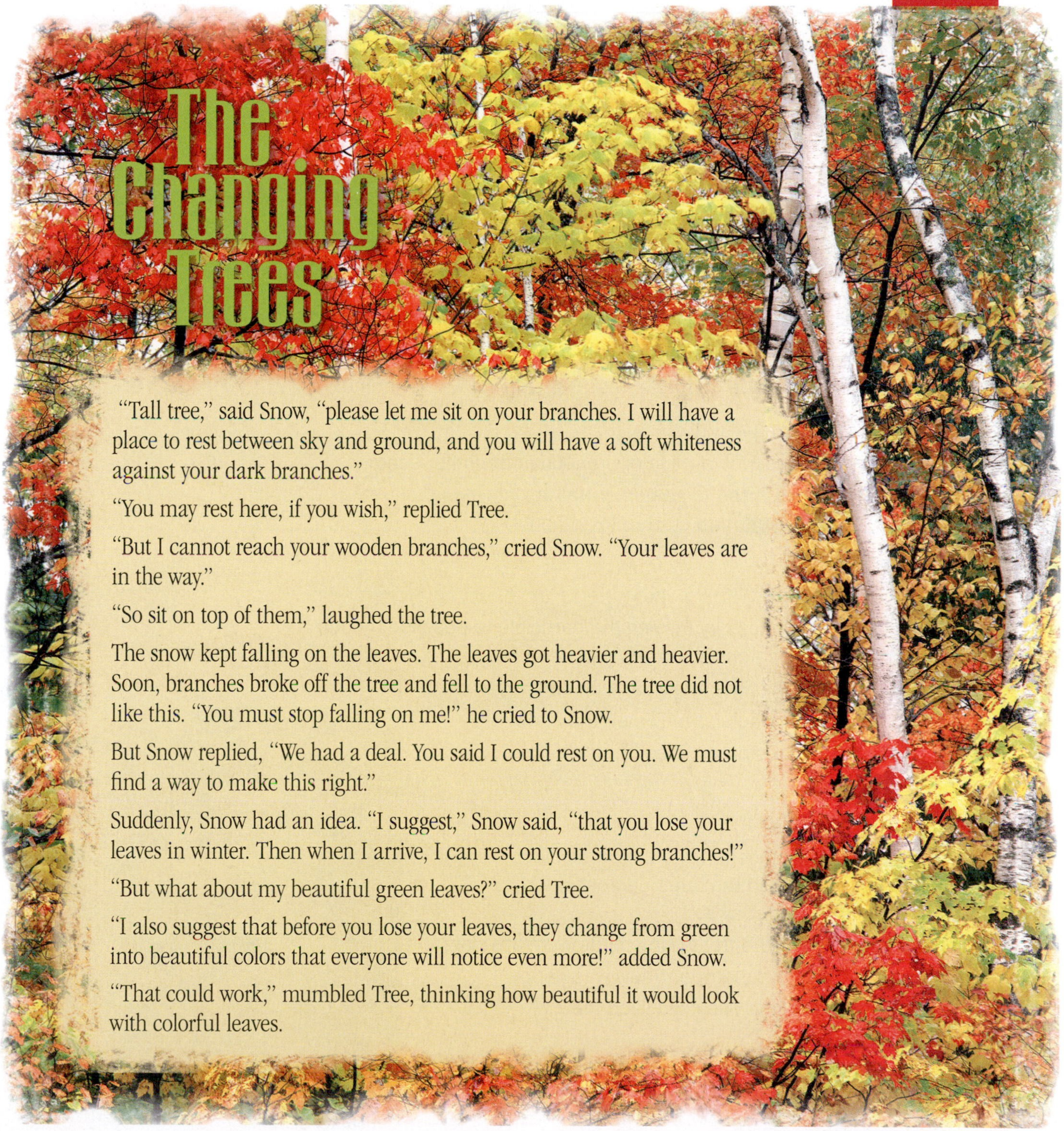

The Changing Trees

"Tall tree," said Snow, "please let me sit on your branches. I will have a place to rest between sky and ground, and you will have a soft whiteness against your dark branches."

"You may rest here, if you wish," replied Tree.

"But I cannot reach your wooden branches," cried Snow. "Your leaves are in the way."

"So sit on top of them," laughed the tree.

The snow kept falling on the leaves. The leaves got heavier and heavier. Soon, branches broke off the tree and fell to the ground. The tree did not like this. "You must stop falling on me!" he cried to Snow.

But Snow replied, "We had a deal. You said I could rest on you. We must find a way to make this right."

Suddenly, Snow had an idea. "I suggest," Snow said, "that you lose your leaves in winter. Then when I arrive, I can rest on your strong branches!"

"But what about my beautiful green leaves?" cried Tree.

"I also suggest that before you lose your leaves, they change from green into beautiful colors that everyone will notice even more!" added Snow.

"That could work," mumbled Tree, thinking how beautiful it would look with colorful leaves.

1 TRY OUT LANGUAGE
2 LEARN GRAMMAR
3 APPLY ON YOUR OWN

Use Participles as Adjectives

Verbs have four principal parts. For example:

Present	Present Participle	Past	Past Participle
fall	falling	fell	fallen
smile	smiling	smiled	smiled

You can use a **participle** in several different ways:

• A participle is often part of a verb phrase. A verb phrase contains a **helping verb** and a participle.

    Present Participle: Snow **was** **falling** from the sky.

    Past Participle: The snow **had** **fallen** on the leaves of the tree.

• A participle can act as an adjective to describe a **noun** or **pronoun**.

    EXAMPLES   The **fallen** **snow** covered the leaves.
                  The boy walked on the leaves. **Smiling**, **he** walked home.

• You can use a **participle** to combine two sentences. Move the participle from one sentence to describe a noun or pronoun in the other sentence.

    EXAMPLE   **The man** started to go home. **He** was **shivering**.
                  The **shivering** man started to go home.

Practice Together

Combine each pair of sentences by moving the <u>participle</u> to describe a noun or a pronoun in the other sentence. Say the new sentence.

    1. The snow was <u>falling</u>. The snow piled up on the ground.
    2. The sun is <u>shining</u>. The sun may melt the snow.
    3. Tree felt its branches break. Tree was <u>crying</u>.

Try It!

Combine each pair of sentences. Move the <u>participle</u> to describe a noun or pronoun in the other sentence. Write the new sentence on a card. Say it.

    4. Some birds flew to the tree. Some birds were <u>chirping</u>.
    5. Snow was <u>resting</u> on the tree. Snow was happy.
    6. The child was <u>smiling</u>. The child liked the grandfather's story.

▲ **Tree agreed to lose its leaves to make room for Snow.**

Let's Agree

NEGOTIATE

When people negotiate, they try to reach an agreement. Usually they have to compromise. This means each person gives up a little of what he or she wants to reach an agreement that seems fair.

Work with a partner. Role-play a parent and teen negotiating an issue, such as going to the movies or having friends visit. Be sure to listen to the other person's views and use polite, respectful language.

Some Polite, Respectful Language		
please	I understand	maybe we could
thank you	I'm sure	how about if we
I'm sorry	would you rather	why don't we

One important word in negotiations is *but*. When you use it, it means there is a certain condition to remember.

EXAMPLE   You can go to the movie, but you must be home for dinner.

Act out your negotiation for a small group of classmates. Talk about the compromise that was made. Then listen to another pair negotiate.

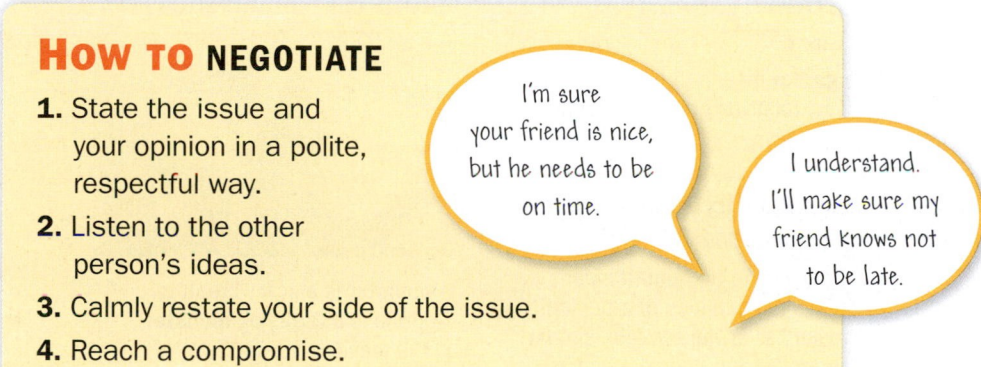

HOW TO NEGOTIATE

1. State the issue and your opinion in a polite, respectful way.
2. Listen to the other person's ideas.
3. Calmly restate your side of the issue.
4. Reach a compromise.

I'm sure your friend is nice, but he needs to be on time.

I understand. I'll make sure my friend knows not to be late.

USE PARTICIPLES AS ADJECTIVES

When you negotiate, you might need to use **participles** as adjectives to describe the people or things you are talking about.

EXAMPLES   Your **chatting** group of friends need to be quieter.
Your **tired** parents need to get some sleep.

Prepare to Read

Learn Key Vocabulary

Study the Words Use the steps below.

1. Pronounce the word. Say it aloud several times. Spell it.
2. Rate your word knowledge.
3. Study the example. Tell more about the word.
4. Practice it. Make the word your own.

Key Words

battle (**bat**-ul) *noun*
▶ page 604

A **battle** is a fight. During the American Civil War, the North was in a **battle** with the South.

council (**kown**-sul) *noun*
▶ page 603

A **council** is a group of people who gather together to make decisions. The student **council** decides where to go for the class trip.

creature (**krē**-chur) *noun*
▶ page 600

A **creature** is an animal. This interesting **creature** can be found in Australia.

destroy (di-**stroi**) *verb*
▶ page 603

When you **destroy** something, it cannot be repaired. Our puppy **destroyed** the newpapers.
Synonyms: **ruin, wreck**
Antonym: **fix**

gather (**gath**-ur) *verb*
▶ page 603

To **gather** means to bring together. All my relatives **gather** at our house on holidays.

human (**hyū**-man) *adjective, noun* ▶ page 600

1 *adjective* To be **human** means to have the qualities of a person. The gorillas at the zoo look almost **human**. **2** *noun* People are also called **humans**.

monster (**mahn**-stur) *noun*
▶ page 600

A **monster** is a scary creature. Godzilla is a terrifying **monster** in the movies.
Related Word: **monstrous**

powerful (**pau**-ur-ful)
adjective ▶ page 604

People are **powerful** when they are strong. This man shows off his **powerful** strength in a competition.
Related Words: **power, powerless**

Practice the Words Make an Idea Web for each Key Word. Write four things the word makes you think of. Share your finished webs with a partner.

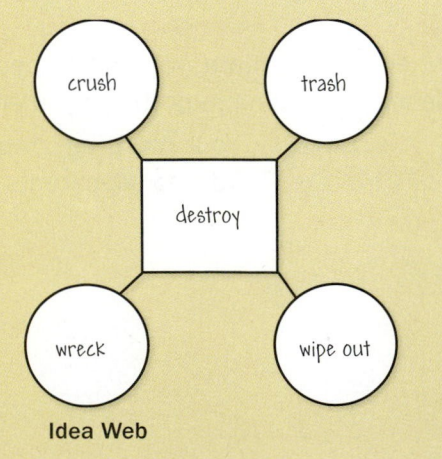

crush

trash

destroy

wreck

wipe out

Idea Web

Analyze Theme

How Do Authors Develop a Theme? You have learned that a theme is the unifying message or lesson of a story. A theme may or may not be directly stated. The author introduces the idea and then continues to develop it using elements of plot, setting, and character. Once you determine the author's theme, reread sections of the text to see not only how the story elements work together to reveal the message, but also how the theme influences these elements.

As you read, look for evidence of a central message or theme.

Reading Strategies

· Plan
· Monitor
· Visualize
· Determine Importance
· Ask Questions
· Make Connections
· Make Inferences

Synthesize Bring together ideas gained from texts and blend them into a new understanding.

Look Into the Text

The skin and the hair of the Yakwawiak were so thick that no arrow could pierce them. The two great tusks of these monsters were as sharp as spears, and their long noses were like great snakes. Yakwawiak hurled down the trees and muddied the springs. They trampled everything underfoot as they went about the land. They crushed the humans and the animals under their feet, and the people had to hide in caves to escape them. Those great monsters did not remember the words of Kitselemukong, who said that all beings on earth should live together. The Yakwawiak had no respect for any other living thing.

> " I think this statement suggests a central message of the story. "

Practice Together

Begin a Theme Chart A Theme Chart can help you analyze how details from the story are used to develop a story's theme. Reread the passage above, and add to the Theme Chart.

Theme: All beings on earth should live together in harmony.

What Happens	How This Develops the Theme
The Yakwawiak hurl down trees, muddy springs, and trample everything; people and animals hide in caves to escape.	Shows how the Yakwawiak's destructive behavior hurts others

Theme Chart

Legend

A legend is a fictional story passed down over time that is told as if it is a true part of history. It may include some element of truth or historic fact, but the events are made to seem bigger and better than they really were.

Legends are often meant to teach a lesson about life or the world. The lesson the hero or heroine learns usually reflects the **cultural beliefs** of the people who created it.

As you read, examine important details from the legend. Use these details, and what you already know or have experienced, to make generalizations about the theme of the legend.

Look Into the Text

Those great monsters did not remember the words of Kitselemukong, who said all beings on earth should live together. . . .

cultural beliefs

At last, one man could take it no longer. This man, whose name was Two Hawks Flying, left the caves . . .

The Legend of the Yakwawiak

by Joseph and James Bruchac

illustrated by Stefano Vitale

Comprehension Coach

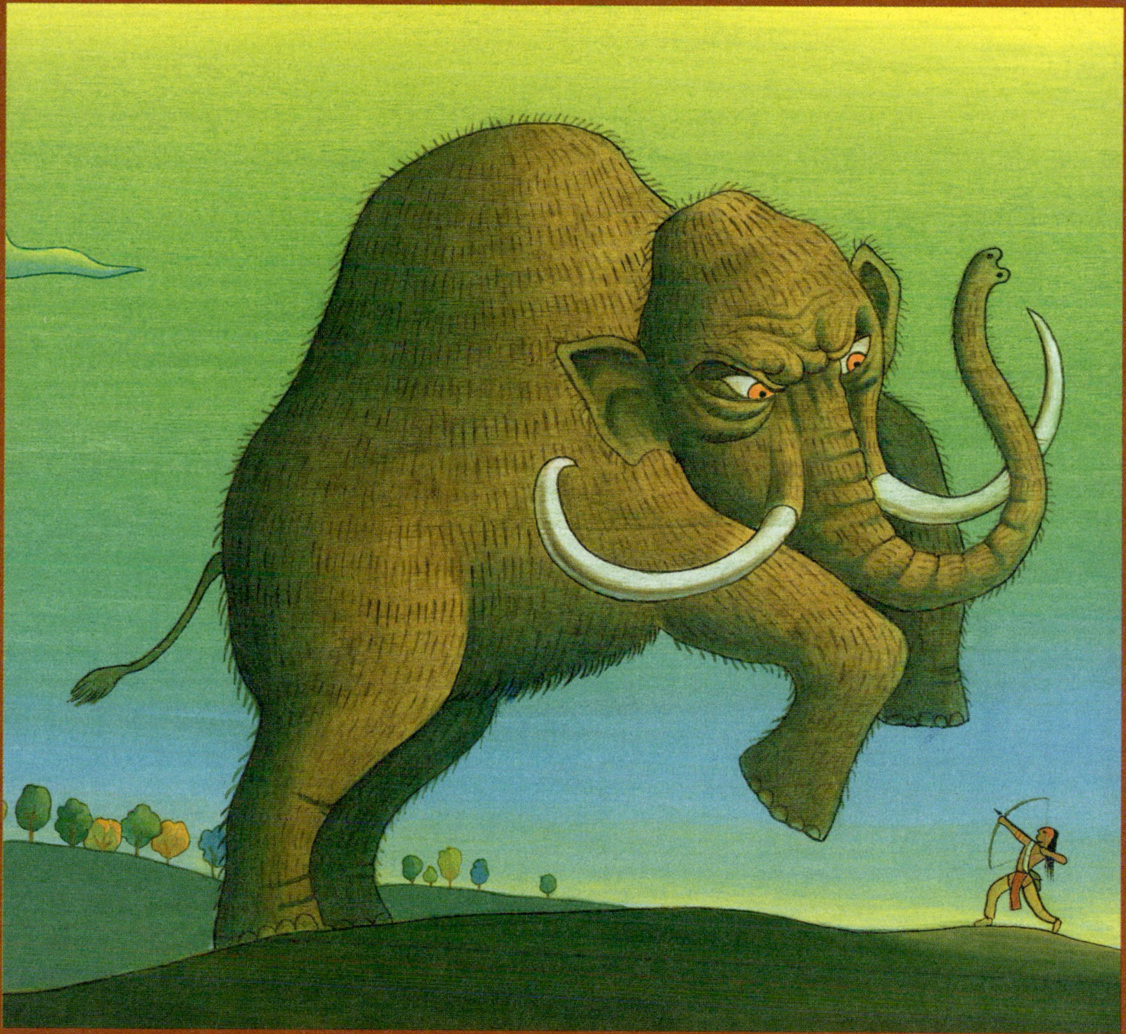

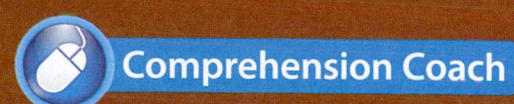

Of all the **creatures** that walked the earth on four legs, the Yakwawiak were the largest. The earth shook under their feet, and the other animals ran from them, for these **monsters** were **bad-tempered** and unfriendly. The **human** beings had been given permission by Kitselemukong, the Great Mystery, to hunt the animals for food. But they too were afraid of the Yakwawiak.

The skin and the hair of the Yakwawiak were so thick that no arrow could **pierce** them. The two great tusks of these monsters were as sharp as spears, and their long noses were like great snakes. The Yakwawiak **hurled** down the trees and muddied the springs.

But they too were afraid of the Yakwawiak.

They **trampled** everything underfoot as they went about the land. They crushed the humans and the animals under their feet, and the people had to hide in caves to escape them. Those great monsters did not remember the words of Kitselemukong, who said that all beings on earth should live together. The Yakwawiak had no respect for any other living thing.

At last, one man **could take it no longer**. This man, whose name was Two Hawks Flying, left the caves where all the people were hiding from the great monsters. He climbed to the top of the highest mountain. He made a fire and prayed to the Creator. He placed tobacco on the **glowing** coals.

Key Vocabulary
creature *n.*, an animal
monster *n.*, an animal that scares people because of how it looks or acts
human *adj.*, having the traits or characteristics of people

In Other Words
bad-tempered mean
pierce cut through
hurled threw
trampled stepped on
could take it no longer decided to do something about the problem
glowing hot

Look Into the Text
1. **Explain** In your own words, describe the Yakwawiak. Why are they considered **monsters**?
2. **Character's Motive** Why does Two Hawks Flying ask Kitselemukong for help?

As the smoke rose up into the sky, he spoke his words to Kitselemukong.

"Great Mystery," Two Hawks Flying said, "you are the one who made all things. You are the one who said that we should all live together and respect each other. But the Yakwawiak have forgotten your words. They wish to kill all of the other beings in the world. Help us, Creator, or we will all be **destroyed**."

Kitselemukong **saw that** this could not continue and decided to **take pity on** the people.

A great light appeared in front of Two Hawks Flying.

"Hear me," said a voice from within that light, which was Kitselemukong. "I will help you. Call all of the people and the animals together. Have them **gather** here at dawn."

"I will do as you say," said Two Hawks Flying.

Then he went to speak to the people and all of the other animals.

"Kitselemukong has told me that all of us must come together in **council**," Two Hawks Flying said. Everyone who heard him, both the humans and the animals, knew that his words were true, and they began to gather.

The wolf and the bear, the moose and the mountain lion, the lynx and the wolverine, the elk and deer and all of the other animals, including many whose names are now forgotten, came together. The human beings came from their hiding places in the caves and joined them. They all gathered on the mountaintop where Two Hawks Flying had prayed.

"You must **drive the Yakwawiak from the land**," the voice of Kitselemukong said from within that great glowing light. "They have forgotten to respect other beings. Now you must all join together and **make war on** them."

So the people and all of the animals began to make war on the Yakwawiak. Side by side, they marched together toward the Yakwawiak, but the Yakwawiak were waiting. The earth shook under their feet as they **charged**, and the fight began.

Key Vocabulary

destroy *v.*, to ruin or make useless

gather *v.*, to come together in a group

council *n.*, a meeting to discuss actions

In Other Words

saw that knew, realized

take pity on help

drive the Yakwawiak from the land make the Yakwawiak leave the places you live

make war on fight

charged ran toward each other

Look Into the Text

1. **Confirm Prediction** Did the Creator come up with a solution you predicted? Explain what people and animals must do.

2. **Inference** Who are the animals whose "names are now forgotten"?

Kitselemukong watched from the top of the highest mountain as they fought. It was a hard **battle**, for the Yakwawiak were strong. The Yakwawiak tried to **crush** the animals and people beneath their huge feet. They stabbed them with their sharp tusks and threw them up into the air with their trunks. The piercing sound of their screams as they fought was terrible to hear. Even when they were wounded and bleeding, the huge monsters continued to fight.

All through that long day, the fight went back and forth. It went from the edge of the great salt water to the wide river that flows through the **heart** of the land. Many of the bravest animals, those who were almost as large and **powerful** as the Yakwawiak, were killed. The giant bear and the great wolf fell,

> . . . the huge monsters continued to fight.

and the huge beaver fell in battle. Only their bones buried in the earth show that they ever lived. Many of the people and the other animals were also killed in the fight, but they still fought bravely. One of the bravest was Two Hawks Flying.

The air was filled with the terrible screams of the Yakwawiak as they fought. Mountains were pushed over and valleys **gouged out** by the monsters as they fought. The earth sank down and became **marshy** as it was trampled under the feet of the huge creatures. Blood soaked into the ground.

But Two Hawks Flying saw that the Yakwawiak were too powerful. The human beings and the animals could not defeat them alone.

"Great One," he shouted, "you must help us now."

Key Vocabulary
battle *n.*, a fight between people or armies
powerful *adj.*, strong

In Other Words
crush flatten, kill
heart middle, center
gouged out dug into the ground; made
marshy wet and muddy

So Kitselemukong began to hurl down lightning from the top of the highest mountain. Each time a bolt of lightning struck, one of the Yakwawiak was killed. Finally, only the largest of the terrible monsters remained. He was so large that the other monsters seemed small in comparison. It seemed that nothing could defeat him. Each time a lightning bolt was hurled at him, he knocked it away with his tusks. But this one **Yakwawi** had been wounded many times, and he was growing weaker. At last he turned and began to run. He ran toward the cold north land, where no trees grow and there is always ice and snow. Some tried to follow him, but Two Hawks Flying called them back.

"No," he said. "That one is the last of his kind. He will no longer bother us."

Some say that the Yakwawi is still hiding there to this day. You may hear his awful cry in the howl of the north wind. Sometimes, it is said, a lone hunter **may chance upon** the Yakwawi in that far northern land. If that hunter has not been a good man, if he has killed animals needlessly and not shared with others, such a hunter never returns to his people.

When we dig into the earth in the places where the battle raged long ago, we find the bones and the giant tusks of the Yakwawiak. Nothing else remains of them in the lands of the Lenape, the human beings.

But Kitselemukong left one other sign on the earth of that great battle. In the marshlands created by that long ago fight, there where the blood soaked into the earth, Kitselemukong made a new berry grow. Its skin is as red as the blood that was shed. It is the cranberry. When the people see it, they remember **the fate of** the Yakwawiak, those great creatures who had no respect for the rest of the creation. ❖

In Other Words
Yakwawi single Yakwawiak
may chance upon might meet
the fate of what happened to

Look Into the Text
1. **Explain** Why is the battle against the Yawawiak so difficult to win?
2. **Confirm Prediction** How are the Yakwawiak destroyed? Was your prediction correct?
3. **Theme** How does the story of the Yawawiak relate to the theme "Global Warnings"?

The Mighty Mastodon

It's true: Yakwawiak really did roam North America more than 10,000 years ago. We know them today as the American mastodon. These huge animals were actually relatives of the modern elephant. Adult mastodon stood approximately ten feet tall. They weighed as much as eight tons. Their tusks were more than eight feet long!

The story of the Yakwawiak warns us of what can happen to those who are disrespectful to the creatures of the Earth. The legend of the Yakwawiak is the Lenape Indians' explanation for how the mastodon disappeared. Many Native American legends were told to explain the history of Earth and to glorify the extraordinary actions of the people who came before them.

◄ Before disappearing, the mastodon roamed the U.S.

Bones have been found in the Midwest, including some in Chicago, Illinois.

About the Author

Joseph and James Bruchac

Joseph Bruchac (1942–) is a world-famous writer and Abenaki Indian storyteller. Bruchac travels the country to discuss Native American culture and tell stories. His son, **James Bruchac**, is a writer and storyteller, as well as a wilderness survival expert. Together, father and son have written several books of Native American tales for young adults.

Cultural Background

Native Americans believed in showing respect to the animals they hunted by only killing what they needed for food or clothing. They asked for permission before killing an animal and for forgiveness once it had been killed.

POSSUM CROSSING
by Nikki Giovanni

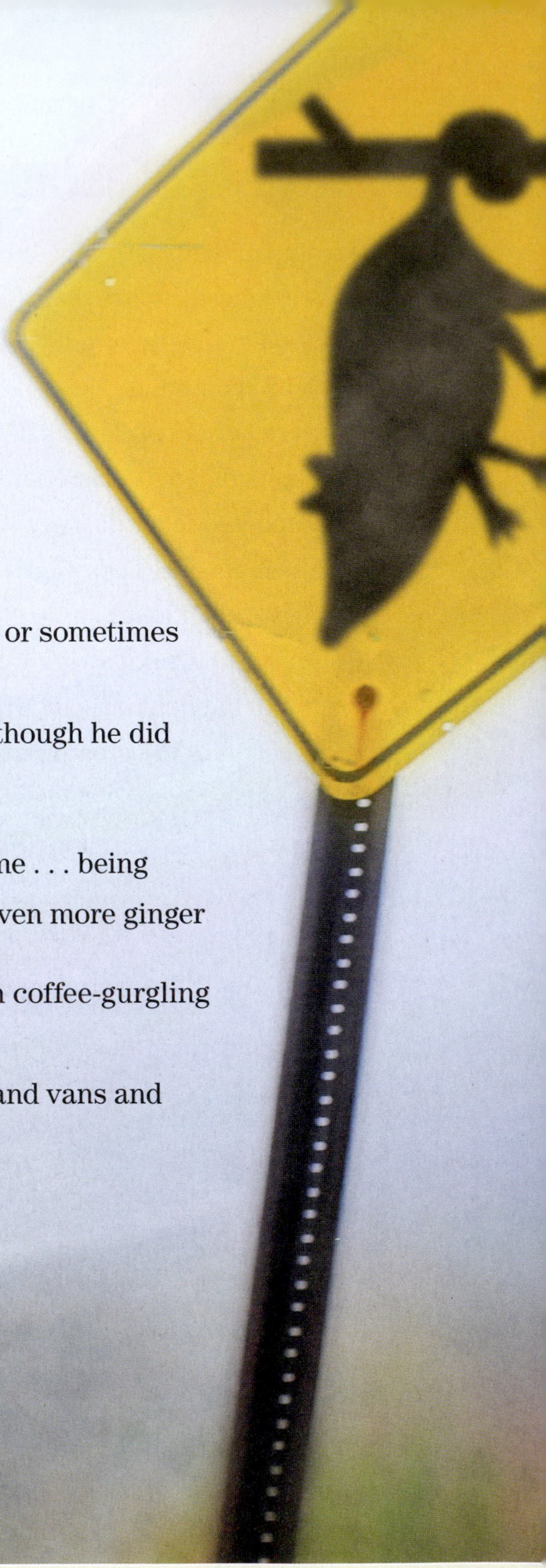

Backing out the driveway
the car lights cast an eerie glow
in the morning fog centering
on movement in the rain slick street

5   Hitting brakes I anticipate a squirrel or a cat or sometimes
a little raccoon
I once braked for a blind little mole who try though he did
could not escape the cat toying with his life

Mother-to-be possum occasionally lopes home . . . being
10   naturally . . . slow her condition makes her even more ginger

We need a sign POSSUM CROSSING to warn coffee-gurgling
neighbors:
we share the streets with more than trucks and vans and
railroad crossings

15   All birds being the living kin of dinosaurs
think themselves invincible and pay no heed
to the rolling wheels while they dine
on an unlucky rabbit

In Other Words
eerie strange
ginger helpless
kin relatives
pay no heed to ignore

I hit brakes for the flutter of the lights hoping it's not a deer

20 or a skunk or a groundhog

coffee splashes over the cup which I quickly put away from me

and into the empty passenger seat

I look . . .

relieved and exasperated . . .

25 to discover I have just missed a big wet leaf

struggling . . . to lift itself into the wind

and live

About the Author

Nikki Giovanni

Nikki Giovanni (1943–) is a writer, an educator, and an activist. She supports topics or social issues that she feels strongly about. Giovanni encourages young writers to trust themselves. She says, "If you know what you're talking about, or if you feel that you do, the reader will believe you."

In Other Words
flutter of the lights thing that moved in front of the car

Look Into the Text

1. **Author's Viewpoint** Why does the speaker want a sign on her street? What does this say about her?

2. **Figurative Language** What does the speaker mean when she says that the leaf was "struggling . . . to lift itself into the wind and live"? (lines 25–27)

Henri Rousseau
1891

The Tyger

by William Blake

Tyger Tyger, burning bright
In the forests of the night,
What immortal hand or eye
Could frame thy fearful symmetry?

5   In what distant deeps or skies,
Burnt the fire of thine eyes?
On what wings dare he aspire?
What the hand dare seize the fire?

And what shoulder, and what art
10   Could twist the sinews of thy heart?
And when thy heart began to beat,
What dread hand and what dread feet?

In Other Words
immortal inhuman, divine
sinews muscles

What the hammer? What the chain?

In what furnace was thy brain?

15   What the anvil? What dread grasp

Dare its deadly terrors clasp?

When the stars threw down their spears,

And water'd heaven with their tears,

Did He smile His work to see?

20   Did He who made the lamb make thee?

Tyger Tyger, burning bright

In the forests of the night,

What immortal hand or eye

Dare frame thy fearful symmetry?

Nature Background

Wild tigers are admired for their beauty and strength. However, they are disappearing from Earth due to illegal hunting and the loss of their natural habitats. It is believed that today only 5,000 to 7,000 tigers remain in the wild.

Look Into the Text

1. **Point of View**
   Who is the speaker in the poem?
2. **Vocabulary** How does the speaker feel about the tiger? What descriptive words show this?

Connect Reading and Writing

Vocabulary
battle

council

creatures

destroyed

gathered

monster

powerful

CRITICAL THINKING

1. SUM IT UP Use the details in your Theme Chart to summarize the key events of the legend.

Theme: All beings on earth should live together in harmony.	
What Happens	**How This Develops the Theme**
The Yakwawiak hurl down trees, muddy springs, and trample everything; people and animals hide in caves to escape.	Shows how the Yakwawiak's destructive behavior hurts others

Theme Chart

2. Discuss Share your Quickwrite with a partner. What do you think the Lenape were curious about when they told the legend of these **monsters**?

3. Describe A legend is a story about the past. What clues tell you that the **battle** with the Yakwawiak took place long ago?

4. Make Judgments Do you think the decision to not **destroy** the last Yakwawiak was a good one? Explain your thinking.

READING FLUENCY

Expression Read the passage on page 661 to a partner. Assess your fluency.

1. My voice never/sometimes/always matched what I read.

2. What I did best in my reading was _____.

READING STRATEGY

What strategy helped you understand this selection? Tell a partner about it.

VOCABULARY REVIEW

Oral Review Read the paragraph aloud. Add the vocabulary words.

My friends and I saw a movie about a frightening _____. The beast was so big and _____ that it picked up smaller _____ with one hand! The city _____ held a meeting to decide what to do. But when they _____ together in city hall, the monster showed up, too! That's when the hero arrived. After a _____, the hero _____ the monster.

Written Review Imagine you discover a giant **creature**. Write a speech to persuade the city **council** that it is not a **monster**, but a new species that should be protected. Use five vocabulary words.

WRITE ABOUT THE GUIDING QUESTION

Explore How We Can Help Earth
How could changing their ways have saved the Yakwawiak from being **destroyed**? Write your opinion. Reread the selection to find examples to support your opinion.

Connect Across the Curriculum

Understand Figurative Language

Academic Vocabulary
- **symbol** (**sim**-bul) *noun*
  A **symbol** is an object that represents something else.

Writers sometimes use **figurative language** to create powerful images. Figurative words and phrases are **symbols** for ideas. In the sentence below, *bones buried in the earth* is a symbol for death.

> Only their <u>bones buried in the earth</u> show that they ever lived.

You can use context clues to figure out the meaning of figurative language. The context clues that help you figure out the death **symbol** are: *bones buried* and *lived* (in the past tense so they are no longer living).

Find Other Examples Review "Possum Crossing" and "The Tyger" with a partner to find more examples of figurative language. Make a list of the examples you find, the meaning of the figurative language, and the context clues that help you determine the meaning.

Analyze Changes in the English Language

Academic Vocabulary
- **definition** (de-fu-**ni**-shun) *noun*
  The meaning of a word is its **definition**.

Learn About Language The English language grows and changes over time. Some words that were common 200 years ago are no longer used today. You use many words today that weren't even invented 200 years ago! Words that had one **definition** 50 years ago have a different **definition** today. This constant changing keeps the English language alive.

Analyze Language The poem "Possum Crossing" was published in 2002. "The Tyger" was published in 1794. Some words in "Possum Crossing" didn't exist or had different **definitions** in 1794. Some words in "The Tyger" are no longer used or spelled differently in 2002.

Re-read each poem. Write down words that you think are either newer words or words that aren't used anymore. Look up each word in a dictionary to find its **definition** and date of origin, or beginning. Discuss what you learn with your class.

Negotiate

Role-Play With a partner, act out a negotiation between two friends who are planning an afternoon together. One wants to go to a movie; the other wants to go skateboarding. Use some participles as adjectives as you negotiate to reach an agreement. Trade roles.

> I have already seen that movie.

> Yes, but this is the sequel. It's not the same. We can skateboard over to the theater if you want.

Write About a Story

Study the Models When you write, you want to make your readers excited about what they are reading. If you add details and combine ideas to vary your sentences, your writing will hold your reader's interest.

JUST OK

> Mother Earth looked around at her land. It was burning. The fire had burned for days. Mother Earth was tired. She breathed a dusty sigh. She listened. Suddenly she heard something. She felt rain. It hit her face. She laughed in the rain. The rain was pouring. She swallowed the rain. She turned it into a lake. The animals returned. They drank from the lake. They thanked Mother Earth. They sang a song of praise.

This writing is very choppy. There aren't that many details, and it's not very interesting.

BETTER

> Mother Earth looked around at her burning land. The fire had burned for days. Mother Earth was tired. Breathing a dusty sigh, she listened. Suddenly she heard something. She felt rain hitting her face and watched as the rain put the fires out. She laughed in the pouring rain. Swallowing the rain, she turned it into a lake. The returning animals drank from the lake. Singing a song of praise, they thanked Mother Earth.

This writer adds details to explain what happened. The writer combines ideas to make the sentences smoother and more interesting.

Add Sentences Think of two sentences to add to the BETTER model above. Use details that will hold your reader's interest.

WRITE ON YOUR OWN Write about another tale or legend you have read or heard. Use details to elaborate on ideas, and combine ideas to vary your sentences.

REMEMBER

You can combine sentences by moving a participle that describes a noun or pronoun:

The animals began <u>dancing</u>.

The animals cheered.

= The <u>dancing</u> animals cheered.

from GRAND CANYON SPEECH by Theodore Roosevelt

Arizona, May 6, 1903

1   In the Grand Canyon, Arizona has a natural wonder which, so far as I know, is **in kind absolutely unparalleled** throughout the rest of the world. I want to ask you to do one thing in connection with it in your own interest and in the interest of the country—to keep this great wonder of nature as it now is.

2   I was delighted to learn of the wisdom of the Santa Fe railroad people in deciding not to build their hotel on the brink of the canyon. I hope you will not have a building of any kind, not a summer cottage, a hotel, or anything else, to **mar the wonderful grandeur, the sublimity,** the great loneliness and beauty of the canyon. Leave it as it is. You cannot improve on it. The ages have been at work on it, and man can only mar it.

3   What you can do is to keep it for your children, your children's children, and for all who come after you, as one of the great sights which every American if he can travel at all should see. We have gotten past the stage, my fellow citizens, when we are to be **pardoned** if we treat any part of our country as something to be skinned for two or three years for the use of the present generation, whether it is the forest, the water, the scenery.

4   Whatever it is, handle it so that your children's children will get the benefit of it. If you deal with irrigation, apply it under circumstances that will make it of benefit, not to the speculator who hopes to get profit out of it for two or three years, but handle it so that it will be of use to the home-maker, to the man who comes to live here, and to have his children stay after him. Keep the forests in the same way.

5   Preserve the forests by use; preserve them for the ranchman and the stockman, for the people of the Territory, for the people of the region **round about.** Preserve them for that use, but use them so that they will not be squandered, that they will not be wasted, so that they will be of benefit to the Arizona of 1953 as well as the Arizona of 1903.

Historical Background
Before they became states, many regions of the Western U.S. were Territories. Land was given away or sold for very little.

In Other Words
in kind absolutely unparalleled unique
mar the wonderful grandeur, the sublimity mess up the wonderful, awesomeness
pardoned forgiven
round about around there

"...keep this great wonder of NATURE as it is now..."

Compare Across Texts

Compare Themes and Symbols

"The Legend of the Yakwawiak," "Possum Crossing," and "Grand Canyon Speech" are different genres of writing, but they all share a common message: respect the natural world. Compare the themes and **symbols** each selection uses to help illustrate their themes.

How It Works

Organize Themes and Symbols To compare themes and **symbols** in both texts, organize them in a chart.

Selection	Theme	Symbol
"Possum Crossing"	Respect all living things.	The possum sign stands for those creatures who are vulnerable to man.
"The Legend of the Yakwawiak"	Respect all living things.	
"Grand Canyon Speech"		

Comparison Chart

Practice Together

Compare Themes and Symbols Use the chart to compare the selections. Here is the beginning of a summary comparing the themes and **symbols**.

> "Possum Crossing" and "The Legend of the Yakwawiak" use symbols to show the importance of respecting all living things. In "Possum Crossing," the possum sign is a symbol of creatures who can be hurt by man. The speaker uses this symbol to show . . .

Try It!

Finish the chart by adding information from Roosevelt's speech. Use this frame to help you.

"The Legend of the Yakwawiak," "Possum Crossing," and "Grand Canyon Speech" all use symbols to better illustrate their theme. In the legend, the _____ reminds others that _____, while in the poem, _____ stands for _____. Roosevelt's speech also uses _____ to _____.

Academic Vocabulary
- **symbol** (sim-bul) *noun*
  A **symbol** is an object that represents something else.

GLOBAL WARNINGS

GUIDING QUESTION How can changing our ways benefit the Earth?

Content Library

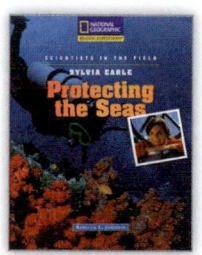

Leveled Library

 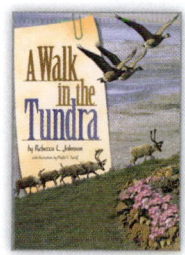 

Reflect on Your Reading

Think back on your reading of the unit selections. Discuss what you did to understand what you read.

Focus on Reading | **Analyze Argument**

In this unit, you learned how writers use techniques to persuade readers. Choose a selection from the unit and create a graphic that shows the persuasive techniques the writer used. It could be a Goal-and-Outcome Chart, a Cause-and-Effect Chart, or any graphic that shows how the writer used the persuasive technique. Explain your graphic organizer to a partner.

Focus Strategy | **Synthesize**

As you read the selections, you learned to synthesize. Explain to a partner how you will use this strategy in the future.

Explore the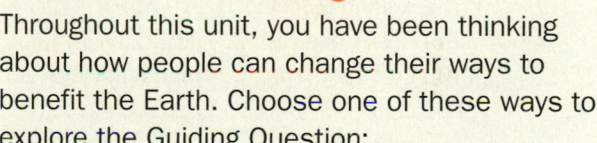

Throughout this unit, you have been thinking about how people can change their ways to benefit the Earth. Choose one of these ways to explore the Guiding Question:

- **Discuss** With a group, discuss a show you've seen on TV that talked about the need to change our ways to benefit the Earth.
- **Create** Create an advertisement to convince people to make a change to benefit the Earth. Share your ad with a group.
- **Write** Write a letter to a newspaper editor that persuades readers to make choices that protect the environment. Include relevant information.

Book Talk

Which Unit Library book did you choose? Explain to a partner what it taught you about protecting the environment.

Resources

Reading Handbook

Reading Strategies

What Are Reading Strategies?

Reading strategies are hints or techniques you can use to help you become a better reader. They help you interact with the text and take control of your own reading comprehension. Reading strategies can be used before, during, and after you read.

Plan and Monitor

Before you read, plan how to approach the selection by using prereading strategies. **Preview** the selection to see what it is about and try to make a prediction about its content. Keep in mind that English is read from left to right, and that text moves from the top of the page to the bottom. **Set a purpose** for reading, or decide why you will read the selection. You might want or need to adjust your purpose for reading as you read. Monitor your reading to check how well you understand and remember what you read.

How to Select and Use Prereading Strategies	
Title:	Surfing the Pipeline
Author:	Christina Rodriguez
Preview the Text	• Look at the title: Surfing the Pipeline. • Look at the organization of the text, including any chapter titles, heads, and subheads. • Look at any photos and captions. • Think about what the selection is about.
Activate Prior Knowledge	• I know many people surf in the ocean on surfboards. • I've seen a film about people trying to surf on huge waves in California.
Ask Questions	• What is the pipeline? • Where is the pipeline? • Who surfs the pipeline? • Why do people try to surf the pipeline?
Set a Purpose for Reading	• I want to read to find out how people surf the pipeline.

How to Make and Confirm Predictions

Making **predictions** about a selection will help you understand and remember what you read. As you preview a selection, **ask questions** and think about any **prior knowledge** you have about the subject. If you do not learn enough additional information from these steps, read the first few paragraphs of the selection.

Think about the events taking place, and then predict what will happen next. If you are reading fiction or drama, you can use what you know about common plot patterns to help you predict what may happen in the story. After you read each section, confirm your predictions, or see if they were correct. Sometimes you will need to revise your predictions for the next section based on what you read.

Preview to Anticipate Read the title. Think about what the selection will be about as you read the first few paragraphs. Look for clues about the selection's content.

Make and Confirm Predictions As you read, predict what will happen next in the selection based on text evidence or personal experience. Take notes while you are reading, and use a **Prediction Chart** to record your ideas. As you continue to read the selection, confirm your predictions. If a prediction is incorrect, revise it.

Surfing the Pipeline

There Uli was, standing on the white, sandy shores of Oahu, Hawaii. Right in front of her was the famous Banzai Pipeline—one of the most difficult and dangerous places to surf in the world. Uli looked out and saw twelve-foot waves crashing toward her.

Uli had been waiting for this day for a long time. She was ready.

Uli grabbed her surfboard and entered the water. The waves were fierce and strong that morning. It took all of Uli's energy to swim out to the surfing location. Uli could see rocks sticking up through the water. She finally found the perfect starting point and waited anxiously to begin surfing.

Prediction Chart

Prediction	Did It Happen?	Evidence
Uli is going to surf at the Banzai Pipeline.	Not yet, but she will soon.	She is at the starting point to begin surfing. (text evidence)
Surfing the Banzai Pipeline will be hard for Uli.	Not yet, but it will soon.	New activities are always hard when I try them for the first time. (personal experience)

How to Monitor Your Reading

When you **monitor your reading**, you are checking to make sure you understand the information you read. You can check your understanding by keeping track of your thinking while reading. Pause while reading to think about images you may be creating in your mind, connections you are making between words or topics within the text, or problems you are having with understanding the text. When you read something that doesn't make sense to you, use these monitoring strategies to help you.

Strategy	How to Use It	Example Text
Reread to Clarify Ideas	Reread silently the passage you do not understand. Then reread the passage aloud. Continue rereading until you feel more confident about your understanding of the passage.	I will silently reread the first paragraph. Then I will read it aloud. The paragraph is more understandable now.
Use Resources to Clarify Vocabulary	Look up confusing words in a dictionary or thesaurus, or ask a classmate for help.	"... dangerous places to surf ..." I'm not sure what "surf" means. I'll look it up.
Read On and Use Context Clues to Clarify Ideas and Vocabulary	Read past the part of the text where you are confused. What does the rest of the information tell you? Are there nearby words or phrases, context clues or visuals that help you understand?	"... looked out and saw twelve-foot waves ..." Maybe "surf" means riding ocean waves.
Adjust Your Reading Rate	Read slowly when something is confusing or difficult. Keep in mind that English is read from left to right and that text runs down the page from the top. If you are having a difficult time understanding what you're reading, first make sure that you're reading it in the right order.	"Right in front of her was the famous Banzai Pipeline ..." I've never heard of the Banzai Pipeline. I'll read slower to find out what it is.
Adjust Your Purpose for Reading	Think of the purpose you set for reading before you started to read. Have you found a new purpose, or reason to read? If so, adjust your purpose and read on.	I originally wanted to read to find out how people surf the pipeline. Now I want to read to see if Uli actually does it.

How to Use Graphic Organizers

Before you read, you can use graphic organizers to prepare for better comprehension. For example, use a **KWL Chart** to record your prior knowledge about the topic.

KWL Chart

WHAT I <u>K</u>NOW	WHAT I <u>W</u>ANT TO KNOW	WHAT I <u>L</u>EARNED

As you read, use a variety of graphic organizers such as diagrams and charts to help keep track of your thinking. Take notes about any ideas or vocabulary that confuse you. Writing down ideas keeps you actively involved in your reading. It also can help clear up any confusion you may have about information in a selection.

Use graphic organizers to capture your thoughts and to help you remember information based on how it was described in the text or based on the text structure. Here are some more examples of graphic organizers:

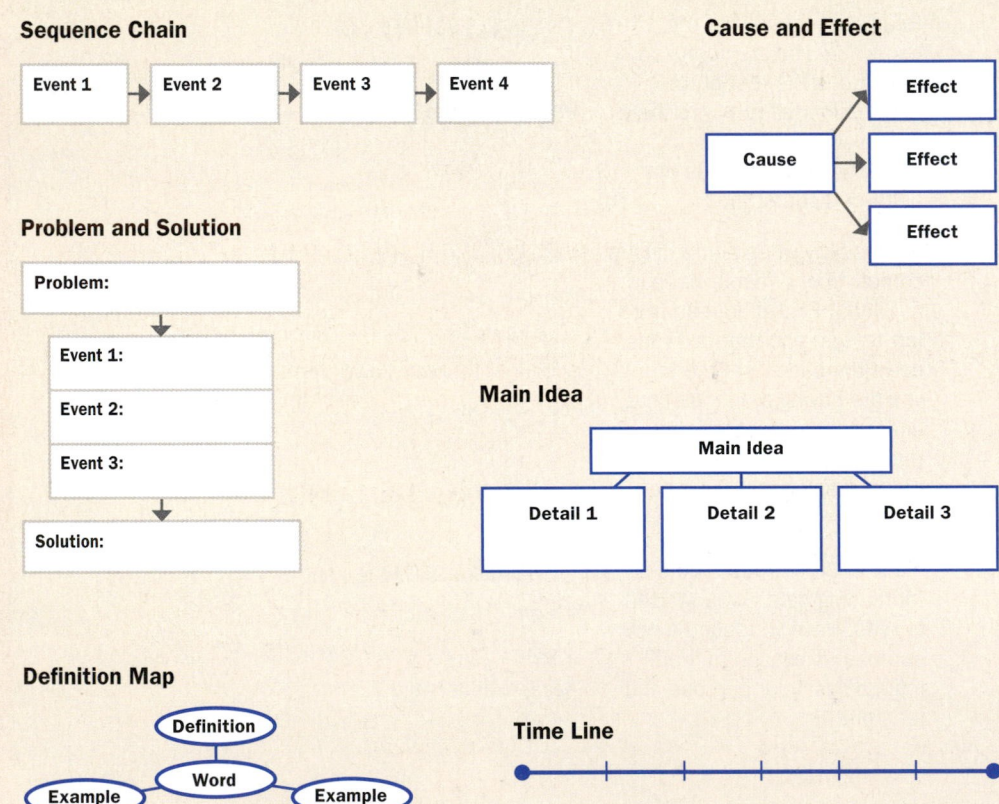

Sequence Chain

Event 1 → Event 2 → Event 3 → Event 4

Cause and Effect

Cause → Effect / Effect / Effect

Problem and Solution

Problem:
↓
Event 1:
Event 2:
Event 3:
↓
Solution:

Main Idea

Main Idea — Detail 1, Detail 2, Detail 3

Definition Map

Definition — Word — Example — Example

Time Line

Determine Importance

Determining importance is a reading strategy you can use to find the most important details or ideas in a selection. A good way to think about what is important in the selections you read is to **summarize**. When you summarize, you state the main idea and only the most important details in a selection, usually in a sentence or two. To summarize, identify the topic of a paragraph or selection, find the main idea and the most important details, and put them in your own words.

Stated Main Ideas

The main idea of a selection is the most important point a writer wants to relate to readers. Writers often state the main idea in a topic sentence near the beginning of a selection.

What's in a Name?

All college sports teams have special names. Many of these names are common, such as the Bears or the Tigers. However, more teams should have names that are unique and express the school's individuality. The University of Arkansas team names are Razorbacks and Lady Razorbacks. Virginia Tech athletes are called Hokies. Purdue has the Boilermakers. My favorite is the University of California at Santa Cruz's Banana Slugs and Lady Slugs. Slugs are unusual creatures. They have soft, slimy bodies and enjoy moist environments. These unique names make the college sports world a more interesting and fun place.

How to Identify Stated Main Ideas	
What is the paragraph about?	• names of college teams
Look for supporting details.	• Some teams have unique names like Razorbacks, Hokies, Boilermakers, and Lady Slugs. • The author feels these names make the college sports world more fun.
Eliminate unnecessary information or details.	• Slugs are slimy and enjoy moist environments.
Summarize the main idea.	• Unique sports team names are better and more fun than common names.

Implied Main Ideas

Sometimes a main idea is implied, or not directly stated. Readers have to figure out the main idea by studying all of the details in a selection.

The Future of Humankind

Many people agree that space exploration is important. However, when government spending is discussed, many people insist there are problems on Earth that need attention and money first. Don't they realize that the future of the human race depends on space exploration? Someday, the Earth's resources may run out. Paying for more exploration will allow us to learn more about space and how we can better care for our planet.

How to Identify Implied Main Ideas	
What is the paragraph about?	• space exploration
Find and list details.	• Many people feel other issues are more important than space exploration. • Our future depends on exploration.
What message is the author trying to convey?	• If we explore space now, we can better take care of ourselves and Earth.
Summarize the implied main idea.	• Space exploration should be paid for because it is just as important as any other issue. We could die without it.

Personal Relevance

An additional way to determine importance while reading a selection is to look for details that have personal relevance to you. These details may be important to you because they remind you of someone or something in your own life. For example, you might relate to "What's in a Name?" because you have a favorite sports team name. You might understand the main point that the writer is trying to make because you might agree that sports team names should be unique.

Make Connections

Making connections is a reading strategy you can use to better understand or enjoy the information presented in a selection.

As you read, think about what the information reminds you of. Have you seen or heard something like this before? Have you read or experienced something like this? Thinking about what you already know helps you make a connection to the new information.

Type of Connection	Description	Example
Text to Self	A connection between the text you are reading and something that has happened in your own life. A text-to-self connection can also be a feeling, such as happiness or excitement, that you feel as you are reading.	This part of the story reminds me of the first time I drove a car. My dad showed me how to turn and stop. I remember how scared I was. Thinking about this memory helps me better understand how the character is feeling as he learns how to drive.
Text to Text	A connection between the text you are reading and another selection you have read, a film you have seen, or a song you have heard. Sometimes the text you are reading might have a similar theme, or message, to something you've read, seen, or heard before. A text may also belong to a genre, such as mystery or biography, that you are familiar with.	This part of the news article reminds me of a movie I saw about space. Astronauts were taking a trip to the moon, but their spaceship lost all power. I can think about the movie as I read about the most recent space shuttle mission.
Text to World	A connection between something you read in the text and something that is happening or has happened in the world. You might also make a connection with the time period or era that a selection takes place in, such as the Great Depression or the 1980s. The setting may also be familiar.	This part of the text reminds me of presidential elections. I remember candidates giving speeches to tell why they should be president. Thinking about this helps me understand why the characters in the selection give speeches.

Use a chart like the one below to help make and record text-to-self, text-to-text, or text-to-world connections as you read.

Make Connections Chart

The text says . . .	This reminds me of . . .	This helps me because . . .

Make Inferences

Making inferences is a reading strategy in which you make educated guesses about the text's content based on experiences that you've had in everyday life or on facts or details that you read.

Sometimes people call making inferences "reading between the lines." This means looking at *how* the text was written along with what is being discussed. When you "read between the lines," you pay attention to the writer's tone, voice, use of punctuation, or emphasis on certain words. Writers can also use irony, dialogue, or descriptions to infer messages.

When you add your prior knowledge or personal experiences to what you are reading, you can make inferences by reading all the clues and making your best guesses.

How to Make Inferences Using Your Own Experience

Read the following paragraph and chart to learn how to make an inference using your own experiences.

The Waiting

Rain pounded against the windows as Sarah stomped up and down the stairs. She only stopped going up and down to check the time on the clock downstairs every five minutes. She had been dressed and ready to go for more than an hour! Sarah had spent weeks picking out her dress and shoes, and she had even paid $50 to have her hair styled. She threw the flower she had so excitedly bought yesterday in the corner beside the camera. Sarah wondered, "Where is he? Will I have to go alone tonight?"

Inferences Based on Your Own Experience	
You read	Sarah had been dressed and ready to go somewhere for more than an hour. She spent a lot of time selecting her dress and shoes. She threw her flower in the corner by the camera.
You know	I know that people spend a lot of time choosing special outfits for events like dances, weddings, or parties. I know that my parents took a photo of me and my date for the prom last year. My date and I both had flowers for our outfits that night.
You infer	Sarah had a date to a special event that night. She was upset because she cared a lot about the event she was going to and didn't want to be late or go alone.

How to Make Inferences Using Text Evidence

Read the following paragraph and chart to learn how to make an inference by using clues that appear in the text.

The Waiting

Rain pounded against the windows as Sarah stomped up and down the stairs. She only stopped going up and down to check the time on the clock downstairs every five minutes. She had been dressed and ready to go for more than an hour! Sarah had spent weeks picking out her dress and shoes, and she had even paid $50 to have her hair styled. She threw the flower she had so excitedly bought yesterday in the corner beside the camera. Sarah wondered, "Where is he? Will I have to go alone tonight?"

Inferences Based on Text Evidence	
You read	Sarah had been dressed and ready to go somewhere for more than an hour. She spent a lot of time selecting her dress and shoes. She threw her flower in the corner by the camera.
You infer	Sarah had plans to go somewhere special that evening and was waiting for her date. She cared a lot about the event she was going to. Someone is late, and she is angry at him.

Ask Questions

You can **ask questions** to learn new information, to clarify, and to understand or figure out what is important in a selection. Asking questions of yourself and the author while reading can help you locate information you might otherwise miss.

How to Self-Question

Ask yourself questions to understand something that is confusing, keep track of what is happening, or think about what you know.

Ask and Write Questions Use a question word such as *Who, What, When, Where, Why,* or *How* to write your questions.

Examples: How can I figure out what this word means? What are the characters doing? Why is this important? Do I agree with this?

Answer the Questions and Follow Up Use the text, photographs, or other visuals to answer your questions. Write your answer next to the question. Include the page number where you found the answer.

How to Question the Author

Sometimes, you may have questions about what the author is trying to tell you in a selection. Write these types of questions, and then try to answer them by reading the text. The answers to these questions are known as "author and you" answers.

Questions to Ask the Author

- What is the author trying to say here?
- Does the author explain his or her ideas clearly?
- What is the author talking about?
- Does the author support his or her ideas or opinions with facts?

How to Find Question-Answer Relationships

Where you find the answers to your questions is very important. Sometimes the answers are located right in the text. Other times, your questions require you to use ideas and information that are not in the text. Some questions can be answered by using your background knowledge on a topic. Read the chart to learn about question-answer relationships.

Type of Answer	How to Find the Answers
"Right There"	Sometimes you can simply point to the text and say that an answer to one of your questions is "right there."
"Think and Search"	Look back at the selection. Find the information the question is asking about. Think about how the information fits together to answer the question.
"Author and You"	Use ideas and information that are not stated directly in the text. Think about what you have read, and create your own ideas or opinions based on what you know about the author.
"On Your Own"	Use your feelings, what you already know, and your own experiences to find these answers.

Synthesize

When you **synthesize**, you gather your thoughts about what you have read to draw conclusions, make generalizations, and compare the information to information you've read in other texts. You form new overall understandings by putting together ideas and events.

How to Draw Conclusions

Reading is like putting a puzzle together. There are many different parts that come together to make up the whole selection. Synthesizing is the process of putting the pieces together while we read. We combine new information with what we already know to create an original idea or to form new understandings.

Read this passage and the text that follows to help you understand how to synthesize what you read.

Distracted Drivers

Cell phone use in cars has steadily risen in the past decade. Studies from the Departments of Highway Safety show that the more distracted drivers are, the more likely they are to be in an accident. Lawmakers in some states have successfully passed laws requiring drivers to use hands-free accessories while a vehicle is moving. This means they may use an earpiece or a speaker-phone device but not hold the phone in their hands. Many people feel that talking on cell phones is not the only distracting activity that should be illegal for drivers.

Use text evidence from the selection and your own experience to draw conclusions as you read.

Drawing Conclusions	
Look for Details	The more distracted a driver is, the more likely he or she is to be involved in an accident. Cell phones are distracting.
Think About What You Know	I know people who have been in car accidents while talking on their cell phones.
Decide What You Believe	Lawmakers should continue to work on laws to stop drivers from being distracted.

How to Make Generalizations

Generalizations are broad statements that apply to a group of people, a set of ideas, or the way things happen. You can make generalizations as you read, using experience and text evidence from a selection to help you.

- **Take notes about the facts or opinions** Look for the overall theme or message of the selection.
- **Add examples** Think about what you know about the topic from your own knowledge and experience.
- **Construct a generalization** Write a statement that combines the author's statements and your own.

  Example: Using a cell phone while driving can make you have an accident.

How to Compare Across Texts

Comparing two or more texts helps you combine ideas, develop judgments, and draw conclusions. Read the following paragraph, and think about how it connects to the paragraph on page 631.

Graduated Driver's License Programs

More and more states are creating graduated driver's license (GDL) laws. Studies show that these programs help teen driver accidents and deaths to decline. The programs differ from state to state, but most GDL programs require an adult with a valid driver's license to be present when a teen is driving, and a teen driver must enroll in a certified driver's education and training course. Each state has various restrictions for teen drivers and punishments for when those restrictions are ignored.

Think About Something You Have Already Read In "Distracted Drivers," you read that cell phones are distracting to drivers and that many people feel it should be illegal to use one while driving.

Think About What You Are Reading Right Now Many states have graduated driver's license programs. Accidents involving teen drivers have declined.

Compare Across Texts and Draw Conclusions Both articles are about laws related to driving. Lawmakers hope that all of the laws they pass related to driving will create safer driving conditions for everyone.

Comparing across texts can help you foster an argument or advance an opinion. Having multiple opinions and facts from different sources makes your argument or opinion more credible.

Visualize

When you **visualize**, you use your imagination to better understand what the author is describing. While reading, create an image or picture in your mind that represents what you are reading about. Look for words that tell how things look, sound, smell, taste, and feel.

My Favorite Car Is a Truck

My name is Stephen, and today was a magical day. I've been working hard and saving money all summer. I finally have enough money for a down payment on a new car. Today my father took me to a car dealership to pick out my car. I immediately found my favorite vehicle. It was a red, shiny pickup truck with gleaming wheels. I climbed inside and looked around. The brown seats were sparkling clean, and the truck still had that new car smell inside the cab. I put the key in the ignition and turned it on. The quiet hum of the engine made me so happy. After a long test-drive, my father and I agreed this was the truck for me.

How to Visualize Using Sketches

- **Read the Text** Look for words that help create pictures in your mind about the characters, setting, and events.
- **Picture the Information in Your Mind** Stop and focus on the descriptive words. Create pictures in your mind using these words.
- **Draw the Events** Sketch pictures to show what is happening. You could draw Stephen climbing inside the pickup truck.

How to Visualize Using Senses

- **Look for Words** Find adjectives and sensory words: smell, look, sound, taste, and feel. Stephen uses the words *red, shiny, with gleaming wheels; brown seats, sparkling clean; new car smell;* and *quiet hum of the engine* to talk about the truck.
- **Create a Picture in Your Mind of the Scene** What do you hear, feel, see, smell, and taste? Examine how these details improve your understanding.

I smell: new car smell	**I hear:** engine humming
I see: red, shiny truck	**I feel:** texture of the seats, the key

How to Recognize Emotional Responses

Do any of the words in the selection make you feel certain emotions? Asking yourself how you feel when you read can help you remember the information.

Example: I feel excited for the main character because I know what it's like to pick out something new.

What Is Reading Fluency?

Reading fluency is the ability to read smoothly and expressively with clear understanding. Fluent readers are able to better understand and enjoy what they read. Use the strategies that follow to build your fluency in these four key areas:

- accuracy and rate
- phrasing
- intonation
- expression

How to Improve Accuracy and Rate

Accuracy is the correctness of your reading. Rate is the speed of your reading.

How to read accurately:

- Use correct pronunciation.
- Emphasize correct syllables.
- Recognize most words.

How to read with proper rate:

- Match your reading speed to what you are reading. For example, if you are reading an exciting story, read slightly faster. If you are reading a sad story, read slightly slower.
- Recognize and use punctuation.

Test your accuracy and rate:

- Choose a text you are familiar with, and practice reading it aloud or silently multiple times.
- Keep a dictionary with you while you read, and look up words you do not recognize.
- Use a watch or clock to time yourself while you read a passage.
- Ask a friend or family member to read a passage for you, so you know what it should sound like.

Use the formula below to measure a reader's accuracy and rate while reading aloud. For passages to practice with, see **Reading Fluency Practice**, pp. 638–661 .

Accuracy and Rate Formula

_____ − _____ = _____
words attempted in one minute — number of errors = words correct per minute (wcpm)

How to Improve Intonation

Intonation is the rise and fall in the pitch or tone of your voice as you read aloud. Pitch and tone both mean the highness or lowness of the sound.

How to read with proper intonation:

- Change the sound of your voice to match what you are reading.
- Make your voice flow, or sound smooth while you read.
- Make sure you are pronouncing words correctly.
- Raise the sound of your voice for words that should be stressed, or emphasized.
- Use proper rhythm and meter.
- Use visual clues. (see box below)

Visual Clue and Meaning	Example	How to Read It
Italics: draw attention to a word to show special importance	She is *smart*.	Emphasize "smart."
Dash: shows a quick break in a sentence	She is—smart.	Pause before saying "smart."
Exclamation: can represent energy, excitement, or anger	She is smart!	Make your voice louder at the end of the sentence.
All capital letters: can represent strong emphasis, or yelling	SHE IS SMART.	Emphasize the whole sentence.
Bold facing: draws attention to a word to show importance	She is **smart**.	Emphasize "smart."
Question mark: shows curiosity or confusion	She is smart?	Raise the pitch of your voice slightly at the end of the sentence.

Use the rubric below to measure how well a reader uses intonation while reading aloud. For intonation passages, see **Reading Fluency Practice**, pp. 638–661.

Intonation Rubric		
1	**2**	**3**
The reader's tone does not change. The reading all sounds the same.	The reader's tone changes sometimes to match what is being read.	The reader's tone always changes to match what is being read.

How to Improve Phrasing

Phrasing is how you use your voice to group words together.

How to read with proper phrasing:

- Use correct rhythm and meter by not reading too fast or too slow.
- Pause for key words within the text.
- Make sure your sentences have proper flow and meter, so they sound smooth instead of choppy.
- Make sure you sound like you are reading a sentence instead of a list.
- Use punctuation to tell you when to stop, pause, or emphasize. (see box below)

Punctuation	How to Use It
. period	stop at the end of the sentence
, comma	pause within the sentence
! exclamation point	emphasize the sentence and pause at the end
? question mark	emphasize the end of the sentence and pause at the end
; semicolon	pause within the sentence between two related thoughts
: colon	pause within the sentence before giving an example or explanation

One way to practice phrasing is to copy a passage, then place a slash (/), or pause mark, within a sentence where there should be a pause. One slash (/) means a short pause. Two slashes (//) mean a longer pause, such as a pause at the end of a sentence.

Read aloud the passage below, pausing at each pause mark. Then try reading the passage again without any pauses. Compare how you sound each time.

There are many ways / to get involved in your school / and community. // Joining a club / or trying out for a sports team/ are a few of the options. // Volunteer work can also be very rewarding. // You can volunteer at community centers, / nursing homes, / or animal shelters. //

Use the rubric below to measure how well a reader uses phrasing while reading aloud. For phrasing passages, see **Reading Fluency Practice**, pp. 638–661.

Phrasing Rubric		
1	**2**	**3**
Reading is choppy. There are usually no pauses for punctuation.	Reading is mostly smooth. There are some pauses for punctuation.	Reading is very smooth. Punctuation is being used properly.

How to Improve Expression

Expression in reading is how you use your voice to express feeling.

How to read with proper expression:

- Match the sound of your voice to what you are reading. For example, read louder and faster to show strong feeling. Read slower and quieter to show sadness or seriousness.
- Match the sound of your voice to the genre. For example, read a fun, fictional story using a fun, friendly voice. Read an informative, nonfiction article using an even tone and a more serious voice.
- Avoid speaking in monotone, which is using only one tone in your voice.
- Pause for emphasis and exaggerate letter sounds to match the mood or theme of what you are reading.

Practice incorrect expression by reading this sentence without changing the tone of your voice: *I am so excited!*

Now read the sentence again with proper expression: *I am so excited!* The way you use your voice while reading can help you to better understand what is happening in the text.

For additional practice, read the sentences below aloud with and without changing your expression. Compare how you sound each time.

- I am very sad.
- That was the most *boring* movie I have ever seen.
- We won the game!

Use the rubric below to measure how well a reader uses expression while reading aloud. For expression passages, see **Reading Fluency Practice**, pp. 638–661.

Expression Rubric

1	2	3
The reader sounds monotone. The reader's voice does not match the subject of what is being read.	The reader is making some tone changes. Sometimes, the reader's voice matches what is being read.	The reader is using proper tones and pauses. The reader's voice matches what is being read.

Practice Intonation: "Hitching a Ride"

Intonation is the rise and fall in the pitch or tone of your voice as you read aloud. Use this passage to practice reading with proper intonation. Print a copy of this passage from **myNGconnect.com** to help you monitor your progress.

The Crittercam team is deep in the bitter cold of Antarctica. It is working here with scientists. They are studying what the world's largest penguin eats. The emperor penguin looks like he is dressed in a fancy suit for a dinner party. But no one really knows just where these penguins eat their meals. That changes when the Crittercam catches it all on film!

Scientists already know that emperor penguins make "yo-yo" dives when they search for food. They dive down for several dozen meters. Then they zoom up near the surface and back down again. Finally, they come up for air. But when were they catching their fish? Was it deep in the water? Was it near the surface? Crittercam has the answer!

From "Hitching a Ride," page 16

Practice Expression: "LAFFF"

Expression in reading is how you use your voice to express feeling. Use this passage to practice reading with proper expression. Print a copy of this passage from myNGconnect.com to help you monitor your progress.

"What are you doing?" I squeaked.

Still in his strange, deep voice, Peter said, "What are *you* doing? After all, this is my garage."

"I was just cutting across your yard to get home. Your parents never complained before."

"I thought you were spying on me," said Peter. "I thought you wanted to know about my machine." He hissed when he said the word *machine*.

Honestly, he was beginning to frighten me. "What machine?" I demanded. "You mean this shower-stall thing?"

He drew himself up and narrowed his eyes, making them into thin slits. "This is my time machine!"

I goggled at him. "You mean . . . you mean . . . this machine can send you forward and backward in time?"

"Well, actually, I can only send things forward in time," admitted Peter, speaking in his normal voice again. "That's why I'm calling the machine LAFFF. It stands for Lu's Artifact For Fast Forward."

From "LAFFF," page 38

Practice Phrasing: "Kids Are Inventors, Too"

Phrasing is how you use your voice to group words together. Use this passage to practice reading with proper phrasing. Print a copy of this passage from myNGconnect.com to help you monitor your progress.

"I wanted to design an automatic rabbit feeder for my school invention project," Reeba Daniel said. "But my teacher told me that automatic pet feeders had already been invented."

Then Reeba's mom gave her a suggestion. "Invent something everyone could use—something that saves time."

A few days later, while Reeba was folding laundry, she thought about how this common household chore is a two-step job. First, the clothes go into the washer. Then, when they're damp and heavy, somebody needs to lift them into the dryer. Reeba thought about inventing a machine that would wash and dry clothes in one step.

The washer could be on top of the dryer and have a trapdoor that opens when the drain cycle is complete. The clothes would drop into the dryer, making it start. A computerized device could time each of the cycles.

From "Kids Are Inventors, Too," page 66

Practice Intonation: "The Challenge"

Intonation is the rise and fall in the pitch or tone of your voice as you read aloud. Use this passage to practice reading with proper intonation. Print a copy of this passage from myNGconnect.com to help you monitor your progress.

José, eager to connect, took a deep breath and said, "I see that you play racquetball. You wanna play a game?"

"Are you good?" Estela asked flatly. She picked up a slice of tomato that had slid out of her sandwich.

"Pretty good," he said without thinking as he slipped into a lie. "I won a couple of tournaments."

He watched as the tomato slice slithered down Estela's throat. She wiped her mouth and said, "Sure. How about after school on Friday."

"That's tomorrow," José said.

"That's right. Today's Thursday and tomorrow's Friday." She flattened the empty milk carton with her fist and slapped her science book closed. Then she hurled the carton and her balled-up lunch bag at the plastic-lined garbage can. "What's your name?"

"Camacho. José Camacho."

"I'm Estela. My friends call me Stinger."

"Stinger?"

"Yeah, Stinger. I'll meet you at the courts at 3:45." She got up and headed toward the library.

From "The Challenge," page 102

Practice Phrasing: "Rachel the Clever"

Phrasing is how you use your voice to group words together. Use this passage to practice reading with proper phrasing. Print a copy of this passage from myNGconnect.com to help you monitor your progress.

Now, one day the king stopped at an inn. There he heard the innkeeper boasting about his daughter, Rachel, who was so clever she could solve any riddle. The king frowned.

"I don't like liars," he told the innkeeper. "I will ask you three riddles. If your daughter can solve them, you will be rewarded. But if she fails, you shall lose your inn. First, what is the fastest thing? Second, what is the richest thing? Third, what is the dearest thing?"

Sadly, the innkeeper went home to his daughter, Rachel, and told her what the king had said. Rachel smiled. "You won't lose the inn, Father. Go to the king and tell him that Thought is the fastest thing. Life-giving Earth is the richest thing. And Love is the dearest thing."

When the king heard these answers, he frowned again. He had vowed to wed only a woman as clever as he. Could that woman be Rachel, a common innkeeper's daughter?

From "Rachel the Clever," page 130

Practice Expression: "A Contest of Riddles"

Expression in reading is how you use your voice to express feeling. Use this passage to practice reading with proper expression. Print a copy of this passage from myNGconnect.com to help you monitor your progress.

KING. Daughter, your happiness means a lot to us. What if we let you choose your own husband?

QUEEN. [*gasps*] What? No girl in our kingdom has ever been allowed to make her own choice. It is the parents' responsibility to make such an important decision. [*aside, with a hint of a smile*] How he spoils that girl!

PRINCESS. Father, I have always wanted to marry someone who enjoys riddles as much as I do. I could marry a man who is as good a riddler as I am. That would make me very happy.

KING. [*suddenly claps his hands happily*] I have an idea! We will have a contest. You will match your skills against young men throughout the kingdom. The one who wins will become your husband. [*speaking to the* QUEEN] This is a plan that works for us all. We make the decision, and at the same time, our daughter gets a clever husband.

QUEEN. [*nods*] So let it be done.

From "A Contest of Riddles," page 148

Practice Intonation: "The Lotus Seed"

Intonation is the rise and fall in the pitch or tone of your voice as you read aloud. Use this passage to practice reading with proper intonation. Print a copy of this passage from myNGconnect.com to help you monitor your progress.

She arrived in a strange new land with blinking lights and speeding cars and towering buildings that scraped the sky and a language she didn't understand.

She worked many years, day and night, and so did her children and her sisters and her cousins, too, living together in one big house.

Last summer my little brother found the special seed and asked questions again and again. He'd never seen a lotus bloom or an emperor on a golden dragon throne.

So one night he stole the seed from beneath the family altar and planted it in a pool of mud somewhere near Bá's onion patch.

Bá cried and cried when she found out the seed was gone. She didn't eat, she didn't sleep, and my silly brother forgot what spot of earth held the seed.

From "The Lotus Seed," page 184

Practice Phrasing: "Immigrants Today"

Phrasing is how you use your voice to group words together. Use this passage to practice reading with proper phrasing. Print a copy of this passage from myNGconnect.com to help you monitor your progress.

The reasons that cause people to come to the United States are as varied and unique as the people who come here. Sometimes, people are forced to escape their countries. They are afraid of what might happen to them because of their races or religions. They are afraid they will be punished for their political beliefs. Refugees come to the United States in order to live their lives free from these types of prejudice and abuse.

Others come to the United States to escape poverty in their home countries. In the United States, people can find jobs that are not available in their home countries. They can also find jobs that pay them more money. Many immigrants seek to improve the quality of their lives, and their children's futures, too. They leave family, friends, and homes because they want more educational opportunities for themselves and their children.

From "Immigrants Today," page 204

Practice Expression: "Brothers in Hope"

Expression in reading is how you use your voice to express feeling. Use this passage to practice reading with proper expression. Print a copy of this passage from myNGconnect.com to help you monitor your progress.

Later that day, as we prepared for sleep, we saw many big trucks approaching. They were moving very fast, and their rumbling tires sent huge dust clouds into the air. Frightened that there were soldiers in the trucks, we ran to hide.

As the trucks drew closer, my heart began to pound so hard I could hear nothing else. I huddled close to my group, covered my face with my hands, and waited.

After a few minutes I gathered my courage and went to peek through the trees. I saw one of the drivers. It was Tom!

"It's safe, it's safe!" I cried. "Tom has come to save us!"

Many of the boys ran out from the forest, and soon the trucks were surrounded by boys. Everyone wanted to be taken to safety.

Tom began to speak. "I'm very sorry, but we cannot take all of you. There is not enough room. For now, we will take only the smallest and those who are too sick to walk.

"The rest of you must keep walking to Kenya. We will show you the way. Your worst days will soon be behind you."

From "Brothers in Hope," page 226

Practice Phrasing: "The Human Machine"

Phrasing is how you use your voice to group words together. Use this passage to practice reading with proper phrasing. Print a copy of this passage from myNGconnect.com to help you monitor your progress.

Your heart pumps blood throughout your body. With every heartbeat, blood surges out of your heart and into tubes called blood vessels. When blood leaves the heart, it enters blood vessels called arteries. The arteries divide into smaller and smaller blood vessels that carry blood to all parts of the body. The smallest kind of blood vessel in your body is the capillary. Capillaries are so small that you need a microscope to examine them. Blood vessels called veins carry blood back to your heart.

Blood always circulates around your body in the same direction. Blood leaves the heart, travels to each of the cells in your body, and returns to the heart with much less oxygen. The heart then pumps this blood to the lungs to get more oxygen. The oxygen-rich blood travels back to the heart, and the cycle begins all over again. Your heart and blood vessels make up your circulatory system.

From "The Human Machine," page 266

Practice Intonation: "The Beat Goes On"

Intonation is the rise and fall in the pitch or tone of your voice as you read aloud. Use this passage to practice reading with proper intonation. Print a copy of this passage from **myNGconnect.com** to help you monitor your progress.

Healthy hearts have four chambers, or sections. The two upper chambers, called atria, receive blood from veins. The ventricles, or lower sections, pump blood into arteries.

That's the plan anyway. But Brian Whitlow's life began differently. "I was born with only one ventricle," he says. Brian's heart couldn't pump blood to his lungs to get oxygen.

But Whitlow's mother didn't give up. Nor did his doctors. When Brian was just a few weeks old, surgeons operated on him.

"We can't rebuild chambers that haven't grown," says Dr. Daniel Bernstein, one of Whitlow's childhood doctors. Instead, the surgeons rearranged his blood vessels to bypass the missing chamber.

After the operation, Whitlow's blood ran straight to his lungs. There it got oxygen, then it flowed back to his heart. Whitlow's single ventricle then sent oxygen-rich blood gushing throughout his body.

That worked pretty well, Whitlow says. "I did all the normal things, including playing Little League baseball." Then things changed.

From "The Beat Goes On," page 286

Practice Expression: "Two Left Feet, Two Left Hands, and Too Left on the Bench"

Expression in reading is how you use your voice to express feeling. Use this passage to practice reading with proper expression. Print a copy of this passage from **myNGconnect.com** to help you monitor your progress.

I followed my teammates to one end of the field. "Lubar!" Mr. Growler shouted at me.

"What?" Wow. I'd already been singled out for attention. I decided I loved football.

"You wanna guard?"

Wow again. He was asking me if I wanted to be a guard. Ten seconds into my sporting career, and I was being given an important assignment. Knowing absolutely nothing about the position of a guard in football, and being a total nerd at heart, I figured I should do the one thing I was good at: seek out information. "Where do I stand?" I asked.

"What?" Mr. Growler seemed puzzled.

"Where does a guard stand?" I asked.

He sighed and stared at me as if I'd just arrived from Pluto. Around me, I could hear kids snickering. Mr. Growler pointed at my head. "Would you like a guard for your glasses?"

"Oh…"

From "Two Left Feet, Two Left Hands, and Too Left on the Bench," page 306

Practice Expression: "Encounter"

Expression in reading is how you use your voice to express feeling. Use this passage to practice reading with proper expression. Print a copy of this passage from myNGconnect.com to help you monitor your progress.

For a while I forgot my dream.

For a while I was not afraid.

So we built a great feasting fire and readied the pepper pot and yams and cassava bread and fresh fish. For though the strangers were not quite human beings, we would still treat them as such.

Our chief rolled tobacco leaves and showed them how to smoke, but they coughed and snorted and clearly did not know about these simple things.

Then I leaned forward and stared into their chief's eyes. They were blue and gray like the shifting sea.

Suddenly, I remembered my dream and stared at each of the strangers in turn. Even those with dark human eyes looked away, like dogs before they are driven from the fire.

So I drew back from the feast, which is not what one should do, and I watched how the sky strangers touched our golden nose rings and our golden armbands but not the flesh of our faces or arms. I watched their chief smile. It was the serpent's smile—no lips and all teeth.

I jumped up, crying, "Do not welcome them."

But the welcome had already been given.

From "Encounter," page 342

Practice Intonation: "Culture Clash"

Intonation is the rise and fall in the pitch or tone of your voice as you read aloud. Use this passage to practice reading with proper intonation. Print a copy of this passage from **myNGconnect.com** to help you monitor your progress.

The Spaniards reached the Aztec capital on November 8, 1519. They found themselves facing thousands of curious eyes. The Aztec examined the Spanish explorers closely. To them, the explorers seemed very different.

For example, the strange visitors appeared to be made of glowing metal. That's because sunlight reflected off their armor.

The Aztec stared especially hard at the visitors' horses. These animals were new to the Aztec. Some even wondered if horse and rider were a single, giant monster.

Despite their confusion, the Aztec welcomed the Spanish. The Aztec king, Moctezuma, even swapped gifts with Cortés. To the Aztec that meant the two men were friends.

What Moctezuma didn't know was that Cortés was a wolf in sheep's clothing. He wanted more than gifts.

From "Culture Clash," page 362

Practice Phrasing: "When Cultures Meet"

Phrasing is how you use your voice to group words together. Use this passage to practice reading with proper phrasing. Print a copy of this passage from myNGconnect.com to help you monitor your progress.

The American elk, a type of deer, roamed much of the United States and southern Canada. Native Americans hunted them. Soon, Europeans began hunting elk, too. They hunted thousands of elk. After a time, elk could only be found west of the Rocky Mountains.

About 50 million buffalo once roamed the North American Plains. The Plains Indians used the buffalo for food, clothing, shelter, tools, fuel, and medicine. European settlers hunted the buffalo, too. Often they hunted for sport or they took the skins and left the meat to rot in the sun. Settlers killed millions of buffalo. By 1889, there were only about 1,000 buffalo in the United States. Soon, the Plains Indians had to change their way of life because too few buffalo remained to support them.

From "When Cultures Meet," page 382

Practice Intonation: "Dogs at Work"

Intonation is the rise and fall in the pitch or tone of your voice as you read aloud. Use this passage to practice reading with proper intonation. Print a copy of this passage from myNGconnect.com to help you monitor your progress.

Fruits, vegetables, meat, and other food items sometimes carry insects and diseases. Food from foreign countries could infect crops or animals in the United States. To prevent that, the U.S. Department of Agriculture created the Beagle Brigade. Furry, four-legged baggage inspectors sniff purses and bags at international airports. The beagle calmly sits down next to anything that smells suspicious. The hound's human partner then checks for illegal items.

Why beagles? They're friendly and cute. They don't scare people as they sniff through the crowds. Beagles have amazing noses. They can sense odors better than many high-tech machines.

Beagles can work for six to ten years. A Beagle Brigade dog can remember up to fifty different odors by the end of its career. Sometimes harmless products, such as lemon-scented shaving cream, fool the dogs. But not often. The Beagle Brigade sniffs out the truth 84 percent of the time.

From "Dogs at Work," page 416

Practice Phrasing: "Angels in the Snow"

Phrasing is how you use your voice to group words together. Use this passage to practice reading with proper phrasing. Print a copy of this passage from myNGconnect.com to help you monitor your progress.

Getting to the victims in arctic Aniak is far more challenging than in an average city. The Dragon Slayers can't just drive an ambulance to the scene of an emergency. Most of the people they help are Yupik Eskimos and Athabascan Indians, like the Dragon Slayers. Aniak is a landlocked village of 600 people. It is surrounded by rivers. The nearest major city is Anchorage. It is 350 miles west. The team uses frozen waterways as roads through early May. They travel in snowmobiles and four-wheelers. They have to rely on boats when the ice melts. "And here, members of the team almost always know the person who's injured or sick. So it's very personal. There's an emotional aspect to knowing the victim your whole life that you don't have in a larger city," Hess says.

Marteney has had to deal with her share of difficult and emotional calls. "After we have a really hard call, we all meet at the fire station. We talk about the person we may have lost, what happened on the call, what we did right," says Marteney. "Then we do a group hug and go for a walk. It really helps."

From "Angels in the Snow," page 434

Practice Expression: "Zlateh the Goat"

Expression in reading is how you use your voice to express feeling. Use this passage to practice reading with proper expression. Print a copy of this passage from myNGconnect.com to help you monitor your progress.

For Reuven the furrier it was a bad year, and after long hesitation he decided to sell Zlateh the goat. She was old and gave little milk. Feivel the town butcher had offered eight gulden for her. Such a sum would buy Hanukkah candles, potatoes and oil for pancakes, gifts for the children, and other holiday necessaries for the house. Reuven told his oldest boy Aaron to take the goat to town.

Aaron understood what taking the goat to Feivel meant, but had to obey his father. Leah, his mother, wiped the tears from her eyes when she heard the news. Aaron's younger sisters, Anna and Miriam, cried loudly. Aaron put on his quilted jacket and a cap with earmuffs, bound a rope around Zlateh's neck, and took along two slices of bread with cheese to eat on the road. Aaron was supposed to deliver the goat by evening, spend the night at the butcher's, and return the next day with the money.

From "Zlateh the Goat," page 450

Practice Phrasing: "Play Ball"

Phrasing is how you use your voice to group words together. Use this passage to practice reading with proper phrasing. Print a copy of this passage from myNGconnect.com to help you monitor your progress.

A few years after the Civil War ended, the first professional baseball league was created. In 1876, the first group of teams officially became the National League.

In 1901, the American League was created. Other leagues had formed throughout the years, but only these two leagues survived. These are the same two leagues that play today.

For a few years, the National League and the American League never played baseball against each other. But, in 1903, things changed. Baseball officials decided to hold a series of games at the end of that year's baseball season. They would call the event the World Series.

The best teams from the National League and the American League would play against each other. They would play nine games. The team who won the most games out of nine would win the series. Today, there are only seven games in the World Series.

The first World Series pitted the Boston Pilgrims (later the Red Sox) against the Pittsburgh Pirates. Pittsburgh won the first game; Boston the second.

From "Play Ball," page 484

Practice Intonation: "Roberto Clemente"

Intonation is the rise and fall in the pitch or tone of your voice as you read aloud. Use this passage to practice reading with proper intonation. Print a copy of this passage from myNGconnect.com to help you monitor your progress.

To his new fans in Pittsburgh, Roberto was like a jolt of *electricity*. He could score from first base on a single. He could hit line drives, bunts, towering home runs, sacrifice flies—whatever was needed. Once he even scored an inside-the-park GRAND SLAM!

Playing right field, he had no equal. He was always leaping, diving, crashing, rolling. Once, trying to catch a pop fly, running full speed, he SLAMMED into the right-field wall—and fell to the ground. At last, slowly, he lifted his glove. The ball was inside.

But it wasn't just how he played. He had *style*. He was *cool*. He had this move he did with his neck before each at bat, creaking it one way, then the other.

Soon kids who wanted to be just like Roberto were doing it, too, twisting their necks this way and that.

Roberto did it to ease the pain he felt from playing his heart out in every game.

"If you don't try as hard as you can," he said, "you are wasting your life."

From "Roberto Clemente," page 508

Practice Expression: "Raymond's Run"

Expression in reading is how you use your voice to express feeling. Use this passage to practice reading with proper expression. Print a copy of this passage from myNGconnect.com to help you monitor your progress.

I spread my fingers in the dirt and crouch over the Get on Your Mark. I am telling myself, Squeaky you must win. The pistol shot explodes in my blood and I am off, flying past the other runners. My arms pump up and down, and the whole world is quiet except for the crunch of gravel in the track. On the other side of the fence is Raymond with his arms down to his side and the palms tucked up behind him, running in his very own style. It's the first time I ever saw that and I almost stop to watch my brother on his first run. But the white ribbon is bouncing toward me. I tear past it, racing into the distance till my feet start digging up footfuls of dirt and brake me short. Then all the kids standing on the side pile on me, banging me on the back and slapping my head with their May Day programs, for I have won again.

From "Raymond's Run," page 526

Practice Intonation: "Handle with Care"

Intonation is the rise and fall in the pitch or tone of your voice as you read aloud. Use this passage to practice reading with proper intonation. Print a copy of this passage from **myNGconnect.com** to help you monitor your progress.

You wad up a piece of paper, take aim, and toss the paper into the wastebasket. It doesn't seem terribly wasteful—but it adds up. The average American makes about ten tons of trash in thirteen years.

Where does that trash go next? Much of our trash ends up in landfills. Landfills take up valuable land and sometimes make the water, air, and land around them dirty. More than a third of the trash in landfills is paper. Reusing and reducing what you throw away can cut down on the need for more landfills. In fact, about 80 percent of household trash can be recycled.

Wastes from certain jobs or activities can also cause problems. Wastes are especially harmful if they are hazardous, or dangerous, to humans and other species. The United States has passed laws to control both the disposal and the storage of hazardous wastes that may be poisonous or cause diseases.

From "Handle with Care," page 556

Practice Phrasing: "Melting Away"

Phrasing is how you use your voice to group words together. Use this passage to practice reading with proper phrasing. Print a copy of this passage from myNGconnect.com to help you monitor your progress.

No one is sure what is causing the worldwide warm-up. Most scientists blame some gases in Earth's atmosphere. They point to one gas in particular—carbon dioxide.

Most people depend on oil, coal, and natural gas. These fuels help run cars, heat homes, and power factories. But they also give off carbon dioxide. Carbon dioxide heats the atmosphere and makes Earth warmer.

Over time, cars and factories have changed the atmosphere. Today, the air has about 30 percent more carbon dioxide than in the days before cars and factories. Other heat-trapping gases have also skyrocketed.

From "Melting Away," page 578

Practice Expression: "The Legend of the Yakwawiak"

Expression in reading is how you use your voice to express feeling. Use this passage to practice reading with proper expression. Print a copy of this passage from myNGconnect.com to help you monitor your progress.

Kitselemukong watched from the top of the highest mountain as they fought. It was a hard battle, for the Yakwawiak were strong. The Yakwawiak tried to crush the animals and people beneath their huge feet. They stabbed them with their sharp tusks and threw them up into the air with their trunks. The piercing sound of their screams as they fought was terrible to hear. Even when they were wounded and bleeding, the huge monsters continued to fight.

All through that long day, the fight went back and forth. It went from the edge of the great salt water to the wide river that flows through the heart of the land. Many of the bravest animals, those who were almost as large and powerful as the Yakwawiak, were killed.

From "The Legend of the Yakwawiak," page 598

Glossary

The definitions in this glossary are for words as they are used in the selections in this book. Use the Pronunciation Key below to help you use each word's pronunciation. Then read about the parts of an entry.

Pronunciation Key

Symbols for Consonant Sounds

b	box	p	pan
ch	chick	r	ring
d	dog	s	bus
f	fish	sh	fish
g	girl	t	hat
h	hat	th	earth
j	jar	th	father
k	cake	v	vase
ks	box	w	window
kw	queen	wh	whale
l	bell	y	yarn
m	mouse	z	zipper
n	pan	zh	treasure
ng	ring		

Symbols for Short Vowel Sounds

a	hat
e	bell
i	chick
o	box
u	bus

Symbols for Long Vowel Sounds

ā	cake
ē	key
ī	bike
ō	goat
yū	mule

Symbols for R-controlled Sounds

ar	barn
air	chair
ear	ear
ïr	fire
or	corn
ur	girl

Symbols for Variant Vowel Sounds

ah	father
aw	ball
oi	boy
ow	mouse
oo	book
ü	fruit

Miscellaneous Symbols

shun	fraction
chun	question
zhun	division

• Academic Vocabulary

Certain words in this glossary have a red dot indicating that they are academic vocabulary words. These are the words that you will use as you study many different subjects in school.

Parts of an Entry

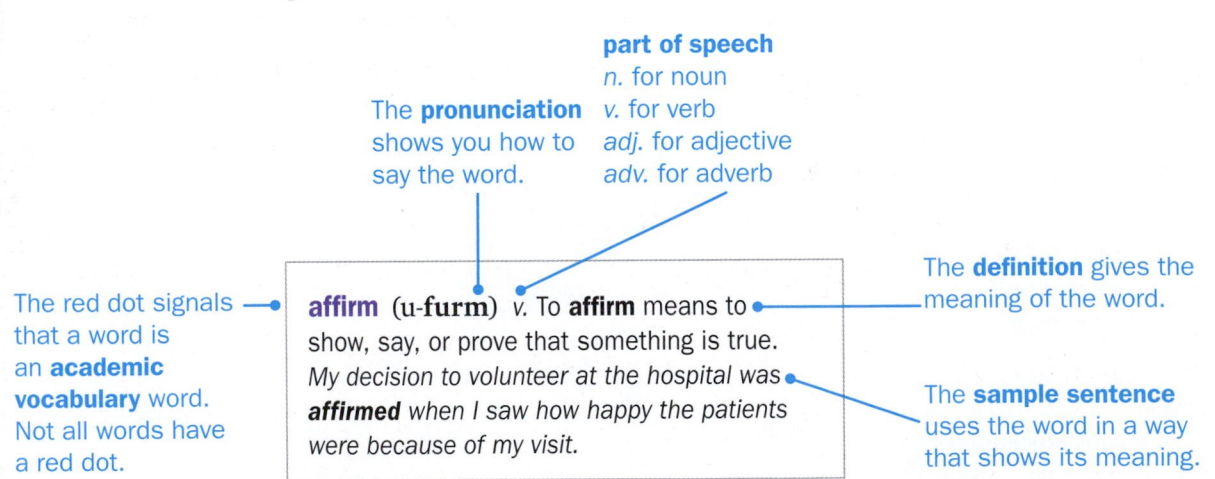

The red dot signals that a word is an **academic vocabulary** word. Not all words have a red dot.

The **pronunciation** shows you how to say the word.

part of speech
n. for noun
v. for verb
adj. for adjective
adv. for adverb

affirm (u-furm) *v.* To **affirm** means to show, say, or prove that something is true. *My decision to volunteer at the hospital was affirmed when I saw how happy the patients were because of my visit.*

The **definition** gives the meaning of the word.

The **sample sentence** uses the word in a way that shows its meaning.

A

ability (u-**bil**-ut-ē) *n*. If you have **ability**, you have the skill to do something. *A gymnast has the **ability** to balance.*

accept (ak-**sept**) *v*. When you **accept** something, you admit that it is true. *The team **accepted** that they had lost.*

accident (**ak**-sud-ent) *n*. An **accident** is a sudden event that causes damage to people or things. *The car **accident** caused $1,000 in damages.*

• **adjust** (ud-**just**) *v*. When you **adjust** to something, you become used to it. *You can **adjust** to cold weather when you go outside.*

• **affect** (u-**fekt**) *v*. When you **affect** someone or something, you cause a change. *Loud music can **affect** your hearing.*

• **aid** (**ād**) *v*. To **aid** someone is to help or give support. *The nurse had to **aid** the patient in getting out of bed.*

• **analyze** (**a**-nu-līz) *v*. When you **analyze** something, you study it closely. *Mark **analyzed** the piece of grass under the microscope.*

• **appeal** (u-**pēl**) *n*. An **appeal** is a strong request for something. *The lawyer made an **appeal** to the judge.*

• **approach** (u-**prōch**) *v*. To **approach** means to come toward someone or something. *The librarian **approached** the student to offer help.*

• **area** (**air**-ē-u) *n*. An **area** is a section of a place often set aside for special use. *Fences are often used to mark **areas** where people are not allowed to go.*

arrive (u-**rīv**) *v*. When you **arrive**, you get to a place. *Some people like to **arrive** early at a party.*

artery (**art**-u-rē) *n*. An **artery** is a type of blood vessel. ***Arteries** carry blood away from the heart.*

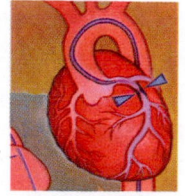

• **assignment** (u-**sīn**-mint) *n*. An **assignment** is a task or job given to someone. *An **assignment** is often more fun to do in pairs.*

• **associate** (u-**sō**-shē-āt) *v*. When you **associate** two things, you connect, or relate, them in your mind. *Tina will always **associate** her backpack with school.*

• **assume** (u-**süm**) *v*. When you **assume**, you guess something is true. *I **assume** you've finished your homework since you're watching TV.*

atmosphere (**at**-mus-fear) *n*. The **atmosphere** is the air that surrounds Earth. *Airplanes fly through the **atmosphere**.*

• **attach** (u-**tach**) *v*. When you **attach** something, you stick it to something else. *Use tape to **attach** a poster to your wall.*

attention (u-**ten**-shun) *n*. When you give someone your **attention**, you listen to what they say or watch what they do. *Pay **attention** to your teacher so you can learn.*

awkward (**aw**-kwurd) *adj*. Someone who is **awkward** feels nervous or clumsy. *The boy feels **awkward** at the dance.*

B

backward (**bak**-wurd) *adv*. To move **backward** is to move toward the back. *You can move some chess pieces **backward**.*

battle (**bat**-ul) *n*. A **battle** is a fight. *During the American Civil War, the North did **battle** with the South.*

• **benefit** (**be**-nu-fit) *v*. When you **benefit** from something, it improves your life or helps you. *You will **benefit** from brushing your teeth two times a day.*

blend (**blend**) *v*. When you **blend** things, you mix them together. *In cooking, you **blend** the ingredients.*

blizzard (**bli**-zurd) *n*. A **blizzard** is a strong snowstorm. *It's hard to see where you're going in a **blizzard**.*

bloom (**blüm**) *v*. To **bloom** means to open up or turn into a flower. *Flowers usually **bloom** in spring.*

• **Academic Vocabulary**

- **bond** (**bahnd**) **1** *n.* A **bond** is something that unites two or more people. *The family **bond** between Lisa and Raul is very strong.* **2** *v.* When you **bond** with someone, you form a close relationship with him or her. *Teammates **bond** with each other when playing sports.*

C

- **capable** (**kā**-pu-bul) *adj.* When you are **capable**, you have the qualities needed to do something. *George is **capable** of climbing the mountain.*

capital (**kap**-ut-ul) *n.* A **capital** is the city where a government is located. *Washington, D.C., is the **capital** of the United States.*

captive (**kap**-tiv) *adj.* A **captive** animal is not free to leave. *Animals in cages are **captive**.*

career (ku-**rēr**) *n.* A **career** is the type of work a person does. *She wants a **career** in architecture.*

- **category** (**ka**-tu-gor-ē) *n.* A **category** is a group of items that have something in common. *Snakes are not part of the rodent **category**.*

celebrate (**sel**-u-brāt) *v.* To **celebrate** means to do something fun because of an important event. *Every year you **celebrate** your birthday.*

cell (**sel**) *n.* A **cell** is the smallest working part of a living thing. *People are made up of millions of **cells**.*

- **challenge** (**chal**-unj) *n.* A **challenge** is something that is hard to do. *It is a **challenge** to run a race.*

champion (**cham**-pē-un) *n.* A **champion** is a winner. *She became **champion** by winning first place in a contest.*

- **chapter** (**chap**-tur) *n.* A **chapter** is one part of something. *A book usually has several **chapters**.*

- **characteristic** (kair-ik-tu-**ris**-tik) *n.* A **characteristic** is a quality of something. *One **characteristic** of a giraffe is its long neck.*

choice (**chois**) *n.* A **choice** is a decision. *You make a **choice** about what to eat each day.*

circulate (**sur**-kū-lāt) *v.* When something **circulates**, it moves along a path that returns to the place it started. *Blood **circulates** throughout your body.*

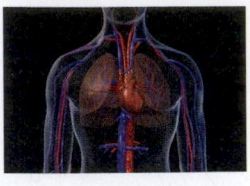

clever (**klev**-ur) *adj.* A **clever** person uses intelligence to do something tricky. *A magician is **clever**.*

clueless (**klü**-lis) *adj.* To be **clueless** means to be confused or not to know something. *The girl was **clueless** about how to answer the question.*

- **communicate** (ku-**myū**-nu-kāt) *v.* When you **communicate**, you give and get information. *The telephone is the easiest way to **communicate** with my relatives in Spain.*

- **community** (ku-**myū**-nu-tē) *n.* A **community** is a group of people who live in one place. *A neighborhood is a kind of **community**.*

- **compare** (kum-**pair**) *v.* When you **compare** two things, you tell how they are alike and different. *We have to **compare** a hill to a mountain in our social studies class.*

compete (kum-**pēt**) *v.* When you **compete**, you take part in a contest. *The athletes **compete** to win the race.*

- **compound** (**kom**-pownd) *adj.* When something is **compound**, it is made of two or more parts. *He has a **compound** fracture in his leg.*

- **concentrate** (**kon**-sun-trāt) *v.* When you **concentrate**, you think about what you do. *You have to **concentrate** when you read.*

confidence (**kahn**-fu-dints) *n.* When you have **confidence**, you believe you can do something. *He has **confidence** that he will win the game.*

- **conflict** (**kahn**-flikt) *n.* A **conflict** is a problem or a disagreement. *A **conflict** often leads to anger.*

congratulate (kun-**grach**-u-lāt) *v.* When you **congratulate** someone, you let that person know you are happy for something they have achieved. *This woman is **congratulated** for finishing school.*

- **Academic Vocabulary**

• **connect** (ku-**nekt**) *v.* When you **connect** things, you show how they are related. *Connect the printer to the computer with the cable.*

conquer (**kahn**-kur) *v.* To **conquer** means to win control of people through force. *Adolf Hitler tried to conquer all of Europe in World War II.*

contact (**kahn**-takt) *n.* **Contact** is the act of meeting or communicating. *The friends stay in contact over the phone because they live so far apart.*

contest (**kahn**-test) *n.* A **contest** is a game or test to see who is the best at something. *The winner of a contest often gets a prize.*

• **context** (**kon**-tekst) **1** *n.* **Context** is the surrounding text near a word or phrase that helps explain its meaning. **2** *adj.* A **context** clue helps you figure out a word's meaning. *Use context clues to help you understand the word.*

continue (kun-**tin**-yū) *v.* To **continue** means to keep doing something. *The runner continues the race for his team by grabbing the baton from the previous runner.*

• **contrast** (kun-**trast**) *v.* When you **contrast** things, you tell how they are different. *Please contrast a desert and a rainforest in your report.*

• **convince** (kun-**vints**) *v.* When you **convince** someone, you make the person agree with you. *I convinced my friend to go to the movies with me.*

council (**kown**-sul) *n.* A **council** is a group of people who gather together to make decisions. *The student council decides where to go for the class trip.*

creature (**krē**-chur) *n.* A **creature** is an animal. *The platypus is an interesting creature that is found in Australia.*

• **credit** (**kred**-ut) *n.* When you are given **credit**, you are noticed for something you have done well. *You want credit from your parents for a good grade.*

crop (**krop**) *n.* A **crop** is a type of plant grown in large amounts to eat or use. *The farmer has a good crop of corn this year.*

cross (**kraws**) *v.* When you **cross** something, you go from one side to another. *The hikers crossed the bridge.*

custom (**kus**-tum) *n.* A **custom** is something that a certain group of people usually do. *In the U.S., it is a custom to shake hands when meeting someone.*

D

damage (**dam**-ij) *v.* To **damage** means to cause harm. *Wind and water from a storm can damage a building.*

dangerous (**dān**-jur-us) *adj.* Something **dangerous** is not safe. *The sign warned people that swimming might be dangerous.*

• **data** (**dā**-tu) *n.* **Data** is factual information. *The data in my report was gathered from library books.*

decide (di-**sīd**) *v.* When you **decide**, you make a choice about something. *He cannot decide what to wear.*

defeat (di-**fēt**) *n.* A **defeat** is a loss. *He felt responsible for his team's defeat.*

• **definition** (de-fuh-**ni**-shun) *n.* The meaning of a word is its **definition**. *Please look up the definition of five words in the dictionary.*

department (di-**part**-ment) *n.* A **department** is a part of a larger group or business. *You get a driver's license at a motor vehicle department.*

dependable (di-**pen**-du-bul) *adj.* A **dependable** person can be trusted to do the right thing. *Parents want dependable babysitters.*

• **design** (di-**zīn**) *v.* When you **design** something, you plan how to make it or do it. *People design things by making drawings first.*

desire (di-**zī**-ur) *v.* When you **desire** something, you really want it. *The child desired the bike in the store window.*

destination (des-tu-**nā**-shun) *n.* A **destination** is a place you plan to go. *The destination for our summer vacation is New York City.*

destroy (di-**stroi**) *v.* When you **destroy** something, it cannot be repaired. *Our dog destroyed the newspapers.*

• **Academic Vocabulary**

determined (di-**tur**-mind) *adj.* When you are **determined**, you try very hard to do something. *Each runner in the race is **determined** to win.*

• **device** (di-**vīs**) *n.* A **device** is a tool. *A remote control is a **device** that changes channels on a TV.*

difficult (**dif**-i-kult) *adj.* Something that is **difficult** is hard to do. *Gymnastics is very **difficult**.*

disaster (diz-**as**-tur) *n.* A **disaster** is a very bad event. *Weather sometimes causes terrible **disasters**.*

• **distinguish** (di-**sting**-wish) *v.* To **distinguish** is to recognize and understand the difference between two or more things. *The children need to **distinguish** between right and wrong.*

dream (drēm) *n.* A **dream** is a thought or an image in your mind when you sleep. *I had a good **dream** last night.*

E

education (ej-u-**kā**-shun) *n.* Your **education** is everything you learn. *Education can come from books, people, or experiences.*

effort (**e**-furt) *n.* When you put **effort** into something, you try harder. *A runner puts **effort** into winning a race.*

• **element** (**e**-lu-ment) *n.* An **element** is a basic part of something. *A light bulb is one **element** of a lamp.*

• **emerge** (i-**murj**) *v.* When you **emerge** from a place, you come out of it. *A swimmer **emerges** from the water for air.*

emergency (i-**mur**-jen-sē) *adj.* An **emergency** service helps people in serious situations. *The **emergency** medical team rides in an ambulance.*

emperor (**em**-pur-ur) *n.* An **emperor** is a ruler. *An **emperor** once ruled Vietman.*

empire (**em**-pī-ur) *n.* An **empire** is a large group of areas ruled by one person. *The Romans had an **empire** that included lands from Europe to Africa.*

employee (em-**ploi**-ē) *n.* An **employee** is a person who works for someone else. *I asked the store **employee** for help.*

• **encounter** (en-**kown**-tur) *n.* An **encounter** is a meeting. *The photographer took pictures of his **encounter** with a bear.*

encourage (en-**kur**-ij) *v.* When you **encourage** people, you give them hope that they can do something. *The father **encouraged** his son to play baseball.*

• **energy** (**e**-nur-jē) *n.* **Energy** is the power or force to do things. *Young children have lots of **energy**.*

• **evaluate** (ē-**val**-yū-wāt) *v.* To **evaluate** is to decide how good or useful something is. *The teachers will **evaluate** the new math program.*

• **evidence** (**e**-vu-dens) *n.* **Evidence** is facts or information that show that something is true. *There is **evidence** that sharks have been around for thousands of years.*

• **exact** (eks-**zact**) *adj.* Something that is **exact** is accurate and specific. *The thermometer gives an **exact** reading of the temperature outside.*

examine (eks-**zam**-un) *v.* When you **examine** something, you look at it very closely. *A doctor **examines** you to make sure you are healthy.*

excellent (eks-**su**-lent) *adj.* When something is **excellent**, it is very good. *The audience thought the play was **excellent**.*

exercise (eks-**sur**-sīz) *n.* **Exercise** is an activity you do to stay fit and healthy. *Many people ride bicycles for **exercise**.*

exist (eks-**zist**) *v.* To **exist** means to be real. *Most people don't believe that ghosts **exist**.*

experience (eks-**spēr**-ē-uns) *n.* **Experience** is knowledge or skill that comes from having already done something. *A chef has a lot of cooking **experience**.*

• **experiment** (eks-**sper**-i-ment) *v.* When you **experiment**, you try an idea. *You can **experiment** in science class.*

• **Academic Vocabulary**

F

fan (**fan**) *n.* A **fan** is someone who supports a particular team or person. *Fans go to games to cheer for their teams.*

• **feature** (**fē**-chur) *n.* A **feature** is a part of something that stands out or is noticeable. *My sister's eyes are her best feature.*

foreign (**for**-in) *adj.* When something is **foreign**, it is from somewhere else. *Last summer, my family and I traveled to a foreign country.*

forever (**for**-e-vur) *adv.* **Forever** means for a time without end. *The road looks like it goes on forever.*

forget (**fur**-get) *v.* When you **forget** something, you no longer know it. *My sister often forgets where she puts her keys.*

forward (**for**-wurd) *adv.* To move **forward** is to move ahead or to the front. *A sign can tell you to move forward.*

future (**fyū**-chur) *n.* The **future** is a time that has not yet happened. *Tomorrow is in the future.*

G

gather (**gath**-ur) *v.* To **gather** means to bring together. *All my relatives gather at our house on holidays.*

genius (**jēn**-yus) *n.* A **genius** is someone who is very smart. *A genius named Thomas Edison invented the lightbulb.*

gesture (**jes**-chur) *n.* A **gesture** is an action done to show how you feel. *Our neighbor made us dinner as a friendly gesture.*

glacier (**glā**-shur) *n.* A **glacier** is a huge body of moving ice. *Many mountains are formed by moving glaciers.*

glory (**glor**-ē) *n.* **Glory** is a moment of great success. *Winning the science award was my greatest moment of glory.*

• **goal** (**gōl**) *n.* A **goal** is a purpose or what you want to happen. *Tim has a goal to read seven books this month.*

H

healthy (**hel**-thē) *adj.* Someone who is **healthy** is not sick. *Exercise will help keep you healthy.*

honest (**ahn**-ust) *adj.* An **honest** person tells the truth. *Abe Lincoln was known as Honest Abe because of his truthfulness.*

honor (**ahn**-ur) *n.* An **honor** is a symbol of high praise from others. *It is an honor to be given an award.*

human (**hyū**-man) **1** *adj.* To be **human** means to have the qualities of a person. *The gorillas at the zoo almost look human.* **2** *n.* People are also called **humans**.

I

• **identify** (ī-**den**-tu-fī) *v.* When you **identify** something, you recognize or discover it. *The fireman was glad to identify the cause of the fire.*

• **illustrate** (i-lus-**trāt**) *v.* To **illustrate** is to use pictures or examples to make something clear. *I will illustrate a book for art class.*

• **image** (**im**-ij) *n.* An **image** is a mental picture of something. *Matthew laughs at the image of his dog eating an ice cream cone.*

• **immigrant** (**im**-i-grint) *n.* An **immigrant** is someone who moves from one country to another country to live. *Many immigrants come to the U.S. to start new lives.*

improve (im-**prüv**) *v.* To **improve** something means to make it better. *Painting a house improves how it looks.*

• **interpret** (in-**tur**-prit) *v.* To **interpret** means to figure out or explain what something means. *The woman interpreted the speech through sign language.*

interrupt (int-u-**rupt**) *v.* To **interrupt** means to break into a conversation or activity. *It is impolite to interrupt a conversation.*

introduce (in-tru-**düs**) *v.* To **introduce** means to present someone by name. *You may introduce one friend to another.*

• **Academic Vocabulary**

invention (in-**ven**-shun) *n.* An **invention** is something that is made for the first time. *The telephone is an invention that lets people talk.*

invitation (in-vu-**tā**-shun) *n.* An **invitation** is a request for you to do something. *People getting married send wedding invitations.*

• **involve** (in-**vahlv**) *v.* To be **involved** means to be part of something. *A team involves people working together.*

J

• **job** (job) *n.* A **job** is work you do. *This person has a job in a restaurant.*

journey (**jur**-nē) *n.* A **journey** is a long trip. *People take a journey across the ocean in a ship.*

• **judgment** (**juj**-mint) *n.* A **judgment** is a decision or ruling. *In a court, a judge makes a judgment about who is right.*

K

knowledge (**nah**-lij) *n.* **Knowledge** is what you know. *When you learn new things, you add to your knowledge.*

L

league (lēg) *n.* A **league** is a group of teams that play the same sport. *My friends and I all play in our neighborhood baseball league.*

local (**lō**-cul) *adj.* **Local** means nearby. *My family goes to the local farmers' market every weekend to buy fresh vegetables.*

• **logical** (**lah**-ji-kul) *adj.* Something that is **logical** seems believable or reasonable. *It is logical to wear a coat when it is cold outside.*

M

machine (mu-**shēn**) *n.* A **machine** is a tool made of parts that does some kind of work. *You can make clothes with a sewing machine.*

marry (**mair**-ē) *v.* To **marry** means to join together. *When two people marry, they join together to make a family.*

melt (melt) *v.* To **melt** means to change from a solid to a liquid. *When the sun is out, the snow begins to melt.*

mighty (**mī**-tē) *adj.* To be **mighty** means to be powerful and strong. *Crocodiles have mighty jaws.*

• **model** (**mod**-ul) *n.* A **model** is a copy of something. *He builds models of motorcycles as a hobby.*

monster (**mahn**-ster) *n.* A **monster** is a scary creature. *The dinosaur was a terrifying monster.*

muscle (**mus**-ul) *n.* A **muscle** is an organ that gives you strength to move. *You can see and feel the muscles in your arm.*

museum (myū-**zē**-um) *n.* In a **museum**, people can look at art or other valuable objects. *Our class saw paintings at the museum.*

N

nonsense (**nahn**-sens) *n.* **Nonsense** is something that makes no sense. *Sometimes riddles are nonsense.*

notice (**nō**-tis) *v.* To **notice** something is to see or hear it. *You may notice the colors in a piece of art.*

O

obedient (ō-**bē**-dē-int) *adj.* When you're **obedient**, you do what you are told to do. *An obedient dog listens to commands.*

obey (ō-**bā**) *v.* To **obey** means to do what you are told. *The dogs obeyed their owner by sitting.*

odor (**ō**-dur) *n.* An **odor** is a smell. *The trash can has a strong odor.*

organ (**or**-gun) *n.* An **organ** is a body part that has a certain job to do. *Your heart and lungs are important organs.*

• **Academic Vocabulary**

- **organize** (**or**-gu-nīz) *v.* To **organize** means to arrange things in a certain order. *Mr. Holmes organizes his books in alphabetical order.*

- **original** (u-**rij**-in-ul) *adj.* Something that is **original** is the first of its kind. *The artist created an original painting for her neighbor.*

- **outcome** (**owt**-kum) *n.* An **outcome** is the result of something. *A scoreboard shows the outcome of a race.*

  oxygen (**ahk**-si-jen) *n.* **Oxygen** is the air we breathe. *We use extra oxygen to exercise.*

P

pastime (**pas**-tīm) *n.* A **pastime** is an activity that you often do for fun. *Cooking is my favorite pastime.*

patiently (**pā**-shent-lē) *adv.* When you do something **patiently**, you do not get upset. *My dog waits patiently outside while I buy a cup of coffee.*

peasant (**pe**-zint) *n.* A **peasant** is a European small farm worker. *Peasants worked hard for the things they had.*

- **perspective** (pur-**spek**-tiv) *n.* A **perspective** is a way of thinking about something. *The teacher and her student have a different perspective on homework.*

popular (**pop**-yū-lur) *adj.* To be **popular** means to be liked by many people. *Popcorn is a popular snack eaten at the movies.*

- **position** (pu-**zish**-un) *n.* Your **position** on an issue is what you think or believe about it. *Her position is that recycling is a good thing to do.*

possession (pu-**zesh**-un) *n.* A **possession** is something that belongs to someone. *A toy may be a child's favorite possession.*

poverty (**pah**-vur-tē) *n.* **Poverty** is the state or condition of being poor. *People who live in poverty may not have enough food to eat.*

powerful (**pow**-ur-ful) *adj.* People are **powerful** when they are strong. *The weightlifter showed off his powerful strength in the competition.*

practice (**prak**-tis) *v.* To **practice** means to do something in order to become better at it. *People must practice to become good musicians.*

- **Academic Vocabulary**

preserve (prē-**zurv**) *v.* To **preserve** means to keep something from being lost. *People celebrate certain holidays to preserve their culture.*

prevent (prē-**vent**) *v.* To **prevent** something means to keep it from happening. *Airbags can prevent injuries in a car crash.*

problem (**prah**-blum) *n.* A **problem** is something to be figured out. *He thought about the problem before he answered it.*

- **professional** (prō-**fesh**-un-ul) *adj.* A **professional** is someone who does a job for money. *My aunt is a professional dancer.*

protect (prō-**tekt**) *v.* To **protect** means to keep safe. *Mothers will do anything to protect their young.*

proud (**prowd**) *adj.* To be **proud** means to feel good about yourself. *You feel proud if you win a trophy.*

pump (**pump**) **1** *v.* To **pump** something is to push liquid from one place to another. *In some places, people pump water from wells.* **2** *n.* A **pump** is also something that pushes liquid. *People also use pumps to deliver water.*

- **purpose** (**pur**-pus) *n.* A **purpose** is a reason for doing something. *His purpose for going to the store was to buy milk.*

R

realize (**rē**-u-līz) *v.* To **realize** means to understand something. *I realized the correct answer too late.*

- **record** (ri-**kord**) *v.* When you **record**, you make a copy. *The singer recorded her song in a studio.*

recycle (rē-**sī**-kul) *v.* To **recycle** means to use again, usually in a different way. *People usually recycle glass, paper, and plastic.*

reef (**rēf**) *n.* A **reef** is a series of rocks or coral near the surface of the ocean. *A reef is home to many ocean animals.*

- **refer** (ri-**fur**) *v.* **Refer** means to relate to something that came before. *I will refer to the last chapter if I have trouble understanding this one.*

- **reflect** (ri-**flekt**) *v.* To **reflect** means to be a sign of something. *Manuel's good grades **reflect** his intelligence.*

- **region** (rē-jun) *n.* A **region** is a specific area. *The Arctic **region** is covered in snow and ice.*

- **release** (ri-**lēs**) *v.* When you **release** something, you let it go. *The woman **released** the balloon into the air.*

  remember (ri-**mem**-bur) *v.* When you **remember** something, you think of it again. *My sister always **remembers** where she puts her keys.*

- **research** (rē-**surch**) *v.* When you **research** something, you look for information about it. *I went to the library to **research** butterflies.*

- **resource** (rē-sors) *n.* A **resource** is something you can use. *Trees are a natural **resource** for wood used in house building.*

  respect (ri-**spekt**) *n.* When you have **respect** for someone, you have a good opinion of that person. *You show **respect** by being polite.*

- **response** (ri-**spons**) *n.* A **response** is an answer or reply. *A **response** can be either spoken or written.*

  riddle (**rid**-ul) *n.* A **riddle** is a puzzle or tricky question. *A person solves a **riddle** by finding the answer.*

- **role** (rōl) *n.* A **role** is a position someone has in a certain situation. *Luke does a great job in his **role** as the class leader.*

- **route** (rowt) *n.* A **route** is a path that leads somewhere. *The bridge is the quickest **route** to the other side of the river.*

  ruler (rü-lur) *n.* A **ruler** is a person who runs a country. *Elizabeth I is known by many as England's greatest **ruler**.*

S

scientist (**sī**-en-tist) *n.* A **scientist** studies things in nature. *The **scientist** used a microscope to look at cells.*

- **search** (surch) **1** *v.* To **search** for something means to look for it. **2** *n.* A **search** is the act of looking for something. *They are on a **search** to find a missing person.*

- **section** (**sek**-shun) *n.* A **section** is one part of something. *I cut the sandwich into equal **sections**.*

  segregate (se-gri-gāt) *v.* **Segregate** means to separate or keep apart. *Gym classes usually **segregate** the boys and girls.*

- **sequence** (sē-kwens) *n.* The **sequence** of events is the order in which the events happen. *I do the same exercises in the same **sequence** every morning.*

  serious (sear-ē-us) *adj.* When you are **serious** about something, you feel that it is important. *Many people are **serious** about their work.*

  service (sur-vis) *n.* A **service** is something done to help someone else. *Free gift-wrapping is a **service** some stores provide.*

  settler (set-lur) *n.* **Settlers** are people who move to a new area to live. *American **settlers** worked hard to survive in their new homes.*

  shelter (shel-tur) *n.* A **shelter** is something that covers and protects you. *A bus **shelter** can protect you from the weather.*

  shore (shor) *n.* A **shore** is the land beside a large body of water. *A **shore** can be rocky or made of sand.*

- **similar** (si-mu-lur) *adj.* Things that are **similar** are almost the same. *The sisters look very **similar** to each other.*

- **situation** (si-chu-wā-shun) *n.* A **situation** is the context in which a word is used. *Some words have different meanings in different **situations**.*

  soil (soil) *n.* **Soil** is the dirt that covers the ground. *Most trees and plants need rich, wet **soil** to help them grow.*

- **solve** (solv) *v.* To **solve** a problem means to find the answer. *The girl **solved** the math problem on the board.*

- **Academic Vocabulary**

source (sors) *n.* A **source** is where something comes from. *Lakes are the **source** for much of our drinking water.*

special (spe-shul) *adj.* When something is **special**, it is different and important. *Your birthday is a **special** day.*

spirit (spear-ut) *n.* Your **spirit** is the kind of person you are. *Everyone likes my brother for his fun-loving **spirit**.*

spread (spred) *v.* When something **spreads**, it moves across a larger area. *Milk **spreads** all over the floor when spilled.*

squeaky (skwē-kē) *adj.* A **squeaky** noise is a high-pitched sound. *Mice make **squeaky** noises.*

starve (starv) *v.* To **starve** means to not have enough food to live. *If you do not eat for a long time, you will **starve**.*

stranger (strānj-ur) *n.* A **stranger** is someone you do not know. *Everyone at the party was a **stranger** to her.*

• **structure** (struk-chur) *n.* The **structure** of something is its arrangement or organization. *The **structure** of the bridge was very complex.*

suggestion (sug-jes-chun) *n.* A **suggestion** is an opinion or idea. *Some restaurants have boxes to leave **suggestions** on paper.*

• **survive** (sur-vīv) *v.* To **survive** means to get through something difficult. *Surgery wasn't fun, but I **survived**.*

• **symbol** (sim-bul) *n.* A **symbol** is an object that represents something else. *A red octagon is a **symbol** meaning "stop" in the United States.*

system (sis-tum) *n.* A **system** is a group of parts that work together to do a job. *People use a **system** of roads to drive to places more quickly.*

T

• **team** (tēm) *n.* A **team** is a group that works together. *The baseball **team** practices together in order to improve.*

temperature (tem-pur-u-chur) *n.* The **temperature** is how hot or cold something is. *The **temperature** in the United States is usually at its highest during the summer.*

tend (tend) *v.* When you **tend** something, you take care of it. *The man **tends** a plant by watering it.*

test (test) *v.* When you **test** something, you try it. *You should **test** your flashlight to see if the batteries work.*

throne (thrōn) *n.* A **throne** is a special chair where a royal person sits. *Kings, queens, and emperors sit on **thrones**.*

tool (tül) *n.* A **tool** is something that makes work easier. *A saw is a **tool** used to cut wood.*

• **topic** (tah-pik) *n.* A **topic** is something that you talk or write about. *The **topic** of the fireman's speech is fire safety.*

train (trān) *v.* When you **train** someone, you teach that person how to do something correctly. *A coach **trains** athletes.*

• **trait** (trāt) *n.* A **trait** is a quality or characteristic of something. *Honesty is an important personality **trait**.*

transplant (trans-plant) **1** *n.* A **transplant** is something taken from one place to another. *Heart **transplants** are becoming more common.* **2** *v.* To **transplant** something means to take it from one place to another. *Trees are sometimes **transplanted** from a forest to a park.*

trust (trust) *v.* To **trust** someone means to believe that they will do what is best for you. *The girl **trusts** her friend to catch her.*

U

• **unique** (yū-nēk) *adj.* Something that is **unique** is unusual or one of its kind. *That hairstyle is very **unique**.*

V

vein (vān) *n.* A **vein** is a blood vessel that carries blood to the heart. *You can see **veins** in your wrist through your skin.*

• **Academic Vocabulary**

ventricle (ven-tri-kul) *n.* A **vetricle** is a lower area of the heart. *The **ventricles** pump blood out of your heart.*

vessel (ves-ul) *n.* A **vessel** is a tube through which liquid travels in a living thing. *The **vessels** in a leaf deliver water to the plant.*

W

warning (wor-ning) *n.* A **warning** lets you know that there is danger ahead. *Traffic signs are **warnings** to drive carefully.*

waste (wāst) *n.* **Waste** is something that is left over or thrown away. *People put their **waste** outside to be picked up each week.*

weight (wāt) *n.* A **weight** is a heavy object used for exercise. *People lift **weights** to make their muscles stronger.*

welcome (wel-kum) *v.* When you **welcome** someone, you greet that person kindly. *We all **welcome** our relatives.*

• Academic Vocabulary Master Word List

adaptation	couple	impact	role
adjust	create	individual	route
adjustment	credit	inevitable	scale
affect	data	integrate	section
aid	debate	interpret	select
amend	decision	involve	sequence
analyze	define	job	series
appeal	definition	judgment	similar
application	demonstrate	literal	situation
appreciate	design	locate	solve
approach	despite	location	source
appropriate	device	logical	space
area	discover	media	specific
arrange	discuss	migrate	structure
assignment	distinguish	model	summarize
assist	effect	modify	support
associate	effectively	narrative	survive
assume	element	negative	symbol
attach	emerge	obvious	team
available	encounter	organize	technical
awareness	energy	origin	technique
belief	ensure	original	technology
benefit	environment	outcome	temporary
bond	equipment	perspective	theme
capable	establish	plan	topic
category	evaluate	position	tradition
challenge	evidence	positive	trait
chapter	exact	predict	unique
characteristic	experiment	professional	vary
classic	expert	promote	
collapse	explain	propaganda	
collect	explanation	purpose	
communicate	fact	react	
community	feature	record	
compare	force	refer	
compound	freedom	reflect	
concentrate	goal	region	
conflict	generate	relate	
connect	globe	release	
connotation	identify	report	
context	illustrate	research	
contrast	image	resource	
convince	immigrant	response	

• **Words in red appear in Level B.**

Literary Terms

A

Alliteration The repetition of the same sounds (usually consonants) at the beginning of words that are close together. **Example:** Molly makes magnificent mousse, though Pablo prefers pecan pie.

> *See also* **Repetition**

Allusion A key form of literary language, in which one text makes the reader think about another text that was written before it. Allusion can also mean a reference to a person, place, thing, or event that is not specifically named. **Example:** When Hannah wrote in her short story that vanity was the talented main character's "Achilles heel," her teacher understood that Hannah was referring to a character in a Greek myth. So, she suspected that the vanity of the main character in Hannah's short story would prove to be the character's greatest weakness.

> *See also* **Connotation; Literature; Poetry**

Argument A type of writing or speaking that supports a position or attempts to convince the reader or listener. Arguments include a claim that is supported by reasons and evidence.

> *See also* **Claim; Reason; Evidence**

Article A short piece of nonfiction writing on a specific topic. Articles appear in newspapers and magazines.

> *See also* **Expository nonfiction; Nonfiction**

Autobiography The story of a person's life, written by that person. **Example:** Mahatma Gandhi wrote an autobiography titled *Gandhi: An Autobiography: The Story of My Experiments With Truth*.

> *See also* **Diary; Journal; Personal narrative**

B

Biographical fiction A fictional story that is based on real events in the life of a real person. **Example:** Although the book *Farmer Boy* by Laura Ingalls Wilder is about her husband's childhood, the conversations between characters are from the author's imagination. They are based on what she thought the characters might have said at the time.

> *See also* **Biography; Fiction**

Biography The story of a person's life, written by another person.

> *See also* **Autobiography; Biographical fiction**

C

Character A person, an animal, or an imaginary creature in a work of fiction.

> *See also* **Characterization; Character traits**

Characterization The way a writer creates and develops a character. Writers use a variety of ways to bring a character to life: through descriptions of the character's appearance, thoughts, feelings, and actions; through the character's words; and through the words or thoughts of other characters.

> *See also* **Character; Character traits; Motive**

Character traits The special qualities of personality that writers give their characters.

> *See also* **Character; Characterization**

Claim A statement that clearly identifies an author's ideas or opinion.

> *See also* **Argument; Reason; Evidence**

Climax The turning point or most important event in a plot.

> *See also* **Falling action; Plot; Rising action**

Complication See **Rising action**

Conflict The main problem faced by a character in a story or play. The character may be involved in a struggle against nature, another character, or society. The struggle may also be between two elements in the character's mind.

> *See also* **Plot**

Connotation The feelings suggested by a word or phrase, apart from its dictionary meaning. **Example:** The terms "used car" and "previously owned vehicle" have different connotations. To most people, the phrase "previously owned vehicle" sounds better than "used car."

> *See also* **Denotation; Poetry**

D

Denotation The dictionary meaning of a word or phrase. Denotation is especially important in functional texts and other types of nonfiction used to communicate information precisely.

> *See also* **Connotation; Functional text; Nonfiction**

Descriptive language Language that creates a "picture" of a person, place, or thing—often using words that appeal to the five senses: sight, hearing, touch, smell, and taste. **Example:** The bright, hot sun beat down on Earth's surface. Where once a vibrant lake cooled the skin of hippos and zebras, only thin, dry cracks remained, reaching across the land like an old man's fingers, as far as the eye could see. The smell of herds was gone, and only silence filled the space.

> *See also* **Imagery**

Dialogue What characters say to each other. Writers use dialogue to develop characters, move the plot forward, and add interest. In most writing, dialogue is set off by quotation marks; in play scripts, however, dialogue appears without quotation marks.

Diary A book written by a person about his or her own life as it is happening. Unlike an autobiography, a diary is not usually meant to be published. It is made up of entries that are written shortly after events occur. The person writing a diary often expresses feelings and opinions about what has happened.

See also **Autobiography; Journal**

Drama A kind of writing in which a plot unfolds in the words and actions of characters performed by actors.

See also **Genre; Play; Plot**

E

Essay A short piece of nonfiction, normally in prose, that discusses a single topic without claiming to do so thoroughly. Its purpose may be to inform, entertain, or persuade.

See also **Nonfiction; Photo-essay; Topic**

Evidence Information provided to support a claim.

See also **Argument; Claim; Reasons**

Exaggeration Figurative language that makes things seem bigger than they really are in order to create a funny image in the reader's mind. **Example:** My eyes are so big they pop out of my face when I get surprised or angry.

See also **Figurative language; Hyperbole**

Exposition The rising action of a story in which characters and the problems they face are introduced.

See also **Rising action**

Expository nonfiction Writing that gives information and facts. It is usually divided into sections that give information about subtopics of a larger topic.

See also **Article; News feature; Nonfiction; Report; Textbook; Topic**

F

Fable A brief fictional narrative that teaches a lesson about life. Many fables have animals instead of humans as characters. Fables often end with a short, witty statement of their lesson. **Example:** "The Tortoise and the Hare" is a famous fable in which a boastful, quick-moving hare challenges a slow-moving tortoise to a race. Because the overconfident hare takes a nap during the race, the tortoise wins. The moral of the fable is that slow and steady wins the race.

See also **Fiction; Folk tale;**

Fairy tale *See* **Fantasy; Folk tale**

Falling action The actions and events in a plot that happen after the climax. Usually, the major problem is solved in some way, so the remaining events serve to bring the story to an end.

See also **Climax; Conflict; Plot, Rising action**

Fantasy Fiction in which imaginary worlds differ from the "real" world outside the text. Fairy tales, science fiction, and fables are examples of fantasy.

See also **Fable; Fiction**

Fiction Narrative writing about imaginary people, places, things, or events.

See also **Biographical fiction; Fable; Fantasy; Folk tale; Historical fiction; Myth; Novel; Realistic fiction; Short story**

Figurative language The use of a word or phrase to say one thing and mean another. Figurative language is especially important in literature and poetry because it gives writers a more effective way of expressing what they mean than using direct, literal language. **Example:** Upon receiving her monthly bills, Victoria complained that she was "drowning in debt."

See also **Exaggeration; Hyperbole; Idiom; Imagery; Literature; Metaphor; Personification; Poetry; Simile; Symbol**

Folk tale A short, fictional narrative shared orally rather than in writing, and thus partly changed through its retellings before being written down. Folk tales include myths, legends, fables, ghost stories, and fairy tales.

See also **Fable; Legend; Myth**

Folklore The collection of a people's beliefs, customs, rituals, spells, songs, sayings, and stories as shared mainly orally rather than in writing.

See also **Folk tale; Legend; Myth**

Functional text Writing in which the main purpose is to communicate the information people need to accomplish tasks in everyday life. **Examples:** résumés, business letters, technical manuals, and the help systems of word-processing programs.

G

Genre A type or class of literary works grouped according to form, style, and/or topic. Major genres include fictional narrative prose (such as short stories and most novels), nonfiction narrative prose (such as autobiographies, diaries, and journals), drama, poetry, and the essay.

See also **Essay; Fiction; Literature; Nonfiction; Poetry; Prose; Style; Topic**

H

Hero or **Heroine** In myths and legends, a man or woman of great courage and strength who is celebrated for his or her daring feats.

See also **Legend; Myth**

Historical fiction Fiction based on events that actually happened or on people who actually lived. It may be written from the point of view of a "real" or an imaginary character, and it usually includes invented dialogue.

See also **Fiction**

Hyperbole Figurative language that exaggerates, often to the point of being funny, to emphasize something. **Example:** When his mother asked how long he had

waited for the school bus that morning, Jeremy grinned and said, "Oh, not long. Only about a million years."
  See also **Exaggeration; Figurative language**

I

Idiom A phrase or expression that means something different from the word or words' dictionary meanings. Idioms cannot be translated word for word into another language because an idiom's meaning is not the same as that of the individual words that make it up. **Example:** "Mind your p's and q's" in English means to be careful, thoughtful, and behave properly.

Imagery Figurative language that communicates sensory experience. Imagery can help the reader imagine how people, places, and things look, sound, taste, smell, and feel. It can also make the reader think about emotions and ideas that commonly go with certain sensations. Because imagery appeals to the senses, it is sometimes called *sensory language*.
  See also **Descriptive language; Figurative language; Symbol**

Interview A discussion between two or more people in which questions are asked and answered so that the interviewer can get information. The record of such a discussion is also called an interview.

J

Jargon Specialized language used by people to describe things that are specific to their group or subject. **Example:** *Mouse* in a computer class means "part of a computer system," not "a rodent."

Journal A personal record, similar to a diary. It may include accounts of actual events, stories, poems, sketches, thoughts, essays, a collection of interesting information, or just about anything the writer wishes to include.
  See also **Diary**

L

Legend A very old story, usually written about a hero or heroine or to explain something in nature. Legends are mostly fiction, but some details may be true.
  See also **Folk tale; Hero or Heroine; Myth**

Literature Works written as prose or poetry.
  See also **Poetry; Prose**

M

Metaphor A type of figurative language that compares two unlike things by saying that one thing is the other thing. **Example:** Dhara says her grandfather can be a real mule when he doesn't get enough sleep.
  See also **Figurative language; Simile; Symbol**

Meter The patterning of language into regularly repeating units of rhythm. Language patterned in this way is called *verse*. By varying the rhythm within a meter, the writer can heighten the reader's attention to what is going on in the verse and reinforce meaning.
  See also **Poetry; Rhythm**

Mood The overall feeling or atmosphere a writer creates in a piece of writing.
  See also **Tone**

Motive The reason a character has for his or her thoughts, feelings, actions, or words. **Example:** Maria's motive for bringing cookies to her new neighbors was to learn what they were like.
  See also **Characterization**

Myth A fictional narrative, often a folk tale, that tells of supernatural events as a way of explaining natural events and their relation to human life. Myths commonly involve gods, goddesses, monsters, and superhuman heroes or heroines.
  See also **Folk tale; Hero** or **Heroine; Legend**

N

Narrative writing Writing that gives an account of a set of real or imaginary events (the story), which the writer selects and arranges in a particular order (the plot). Narrative writing includes nonfiction works such as news articles, autobiographies, and journals, as well as fictional works such as short stories, novels, and plays.
  See also **Autobiography; Fiction; Journal; Narrator; Nonfiction; Plot; Story**

Narrator Someone who gives an account of events. In fiction, the narrator is the teller of a story (as opposed to the real author, who invented the narrator as well as the story). Narrators differ in how much they participate in a story's events. In a first-person narrative, the narrator is the "I" telling the story. In a third-person narrative, the narrator is not directly involved in the events and refers to characters by name or as *he*, *she*, *it*, or *they*. Narrators also differ in how much they know and how much they can be trusted by the reader.
  See also **Character; Point of view**

News feature A nonfiction article that gives facts about real people and events.
  See also **Article; Expository nonfiction; Nonfiction**

Nonfiction Written works about events or things that are not imaginary; writing other than fiction.
  See also **Autobiography; Biography; Diary; Essay; Fiction; Journal; Personal narrative; Photo-essay; Report; Textbook**

Novel A long, fictional narrative, usually in prose. Its length enables it to have more characters, a more complicated plot, and a more fully developed setting than shorter works of fiction.
  See also **Character; Fiction; Plot; Prose; Setting; Short story**

O

Onomatopoeia The use of words that imitate the sounds they refer to. **Examples:** *buzz*, *slam*, *hiss*

P

Personal narrative An account of a certain event or set of events in a person's life, written by that person.
> *See also* **Autobiography; Diary; Journal**

Personification Figurative language that describes animals, things, or ideas as having human traits. **Examples:** In the movie *Babe* and in the book *Charlotte's Web*, the animals are all personified.
> *See also* **Figurative language**

Persuasive writing Writing that attempts to get someone to do or agree to something by appealing to logic or emotion. Persuasive writing is used in advertisements, editorials, and political speeches.

Photo-essay A short nonfiction piece made up of photographs and captions. The photographs are as important as the words in presenting information.
> *See also* **Essay; Nonfiction**

Play A work of drama, especially one written to be performed on a stage. **Example:** Lorraine Hansberry's *A Raisin in the Sun* was first performed in 1959.
> *See also* **Drama**

Plot The pattern of events and situations in a story or play. Plot is usually divided into four main parts: *conflict* (or *problem*), *rising action* (or *exposition* or *complication*), *climax*, and *falling action* (or *resolution*).
> *See also* **Climax; Conflict; Drama; Falling action; Fiction; Rising action; Story**

Poetry A form of literary expression that uses line breaks for emphasis. Poems often use connotation, imagery, metaphor, symbol, allusion, repetition, and rhythm. Word patterns in poetry include rhythm or meter, and often rhyme and alliteration.
> *See also* **Alliteration; Connotation; Figurative language; Meter; Repetition; Rhyme; Rhythm**

Point of view The position from which the events of a story seem to be observed and told. A first-person point of view tells the story through what the narrator knows, experiences, concludes, or can find out by talking to other characters. A third-person point of view may be *omniscient*, giving the narrator unlimited knowledge of things, events, and characters, including characters' hidden thoughts and feelings. Or it may be *limited* to what one or a few characters know and experience. **Example** of First-Person Point of View: I'm really hungry right now, and I can't wait to eat my lunch. **Example** of Third-Person Limited Point of View: Olivia is really hungry right now and she wants to eat her lunch. **Example** of Third-Person Omniscient Point of View: Olivia is really hungry right now and she wants to eat her lunch. The other students are thinking about their weekend plans.

The teacher is wondering how she will finish the lesson before the bell rings.
> *See also* **Character; Fiction; Narrator**

Propaganda A type of persuasion that twists or doesn't tell the whole truth. Types of propaganda include *glittering generalities* (using impressive words to skip past the truth), *transfers* (using appealing ideas or symbols that aren't directly related to the topic), *testimonials* (using the words of famous people), *plain folks* (showing that a product or idea has the same values as the audience), *bandwagon* (claiming that everyone else is doing it), and *name calling*.
> *See also* **Persuasive writing**

Prose A form of writing in which the rhythm is less regular than that of verse and more like that of ordinary speech.
> *See also* **Poetry; Rhythm**

Proverb A short saying that expresses a general truth. Proverbs are found in many different languages and cultures. **Example:** An apple a day keeps the doctor away.

Purpose An author's reason for writing. Most authors write to entertain, inform, or persuade. **Example:** An author's purpose in an editorial is to persuade the reader to think or do something.
> *See also* **Expository nonfiction; Narrative writing; Persuasive writing**

R

Realistic fiction Fiction in which detailed handling of imaginary settings, characters, and events produces a lifelike illusion of a "real" world. **Example:** Although Upton Sinclair's *The Jungle* is a work of fiction, the author's graphic, detailed descriptions of the slaughterhouse workers' daily lives led to real changes in the meatpacking industry.
> *See also* **Fiction**

Reason A logical explanation that connects a piece of evidence to a writer or speaker's claim.
> *See also* **Argument; Claim; Evidence**

Repetition The repeating of individual vowels and consonants, syllables, words, phrases, lines, or groups of lines. Repetition can be used because it sounds pleasant, to emphasize the words in which it occurs, or to help tie the parts of a text into one structure. It is especially important in creating the musical quality of poetry, where it can take such forms as alliteration and rhyme.
> *See also* **Alliteration; Poetry; Rhyme**

Report A usually short piece of nonfiction writing on a particular topic. It differs from an essay in that it normally states only facts and does not directly express the writer's opinions.
> *See also* **Essay; Nonfiction; Topic**

Resolution See **Falling action**

Rhyme The repetition of ending sounds in different words. Rhymes usually come at the end of lines of verse, but they may also occur within a line.
Examples: *look, brook, shook*
  See *also* **Poetry; Repetition; Rhyme scheme**

Rhyme scheme The pattern of rhymed line endings in a work of poetry or a stanza. It can be represented by giving a certain letter of the alphabet to each line ending on the same rhyme. **Example:** Because the end word of every other line rhymes in the following poem, the rhyme scheme is *abab*:

Winter night falls quick (a)
The pink sky gone, blackness overhead (b)
Looks like the snow will stick (a)
Down the street and up the hill I tread (b)
  See *also* **Poetry; Rhyme; Stanza**

Rhythm The natural rise and fall, or "beat," of language. Rhythm is present in all language, including speech and prose, but it is most obvious in poetry.
  See *also* **Meter; Poetry; Prose**

Rising action The part of a plot that presents actions or events that lead to the climax.
  See *also* **Climax; Conflict; Exposition; Falling action; Plot**

S

Setting The time and place in which the events of a story occur.

Short story A brief, fictional narrative. Like the novel, it organizes the action, thought, and dialogue of its characters into a plot. But it tends to focus on fewer characters and to center on a single event.
  See *also* **Character; Fiction; Novel; Plot; Story**

Simile A type of figurative language that compares two unlike things by using a word or phrase such as *like, as, than, similar to, resembles,* or *seems.*
Examples: The tall, slim man had arms as willowy as a tree's branches. The woman's temper is like an unpredictable volcano.
  See *also* **Figurative language; Metaphor**

Song lyrics Words meant to be sung. Lyrics have been created for many types of songs, including love songs, religious songs, work songs, sea chanties, and children's game songs. Lyrics for many songs were shared orally for generations before being written down. Not all song lyrics are lyrical like poems; some are the words to songs that tell a story. Not all poems called songs were written to be sung.
  See *also* **Folklore; Poetry**

Speech A message on a specific topic, spoken before an audience; also, spoken (not written) language.

Stanza A group of lines that forms a section of a poem and has the same pattern (including line lengths, meter, and usually rhyme scheme) as other sections of the same poem. In printed poems, stanzas are separated from each other by a space.
  See *also* **Meter; Poetry; Rhyme scheme**

Story A series of events (actual or imaginary) that can be selected and arranged in a certain order to form a narrative or dramatic plot. It is the raw material from which the finished plot is built. Although there are technical differences, the word *story* is sometimes used in place of *narrative.*
  See *also* **Drama; Plot**

Style The way a writer uses language to express the feelings or thoughts he or she wants to convey. Just as no two people are alike, no two styles are exactly alike. A writer's style results from his or her choices of vocabulary, sentence structure and variety, imagery, figurative language, rhythm, repetition, and other resources.
  See *also* **Figurative language; Genre; Imagery; Repetition; Rhythm**

Symbol A word or phrase that serves as an image of some person, place, thing, or action but that also calls to mind some other, usually broader, idea or range of ideas. **Example:** An author might describe doves flying high in the sky to symbolize peace.
  See *also* **Figurative language; Imagery**

T

Textbook A book prepared for use in schools for the study of a subject.

Theme The underlying message or main idea of a piece of writing. It expresses a broader meaning than the topic of the piece.
  See *also* **Topic**

Tone A writer's or speaker's attitude toward his or her topic or audience or toward him- or herself. A writer's tone may be positive, negative, or neutral. The words the writer chooses, the sentence structure, and the overall pattern of words convey the intended tone.
  See *also* **Connotation; Figurative language; Literature; Mood; Rhythm; Topic**

Topic What or who is being discussed in a piece of writing; the subject of the piece.
  See *also* **Theme**

Index of Skills

A

Academic vocabulary 6, 8, 90, 91, 94, 101, 122, 129, 140, 164, 170, 174, 176, 183, 196, 203, 218, 225, 248, 252, 258, 265, 278, 285, 305, 320, 326, 330, 334, 341, 361, 381, 402, 406, 408, 415, 426, 433, 442, 449, 466, 470, 474, 476, 483, 500, 518, 525, 538, 542, 546, 548, 555, 570, 577, 590, 597, 614, 618, 672

Adjectives 180–181, 197, 200, 222
  comparative 200–201, 219
  descriptive 615
  participles as 594–595
  possessive 282–283, 299

Adverbs 222–223, 249

Analyze 121, 183, 253, 402, 569

Antonyms 164, 298

Argument 546–547, 555, 556, 577, 619

Ask questions 11, 13, 15, 31, 143, 145, 165, 341, 361, 381, 403, 471, 630

Author's purpose 120, 415, 424

Author's style 276, 532

Author's viewpoint 406–407, 433, 471, 538, 609

B

Base words 8–9, 176–177

Book talk 87, 171, 253, 327, 403, 471, 543, 619

Build background 10, 32, 60, 96, 124, 142, 178, 198, 220, 260, 280, 300, 336, 356, 376, 410, 428, 444, 478, 502, 520, 550, 572, 592

C

Cause and effect 15, 73, 78, 189, 203, 209, 217, 272, 291, 293, 296, 348, 369, 389, 395, 437, 440, 464, 487, 491, 559, 563, 585

Character 49, 90–93, 129, 130, 133, 157, 162, 171, 189, 196, 341, 470, 533
  actions 91, 129, 196
  motives 117, 133, 157, 345, 453, 600
  traits 91, 129
  viewpoint 43, 53, 112, 117, 162, 192, 457, 525, 529

Characterization 91

Chorus 147

Chronological order 256–257, 305, 327, 474–475, 483, 543

Clarify and verify 429, 431, 443

Clauses 504, 522

Compare 29, 79, 195–196, 199–201, 219, 247, 277, 319, 337–339, 355, 357, 359, 375, 397, 402, 465, 499, 569
  author's style 542
  characters 196, 470
  details 25
  fiction and nonfiction 225, 374, 403, 542
  media 507
  setting 470
  themes 170, 618
  topics 326, 361
  writing on the same topic 86, 252

Compare across text 86, 170, 217, 225, 252, 326, 402, 632

Compare and contrast 21, 69, 77, 112, 238, 246, 275, 291, 317, 331, 345, 372, 385, 439, 487

Compound words 8–9, 30

Conclusions, draw 23, 47, 57, 79, 135, 139, 164, 209, 211, 215, 247, 269, 293, 352, 365, 367, 369, 372, 391, 421, 424, 489, 495, 498, 513, 533, 536, 631

Connections, make 37, 415, 433, 449, 627

Connotation/denotation 570

Content library 1, 87, 89, 171, 173, 253, 255, 327, 329, 403, 405, 471, 473, 543, 545, 619

Context clues 107, 120, 298, 396, 398, 437, 491
  definition 258–259, 278
  example 258–259, 320
  multiple-meaning words 476–477, 500, 538
  restatement 258–259, 278
  specialized vocabulary 548–549

Conversation 97, 99, 248

Critical thinking
  analyze 121, 569
  compare 29, 79, 163, 195, 217, 247, 277, 319, 397, 425, 465, 499, 569
  describe 29, 297, 373, 613
  draw conclusions 57, 79, 139, 247
  evaluate 121, 247, 319, 373, 441, 517, 537
  explain 29, 57, 139, 163, 217, 297, 353, 397, 425, 499, 589
  infer 195, 277, 441, 537
  interpret 195, 373, 537
  make judgments 57, 79, 121, 139, 163, 217, 277, 353, 397, 425, 499, 569, 613
  paraphrase 319, 441, 465, 589
  speculate 29, 297, 517, 589
  summarize 29, 57, 79, 121, 139, 163, 195, 217, 247, 277, 297, 319, 353, 373, 397, 425, 441, 465, 499, 517, 537, 569, 589, 613

Critical viewing 140, 151, 153, 157, 159, 194, 229, 230, 232, 234, 237, 239, 241, 313, 368, 396, 401, 496, 529, 531, 532–533

D

Define and explain 261, 263, 279

Describe 29, 47, 179, 181, 197, 221, 223, 297, 345, 373, 613

Details 28, 457, 587

Dialogue 147

Differences, explore 201, 263, 339

Digital library 10, 32, 60, 96, 124, 142, 178, 198, 220, 260, 280, 300, 336, 356, 376, , 410, 428, 444, 478, 502, 520, 550, 572, 592

Directions, give and follow 281, 283, 299

Discuss 87, 171, 253, 327, 353, 403, 465, 471, 517, 543, 613, 619

Discussion 301, 303, 321, 595

Drama, analyze elements of 147, 169, 612

Draw 87, 253, 327, 403, 471, 543

E

Elaborate 521, 523, 539

Evaluate 121, 247, 319, 373, 441, 517, 537

Evidence 47, 211, 352, 367, 391, 424, 513, 518, 556, 577, 578

Explain 25, 28, 29, 43, 49, 57, 73, 139, 163, 207, 209, 216, 217, 238, 289, 296, 297, 353, 393, 397, 419, 439, 464, 499, 563, 589, 600, 606

F

Fact and opinion 529

Fiction, elements of *see* Character, Plot, Setting

Figurative language 151, 238, 334–335, 396, 497, 548, 609, 614
  idioms 334–335, 374, 398
  metaphor 194, 233, 276, 317, 334–335, 391
  personification 334–335, 354, 398
  simile 318, 334–335

G

Generalizations, make 632

Genre
  article 244, 434, 435
  autobiography 306
  biographical fiction 226
  biography 508
  city profile 370
  classic short story 450
  drama 148
  environmental report 578
  fiction 166
  folk tale 130, 141
  historical fiction 342
  history article 362, 484
  history textbook 382
  informational text 538
  interview 566
  legend 598
  log 400
  magazine article 66, 416
  myth 161
  narrative nonfiction 474
  nonfiction 82, 322, 400, 468, 469, 540
  online news article 434
  personal narrative 216
  persuasive essay 556
  persuasive writing 546, 555
  photo-essay 459
  play 148
  poetry 194, 250, 276, 318, 320, 396, 424, 496–497, 608, 610–611
  realistic fiction 184
  science article 16, 266, 286
  short story 38, 102, 526
  social science textbook 204
  song lyrics 33, 221, 281, 498
  speech 616
  technical directions 588

Glossary 662

Grammar
  clauses 504, 522
  participles 594–595
  predicates 62–63, 81, 412–413, 446–447, 480–481, 501

Index of Authors and Titles

Index of Art and Artists

Acknowledgments, continued from page ii

Grateful acknowledgement is also given for permission to provide audio recordings of literature and informational text selections included in this book.

John Agard c/o Caroline Sheldon Literary Agency: Excerpt from *Old World New World* by John Agard. copyright © 2002 by John Agard reproduced by kind permission of John Agard c/o Caroline Sheldon Literary Agency Limited.

Connect for Kids: Adapted from "Angels in the Snow" by Holly St. Lifer from Connect for Kids, managed by the Forum for Youth Investment. Used by permission.

Darby Creek Publishing: "Two Left Feet, Two Left Hands, and Too Left on the Bench" by David Lubar. Copyright © 2005 by David Lubar by arrangement with Darby Creek Publishing.

Amelia Fusion: Excerpt from *The Log of Christopher Columbus*, translated by Robert H. Fusion. Copyright © 1987 by Robert H. Fusion. Reprinted by permission of Amelia Fusion

HarperCollins Publishers: "Zlateh the Goat," by Isaac Bashevis Singer from *Zlateh the Goat and Other Stories*. Text copyright © 1966 by Isaac Bashevis Singer, copyright renewed 1994 by Alma Singer, Used by permission of HarperCollins Publishers.

"Possum Crossing" by Nikki Giovanni from *Quilting the Black-Eyed Pea*. Copyright © 2002 by Nikki Giovanni. Reprinted by permission of HarperCollins Publishers, William Morrow.

Houghton Mifflin Harcourt Publishing Company: "The Challenge" by Gary Soto from *Local News*. Copyright © 1993 by Gary Soto. Reprinted by permission of Houghton Mifflin Harcourt Publishing Company. All rights reserved.

Excerpt from *Encounter* by Jane Yolen. Text copyright © 1992 by Jane Yolen, illustrations copyright © 1992 by David Shannon. Reproduced by permission of Houghton Mifflin Harcourt Publishing Company.

Excerpt from *The Lotus Seed* by Sherry Garland. Text copyright © 1993 by Sherry Garland, illustrations copyright © 1993 by Tatsuro Kiuchi. Reproduced by permission of Houghton Mifflin Harcourt Publishing Company. All rights reserved.

Excerpts from *The Hobbit* by J.R.R. Tolkein. Copyright © 1937 by George Allen & Unwin Ltd., © 1966 by J.R.R. Tolkein, © renewed 1994 by Christopher R. Tolkein, John F.R. Tolkein. Copyright © restored 1996 by the Estate of J.R.R. Tolkein, assigned 1997 to the J.R.R. Tolkein Copyright Trust. Reprinted by permission of Houghton Mifflin Harcourt Publishing Company and HarperCollins, Ltd. All rights reserved.

Lee and Low Books, Inc.: Excerpt from *Brothers in Hope: The Story of the Lost Boys of the Sudan* by Mary Williams. Text copyright © 2005 by Mary Williams. Permission arranged with Lee & Low Books, Inc., New York, NY 10016.

Lensey Namioka: "Laff" by Lensey Namioka from *Within Reach*, edited By Donald R. Gallo. Copyright 1993 by Lensey Namioka. Reprinted by permission of Lensey Namioka. All rights are reserved by the author.

Lerner Publishing Group, Inc.: "The Kids' Invention Book" by Arlene Erlbach. Copyright © 1997 by Arlene Erlbach. Reprinted with the permission of Lerner Publications Company, a division of Lerner Publishing Group, Inc. All rights reserved. No part of this excerpt may be used or reproduced in any manner whatsoever without the prior written permission of Lerner Publishing Group, Inc.

Literary Estate of May Swenson: "Analysis Baseball" by May Swenson. Copyright © 1978 by May Swenson. Reprinted with the permission of the Literary Estate of May Swenson.

LifeTime Media, Inc.: Excerpt from *Pressure is a Privilege* by Billie Jean King, foreword by Christine Brennan. Copyright © 2008 by Billie Jean King. Reprinted by permission by LifeTime Media, Inc. All rights reserved.

National Geographic Society: "Going Green with Cameron Diaz" by Rachel Buchholz, from "Welcome to the Green Issue" by Rachel Buchholz, from *National Geographic Kids*, October 2007. Used by permission of National Geographic Image Collection.

"Bionics" by John Fishman from *National Geographic*, January 2010. Copyright © 2010 by the National Geographic Society. Reprinted by permission of the National Geographic Society. All rights reserved.

Excerpt from "A Conflict Close to Home" from *A Blog for Peace in Israel-Palestine* by Aziz Abu Sarah. from NationalGeographic.com. Reprinted by permission of the National Geographic Society. All rights reserved.

Penguin Group (USA), Inc.: "The Wonder Dog" by from *Heroes and She-Roes: Poems of Amazing Everyday Heroes* by J. Patrick Lewis. Copyright © 2005 by J. Patrick Lewis. Used by permission of Dial Books for Young Readers, A Division of Penguin Young Readers Group, A Member of Penguin Group (USA) Inc., 345 Hudson Street, New York, NY 10014. All rights reserved.

"How Coach Told Me I Didn't Make the Cut" by Gary Soto from *Fearless Fernie: Hanging Out with Fernie and Me*. Copyright © 2002 by Gary Soto. Used by permission of G.P. Putnam's Sons, A Division of Penguin Young Readers Group, A Member of Penguin Group (USA) Inc., 345 Hudson Street, New York, NY 10014. All rights reserved.

Random House, Inc.: Excerpt and adaptation of "Raymond's Run" by Toni Cade Bambara from *Gorilla, My Love*. Copyright © 1971 by Toni Cade Bambara. Used by permission of Random House, Inc.

Marian Reiner: Excerpt rom *Rachel the Clever and Other Jewish Folktales* by Josepha Sherman. Copyright © 1993 by Josepha Sherman. Published by August House Publishers. Reprinted by permission of Marian Reiner on their behalf.

Alberto Alvaro Ríos: "The Lemon Story" from *Capriotada: A Nogales Memoir* by Alberto Alvaro Ríos. Copyright © 1999 by Alberto Alvaro Ríos. Used by permission of the author.

Simon & Schuster, Inc.: Excerpt from *Roberto Clemente* by Jonah Winter, illustrated by Raul Colon. Text copyright © 2005 by Jonah Winter. Illustrations copyright © 2005 by Raul Colon. Reprinted by arrangement with Atheneum, an Imprint of Simon & Schuster Children's Publishing Division. All rights reserved.

Excerpt from *Abundance: The Future is Better than You Think* by Peter H. Diamandis and Steven Kotler. Copyright © 2012 by Peter H. Diamandis and Steven Kotler. Reprinted with the permission of Free Press of Simon & Schuster. All rights reserved.

TIME for Kids: "Refugees Find New Lives" by Ritu Upadhyay from "Sudan's Lost Boys Find a Home: Young survivors start a new life in the U.S." by Ritu Upadhyay from *Time for Kids*, February 22, 2002. Copyright © 2002 by Time, Inc. By permission of Time, Inc. All rights reserved.

Walker and Company, Inc.: "Yakwawiak" by Joseph and James Bruchac from *When the Chenoo Howls: Native American Tales of Terror*. Reprinted by permission of Walker & Co.

Janet Wong: "A Suitcase of Seaweed" *A Suitcase Full of Seaweed* by Janet S. Wong. Copyright © 1996 by Janet S. Wong. Reprinted by permission of the author.

Photography

Cover, Back cover Andrew Masur/Getty Images. **1** ©Thomas Hoepker/Magnum Photos. **4** ©Aleksandr Markin/Shutterstock.com. **5** ©Andersen Ross/Blend Images/Jupiter Images. **6** ©a katz/Shutterstock.com. **9** ©C Squared Studios/ Photodisc/Getty Images. **9** ©Bettmann/ Bettmann Premium/Corbis. **10** ©Nick Caloyianis. **11** ©The Image Bank (Mike Kelly)/Getty Images. **11** ©Warren Morgan/Corbis. **12** ©Brian J. Skerry/ National Geographic. **12** ©Paul Nicklen/National Geographic. **12** ©Mike Parry/Minden Pictures/ Getty Images. **13** ©Erick Higuera Baja Mexico/ Flickr/Getty Images. **13** ©Wolfgang Poelzer/ WaterFrame/Getty Images. **13** ©Reinhard Dirscherl/WaterFrame/Getty Images. **14** ©Plush Studios/Blend Images/Alamy. **14** ©LWA/Dann Tardif/Blend Images/Getty Images. **14** ©Steve Winter/National Geographic. **14** ©Randy Faris/ Cardinal/Corbis. **14** ©Randy Faris/Corbis. **14** ©Scott Indermaur/Jupiterimages. **14** ©Melissa King/iStockphoto. **14** ©Joyce and Frank Burek/ AnimalsAnimals. **16–17, 18** ©Jonathan Bird/Peter Arnold/Getty Images. **19** ©James Watt/Animals Animals. **19** ©Birgit Buhleier/National Geographic Remote Imaging. **20–21** ©Greg Marshall/National Geographic Remote Imaging. **22** ©Nick Caloyianis/ National Geographic Remote Imaging. **23** ©Greg Marshall/National Geographic Remote Imaging. **23** ©Mehdi Bakhtiari/National Geographic Remote Imaging. **24** ©Joel Sartore/National Geographic. **25** ©Courtesy of Shark Research Center Iziko Museums of Cape Town South Africa. **25** ©Kira Fuchs/National Geographic Remote Imaging. **25** ©Allan Ligon/National Geographic Remote Imaging. **26** ©National Geographic Remote Imaging. **26** ©Bob Cranston/Animals Animals. **27** ©Marshall Greg/National Geographic. **28** ©Marshall Greg/National Geographic. **34** ©Ocean/ Corbis. **36** ©Tim Ridley/Dorling Kindersley/Getty Images. **36** ©Paul Barton/Corbis. **36** ©Bettmann/ Corbis. **36** ©Chad Ehlers/Alamy. **36** ©Randy Faris/ Cardinal/Corbis. **36** ©Barry St Photography/Alamy. **36** ©Westend61/Getty Images. **56** ©R C. Pian. **59** ©Lambert/Archive Photos/Getty Images. **60** ©Michael Goulding KRT/Newscom. **60, 67** ©Gala Narezo/Getty Images. **60, 67** ©Lauren Nicole/ Digital Vision/Getty Images. **61** ©John A. Rizzo/ Photodisc/Getty Images. **61** ©Hugh Threlfall/ Alamy. **61** ©Michael Newman/PhotoEdit. **61** ©LWA–Sharie Kennedy/Corbis. **62** ©Jutta Klee/ Comet/Corbis. **64** ©Peter Dazeley/Photographer's Choice/Getty Images. **64** ©Tetra Images/Jupiter Images. **64** ©Tetra Images/Corbis. **64** ©Construction Photography/Ramble/Corbis. **64** ©Somos/Veer/Getty Images. **64** ©Polka Dot Images/Jupiterimages. **64** ©Thinkstock/ Jupiterimages/Alamy. **66** ©rubberball/Getty Images. **68** ©Siede Preis/Photodisc. **68** ©Greater Farmington Chamber of Commerce. **69** ©rubberball/Getty Images. **69** ©James Woodson/ Photodisc/Getty Images. **69** ©United States Patent and Trademark Office. **70** ©Stockbyte/Getty Images. **70** ©Lerner Publishing Group. **70–71** ©Sergey Shlyaev/Fotolia. **71** ©Stockbyte/Getty Images. **72** ©Thomas Northcut/Photodisc/Getty Images. **72** ©Thomas Northcut/Photodisc/Getty Images. **72** ©Lerner Publishing Group. **73** ©Chemistry/Photographer's

Common Core State Standards

Unit 1   Imagine the Possibilities

Unit Launch

Pages	Lesson	Code	Standards Text
0–1	**Unit Opener**	SL.7.1	Engage effectively in a range of collaborative discussions (one-on-one, in groups, and teacher-led) with diverse partners on grade 7 topics, texts, and issues, building on others' ideas and expressing their own clearly.
2–7	**Focus on Reading** **Reading Strategies:** Plan, Monitor, Visualize, Determine Importance, Ask Questions, Make Connections, Make Inferences, Synthesize	RI.7.1	Cite several pieces of textual evidence to support analysis of what the text says explicitly as well as inferences drawn from the text.
		RL.7.1	Cite several pieces of textual evidence to support analysis of what the text says explicitly as well as inferences drawn from the text.
	Literary Analysis:	RL.7.2	Determine a theme or central idea of a text and analyze its development over the course of the text; provide an objective summary of the text.
	Use Text Evidence, Determine Main Idea, Use Context Clues, Make Inferences	RL.7.10	By the end of the year, read and comprehend literature, including stories, dramas, and poems, in the grades 6–8 text complexity band proficiently, with scaffolding as needed at the high end of the range.
8–9	**Focus on Vocabulary** Use Word Parts	RL.7.4	Determine the meaning of words and phrases as they are used in a text, including figurative and connotative meanings; analyze the impact of rhymes and other repetitions of sounds (e.g., alliteration) on a specific verse or stanza of a poem or section of a story or drama.
		RI.7.4	Determine the meaning of words and phrases as they are used in a text, including figurative, connotative, and technical meanings; analyze the impact of a specific word choice on meaning and tone.
		L.7.4.b	Determine or clarify the meaning of unknown and multiple-meaning words and phrases based on grade 7 reading and content, choosing flexibly from a range of strategies. Use common, grade-appropriate Greek or Latin affixes and roots as clues to the meaning of a word (e.g., *belligerent, bellicose, rebel*).

Selection 1 Hitching a Ride

Pages	Lesson	Code	Standards Text
10	**Connect**	SL.7.2	Analyze the main ideas and supporting details presented in diverse media and formats (e.g., visually, quantitatively, orally) and explain how the ideas clarify a topic, text, or issue under study.
11–13	**Language & Grammar** Ask and Answer Questions	SL.7.1.c	Engage effectively in a range of collaborative discussions (one-on-one, in groups, and teacher-led) with diverse partners on grade 7 topics, texts, and issues, building on others' ideas and expressing their own clearly. Pose questions that elicit elaboration and respond to others' questions and comments with relevant observations and ideas that bring the discussion back on topic as needed.
	Use Different Kinds of Sentences	L.7.1	Demonstrate command of the conventions of standard English grammar and usage when writing or speaking.
		L.7.2	Demonstrate command of the conventions of standard English capitalization, punctuation, and spelling when writing.
14	**Key Vocabulary**	RI.7.4	Determine the meaning of words and phrases as they are used in a text, including figurative, connotative, and technical meanings; analyze the impact of a specific word choice on meaning and tone.
15	**Reading Strategy** Plan, Monitor, and Ask Questions	RI.7.1	Cite several pieces of textual evidence to support analysis of what the text says explicitly as well as inferences drawn from the text.
	Literary Analysis Use Text Evidence	RI.7.10	By the end of the year, read and comprehend literary nonfiction in the grades 6–8 text complexity band proficiently, with scaffolding as needed at the high end of the range.

Common Core State Standards, continued

Selection 1 Hitching a Ride, continued

Pages	Lesson	Code	Standards Text
16–28	**Reading Selection**	RI.7.1	Cite several pieces of textual evidence to support analysis of what the text says explicitly as well as inferences drawn from the text.
		RI.7.2	Determine two or more central ideas in a text and analyze their development over the course of the text; provide an objective summary of the text.
		RI.7.10	By the end of the year, read and comprehend literary nonfiction in the grades 6–8 text complexity band proficiently, with scaffolding as needed at the high end of the range.
29	**Connect Reading and Writing** Critical Thinking	RI.7.1	Cite several pieces of text evidence to support analysis of what the text says explicitly as well as inferences drawn from the text.
		RI.7.2	Determine two or more central ideas in a text and analyze their development over the course of the text; provide an objective summary of the text.
	Vocabulary Review	L.7.6	Acquire and use accurately grade-appropriate general academics and domain-specific words and phrases; gather vocabulary knowledge when considering a word or phrase important to comprehension or expression.
	Write About the GQ	W.7.9	Draw evidence from literary or informational texts to support analysis, reflection, and research.
		W.7.10	Write routinely over extended time frames (time for research, reflection, and revision) and shorter time frames (a single sitting or a day or two) for a range of discipline-specific tasks, purposes, and audiences.
30	**Vocabulary Study** Use Compound Words	RI.7.4	Determine the meaning of words and phrases as they are used in a text, including figurative, connotative, and technical meanings; analyze the impact of a specific word choice on meaning and tone.
30	**Researching/Speaking** Study an Endangered Species	SL.7.1.a	Engage effectively in a range of collaborative discussions (one-on-one, in groups, and teacher-led) with diverse partners on grade 7 topics, texts, and issues, building on others' ideas and expressing their own clearly. Come to discussions prepared, having read or researched material under study; explicitly draw on that preparation by referring to evidence on the topic, text, or issue to probe and reflect on ideas under discussion.
		SL.7.2	Analyze the main ideas and supporting details presented in diverse media and formats (e.g., visually, quantitatively, orally) and explain how the ideas clarify a topic, text, or issue under study.
		SL.7.5	Include multimedia components and visual displays in presentations to clarify claims and findings and emphasize salient points.
31	**Language and Grammar** Ask and Answer Questions	SL.7.1.c	Engage effectively in a range of collaborative discussions (one-on-one, in groups, and teacher-led) with diverse partners on grade 7 topics, texts, and issues, building on others' ideas and expressing their own clearly. Pose questions that elicit elaboration and respond to others' questions and comments with relevant observations and ideas that bring the discussion back on topic as needed.
		L.7.1	Demonstrate command of the conventions of standard English grammar and usage when writing or speaking.

Selection 1 Hitching a Ride, continued

Pages	Lesson	Code	Standards Text
31	**Writing and Grammar** Write About New Ideas	W.7.3.d	Write narratives to develop real or imagined experiences or events using effective technique, relevant descriptive details, and well-structured event sequences. Use precise words and phrases, relevant descriptive details, and sensory language to capture the action and convey experiences and events.
		L.7.1	Demonstrate command of the conventions of standard English grammar and usage when writing or speaking.
		L.7.2	Demonstrate command of the conventions of standard English capitalization, punctuation, and spelling when writing.

Selection 2 LAFFF

Pages	Lesson	Code	Standards Text
32	**Connect**	SL.7.2	Analyze the main ideas and supporting details presented in diverse media and formats (e.g., visually, quantitatively, orally) and explain how the ideas clarify a topic, text, or issue under study.
33–35	**Language & Grammar** Express Ideas and Feelings	SL.7.1	Engage effectively in a range of collaborative discussions (one-on-one, in groups, and teacher-led) with diverse partners on grade 7 topics, texts, and issues, building on others' ideas and expressing their own clearly.
		SL.7.5	Include multimedia components and visual displays in presentations to clarify claims and findings and emphasize salient points.
	Use Nouns	L.7.1	Demonstrate command of the conventions of standard English grammar and usage when writing or speaking.
		L.7.2	Demonstrate command of the conventions of standard English capitalization, punctuation, and spelling when writing.
		L.7.2.b	Demonstrate command of the conventions of standard English capitalization, punctuation, and spelling when writing. Spell correctly.
		L.7.3.a	Use knowledge of language and its conventions when writing, speaking, reading, or listening. Choose language that expresses ideas precisely and concisely, recognizing and eliminating wordiness and redundancy.
36	**Key Vocabulary**	RL.7.4	Determine the meaning of words and phrases as they are used in a text, including figurative and connotative meanings; analyze the impact of rhymes and other repetitions of sounds (e.g., alliteration) on a specific verse or stanza of a poem or section of a story or drama.
37	**Reading Strategy** Make Connections, Make Inferences, Visualize **Literary Analysis** Use Text Evidence, Make Inferences	RL.7.1	Cite several pieces of textual evidence to support analysis of what the text says explicitly as well as inferences drawn from the text.
		RL.7.10	By the end of the year, read and comprehend literature, including stories, dramas, and poems, in the grades 6–8 text complexity band proficiently, with scaffolding as needed at the high end of the range.

Common Core State Standards, continued

Pages	Lesson	Code	Standards Text
38–56	**Reading Selection**	RL.7.1	Cite several pieces of textual evidence to support analysis of what the text says explicitly as well as inferences drawn from the text.
		RL.7.2	Determine a theme or central idea of a text and analyze its development over the course of the text; provide an objective summary of the text.
		RL.7.3	Analyze how particular elements of a story or drama interact (e.g., how setting shapes the characters or plot).
		RL.7.6	Analyze how an author develops and contrasts the points of view of different characters or narrators in a text.
		RL.7.10	By the end of the year, read and comprehend literature, including stories, dramas, and poems, in the grades 6–8 text complexity band proficiently, with scaffolding as needed at the high end of the range.
57	**Connect Reading and Writing** Critical Thinking	RL.7.2	Determine a theme or central idea of a text and analyze its development over the course of the text; provide an objective summary of the text.
	Vocabulary Review	L.7.6	Acquire and use accurately grade-appropriate general academic and domain-specific words and phrases; gather vocabulary knowledge when considering a word or phrase important to comprehension or expression.
	Write About the GQ	W.7.9	Draw evidence from literary or informational texts to support analysis, reflection, and research.
		W.7.10	Write routinely over extended time frames (times for research, reflection, and revision) and shorter time frames (a single sitting or a day or two) for a range of discipline-specific tasks, purposes, and audiences.
58	**Vocabulary Study** Use Prefixes	RL.7.4	Determine the meaning of words and phrases as they are used in a text, including figurative and connotative meanings; analyze the impact of rhymes and of repetitions of sounds (e.g. alliteration) on a specific verse or stanza of a poem or section of a story or drama.
		L.7.4.b	Determine or clarify the meaning of unknown and multiple-meaning words and phrases based on grade 7 reading and content, choosing flexibly from a range of strategies. Use common, grade-appropriate Greek or Latin affixes and roots as clue to the meaning of words (e.g., *belligerent, bellicose, rebel*).
58	**Literary Analysis** Analyze Plot	RL.7.3	Analyze how particular elements of a story or drama interact (e.g., how setting shapes the characters or plot).
59	**Language and Grammar** Express Ideas and Feelings	SL.7.1	Engage effectively in a range of collaborative discussions (one-on-one, in groups, and teacher-led) with diverse partners on grade 7 topics, texts, and issues, building on others' ideas and expressing their own clearly.
		L.7.3.a	Use knowledge of language and its conventions when writing, speaking, reading, or listening. Choose language that expresses ideas precisely and concisely, recognizing and eliminating wordiness and redundancy.

Selection 2 LAFFF, continued

Pages	Lesson	Code	Standards Text
59	**Writing and Grammar** Write About Time Travel	W.7.3.d	Write narratives to develop real or imagined experiences or events using effective technique, relevant descriptive details, and well-structured event sequences. Use precise words and phrases, relevant descriptive details, and sensory language to capture the action and convey experiences and events.
		L.7.1	Demonstrate command of the conventions of standard English grammar and usage when writing or speaking.
		L.7.2	Demonstrate command of the conventions of standard English capitalization, punctuation, and spelling when writing.
		L.7.3.a	Use knowledge of language and its conventions when writing, speaking, reading, or listening. Choose language that expresses ideas precisely and concisely, recognizing and eliminating wordiness and redundancy.

Selection 3 Kids Are Inventors, Too

Pages	Lesson	Code	Standards Text
60	**Connect**	SL.7.2	Analyze the main ideas and supporting details presented in diverse media and formats (e.g., visually, quantitatively, orally) and explain how the ideas clarify a topic, text, or issue under study.
61–63	**Language & Grammar** Give Information	SL.7.1.a	Engage effectively in a range of collaborative discussions (one-on-one, in groups, and teacher-led) with diverse partners on grade 7 topics, texts, and issues, building on others' ideas and expressing their own clearly. Come to discussions prepared, having read or researched material under study; explicitly draw on that preparation by referring to evidence on the topic, text, or issue to probe and reflect on ideas under discussion.
		SL.7.2	Analyze the main ideas and supporting details presented in diverse media and formats (e.g., visually, quantitatively, orally) and explain how the ideas clarify a topic, text, or issue under study.
		SL.7.4	Present claims and findings, emphasizing salient points in a focused, coherent manner with pertinent descriptions, facts, details, and examples; use appropriate eye contact, adequate volume, and clear pronunciation.
	Use Complete Sentences	L.7.1	Demonstrate command of the conventions of standard English grammar and usage when writing or speaking.
64	**Key Vocabulary**	RI.7.4	Determine the meaning of words and phrases as they are used in a text, including figurative, connotative, and technical meanings; analyze the impact of a specific word choice on meaning and tone.
65	**Reading Strategy** Determine Importance and Synthesize	RI.7.1	Cite several pieces of textual evidence to support analysis of what the text says explicitly as well as inferences drawn from the text.
	Literary Analysis Determine Main Idea, Make Inferences	RI.7.2	Determine two or more central ideas in a text and analyze their development over the course of the text; provide an objective summary of the text.
66–78	**Reading Selection**	RI.7.1	Cite several pieces of textual evidence to support analysis of what the text says explicitly as well as inferences drawn from the text.
		RI.7.4	Determine the meaning of words and phrases as they are used in a text, including figurative, connotative, and technical meanings; analyze the impact of a specific word choice on meaning and tone.
		RI.7.10	By the end of the year, read and comprehend literary nonfiction in the grades 6–8 text complexity band proficiently, with scaffolding as needed at the high end of the range.

Common Core State Standards, continued

Selection 3 Kids Are Inventors, Too, continued

Pages	Lesson	Code	Standards Text
79	**Connect Reading and Writing** Critical Thinking	RI.7.1	Cite several pieces of textual evidence to support analysis of what the text says explicitly as well as inferences drawn from the text.
		RI.7.2	Determine two or more central ideas in a text and analyze their development over the course of the text; provide an objective summary of the text.
	Vocabulary Review	L.7.6	Acquire and use accurately grade-appropriate general academic and domain-specific words and phrases; gather vocabulary knowledge when considering a word or phrase important to comprehension or expression.
	Write About the GQ	W.7.9	Draw evidence from literary or informational texts to support analysis, reflection, and research.
		W.7.10	Write routinely over extended time frames (time for research, reflection, and revision) and shorter time frames (a single sitting or a day or two) for a range of discipline-specific tasks, purposes, and audiences.
80	**Vocabulary Study** Use Suffixes	L.7.4.b	Determine or clarify the meaning of unknown and multiple-meaning words and phrases based on grade 7 reading and content, choosing flexibly from a range of strategies. Use common, grade-appropriate Greek or Latin affixes and roots as clues to the meaning of a word (e.g., *belligerent, bellicose, rebel*).
80	**Research/Speaking** Make a Diagram	SL.7.4	Present claims and findings, emphasizing salient points in a focused, coherent manner with pertinent descriptions, facts, details, and examples; use appropriate eye contact, adequate volume, and clear pronunciation.
		SL.7.5	Include multimedia components and visual displays in presentations to clarify claims and findings and emphasize salient points.
81	**Language and Grammar** Give Information	SL.7.1.a	Engage effectively in a range of collaborative discussions (one-on-one, in groups, and teacher-led) with diverse partners on grade 7 topics, texts, and issues, building on others' ideas and expressing their own clearly. Come to discussions prepared, having read or researched material under study; explicitly draw on that preparation by referring to evidence on the topic, text, or issue to probe and reflect on ideas under discussion.
		SL.7.4	Present claims and findings, emphasizing salient points in a focused, coherent manner with pertinent descriptions, facts, details, and examples; use appropriate eye contact, adequate volume, and clear pronunciation.
		L.7.1	Demonstrate command of the conventions of standard English grammar and usage when writing or speaking.
81	**Writing and Grammar** Write Using Effective Sentences	L.7.1	Demonstrate command of the conventions of standard English grammar and usage when writing or speaking.
		W.7.3.d	Write narratives to develop real or imagined experiences or events using effective technique, relevant descriptive details, and well-structured event sequences. Use precise words and phrases, relevant descriptive details, and sensory language to capture the action and convey experiences and events.
82–85	**Close Reading**	RI.6.10	By the end of the year, read and comprehend literary nonfiction in the grades 6–8 text complexity band proficiently, with scaffolding as needed at the high end of the range.

Compare Across Texts

Pages	Lesson	Code	Standards Text
86	Compare Writing	RI.7.9	Analyze how two or more authors writing about the same topic shape their presentations of key information by emphasizing different evidence or advancing different interpretations of facts.

Unit Wrap-Up

Pages	Lesson	Code	Standards Text
87	Reflect on Your Reading	RL.7.2	Determine a theme or central idea of a text and analyze its development over the course of the text; provide an objective summary of the text.
		RL.7.10	By the end of the year, read and comprehend literature, including stories, dramas, and poems, in the grades 6–8 text complexity band proficiently, with scaffolding as needed at the high end of the range.
		RI.7.2	Determine two or more central ideas in a text and analyze their development over the course of the text; provide an objective summary of the text.
		RI.7.4	Determine the meaning of words and phrases as they are used in a text, including figurative, connotative, and technical meanings; analyze the impact of a specific word choice on meaning and tone.
		RI.7.10	By the end of the year, read and comprehend literary nonfiction in the grades 6–8 text complexity band proficiently, with scaffolding as needed at the high end of the range.
	Explore the GQ/Book Talk	W.7.10	Write routinely over extended time frames (time for research, reflection, and revision) and shorter time frames (a single sitting or a day or two) for a range of discipline-specific tasks, purposes, and audiences.
		SL.7.1	Engage effectively in a range of collaborative discussions (one-on-one, in groups, and teacher-led) with diverse partners on grade 7 topics, texts, and issues, building on others' ideas and expressing their own clearly.
		SL.7.5	Include multimedia components and visual displays in presentations to clarify claims and findings and emphasize salient points.

Unit 2   Play to Your Strengths

Unit Launch

Pages	Lesson	Code	Standards Text
88–89	Unit Opener	SL.7.1	Engage effectively in a range of collaborative discussions (one-on-one, in groups, and teacher-led) with diverse partners on grade 7 topics, texts, and issues, building on others' ideas and expressing their own clearly.
90–93	Focus on Reading Plot, Character, Setting	RL.7.3	Analyze how particular elements of a story or drama interact (e.g., how setting shapes the characters or plot).
94–95	Focus on Vocabulary Relate Words	RL.7.4	Determine the meaning of words and phrases as they are used in a text, including figurative and connotative meanings; analyze the impact of rhymes and other repetitions of sounds (e.g., alliteration) on a specific verse or stanza of a poem or section or drama.
		L.7.5	Demonstrate understanding of figurative language, word relationships, and nuances in word meanings.
		L.7.5.b	Use relationship between particular words (e.g., synonym/antonym, analogy) to better understand each of the words.
		L.7.5.c	Distinguish among the connotations (associations) of words with similar denotations (definitions) (e.g., *refined, respectful, polite, diplomatic, condescending*).

Common Core State Standards, continued

Selection 1 The Challenge

Pages	Lesson	Code	Standards Text
96	**Connect**	SL.7.2	Analyze the main ideas and supporting details presented in diverse media and formats (e.g., visually, quantitatively, orally) and explain how the ideas clarify a topic, text, or issue under study.
97–99	**Language & Grammar** Engage in Conversation	L.7.1	Demonstrate command of the conventions of standard English grammar and usage when writing or speaking.
		SL.7.1	Engage effectively in a range of collaborative discussions (one-on-one, in groups, and teacher-led) with diverse partners on grade 7 topics, texts, and issues, building on others' ideas and expressing their own clearly.
		SL.7.1.b	Follow rules for collegial discussions, track progress toward specific goals and deadlines, and define individual roles as needed.
	Use Pronouns as Subjects	L.7.1	Demonstrate command of the conventions of standard English grammar and usage when writing or speaking.
100	**Key Vocabulary**	RL.7.4	Determine the meaning of words and phrases as they are used in a text, including figurative and connotative meanings; analyze the impact of rhymes and other repetitions of sounds (e.g. alliteration) on a specific verse or stanza of a poem or section of a story or drama.
101	**Reading Strategy** Monitor	RL.7.10	By the end of the year, read and comprehend literary nonfiction in the grades 6–8 text complexity band proficiently, with scaffolding as needed at the high end of the range.
	Literary Analysis Analyze Plot	RL.7.3	Analyze how particular elements of a story or drama interact (e.g., how setting shapes the characters or plot).
102–120	**Reading Selection**	RL.7.6	Analyze how an author develops and contrasts the points of view of different characters or narrators in a text.
		RL.7.10	By the end of the year, read and comprehend literature, including stories, dramas, and poems, in the grades 6–8 text complexity band proficiently, with scaffolding as needed at the high end of the range.
121	**Connect Reading and Writing** Critical Thinking	RL.7.2	Determine a theme or central idea of a text and analyze its development over the course of the text; provide an objective summary of the text.
		RL.7.3	Analyze how particular elements of a story or drama interact (e.g., how setting shapes the characters or plot).
	Vocabulary Review	L.7.6	Acquire and use accurately grade-appropriate general academic and domain-specific words and phrases; gather vocabulary knowledge when considering a word or phrase important or comprehension or expression.
	Write About the GQ	W.7.9	Draw evidence from literacy or informational texts to support analysis, reflection, and research.
		W.7.10	Write routinely over extended time frames (time for research, reflection, and revision) and shorter time frames (a single sitting or a day or two) for a range of discipline-specific tasks, purposes, and audiences.

Selection 1 The Challenge, continued

Pages	Lesson	Code	Standards Text
122	Vocabulary Study	L.7.5	Demonstrate understanding of figurative language, word relationships, and nuances in word meanings.
		L.7.5.b	Use the relationship between particular words (e.g., synonym/antonym, analogy) to better understand each of the words.
	Media/Viewing	RI.7.7	Compare and contrast text to an audio, video or multimedia version of the text, analyzing each medium's portrayal of the subject (e.g., how the delivery of a speech affects the impact of the words).
		SL.7.1.a	Engage effectively in a range of collaborative discussions (one-on-one, in groups, and teacher-led) with diverse partners on grade 7 topics, texts, and issues, building on others' ideas and expressing their own clearly. Come to discussions prepared, having read or researched material under study; explicitly draw on that preparation by referring to evidence on the topic, text, or issue to probe and reflect on ideas under discussion.
123	Language and Grammar Engage in Conversation	SL.7.1	Engage effectively in a range of collaborative discussions (one-on-one, in groups, and teacher-led) with diverse partners on grade 7 topics, texts, and issues, building on others' ideas and expressing their own clearly.
		SL.7.1.b	Follow rules for collegial discussions, track progress toward specific goals and deadlines, and define individual roles as needed.
		L.7.1	Demonstrate command of the conventions of standard English grammar and usage when writing or speaking.
123	Writing and Grammar Write About a Friend	W.7.3.d	Write narratives to develop real or imagined experiences or events using effective technique, relevant descriptive details, and well-structured event sequences. Use precise words and phrases, relevant descriptive details, and sensory language to capture the action and convey experiences and events.
		L.7.1	Demonstrate command of the conventions of standard English grammar and usage when writing or speaking.
		L.7.3.a	Use knowledge of language and its conventions when writing, speaking, reading, or listening. Choose language that expresses ideas precisely and concisely, recognizing and eliminating wordiness and redundancy.

Selection 2 Rachel the Clever

Pages	Lesson	Code	Standards Text
124	Connect	SL.7.2	Analyze the main ideas and supporting details presented in diverse media and formats (e.g., visually, quantitatively, orally) and explain how the ideas clarify a topic, text, or issue under study.
125–127	Language & Grammar Retell a Story	L.7.1	Demonstrate command of the conventions of standard English grammar and usage when writing or speaking.
		SL.7.1	Engage effectively in a range of collaborative discussions (one-on-one, in groups, and teacher-led) with diverse partners on grade 7 topics, texts, and issues, building on others' ideas and expressing their own clearly.
	Use Forms of the Verb *Be*	L.7.1	Demonstrate command of the conventions of standard English grammar and usage when writing or speaking.
128	Key Vocabulary	RL.7.4	Determine the meaning of words and phrases as they are used in a text, including figurative and connotative meanings; analyze the impact of rhymes and other repetitions of sounds (e.g., alliteration) on a specific verse or stanza of a poem or section of a story or drama.

Common Core State Standards, continued

Pages	Lesson	Code	Standards Text
129	**Reading Strategy** Monitor	RL.7.10	By the end of the year, read and comprehend literature, including stories, dramas, poems, in the grades 6–8 text complexity band proficiently, with scaffolding as needed at the high end of the range.
	Literary Analysis Analyze Character	RL.7.3	Analyze how particular elements of a story or drama interact (e.g., how setting shapes the character or plot).
130–138	**Reading Selection**	RL.7.1	Cite several pieces of textual evidence to support analysis of what the text says explicitly as well as inferences drawn from the text.
		RL.7.3	Analyze how particular elements of a story or drama interact (e.g., how setting shapes the character or plot).
		RL.7.10	By the end of the year, read and comprehend literature, including stories, dramas, poems, in the grades 6–8 text complexity band proficiently, with scaffolding as needed at the high end of the range.
139	**Connect Reading and Writing** Critical Thinking	RL.7.2	Determine a theme or central idea of a text and analyze its development over the course of the text; provide an objective summary of the text.
		RL.7.3	Analyze how particular elements of a story or drama interact (e.g., how setting shapes the characters or plot).
	Vocabulary Review	L.7.6	Acquire and use accurately grade-appropriate general academic and domain-specific words and phrases; gather vocabulary knowledge when considering a word or phrase important to comprehension or expression.
	Write About the GQ	W.7.9	Draw evidence from literary or informational texts to support analysis, reflection, and research.
		W.7.10	Write routinely over extended time frames (time for research, reflection, and revision) and shorter time frames (a single sitting or a day or two) for a range of discipline-specific tasks, purposes, and audiences.
140	**Vocabulary Study** Use Synonyms	RL.7.4	Determine the meaning of words and phrases as they are used in a text, including figurative and connotative meanings; analyze the impact of rhymes and other repetitions of sounds (e.g., alliteration) on a specific verse or stanza of a poem or section of a story or drama.
		L.7.4.c	Determine or clarify the meaning of unknown and multiple-meaning words and phrases based on grade 7 reading and content, choosing flexibly from a range of strategies. Consult general and specialized reference materials (e.g., dictionaries, glossaries, thesauruses), both print and digital, to find the pronunciation of a word or determine or clarify its precise part of speech.
		L.7.5	Demonstrate understanding of figurative language, word relationships, and nuances in word meanings.
		L.7.5.b	Use the relationship between particular words (e.g., synonym/antonym, analogy) to better understand each of the words.
140	**Viewing/Speaking** Illustrate Character Traits	SL.7.5	Include multimedia components and visual displays in presentations to clarify claims and findings and emphasize salient points.
141	**Language and Grammar** Retell a Story	SL.7.1	Engage effectively in a range of collaborative discussions (one-on-one, in groups, and teacher-led) with diverse partners on grade 7 topics, texts, and issues, building on others' ideas and expressing their own clearly.
		L.7.1	Demonstrate command of the conventions of standard English grammar and usage when writing or speaking.

Selection 2 Rachel the Clever, continued

Pages	Lesson	Code	Standards Text
141	**Writing and Grammar** Write About a Folk Tale	W.7.3.d	Write narratives to develop real or imagined experiences or events using effective technique, relevant descriptive details, and well-structured event sequences. Use precise words and phrases, relevant descriptive details, and sensory language to capture the action and convey experiences and events.
		L.7.1	Demonstrate command of the conventions of standard English grammar and usage when writing or speaking.
		L.7.2	Demonstrate command of the conventions of standard English capitalization, punctuation, and spelling when writing.

Selection 3 A Contest of Riddles

Pages	Lesson	Code	Standards Text
142	**Connect**	SL.7.2	Analyze the main ideas and supporting details presented in diverse media and formats (e.g., visually, quantitatively, orally) and explain how the ideas clarify a topic, text, or issue under study.
143–145	**Language & Grammar** Ask for and Give Information	SL.7.1.c	Engage effectively in a range of collaborative discussions (one-on-one, in groups, and teacher-led) with diverse partners on grade 7 topics, texts, and issues, building on others' ideas and expressing their own clearly. Pose questions that elicit elaboration and respond to others' questions and comments with relevant observations and ideas that bring the discussion back on topic as needed.
	Use Subjects and Verbs	L.7.1	Demonstrate command of the conventions of standard English grammar and usage when writing or speaking.
		L.7.2	Demonstrate command of the conventions of standard English capitalization, punctuation, and spelling when writing.
		L.7.2.b	Spell correctly.
146	**Key Vocabulary**	RL.7.4	Determine the meaning of words and phrases as they are used in a text, including figurative and connotative meanings; analyze the impact of rhymes and other repetitions of sounds (e.g., alliteration) on a specific verse or stanza of a poem or section of a story or drama.
147	**Reading Strategy** Monitor: Clarify Vocabulary	RL.7.1	Cite several pieces of textual evidence to support analysis of what the text says explicitly as well as inferences drawn from the text.
	Literary Analysis Analyze Elements of Drama	RL.7.5	Analyze how a drama's or poem's form or structure (e.g., soliloquy, sonnet) contributes to its meaning
148–162	**Reading Selection**	RL.7.1	Cite several pieces of textual evidence to support analysis of what the text says explicitly as well as inferences drawn from the text.
		RL.7.3	Analyze how particular elements of a story or drama interact (e.g. how setting shapes the characters or plot).
		RL.7.10	By the end of the year, read and comprehend literature, including stories, dramas, and poems, in grades 6–8 text complexity band proficiently, with scaffolding as needed at the high end of the range.

Common Core State Standards, continued

Selection 3 A Contest of Riddles, continued

Pages	Lesson	Code	Standards Text
163	**Connect Reading and Writing** Critical Thinking	RL.7.2	Determine a theme or central idea of a text and analyze its development over the course of the text; provide an objective summary of the text.
		RL.7.5	Analyze how a drama's or poem's form or structure (e.g., soliloquy, sonnet) contributes to its meaning.
	Vocabulary Review	L.7.6	Acquire and use accurately grade-appropriate general academic and domain-specific words and phrases; gather vocabulary knowledge when considering a word or phrase important to comprehension or expression.
	Write About the GQ	W.7.9	Draw evidence from literary or informational texts to support analysis, reflection, and research
		W.7.10	Write routinely over extended time frames (time for research, reflection, and revision) and shorter time frames (a single sitting or a day or two) for a range of discipline-specific tasks, purposes, and audiences.
164	**Vocabulary Study** Use Synonyms and Antonyms	L.7.4.c	Determine or clarify the meaning of unknown and multiple-meaning words and phrases based on grade 7 reading and content, choosing flexibly from a range of strategies. Consult general and specialized reference materials (e.g., dictionaries, glossaries, thesauruses), both print and digital, to find the pronunciation of a word or determine or clarify its precise meaning or its part of speech.
		L.7.5	Demonstrate understanding of figurative language, word relationships, and nuances in word meanings.
		L.7.5.b	Demonstrate understanding of figurative language, word relationships, and nuances in word meanings. Use the relationship between particular words (e.g., synonym/antonym, analogy) to better understand each of the words.
		L.7.5.c	Demonstrate understanding of figurative language, word relationships, and nuances in word meanings. Distinguish among the connotations (associations) of words with similar denotations (definitions) (e.g., *refined, respectful, polite, diplomatic, condescending*).
	Listening/Speaking Act Out a Scene	RL.7.7	Compare and contrast a written story, drama, or poem to its audio, filmed, staged, or multimedia version, analyzing the effects of techniques unique to each medium (e.g., lighting, sound, color, or camera focus and angles in a film).
165	**Language and Grammar** Ask for and Give Information	SL.7.1.c	Engage effectively in a range of collaborative discussions (one-on-one, in groups, and teacher-led) with diverse partners on grade 7 topics, texts, and issues, building on others' ideas and expressing their own clearly. Pose questions that elicit elaboration and respond to others' questions and comments with relevant observations and ideas that bring the discussion back on topic as needed.
		L.7.3.a	Use knowledge of language and its conventions when writing, speaking, reading, or listening. Choose language that expresses ideas precisely and concisely, recognizing and eliminating wordiness and redundancy.
165	**Writing and Grammar** Write About a Play	L.7.1	Demonstrate command of the conventions of standard English grammar and usage when writing or speaking.
		L.7.3.a	Use knowledge of language and its conventions when writing, speaking, reading, or listening. Choose language that expresses ideas precisely and concisely, recognizing and eliminating wordiness and redundancy.
		W.7.3.d	Use precise words and phrases, relevant descriptive details, and sensory language to capture the action and convey experiences and events.

Selection 3 A Contest of Riddles, continued

Pages	Lesson	Code	Standards Text
166–169	Close Reading	RL.7.10	By the end of the year, read and comprehend literature, including stories, dramas, and poems, in the grades 6–8 text complexity band proficiently, with scaffolding as needed at the high end of the range.

Compare Across Texts

170	Compare Themes in Literature	RL.7.2	Determine a theme or central idea of a text and analyze its development over the course of the text; provide an objective summary of the text.

Unit Wrap-Up

171	Reflect on Your Reading	RL.7.3	Analyze how particular elements of a story or drama interact (e.g., how setting shapes the characters or plot).
		W.7.10	Write routinely over extended time frames (time for research, reflection, and revision) and shorter time frames (a single sitting or a day or two) for a range of discipline-specific tasks, purposes, and audiences.
	Explore the GQ/Book Talk	SL.7.1	Engage effectively in a range of collaborative discussions (one-on-one, in groups, and teacher-led) with diverse partners on grade 7 topics, texts, and issues, building on others' ideas and expressing their own clearly.

Unit 3   A New Chapter

Unit Launch

Pages	Lesson	Code	Standards Text
172–173	Unit Opener	SL.7.1	Engage effectively in a range of collaborative discussions (one-on-one, in groups, and teacher-led) with diverse partners on grade 7 topics, texts, and issues, building on others' ideas and expressing their own clearly.
174–175	Focus on Reading Analyze Interactions	RL.7.3	Analyze how particular elements of a story or drama interact (e.g., how setting shapes the characters or plot).
		RI.7.3	Analyze the interactions between individuals, events, and ideas in a text (e.g., how ideas influence individuals or how individuals influence ideas or events).
176–177	Focus on Vocabulary Use Word Parts	L.7.4.b	Determine or clarify the meaning of unknown and multiple-meaning words and phrases based on grade 7 reading and content, choosing flexibly from a range of strategies. Use common grade-appropriate Greek or Latin affixes and roots as clues to the meaning of a word (e.g., *belligerent, bellicose, rebel*).
		RL.7.4	Determine the meaning of words and phrases as they are used in a text, including figurative and connotative meanings; analyze the impact of rhymes and other repetitions of sounds (e.g., alliteration) on a specific verse or stanza of a poem or section of a story or drama.
		RI.7.4	Determine the meaning of words and phrases as they are used in a text, including figurative, connotative, and technical meanings; analyze the impact of a specific word choice on meaning and tone.

Selection 1 The Lotus Seed

178	Connect	SL.7.2	Analyze the main ideas and supporting details presented in diverse media and formats (e.g., visually, quantitatively, orally) and explain how the ideas clarify a topic, text, or issue under study.

Common Core State Standards, continued

Pages	Lesson	Code	Standards Text
179–181	**Language & Grammar** Describe People, Places, and Things	SL.7.1	Engage effectively in a range of collaborative discussions (one-on-one, in groups, and teacher-led) with diverse partners on grade 7 topics, texts, and issues, building on others' ideas and expressing their own clearly.
	Use Adjectives That Describe	L.7.2.a	Demonstrate command of the conventions of standard English capitalization, punctuation, and spelling when writing. Use a comma to separate coordinate adjectives (e.g., It was a fascinating, enjoyable movie but not He wore an old[,] green shirt).
		L.7.3.a	Use knowledge of language and its conventions when writing, speaking, reading, or listening. Choose language that expresses ideas precisely and concisely, recognizing and eliminating wordiness and redundancy
182	**Key Vocabulary**	RL.7.4	Determine the meaning of words and phrases as they are used in a text, including figurative and connotative meanings; analyze the impact of rhymes and other repetitions of sounds (e.g., alliteration) on a specific verse or stanza of a poem or section of a story or drama.
183	**Reading Strategy** Visualize	RL.7.10	By the end of the year, read and comprehend literature, including stories, dramas, and poems, in the grades 6–8 text complexity band proficiently, with scaffolding as needed at the high end of the range.
	Literary Analysis Analyze Plot	RL.7.3	Analyze how particular elements of a story or drama interact (e.g., how setting shapes the characters or plot).
184–194	**Reading Selection**	RL.7.1	Cite several pieces of textual evidence to support analysis of what the text says explicitly as well as inferences drawn from the text.
		RL.7.3	Analyze how particular elements of a story or drama interact (e.g., how setting shapes the characters or plot).
		RL.7.6	Analyze how an author develops and contrasts the points of view of different characters or narrators in a text.
		RL.7.10	By the end of the year, read and comprehend literature, including stories, dramas, and poems, in the grades 6–8 text complexity band proficiently, with scaffolding as needed at the high end of the range.
195	**Connect Reading and Writing** Critical Thinking	RL.7.1	Cite several pieces of textual evidence to support analysis of what the text says explicitly as well as inferences drawn from the text.
		RL.7.2	Determine a theme or central idea of a text and analyze its development over the course of the text; provide an objective summary of the text.
	Vocabulary Review	L.7.6	Acquire and use accurately grade-appropriate general academic and domain-specific words and phrases; gather vocabulary knowledge when considering a word or phrase important to comprehension or expression.
	Write About the GQ	W.7.9	Draw evidence from literary or informational texts to support analysis, reflection, and research.
		W.7.10	Write routinely over extended time frames (time for research, reflection, and revision) and shorter time frames (a single sitting or a day or two) for a range of discipline-specific tasks, purposes, and audiences.
196	**Vocabulary Study** Use Prefixes	L.7.4.b	Determine or clarify the meaning of unknown and multiple-meaning words and phrases based on grade 7 reading and content, choosing flexibly from a range of strategies. Use common, grade-appropriate Greek or Latin affixes and roots as clues to the meaning of a word (e.g., *belligerent, bellicose, rebel*).

Selection 1 The Lotus Seed, continued

Pages	Lesson	Code	Standards Text
196	**Literary Analysis** Compare Characters	RL.7.6	Analyze how an author develops and contrasts the point of view of different characters or narrators in a text.
197	**Language and Grammar** Describe People, Places, and Things	SL.7.1	Engage effectively in a range of collaborative discussions (one-on-one, in groups, and teacher-led) with diverse partners on grade 7 topics, texts, and issues, building on others' ideas and expressing their own clearly.
197	**Writing and Grammar** Write About People, Places, and Things	L.7.2.a	Demonstrate command of the conventions of standard English capitalization, punctuation, and spelling when writing. Use a comma to separate coordinate adjectives (e.g., It was a fascinating, enjoyable movie but not He wore an old[,] green shirt).
		W.7.3.d	Write narratives to develop real or imagined experiences or events using effective technique, relevant descriptive details, and well-structured event sequences. Use precise words and phrases, relevant descriptive details, and sensory language to capture the action and convey experiences and events.
		L.7.1	Demonstrate command of the conventions of standard English grammar and usage when writing or speaking.

Selection 2 Immigrants Today

Pages	Lesson	Code	Standards Text
198	**Connect**	SL.7.2	Analyze the main ideas and supporting details presented in diverse media and formats (e.g., visually, quantitatively, orally) and explain how the ideas clarify a topic, text, or issue under study.
199–201	**Language & Grammar** Make Comparisons	SL.7.1	Engage effectively in a range of collaborative discussions (one-on-one, in groups, and teacher-led) with diverse partners on grade 7 topics, texts, and issues, building on others' ideas and expressing their own clearly.
		SL.7.1.a	Come to discussions prepared, having read or researched material under study; explicitly draw on that preparation by referring to evidence on the topic, text, or issue to probe and reflect on ideas under discussion.
		SL.7.5	Include multimedia components and visual displays in presentations to clarify claims and findings and emphasize salient points.
	Use Adjectives That Compare	L.7.1	Demonstrate command of the conventions of standard English grammar and usage when writing or speaking.
		L.7.2	Demonstrate command of the conventions of standard English capitalization, punctuation, and spelling when writing.
		L.7.2.b	Spell correctly.
202	**Key Vocabulary**	RI.7.4	Determine the meaning of words and phrases as they are used in a text, including figurative, connotative, and technical meanings; analyze the impact of a specific word choice on meaning and tone.
203	**Reading Strategy** Visualize	RI.7.4	Determine the meaning of words and phrases as they are used in a text, including figurative, connotative, and technical meanings; analyze the impact of a specific word choice on meaning and tone
	Literary Analysis Analyze Interactions Among Ideas	RI.7.3	Analyze interactions between individuals, events, and ideas, in a text (e.g., how ideas influence individuals or events, or how individuals influence ideas or events).

Common Core State Standards, continued

Selection 2 Immigrants Today, continued

Pages	Lesson	Code	Standards Text
204–216	**Reading Selection**	RI.7.1	Cite several pieces of textual evidence to support analysis of what the text says explicitly as well as inferences drawn from the text.
		RI.7.2	Determine two or more central ideas in a text and analyze their development over the course of the text; provide an objective summary of the text.
		RI.7.10	By the end of the year, read and comprehend literary nonfiction in the grades 6–8 text complexity band proficiently, with scaffolding as needed at the high end of the range.
217	**Connect Reading and Writing** Critical Thinking	RI.7.2	Determine two or more central ideas in a text and analyze their development over the course of the text; provide an objective summary of the text.
	Vocabulary Review	L.7.6	Acquire and use accurately grade-appropriate general academic and domain-specific words and phrases; gather vocabulary knowledge when considering a word or phrase important to comprehension or expression.
	Write About the GQ	W.7.9	Draw evidence from literary or informational texts to support analysis, reflection, and research.
		W.7.10	Write routinely over extended time frames (time for research, reflection, and revision) and shorter time frames (a single sitting or a day or two) for a range of tasks, purposes, and audiences.
218	**Vocabulary Study** Use Prefixes and Suffixes	RI.7.4	Determine the meaning of words and phrases as they are used in a text, including figurative, connotative, and technical meanings; analyze the impact of a specific word choice on meaning and tone.
		L.7.4.b	Determine or clarify the meaning of unknown and multiple-meaning words and phrases based on grade 7 reading and content, choosing flexibly from a range of strategies. Use common grade-appropriate Greek or Latin affixes and roots as clues to the meaning of a word (e.g., *belligerent, bellicose, rebel*)
218	**Researching/Speaking** Make an Immigration Graph	SL.7.5	Includes multimedia components and visual displays in presentations to clarify claims and findings and emphasize salient points.
219	**Language and Grammar** Make Comparisons	SL.7.1	Engage effectively in a range of collaborative discussions (one-on-one, in groups, and teacher-led) with diverse partners on grade 7 topics, texts, and issues, building on others' ideas and expressing their own clearly.
		L.7.1	Demonstrate command of the conventions of standard English grammar and usage when writing or speaking.
219	**Writing and Grammar** Write to Compare	W.7.3.d	Write narratives to develop real or imagined experiences or events using effective technique, relevant descriptive details, and well-structured event sequences. Use precise words and phrases, relevant descriptive details, and sensory language to capture the action and convey experiences and events.
		L.7.1	Demonstrate command of the conventions of standard English grammar and usage when writing or speaking.
		L.7.2	Demonstrate command of the conventions of standard English capitalization, punctuation, and spelling when writing.
		L.7.2.b	Spell correctly.

Selection 3 Brothers in Hope

Pages	Lesson	Code	Standards Text
220	**Connect**	SL.7.2	Analyze the main ideas and supporting details presented in diverse media and formats (e.g., visually, quantitatively, orally) and explain how the ideas clarify a topic, text, or issue under study.

Pages	Lesson	Code	Standards Text
221–223	Language & Grammar Describe an Event or Experience	SL.7.1	Engage effectively in a range of collaborative discussions (one-on-one, in groups, and teacher-led) with diverse partners on grade 7 topics, texts, and issues, building on others' ideas and expressing their own clearly.
		SL.7.1.a	Come to discussions prepared, having read or researched material under study; explicitly draw on that preparation by referring to evidence on the topic, text, or issue to probe and reflect on ideas under discussion.
		SL.7.5	Include multimedia components and visual displays in presentations to clarify claims and findings and emphasize salient points.
	Use Adverbs	L.7.1	Demonstrate command of the conventions of standard English grammar and usage when writing or speaking.
224	Key Vocabulary	RL.7.4	Determine the meaning of words and phrases as they are used in a text, including figurative and connotative meanings; analyze the impact of rhymes and other repetitions of sounds (e.g., alliteration) on a specific verse or stanza of a poem or section of a story or drama.
225	Reading Strategy Visualize	RL.7.10	By the end of the year, read and comprehend literature, including stories, dramas, and poems, in the grades 6–8 text complexity band proficiently, with scaffolding as needed at the high end of the range.
	Literary Analysis Compare Fiction and Nonfiction	RL.7.1	Cite several pieces of textual evidence to support analysis of what the text says explicitly as well as inferences drawn from the text.
		RL.7.9	Compare and contrast a fictional portrayal of a time, place, or character and a historical account of the same period as a means of understanding how authors of fiction use or alter history.
226–246	Reading Selection	RL.7.4	Determine the meaning of words and phrases as they are used in a text, including figurative and connotative meanings; analyze the impact of rhymes and other repetitions of sounds (e.g., alliteration) on a specific verse or stanza of a poem or section of a story or drama.
		RL.7.10	By the end of the year, read and comprehend literature, including stories, dramas, and poems, in the grades of 6-8 text complexity band proficiently, with scaffolding as needed at the high end of the range.
		L.7.5.a	Demonstrate understanding of figurative language, word relationships, and nuances in word meanings. Interpret figures of speech (e.g., literary, biblical, and mythological allusions) in context.
247	Connect Reading and Writing Critical Thinking	RL.7.1	Cite several pieces of textual evidence to support analysis of what the text says explicitly as well as inferences drawn from the text.
		RL.7.2	Determine a theme or central idea of a text and analyze its development over the course of the text; provide an objective summary of the text.
	Vocabulary Review	L.7.6	Acquire and use accurately grade-appropriate general academic and domain-specific words and phrases; gather vocabulary knowledge when considering a word or phrase important to comprehension or expression.
	Write About the GQ	W.7.9	Draw evidence from literary or informational texts to support analysis, reflection, and research.
		W.7.10	Write routinely over extended time frames (time for research, reflection, and revision) and shorter time frames (a single sitting or a day or two) for a range of discipline-specific tasks, purposes, and audiences.
248	Vocabulary Study Use Word Parts: Roots	L.7.4.b	Determine or clarify the meaning of unknown and multiple-meaning words and phrases based on grade 7 reading and content, choosing flexibly from a range of strategies. Use common, grade-appropriate Greek or Latin affixes and roots as clues to the meaning of a word (e.g., *belligerent, bellicose, rebel*).

Common Core State Standards, continued

Selection 3 Brothers in Hope, continued

Pages	Lesson	Code	Standards Text
248	**Listening/Speaking** Role-Play a Conversation	SL.7.1	Engage effectively in a range of collaborative discussions (one-on-one, in groups, and teacher-led) with diverse partners on grade 7 topics, texts, and issues, building on others' ideas and expressing their own clearly.
249	**Language and Grammar** Describe an Event or Experience	SL.7.1	Engage effectively in a range of collaborative discussions (one-on-one, in groups, and teacher-led) with diverse partners on grade 7 topics, texts, and issues, building on others' ideas and expressing their own clearly.
		L.7.1	Demonstrate command of the conventions of standard English grammar and usage when writing or speaking.
249	**Writing and Grammar** Write About an Event	W.7.3.d	Use precise words and phrases, relevant descriptive details, and sensory language to capture the action and convey experiences and events. Write narratives to develop real or imagined experiences or events using effective technique, relevant descriptive details, and well-structured event sequences.
		L.7.1	Demonstrate command of the conventions of standard English grammar and usage when writing or speaking.
250–251	**Close Reading**	RL.7.10	By the end of the year, read and comprehend literature, including stories, dramas, and poems, in the grades 6–8 text complexity band proficiently, with scaffolding as needed at the high end of the range.

Compare Across Texts

Pages	Lesson	Code	Standards Text
252	**Compare Writing on the Same Topic**	RL.7.9	Compare and Contrast a fictional portrayal of a time, place, or character and a historical account of the same period as a means of understanding how authors of fiction use or alter history.

Unit Wrap-Up

Pages	Lesson	Code	Standards Text
253	**Reflect on Your Reading**	RL.7.3	Analyze how particular elements of a story or drama interact (e.g., how setting shapes the characters or plot).
		RI.7.3	Analyze the interactions between individuals, events, and ideas in a text (e.g., how ideas influence individuals or events, or how individuals influence ideas or events).
		RL.7.10	By the end of the year, read and comprehend literature, including stories, dramas, and poems, in the grades 6–8 text complexity band proficiently, with scaffolding as needed at the high end of the range.
		RI.7.4	Determine the meaning of words and phrases as they are used in a text, including figurative, connotative, and technical meanings; analyze the impact of a specific word choice on meaning and tone.
	Explore the GQ/Book Talk	W.7.10	Write routinely over extended time frames (time for research, reflection, and revision) and shorter time frames (a single sitting or a day or two) for a range of discipline-specific tasks, purposes, and audiences.
		SL.7.1	Engage effectively in a range of collaborative discussions (one-on-one, in groups, and teacher-led) with diverse partners on grade 7 topics, texts, and issues, building on others' ideas and expressing their own clearly.
		SL.7.5	Include multimedia components and visual displays in presentations to clarify claims and findings and emphasize salient points.

Unit 4 Everybody Is a Winner

Unit Launch

Pages	Lesson	Code	Standards Text
254–255	**Unit Opener**	SL.7.1	Engage effectively in a range of collaborative discussions (one-on-one, in groups, and teacher-led) with diverse partners on grade 7 topics, texts, and issues, building on others' ideas and expressing their own clearly.
256–257	**Focus on Reading** Text Structure: Main Idea and Chronological Order	RL.7.5	Analyze how a drama's or poem's form or structure (soliloquy, sonnet) contributes to its meaning.
		RI.7.5	Analyze the structure an author uses to organize a text, including how the major sections contribute to the whole and to the development of ideas.
258–259	**Focus on Vocabulary** Use Context Clues	RI.7.4	Determine the meaning of words and phrases as they are used in a text, including figurative, connotative, and technical meanings, analyze the impact of a specific word choice on meaning and tone.
		L.7.4	Determine or clarify the meaning of unknown and multiple-meaning words and phrases based on grade 7 reading and content, choosing flexibly from a range of strategies.
		L.7.4.a	Use context (e.g., the overall meaning of a sentence or paragraph; a word's position or function in a sentence) as a clue to the meaning of a word or phrase.
		L.7.4.d	Verify the preliminary determination of the meaning of a word or phrase (e.g., by checking the inferred meaning in context or in a dictionary.)

Selection 1 The Human Machine

Pages	Lesson	Code	Standards Text
260	**Connect**	SL.7.2	Analyze the main ideas and supporting details presented in diverse media and formats (e.g., visually, quantitatively, orally) and explain how the ideas clarify a topic, text, or issue under study.
261–263	**Language & Grammar** Define and Explain	SL.7.1	Engage effectively in a range of collaborative discussions (one-on-one, in groups, and teacher-led) with diverse partners on grade 7 topics, texts, and issues, building on others' ideas and expressing their own clearly.
		SL.7.1.a	Come to discussions prepared, having read or researched material under study; explicitly draw on that preparation by referring to evidence on the topic, text, or issue to probe and reflect on ideas under discussion.
		SL.7.5	Include multimedia components and visual displays in presentations to clarify claims and findings and emphasize salient points.
	Use Possessive Nouns	L.7.1	Demonstrate command of the conventions of standard English grammar and usage when writing or speaking.
		L.7.2	Demonstrate command of the conventions of standard English capitalization, punctuation, and spelling when writing.
264	**Key Vocabulary**	RI.7.4	Determine the meaning of words and phrases as they are used in a text, including figurative, connotative, and technical meanings; analyze the impact of a specific word choice on meaning and tone.
265	**Reading Strategy** Determine Importance: Main Idea and Details	RI.7.2	Determine two or more central ideas in a text and analyze their development over the course of the text; provide an objective summary of the text.
	Literary Analysis Text Structure: Main Idea and Details	RI.7.5	Analyze the structure an author uses to organize a text, including how the major sections contribute to the whole and to the development of the ideas.

Common Core State Standards, continued

Pages	Lesson	Code	Standards Text
266–276	**Reading Selection**	RI.7.1	Cite several pieces of textual evidence to support analysis of what the text says explicitly as well as inferences drawn from the text.
		RI.7.2	Determine two or more central ideas in a text and analyze their development over the course of the text; provide an objective summary of the text.
		RI.7.10	By the end of the year, read and comprehend literary nonfiction in the grades 6–8 text complexity band proficiently, with scaffolding as needed at the high end of the range.
		L.7.5.a	Demonstrate understanding of figurative language, word relationships, and nuances in word meanings. Interpret figures of speech (e.g, literary, biblical, and mythological allusions) in context
277	**Connect Reading and Writing** Critical Thinking	RI.7.1	Cite several pieces of textual evidence to support analysis of what the text says as well as inferences drawn from the text.
		RI.7.2	Determine two or more central ideas in a text and analyze their development over the course of the text; provide an objective summary of the text.
	Vocabulary Review	L.7.6	Acquire and use accurately grade-appropriate general academic and domain-specific words and phrases; gather vocabulary knowledge when considering a word or phrase important to comprehension or expression.
	Write About the GQ	W.7.9	Draw evidence from literary and informational texts to support analysis, reflection, and research.
		W.7.10	Write routinely over extended time frames (time for research, reflection, and revision) and shorter time frames (a single sitting or a day or two) for a range of discipline-specific tasks, purposes, and audiences.
278	**Vocabulary Study** Use Context Clues: Definition and Restatement	RI.7.4	Determine the meaning of words and phrases as they are used in a text, including figurative, connotative, and technical meanings; analyze the impact of a specific word choice on meaning and tone.
		L.7.4.a	Determine or clarify the meaning of unknown and multiple-meaning words and phrases based on grade 7 reading and content, choosing flexibly from a range of strategies. Use context (e.g., the overall meaning of a sentence or paragraph; a word's position or function in a sentence) as a clue to the meaning of a word or phrase.
		L.7.4.d	Determine or clarify the meaning of unknown and multiple-meaning words and phrases based on grade 7 reading and content, choosing flexibly from a range of strategies. Verify the preliminary determination of the meaning of a word or phrase (e.g., by checking the inferred meaning in context or in a dictionary).
278	**Listening/Speaking** Deliver an Informative Presentation	SL.7.4	Present claims and findings, emphasizing salient points in a focused, coherent manner with pertinent descriptions, facts, details, and examples; use appropriate eye contact, adequate volume, and clear pronunciation.
279	**Language and Grammar** Define and Explain	SL.7.1	Engage effectively in a range of collaborative discussions (one-on-one, in groups, and teacher-led) with diverse partners on grade 7 topics, texts, and issues, building on others' ideas and expressing their own clearly.
		L.7.1	Demonstrate command of the conventions of standard English grammar and usage when writing or speaking.

Selection 1 The Human Machine, continued

Pages	Lesson	Code	Standards Text
279	**Writing and Grammar** Write About Athletes	W.7.3.d	Write narratives to develop real or imagined experiences or events using effective technique, relevant descriptive details, and well-structured event sequences. Use precise words and phrases, relevant descriptive details, and sensory language to capture the action and convey experiences and events.
		L.7.1	Demonstrate command of the conventions of standard English grammar and usage when writing or speaking.
		L.7.2	Demonstrate command of the conventions of standard English capitalization, punctuation, and spelling when writing.

Selection 2 The Beat Goes On

Pages	Lesson	Code	Standards Text
280	**Connect**	SL.7.2	Analyze the main ideas and supporting details presented in diverse media and formats (e.g., visually, quantitatively, orally) and explain how the ideas clarify a topic, text, or issue under study.
281–283	**Language & Grammar** Give and Follow Directions	SL.7.1	Engage effectively in a range of collaborative discussions (one-on-one, in groups, and teacher-led) with diverse partners on grade 7 topics, texts, and issues, building on others' ideas and expressing their own clearly.
	Use Possessive Adjectives	L.7.1	Demonstrate command of the conventions of standard English grammar and usage when writing or speaking.
284	**Key Vocabulary**	RI.7.4	Determine the meaning of words and phrases as they are used in a text, including figurative, connotative, and technical meanings; analyze the impact of a specific word choice on meaning and tone.
285	**Reading Strategy** Determine Importance: Summarize	RI.7.2	Determine two or more central ideas in a text and analyze their development over the course of the text; provide an objective summary of the text.
	Literary Analysis Text Structure: Main Idea and Details	RI.7.5	Analyze the structure an author uses to organize a text, including how the major sections contribute to the whole and to the development of the ideas.
286–296	**Reading Selection**	RI.7.1	Cite several pieces of textual evidence to support analysis of what the text says explicitly as well as inferences drawn from the text.
		RI.7.10	By the end of the year, read and comprehend literary nonfiction in the grades 6–8 text complexity band proficiently, with scaffolding as needed at the high end of the range.
		RI.7.2	Determine two or more central ideas in a text and analyze their development over the course of the text; provide an objective summary of the text.
297	**Connect Reading and Writing** Critical Thinking	RI.7.1	Cite several pieces of textual evidence to support analysis of what the text says explicitly as well as inferences drawn from the text.
		RI.7.2	Determine two or more central ideas in a text and analyze their development over the course of the text; provide an objective summary of the text.
	Vocabulary Review	L.7.6	Acquire and use accurately grade-appropriate general academic and domain-specific words and phrases; gather vocabulary knowledge when considering a word or phrase important to comprehension or expression.
	Write About the GQ	W.7.9	Draw evidence from literary or informational texts to support analysis, reflection, and research.
		W.7.10	Write routinely over extended time frames (time for research, reflection, and revision) and shorter time frame (a single sitting or a day or two) for a range of discipline-specific tasks, purposes, and audiences.

Common Core State Standards, continued

Selection 2 The Beat Goes On, continued

Pages	Lesson	Code	Standards Text
298	**Vocabulary Study** Use Context Clues	RI.7.4	Determine the meaning of words and phrases as they are used in a text, including figurative, connotative, and technical meanings; analyze the impact of a specific word choice on meaning and tone.
		L.7.4.a	Determine or clarify the meaning of unknown and multiple-meaning words and phrases based on grade 7 reading and content, choosing flexibly from a range of strategies. Use context (e.g., the overall meaning of a sentence or paragraph; a word's position or function in a sentence) as a clue to the meaning of a word or phrase.
298	**Research/Technology** Make a Public Service Announcement	SL.7.3	Delineate a speaker's argument and specific claims, evaluating the soundness of the reasoning and the relevance and sufficiency of the evidence.
		SL.7.4	Present claims and findings, emphasizing salient points in a focused, coherent manner with pertinent descriptions, facts, details, and examples; use appropriate eye contact, adequate volume, and clear pronunciation.
		SL.7.5	Include multimedia components and visual displays in presentations to clarify claims and findings and emphasize salient points.
299	**Language and Grammar** Give and Follow Directions	SL.7.1	Engage effectively in a range of collaborative discussions (one-on-one, in groups, and teacher-led) with diverse partners on grade 7 topics, texts, and issues, building on others' ideas and expressing their own clearly.
		L.7.1	Demonstrate command of the conventions of standard English grammar and usage when writing or speaking.
299	**Writing and Grammar** Write Directions to a Place	W.7.3.d	Write narratives to develop real or imagined experiences or events using effective technique, relevant descriptive details, and well-structured event sequences. Use precise words and phrases, relevant descriptive details, and sensory language to capture the action and convey experiences and events.
		L.7.1	Demonstrate command of the conventions of standard English grammar and usage when writing or speaking.

Selection 3 Two Left Feet, Two Left Hands, and Too Left on the Bench

Pages	Lesson	Code	Standards Text
300	**Connect**	SL.7.2	Analyze the main ideas and supporting details presented in diverse media and formats (e.g., visually, quantitatively, orally) and explain how the ideas clarify a topic, text, or issue under study.

Selection 3 Two Left Feet, Two Left Hands, and Too Left on the Bench, continued

Pages	Lesson	Code	Standards Text
301–303	**Language & Grammar** Engage in Discussion	SL.7.1.a	Engage effectively in a range of collaborative discussions (one-on-one, in groups, and teacher-led) with diverse partners on grade 7 topics, texts, and issues, building on others' ideas and expressing their own clearly. Come to discussions prepared, having read or researched material under study; explicitly draw on that preparation by referring to evidence on the topic, text, or issue to probe and reflect on ideas under discussion.
		SL.7.1.b	Engage effectively in a range of collaborative discussions (one-on-one, in groups, and teacher-led) with diverse partners on grade 7 topics, texts, and issues, building on others' ideas and expressing their own clearly. Follow rules for collegial discussions, track progress toward specific goals and deadlines, and define individual roles as needed.
		SL.7.1.c	Engage effectively in a range of collaborative discussions (one-on-one, in groups, and teacher-led) with diverse partners on grade 7 topics, texts, and issues, building on others' ideas and expressing their own clearly. Pose questions that elicit elaboration and respond to others' questions and comments with relevant observations and ideas that bring the discussion back on topic as needed.
		SL.7.1.d	Engage effectively in a range of collaborative discussions (one-on-one, in groups, and teacher-led) with diverse partners on grade 7 topics, texts, and issues, building on others' ideas and expressing their own clearly. Acknowledge new information expressed by others and, when warranted, modify their own views.
	Use Indefinite Pronouns	L.7.1	Demonstrate command of the conventions of standard English grammar and usage when writing or speaking.
304	**Key Vocabulary**	RI.7.4	Determine the meaning of words and phrases as they are used in a text, including figurative, connotative, and technical meanings; analyze the impact of a specific word choice on meaning and tone.
305	**Reading Strategy** Determine Importance	RI.7.2	Determine two or more central ideas in a text and analyze their development over the course of the text; provide an objective summary of the text.
	Text Structure Chronological Order	RI.7.5	Analyze the structure an author uses to organize a text, including how the major sections contribute to the whole and to the development of ideas.
306–318	**Reading Selection**	RI.7.2	Determine two or more central ideas of a text and analyze its development over the course of the text; provide an objective summary of the text.
		RI.7.4	Determine the meaning of words and phrases as they are used in a text, including figurative, connotative, and technical meanings; analyze the impact of a specific word choice on meaning and tone.
		RI.7.10	By the end of the year, read and comprehend literary nonfiction in the grades 6-8 text complexity band proficiently, with scaffolding as needed at the high end of the range.

Common Core State Standards, continued

Pages	Lesson	Code	Standards Text
319	**Connect Reading and Writing** Critical Thinking	RL.7.2	Determine a theme or central idea of a text and analyze its development over the course of the text; provide an objective summary of the text.
	Vocabulary Review	L.7.6	Acquire and use accurately grade-appropriate general academic and domain-specific words and phrases; gather vocabulary knowledge when considering a word or phrase important to comprehension or expression.
	Write About the GQ	W.7.9	Draw evidence from literary or informational texts to support analysis, reflection, and research.
		W.7.10	Write routinely over extended time frames (time for research, reflection, and revision) and shorter time frames (a single sitting or a day or two) for a range of discipline-specific tasks, purposes, and audiences.
320	**Vocabulary Study** Use Context Clues	RI.7.4	Determine the meaning of words and phrases as they are used in a text, including figurative, connotative, and technical meanings; analyze the impact of a specific word choice on meaning and tone.
		L.7.4	Determine or clarify the meaning of unknown and multiple-meaning words and phrases based on grade 7 reading and content, choosing flexibly from a range of strategies.
		L.7.4.a	Use context (e.g., the overall meaning of a sentence or paragraph; a word's position or function in a sentence) as a clue to the meaning of a word or phrase.
		L.7.4.d	Verify the preliminary determination of the meaning of a word or phrase (e.g., checking the inferred meaning in context or in a dictionary).
320	**Literary Analysis** Analyze Structure: Poetry	RL.7.5	Analyze how a drama's or poem's form or structure (e.g., soliloquy, sonnet) contributes to its meaning.
321	**Language and Grammar** Engage in Discussion	SL.7.1.b	Engage effectively in a range of collaborative discussions (one-on-one, in groups, and teacher-led) with diverse partners on grade 7 topics, texts, and issues, building on others' ideas and expressing their own clearly. Follow rules for collegial discussions, track progress toward specific goals and deadlines, and define individual roles as needed.
		SL.7.1.c	Engage effectively in a range of collaborative discussions (one-on-one, in groups, and teacher-led) with diverse partners on grade 7 topics, texts, and issues, building on others' ideas and expressing their own clearly. Pose questions that elicit elaboration and respond to others' questions and comments with relevant observations and ideas that bring the discussion back on topic as needed.
		SL.7.1.d	Engage effectively in a range of collaborative discussions (one-on-one, in groups, and teacher-led) with diverse partners on grade 7 topics, texts, and issues, building on others' ideas and expressing their own clearly. Acknowledge new information expressed by others and, when warranted, modify their own views.
		L.7.1	Demonstrate command of the conventions of standard English grammar and usage when writing or speaking.
321	**Writing and Grammar** Write About a School Sports Team	W.7.3.d	Write narratives to develop real or imagined experiences or events using effective technique, relevant descriptive details, and well-structured event sequences. Use precise words and phrases, relevant descriptive details, and sensory language to capture the action and convey experiences and events.
		L.7.1	Demonstrate command of the conventions of standard English grammar and usage when writing or speaking.
322–325	**Close Reading**	RI.7.10	By the end of the year, read and comprehend literary nonfiction in the grades 6–8 text complexity band proficiently, with scaffolding as needed at the high end of the range.

Unit 4 Everybody Is a Winner, continued

Compare Across Texts

Pages	Lesson	Code	Standards Text
326	Compare Topics	RI.7.9	Analyze how two or more authors writing about the same topic shape their presentations of key information by emphasizing different evidence or advancing different interpretations of facts.

Unit Wrap-Up

Pages	Lesson	Code	Standards Text
327	Reflect on Your Reading	RL.7.2	Determine a theme or central idea of a text and analyze its development over the course of the text; provide an objective summary of the text.
		RL.7.5	Analyze how a drama's or poem's form or structure (e.g., soliloquy, sonnet) contributes to its meaning.
		RI.7.2	Determine two or more central ideas in a text and analyze their development over the course of the text; provide an objective summary of the text.
		RI.7.5	Analyze the structure an author uses to organize a text, including how the major sections contribute to the whole and to the development of ideas.
	Explore the GQ/Book Talk	W.7.10	Write routinely over extended time frames (time for research, reflection, and revision) and shorter time frames (a single sitting or a day or two) for a range of discipline-specific tasks, purposes, and audiences.
		SL.7.1	Engage effectively in a range of collaborative discussions (one-on-one, in groups, and teacher-led) with diverse partners on grade 7 topics, texts, and issues, building on others' ideas and expressing their own clearly.

Unit 5 Close Encounters

Unit Launch

Pages	Lesson	Code	Standards Text
328–329	Unit Opener	SL.7.1	Engage effectively in a range of collaborative discussions (one-to-one, in groups, and teacher-led) with diverse partners on grade 7 topics, tests, and issues, building on others' ideas and expressing their own clearly.
330–333	Focus on Reading Compare Fiction and Nonfiction	RL.7.9	Compare and contrast a fictional portrayal of a time, place, or character and a historical account of the same time period as a means of understanding how authors use or alter fiction.
		RI.7.9	Analyze how two or more authors writing about the same topic shape their presentation of key information by emphasizing different evidence or advancing different interpretations of facts.
334–335	Focus on Vocabulary Interpret Figurative Language	RL.7.4	Determine the meaning of words and phrases as they are used in a text, including figurative and connotative meanings; analyze the impact of rhymes and other repetitions of sounds (e.g., alliteration) on a specific verse or stanza of a poem or section of a story or drama.
		RI.7.4	Determine the meaning of words and phrases as they are used in a text, including figurative, connotative, and technical meanings; analyze the impact of a specific word choice on meaning and tone.
		L.7.4.a	Determine or clarify the meaning of unknown and multiple-meaning words and phrases based on grade 7 reading and content, choosing flexibly from a range of strategies. Use context (e.g., the overall meaning of a sentence or paragraph; a word's position or function in a sentence) as a clue to the meaning of a word or phrase.
		L.7.5.a	Demonstrate understanding of figurative language, word relationships, and nuances in word meanings. Interpret figures of speech (e.g., literary, biblical, and mythological allusions) in context.

Common Core State Standards, continued

Selection 1 Encounter

Pages	Lesson	Code	Standards Text
336	**Connect**	SL.7.2	Analyze the main idea and supporting details presented in diverse media and formats (e.g., visually, quantitatively, orally) and explain how the ideas clarify a topic, text, or issue under study.
337–339	**Language & Grammar** Make Comparisons	SL.7.1	Engage effectively in a range of collaborative discussions (one-on-one, in groups, and teacher-led) with diverse partners on grade 7 topics, texts, and issues, building on others' ideas and expressing their own clearly.
		SL.7.1.a	Come to discussions prepared, having read or researched material under study; explicitly draw on that preparation by referring to evidence on the topic, text, or issue to probe and reflect on ideas under discussion.
	Use Verbs in the Present Tense	L.7.1	Demonstrate command of the conventions of standard English grammar and usage when writing or speaking.
		L.7.2	Demonstrate command of the conventions of standard English capitalization, punctuation, and spelling when writing.
340	**Key Vocabulary**	RL.7.4	Determine the meaning of words and phrases as they are used in a text, including figurative and connotative meanings; analyze the impact of rhymes and other repetitions of sounds (e.g., alliteration) on a specific verse or stanza of a poem or section of a story or drama.
341	**Reading Strategy** Ask Questions	RL.7.1	Cite several pieces of textual evidence to support analysis of what the text says explicitly as well as inferences drawn from the text.
	Literary Analysis Analyze Plot, Character, and Setting	RL.7.3	Analyze how particular elements of a story or drama interact (e.g., how setting shapes the characters or plot).
342–352	**Reading Selection**	RL.7.1	Cite several pieces of textual evidence to support analysis of what the text says explicitly as well as inferences drawn from the text.
		RL.7.6	Analyze how an author develops and contrasts the points of view of different characters or narrators in a text.
		RL.7.10	By the end of the year, read and comprehend literature, including stories, dramas, and poems, in the grades 6–8 text complexity band proficiently, with scaffolding as needed at the high end of the range.
353	**Connect Reading and Writing** Critical Thinking	RL.7.2	Determine a theme or central idea of a text and analyze its development over the course of the text; provide an objective summary of the text.
	Vocabulary Review	L.7.6	Acquire and use accurately grade-appropriate general academic and domain-specific words and word phrases important to comprehension or expression.
	Write About the GQ	W.7.9	Draw evidence from literary or informational texts to support analysis, reflection, and research
		W.7.10	Write routinely over extended time frames (time for research, reflection, and revision) and shorter time frames (a single sitting or a day or two) for a range of discipline-specific tasks, purposes, and audiences.
354	**Vocabulary Study** Analyze Personification	RL.7.4	Determine the meaning of words and phrases as they are used in a text, including figurative and connotative meanings; analyze the impact of rhymes and other repetitions of sounds (e.g., alliteration) on a specific verse or stanza of a poem or section of a story or drama.
		L.7.5	Demonstrate understanding of figurative language, word relationships, and nuances in word meanings.
354	**Listening and Speaking** Give an Oral Response to Literature	SL.7.4	Present claims and findings, emphasizing salient points in a focused, coherent manner with pertinent descriptions, facts, details, and examples; use appropriate eye contact, adequate volume, and clear pronunciation.

Selection 1 Encounter, continued

Pages	Lesson	Code	Standards Text
355	**Language and Grammar** Make Comparisons	SL.7.1	Engage effectively in a range of collaborative discussions (one-on-one, in groups, and teacher-led) with diverse partners on grade 7 topics, texts, and issues, building on others' ideas and expressing their own clearly.
		L.7.1	Demonstrate command of the conventions of standard English grammar and usage when writing or speaking.
355	**Writing and Grammar** Write About Events	W.7.3.d	Write narratives to develop real or imagined experiences or events using effective technique, relevant descriptive details, and well-structured event sequences. Use precise words and phrases, relevant descriptive details, and sensory language to capture the action and convey experiences and events.
		L.7.1	Demonstrate command of the conventions of standard English grammar and usage when writing or speaking.
		L.7.2	Demonstrate command of the conventions of standard English capitalization, punctuation, and spelling when writing.

Selection 2 Culture Clash

Pages	Lesson	Code	Standards Text
356	**Connect**	SL.7.2	Analyze the main ideas and supporting details presented in diverse media and formats (e.g., visually, quantitatively, orally) and explain how the ideas clarify a topic, text, or issue under study.
357–359	**Language & Grammar** Make Comparisons	SL.7.1	Engage effectively in a range of collaborative discussions (one-on-one, in groups, and teacher-led) with diverse partners on grade 7 topics, texts, and issues, building on others' ideas and expressing their own clearly.
		SL.7.1.a	Come to discussions prepared, having read or researched material under study; explicitly draw on that preparation by referring to evidence on the topic, text, or issue to probe and reflect on ideas under discussion.
	Use Verbs in the Past Tense	L.7.1	Demonstrate command of the conventions of standard English grammar and usage when writing or speaking.
		L.7.2	Demonstrate command of the conventions of standard English capitalization, punctuation, and spelling when writing.
		L.7.2.b	Demonstrate command of the conventions of standard English capitalization, punctuation, and spelling when writing. Spell correctly.
360	**Key Vocabulary**	RI.7.4	Determine the meaning of words and phrases as they are used in a text, including figurative, connotative, and technical meanings; analyze the impact of a specific word choice on meaning and tone.
361	**Reading Strategy** Ask Questions	RI.7.1	Cite several pieces of textual evidence to support analysis of what the text says explicitly as well as inferences drawn from the text.
	Literary Analysis Compare a Topic	RI.7.9	Analyze how two or more authors writing about the same topic shape their presentations of key information by emphasizing different evidence or advancing different interpretations of facts.
362–372	**Reading Selection**	RI.7.1	Cite several pieces of textual evidence to support analysis of what the text says explicitly as well as inferences drawn from the text.
		RI.7.2	Determine two or more central ideas in a text and analyze their development over the course of the text; provide an objective summary of the text.
		RI.7.10	By the end of the year, read and comprehend literary nonfiction in the grades 6–8 text complexity band proficiently, with scaffolding as needed at the high end of the range.

Common Core State Standards, continued

Selection 2 Culture Clash, continued

Pages	Lesson	Code	Standards Text
373	**Connect Reading and Writing** Critical Thinking	RI.7.1	Cite several pieces of textual evidence to support analysis of what the text says explicitly as well as inferences drawn from the text.
		RI.7.2	Determine two or more central ideas in a text and analyze their development over the course of the text; provide an objective summary of the text.
	Vocabulary Review	L.7.6	Acquire and use accurately grade-appropriate general academic and domain-specific words and phrases; gather vocabulary knowledge when considering a word or phrase important to comprehension or expression.
	Write About the GQ	W.7.9	Draw evidence from literary or informational texts to support analysis, reflection, and research.
		W.7.10	Write routinely over extended time frames (time for research, reflection, and revision) and shorter time frames (a single sitting or a day or two) for a range of discipline-specific tasks, purposes, and audiences.
374	**Vocabulary Study** Understand Idioms	RI.7.4	Determine the meaning of words and phrases as they are used in a text, including figurative, connotative, and technical meanings; analyze the impact of a specific word choice on meaning and tone.
		L.7.5.a	Demonstrate understanding of figurative language, word relationships, and nuances in word meanings. Interpret figures of speech (e.g., literary, biblical, and mythological allusions) in context.
374	**Literary Analysis** Compare Fiction and Nonfiction	RL.7.9	Compare and contrast a fictional portrayal of a time, place, or characters and a historical account of the same period as a means of understanding how authors of fiction use or alter history.
375	**Language and Grammar** Make Comparisons	SL.7.1	Engage effectively in a range of collaborative discussions (one-on-one, in groups, and teacher-led) with diverse partners on grade 7 topics, texts, and issues, building on others' ideas and expressing their own clearly.
		L.7.1	Demonstrate command of the conventions of standard English grammar and usage when writing or speaking.
375	**Writing and Grammar** Write About Past Events	W.7.3.d	Write narratives to develop real or imagined experiences or events using effective technique, relevant descriptive details, and well-structured event sequences. Use precise words and phrases, relevant descriptive details, and sensory language to capture the action and convey experiences and events.
		L.7.1	Demonstrate command of the conventions of standard English grammar and usage when writing or speaking.
		L.7.2.b	Demonstrate command of the conventions of standard English capitalization, punctuation, and spelling when writing. Spell Correctly.

Selection 3 When Cultures Meet

Pages	Lesson	Code	Standards Text
376	**Connect**	SL.7.2	Analyze the main ideas and supporting details presented in diverse media and formats (e.g., visually, quantitatively, orally) and explain how the ideas clarify a topic, text, or issue under study.

Selection 3 When Cultures Meet, continued

Pages	Lesson	Code	Standards Text
377–379	**Language & Grammar** Summarize	RI.7.2	Determine two or more central ideas in a text and analyze their development over the course of the text; provide an objective summary of the text.
		SL.7.1.d	Engage effectively in a range of collaborative discussions (one-on-one, in groups, and teacher-led) with diverse partners on grade 7 topics, texts, and issues, building on others' ideas and expressing their own clearly. Acknowledge new information expressed by others and, when warranted, modify their own views.
		SL.7.2	Analyze the main ideas and supporting details presented in diverse media and formats (e.g., visually, quantitatively, orally) and explain how the ideas clarify a topic, text, or issue under study
		SL.7.3	Delineate a speaker's argument and specific claims, evaluating the soundness of the reasoning and the relevance and sufficiency of the evidence.
		SL.7.4	Present claims and findings, emphasizing salient points in a focused, coherent manner with pertinent descriptions, facts, details, and examples; use appropriate eye contact, adequate volume, and clear pronunciation.
	Use Verbs in the Past Tense	L.7.1	Demonstrate command of the conventions of standard English grammar and usage when writing or speaking.
		L.7.2	Demonstrate command of the conventions of standard English capitalization, punctuation, and spelling when writing.
380	**Key Vocabulary**	RI.7.4	Determine the meaning of words and phrases as they are used in a text, including figurative, connotative, and technical meanings; analyze the impact of a specific word choice on meaning and tone.
381	**Reading Strategy** Ask Questions	RI.7.1	Cite several pieces of textual evidence to support analysis of what the text says explicitly as well as inferences drawn from the text.
	Literary Analysis Analyze Text Features	RI.7.7	Compare and contrast a text to an audio, video, or multimedia version of the text, analyzing each medium's portrayal of the subject (e.g., how the delivery of a speech affects the impact of the words)
382–396	**Reading Selection**	RL.7.4	Determine the meaning of words and phrases as they are used in a text, including figurative and connotative meanings; analyze the impact of rhymes and other repetitions of sounds (e.g., alliteration) on a specific verse or stanza of a poem or section of a story or drama.
		RI.7.2	Determine two or more central ideas in a text and analyze their development over the course of the text; provide an objective summary of the text.
		RI.7.4	Determine the meaning of words and phrases as they are used in a text, including figurative, connotative, and technical meanings; analyze the impact of a specific word choice on meaning and tone.
		RI.7.10	By the end of the year, read and comprehend literary nonfiction in the grades 6-8 text complexity band proficiently, with scaffolding as needed at the high end of the range.
		L.7.5.a	Demonstrate understanding of figurative language, word relationships, and nuances in word meanings. Interpret figures of speech (e.g., literary, biblical, and mythological allusions) in context.

Common Core State Standards, continued

Selection 3 When Cultures Meet, continued

Pages	Lesson	Code	Standards Text
397	**Connect Reading and Writing** Critical Thinking	RI.7.2	Determine two or more central ideas in a text and analyze their development over the course of the text; provide an objective summary of the text.
	Vocabulary Review	L.7.6	Acquire and use accurately grade-appropriate general academic and domain-specific words and phrases; gather vocabulary knowledge when considering a word or phrase important to comprehension or expression.
	Write About the GQ	W.7.9	Draw evidence from literary or informational texts to support analysis, reflection, and research.
		W.7.10	Write routinely over extended time frames (time for research, reflection, and revision) and shorter time frames (a single sitting or a day or two) for a range of discipline-specific tasks, purposes, and audiences.
398	**Vocabulary Study** Analyze Idioms	RI.7.4	Determine the meaning of words and phrases as they are used in a text, including figurative, connotative, and technical meanings; analyze the impact of a specific word choice on meaning and tone.
		L.7.4.a	Determine or clarify the meaning of unknown and multiple-meaning words and phrases based on grade 7 reading and content, choosing flexibly from a range of strategies. Use context (e.g., the overall meaning of a sentence or paragraph; a word's position or function in a sentence) as a clue to the meaning of a word or phrase.
		L.7.5.a	Demonstrate understanding of figurative language, word relationships, and nuances in word meanings. Interpret figures of speech (e.g., literary, biblical, and mythological allusions) in context.
398	**Literary Analysis** Analyze Personification	RI.7.4	Determine the meaning of words and phrases as they are used in a text, including figurative, connotative, and technical meanings; analyze the impact of a specific word choice on meaning and tone.
399	**Language and Grammar** Summarize	RI.7.2	Determine two or more central ideas in a text and analyze their development over the course of the text; provide an objective summary of the text.
		SL.7.4	Present claims and findings, emphasizing salient points in a focused, coherent manner with pertinent descriptions, facts, details, and examples; use appropriate eye contact, adequate volume, and clear pronunciation.
		L.7.1	Demonstrate command of the conventions of standard English grammar and usage when writing or speaking.
399	**Writing and Grammar** Write About Past Events	W.7.3.d	Write narratives to develop real or imagined experiences or events using effective technique, relevant descriptive details, and well-structured event sequences. Use precise words and phrases, relevant descriptive details, and sensory language to capture the action and convey experiences and events.
		L.7.1	Demonstrate command of the conventions of standard English grammar and usage when writing or speaking.
		L.7.2	Demonstrate command of the conventions of standard English capitalization, punctuation, and spelling when writing.
400-401	**Close Reading**	RI.7.10	By the end of the year, read and comprehend literary nonfiction in the grades 6–8 text complexity band proficiently, with scaffolding as needed at the high end of the range.

Compare Across Texts

Pages	Lesson	Code	Standards Text
402	Analyze Word Choice and Tone	RI.7.4	Determine the meaning of words and phrases as they are used in a text, including figurative, connotative, and technical meanings; analyze the impact of a specific word choice on meaning and tone.
		RL.7.4	Determine the meaning of words and phrases as they are used in a text, including figurative and connotative meanings; analyze the impact of rhymes and other repetitions of sounds (e.g., alliteration) on a specific verse or stanza of a poem or section of a story or drama.

Unit Wrap-Up

Pages	Lesson	Code	Standards Text
403	Reflect on Your Reading	RI.7.1	Cite several pieces of textual evidence to support analysis of what the text says explicitly as well as inferences drawn from the text.
		RI.7.9	Analyze how two or more authors writing about the same topic shape their presentations of key information by emphasizing different evidence or advancing different interpretations of facts.
	Explore the GQ/Book Talk	SL.7.1	Engage effectively in a range of collaborative discussions (one-on-one, in groups, and teacher-led) with diverse partners on grade 7 topics, texts, and issues, building on others' ideas and expressing their own clearly.
		SL.7.5	Include multimedia components and visual displays in presentations to clarify claims and findings and emphasize salient points.

Unit 6   To the Rescue

Unit Launch

Pages	Lesson	Code	Standards Text
404–405	Unit Opener	SL.7.1	Engage effectively in a range of collaborative discussions (one-on-one, in groups, and teacher-led) with diverse partners on grade 7 topics, texts, and issues, building on others' ideas and expressing their own clearly.
406–407	Focus on Reading Determine Viewpoints	RL.7.6	Analyze how an author develops and contrasts the points of view of different characters or narrators in a text.
		RI.7.6	Determine an author's point of view or purpose in a text and analyze how the author distinguishes his or her position from that of others.
408–409	Focus on Vocabulary Use Word Origins	RI.7.4	Determine the meaning of words and phrases as they are used in a text, including figurative, connotative, and technical meanings; analyze the impact of a specific word choice on meaning and tone.
		L.7.4.b	Determine or clarify the meaning of unknown and multiple-meaning words and phrases based on grade 7 reading and content, choosing flexibly from a range of strategies. Use common, grade-appropriate Greek or Latin affixes and roots as clues to the meaning of a word (e.g., *belligerent, bellicose, rebel.*)
		L.7.5.b	Demonstrate understanding of figurative language, word relationships, and nuances in word meanings. Use the relationship between particular words (e.g., synonym/antonym, analogy) to better understand each of the words.

Selection 1 Dogs At Work

Pages	Lesson	Code	Standards Text
410	Connect	SL.7.2	Analyze the main ideas and supporting details presented in diverse media and formats (e.g., visually, quantitatively, orally) and explain how the ideas clarify a topic, text, or issue under study.

Common Core State Standards, continued

Selection 1 Dogs At Work, continued

Pages	Lesson	Code	Standards Text
411-413	**Language & Grammar** Summarize	SL.7.1.a	Engage effectively in a range of collaborative discussions (one-on-one, in groups, and teacher-led) with diverse partners on grade 7 topics, texts, and issues, building on others' ideas and expressing their own clearly. Come to discussions prepared, having read or researched material under study; explicitly draw on that preparation by referring to evidence on the topic, text, or issue to probe and reflect on ideas under discussion.
		RI.7.2	Determine two or more central ideas in a text and analyze their development over the course of the text; provide an objective summary of the text.
		SL.7.2	Analyze the main ideas and supporting details presented in diverse media and formats (e.g., visually, quantitatively, orally) and explain how the ideas clarify a topic, text, or issue under study.
		SL.7.4	Present claims and findings, emphasizing salient points in a focused, coherent manner with pertinent descriptions, facts, details, and examples; use appropriate eye contact, adequate volume, and clear pronunciation.
	Use Nouns in the Subject and Predicate	L.7.1	Demonstrate command of the conventions of standard English grammar and usage when writing or speaking.
414	**Key Vocabulary**	RI.7.4	Determine the meaning of words and phrases as they are used in a text, including figurative, connotative, and technical meanings; analyze the impact of a specific word choice on meaning and tone.
415	**Reading Strategy** Make Connections	RI.7.1	Cite several pieces of textual evidence to support analysis of what the text says explicitly as well as inferences drawn from the text.
	Literary Analysis Analyze Author's Purpose and Tone	RI.7.4	Determine the meaning of words and phrases as they are used in a text, including figurative, connotative, and technical meanings; analyze the impact of a specific word choice on meaning and tone.
		RI.7.6	Determine an author's point of view or purpose in a text and analyze how the author distinguishes his or her position from that of others
416–424	**Reading Selection**	RI.7.2	Determine two or more central ideas in a text and analyze their development over the course of the text; provide an objective summary of the text.
		RI.7.10	By the end of the year, read and comprehend literary nonfiction in the grades 6–8 text complexity band proficiently, with scaffolding as needed at the high end of the range.
425	**Connect Reading and Writing** Critical Thinking	RI.7.1	Cite several pieces of textual evidence to support analysis of what the text says explicitly as well as inferences drawn from the text.
	Vocabulary Review	L.7.6	Acquire and use accurately grade-appropriate general academic and domain-specific words and phrases; gather vocabulary knowledge when considering a word or phrase important to comprehension or expression.
	Write About the GQ	W.7.9	Draw evidence from literary or information texts to support analysis, reflection, and research.
		W.7.10	Write routinely over extended time frames (time for research, and revisions) and short time frames (a single sitting or a day or two) for a range of discipline-specific tasks, purposes, and audiences.

Selection 1 Dogs At Work, continued

Pages	Lesson	Code	Standards Text
426	**Vocabulary Study** Use Words and Phrases from Mythology	RI.7.4	Determine the meaning of words and phrases as they are used in a text, including figurative, connotative, and technical meanings; analyze the impact of a specific word choice on meaning and tone.
		L.7.4.b	Determine or clarify the meaning of unknown and multiple-meaning words and phrases based on grade 7 reading and content, choosing flexibly from a range of strategies. Use common, grade-appropriate Greek or Latin affixes and roots as clues to the meaning of a word (e.g., *belligerent, bellicose, rebel*).
		L.7.5.a	Demonstrate understanding of figurative language, word relationships, and nuances in word meanings. Interpret figures of speech (e.g., literary, biblical, and mythological allusions) in context.
426	**Literary Analysis** Analyze Poetry	RL.7.4	Determine the meaning of words and phrases as they are used in a text, including figurative and connotative meanings; analyze the impact of rhymes and other repetitions of sounds (e.g., alliteration) on a specific verse or stanza of a poem or section of a story or drama.
427	**Language and Grammar** Summarize	RI.7.2	Determine two or more central ideas in a text and analyze their development over the course of the text; provide an objective summary of the text.
		SL.7.4	Present claims and findings, emphasizing salient points in a focused, coherent manner with pertinent descriptions, facts, details, and examples; use appropriate eye contact, adequate volume, and clear pronunciation.
		L.7.1	Demonstrate command of the conventions of standard English grammar and usage when writing or speaking.
427	**Writing and Grammar** Write About People, Places, and Things	L.7.1	Demonstrate command of the conventions of standard English grammar and usage when writing or speaking.
		W.7.3.d	Write narratives to develop real or imagined experiences or events using effective technique, relevant descriptive details, and well-structured event sequences. Use precise words and phrases, relevant descriptive details, and sensory language to capture the action and convey experiences and events.

Selection 2 Angels in the Snow

Pages	Lesson	Code	Standards Text
428	**Connect**	SL.7.2	Analyze the main ideas and supporting details presented in diverse media and formats (e.g., visually, quantitatively, orally) and explain how the ideas clarify a topic, text, or issue under study.
429–431	**Language & Grammar** Clarify and Verify	SL.7.1	Engage effectively in a range of collaborative discussions (one-on-one, in groups, and teacher-led) with diverse partners on grade 7 topics, texts, and issues, building on others' ideas and expressing their own clearly.
		SL.7.1.a	Come to discussions prepared, having read or researched material under study; explicitly draw on that preparation by referring to evidence on the topic, text, or issue to probe and reflect on ideas under discussion.
	Use Prepositions	L.7.1.a	Demonstrate command of the conventions of standard English grammar and usage when writing or speaking. Explain the function of phrases and clauses in general and their function in specific sentences.
432	**Key Vocabulary**	RI.7.4	Determine the meaning of words and phrases as they are used in a text, including figurative, connotative, and technical meanings; analyze the impact of a specific word choice on meaning and tone.

Common Core State Standards, continued

Pages	Lesson	Code	Standards Text
433	**Reading Strategy** Make Connections	RI.7.1	Cite several pieces of textual evidence to support analysis of what the text says explicitly as well as inferences drawn from the text.
	Literary Analysis Analyze Author's Viewpoint	RI.7.6	Determine an author's point of view or purpose in a text and analyze how the author distinguishes his or her position from that of others.
434–440	**Reading Selection**	RI.7.4	Determine the meaning of words and phrases as they are used in a text, including figurative, connotative, and technical meanings; analyze the impact of a specific word choice on meaning and tone.
		RI.7.10	By the end of the year, read and comprehend literary nonfiction in the grades 6–8 text complexity band proficiently, with scaffolding as needed at the high end of the range.
441	**Connect Reading and Writing** Critical Thinking	RI.7.2	Determine two or more central ideas in a text and analyze their development over the course of the text; provide an objective summary of the text.
		RI.7.4	Determine the meaning of words and phrases as they are used in a text, including figurative, connotative, and technical meanings; analyze the impact of a specific word choice on meaning and tone.
	Vocabulary Review	L.7.6	Acquire and use accurately grade-appropriate general academic and domain-specific words and phrases; gather vocabulary knowledge when considering a word or phrase important to comprehension or expression.
	Write About the GQ	W.7.9	Draw evidence from literary or informational texts to support analysis, reflection, and research.
		W.7.10	Write routinely over extended time frames (time for research, and revision) and shorter time frames (a single sitting or a day or two) for a range of discipline-specific tasks, purposes, and audiences.
442	**Vocabulary Study** Use Greek, Latin, and Anglo-Saxon Roots	RI.7.4	Determine the meaning of words and phrases as they are used in a text, including figurative, connotative, and technical meanings; analyze the impact of a specific word choice on meaning and tone.
		L.7.4.b	Determine or clarify the meaning of unknown and multiple-meaning words and phrases based on grade 7 reading and content, choosing flexibly from a range of strategies. Use common, grade-appropriate Greek or Latin affixes and roots as clues to the meaning of a word (e.g., *belligerent, bellicose, rebel*).
		L.7.5.b	Demonstrate understanding of figurative language, word relationships, and nuances in word meanings. Use the relationship between particular words (e.g., synonym/antonym, analogy) to better understand each of the words.
442	**Media/Viewing** Analyze Media	RI.7.7	Compare and contrast a text to an audio, video, or multimedia version of the text, analyzing each medium's portrayal of the subject (e.g., how the delivery of a speech affects the impact of the words).
		SL.7.2	Analyze the main ideas and supporting details presented in diverse media and formats (e.g., visually, quantitatively, orally) and explain how the ideas clarify a topic, text, or issue under study.

Selection 2 Angels in the Snow, continued

Pages	Lesson	Code	Standards Text
443	**Language and Grammar** Clarify and Verify	SL.7.1	Engage effectively in a range of collaborative discussions (one-on-one, in groups, and teacher-led) with diverse partners on grade 7 topics, texts, and issues, building on others' ideas and expressing their own clearly.
		L.7.1.a	Demonstrate command of the conventions of standard English grammar and usage when writing or speaking. Explain the function of phrases and clauses in general and their function in specific sentences.
443	**Writing and Grammar** Write to Add Important Details	W.7.3.d	Write narratives to develop real or imagined experiences or events using effective technique, relevant descriptive details, and well-structured event sequences. Use precise words and phrases, relevant descriptive details, and sensory language to capture the action and convey experiences and events.
		L.7.1.a	Demonstrate command of the conventions of standard English grammar and usage when writing or speaking. Explain the function of phrases and clauses in general and their function in specific sentences.

Selection 3 Zlateh the Goat

Pages	Lesson	Code	Standards Text
444	**Connect**	SL.7.2	Analyze the main ideas and supporting details presented in diverse media and formats (e.g., visually, quantitatively, orally) and explain how the ideas clarify a topic, text, or issue under study.
445–447	**Language & Grammar** Tell an Original Story	SL.7.1	Engage effectively in a range of collaborative discussions (one-on-one, in groups, and teacher-led) with diverse partners on grade 7 topics, texts, and issues, building on others' ideas and expressing their own clearly.
	Use Pronouns in the Subject and the Predicate	L.7.1	Demonstrate command of the conventions of standard English grammar and usage when writing or speaking.
448	**Key Vocabulary**	RL.7.4	Determine the meaning of words and phrases as they are used in a text, including figurative and connotative meanings; analyze the impact of rhymes and other repetitions of sounds (e.g., alliteration) on a specific verse or stanza of a poem or section of a story or drama.
449	**Reading Strategy** Make Connections	RL.7.2	Determine a theme or central idea of a text and analyze its development over the course of the text; provide an objective summary of the text.
	Literary Analysis Analyze Plot and Theme	RL.7.3	Analyze how particular elements of a story or drama interact (e.g., how setting shapes the characters or plot).
450–464	**Reading Selection**	RL.7.1	Cite several pieces of textual evidence to support analysis of what the text says explicitly as well as inferences drawn from the text.
		RL.7.10	By the end of the year, read and comprehend literature, including stories, dramas, and poems, in the grades 6-8 text complexity band proficiently, with scaffolding as needed at the high end of the range.
		RI.7.1	Cite several pieces of textual evidence to support analysis of what the text says explicitly as well as inferences drawn from the text

Common Core State Standards, continued

Selection 3 Zlateh the Goat, continued

Pages	Lesson	Code	Standards Text
465	**Connect Reading and Writing** Critical Thinking	RL.7.2	Determine a theme or central idea of a text and analyze its development over the course of the text; provide an objective summary of the text.
	Vocabulary Review	L.7.6	Acquire and use accurately grade-appropriate general academic and domain-specific words and phrases; gather vocabulary knowledge when considering a word or phrase important to comprehension or expression.
	Write About the GQ	W.7.9	Draw evidence from literary or informational texts to support analysis, reflection, and research.
		W.7.10	Write routinely over extended time frames (time for research, reflection, and revision) and shorter time frames (a single sitting or a day or two) for a range of discipline-specific tasks, purposes, and audiences.
466	**Vocabulary Study** Borrowed Words	L.7.4.d	Determine or clarify the meaning of unknown and multiple-meaning words and phrases based on grade 7 reading and content, choosing flexibly from a range of strategies. Verify the preliminary determination of the meaning of a word or phrase (e.g., by checking the inferred meaning in context or in a dictionary).
466	**Listening/Speaking** Respond to Literature	SL.7.4	Present claims and findings, emphasizing salient points in a focused, coherent manner with pertinent descriptions, facts, details, and examples; use appropriate eye contact, adequate volume, and clear pronunciation.
467	**Language and Grammar** Tell an Original Story	SL.7.1	Engage effectively in a range of collaborative discussions (one-on-one, in groups, and teacher-led) with diverse partners on grade 7 topics, texts, and issues, building on others' ideas and expressing their own clearly.
		L.7.1	Demonstrate command of the conventions of standard English grammar and usage when writing or speaking.
467	**Writing and Grammar** Write an Original Story	L.7.1	Demonstrate command of the conventions of standard English grammar and usage when writing or speaking.
		W.7.3.d	Write narratives to develop real or imagined experiences or events using effective technique, relevant descriptive details, and well-structured event sequences. Use precise words and phrases, relevant descriptive details, and sensory language to capture the action and convey experiences and events.
468–469	**Close Reading**	RI.7.10	By the end of the year, read and comprehend literary nonfiction in the grades 6-8 text complexity band proficiently, with scaffolding as needed at the high end of the range.

Compare Across Texts

Pages	Lesson	Code	Standards Text
470	**Compare Characters** **and Setting**	RL.7.3	Analyze how particular elements of a story or drama interact (e.g., how setting shapes the characters or plot).

Unit Wrap-Up

Pages	Lesson	Code	Standards Text
471	Reflect on Your Reading	RI.7.6	Determine an author's point of view or purpose in a text and analyze how the author distinguishes his or her position from that of others.
		RL.7.6	Analyze how an author develops and contrasts the points of view of different characters or narrators in a text.
	Explore the GQ/Book Talk	W.7.10	Write routinely over extended time frames (time for research, reflection, and revision) and shorter time frames (a single sitting or a day or two) for a range of discipline-specific tasks, purposes, and audiences.
		SL.7.1	Engage effectively in a range of collaborative discussions (one-on-one, in groups, and teacher-led) with diverse partners on grade 7 topics, texts, and issues, building on others' ideas and expressing their own clearly.
		SL.7.5	Include multimedia components and visual displays in presentations to clarify claims and findings and emphasize salient points.

Unit 7   More Than a Game

Unit Launch

Pages	Lesson	Code	Standards Text
472–473	Unit Opener	SL.7.1	Engage effectively in a range of collaborative discussions (one-on-one, in groups, and teacher-led) with diverse partners on grade 7 topics, texts, and issues, building on others' ideas and expressing their own clearly.
474–475	Focus on Reading Text Structure: Chronological Order	RI.7.5	Analyze how the structure an author uses to organize a text, including how the major sections contribute to the whole and to the development of ideas.
476–477	Focus on Vocabulary Use Context Clues: Multiple Meaning Words	RI.7.4	Determine the meaning of words and phrases as they are used in a text, including figurative, connotative, and technical meanings; analyze the impact of a specific word choice on meaning and tone.
		L.7.4	Determine or clarify the meaning of unknown and multiple-meaning words and phrases based on grade 7 reading and content, choosing flexibly from a range of strategies.
		L.7.4.a	Use context (e.g., the overall meaning of a sentence or paragraph; a word's position or function in a sentence) as a clue to the meaning of a word or phrase.
		L.7.4.c	Consult general and specialized reference materials (e.g., dictionaries, glossaries, thesauruses) both print and digital, to find the pronunciation of a word or determine or clarify its precise meaning or its part of speech.

Selection 1 Play Ball!

Pages	Lesson	Code	Standards Text
478	Connect	SL.7.2	Analyze the main ideas and supporting details presented in diverse media and formats (e.g., visually, quantitatively, orally) and explain how the ideas clarify a topic, text, or issue under study.
479–481	Language & Grammar Express Opinions	SL.7.1	Engage effectively in a range of collaborative discussions (one-on-one, in groups, and teacher-led) with diverse partners on grade 7 topics, texts, and issues, building on others' ideas and expressing their own clearly.
		SL.7.1.a	Come to discussions prepared, having read or researched material under study; explicitly draw on that preparation by referring to evidence on the topic, text, or issue to probe and reflect on ideas under discussion.
	Use Complete Sentences	L.7.1.b	Demonstrate command of the conventions of standard English grammar and usage when writing or speaking. Choose among simple, compound, complex, and compound-complex sentences to signal differing relationships among ideas.

Common Core State Standards, continued

Selection 1 Play Ball!, continued

Pages	Lesson	Code	Standards Text
482	**Key Vocabulary**	RI.7.4	Determine the meaning of words and phrases as they are used in a text, including figurative, connotative, and technical meanings; analyze the impact of a specific word choice on meaning and tone.
483	**Reading Strategy** Make Inferences	RI.7.1	Cite several pieces of textual evidence to support analysis of what the text says explicitly as well as inferences drawn from the text.
	Literary Analysis Text Structure: Chronological Order	RI.7.5	Analyze the structure an author uses to organize a text, including how the major sections contribute to the whole and to the development of the ideas.
484–498	**Reading Selection**	RI.7.1	Cite several pieces of textual evidence to support analysis of what the text says explicitly as well as inferences drawn from the text.
		RI.7.10	By the end of the year, read and comprehend literary nonfiction in the grades 6–8 text complexity band proficiently, with scaffolding as needed at the high end of the range.
		L.7.5.a	Demonstrate understanding of figurative language, word relationships, and nuances in word meanings. Interpret figures of speech (e.g., literary, biblical, and mythological allusions) in context.
499	**Connect Reading and Writing** Critical Thinking	RI.7.2	Determine two or more central ideas in a text and analyze their development over the course of the text; provide an objective summary of the text.
	Vocabulary Review	L.7.6	Acquire and use accurately grade-appropriate general academic and domain-specific words and phrases; gather vocabulary knowledge when considering a word or phrase important to comprehension or expression.
	Write About the GQ	W.7.9	Draw evidence from literary or informational texts to support analysis, reflection, and research.
		W.7.10	Write routinely over extended time frames (time for research, reflection, and revision) and shorter time frames (a single sitting or a day or two) for a range of discipline-specific tasks, purposes, and audiences.
500	**Vocabulary Study** Use Multiple-Meaning Words Across Content Areas	RI.7.4	Determine the meaning of words and phrases as they are used in a text, including figurative, connotative, and technical meanings; analyze the impact of a specific word choice on meaning and tone.
	Literary Analysis Analyze Language	L.7.4.a	Determine or clarify the meaning of unknown and multiple-meaning words and phrases based on grade 7 reading and content, choosing flexibly from a range of strategies. Use context (e.g., the overall meaning of a sentence or paragraph; a word's position or function in a sentence) as a clue to the meaning of a word or phrase.
		L.7.4.c	Determine or clarify the meaning of unknown and multiple-meaning words and phrases based on grade 7 reading and content, choosing flexibly from a range of strategies. Consult general and specialized reference materials (e.g., dictionaries, glossaries, thesauruses), both print and digital, to find the pronunciation of a word, or determine or clarify its precise meaning or its part of speech.
501	**Language and Grammar** Express Opinions	SL.7.1	Engage effectively in a range of collaborative discussions (one-on-one, in groups, and teacher-led) with diverse partners on grade 7 topics, texts, and issues, building on others' ideas and expressing their own clearly.
		L.7.1.b	Demonstrate command of the conventions of standard English grammar and usage when writing or speaking. Choose among simple, compound, complex, and compound-complex sentences to signal differing relationships among ideas.

Selection 1 Play Ball!, continued

Pages	Lesson	Code	Standards Text
501	**Writing and Grammar** Write Complete Sentences	W.7.3.d	Write narratives to develop real or imagined experiences or events using effective technique, relevant descriptive details, and well-structured event sequences. Use precise words and phrases, relevant descriptive details, and sensory language to capture the action and convey experiences and events.
		L.7.1.b	Demonstrate command of the conventions of standard English grammar and usage when writing or speaking. Choose among simple, compound, complex, and compound-complex sentences to signal differing relationships among ideas.

Selection 2 Roberto Clemente

Pages	Lesson	Code	Standards Text
502	**Connect**	SL.7.2	Analyze the main ideas and supporting details presented in diverse media and forms (e.g., visually, quantitatively, orally) and explain how the ideas clarify a topic, text, or issue under study.
503–505	**Language & Grammar** Justify	SL.7.1.a	Engage effectively in a range of collaborative discussions (one-on-one, in groups, and teacher-led) with diverse partners on grade 7 topics, texts, and issues, building on others' ideas and expressing their own clearly. Come to discussions prepared, having read or researched material under study; explicitly draw on that preparation by referring to evidence on the topic, text, or issue to probe and reflect on ideas under discussion.
		SL.7.4	Present claims and findings, emphasizing salient points in a focused, coherent manner with pertinent descriptions, facts, details, and examples; use appropriate eye contact, adequate volume, and clear pronunciation.
	Use Compound Sentences	L.7.1.a	Demonstrate command of the conventions of standard English grammar and usage when writing or speaking. Explain the function of phrases and clauses in general and their functions in specific sentences.
		L.7.1.b	Demonstrate command of the conventions of standard English grammar and usage when writing or speaking. Choose among simple, compound, complex, and compound-complex sentences to signal differing relationships among ideas.
		L.7.1.c	Demonstrate command of the conventions of standard English grammar and usage when writing or speaking. Place phrases and clauses within a sentence, recognizing and correcting misplaced and dangling modifiers.
506	**Key Vocabulary**	RI.7.4	Determine the meaning of words and phrases as they are used in a text, including figurative, connotative, and technical meanings; analyze the impact of a specific word choice on meaning and tone.
507	**Reading Strategy** Make Inferences	RI.7.1	Cite several pieces of textual evidence to support analysis of what the text says explicitly as well as inferences drawn from the text.
	Literary Analysis Compare Media	RI.7.7	Compare and contrast a text to an audio, video, or multimedia version of the text, analyzing each medium's portrayal of the subject (e.g., how the delivery of a speech affects the impact of the words
508–516	**Reading Selection**	RI.7.1	Cite several pieces of textual evidence to support analysis of what the text says explicitly as well as inferences drawn from the text.
		RI.7.10	By the end of the year, read and comprehend literary nonfiction in the grades 6–8 text complexity band proficiently, with scaffolding as needed at the high end of the range.

Common Core State Standards, continued

Pages	Lesson	Code	Standards Text
517	**Connect Reading and Writing** Critical Thinking	RI.7.2	Determine two or more central ideas in a text and analyze their development over the course of the text; provide an objective summary of the text.
	Vocabulary Review	L.7.6	Acquire and use accurately grade-appropriate general academic and domain-specific words and phrases; gather vocabulary knowledge when considering a word or phrase important to comprehension or expression.
	Write About the GQ	W.7.9	Draw evidence from literary or informational texts to support analysis, reflection, and research.
		W.7.10	Write routinely over extended time frames (time for research, reflection, and revision) and shorter time frames (a single sitting or a day or two) for a range of discipline-specific tasks, purposes, and audiences.
518	**Vocabulary Study** Interpret Jargon	RI.7.4	Determine the meaning of words and phrases as they are used in a text, including figurative, connotative, and technical meanings; analyze the impact of a specific word choice on meaning and tone.
		L.7.4.a	Determine or clarify the meaning of unknown words and multiple-meaning words and phrases based on grade 7 reading and content, choosing flexibly from a range of strategies. Use context (e.g., the overall meaning of a sentence or paragraph; a word's position or function in a sentence) as a clue to the meaning of a word or phrase.
		L.7.4.d	Determine or clarify the meaning of unknown words and multiple-meaning words and phrases based on grade 7 reading and content, choosing flexibly from a range of strategies. Verify the preliminary determination of the meaning of a word or phrase (e.g., by checking the inferred meaning in context or in a dictionary.)
		L.7.5.a	Demonstrate understanding of figurative language, word relationships, and nuances in word meanings. Interpret figures of speech (e.g., literary, biblical, and mythological allusions) in context.
518	**Literary Analysis** Infer the Main Idea	RI.7.1	Cite several pieces of textual evidence to support analysis of what the text says explicitly as well as inferences drawn from the text.
		RI.7.2	Determine two or more central ideas in a text and analyze their development over the course of the text; provide an objective summary of the text.
519	**Language and Grammar** Justify	SL.7.4	Present claims and findings, emphasizing salient points in a focused, coherent manner with pertinent descriptions, facts, details, and examples; use appropriate eye contact, adequate volume, and clear pronunciation.
		L.7.1.b	Demonstrate command of the conventions of standard English grammar and usage when writing or speaking. Choose among simple, compound, complex, and compound-complex sentences to signal differing relationships among ideas.

Selection 2 Roberto Clemente, continued

Pages	Lesson	Code	Standards Text
519	**Writing and Grammar** Combine Your Ideas	W.7.3.d	Write narratives to develop real or imagined experiences or events using effective technique, relevant descriptive details, and well-structured event sequences. Use precise words and phrases, relevant descriptive details, and sensory language to capture the action and convey experiences and events.
		L.7.1.b	Demonstrate command of the conventions of standard English grammar and usage when writing or speaking. Choose among simple, compound, complex, and compound-complex sentences to signal differing relationships among ideas.
		L.7.1.c	Demonstrate command of the conventions of standard English grammar and usage when writing or speaking. Place phrases and clauses within a sentence, recognizing and correcting misplaced and dangling modifiers

Selection 3 Raymond's Run

Pages	Lesson	Code	Standards Text
520	**Connect**	SL.7.2	Analyze the main ideas and supporting details presented in diverse media and formats (e.g., visually, quantitatively, orally) and explain how the ideas clarify a topic, text, or issue under study.
521–523	**Language & Grammar** Elaborate	SL.7.1.a	Engage effectively in a range of collaborative discussions (one-on-one, in groups, and teacher-led) with diverse partners on grade 7 topics, texts, and issues, building on others' ideas and expressing their own clearly. Come to discussions prepared, having read or researched material under study; explicitly draw on that preparation by referring to evidence on the topic, text, or issue to probe and reflect on ideas under discussion.
		SL.7.1.c	Engage effectively in a range of collaborative discussions (one-on-one, in groups, and teacher-led) with diverse partners on grade 7 topics, texts, and issues, building on others' ideas and expressing their own clearly. Pose questions that elicit elaboration and respond to others' questions and comments with relevant observations and ideas that bring the discussion back on topic as needed.
	Use Complex Sentences	L.7.1.a	Demonstrate command of the conventions of standard English grammar and usage when writing or speaking. Explain the function of phrases and clauses in general and their functions in specific sentences.
		L.7.1.b	Demonstrate command of the conventions of standard English grammar and usage when writing or speaking. Choose among simple, compound, complex, and compound-complex sentences to signal differing relationships among ideas.
		L.7.1.c	Demonstrate command of the conventions of standard English grammar and usage when writing or speaking. Place phrases and clauses within a sentence, recognizing and correcting misplaced and dangling modifiers.
524	**Key Vocabulary**	RL.7.4	Determine the meaning of words and phrases as they are used in a text, including figurative and connotative meanings; analyze the impact of rhymes and other repetitions of sounds (e.g., alliteration) on a specific verse or stanza of a poem or section of a story or drama.
525	**Reading Strategy** Make Inferences	RL.7.1	Cite several pieces of textual evidence to support analysis of what the text says explicitly as well as inferences drawn from the text.
	Literary Analysis Determine Viewpoint	RL.7.6	Analyze how an author develops and contrasts the points of view of different characters or narrators in a text.

Common Core State Standards, continued

Pages	Lesson	Code	Standards Text
526–536	**Reading Selection**	RL.7.1	Cite several pieces of textual evidence to support analysis of what the text says explicitly as well as inferences drawn from the text.
		RL.7.10	By the end of the year, read and comprehend literature, including stories, dramas, and poems, in the grades 6-8 text complexity band proficiently, with scaffolding as needed at the high end of the range.
537	**Connect Reading and Writing** Critical Thinking	RL.7.2	Determine a theme or central idea of a text and analyze its development over the course of the text; provide an objective summary of the text.
		RL.7.1	Cite several pieces of textual evidence to support analysis of what the text says explicitly as well as inferences drawn from the text.
	Vocabulary Review	L.7.6	Acquire and use accurately grade-appropriate general academic and domain-specific words and phrases; gather vocabulary knowledge when considering a word or phrase important to comprehension or expression.
	Write About the GQ	W.7.9	Draw evidence from literary or informational texts to support analysis, reflection, and research.
		W.7.10	Write routinely over extended time frames (time for research, reflection, and revision) and shorter time frames (a single sitting or a day or two) for a range of discipline-specific tasks, purposes, and audiences.
538	**Vocabulary Study** Use Context Clues: Multiple-Meaning Words	L.7.4.a	Determine or clarify the meaning of unknown and multiple-meaning words and phrases based on grade 7 reading and content, choosing flexibly from a range of strategies. Use context (e.g. the overall meaning of a sentence or paragraph; a word's position or function in a sentence) as a clue to the meaning of a word or phrase.
		L.7.4.d	Determine or clarify the meaning of unknown and multiple-meaning words and phrases based on grade 7 reading and content, choosing flexibly from a range of strategies. Verify the preliminary determination of the meaning of a word or phrase (e.g., by checking the inferred meaning in context or in a dictionary).
538	**Literary Analysis** Evaluate Informational Text	RI.7.6	Determine an author's point of view or purpose in a text and analyze how the author distinguishes his or her position from that of others.
539	**Language and Grammar** Elaborate	SL.7.1.c	Engage effectively in a range of collaborative discussions (one-on-one, in groups, and teacher-led) with diverse partners on grade 7 topics, texts, and issues, building on others' ideas and expressing their own clearly. Pose questions that elicit elaboration and respond to others' questions and comments with relevant observations and ideas that bring the discussion back on topic as needed.
		L.7.1.b	Demonstrate command of the conventions of standard English grammar and usage when writing or speaking. Choose among simple, compound, complex, and compound-complex sentences to signal differing relationships among ideas.

Selection 3 Raymond's Run, continued

Pages	Lesson	Code	Standards Text
539	**Writing and Grammar** Use a Variety of Sentences	L.7.1.b	Demonstrate command of the conventions of standard English grammar and usage when writing or speaking. Choose among simple, compound, complex, and compound-complex sentences to signal differing relationships among ideas.
		L.7.1.c	Demonstrate command of the conventions of standard English grammar and usage when writing or speaking. Place phrases and clauses within a sentence, recognizing and correcting misplaced and dangling modifiers.
		W.7.3.d	Write narratives to develop real or imagined experiences or events using effective technique, relevant descriptive details, and well-structured event sequences. Use precise words and phrases, relevant descriptive details, and sensory language to capture the action and convey experiences and events.
540–541	**Close Reading**	RI.7.10	By the end of the year, read and comprehend literary nonfiction in the grades 6–8 text complexity band proficiently, with scaffolding as needed at the high end of the range.

Compare Across Texts

Pages	Lesson	Code	Standards Text
542	**Compare Authors' Styles**	RI.7.6	Determine an author's point of view or purpose in a text and analyze how the author distinguishes his or her position from that of others.

Unit Wrap-Up

Pages	Lesson	Code	Standards Text
543	**Reflect on Your Reading**	RI.7.5	Analyze the structure an author uses to organize a text, including how the major sections contribute to the whole and to the development of the ideas.
	Explore the GQ/Book Talk	W.7.10	Write routinely over extended time frames (time for research, reflection, and revision) and shorter time frames (a single sitting or a day or two) for a range of discipline-specific tasks, purposes, and audiences.
		SL.7.1	Engage effectively in a range of collaborative discussions (one-on-one, in groups, and teacher-led) with diverse partners on grade 7 topics, texts, and issues, building on others' ideas and expressing their own clearly.
		SL.7.5	Include multimedia components and visual displays in presentations to clarify claims and findings and emphasize salient points.

Unit 8 Global Warnings

Unit Launch

Pages	Lesson	Code	Standards Text
544–545	**Unit Opener**	SL.7.1	Engage effectively in a range of collaborative discussions (one-to-one, in groups, and teacher-led) with diverse partners on grade 7 topics, texts, and issues, building on others' ideas and expressing their own clearly.
546–547	**Focus on Reading** Analyze Argument	RI.7.8	Trace and evaluate the argument and specific claims in a text, assessing whether the reasoning is sound and the evidence is relevant and sufficient to support the claims.

Common Core State Standards, continued

Pages	Lesson	Code	Standards Text
548–549	**Focus on Vocabulary** Use Context Clues	L.7.4.a	Determine or clarify the meaning of unknown and multiple-meaning words and phrases based on grade 7 reading and content, choosing flexibly from a range of strategies. Use context (e.g., the overall meaning of a sentence or paragraph; a word's position or function in a sentence) as a clue to the meaning of a word or phrase.
		L.7.4.d	Determine or clarify the meaning of unknown and multiple-meaning words and phrases based on grade 7 reading and content, choosing flexibly from a range of strategies. Verify the preliminary determination of the meaning of a word or phrase (e.g., by checking the inferred meaning in context or in a dictionary).
		L.7.5.a	Demonstrate understanding of figurative language, word relationships, and nuances in word meanings. Interpret figures of speech (e.g., literary, biblical, and mythological allusions) in context
		L.7.5.c	Demonstrate understanding of figurative language, word relationships, and nuances in word meanings. Distinguish among the connotations (associations) of words with similar denotations (definitions) (e.g., *refined, respectful, polite, diplomatic, condescending*)
Selection 1 Handle with Care			
550	**Connect**	SL.7.2	Analyze the main ideas and supporting details presented in diverse media and formats (e.g., visually, quantitatively, orally) and explain how the ideas clarify a topic, text, or issue under study.
551–553	**Language & Grammar** Persuade	SL.7.3	Delineate a speaker's argument and specific claims, evaluating the soundness of the reasoning and the relevance and sufficiency of the evidence.
		SL.7.4	Present claims and findings, emphasizing salient points in a focused, coherent manner with pertinent descriptions, facts, details, and examples; use appropriate eye contact, adequate volume, and clear pronunciation.
		SL.7.1.a	Engage effectively in a range of collaborative discussions (one-on-one, in groups, and teacher-led) with diverse partners on grade 7 topics, texts, and issues, building on others' ideas and expressing their own clearly. Come to discussions prepared, having read or researched material under study; explicitly draw on that preparation by referring to evidence on the topic, text, or issue to probe and reflect on ideas under discussion.
	Use Verbs in the Present, Past, and Future Tense	L.7.1	Demonstrate command of the conventions of standard English grammar and usage when writing or speaking.
		L.7.2	Demonstrate command of the conventions of standard English capitalization, punctuation, and spelling when writing.
554	**Key Vocabulary**	RI.7.4	Determine the meaning of words and phrases as they are used in a text, including figurative, connotative, and technical meanings; analyze the impact of a specific word choice on meaning and tone.
555	**Reading Strategy** Synthesize	RI.7.1	Cite several pieces of textual evidence to support analysis of what the text says explicitly as well as inferences drawn from the text.
	Literary Analysis Analyze Argument and Reasons	RI.7.8	Trace and evaluate the argument and specific claims in a text, assessing whether the reasoning is sound and the evidence is relevant and sufficient to support the claims

Pages	Lesson	Code	Standards Text
556–568	**Reading Selection**	RI.7.2	Determine two or more central ideas in a text and analyze their development over the course of the text; provide an objective summary of the text.
		RI.7.10	By the end of the year, read and comprehend literary nonfiction in the grades 6–8 text complexity band proficiently, with scaffolding as needed at the high end of the range.
		SL.7.2	Analyze the main ideas and supporting details presented in diverse media and formats (e.g, visually, quantitatively, orally) and explain how the ideas clarify a topic, text, or issue under study.
569	**Connect Reading and Writing** Critical Thinking	RI.7.2	Determine a theme or central idea of a text and analyze the development over the course of the text; provide an objective summary of the text.
	Vocabulary Review	L.7.6	Acquire and use accurately grade-appropriate general academic and domain-specific words and phrases; gather vocabulary knowledge when considering a word or phrase important to comprehension or expression.
	Write About the GQ	W.7.9	Draw evidence from literary or informational texts to support analysis, reflection, and research.
		W.7.10	Write routinely over extended time frames (time for research, reflection, and revision) and shorter time frames (a single sitting or a day or two) for a range of discipline-specific tasks, purposes, and audiences.
570	**Vocabulary Study** Understand Denotation and Connotation	RI.7.4	Determine the meaning of words and phrases as they are used in a text, including figurative, connotative, and technical meanings; analyze the impact of a specific word choice on meaning and tone.
		L.7.4.a	Determine or clarify the meaning of unknown and multiple-meaning words and phrases based on grade 7 reading and content, choosing flexibly from a range of strategies. Use context (e.g., the overall meaning of a sentence or paragraph; a word's position or function in a sentence) as a clue to the meaning of a word or phrase.
		L.7.5.c	Demonstrate understanding of figurative language, word relationships, and nuances in word meanings. Distinguish among the connotations (associations) of words with similar denotations (definitions) (e.g., *refined, respectful, polite, diplomatic, condescending*).
570	**Media/Viewing** Analyze Propaganda in the Media	SL.7.1.a	Engage effectively in a range of collaborative discussions (one-on-one, in groups, and teacher-led) with diverse partners on grade 7 topics, texts, and issues, building on others' ideas and expressing their own clearly. Come to discussions prepared, having read or researched material under study; explicitly draw on that preparation by referring to evidence on the topic, text, or issue to probe and reflect on ideas under discussion.
571	**Language and Grammar** Persuade	SL.7.3	Delineate a speaker's argument and specific claims, evaluating the soundness of the reasoning and the relevance and sufficiency of the evidence.
		SL.7.4	Present claims and findings, emphasizing salient points in a focused, coherent manner with pertinent descriptions, facts, details, and examples; use appropriate eye contact, adequate volume, and clear pronunciation.
		L.7.1	Demonstrate command of the conventions of standard English grammar and usage when writing or speaking.

Common Core State Standards, continued

Selection 1 Handle with Care, continued

Pages	Lesson	Code	Standards Text
571	**Writing and Grammar** Write About Community Action	L.7.1	Demonstrate command of the conventions of standard English grammar and usage when writing or speaking.
		L.7.2	Demonstrate command of the conventions of standard English capitalization, punctuation, and spelling when writing.
		W.7.3.d	Write narratives to develop real or imagined experiences or events using effective technique, relevant descriptive details, and well-structured event sequences. Use precise words and phrases, relevant descriptive details, and sensory language to capture the action and convey experiences and events.

Selection 2 Melting Away

Pages	Lesson	Code	Standards Text
572	**Connect**	SL.7.2	Analyze the main ideas and supporting details presented in diverse media and formats (e.g., visually, quantitatively, orally) and explain how the ideas clarify a topic, text, or issue under study.
573–575	**Language & Grammar** Use Appropriate Language	SL.7.1.a	Engage effectively in a range of collaborative discussions (one-on-one, in groups, and teacher-led) with diverse partners on grade 7 topics, texts, and issues, building on others' ideas and expressing their own clearly. Come to discussions prepared, having read or researched material under study; explicitly draw on that preparation by referring to evidence on the topic, text, or issue to probe and reflect on ideas under discussion.
		SL.7.6	Adapt speech to a variety of contexts and tasks, demonstrating command of formal English when indicated or appropriate.
	Use Verbs in the Present Perfect Tense	L.7.1	Demonstrate command of the conventions of standard English grammar and usage when writing or speaking.
		L.7.2	Demonstrate command of the conventions of standard English capitalization, punctuation, and spelling when writing.
576	**Key Vocabulary**	RI.7.4	Determine the meaning of words and phrases as they are used in a text, including figurative, connotative, and technical meanings; analyze the impact of a specific word choice on meaning and tone.
577	**Reading Strategy** Synthesize	RI.7.1	Cite several pieces of textual evidence to support analysis of what the text says explicitly as well as inferences drawn from the text.
	Literary Analysis Analyze Argument and Evidence	RI.7.8	Trace and evaluate the argument and specific claims in a text, assessing whether the reasoning is sound and the evidence is relevant and sufficient to support the claims.
578–588	**Reading Selection**	RI.7.1	Cite several pieces of textual evidence to support analysis of what the text says explicitly as well as inferences drawn from the text.
		RI.7.2	Determine two or more central ideas in a text and analyze their development over the course of the text; provide an objective summary of the text.
		RI.7.10	By the end of the year, read and comprehend literary nonfiction in the grades 6–8 text complexity band proficiently, with scaffolding as needed at the high end of the range.

Pages	Lesson	Code	Standards Text
589	**Connect Reading and Writing** Critical Thinking	RI.7.2	Determine two or more central ideas in a text and analyze their development over the course of the text; provide an objective summary of the text.
	Vocabulary Review	L.7.6	Acquire and use accurately grade-appropriate general academic and domain-specific words and phrases; gather vocabulary knowledge when considering a word or phrase important to comprehension or expression.
	Write About the GQ	W.7.9	Draw evidence from literary or information texts to support analysis, reflection, and research.
		W.7.10	Write routinely over extended time frames (time for research, reflection, and revision) and shorter time frames (a single sitting or a day or two) for a range of discipline-specific tasks, purposes, and audiences.
590	**Vocabulary Study** Understanding Technical Language	RI.7.4	Determine the meaning of words and phrases as they are used in a text, including figurative, connotative, and technical meanings; analyze the impact of a specific word choice on meaning and tone.
		L.7.4.a	Determine or clarify the meaning of unknown and multiple-meaning words and phrases based on grade 7 reading and content, choosing flexibly from a range of strategies. Use context (e.g., the overall meaning of a sentence or paragraph; a word's position or function in a sentence) as a clue to the meaning of a word or phrase.
		L.7.4.d	Determine or clarify the meaning of unknown and multiple-meaning words and phrases based on grade 7 reading and content, choosing flexibly from a range of strategies. Verify the preliminary determination of the meaning of a word or phrase (e.g., by checking the inferred meaning in context or in a dictionary.)
590	**Listening/Speaking** Give a Persuasive Speech	SL.7.3	Delineate a speaker's argument and specific claims, evaluating the soundness of the reasoning and the relevance and sufficiency of the evidence.
		SL.7.4	Present claims and findings, emphasizing salient points in a focused, coherent manner with pertinent descriptions, facts, details, and examples; use appropriate eye contact, adequate volume, and clear pronunciation.
		SL.7.5	Include multimedia components and visual displays in presentations to clarify claims and findings and emphasize salient points.
591	**Language and Grammar** Use Appropriate Language	SL.7.6	Adapt speech to a variety of contexts and tasks, demonstrating command of formal English when indicated or appropriate.
		L.7.1	Demonstrate command of the conventions of standard English grammar and usage when writing or speaking.
591	**Writing and Grammar** Write About Actions	W.7.3.d	Write narratives to develop real or imagined experiences or events using effective technique, relevant descriptive details, and well-structured event sequences. Use precise words and phrases, relevant descriptive details, and sensory language to capture the action and convey experiences and events.
		L.7.1	Demonstrate command of the conventions of standard English grammar and usage when writing or speaking.
		L.7.2	Demonstrate command of the conventions of standard English capitalization, punctuation, and spelling when writing.

Common Core State Standards, continued

Pages	Lesson	Code	Standards Text
592	**Connect**	SL.7.2	Analyze the main ideas and supporting details presented in diverse media and formats (e.g., visually, quantitatively, orally) and explain how the ideas clarify a topic, text, or issue under study.
593–595	**Language & Grammar** Negotiate	SL.7.1.a	Engage effectively in a range of collaborative discussions (one-on-one, in groups, and teacher-led) with diverse partners on grade 7 topics, texts, and issues, building on others' ideas and expressing their own clearly.
			Come to discussions prepared, having read or researched material under study; explicitly draw on that preparation by referring to evidence on the topic, text, or issue to probe and reflect on ideas under discussion.
		SL.7.1.d	Engage effectively in a range of collaborative discussions (one-on-one, in groups, and teacher-led) with diverse partners on grade 7 topics, texts, and issues, building on others' ideas and expressing their own clearly.
			Acknowledge new information expressed by others and, when warranted, modify their own views.
		SL.7.4	Present claims and findings, emphasizing salient points in a focused, coherent manner with pertinent descriptions, facts, details, and examples; use appropriate eye contact, adequate volume, and clear pronunciation.
		SL.7.6	Adapt speech to a variety of contexts and tasks, demonstrating command of formal English when indicated or appropriate.
	Use Participles as Adjectives	L.7.1.c	Demonstrate command of the conventions of standard English grammar and usage when writing or speaking.
			Place phrases and clauses within a sentence, recognizing and correcting misplaced and dangling modifiers
596	**Key Vocabulary**	RL.7.4	Determine the meaning of words and phrases as they are used in a text, including figurative and connotative meanings; analyze the impact of rhymes and other repetitions of sounds (e.g., alliteration) on a specific verse or stanza of a poem or section of a story or drama.
597	**Reading Strategy** Synthesize	RL.7.1	Cite several pieces of textual evidence to support analysis of what the text says explicitly as well as inferences drawn from the text.
	Literary Analysis Analyze Theme	RL.7.2	Determine a theme or central idea of a text and analyze its development over the course of the text; provide an objective summary of the text.
598–612	**Reading Selection**	RL.7.2	Determine a theme or central idea of a text and analyze its development over the course of the text; provide an objective summary of the text.
		RL.7.10	By the end of the year, read and comprehend literature, including stories, dramas, and poems, in the grades 6-8 text complexity band proficiently, with scaffolding as needed at the high end of the range.
613	**Connect Reading and Writing** Critical Thinking	RL.7.2	Determine a theme or central idea of a text and analyze its development over the course of the text; provide an objective summary of the text.
	Vocabulary Review	L.7.6	Acquire and use accurately grade-appropriate general academic and domain-specific words and phrases; gather vocabulary knowledge when considering a word or phrase important to comprehension or expression.
	Write About the GQ	W.7.9	Draw evidence from literary or informational texts to support analysis, reflection, and research.
		W.7.10	Write routinely over extended time frames (time for research, reflection, and revision) and shorter time frames (a single sitting or a day or two) for a range of discipline-specific tasks, purposes, and audiences.

Selection 3 The Legend of the Yakwawiak, continued

Pages	Lesson	Code	Standards Text
614	**Vocabulary Study** Understand Figurative Language	L.7.4.a	Determine or clarify the meaning of unknown and multiple-meaning words and phrases based on grade 7 reading and content, choosing flexibly from a range of strategies. Use context (e.g. the overall meaning of a sentence or paragraph; a word's position or function in a sentence) as a clue to the meaning of a word or phrase.
		L.7.5.a	Demonstrate understanding of figurative language, word relationships, and nuances in word meanings. Interpret figures of speech (e.g., literary, biblical, and mythological allusions) in context.
614	**Literary Analysis** Analyze Changes in the English Language	L.7.4.d	Determine or clarify the meaning of unknown and multiple-meaning words and phrases based on grade 7 reading and content, choosing flexibly from a range of strategies. Verify the preliminary determination of the meaning of a word or phrase (e.g., by checking the inferred meaning in context or in a dictionary).
615	**Language and Grammar** Negotiate	SL.7.1.d	Engage effectively in a range of collaborative discussions (one-on-one, in groups, and teacher-led) with diverse partners on grade 7 topics, texts, and issues, building on others' ideas and expressing their own clearly. Acknowledge new information expressed by others and, when warranted, modify their own views.
		SL.7.4	Present claims and findings, emphasizing salient points in a focused, coherent manner with pertinent descriptions, facts, details, and examples; use appropriate eye contact, adequate volume, and clear pronunciation.
		SL.7.6	Adapt speech to a variety of contexts and tasks, demonstrating command of formal English when indicated or appropriate.
		L.7.1.c	Demonstrate command of the conventions of standard English grammar and usage when writing or speaking. Place phrases and clauses within a sentence, recognizing and correcting misplaced and dangling modifiers.
615	**Writing and Grammar** Write About a Story	W.7.3.d	Write narratives to develop real or imagined experiences or events using effective technique, relevant descriptive details, and well-structured event sequences. Use precise words and phrases, relevant descriptive details, and sensory language to capture the action and convey experiences and events.
		L.7.1.c	Demonstrate command of the conventions of standard English grammar and usage when writing or speaking. Place phrases and clauses within a sentence, recognizing and correcting misplaced and dangling modifiers.
616–617	**Close Reading**	RI.7.10	By the end of the year, read and comprehend literary nonfiction in the grades 6–8 text complexity band proficiently, with scaffolding as needed at the high end of the range.
Compare Across Texts			
618	**Compare Themes and Symbols**	RL.7.2	Determine a theme or central idea of a text and analyze its development over the course of the text; provide an objective summary of the text.

Common Core State Standards, continued

Unit Wrap-Up

Pages	Lesson	Code	Standards Text
619	**Reflect on Your Reading**	RI.7.8	Trace and evaluate the argument and specific claims in a text, assessing whether the reasoning is sound and the evidence is relevant and sufficient to support the claims.
	Explore the GQ/Book Talk	W.7.10	Write routinely over extended time frames (time for research, reflection, and revision) and shorter time frames (a single sitting or a day or two) for a range of discipline-specific tasks, purposes, and audiences.
		SL.7.1	Engage effectively in a range of collaborative discussions (one-on-one, in groups, and teacher-led) with diverse partners on grade 7 topics, texts, and issues, building on others' ideas and expressing their own clearly.
		SL.7.5	Include multimedia components and visual displays in presentations to clarify claims and findings and emphasize salient points.

Reading Handbook

Pages	Lesson	Code	Standards Text
621–633	**Reading Strategies:** Plan and Monitor	RL.7.1	Cite several pieces of textual evidence to support analysis of what the text says explicitly as well as inferences drawn from the text.
	Determine Importance Make Connections	RI.7.1	Cite several pieces of textual evidence to support analysis of what the text says explicitly as well as inferences drawn from the text.
	Make Inferences Ask Questions	RI.7.2	Determine two or more central ideas in a text and analyze their development over the course of the text; provide an objective summary of the text.
	Synthesize Visualize	RL.7.10	By the end of the year, read and comprehend literature, including stories, dramas, and poems, in the grades 6–8 text complexity band proficiently, with scaffolding as needed at the high end of the range.
		RI.7.10	By the end of the year, read and comprehend literary nonfiction in the grades 6–8 text complexity band proficiently, with scaffolding as needed at the high end of the range.